THE GODDESS AND
THE AMERICAN GIRL

THE GODDESS AND THE AMERICAN GIRL

*The Story of Suzanne Lenglen
and Helen Wills*

Larry Engelmann

New York   Oxford
OXFORD UNIVERSITY PRESS
1988

Oxford University Press

Oxford New York Toronto
Delhi Bombay Calcutta Madras Karachi
Petaling Jaya Singapore Hong Kong Tokyo
Nairobi Dar es Salaam Cape Town
Melbourne Auckland

and associated companies in
Beirut Berlin Ibadan Nicosia

Library of Congress Cataloging-in-Publication Data
Engelmann, Larry.
The goddess and the American girl.
Bibliography: p. Includes index.
1. Lenglen, Suzanne. 2. Tennis players—France—Biography. 3. Wills, Helen.
4. Tennis players—United States—Biography. I. Title.
GV994.L4E54 1988   796.342′092′2 [B]   87-31556
ISBN 0-19-504363-4

1 3 5 7 9 8 6 4 2
Printed in the United States of America
on acid-free paper

For
Marya and Erika
my goddess and my American girl

PREFACE

The first time I saw a reference to Suzanne Lenglen was in an American literature class at the University of Michigan. The class was reading Ernest Hemingway's 1926 novel *The Sun Also Rises*. In chapter VI of that novel, Hemingway described one of his principal fictional characters, Robert Cohn, by writing that "he loved to win at tennis. He probably loved to win as much as Lenglen, for instance."

I remember someone in the class asking about the "Lenglen" character: "Who was he? What did he do? How did Hemingway know about him?" The instructor didn't know. We were to assume that it really wasn't that important. But whoever he was, we were assured, he loved to win at something. If he didn't, then Hemingway, quite obviously, would never have included the reference.

And so we moved on to other parts of the text.

I underlined that passage and put a question mark in the margin of the page. Later I searched through several celebrated histories of the 1920s and found not a single reference to Lenglen. Not one. I drew the conclusion that this Lenglen person was some obscure figure of the Twenties who, in the eyes of historians, was quite obviously not as important as Floyd Collins, Al Smith, Jack Dempsey, Billy Sunday, Gene Tunney, Charles Ponzi, Aimee Semple McPherson, Herbert Hoover, Ruth Snyder, Sacco and Vanzetti, Izzy Einstein, William Jennings Bryan, Ruth Elder, John Scopes, Charles Lindbergh, Gertrude Ederle, Babe Ruth, Bobby Jones, Fatty Arbuckle, Al Capone, Queen Marie of Roumania, and a whole host of other characters who were commonly discussed at length in nearly every published history of the decade. And so for the time being I forgot about Hemingway's mysterious Lenglen.

Not long after that, in an American history class, I watched a popular documentary film entitled "The Golden Twenties." In that film I saw and heard for the first time a reference to Helen Wills. She was given only a brief moment in the film, which delegated much more time to clips of Charleston contests and flappers and Flaming Youth. Yet just that moment was enough to arouse my curiosity. Wills was shown holding a tennis racket, staring into the camera. She looked away for an instant, betraying what appeared to be a shy uneasiness, then she glanced up again and smiled. She was, it was clear, strikingly beautiful. The film gave no information on her accomplishments or her importance. She was, it was implied, merely another of the colorful figures from America's past. Another quick search through the standard histories of the 1920s turned up not a single reference to Helen Wills. Jess Willard and Harry Wills, prize-fighters, turned up again and again in the "W" section of indexes. But there wasn't a sign of Helen Wills. I concluded that she was probably about as unimportant as Hemingway's Lenglen.

Then, in the mid-1970s, I began work on my first book, *Intemperance: The Lost War Against Liquor* (Free Press, 1979), a history of the efforts to enforce prohibition in the 1920s. During my research I read hundreds of newspapers and magazine articles from the 1920s and the early 1930s. It was at that time that I was surprised to discover that Lenglen was not a "Mr." but a "Mlle." and that she was in fact a major figure of the 1920s and 1930s. And I found, much to my surprise, that the name of Helen Wills appeared almost daily in American newspapers and magazines in the 1920s—and not just on the sports pages. Wills was a front-page story, and she twice appeared on the cover of *Time* magazine in that decade.

I became enthralled by Lenglen and Wills as I read about them in the papers, and I decided to write about them when I had finished *Intemperance*.

I am still not sure why American historians have ignored these two extraordinary women. I thought, for a time, that it was perhaps due to the unexamined bias that historians share towards individuals whose primary renown is in sports or entertainment rather than in politics or literature. But then I found that many other sports figures had in fact been examined at length by historians and biographers and held up as central figures of American culture and values of the past—Ruth, Gehrig, Dempsey, Jim Thorpe, Joe Louis, and Jackie Robinson among others. I was left with no answer to the mystery of the omission of Lenglen and Wills from the standard chronicles of the past.

When I spoke with those who remembered the 1920s and the 1930s I found that all of them fondly recalled memories of Helen Wills and Suzanne Lenglen, and they asked the same question I had asked: "Why hasn't anybody written about them?"

Wills and Lenglen represent a curious consequence of the tunnel vision of historians. Both were better known and more admired than any movie stars, novelists, writers, artists, or politicians of the 1920s and the 1930s. Young men and women taped pictures of Lenglen and Wills on their walls, and crowds turned out by the tens of thousands to see them. What they wore on a given day set styles for the rest of the nation. What they said and did was reported in meticulous detail in the daily papers. Young women sought their advice on everything from diet and exercise to marriage and careers. The great artists of the day—including Augustus John, Alexander Calder, and Diego Rivera—found Helen Wills a perfect subject for their work. In compiling a book of contemporary thought on the 1930s, philosopher Will Durant sought out Helen

Wills as a contributor. Herbert Hoover asked Helen Wills to campaign for him in 1928 in order to win the younger voters of the country to his cause. Benito Mussolini invited Helen Wills to visit Italy in order to attract public attention to his new regime. Charlie Chaplin wrote that the most beautiful thing he had ever seen was Helen Wills playing tennis. Suzanne Lenglen stole crowds away from the President of Switzerland in his own country and toured the United States in 1926 and 1927 gathering bigger crowds and more money for her appearances than any other political or sports figure of the time—in 1927 she earned nearly three times as much in professional sports as Babe Ruth did. In order to attract Suzanne Lenglen to America in 1921, the officers of the United States Lawn Tennis Association conspired to violate the Eighteenth Amendment to the Constitution and to provide her with contraband wine and cognac, which she said she needed in order to play tennis properly. Never before or since have such respected individuals conspired to break the law just to guarantee the appearance of an amateur athlete in a tournament. Shouldn't just one or two of these facts have gained the attention of some historian in the past half-century?

The fame of Wills and Lenglen stemmed from their athletic accomplishments, of course. They were two of the finest athletes that the world has ever seen. Between 1919 and 1938 they won fourteen singles titles at Wimbledon. Not until the summer of 1987 did Martina Navratilova break Suzanne Lenglen's long-standing record of five consecutive wins at Wimbledon and tie Helen Wills's record of eight singles wins in the tournament. The Lenglen record stood unbroken for sixty-three years, the Wills record for forty-nine. No one has yet broken the record of sequential victories that Wills and Lenglen set in tennis. Between 1919 and 1926, when she retired from amateur tennis, Suzanne Lenglen lost only two sets in singles and won 269 of 270 matches. And from 1927 until 1933, Helen Wills lost no sets in singles competition anywhere in the world, and she became the first tennis player to win the national titles of France, England, and the United States. She accomplished that feat first in 1928 and then did it again in 1929. She won 180 matches in a row and won the Wimbledon singles title every time she played there after 1926.

Lenglen and Wills became celebrities and were lauded enthusiastically as the glory of their times. Lenglen was referred to as "The Goddess" by her countrymen, and she was regarded as the greatest Frenchwoman since Joan of Arc. Wills was called "The American Girl," and one New York newspaper editor observed that every male in America from "six to sixty" was in love with her. If the title of Miss America had been put to a popular vote, there is little doubt that Helen Wills would have won that title year after year in the 1920s.

The two women carried a good deal of symbolic baggage in the 1920s. While Suzanne Lenglen came to represent the glory of resurgent, romantic, postwar France, Helen Wills represented the greatness and energy of young, democratic America. The only confrontation, in 1926 in France, advertised as the struggle of the Old World against the New World, remains to this day the most dramatic and significant tennis match ever played.

So, not only did Hemingway's Lenglen love to win, she won more than anybody else in sports. Had Hemingway written his novel a few years later he could have written that Robert Cohn loved to win as much as Wills loved to win. Yet later students of American literature—and history—would still have found the reference obscure. Until now.

Lenglen and Wills are important not alone because they won the tennis matches in which they played and were celebrated symbols of the greatness of the countries from which they came. They are important and admirable because they accepted enormous challenges and difficulties in establishing themselves as champions. In countless tests and contests, and often in the face of harrowing circumstances, they struggled to do their best and to challenge the conventional wisdom of the day concerning the physical and emotional limitations of women. Each paid a very high price for the victories won.

Eventually, they became outspoken champions of the right of self-determination for athletes. They sought independence from male-dominated associations and organizations that controlled tennis and other sports. As a result, all athletes today, male and female, are the beneficiaries of their pioneering efforts.

What follows, then, is the story of two women who rewrote the record books in tennis, set aflutter the hearts of millions of young men, inspired millions of young women, were idolized by their contemporaries, and who were pioneers in expanding the freedom of athletes to control their own careers. Yet it is important to keep in mind that the records they set might have been even more incredible if Lenglen and Wills had been more ambitious. When the chance came to break records at Forest Hills and Wimbledon, Wills decided to pass up those tournaments to do something else—vacation in Europe one year and study art another. And Suzanne Lenglen abandoned amateur tennis to become a pioneer in professional sports. She probably could have won a dozen or more national titles had she remained an amateur. So, extraordinary as their records are, they represent also a lack of obsession with record-breaking.

Helen Wills wrote in the 1930s that what was important in life was not simply winning titles or putting a list of records in a book. What was important was the way in which one lived and played. The enduring things, she wrote, are the things of the spirit. The goal is never as important as the manner in which it is achieved, she believed. And she warned that, in the overly ambitious pursuit of victories, an athlete may find that what is won, in the end, is as hollow as a victory cup. Helen Wills wanted no hollow victories. She said that she played tennis only because she loved the game. Winning was important. But far more important was the way in which victory was achieved. Lenglen, too, loved to win. But she also realized that what was important, in the end, was the game itself. In the decade after she retired from amateur tennis, Suzanne Lenglen supervised a tennis school for youngsters in France in order to teach them the game that she had mastered as a child.

Robert Cohn loved to win at tennis. "He probably loved to win as much as Lenglen, for instance." On the other hand, Hemingway points out, "He was not angry at being beaten."

There is a large supporting cast in this narrative made up of women who lost many tennis matches to Lenglen and Wills and who "were not angry at being beaten." In sports, as in politics, there are several losers for each winner. And in sports, it is the worthy losers who provide the competition that gives the new records credibility. Helen Hull Jacobs, Alice Marble, Elizabeth Ryan, Kitty McKane, Marjorie Morrill Painter, Edith Sigourney, Edith Cross, Leslie Bancroft Aeschliman, Dorothy Round, Dorothy Wightman, Sarah Palfrey, Carolyn and Dorothea Swarz, and Anna Harper, all lost to Suzanne Lenglen or Helen Wills. And they also won many victories and titles. But they were the players in matches in which the greatness of Wills and Lenglen was defined. When I contacted them they were generous, articulate, cooperative, and happy to tell about their tennis years. And they enjoyed those years, remembering their losses with as much zest and enjoyment as their victories over others. I found in their stories, as in the stories of Lenglen and Wills, the same simple principle asserted again and again: It matters if you win or lose, but far more important is how you play the game. There is an undeniable nobility in a dedicated effort that might fall short of victory. That collective wisdom, I believe, is worth pointing out today.

By the time I had completed this manuscript, my youngest daughter, Erika, was reading *The Sun Also Rises* in her senior high school English class. When someone asked about Hemingway's allusion to Lenglen, she explained it. I hope that this book will explain it for everyone else.

San Jose, California   Larry Engelmann
January 1, 1988

ACKNOWLEDGMENTS

From the beginning of my research on Helen Wills and Suzanne Lenglen I enjoyed the cooperation, help, and advice of several talented individuals. Their contributions to my research were crucial.

King Wah Ng Moberg, an energetic and imaginative librarian at San Jose State University, was able to provide me with all of the articles and books that I requested. Through the incredible workings of the interlibrary loan system she made available to me many vital and difficult-to-locate articles and books and, consequently, much of the information essential to a complete telling of the Wills-Lenglen stories. Over the course of several years Mrs. Moberg gave me advice and encouragement on this project and suggested resources with which I was unfamiliar. I was fortunate, indeed, to have King Wah working with me and for me. She set high standards for herself and lived up to them. Without her help this project certainly would have been less complete.

Several other staff members of the library at San Jose State University also helped me and provided efficient and friendly service. I was generously given the use of a special room for going over microfilms and interlibrary loan materials. And my hours of research were made both more pleasant and more productive thanks to the competence and patience of the SJSU library staff.

The staff of the Bancroft Library at the University of California also provided superb help day after day for me. And the staff of the Palo Alto Public Library allowed me to use the original copies of *Collier's* magazine, which carried some of the best tennis writing in the 1920s and the 1930s.

Several research assistants also provided me with some suggestions, criticism, and encouragement. Jennifer Keim first helped me assemble a complete bibliography on Wills and Lenglen and helped locate many archival materials. I also enjoyed the help of Melissa Pham and Cheryl Bedrosian. Some outstanding female athletes also read parts of the story and gave me suggestions and criticism. Among them were Kim Purcell, Janet Arlene Harman, Christa Cook, and Jodi Bredding. Kathryn Lydia Briggs also read parts of the manuscript and suggested some changes, as did my daughters, Marya and Erika.

Margaret Adams, a free-lance editor, offered advice and encouragement over the course of several years, as did Kathy Rebello of *USA Today*.

Elizabeth Walters, librarian of the San Jose *Mercury News,* offered advice on the use of newspaper clippings files and on the location of various resources. Her sensitivity to women's issues in particular was helpful to me, also.

Jeffrey Klein, editor of *West* magazine, published part of this manuscript in 1984 and offered encouragement.

The late Elmer Griffin granted me several lengthy interviews and then put me in touch with a dozen other primary sources for my work. Edward Chandler and Gerald Stratford also provided information over the course of several years. Alice Marble spoke with me at length during the course of two days and helped me re-create the tennis world of the 1930s. And the late Fred Moody provided me with some detailed and sometimes scandalous information which, I am sure, he knew could not be printed in this book. My long afternoon conversation with Fred was simply priceless.

John Gardiner let me watch his priceless films of Helen Wills and Suzanne Lenglen playing on the French Riviera in 1926.

My colleagues at San Jose State, Gerald Wheeler and George Moore, also helped me get reasonable teaching schedules that made my research and travel more manageable. Jim Walsh, a fine historian and writer, located information on Helen Wills in the James Phelan papers for me and also pointed out many other possible sources on the subject. History department secretaries Lynn Cole and Joan Bloch also generously helped me with typing and Xeroxing and preparing this manuscript.

Thanks also to John and Mary Carol Pamperin, Rodney Kopp, Barbara Briggs, Robin White, Paul D. Campbell, Debra Lo, Margo Morris, James A. Darby, Diana Killian, Bui Le Ha, Sarah Briggs, Michael Malone, Kerrie McCaffrey, Pat Henry Yeomans, Tom Carter, Ron Rapoport, Paul Campbell, Sidney Fine, Bill Bellows, Amy Thompson, Maree Taylor, Kasie Cheung, Lina Lim, John Snetsinger, Glenna Matthews, Colleen Engelmann, Delores Barnett, Anna McCune Harper, and the late Edith Cross Jensen.

Finally, my agent, Emilie Jacobson, believed in this book through several years of research and writing and never let me remain discouraged for long about the difficulties of research, writing, or publication. Her understanding and patience over the past several years have been deeply appreciated.

L.E.

CONTENTS

THE GODDESS AND
THE AMERICAN GIRL

CHAPTER
·⊷◄ I ►⊶·

THE GODDESS

"This world of ours is only formed for ostentation;
men are only puffed up with wind and are bandied
to and fro like tennis balls."   —Montaigne

"I just throw dignity to the winds and think of
nothing but the game."   —Suzanne Lenglen

"When you play tennis you take chances."
Molla Bjursted Mallory

"America had its day yesterday; this is France's day."
—Suzanne Lenglen

Paris. January 1926. Day after day an unusual warm rain fell, and the Seine rose to its highest level in fifteen years. Then came the lowest temperatures in memory and a heavy snowfall that virtually paralyzed the city. Snow was also reported in Florence, and ice in Nice. The seasonal migration of the rich to the Riviera was postponed, and thousands of Parisians who had expected to be playing in Monte Carlo or Cannes found themselves in the city awaiting a change in the weather. It was not the weather alone, however, that draped a dispiriting pall over the city. Government, the economy, and culture seemed daily to slip from relative absurdity toward absolute vulgarity. And critics chorused agreement that the available public entertainment was the worst ever. The music halls had abandoned everything but nudity. Art had reached a nadir, and the reputable modistes conspired to attire women in styles to match the ghastly weather. Costumed in the latest fashions, women by day looked like boys and by night like female impersonators.

A severe financial crisis sliced the franc to a slender fraction of its pre-war value. French governments, incapable of solving the crisis, collapsed with frightening regularity, and revolution loomed as an increasingly attractive alternative to the existing madness. Mobs gathered outside the Chamber of Deputies, and people on the street grumbled openly.

To make matters even worse, France was invaded by battalions of American tourists and expatriates intent upon taking advantage of the favorable exchange rate. A popular journalist summed up the prevailing French attitude toward the invaders when he warned that "there are too many of these parasites here, eating our food, drinking our wine, going untaxed and paying ridiculously little for everything they consume." The

3

same writer threatened to form a Joan of Arc Society to boot the Americans out of France. "We have got to teach these unwelcome visitors that they are not wanted here," he warned.

Everything, from the weather to the Americans, vexed and distressed the French in the first weeks of 1926. The glory that had accompanied victory in the Great War seemed suddenly remote, and hopes for security and prosperity were grudgingly abridged. Yet there remained in the midst of this plague of troubles one shining symbol of the indomitable spirit of France. That luminous symbol and unfailing inspiration was Suzanne Lenglen, acclaimed by all of her countrymen as "The Goddess."

She was not a child of any royal family. She inherited no regal empire, no palace, no uniformed armies, no official titles, no scepter, no great seal of state. Yet from 1919 until 1927 Suzanne Lenglen enjoyed all of the influence, prestige, and popularity previously the exclusive realm of the most esteemed hereditary rulers. She radiated an unparalleled imperiousness and was the dazzling cynosure of whatever domain she occupied at a given moment. Every European nation saw evidence of her majesty and appeal. She was greeted everywhere by masses of awed and adoring fans. She traveled exclusively by chauffeured limousine or private rail car. She draped herself fittingly in the white ermine of royalty and crowned herself with a unique jeweled bandeau. Her wardrobe was created by France's leading designer, and what she wore set the style for women throughout the Western world. What she said, did, ate, how she felt, and where she lived were all reported in painstaking and adoring detail in the newspapers. She was the best known and most admired woman in Europe—perhaps in the world. To see her was the rage. To speak with her—the exchange of only a word—set one apart. To France she was a national heroine, as great as Joan of Arc. And when people spoke of her, more often than not they used one of her mythic appellations rather than her name. She was "la belle Suzanne," "notre gracieuse championne," "The Maid Marvel," "The Little Sorceress," and "The Queen." But the deific reference to Suzanne as "The Goddess" perhaps best expressed the feelings of France.

Suzanne Lenglen rose to prominence initially by her extraordinary athletic skill at tennis. But it would be an error simply to say that Suzanne "played" tennis. Others played tennis. Suzanne Lenglen performed tennis. She danced tennis. She celebrated tennis. She laughed and she sang tennis. And there were times when Suzanne suffered tennis. But because she was so unlike any other tennis player in the world, no one ever said that this goddess played tennis. For to say such a thing might bring a comparison with other players, and that would be to miss completely her singular virtuosity and spell.

Lenglen's career was a grimly and gloriously national affair in France. It was a brave journalist indeed who dared to write one word of criticism concerning her activities. Reports of her contests printed in French newspapers were always adulatory. When she lost a game or played an extended set—a rare occurrence—reporters explained faithfully why such an outrageous thing had happened. A close contest in doubles was invariably the fault of her partner. In singles she might lose a game or two because she was preoccupied by a concern for the health of her father or her dog.

And whenever some journalist did make a rare error in judgment and published something even slightly unflattering about the Goddess, he was immediately denounced by other journalists and his story passionately refuted. Such a newsman was ridiculed not simply as a fool but as an enemy of Suzanne Lenglen, of sport, and of France. Consequently, French newspapers served almost exclusively as a public relations firm for the Goddess. Journalists were reduced to silence or sycophancy. Suzanne's publicity, American correspondents found, was "publicity gone mad," and many of them wondered how the laudatory Lenglen stories could be printed year after year and still retain any credibility with the public. "One would have thought Lenglen would have stopped this kind of thing long ago," one of them complained.

But Lenglen did not stop it. For more than a decade, from 1914 until 1926, she encouraged it and abetted those who composed the fables. Indeed, she lived in ecstatic symbiosis with her nation's newsmen, providing pleasant and often dramatic materials for inquiring reporters and then basking in the public attention that followed the publication of such accounts. Few editors could resist describing in colorful detail her most recent athletic contests or alleged romantic liaisons. Flattering photographs appeared weekly in the rotogravure sections of the Sunday papers. In Suzanne Lenglen journalists had at last stumbled upon a subject commensurate with their capacity for hyperbole.

Lenglen mesmerized not just journalists but almost everyone who watched her. Tennis star René Lacoste remembered first falling under her spell in 1921. In the spring of that year young Lacoste traveled with his parents to Saint-Cloud. After promising to return in a few minutes, Lacoste was permitted to enter the Stade Français to watch part of the final match for the World Hard Court Championship between Suzanne Lenglen and the American champion, Molla Mallory. Lacoste, a perceptive student of tennis, kept a detailed notebook in which he analyzed the strengths and weaknesses of various leading players, information he used to improve his own performance. Perhaps there was something he could learn by watching Lenglen. "At first," Lacoste said of his initial glimpse of the French woman, "I was disappointed, as were most of those who saw her for the first time after having heard so much about her." He expected to see a woman execute extraordinary tennis strokes. But Suzanne did not. He found "she played with marvelous ease the simplest strokes in the world. It was only after several games that I understood what harmony was concealed by her simplicity, what wonderful mental and physical balance was hidden by the facility of her play." Lacoste was spellbound by her simple perfection. In his head he had a vague notion of the way the game should be played. But not until he watched Suzanne did Lacoste see the ideal made real. "I had promised to stay a few minutes," he recalled, "but I remained there a long time without being able to depart, looking at this admirable spectacle with wide-open eyes."

Grantland Rice watched the same match at Saint-Cloud and was hardly less restrained in his enthusiasm for the Maid Marvel: "An amazingly symmetrical figure, replete with grace and litheness, arrayed in a white silk dress that barely flutters below the knees. White silk stockings and white shoes. Above this background of white, hair as black as a raven's wing, bound with a brilliant orange band. Perfectly molded arms, bare and brown from many suns—the entire effect being one of extreme vividness—an effect immediately to catch and hold the eye." But even this description, Rice readily confessed, failed to do the Goddess justice. Her movement, her deific grace, the ineffable wonder of her, defied description. Rice watched her "astounding mid-air flutterings, as of some brilliantly colored bird, with the orange band flashing like a flame of yellow fire," and he could only think that "Solomon meeting the Queen of Sheba beat us to it with the proper phrase—'The better half has never been told.'"

A writer for the *New York Times,* seeing her in 1921 for the first time, concluded simply that Lenglen was "one of the most wonderful machines that have ever been created out of a woman's body."

On the pink clay courts of the Riviera and the indoor hard wood surfaces of Paris, Lenglen's performances were graceful enough to be set to music, even were music themselves. Her game was not just serve and volley and forehand and backhand, but rather toccata and cadenza and sometimes, during long rallies, rhapsody. She appeared to play as well as many men but she played with a poetry of motion, a fluency, a bravura, that no male or female had previously even attempted. She reduced the intensity and intricacy of athletics to simplicity and then rechoreographed them so that the prosaic basics of play were surprisingly transformed. And what made all of this even more extraordinary was that she made it appear so easy. While those across the net from her scrambled frantically and huffed and puffed, working themselves to exhaustion, the goddess moved with seeming effortlessness and efficiency like a beautiful gliding bird in flight.

There was a fabled quality to the rise of Suzanne Lenglen. And nearly every Frenchman could provide in precise and painstaking detail stories of her childhood, training, and career whether they actually happened or not. Even Suzanne and her parents had trouble keeping their stories straight on how she had trained, how she had won, and how difficult this or that contest had been. There was unanimous agreement, however, on one central aspect of her career. Although all of France now claimed her, "notre Suzanne" was really the result of the dream of one man, Charles Lenglen. He was Suzanne's father, teacher, trainer, adviser, coach, agent, manager, protector, mentor, and at times even her tormentor.

When asked, Papa Lenglen, a heavyset bear of a man, usually began his somber version of the creation of the goddess with a prophetic mystical incident that took place during a vaudeville performance in the Casino Municipal de Nice in 1912. Among the entertainers during that evening, Papa remembered, was a hypnotist accompanied by a medium who served as his subject. The couple performed demonstrations of mental telepathy, thought-reading, and fortune-telling. The medium, with her eyes blind-folded, said she would answer any question in the mind of any person in the audience. Papa Lenglen concentrated on the question, "Will my daughter one day become champion of France?" Within a few seconds the medium answered, "Better than that—better than that." The success of Suzanne was then something foretold, Papa insisted. But he also knew of the enormous and trying effort and the painful dedication that went into making that which was foretold and destined into actual fact.

Suzanne Rachel Flore Lenglen was born in Compiègne, France, on May 24, 1899. The Lenglen family claimed to be of Franco-Flemish origins, but even this was uncertain. American journalists described Suzanne as a "Provençal type intermingled with a Semitic strain." Papa Lenglen, a businessman of some means, managed the omnibus concession he had in-herited from his father. The enterprise prospered, and soon after Suzanne's birth Papa sold it and moved with his wife, Anais, and their daughter to a rustic villa in Maretz-sur-Matz near Compiègne. There the Lenglens enjoyed a life of pleasant leisure, dividing their time between the new home in the Oise and a small vacation villa in Nice.

At an early age Suzanne demonstrated unusual athletic ability. She was a large-boned and strong girl with superb coordination. At eight she was an accomplished cyclist and a strong swimmer. She could run faster, jump higher, and throw a ball farther than boys her age. And while the family wintered in Nice, Suzanne developed a passion for diabolo, a game that became the rage among European children early in the century. In diabolo, a spinning top is balanced and manipulated on a string held between two sticks. Talented diabolo players, like little Suzanne, could throw the top high into the air and then catch it on the string, or with another player could throw the top back and forth and play what was called "diabolo tennis." In Nice, Suzanne played the game daily on the Promenade des Anglais and became so skillful at it and displayed such unusual panache that crowds of tourists would gather to watch. In time she became such a leading attraction on the street that people asked at what hour the little girl would perform. When she arrived there was applause from those who had gathered to watch. Years later, in recounting the important influences in Suzanne's life, Papa attributed her poise before large crowds to her early experience playing diabolo before the adoring tourists of Nice.

Suzanne studied at the Institute Massena in Nice, where among her courses was one in classic Greek dance. Later, when her movements in tennis were described as like those of a dancer, it was rumored that she had studied with the Ballet Russe de Monte Carlo. But she had not. The single dance course at the Institute was the basis for the grace of movement she so expertly transferred to endeavors in other areas.

While on the Riviera, Papa Lenglen had the opportunity to watch some of the world's best tennis players. Competitors from America, the British Empire, and the Continent began their annual campaigns each winter in the club tournaments on the Riviera. From there they moved on to Saint-Cloud for the World Hard Court Championships in the spring and then to Wimbledon for the World Championships in June. Papa had batted tennis balls around for recreation but was never an accomplished player. He became instead an interested and well-informed observer of the game. He was fascinated by the tactics and maneuvers of tennis, and he was especially impressed by the deference paid to the men and women accomplished in the sport, who were treated like aristocrats. They were housed and fed in the grand hotels and the finest restaurants, escorted back and forth between tournaments by limousine, lionized by the society of sybarites who ranged the Riviera, and invited to party and play with statesmen, monarchs, titled aristocrats, and wealthy industrialists. They were welcomed aboard the most expensive yachts and were pointed out on the street. Dressed in their spotless tennis whites, they were a little like demigods cavorting in play beside this azure sea. (Years later, Jack Kramer wrote of men's tennis attire: "If you never saw tennis players in their long white flannels, I cannot begin to explain to you how majestic they appeared. . . . Tennis clothes were a rare elegance that could transform a man.") Papa envied them. He had a restless passion for fame, and he would have liked to enter the select sporting coterie of the Riviera. Too far past his prime to join that select brotherhood, he watched and fantasized instead.

In time Suzanne came to share Papa's interest in tennis. She expressed a desire to learn the game after seeing her parents play a set on the lawn of their Martez-sur-Matz villa. Papa later remembered the fateful day—in June, 1910—when he presented his daughter with her first tennis racket. It was an inexpensive instrument that he had purchased in a toy shop in Compiègne. He expected his daughter to amuse herself with it for a time and then tire of tennis.

Papa patiently outlined a tennis court on the lawn where Suzanne played with friends and seemed to enjoy the exercise. She did not tire of the game, and within a month Papa noticed that she had learned to handle her racket quite well, striking the ball with unusual dexterity. So Papa purchased another one from a manufacturer in Paris, a racket that was light and properly balanced for a youngster of Suzanne's stature. To get a better idea of her capabilities, Papa played against Suzanne on the family lawn and was pleasantly surprised. "Even at that youthful age," he later recalled, "she showed signs of her developing genius for tactical execution."

Papa next concocted a special backboard for Suzanne to hit against, a board with warps and cracks in it so the ball came off in surprising ways unless it hit certain small even spots. He painted targets on the even areas. Suzanne thrashed away energetically at the board, memorizing its surface geography and eventually mastering it so she could play steadily against the board, smacking back the ball again and again and again to precisely the same spot.

Three months after Suzanne began to play, Papa took her to see a friend, Dr. Cizelly, who lived near Chantilly. Cizelly was a tennis enthusiast and the owner of a good clay court on which Suzanne played her first set on a hard surface before a gallery. She was skilled enough for Dr. Cizelly to suggest she be entered in a local tournament. Suzanne competed in the event, won four rounds, and captured second place.

Papa was encouraged enough to start giving Suzanne some serious tennis instruction. But what should he teach her? And how? With only a few teaching professionals available on the Continent most tennis players taught themselves the game through a slow process of observation and imitation. So Papa began observing in order to teach Suzanne to imitate.

On the Riviera that winter he studied the tennis of the Englishwomen. Their game was played over an extended period of time and consisted of ground strokes and slow tactical maneuvering from the baseline. The game was extremely civilized and unhurried and depended more than anything else upon patience and success at meticulous placement. After a few weeks Papa gave up teaching such play to Suzanne. It was undramatic and tedious and dreadfully boring, and it was totally unsuited for a girl so filled with enthusiasm and energy.

Papa turned then to the game of the men who astounded him "by the remarkable superiority of their methods." "Why, then, should not women adopt the masculine method? It seemed to me that with a well-directed course of training any woman could be taught the game as it was played by the men, although naturally she would be unable to play with the same degree of force."

And so Papa studied more closely the ground strokes and styles and strategies of the all-court game of the leading male players. He visited the courts of the various Riviera clubs more frequently and with a new purpose, and he watched and listened and questioned the players and took careful mental notes. Then he taught Suzanne the strongest features of each player: the forehand of this one, the backhand of that one, and the services of three or four others. He experimented in order to see exactly how much of the men's game a young woman might learn. Without actually intending to do so, he revolutionized women's tennis.

As Suzanne's tennis skills improved, Papa's aspirations increased. The fame and attention and deference he saw bestowed upon tennis players on the Riviera might some day be his through Suzanne. His daughter could accomplish things that no woman had ever before imagined possible. Old assumptions concerning the physical strength, ability, fragility, speed, and expertise of women had never really been tested, Papa believed. Need anatomy actually be destiny? What were the real limitations for a woman athlete? Papa set out to discover for himself. There was no feminine model he could hold up as an inspiration for Suzanne, no woman who stood high above the common crowd of competitors in sport. Papa had only a dream to guide him in his efforts. He dreamed of something entirely new in women's sports—the perfect union of athletics and art. He dreamed of a woman who was the master of every stroke and tactic of the men's all-court game, but a woman who played that game better than any man and who played it with the effortless physical grace and ease of an accomplished dancer.

In late fall 1910, when the Lenglens took up their seasonal residence on the Riviera, Papa applied for the admission of Suzanne to the prestigious Nice Tennis Club, to which he already belonged. The Nice Club was one of the principal sites for winter tournaments on the Riviera, and the best male and female players in the world played on the club's clay courts. Children had not previously been allowed on the courts, but now, by special dispensation, Suzanne was granted limited access.

Papa practiced with Suzanne at the Nice Club, and in a short time his training methods became legendary. Suzanne practiced a single stroke from a set position on the court hour after hour while Papa or a club professional hit balls to her. After Papa sensed that the mechanics of the stroke had been mastered, control and placement became the goal. Papa placed a handkerchief on the court across the net from Suzanne, and the youngster aimed her shots at the small silk target. Gradually, no matter what the bound or speed or angle of the shot, Suzanne could return the ball to the target. Then Papa decreased the size of the target, folding and refolding the handkerchief, and eventually he replaced it with a coin. To the delight and disbelief of observers, Suzanne was soon capable of striking a coin anywhere on the court. On occasion she could hit a coin five times in a row while moving about the court and keeping the ball in play. Some days Papa divided the inner fringe of the court into squares like a chessboard. Suzanne then practiced striking certain squares in sequence from various positions across the net. The drill was repeated again and again, Suzanne returning up to three hundred shots in a row without a break.

Photographer Jacques Henri Lartigue watched Papa training Suzanne, and he recorded in his journal, "Father Lenglen is very severe and it is easy to see he would really like his daughter to be a boy. Mother Lenglen, with her huge eyes and friendly smile, apparently feels differently. She would much prefer it if her daughter would just play and amuse herself like all the other young girls around here. But Suzanne wants to be a champion and that's why she spends every free moment hitting balls into the small squares which have been marked out for her on the tennis court."

Papa prescribed an equally rigorous system of physical conditioning off the court. Conditioning was imperative, he insisted, because fully half of tennis was footwork and speed. So Suzanne swam, ran sprints, and jumped rope every day. Eventually these exercises brought her fame in athletic activities other than tennis. By 1919 she was the high jump champion among French women with a leap of four feet six inches—a mark within four inches of the world record for women at the time. She could jump over the tennis net from a standing position while keeping her feet together. She could run the eighty-meter dash in less than eleven seconds. This was all accomplished at a time when few women athletes trained strenuously. Typical of the conventional wisdom of the day was the attitude Molla Mallory a former singles champion of Norway who dominated the women's singles competition in America for nearly a decade after 1914. Mallory, a chain smoker and enthusiastic party-goer, affirmed, "I held that too serious training took more out of a girl nervously than she gained physically."

On Sunday afternoons Papa packed up the entire family and drove to tournaments at the various Riviera clubs. Suzanne watched and listened while Papa analyzed the strengths and weaknesses of each player. This was followed by a post-match discussion between father and daughter with detailed questions about the mobility and strokes of this or that player. Then back to the Nice courts and the handkerchiefs and coins and chessboard squares and dreams.

Papa did not work alone in developing Suzanne's tennis skills. He unabashedly solicited the best male players on the Riviera to practice with his daughter. His cry, *"Voulez-vous jouer avec ma fille?"* (Will you play with my daughter?) became a familiar appeal to many Riviera tennis regulars who took time to rally with the little girl and stayed to answer her father's endless questions.

Alvardo Rice, secretary of the Nice Tennis Club, also took an interest in Suzanne's athletic progress and found accomplished male players to hit with the eager little girl. He also served as Papa's assistant in training and conditioning Suzanne. Finally, the resident professional of the Nice Tennis Club, J. Negro, worked regularly with her. Because of his uncanny ball control, Negro was a particularly valuable addition to the Lenglen team. Negro's game was full of tricks and surprises, spins and slices. One amazed spectator concluded of Negro's abilities: "If you told me he could make the ball sit up and beg, I wouldn't be the least bit surprised." Negro was nothing less than a sorcerer of tennis, and little Suzanne became his studious apprentice.

Papa insisted that Suzanne master every maneuver and every shot, that there not be even a hint of a weakness in any part of her game. When a difficult stroke troubled the little girl, Papa worked on it with her for days or weeks, analyzing and practicing until the problem was solved. Late in her career Suzanne recalled that during those early training days on the Riviera the backhand return straight down the line rather than cross court had once given her real problems. She practiced the shot over and over again, but just could not execute it effectively. She telegraphed the shot or hit it long or patted it back weakly. She started to avoid the shot, to play around it, but Papa refused to let her. She must not just learn the shot, he insisted, she must perfect it! Suzanne resorted to tantrums and tears to resist, but Papa prevailed. Suzanne learned it and practiced it until it became one of the many deadly strokes in her arsenal. The shot was particularly effective when Suzanne fired it from a half volley. Eventually she could announce with confidence: "A favorite shot of mine is the backhand drive down the line."

On occasion Papa told the truth about Suzanne's strenuous training. "It was necessary for my daughter to do an enormous amount of work before she could show any appreciable results in playing with masculine methods," he wrote in 1926. "She had need of all her tenacity of purpose and all the help given her by her comrades at the Nice Club." At other times, however, he dismissed the time and effort that went into the making of his little athletic virtuoso and stressed instead Suzanne's natural genius and his own constant concern for his daughter's physical and emotional health. He said Suzanne had practiced on the courts of the Nice Club for just one hour each day. Such testimony, no doubt, was intended to enhance the myth of Suzanne by attributing her skills to nature rather than to hard work—a champion born, not made. God provided the raw skills, Papa merely polished them. But far too many had watched as Papa's little girl practiced to exhaustion to give credence to such stuff.

Many of those who watched Suzanne's practice sessions expressed dismay at the way Papa and Mama Lenglen callously utilized emotion to keep their daughter practicing and working and running hour after hour and day after day. When Suzanne did well, when she learned a stroke or maneuver quickly and correctly, Papa and Mama were happy and proud and expressed their approval and affection loudly. When Suzanne had trouble with a shot or was slow on getting into position or made unforced errors, Papa and Mama were quick to express their impatience and disgust with unrestrained volume. In the early days of her training, Suzanne's mistakes were punished by Papa's withholding a treat from her, such as jam with her tea. She was rewarded by treats also, just as a trainer might reward a dancing dog or a horn-playing seal. Papa quickly discovered much more severe and emotionally destructive ways to motivate his little girl. He assaulted and battered the child's self-esteem, ridiculed her in front of spectators, and reduced her to tears and hysterics. Following pandemics of deprecation he embraced and comforted her and sent her back onto the court for another try at winning his love by doing exactly what was expected of her. When Suzanne erred, Mama too openly expressed her dissatisfaction, hissing, "Stupid girl! Keep your eye on the ball!"

Love—the offering or the withholding of it—became the whip Papa snapped. Papa stressed the importance of practice and perfection. Suzanne was not working for herself alone, but for the family. When she failed, she failed Papa or Mama. When she failed, she did not deserve their love and affection or should she expect it. And so Papa advised, directed, teased, criticized, cajoled, denounced, decried, praised and condemned his little girl without ever seeming to be really aware of the pulverizing emotional effect of his methods. His critical, unforgiving eye followed her every move, missing no mistake. And while Suzanne's tennis skills flowered, her emotional growth was stunted. She became athletically formidable and emotionally tattered.

It was ironic that long after Suzanne Lenglen was almost universally acknowledged as the avatar of tennis perfection, she still lacked normal self-confidence. She remained morbidly afraid of failure. She trumpeted self-assurance but there was a parchment-thin quality to that assurance. Just beneath the surface of her certitude was a fear of failing that stemmed not from reality but from childhood conditioning. The person who doubted Suzanne most was Suzanne. At any moment she might become the terrified child clutching for the daddy who might not be there. Her emotional structure was neither strong nor resilient, but a crystal web easily fractured. And time after time the servomechanism that made her nerves and muscles work in harmony went crazy for no good reason.

Papa and Mama Lenglen kept up their criticism at courtside throughout Suzanne's amateur career. Englishman Ted Tinling, who officiated some of Suzanne's matches on the Riviera, recalled that "Papa and Mama Lenglen chattered incessantly on the bench below me," during one of Suzanne's matches. "At that age I spoke better French than English," Tinling wrote, "and my thoughts wandered repeatedly as I overheard, fascinated, their running commentary on Suzanne's every movement. 'She's not arching her back on her serve today,' from Papa Lenglen. 'I liked last year's cardigans without sleeves much better,' from Mama."

For many spectators this was but one part of the unusual ambience created by the presence of the Lenglens. Mama provided yet another daft aspect by her very physiognomy. Mama had such an acute astigmatism, according to Tinling, "that both eyes looked outward in opposite directions, saving her the need to turn her head when following Suzanne's shots during the million hours she spent clucking over her daughter from the sidelines."

For Suzanne there was but one escape from the rigid exhausting routine and the endless ridicule—a flight into illness. Early in her career she learned of the temporary respite to be gained over Papa and Mama through sickness or collapse. Only when she was clearly ailing did she receive rewards of sweet, unsolicited parental affection. As a result, from an early age, Suzanne enjoyed poor health. Only through illness could she slip away from the insistent tyranny of Papa, the tedious practice drills, and the tournaments.

By the early 1920s Suzanne was clearly neurasthenic. And when her physical health really did deteriorate, it became impossible for fans or officials to distinguish between her idiopathic behavior and more serious maladies. At times this led to cruelly unfair criticism of her behavior on and off the tennis courts, which only deepened her fears and uncertainties.

Papa cautiously managed Suzanne's career the way one might guide a promising young boxer up through the ranks of more experienced competitors. She was entered in selected local tournaments, where she won more than she lost. But, win or lose, she always learned. She won the regional championship of Picardy in singles and in doubles in 1912 and went on to win several other local championships. She maintained at the time certain disconcerting childish mannerisms. At the Picardy championships, for example, one of her opponents refused for a while to play against a child who spent her time off the court not in watching other matches or practicing ground strokes but in galloping around on the lawns attracting birds by imitating their calls.

In 1913 Suzanne Lenglen was the surprise winner of the club championship of the Nice Tennis Club. She was then selected as the representative of the club in a match against the Italian Bordighera Club. In Italy, Mama Lenglen was greeted as the representative of the Nice Club and was directed to the dressing room. To the disbelief of the tournament officials, the diminutive Suzanne was then introduced as the actual French competitor; then to their dismay and delight, she won match after match. By the end of the summer of 1913, English travelers were returning from the Riviera with incredible stories about the young tennis thaumaturge they had watched shellac veteran players on the French and Italian clay.

In early 1914 Papa entered Suzanne in the Carlton Club tournament in Cannes for her first real test against top women's competition. She breezed through to the finals, where she outlasted Mrs. R. J. Winch, a ranking English player and a Wimbledon veteran. Lenglen and her partner, the legendary Anthony Wilding, took the mixed doubles title in the tournament.

During the course of her long three-set match against Mrs. Winch, an incident occurred that Papa was fond of describing. At the beginning of the final set Suzanne seemed exhausted, and she told Papa that she could not continue. It was not the first time that the little girl would ask her Papa to allow her to leave the court. And it was not the first time that he absolutely refused. Instead of providing permission to default, Papa provided Suzanne with stern words of warning and encouragement and reminded her that her opponent was also tired. According to Papa, Suzanne concluded before returning to the court: "Then it is not good tennis, it is courage that will win this match." That was the true spirit of Suzanne, Papa pointed out. Courage. And in the end Suzanne's superior courage had indeed brought her the victory. She was not just the best tennis player in the world, she was also the most courageous.

The fall of Mrs. Winch to the little French girl caused a flurry of excitement in tennis circles both on the Continent and in England. The directors of the Carlton Club frankly admitted that they believed Suzanne Lenglen had faced an impossible task in her fight against Mrs. Winch. But Suzanne was now making a habit of winning impossible contests. And all of France was beginning to take notice.

Following her surprising Riviera victory, Suzanne Lenglen traveled to Saint-Cloud for the World Hard Court Championships at the Stade Français. She celebrated her fifteenth birthday at the tournament. Many spectators who now got their first glimpse of the rising star were enthralled by her. Suzanne seemed to stand no taller than her tennis racket, yet she managed to win match after match. And after each victory the crowds delighted in seeing the talented child skip excitedly into the proud embrace of her Papa. English correspondent A. Wallis Myers noticed that during each match Papa and Mama Lenglen sustained Suzanne "by communicating their own partisanship to her youthful spirit." Myers also found that Suzanne's movement across the court was already extraordinarily fluid. She was, he wrote, "a child of the bounding stride who defied ordinary mobility." At Saint-Cloud, Suzanne won world titles in singles and doubles and placed second with her partner in mixed doubles. After that it was clear that she was fast becoming the most popular sports personality in France. To the public she now became the amazing "Bébé Peugot." She was, others suggested, the reincarnation of the fifteenth-century Lady Margot, who came to Paris from the country of Hainault in 1427, and who was a master of *jeu de paume,* a primitive form of tennis, which she played far better than any man. Her reputation for skill in the sport was so great, in fact, that she was invited to play before the royal court of Scotland. There, thanks to her exceptional control and versatility in stroke production, she handily defeated every one of her male opponents. At the time of her visit to Scotland, Margot was but fifteen. Now at the age of fifteen it seemed that Suzanne might match Margot's feat by crossing the English Channel to challenge the best English tennis players at Wimbledon.

But Papa Lenglen refused. Suzanne was not ready yet for the fast grass courts of England, he believed. Wimbledon would have to wait one more year. Papa had seen Dorothea Lambert Chambers, winner of six Wimbledon singles titles, when she played on the Riviera. She was a big, powerful, and tireless woman and a superb court tactician, a master of the backcourt game. This year she would be seeking her seventh Wimbledon singles title, and surely she would overpower Papa Lenglen's little girl. This was not Suzanne's year. She needed more practice and more experience. To push her at this time against a woman so clearly her superior on grass might do irreparable damage to her frail self-confidence and jeopardize her future.

At Wimbledon that year the indomitable Mrs. Lambert Chambers won her seventh singles title, just as Papa expected. Then, even before summer's end, the Great War began in Europe, and Papa's plans for Suzanne's athletic triumphs were postponed indefinitely. The international tournaments at Saint-Cloud and Wimbledon were suspended from 1915 through 1918. These were good years in Suzanne's development, years when she had the stamina and the youthful energy and desire to play and to win. Her health was never better. Later, although they seldom discussed it with others, the Lenglens realized that the wartime hiatus had robbed Suzanne of the chance to capture several national and international titles. In the absence of the big tournaments, however, there was little that Suzanne could do but practice and wait and dream and regret.

In these years legends concerning Suzanne's dedication to France were formulated by the Lenglens for later distribution. One account of the Lenglens' life during the war years indicated that even the Germans recognized and admired Bébé Peugot. During the German invasion of the Oise, Suzanne left the family home and wandered curiously into the street. A German officer stopped and saluted her. "You are little Suzanne, unless I am mistaken," he said in halting French. After Suzanne confirmed her identity, the officer warned, "I beg you to leave immediately while there is time." And so Suzanne hurried home with the alarm. Her trophies were buried to keep them from falling into enemy hands, and the Lenglens retreated to their villa on the Riviera for the duration of the war.

Later, by way of emphasizing Suzanne's patriotic fervor, Mama and Papa insisted that during the war years Suzanne, like all good daughters of France, had been very concerned with the military situation. She played tennis, they "admitted," perhaps only a dozen times between 1914 and 1918, but she spent most of the time during those years knitting socks or rolling bandages for the soldiers.

There was, of course, disagreement with this account. Observers on the Riviera noticed that Suzanne appeared to practice continually during the war years with a routine even more rigorous than before. From early morning until late afternoon she was seen drilling and practicing her strokes and footwork on the courts of the Nice Tennis Club. The war years on the Riviera provided her with an unusual advantage. Soldiers from Australia, England, America, and the Continent convalesced there, and among them were some of the premier players of the world, many of whom played in exhibition matches for the Red Cross. Included among the exhibition players were Richard Norris Williams, the American singles champion, and Clarence "Peck" Griffin, the national doubles champion.

Suzanne watched the servicemen's tournaments and played in some of the exhibition matches with the American and English players. All of those who hit with her were impressed by her precocious expertise, and they returned to their native countries with still more stories of the Riviera darling who danced her way through matches, who kept the ball in play indefinitely until her opponent made an error, the little girl who understood all of the fine points of the game, whose mind comprehended every nuance of strategy and tactics, who was court-wise as no other woman, who hit the ball and covered the court like a man, and whose father was always at courtside encouraging, beseeching, cajoling, and criticizing her. Griffin and Williams were so struck by the young prodigy that they returned to America saying they believed she might beat several of the men ranked among America's top ten players.

Following the war, Europe and America were caught up in a sports mania, and Suzanne Lenglen quickly became a dramatic focal point for the enthusiasm. She undoubtedly benefited from the new interest in sports and also nurtured it by demonstrating her own unique athletic talents. In 1919 the world was at last ready for her.

In describing the temper of the postwar world, Arthur Wallis Myers wrote that "when the Prussian heel was raised there was discovered below, so it seemed, an athlete in embryo." French athletes led the way in the revival of competitive sport, but the epidemic eventually affected every nation in the Western world. In *The Nation*, writer Ida Treat discussed the athletic renaissance and wrote that "the nations have not lost their war psychology: they have carried it over into their sports. France, always the frankest of nations, shows this with greater clearness than other, more reticent countries." Some writers concluded that sport had become literally the extension of war athletically. "Sport today is national as war is; it is even more chauvinistic." And this seemed true even if the athletic opponent had only a few months earlier been an ally. For these sporting wars were even more nationalistic than the shooting ones because there were no alliances or balances of power. Each nation now stood alone.

In this newly charged competitive atmosphere, Suzanne Lenglen's athletic prowess became of great national importance. The French government encouraged athletic competition for French women, and Suzanne stood as the living example of the ideal to be pursued. Sports and athletics were introduced into school programs for girls. The idle comfortable lives lived by so many French women for decades, lives "without adequate physical development," were condemned by hygienists and nationalists. The endemic invalidism and nervousness of French women were attributed to physical inactivity which was "harmful to the race." Competitive athletics for women was no longer repugnant but rather was absolutely necessary for the resurgence of the nation. The inevitable result of strenuous athletic activity, according to government officials, would be "a healthy, intelligent womanhood."

Suzanne and Papa were ready for Wimbledon in 1919. For the Lenglens the tournament was vested with more importance than any of Suzanne's previous contests. It was to be a test not only of the thousands of hours of practice, but also a vindication of Papa's theories about the capabilities of a woman in sport. It was also to be a vindication of the French nation. Out of the carnage and waste of the war might now arise a powerful and glorious phoenix who could embody the soaring spirit that was France itself. A nation hungry for heroics turned its eyes across the Channel as its little champion prepared for her greatest test. Papa did not want Suzanne to falter at this critical juncture of her career. He was spared that annoyance.

Years of stories about the wonders of the little French girl had aroused great popular curiosity about her in England. For the first time in the history of the All-England Lawn Tennis Club spectators were turned away at the gate. Commander George Hillyard, secretary of the club, noticed that there was suddenly "a phenomenal interest in her play and in her personality. It did not seem to matter against whom she played or where, it was all the same to the crowd. It was necessary to put as many of her matches as possible on the Centre Court, for when she played on another court, eager and careless spectators trampled the shrubbery to get a closer look at her."

Little Suzanne was attired like most of the other women on the courts for the 1919 Lawn Tennis Championships. She wore a mid-calf length white cotton skirt, a short-sleeved middy blouse, and a small wide-brimmed bonnet to protect her from the sun. Only in her style of play did she distinguish herself.

Gate receipts at the All-England Club increased dramatically with Suzanne's appearance, and the club became the first of countless tennis organizations to cash in grandly on the appeal of the new wonder woman. Even as Lenglen played her way through the 1919 Wimbledon tournament, club officials launched new plans for building larger tennis facilities to accommodate the new masses of tennis fans.

In 1919 Suzanne Lenglen had her first chance to demonstrate her invincibility to the general public in England. There were still many skeptics who doubted the stories of her expertise and, as a result, this was to be the only Wimbledon tournament in which Suzanne had to face opposition from players who were not yet afraid of her. The defending Wimbledon singles champions still played only in the Challenge Round of the tournament in 1919. The other players fought their way through preliminary qualifying rounds, while the defending champion stood aside waiting to see who might emerge victorious from the pack. In this year, Dorothea Lambert Chambers watched warily as Lenglen stroked her way toward the defending champion and the Challenge Round. Suzanne proceeded without much difficulty through the early rounds of the tournament, but faced a real test in her semifinal match against Elizabeth Ryan, an American who made her home in England. Although Ryan had never won a singles title at Wimbledon—and she never would, although she eventually captured nineteen doubles titles there—she was a determined and deadly challenger. Ryan took four games in the opening set of their match, and the enthusiastic partisan applause indicated that the crowd was with the veteran player. In the second set Suzanne stayed in control until she reached 5–2 and double match point. At that moment Ryan displayed unusual tenacity and battled back. She not only saved the match points and took the game, she then went on to win her own service and broke Lenglen's to pull to five-all. Suzanne was clearly shaken by Ryan's resistance and resurgence. She had lost the momentum in the match. A suspicion arose that she was like all other players—she could be beaten. The acknowledgment was something neither Suzanne nor Papa could face. The eleventh game of the match went to 30–30 before play was halted by rain.

The match was postponed for one hour and during the suspension of play Suzanne listened to one of Papa's dithyrambs, an interesting blend of encouragement, analysis, and threat. When play resumed, Ryan's attack seemed to have lost its edge, while Lenglen hit with renewed resolve. She quickly took two games and the match.

Referee Burrow commented on the match, "I was sorry for Miss Ryan; she made a grand fight; and if that rain had not come when it did, I think she might well have stopped Suzanne's career." But that rain did come when it did, and Suzanne was granted the chance to renew her strength and her concentration. Even nature, it appeared, conspired to favor the little sorceress.

During the preliminary matches Papa was always at courtside observing, analyzing, directing, giving hand signals to Suzanne, and impatiently calling out directions that she never failed to heed. When she changed courts, the youngster looked at Papa as he formed words with his lips or made exaggerated gestures indicating that this or that tactic should be pursued. His intercession and advice were often distracting to those on or near the court, yet no one interrupted the earnest and intense efforts of the man. Nobody asked him to shut up.

After easily dispatching an English opponent in the preliminary final, Suzanne Lenglen at last faced Mrs. Lambert Chambers in the Challenge Round. The match stands in the memory of many veteran Wimbledon spectators as the greatest and most exciting women's final ever played.

"Nobody who saw it will ever forget this match," Burrow remembered. "I say without hesitation that I have never seen a finer since." "People who had watched at Wimbledon for several years said that they would never have believed that women could play such tennis," he said. And correspondent Arthur Wallis Myers wrote that it was "the greatest Ladies' Challenge Round in the history of lawn tennis."

In 1919 Mrs. Lambert Chambers had an unparalleled Wimbledon record. She had won seven singles titles and was favored to take an unprecedented eighth in this tournament. Although she was forty years old, twice Suzanne's age, that statistic was deceptive. By 1919 rules Mrs. Lambert Chambers had not been required to play through the tournament. She played a single match, the Challenge Round. Consequently, those tiring preliminary competitions became a great equalizer. On a single afternoon before a partisan English crowd Mrs. Lambert Chambers could concentrate her effort and determination and play like one twenty years younger while still having the advantage of years of championship match experience. Under such circumstances a woman of forty might seem indecently untouched by time.

Mrs. Lambert Chambers's game was comfortingly traditional. She still used the underhand service. And she was a baseliner who won points through accurate groundstrokes delivered from the outer edge of the squared turf. She hit hard and her passing shots were deadly. But now for the first time in her competitive career she faced a superb, resourceful, energetic young woman who was terrified of losing.

The 1919 Challenge Round was played on a perfect tennis day. There was no wind, the sky was slightly overcast, and the temperature was comfortably mild. A crowd of more than 8000 highly animated enthusiasts—among them the King and Queen and Princess Mary, Lord Curzon and Admiral Beatty—filled the gallery around the Centre Court.

In the opening game Lenglen was clearly skittish. She played a defensive game and seemed more than anything else determined not to lose. But she did lose, dropping her own service at love. Mrs. Lambert Chambers, it seemed, was playing her best, hitting long drives deep to the corners and covering the court well with her loping stride and the self-assured authority that befit someone with seven Wimbledon singles titles.

In the second game Lenglen found her range, and the timidity she betrayed in the opening game evaporated. She broke her opponent's service, won her own, broke again, and held her own again. She smiled through this four-game streak as if to communicate to the audience, "Here is the pace I enjoy. Here is beautiful length against which I have practiced on the Continent. Here is the greatest crowd to please." But then at 4–1 Mrs. Lambert Chambers surged back. She reduced the Lenglen lead to a single game and broke her service in the seventh game, as in the first, at love.

In losing her own service a second time Suzanne Lenglen revealed a tactical weakness in her game attributable, no doubt, to overconfidence. She came to the net to volley at inopportune moments, following in weak approach shots. She was consequently passed cleanly several times while making leaps with both grace and desperation, but leaps that did not get her racket into position to block the Englishwoman's long low drives. By utilizing a bit more caution, Suzanne won the eighth game and then surged ahead to set point in the ninth.

At that point Mrs. Lambert Chambers shifted the pace of her game and chopped some extremely effective drop shots over the net, which upset her opponent's timing. The English champion then managed to pull herself out of a desperate situation, take the ninth game, and hold her own service in the tenth game to pull even at 5–5.

For a few minutes Lenglen appeared shaken by the new tactical ploy of her opponent. Again she became reckless and followed several weak approach shots to the net. Mrs. Lambert Chambers fired back a fusillade of effective passing shots and took the lead at 6–5. In the twelfth game Mrs. Lambert Chambers moved to set point. But Lenglen found her own range again and delivered a series of well-placed volleys to save the point and the game. She then won her own service in the thirteenth game.

While changing courts after the thirteenth game, Lenglen hesitated near the umpire's chair to exchange words with Mama. No bystanders understood the rapid exchange of expletives, but the effect clearly was to break Suzanne's concentration. She dropped the next game at love. She again held her own service in the fifteenth game, and Mrs. Lambert Chambers held hers in the sixteenth. Then, in a final energetic surge, Lenglen held her own service one more time in the seventeenth game and broke Mrs. Chambers in the eighteenth to win the first set, 10–8.

If Suzanne and Papa had expected the lanky antique defending champion to fade in the second set they were unpleasantly surprised. Mrs. Lambert Chambers continued to hit with the same pace and accuracy as in the first set. It was, in fact, Lenglen who appeared to fade now. She gave up coming to the net at all and tried to rest in the backcourt and to win points off her ground strokes alone. At the same time she lost confidence in her service and double-faulted several times. Suzanne manifested her increasing distress by giving Papa pathetically dolorous glances after each point, unmistakable adumbrations of impending doom. Papa glared back at her, fidgeting in his seat, strangling his umbrella and occasionally pounding it against the ground whenever Mrs. Chambers scored. He maintained a constant *sotto voce* monologue and now and then flashed frantic signals to Suzanne.

As the two women changed courts at the end of the fifth game, Papa suddenly stood up and tossed a small vial out onto the apron of the court—an unprecedented action. Perhaps because this had never happened before, and everyone seemed a bit confused by exactly what was taking place, no official intercepted the object. Suzanne bent down and retrieved the vial, opened it, and sipped from it. Then she deposited it at courtside near the umpire's chair. Following the match reporters were told that the vial contained a sugar solution. But Suzanne and Papa still later said that it contained Suzanne's special stimulant—iced and sugared cognac. With the potion Suzanne clearly drank in renewed resolve, and the effect was dramatic. From the 1–4 deficit Suzanne evened the score at 4–4. But then the spell wore off, and Mrs. Lambert Chambers took two more games and with them the second set.

At one set each the momentum of the match appeared to have swung back to the defending champion. The second set had, ironically, inspired rather than tired Mrs. Chambers. She was now both energetic and anxious for the third set to get under way. Lenglen, on the other hand, now seemed completely exhausted. She requested and received more cognac from Papa. Then she asked a linesman to give up his chair so that she might sit for a moment. She remained seated for longer than the allotted time and had to be summoned back onto the court by Mrs. Lambert Chambers. She rose slowly and painfully, as though she had to lift a large weight with her shoulders. Then she walked to the baseline to continue this ordeal, head down, with all of the enthusiasm of a woman on her way to the gallows.

Once play started in the third set Suzanne Lenglen again drew renewed vitality from her cognac. She took a 4–1 lead. Each point was particularly intense now, and each game went to deuce. Then Suzanne's strength again gave out, while Mrs. Lambert Chambers remained strong as ever. To the accompaniment of enthusiastic shouting and applause, Mrs. Lambert Chambers took the sixth, seventh, eighth, and ninth games to lead at 5–4. Lenglen struggled and won the tenth game to even the score at 5–5.

The crowd had become so animated and demonstrative now that the referee called out for silence after each point. Even the royal family was uncharacteristically caught up in the suspense and drama of the match, smiling and talking to others and thoroughly enthralled by this incomparable contest.

Mrs. Lambert Chambers won the eleventh game and then jumped out to double match point in the thirteenth game. On the next point Lenglen came to the net behind a deep drive that pulled Mrs. Lambert Chambers far beyond the baseline. The Englishwoman responded with a strong, sharply angled cross-court shot that seemed clearly a winner. The shot should have ended the match. But it didn't. Suzanne lunged desperately for the ball and touched it with the wooden tip of her racket. The ball fluttered over the net like a wounded bird, dropped to the turf, and died. Mrs. Lambert Chambers remained unruffled and went for the second match point with iron-willed determination. But after a short rally Lenglen suddenly blasted a perfectly disguised backhand drive down the line that left Mrs. Lambert Chambers standing flatfooted in the middle of the baseline ("A favorite shot of mine is the backhand drive down the line"). The French girl continued to assert herself now, pressing Mrs. Chambers, keeping her far beyond the baseline. All the shots that should have won for the Englishwoman kept coming back. Suzanne took the twelfth game and then won the thirteenth to take the lead. She was strong and confident again, dancing over the grass, dashing to the net, returning everything Mrs. Lambert Chambers dished out. The fourteenth and final game Suzanne Lenglen took at love. (The match had required 44 games— a record that stood until 1970, when Margaret Court beat Billie Jean King in 46 games.)

At the completion of the final point of the match Suzanne Lenglen swept off her sunbonnet and ran toward the net to shake hands with the former champion. A French partisan galloped across the court to embrace Suzanne, and Papa and Mama Lenglen danced out to kiss and caress their victorious child. Observing the hoopla, Arthur Wallis Myers wrote that "the deliverance of France's lost provinces did not produce stronger emotion than the deliverance of Suzanne from what looked like certain defeat."

After the match each player expressed satisfaction in the way she had played. Mrs. Lambert Chambers, in fact, insisted that she had never played better tennis in her life. Years later, though, she confessed to a friend that she considered the match a tragedy for both herself and Suzanne. Tragic for herself, she said, because she was twice deprived, by a single stroke, of her eighth Wimbledon title. But tragic also for Suzanne Lenglen, because the victory brought with it a taste of invincibility "and a subsequent compulsion for it, which brought endless sacrifices and unnatural unhappiness, out of all proportion to the rewards of her fame."

But for the moment the victory was to be savored. Suzanne had won an extremely difficult match, had surged from almost certain defeat with double match point against her. Could anyone now possibly doubt Papa's assertions? He said that Suzanne would win, and he said she was courageous, and he said she was the greatest tennis player in the world. Now the world knew. Suzanne Lenglen was the first Gallic invader to win the singles title at Wimbledon—the first non-English-speaking champion. A. Wallis Myers wrote that her victory proved to the world at large "that France possessed the will to conquer."

A star was born at Wimbledon in 1919, and it was obvious that the sponsors of the prestigious competition had a show-business bonanza on their hands. Never before had there been such crowds at the All-England Club. Never before had there been such enthusiasm and excitement. There was a tennis revolution on the horizon. A revolution for women in sports was under way. In the past there had been toleration of the women on the Centre Court. No longer. Now they were welcome.

Following the fall of Mrs. Lambert Chambers the British press took Suzanne to its heart. Typical of the comments was that of A. E. Crawley, who wrote, "I have never seen on a lawn tennis court either man or woman move with such mechanical and artistic perfection and poise.

Whether her objective is the ball or merely changing sides, she reminds you of the movement of fire over prairie grass." "She serves with all the male athlete's power," Crawley found. "She smashes with the same loose and rapid action, the release of a spring of steel. Her volley is not a timid push, but an arrow from the bow. And an arrow from the bow is Suzanne herself." She was "The Diana of Tennis."

Other reporters wanted to know about Lenglen's method of play. Suzanne replied, "My method? I don't think I have any. I just throw dignity to the winds and think of nothing but the game. I try to hit the ball with all my force and send it where my opponent is not."

The triumph provided her with a tremendous psychological boost and gave her self-confidence some much needed strength. She played now with new authority and panache. The next year she captured all three World Hard Court titles at Saint-Cloud. And when she appeared at Wimbledon in the late spring of 1920 to defend her title, she was a far different figure from the "little girl" who had played there in 1919. She had been transformed, almost miraculously. The transformation was Papa's idea. If Suzanne was really a goddess, he believed, then she must dress and act the part.

In 1919 Suzanne Lenglen had surprised only a few spectators by her modified costume—she wore neither the corset nor the thick undergarments that were part of the customary attire. In 1920 she made a liberating quantum leap in fashion and demonstrated for the first time her passion for appearances. She now had her own couturier, Jean Patou, and he had new ideas about women's fashions and women's sports. In place of the hat she had worn for protection from the sun the previous spring, Suzanne wore a bandeau of two yards of bright silk, fastened in front by a large diamond pin. In place of the long cotton skirt she had worn in 1919, she wore a short pleated silk skirt very much like that of a ballet dancer. The length—it fell just below her knees—was shockingly short for the times. She wore silk stockings that were rolled just above the knee. Over her sleeveless silk blouse she wore one or two light pastel sweaters color-coordinated with her bandeau. Her clothes were not merely stylish, they were functional. Papa and Patou had agreed on that. Suzanne was now much freer in her movement, less restricted, and literally less strait-laced than the other women. She was free to leap and to dance and to whirl and to win. Now she could display the style and the fluency that would, in the future, distinguish the genuine royalty of the court.

Off the court—in place of the sweatsuit of half a century later—Suzanne wore an oversized coat of white ermine or mink. The ermine was Papa's idea—denoting the royalty of his daughter, the Queen. No matter the temperature, Suzanne was seldom without her costly coat.

Lenglen also appeared on the courts now in full make-up, the first player to do so, and above her left elbow she wore a gold bracelet. She also popularized the healthy, tanned look as opposed to the porcelain white complexion favored earlier by the more genteel players.

The effect of all of this was dramatic. All the Victorian decorum of women's tennis was suddenly shattered by the French woman. Now, from the moment she made an appearance anywhere, Lenglen became the center of attraction, the radiant sun around which all other bodies seemed to orbit. Yet to many people there was something repulsive in all of this. It represented a marriage for the first time of show business and sport both on and off the court. Could this possibly be good for the game? Bill Tilden, the American champion, utterly loathed Suzanne Lenglen's attire and affectations. Upon seeing her in 1921 he reported that "her costume struck me as a cross between a prima donna's and a streetwalker. She wore a white fur cape over her white tennis costume and around her head a crimson band so flaming that I earnestly hoped no bull was in the neighborhood."

The Goddess had arrived.

In 1920 Suzanne and Papa declared their independence from more than traditional fashion and decorum. They asserted their freedom from the dictates of the French Tennis Federation, an organization controlled by men of little vision who simply did not appreciate the strivings and aspirations and agenda of the Lenglens. When the Federation insisted that Suzanne play with one of her countrymen in the mixed doubles at Wimbledon, Suzanne replied that she wished to be paired instead with the Australian Gerald Patterson. In order to get its way, the Association threatened to withhold sponsorship of Suzanne's trip to Wimbledon. Suzanne and Papa reacted by refusing to accept the sponsorship and instead financed their own trip. Lenglen, partnered with Patterson, won the doubles title, and the French Tennis Federation learned a lesson. In the future it would bend more readily to Suzanne's requirements when they saw it was necessary.

As the defending singles champion in 1920, Suzanne Lenglen had only to play in the Challenge Round. Consequently, she stood aside while a score of contenders battled for the privilege of facing her. Dorothea Lambert Chambers, who managed impressive wins over both Elizabeth Ryan and the American champion Molla Mallory, earned the right to play Lenglen again for the singles crown. But playing through the crowd of contenders had taken a severe physical toll on the English veteran. She had no chance at all against Lenglen now. In an uneventful and unexciting match, the French girl successfully defended her title and won the Challenge Round in straight sets, 6–3, 6–0. She also repeated her win in the women's doubles with Elizabeth Ryan and triumphed in the mixed doubles with Patterson.

From Wimbledon, Suzanne and Papa proceeded to Antwerp to represent France in the tennis competition of the Olympic Games. There she won the gold medal in women's singles, losing only four of the sixty-four games she played. At the Olympic Games, Suzanne introduced herself to newsmen without hesitation or embarrassment as "the Great Lenglen," a title everyone seemed willing to concede to her. She was in a class all her own now, and in France they were starting to say that not only was no one her equal, but there was no one who should even be ranked second to her. And in subsequent French tournaments in which Suzanne Lenglen was an entrant, while other women were ranked, after Suzanne's name was the term *hors classe,* or beyond classification. American journalists often had fun with the term, playfully altering the pronunciation of it and then suggesting, with their American twist, that it also aptly described Suzanne's style of dress and behavior.

In 1921 the English adored Suzanne Lenglen almost as much as their own players. They responded ecstatically when she appeared on the tennis court. Hoi polloi wanted to see only her. Long lines formed outside the tournament grounds on the mornings when she was scheduled to play, and the lines were soon referred to as the "Lenglen trail-a-winding." Suddenly there were droves of common folk who elbowed their way into the club grounds, who came to watch her play, watch her run, watch her dance, watch her win, hear her laugh, and then to dream of her after she had gone. The English now referred to her as "The Pavlova of Tennis" and swooned at the familiar lilt and float and flow of her movements.

The world was suddenly a wonderful place for the Lenglens. There seemed no end in sight for Suzanne's lengthening list of conquests. She marched through the Riviera tournaments in early 1921 with her usual dominance. She won every contest she entered and gave up only a game or two along the way.

At Saint-Cloud in 1921 Suzanne Lenglen experienced for the first time the unusual and unwarranted animosity of Americans. The United States Lawn Tennis Association (USLTA) had sent Big Bill Tilden and Molla Mallory to the French tournament as a friendly gesture in the hope that the French Tennis Federation would reciprocate and send Lenglen to America in late summer. Before the tournament Lenglen ventured by the practice courts and sat to watch Tilden practice against Mallory. Lenglen was completely unaware at the time that Tilden, who was upset by what he considered to be the outlandish newspaper reports describing Suzanne's athletic skill, was spoiling for a match with her. "Some amazing and ridiculous statements had been printed," Tilden said, "holding that Suzanne was equal or superior to any man playing tennis." He wanted to end such speculation as soon as possible. Now with Lenglen he saw his chance. "I was hitting rather badly and the thought came to me that if I looked enough off my game, Suzanne might ask me to play her," Tilden recalled. "I proceeded to be really lousy and sure enough, Suzanne called on me."

Word spread quickly through the grounds that Suzanne Lenglen was going to play a set against "Beeg Beel." The reporters arrived *en masse* to witness the fireworks.

"As I look back at it I am not particularly proud of the fact that with deliberate intent and quite mercilessly I opened up and ran six straight games to win 6-0," Tilden wrote later. "But at the time it seemed the only way to settle once and for all the relative ability of the top women and the top men."

When the six games were over, Tilden sweetly asked Suzanne, "Will you play another?"

"No!" she responded. "You hit too hard."

The reporters rushed on to the court to question Lenglen. She answered their questions by stating, "Yes, Mr. Tilden and I played, but whether he won six games or I did, I really don't know."

Suzanne Lenglen was given the opportunity for revenge in an indirect way when she played against Tilden's close friend Molla Mallory in the finals at Saint-Cloud. Suzanne made the tournament the most popular in France. Tickets for the tournament rose to 500 francs, and 5000 potential spectators were turned away after the tournament had been sold out. Mallory was not at her best in France, where the slow clay courts and the soft tennis balls neutralized her power. Lenglen studied the American champion's style through the week of the tournament and concluded that, if she merely returned Mallory's shots, Mallory would find some way to beat herself. But just before Suzanne entered the court to play, Tilden walked up to her and announced, "No woman in the world can beat Mrs. Mallory today!" Suzanne turned on him and snapped back, "America had its day yesterday! This is France's day." And she was right. Suzanne Lenglen beat Molla Mallory in straight sets, 6-2, 6-3. Then she took the trouble to explain to reporters that she had given up five games only because she was having trouble with her shoes. Halfway through the first set her feet had begun to slip in her shoes, and she had developed blisters. Her mobility and concentration had suffered severely because of the pain.

In fact, Suzanne Lenglen was in deeper trouble than she later acknowledged during the second set against the American titleholder. Each player held her service through the first five games of the set. Then in the sixth game Mallory moved to break point against Lenglen and was close to a 4–2 lead with her own serve coming up. Lenglen realized that she was in jeopardy. Her confidence began to waver, and she looked to Papa in the bleachers for help. He glared back at her and said nothing. She then stopped the game and complained about her feet. She hobbled slowly to the umpire's chair, Tilden believed, "with the obvious intent of defaulting." But Papa would have none of it. He jumped to his feet and roared loudly enough for everyone to hear, "Go back and finish! Go back and finish or I'll disinherit you!" Suzanne gave a long rueful look to Papa and then turned and walked back onto the court. She served slowly and without much spirit. But her own hesitation caused Mallory to miscalculate. The American now went rather carelessly for outright winners on every shot. And in so doing she upset her own timing and lost her touch. She smashed with all of her might, trying to put everything away. Everything she hit went long. Had Mallory merely managed to keep the ball in play, Tilden concluded, she certainly would have shattered Lenglen's deflated confidence. But she did not keep the ball in play and so lost three straight points and with them the game. Lenglen went on to win the remaining games of the set and saved herself from not only defeat but disinheritance.

Following the match, though, Molla Mallory told Tilden, "Bill, I can beat her! The next time I play her I'll beat her!"

Mallory expected to get her second chance against Lenglen at Wimbledon that summer, but was eliminated in an early round by Elizabeth Ryan. In the Challenge Round, Lenglen defeated Ryan in routine fashion, 6–2, 6–0, before a capacity crowd that included the royal family, now all fans of the Goddess. The match was disappointing to spectators because of the ease with which Suzanne defeated her opponent. After the match Lenglen teamed up with Ryan to win the women's doubles.

By the summer of 1921 Suzanne Lenglen's dominance of women's tennis was complete. There appeared to be no woman in the world capable of really testing her. Her opponents were becoming more and more merely gracious victims incapable of providing the proper foil for the goddess. As a result, several sportswriters suggested that the Frenchwoman compete against male opponents. One such appeal in the *New York Times* listed Lenglen's court victims and suggested that despite her unpromising showing against Tilden, she participate in the men's competition in select future tournaments. The writer recommended, in fact, that Suzanne enter the fortieth Lawn Tennis Championships for men at Forest Hills in late summer. No woman's name had ever before been entered in the tournament. On the other hand, there was no written rule preventing such an entry. Tradition alone stood in the way, and Suzanne Lenglen was one to shatter tradition. "Why should she not make the plunge?" the writer asked. "It is a new idea." And "even if she did not win the tournament," he concluded, "she would have at least tried something that no American woman has ever attempted."

Although Lenglen did not seriously entertain the idea of competing against the American men at Forest Hills, she was interested in playing against the American women there in 1921. America, after all, had not yet witnessed firsthand the wonders of the goddess. For Suzanne, America loomed like a last unconquered province. She wrote following her initial victory at Wimbledon in 1919, "I was thrilled with my success, yet I was not satisfied." She wanted more than the Wimbledon title of "World Champion." Since the USLTA did not subscribe to the agreement acknowledging Wimbledon winners as world champions, "I knew in my own heart that there was something I must do before I could feel satisfied that the title had been bestowed without a single string attached." Until she won the American championship, "America could properly question whether I was in reality a world champion." And so, "I knew I must come to America and meet your best players before the title was flawless—that is, flawless according to my notion of it." In the two years after 1919 she thought of little else, she insisted. And "all of the long hours of training, the constant practicing in the effort to improve" were made with the journey to America in mind. "It had been my one great inspiration."

Suzanne Lenglen's opportunity to play in America and fulfill her dream of an untarnished world title came soon after the completion of the 1921 Wimbledon tournament. Because of the adverse exchange rate at the time, the French Tennis Federation disclosed that it could not afford to send Suzanne to America and repay the courtesy of the USLTA in sending America's top players to the Hard Court Championships at Saint-Cloud. But then Anne Morgan, a sister of the younger J. P. Morgan and head of the American Committee for Devastated France, stepped forward with another proposal. She suggested that her committee finance Suzanne's voyage to America. In the United States, Lenglen could play a series of exhibition matches against some of the leading American women players. Proceeds from the ticket sales for the matches would pay for Lenglen's journey, and the remainder would be turned over to the French government to aid regions of France ravaged by the war. Morgan's proposal was accepted by both the French Tennis Federation and by the Lenglens. When news of the impending Lenglen visit was confirmed, Julian Myrick, president of the USLTA, announced that Lenglen's appearance was certain to "strengthen still further the bonds of friendship between the two nations." Nothing could have been further from the truth.

With the acceptance of the Morgan offer, American clubs began bidding for exhibition appearances by the European champion. The initial plans for her journey included departing from France on July 23 and playing in the American Women's Championship tournament at Forest Hills beginning on August 15 and then in the mixed doubles National Championships in Boston at Longwood on August 22. Other than those two national competitions she would play only in exhibition matches.

By mid-July so many requests for a Lenglen appearance had been made to the USLTA that it was clear only a small fraction of the organizations wishing to sponsor exhibitions could be accommodated. The USLTA thoughtfully arranged for all the exhibition matches prior to the Forest Hills tournament to be played on the grass courts in southern New England in order to eliminate the need for excessive travel by the French star and to allow her the chance to adjust to the surface on which the National Championships would be played. Her first match was scheduled for the Greenwich Field Club in Greenwich, Connecticut, her opponent to be either the fifth-ranked American woman Eleanor Goss or the second-ranked Marion Zinderstein Jessup. As soon as the announcement of the match was made, the Greenwich Club initiated construction of new bleachers to accommodate the large crowd expected. Ticket sales in New York and Connecticut were promisingly brisk, and the American public seemed to be as eager to see the Goddess as the French and the English had been.

Before any more exhibition matches could be arranged, complications arose. From France came an announcement that Lenglen's departure would be delayed until July 30. No reason was given. The announcement brought a readjustment of Lenglen's exhibition schedule and the cancellation of four exhibition matches, including the one in Greenwich.

Shortly after getting news of the postponement, the USTLA received a telegram from Anne Morgan informing them that Suzanne Lenglen was suffering from "serious indisposition caused by heat." In Europe, at the same time, Suzanne was telling friends that her illness was due to an attack of grippe which followed a swim in the cold ocean. The USLTA was also advised that Lenglen wished to play no exhibition matches prior to the Forest Hills tournament and that she would be accompanied on her journey to America by Mama Lenglen and Albert de Joannis, vice president of the French Tennis Federation. A brief apology accompanied the message.

But where was Papa? He had always been at courtside for Suzanne's matches, and his antics would certainly be an intriguing novelty for American audiences. How could Suzanne possibly compete in such an important tournament without Papa's advice and encouragement? There were unsubstantiated stories about a blowup in the Lenglen household. Papa had insisted that Suzanne cancel her tour, it was whispered. He had experienced a premonitory vision of catastrophe in America. Pressure was exerted by the French Tennis Federation and the American sponsors of the trip, it was alleged, and Suzanne agreed to travel, but Papa refused either to accompany her or to give his consent for the American adventure. Much later, it was said that Papa had secured from her a promise that she would not play in the Forest Hills tournament, scheduled to begin only a few days after her arrival. Yet the stories were of dubious credibility. They were given widespread circulation only after Suzanne's American visit. And they created a convenient villain for the American fiasco—the halpess Albert de Joannis. It was he who was responsible for pushing Lenglen into the Forest Hills tournament "against her better judgment," it was charged.

Yet the simple fact was that Papa, who disliked long ocean voyages, was not in good health. Long before Suzanne began her journey her name had been entered in the Forest Hills tournament. She said she expected to play there, and she expected to win without difficulty.

Following still further delays, Suzanne Lenglen departed for America on August 6. A special deck tennis court was installed on the luxury liner *Paris* especially for her practice during the voyage. Shortly after embarking on her journey, she wired friends that her indisposition had disappeared and that she was recovering nicely. She played tennis only once during the voyage and instead chose to keep fit by dancing nightly. She arrived in New York on August 13. "I was not superstitious then," she recalled later. "But now I believe in the bad luck of that number 13."

Suzan Lenglen was greeted in New York by an army of curious questioning reporters and a mob of spectators. Passengers who preceded her leaving the *Paris* announced that they had been overawed by her presence during the voyage. She was without question the dominating personality aboard ship. Men watched every move she made, and women tried to keep count of the different outfits she wore during the voyage.

When she finally stepped ashore reporters were surprised by Suzanne's size and appearance. A correspondent for the *New York Times* reported that she stood about 5 feet 10 inches in her heels and weighed perhaps 130 pounds. She was not particularly small, he found, "especially for a Frenchwoman." And when she was not speaking there was no suggestion at all of the athlete in her. But when she talked and moved there was "an alertness and a spring in her walk that made her seem unusual and perhaps athletic."

Lenglen announced immediately that she would play her first match at Forest Hills as scheduled, even though she had gone a month and eight days without playing serious tennis. When asked about her training she both delighted and shocked the reporters by confessing that she drank wine before each match "as a tonic." Then she revealed a shocker: as part of the agreement for her appearances in America, the USLTA had agreed, secretly, to see that all 18th Amendment prohibition regulations were waived by enforcement authorities so that she might consume alcoholic beverages before and during her matches. This is the only documented case in which an established respectable American sports group conspired to violate an amendment to the U.S. Constitution in order to assure the appearance of a star performer. Of course it was unusual and illegal. And of course Suzanne had no idea of the criminal lengths to which the gentlemen rulers of the USLTA had gone to get her to Forest Hills. And she appeared to believe that a conspiracy to violate the prohibition laws of the United States was really not an unusual act for gentlemen to commit if they wished to see the Great Lenglen. As to the virtues of wine, "nothing is so fine for the nerves, for the strength, for the morale," she told reporters. "A little wine tones up the system just right. One cannot always be serious. There must be some sparkle, too." Asked to describe her play in a single word, Suzanne Lenglen said after a pause, "Pep!"

When questioned about her matches in America and the possibility of playing Molla Mallory again, she said she looked forward to a rematch with the American champion. She was unhappy with the earlier contest, she confessed, because she had not been near top form in beating Molla. "I was not at my best because I had blisters on my feet," she again claimed. In fact, when she whipped Mallory her blistered feet hurt so much that "I was really not playing at all."

Her confidence impressed all those present. She seemed to have no doubt at all that she would simply waltz through any American opposition during her ten-week stay. She found it rather amusing that Americans feigned shock at her practice of predicting victory before her matches. Yet it was neither egotism nor false pride that inspired such predictions. "When I am asked a question I endeavor to give a frank answer. If I know I am going to win, what harm is there in saying so? Should I fail there is no one to suffer but myself. Never before in my life have I failed to say to some one, perhaps to my mother or father, that I would win."

Yet, when reporters asked directly if she would win at Forest Hills, Suzanne Lenglen refrained from a positive response. She said she was worried about her health. "I caught a violent cold in Paris before I sailed and I was seasick for three days after leaving Havre. I am eager to have everyone understand that I am not putting my alibi early when I say it would have been more pleasing to me had I been in perfect health at this time," Suzanne confided. "Just at the moment I was wavering about the trip here, I suffered a severe attack of bronchitis from which I have not entirely recovered. It is impossible for me to tell just how much this illness has affected me until I play a practice game tomorrow. I am hoping that it will amount to nothing and that I shall find my strength entirely sufficient to meet the exacting task I am facing."

Lenglen's disclaimers and warnings and her ambiguous attitude toward her American opposition were almost completely overlooked by reporters. She looked wonderful, they found. Certainly she could not be in less than perfect health. In subsequent weeks and years writers who detailed her American visit continued to ignore her clearly stated initial misgivings about her health. Ironically, despite cautionary statements regarding her health, Suzanne continued to exude both restrained and unrestrained confidence in her ability to win all of her matches in America. At one point she announced optimistically that, despite her imperfect health and her lack of familiarity with American grass surfaces, she fully intended to return to France with the Women's National Singles title! Her long string of tournament victories would be interrupted by no American player. Sick or healthy, she implied, she could beat any American woman.

Reporters discovered that she was almost blissfully unconcerned with the fact that her first opponent in the unseeded draw at Forest Hills would be America's fifth-ranked female player, Eleanor Goss. And by an unfortunate accident of the draw, in the second round she was scheduled to meet the defending American champion, Molla Mallory. USLTA officials were deeply disappointed by the draw that put their two stars opposite each other in the second round rather than in the final, but they confessed that there was nothing they could do about it. And Suzanne appeared unconcerned by the prospect. Her attitude seemed to be that any and all opponents were pretty much the same when she was on the court. Be it Mallory or someone else, all eyes, she felt sure, would be on the Great Lenglen alone.

Although her candor often seemed slightly carnivorous, most reporters found Lenglen enormously attractive. "Like her fellow countryman, Carpentier, you liked her instantly when you saw her," one of them wrote. And "the more she talked and gestured and acted the more you liked her. Rather than a great athlete, possibly the outstanding woman athlete of today, she appeared to be a little girl full of enthusiasm of life and the joy of living," it was discovered. In her appearance and demeanor was "the sparkle that is France. Seeing her, those who came to greet her caught some of the same spirit that caused an American crowd to cheer for Carpentier at Jersey City on July 2." Despite the American cheers for heavyweight boxer Georges Carpentier, however, the Frenchman had been knocked unconscious by Jack Dempsey.

The reception prepared for Suzanne Lenglen by the leading American female tennis players was hardly as warm as that of the newsmen. Journalist Al Laney found that the best American players had been called up "to repel this French invader." Her appearance, he wrote, "was considered not so much a friendly visit as an invasion by an enemy." From California, ex-champions May Sutton Bundy and Mary K. Browne had been summoned to New York to compete against the French visitor.

Lenglen's opening match at Forest Hills was scheduled for Tuesday, August 16. But shortly before the match was to begin her opponent, Eleanor Goss, defaulted. This was of more than passing importance since Lenglen needed the workout before facing the American champion in the second round. Several newspapermen immediately charged that Goss had been pressured to withdraw so that "the invader" would be forced to go up against Mallory with the additional handicap of never having played a single competitive match in America. Laney was one of the journalists who believed at the time that the Goss default was part of a premeditated strategy to bring Suzanne Lenglen down. And tennis historian Edward Potter recorded: "Miss Goss had been prevailed upon by the American committee to scratch."

The tournament committee, not wanting to deny the Tuesday ticket-holders the privilege of seeing Suzanne Lenglen play, scheduled her match against Molla Mallory for opening day. And although she/had whipped Mallory at Saint-Cloud while playing with blistered and bleeding feet, she now complained that Mallory was "in good health, she was used to the climate, and she had all the other players and the public as well, to support her." Lenglen began to sense that the Americans were ganging up on her, setting up an ambush. And Papa was not present to give encouragement and advice. Mallory, on the other hand, remembered later that both players had been consulted concerning the rescheduling and both had agreed to play on Tuesday. Lenglen had been given every opportunity to veto the rescheduling and had chosen to play.

On Monday, Suzanne Lenglen practiced against an American male player before a large gallery of interested spectators. Those who watched her noticed that she lacked the dash and the spirit—the "pep!"—that they expected to see. She seemed listless and even lackadaisical. Early Tuesday morning she warmed up for a short time with Sam Hardy, a California doubles specialist. Hardy also noticed that she did not seem "very keen" for the approaching match with Mallory, and he mentioned that fact to friends.

Lenglen was starting to have some serious doubts herself. She was haunted by the statement uttered to her by a gloating Bill Tilden after her defeat of Molla Mallory at Saint-Cloud: "Suzanne, she will beat you!" Tilden had warned. Tilden was present on this day, and Lenglen knew that he would like nothing better than to see her beaten badly—even humiliated—before the American crowd.

Tilden recounted that in the period before the big match on Tuesday, Mallory was eager and "straining at the leash" to get her revenge. An hour before the match, she was dressed and eager to play. "I managed to get her away from the crowd," Tilden said, "settling her in an armchair in the clubhouse in the corner where no one could reach her. There we sat and talked." Knowing Molla's temperament, Tilden reminded her of everything that Suzanne had said and done since their meeting in Saint-Cloud. He brought up certain Lenglen "eccentricities" that both he and Mallory found repulsive. And he repeated over and over again that no woman—not even Lenglen—had a chance against "Iron" Molla on this day. Tilden sensed Molla's increasing animosity and her resolve to win strengthening as he spoke. He did not let her move away until the match was announced. Then she stood, determined and confident and angered and walked to her dressing room to gather up her rackets.

Tilden proceeded to the porch of the clubhouse to await Mallory's return. There he found Suzanne Lenglen. "How are you, Suzanne?" he asked. "I am wonderful," Tilden remembered her reply, "with her usual modesty." And then she predicted for Tilden, "I'll beat her six love, six love." "No one can beat Molla," Tilden shot back. "Least of all you!" At that moment Mallory returned to the porch and asked "Are you ready?" Tilden thought that if Suzanne had possessed "the brains of a gnat" she would have read the unexpressed completion of the question, "for the licking I'm going to give you?"

While Molla Mallory had been in the clubhouse listening to Tilden's diatribe, Suzanne Lenglen had watched a very long and boring match between two women, a match that took until late in the afternoon to complete. And as she sat and watched, Al Laney wrote, "the rest of us watched her." He also realized that watching like that was hardly the proper preparation for her own match.

Although she exuded confidence in her pre-match exchange with Tilden, Lenglen had complained to a group of friends on the clubhouse porch only moments earlier that she did not feel equal to the occasion. She had passed a sleepless night and was bothered by the hacking cough that had troubled her since her arrival in America. Yet she said she was still willing to see this match through because she did not want to disappoint the crowd of 8000 that had waited throughout the long hot afternoon to see her play. "It is impossible for me to disappoint this crowd," she said. "I should feel that I had lured them here under false pretenses." Nobody disagreed with her at that moment.

Mama was worried, too. "Are you sure, Suzanne," she asked, "that you will be able to play the entire match if you start? It would be a calamity if you would have to stop after it started."

"I am going to play!" was Suzanne's terse reply.

But Mama said to those around her that she was sure that Suzanne would be unable to finish an entire match.

Journalist Arthur Wallis Myers described the ensuing match that he watched from a seat below the umpire's chair. Because of the length of the prior match, Myers recalled, play did not begin between Mallory and Lenglen until nearly 5:00 P.M.

Molla Mallory opened the set with her own service. Suzanne Lenglen seemed tired and heavy-footed and simply tapped back the returns. She lost the first game after taking but a single point, and then she dropped her own service at love. The crowd became somewhat restless and waited for Suzanne to spring to life and to display some of the fluency and panache so many newsmen rhapsodized over. Myers noticed from his courtside seat that Suzanne was having difficulty breathing. He realized that she was not well. She began to cough, clutched her throat and chest several times, and gave a concerned glance at Mama.

For a few minutes, Lenglen came alive, fought an extended rally and won a game. The coughing ceased. The crowd became a bit more animated. But then Mallory came right back and took two more games. Suzanne began coughing again; she was offered ice water and refused it. Despite the promises of the USLTA, there was no wine or iced cognac available at courtside as a tonic for the faltering Goddess.

Lenglen succeeded in winning one more game before dropping the opening set, 6–2. It was the only set she had lost in competitive singles since her 1919 Challenge Round match against Mrs. Lambert Chambers. Still, most of the crowd expected her to bounce right back, and the prevailing sentiment among the journalists was that this would now be a three-set match with Lenglen the victor.

Mallory had played that first set like a woman on fire. "I seemed to have wings on my feet," she remembered. She hit every ball with all of her strength and sent them deep into the corners where they fell in for winners. Her combination of power and accuracy kept Lenglen off balance and unable to get her game started. Mallory ended rally after rally with deadly unreturnable drives down the line. Her concentration was so complete that she lost sight of the score and became totally submerged in the play of each point.

By the end of the first set, Suzanne Lenglen had fallen into complete despair. Self-doubt had replaced self-confidence. Her nervous system was overheating and her fragile emotions were starting to disintegrate. Her mind and her muscles no longer worked smoothly together. She was confused, and she was frightened, and she lost confidence in all her shots. When she served the first ball of the second set, Mallory blasted it back for a winner. Then Lenglen served a double fault. She could no longer clear the net. And that ended the match. She paused for a moment and then walked slowly to the umpire's chair and whispered, "I cannot go on. I am really too ill."

Molla Mallory approached the chair, spoke a few words, hesitated a moment, and then ran slowly toward the clubhouse. No announcement was necessary. The crowd knew. Al Laney remembered that there was "a mild burst of applause for the American victory." Suzanne Lenglen collapsed for a moment in one of the judge's chairs while photographers rushed around her. Then she stood and was assisted by de Joannis across the court and toward the clubhouse. As she walked away the crowd remained seated, and there was "a faint but distinct hissing" from many spectators. Laney described it oxymoronically as "a polite sort of hissing," but he also knew that Suzanne Lenglen heard it and knew what it meant—to the American crowd Suzanne was a quitter. Leaving the stadium on that day Laney heard many spectators say "the nastiest things about Suzanne."

On the next morning the *New York Times* commented: "the affair may be summed up this way. Mlle. Lenglen was not herself in the match. She was ill and far from being 'Suzanne the Magnificent,' and she will not be content until she shows American tennis followers that she is capable of a better brand of tennis than she displayed." But most other news accounts were far less charitable. The consensus of sportswriters seemed to be that Suzanne quit when she found that she could not win. Many of them used a phrase that became a common American idiom in the following years—"cough and quit"—which meant to use bad health as an excuse for squirming out of a losing situation.

The Nation suggested that Suzanne Lenglen should have done "what was obviously difficult and perhaps impossible for her to do." If she had been willing to play out the set and "to take the thorough beating which was evidently to be hers, the gallery would have established its own alibis for her," and Mallory would have received no credit "for her brilliant playing and the French star would have twinkled more like a diamond in the sky than ever." Or, the magazine suggested, she could have chosen another alternative. She could "shake hands prettily, wave a deprecating hand to the gallery, and retire in good order." After all, "The only really safe way to stop short in the midst of a game is to be so badly injured as to have to be carried from the field; the requirement may be heroic but the gallery's approval is assured."

After the default, Arthur Wallis Myers visited Lenglen in her room at the Forest Hills Inn. He expected to find her very ill. Instead, however, she appeared to be in high spirits, calling for a mirror to examine her own beaming face. *"Suzanne est coquette toujours,"* Mama explained to Myers. Myers found Suzanne's appearance and behavior totally inconsistent with the pitiable complaints of ill health made only minutes earlier. And he was disturbed by the inconsistency and the apparent disingenuousness of Suzanne and Mama. A physician had been summoned for Suzanne and, according to an account given later by the Lenglens, he forbade her to play tennis for at least eight days. And, Suzanne added, "even if I had wished to run counter to his prescriptions, I was incapable of holding my racket. I had, moreover, not the least appetite and refused all nourishment. Champagne was all that kept me up. I coughed with as much regularity as before," she said. "Wretched headaches made me think I had a jazz band in my head. I was delirious and my temperature went up to 104°."

Perhaps it was the music of that jazz band in her head that gave Suzanne Lenglen the overpowering urge to dance. After Myers left, Suzanne and Mama visited a nightclub, where Suzanne danced away the rest of the evening. She was seen dancing by one USLTA official and numerous other people who recognized her and marveled at her miraculously rapid recovery.

In the next week Lenglen made an effort to keep part of her tennis exhibition schedule and even scheduled another match against Molla Mallory. She played mixed doubles at the Nassau Country Club in Glen Cove, where her performance was warmly received. But after the match, she said, her fever returned. She practiced a little, played another exhibition doubles match, and then gave up trying. Her remaining matches were canceled, including an exhibition match against Mallory and an appearance with Little Bill Johnston in the National Doubles tournament at Longwood. And yet, during all this time, off the court she always appeared vivacious and healthy and ever eager to party. Tennis alone made her sick and reporters and spectators alike noticed this and complained.

One prankster wired the Newport Club, where Suzanne Lenglen was expected to play an exhibition match. The message, which read, "Arriving Newport 6:00 P.M. Arrange for suite for self, mother and maid, accommodation for dog, and suitable dancing partners," sent a surge of hope through the club. Officials actually began meeting the requests of the telegram before the hoax was detected.

The American press continued to chip away at the claims of illness long after the Frenchwoman returned home. Suzanne, who concluded that "America is truly cruel to French athletes," wrote from France that "the attitude of those Americans conducting this campaign against me would be quite inexplicable but for the fact that the principal directors are actuated by pro-Boche sentiments." She acquired a deep animosity for American crowds and American writers and a dark, brooding hatred for Molla Mallory in particular. As to those who were writing and saying all those terrible things about her behavior, "May the weight of their evil action fall on themselves," she prayed.

In time, additional evidence was offered indicating that Lenglen had indeed faked the seriousness of her indisposition both at Forest Hills and after. Dr. Malcolm Goodridge, who examined her following the default, announced that he had found absolutely nothing amiss. Lenglen reacted by threatening to sue for libel. Then Albert de Joannis delivered what was certainly the unkindest cut of all. His story was published after the directors of the French Tennis Federation issued a statement blaming the directors of the USLTA for unjustified critical commentaries on the sporting spirit of Suzanne Lenglen and, indirectly, of France. De Joannis was criticized in the statement for having urged Suzanne "to engage in tennis matches while physically unfit to do so." He responded by resigning as vice president of the Federation and then offered his own version of the American debacle. De Joannis said that Lenglen had been "perfectly well when she met Mrs. Molla Bjursted Mallory at Forest Hills. Mlle. Lenglen was defeated by a player who on that day showed a better brand of tennis."

"I shook hands with Mlle. Lenglen before she entered the court," he said. "Her hand was cool and her pulse normal. She was confident. She only commenced coughing after having lost games. I blame her for absolutely refusing to continue when I could have obtained a recess of half an hour, perhaps an hour, through the sporting spirit of the tennis officials and the large crowd." He protested any denunciations of the USLTA. In America, de Joannis pointed out, Suzanne Lenglen had been received "like a little queen and treated with the utmost courtesy. Her every whim and mood were satisfied." He concluded that "she knows how to win, but she does not know how to lose gracefully," a judgment shared, it seemed, by a large part of the American public. "She placed the personality of Suzanne before the good name of the sporting world of her country and could not face defeat. The attitude of the United States Lawn Tennis officials and the public in the face of the repeated defaults by Mlle. Lenglen was very lenient and above all blame," de Joannis claimed. "Carpentier is a hero in America, despite his defeat, because he showed grit and went down fighting, while Mlle. Lenglen placed France before the American public as preferring to quit rather than to face defeat. France never quits!"

After the de Joannis revelation, Joseph Jennings, treasurer of the USLTA, made a defense of the American organization. "Mlle. Lenglen suffered no physical collapse while here," Jennings said. "In her first match against Mrs. Mallory I talked with her myself just before she went on the courts. We were particular to inquire regarding her health. She had been prancing about in high spirits. There was not a trace of a cough. She assured me she never felt better in her life. Then, as she saw she was facing defeat, the coughing appeared whenever she lost a point and in the face of defeat she just plain quit. In the evening she danced for several hours." Jennings said that on the day after the Mallory match, Suzanne came to him and apologized and promised to go ahead with the remainder of her schedule. Then, he said, "she quit cold in every engagement. We kept track of her and found she continually displayed great activity and strength except when called upon to play tennis."

Jennings was particularly upset by Suzanne's failure to appear in an exhibition match on the first day of Davis Cup competition. A large crowd had turned out for the exhibition and "we warned her that she must give her solemn promise to play and she gave her word repeatedly. Shortly before playing time she suddenly announced another collapse. We had watched and that afternoon she started dancing at five o'clock and continued until midnight." When an official of the USLTA asked Suzanne how it was that she could dance so vigorously when she was too sick to play tennis, she replied, "Oh, it is because I love to dance. It is more exciting." Jennings confessed, "That ended her for our organization and all players sufficiently close to the leaders know the facts."

Despite the accusations from America, the French Tennis Federation supported Lenglen and absolved her of all blame in her default against Mallory. She herself made a tactful retreat from the controversy. But this retreat into illness was not as effective as her previous escapes.

Suzanne Lenglen's claim to the title of "World Champion" was badly tarnished rather than embellished by her American visit. She would have to start rebuilding her reputation in 1922. And in order to make a really convincing comeback both she and Papa realized that she would have to face Molla Mallory again. She might prepare herself physically for such a contest, but mental preparation was something else again. Molla scared Suzanne because Molla no longer believed in the invincibility of the Goddess. Mallory came on like a tiger on the courts, relentlessly, and with firm determination to tear Lenglen's game to shreds. Such a strategy worked at Forest Hills. It ripped Suzanne's will apart and destroyed her self-confidence and concentration at a moment when Papa was not present to act as a restorative. She must again believe in herself as Papa believed in her. She must not doubt. She must not waver. And she must win.

Suzanne Lenglen opened her 1922 campaign by displaying her customary lilt and float and flow in several Riviera tournaments, taking titles almost effortlessly wherever she played. Then on to Saint-Cloud and three

World Hard Court titles. Lenglen showed at the tournament that she still held a grudge against the American press. She was watching a match between Jean Borotra, her friend, and the veteran Max Decugis. At the end of the fourth set, Decugis walked to her chair for a moment and said, "I am just ready to drop." "Don't give up," Suzanne told him. "There are American correspondents here and they will say you 'quit.' "

--•⊰ 4 ⊱•--

Then, once more, Wimbledon and the Lawn Tennis Championships. In 1922 it was still Lenglen's privilege as the defending champion to stand aside until the Challenge Round and to meet the winner in that single match of the earlier rounds of the tournament. But she now said she would not wait for the Challenge Round. She would play through the tournament, from the first to the last round. Her decision led Wimbledon officials to drop the Challenge Round altogether. Every player was seeded. As the first defending champion to play through, Lenglen demonstrated nearly incomparable invincibility and flair. She lost no sets and dropped but twenty games in the first six rounds. In doubles with Elizabeth Ryan she lost no sets, and she lost none in the mixed doubles with her Australian partner, Pat O'Hara Wood.

In the singles category, attention was divided between Suzanne Lenglen slashing her way through one bracket of players and Molla Mallory battering her way through the other. Each woman moved gradually toward a fateful rematch, this time on the Centre Court. There was a special score to be settled now, the newspapers pointed out, a feud that would reach a climax on the court. American correspondents, confident of the abilities of their hard-hitting national champion, wrote home that the final match at Wimbledon would decide once and for all who was world champion in women's tennis and which nation deserved the glory of claiming that champion. Confident of his wife's superiority, Franklin Mallory bet $10,000 that she would win.

As expected, the final match at Wimbledon in 1922 brought Lenglen and Mallory face to face. Rain postponed their confrontation until early evening, shortly before 7:00 P.M. Suzanne waited in her dressing room during the long delay, where the pressure apparently overwhelmed her. She showed signs of the onset of a serious nervous collapse. She argued bitterly with Mama and frantically sent out friends to fetch Elizabeth Ryan. She was haunted again by the specter of defeat, of the crowd hissing, of Papa denouncing her—the whole phantasmic vision of collapse and humiliation and defeat. She changed costumes and reapplied her make-up several times, paced and muttered and cried. She finally pulled herself together emotionally only moments before the match was announced.

The first two games of the final match duplicated the opening games of the Lenglen-Mallory match at Forest Hills. Molla took her own service and broke Suzanne's to take a two–love lead. At the net, for the first time in memory, as officials watched, the two women exchanged bitter words, and it appeared, at one moment, as if they would attempt to strike each other. Mallory smiled broadly and confidently as the third game began, apparently sensing again the shattered confidence and the pathetic vulnerability of the Maid Marvel.

Then there was a sudden dramatic transformation in Lenglen's play. Listening to the steady encouragement and direction from Papa at courtside, Suzanne found her confidence and her range at the same time. Her shots started dropping in along the baseline just as though Papa had placed invisible target-coins there for her to strike. Now she had Mallory on the run, had her stretching awkwardly and helplessly for Suzanne's superb placements, had her arriving at the ball a fraction of a second too late, beat her by a step on every shot, and left her standing flatfooted by chopping short when she was anticipating long.

Suzanne Lenglen now displayed her full repertoire of fluent, imaginative shots and hit winner after winner. It was all over in twenty minutes. She took twelve consecutive games and made the premier American player look like a student before a master. And then, as a final reminder of the score that had just been settled, Lenglen trotted to the net, touched Mallory's outstretched hand, smiled, and turned away and coughed. Then she turned and gave her opponent one last triumphant grin, waved her racket above her head and announced, "Now, Mrs. Mallory, I have proved to you today what I could have done in New York last year." And Molla replied coldly, "Mlle. Lenglen, you have done to me today what I did to you in New York last year; you have beaten me."

A week later in New York, Molla Mallory lit into the American press. They had blown her feud with Suzanne Lenglen way out of proportion, she declared. Then she said that the stories they printed were ridiculous. And some of them openly favored Suzanne! "The newspapers are the dirtiest, filthiest things that ever happened," she said. "I don't want my name in the papers. I have a better chance on the courts than in the newspapers of my own country." When asked if she would play Lenglen again, Mallory shot back, "She won't come over here!" But what if she did come over here in the summer of 1923? "Maybe next summer," Mallory said bitterly. "Nobody knows if we'll be alive next summer. But if she comes over I'll play her again." And when someone asked if she was anxious to meet Lenglen on the courts again, she said, "Yes, I am anxious to meet her again. When you play tennis you take chances."

Molla Mallory was still not a true believer in Lenglen's invincibility.

She believed she had her number, still thought she could trounce her if given just one more chance. And so in the fall of 1922, after successfully defending her American title against the upstart California prodigy, Helen Wills, Mallory traveled to the Riviera for the chance to challenge Lenglen on her home courts. On the Riviera, Mallory entered and won half a dozen tournaments. For several weeks she seemed to be hot on Suzanne's trail, trying to catch her in a tournament but never quite succeeding. The Maid Marvel appeared to be reluctant—some said scared—to confront the American poacher. And whenever the names of both women were entered in the singles of the same tournament, Lenglen withdrew. When she scratched her name from the tournament at the La Festa Club in Monte Carlo, rumors were revived that Wimbledon had been a fluke, that Molla Mallory was indeed the better player of the two, and their relative talents had been reflected more accurately at Forest Hills.

But under Papa's guidance, Suzanne was now merely playing a game of cat and mouse, allowing public interest and the potential gate for the match to build. She and Papa both knew that Molla Mallory simply could not touch her on the familiar home clay of the Riviera. Following Papa's wise counsel, Suzanne waited for the proper moment to pounce on her prey. Whom the Goddess would destroy, she first teased to unwarranted vanity.

The moment for the confrontation came at the end of January at the Nice Tennis Club, where Papa now served as secretary and Suzanne as chief fund-raising attraction. The names of the two women were entered in the singles in the tournament, and neither withdrew. Seeded in opposite halves of the draw, each moved easily into the final. Then before a large noisy and partisan crowd on her home club courts Suzanne Lenglen showed the dazzle of her superior athletic ability. From the moment her first service dug into the clay she was in complete control. She gave up only 18 scattered points and won the match in two love sets. Molla Mallory, seven times the American champion, again looked like a heavy-footed novice before Lenglen's merciless masterful assault. The match was more than a simple defeat for Mallory. It was a final push from the top rungs of tennis. At Forest Hills later that year she lost her American championship to young Helen Wills. Molla Mallory never again earned the chance to play against Suzanne Lenglen.

No sooner had Lenglen whipped Mallory again than she received professional offers. An American promoter offered her 200,000 francs to play a series of twelve exhibition matches in America, and representatives of the town of Durham in England offered her forty pounds to play an exhibition in their town. Lenglen turned down both offers. She would not play in America, she said. "The Americans! They must lose sight of the fact that I would forfeit my standing as an amateur if I accepted their offer. And as for Durham, that town must be near the Scotch border."

Following her Riviera triumph, Suzanne Lenglen went to Saint-Cloud to defend all three of her World Hard Court titles. She won in the singles and mixed doubles, but lost out in the finals of the women's doubles. The big news of the tournament, however, was not her victories, but her collapse. During the mixed doubles final she fainted and was carried from the court. A heart and lung specialist examined her and said her collapse was due to overexertion and excitement from playing in three matches in one day. "It was a silly stunt," Suzanne said of her effort to win the triple crown in a single afternoon. "Never again."

A short time later it was announced that Lenglen was suffering from a serious heart ailment and would be unable to defend her title at Wimbledon.

Yet a more serious problem surfaced in the World Indoor Tournament in Paris—the crowd response. In the second set of Lenglen's final match in the singles of the Paris Tournament, she trailed Mlle. Golding, 0–4. A line call that went against Golding brought forth a loud demonstration from the crowd and after that the crowd seemed to favor Golding. When each of Suzanne's points was booed Suzanne stopped and walked over to her parents and asked them what she should do. "Continue," Papa said. She continued and won. Later Papa said that Suzanne would never again play tennis in Paris.

But she did play again in Paris, and she played at Wimbledon that summer. She danced through the preliminary rounds at Wimbledon with incredible ease. She gave up no more than three games in any single preliminary match, and in the final against the English champion Kitty McKane lost only four games. She again won the doubles title with Elizabeth Ryan.

Suzanne Lenglen appeared to continue to improve in 1924, and it was expected that the best was yet to come. Her future opponents, at least among the women, would be no more than an anonymous group of gracious victims, sacrificial pawns for the wondrous queen of the court. Her matches were becoming more and more solo recitals as she soared toward absolute perfection in her sport. Again she won titles in every Riviera tournament she entered; again she won the World Hard Court titles and moved on to Wimbledon for what looked like a repetition of her past performances there. Indeed, never before (or since) did a player so dominate at Wimbledon as Suzanne Lenglen did in the preliminary rounds in 1924. In her first three matches she won thirty-six consecutive games. Among her victims was the three-time American champion Hazel Wightman. Lenglen also won two rounds of the doubles and three of the mixed doubles without any apparent strain. Wimbledon was hers alone and the Centre Court had become her theater.

But then, without warning, it ended.

In the spring she had gone to Spain for a vacation and played several exhibitions. She also contracted a serious case of jaundice. She remained bedridden for several days, and when time for Wimbledon came round she had not entirely recovered. She was still very ill, but fought to conceal her illness from Papa and from the English gallery. She won her early matches quickly because she had to—a few fans noticed and then for a time forgot what they thought as an unusual urgency in her play, a certain fragility to her walk, fewer smiles. She came to the net only rarely, choosing instead to maneuver along the baseline and win with her superb ground strokes alone. In the fourth round of the tournament she played her regular doubles partner, Elizabeth Ryan. Lenglen took the first set from Ryan easily, 6–2. Then, incredibly, she dropped the second set, 6–8. The loss caused her confidence to waver badly. There were no assurances. Any day and in any match and on any court the end might come. Everything might just slide away. She needed Papa now. He sat at courtside, encouraging, demanding, blessing, condemning, muttering directions to Suzanne. As the third set began, it appeared to the spectators that Suzanne was on the verge of complete physical collapse. She gave Papa her familiar morose look, the look that was her pathetic plea for his permission to default. Many people then saw Papa form the words with his lips, *"Il faut continuer!"* She must continue. There could be no retreat into illness at this point. This was not Forest Hills. Papa commanded her to continue and to win. Like the little girl who two decades earlier skipped on the clay and who danced to her Papa's demands, Suzanne returned to the struggle not to try, but to do. She found within herself the energy and the skill to make a last-gasp effort. She transformed her fear into strength and played well enough to take the third set, 6–4. Ryan had never played more brilliantly and by her tenacity and her refusal to let go, had totally exhausted Suzanne.

The win over Ryan was very costly both physically and emotionally for Suzanne. Her strength was gone. Her will to play was gone. On the next morning she announced her retirement from the singles division of the tournament. Later that day she withdrew from both the doubles and the mixed doubles. Her Wimbledon title went to Kitty McKane, a finalist the previous year against her, when McKane beat Helen Wills in a thrilling three-set match.

Suzanne Lenglen had not recovered by midsummer and was unable to defend her Olympic tennis title in the Games just outside Paris. The gold medalist in the women's singles in the Games was Helen Wills of America.

In 1925 Lenglen undertook yet another comeback. Again she displayed her old brilliance. She retained her World Hard Court titles and proceeded to Wimbledon, where she won titles in singles, doubles, and mixed doubles. Rumors that her health had been irreparably damaged were dispelled by her incredible play. In her opening singles match she crushed Ryan, 6–2, 6–0. She went on to win thirty-six of thirty-seven games in the next three rounds of the singles. In the semifinals she utterly demolished the defending champion McKane in love sets, and in the final against nineteen-year-old Joan Fry of England she gave up only two games.

And so, in winning the singles title at Wimbledon in 1925 Lenglen lost only five games in all the matches she played, a record unequaled in the history of the tournament. She also won the doubles that year with Ryan and the mixed doubles with her fellow countryman Jean Borotra. It was the third time she was a triple winner at Wimbledon (she won all three titles in 1920 and again in 1922). Yet even more extraordinary was her 1925 record in all three categories. Suzanne Lenglen played and won thirty-four sets in the tournament (five in singles, and six each in doubles and mixed doubles) and lost but one set in the mixed doubles. In all three categories she won 209 games and lost fifty-two (60-5 in the singles, 72-16 in the doubles, 77-31 in the mixed doubles) for an average loss of games per set in the tournament of 1.485. The previous record low of 1.735 was held by Lenglen from the 1922 tournament. And before that time the record of 1.875 was Lenglen's from the 1920 tournament. No other triple champion has averaged fewer than 2.4 lost games per set. Suzanne Lenglen was truly incomparable in 1925.

By the end of summer 1925 Lenglen had established a record of dominance in tennis unequaled in that or any other sport. In seven years she had defaulted in one match and suffered what most Frenchmen now considered a technical loss. With the single exception of the tragic interlude at Forest Hills, Lenglen had not lost a match in singles competition in seven years of tournament play. In those seven years she had lost only two sets in singles. At Wimbledon she had played ninety-two matches in three categories and had won eighty-nine. She had also won fifteen World Hard Court Championships, fifteen French National Championships, six Wimbledon singles titles, and two Olympic gold medals.

The effect of all of this on France was to give an enormous boost to national pride. Suzanne Lenglen was unquestionably the great national heroine now. Indeed, some Frenchmen said she was even greater than Joan of Arc. Writing in *Le Journal*, Clement Vautel announced that "an Englishman told me, 'The two greatest French women are Joan of Arc and Suzanne.' I replied, 'You burned the former, but you have not yet beaten the latter;' " Vautel's pride was indicative of the national sentiment that surrounded Suzanne Lenglen. They had not beaten her. They would never beat her! Every Frenchman knew that. And Vautel, along with the overwhelming majority of his countrymen, believed that the Americans had utilized deception and a base conspiracy to confuse and humiliate her when she was not well. What happened in America had nothing whatever to do with Lenglen's greatness but very much to do with the hypocritical American spirit. It was typical of the kind of behavior the French were beginning to expect more and more from their former ally, thanks to the highly impassioned controversy over the repayment of war debts. Could a nation that insisted on bleeding France nearly to death during her financial crisis be expected not to take advantage of the single most glorious symbol of French courage? The Americans! Their greed blinded them to true beauty.

By 1925 Lenglen's fame had spread far beyond the sporting world. She was the first female athlete to be acknowledged as a celebrity outside her particular sport. People who cared little for tennis or who knew nothing of the game now applauded her struggles and triumphs because they were beautiful allegories of France's struggles and triumphs. The masses scrambled to see her. In unison they chanted her name in order to be recognized as part of the great civilization that produced such a wonderful woman.

But it was not just the common crowd that bowed down to the Goddess now. The great and the near great also sang hosannas. A visit by celebrities to the Riviera without an audience with Suzanne was like a visit to Rome without an audience with the Pope. Prosperous industrialists, war profiteers, politicians, writers, movie stars, maharajahs, kings, ex-kings, and pretenders competed for her attention. King Gustav V of Sweden was an unabashed admirer, as was ex-king Manuel of Portugal. Douglas Fairbanks and Mary Pickford visited the Lenglen villa, as did Rudolph Valentino, Georges Carpentier, and scores of lesser lights.

What did Suzanne Lenglen think of the crowds in the streets and in the galleries and the wealthy camp followers who sought her company? She believed that some were in love with her, "others are content with good friendship, while a large percentage are attracted by the reflected glory which comes to them from the association with so famous a personage. They like the limelight even when not directed full upon themselves." She wrote somewhat wistfully that she distributed her attentions and smiles "with royal impartiality." "It is what is expected by the public," she believed, and so she had to make some return for the flattery and the adulation showered upon her.

Of herself, Lenglen revealed that she was "human enough to react joyfully to this new atmosphere." She "enjoyed the interest in people's eyes, the new respect in their voices." She found that it was thrilling to find herself "in the very warm center of things instead of standing outside in the cold circumference; to have her opinion asked, her advice taken; to hear the language of compliment instead of disdain; to feel that wherever she went she made a stir."

Lenglen intimated that she had made an indelible mark in two kingdoms—beauty and sport. Yet anyone who saw her realized that such a conviction was based largely upon illusion. No matter how enchanting her performances on the courts of Europe, no one ever made the mistake of saying Suzanne Lenglen was a beauty. To do so was merely to demonstrate an extraordinary capacity for self-delusion.

Suzanne Lenglen stood about five and a half feet tall. She was a muscular, large-boned girl with gray eyes, raven hair, and a sharp, birdlike profile. She had an unusually long nose and large irregular teeth that protruded unhandsomely from her mouth when she smiled. Paul Gallico recalled that she had "a hatchet face and a hook nose"; while Hazel Wightman, a lifelong friend of Suzanne, described her by simply saying, "She was so homely—you can't imagine a homelier face." Bill Tilden summed up her appearance charitably by observing, "Heaven knows no one could call her beautiful."

Yet despite her physiognomy, she had a rather attractive and healthy demeanor in the early 1920s. Because she eschewed the traditional long-sleeved blouse and wide-brimmed hat of the other players, her face and arms were deeply tanned. But the pressure of practice and of play gradually eroded her physical health as well as her emotional stability. By the mid-1920s, when she stood at the pinnacle of her career, she looked thirty years older than her actual age. There were deep dark circles under her eyes and her skin was wrinkled and creased. The constant exposure to the sun caused her complexion to deteriorate rapidly. She found it necessary to wear ever heavier layers of powder and makeup. Al Laney noticed in the mid-1920s that she had a dull, almost sallow, colorless skin. Under the powder her face appeared puffed, her eyes were rheumy and conveyed the deep inner loneliness of a woman who had an awareness of the inadequacies of athletic genius before the tireless assaults of time.

Ted Tinling, a close friend of the Lenglen family, attributed her premature physical and emotional deterioration to Papa, who "drove her relentlessly toward the goal of absolute supremacy, which was compulsive to both their egos. To maintain this," Tinling wrote, "Suzanne began very early to deprive herself of all the joys of a normal existence." To maintain her athletic supremacy she realized, Tinling found, that there would have to be "the total sacrifice of all natural life." Consequently, even before she turned twenty-five, "her face and expression had already the traces of deep emotional experiences far beyond the normal for her age."

And yet nearly everyone who watched her perform pirouettes on the tennis court remarked that her lack of physical beauty was largely overcome by her grace and poise and movement. There was a remarkable transformation in Suzanne when she stepped onto the court, as though the area within the chalked rectangles was an enchanted kingdom in which the ugly duckling became, for a time, a beautiful swan, or, as one writer referred to her, "an insouciant butterfly." Scores of observers commented on this very fact—the impact of the kinetic upon the aesthetic in the metamorphosis of the mortal Suzanne into the Great Lenglen, the Goddess. Paul Gallico found that "she dressed divinely and her ugliness became almost an asset." It was the movement that held the spectator in thrall, that satisfied the lust of the eye, and for a while disguised her lack of beauty. Suzanne communicated a singular *joi de vivre,* a bubbling *bonhomie* on grass or clay when things went her way, and they almost always went her way. In a world recovering from the horrors of a world war, this gliding goddess by her every move compellingly and enticingly proclaimed, "Behold, I'm absolutely wonderful, come have a look." And the whole world did.

Accurately describing her motion was difficult and tested the rhetorical capabilities of countless spectators. C. C. Pyle, the hard-boiled American promoter, searched for the right words to describe her graceful glissades. "Why, if she were merely to rise from this chair and walk over to the door—it would be, well, it would be like a seagull leaving a wave." Perhaps it was the peculiar slant of the Riviera sunshine, or maybe the effect of ingesting champagne in the casinos in the early afternoon, or both, but the adoring crowds who watched Suzanne in competition in Nice and Cannes every spring suggested that she appeared to glide above the clay, suspended like a beautiful bird in flight. She swooped after the ball, now a floating seagull and then in an instant a falcon diving with deadly speed for the kill. And between points she pranced around on her toes—on her toes—reminding spectators of a prima donna positioning herself for a dance. To many people seeing her for the first time, this seemed a distracting and unnecessary affectation. But Suzanne believed it important never to let her heels touch the court, to be prepared to leap for the ball at any moment and to be, as she once described it, "like a cat walking on hot bricks." Tennis was, after all, a performing art when executed by the Great Lenglen.

A. Wallis Myers felt that the English grass "permitted the best expression of a refined art" when Suzanne played tennis. "Fluency of footwork, at which the French excel, reveled in the lighter and easier tread, the softer carpet for swift toe work. The delicate volley, the application of check or slice, the strokes that satisfied finesse rather than force—these were better displayed on green and yielding turf." England, he felt, provided the Goddess with a better stage than did France.

Even when Lenglen bent down to pick up a ball, her movement was lithe and lambent and memorable. Her turns were not prosaic mechanical maneuvers, they were poetic pirouettes. And all of this was accentuated by her adoption of a dancer's gown for tennis. Her costumes were all of light silk, and she seldom wore a slip under them. Consequently, there was an additional titillating appeal to her movement, for when she leaped high on the court, with the sunlight behind her, her clothing became transparent and the "naughty old gentlemen" at courtside got a delicious peak at the outlines of the body beneath the silk. Sometimes, Ted Tinling recalled, spectators got more than a peak at the outlines. "When she was in flowing stride," Tinling recalled of Suzanne on the Riviera, "it wasn't unusual for one of Suzanne's breasts to pop out."

She was simply incomparable, a singular, odd, suspended phantom of delight, a lovely, haunting apparition who startled the hearts of all who watched her. But neither the costume nor the grace of Suzanne Lenglen made her tennis extraordinary. Those were simply frills. It was rather her absolute mastery of the fundamentals of the game that produced her singular virtuosity. She played a basically simple and crisply efficient game. Young Helen Wills concluded that "the printed word can hardly convey an idea of her efficiency on the court. When you saw her play you did not know how good she was because it looked so easy. It was only from the other side of the net that you realized how really good she was. Her control and delicacy of placement will probably never be equalled."

On the court, Lenglen's primary concern was ball control rather than speed, even though she was capable of hitting consistently with the deceptive power of most male players. Most of her opponents commented on the softness of the drives as well as on the height at which they passed above the net—always about one meter. Papa had drilled into Suzanne the importance of keeping the ball in play by clearing the net. If the ball were hit over the net, even if it were hit hard enough to fall beyond the baseline, there was still the chance that the opponent might play it. But a ball hit into the net was always a lost point. Thus Papa taught Suzanne to observe a "margin of safety" in clearing the net and keeping the ball in play. When she failed to clear the net Papa ridiculed her mercilessly. She learned to remember and regret every netted ball she hit. Sportswriter Al Laney spoke with her during a 1924 Riviera tournament and was impressed by the few times she netted the ball—four times in four matches. When he mentioned that fact to Suzanne, she replied condescendingly, "But of course, my little one. . . . I have been careless this week, *n'est ce pas?*"

Because of that margin of safety, it seemed that Suzanne Lenglen would be vulnerable to a serve and volley player, an easy victim to the player who could rush the net and cut off those enticingly high returns. That was inevitably a miscalculation of many challengers. As if by mental telepathy, she seemed able to anticipate such a move on the part of any opponent. Her sense of anticipation was extraordinarily fine and, when an opponent moved toward the net to volley, her passing shots—perfectly disguised— were almost always winners.

Mary K. Browne pointed out an uncanny aspect of Lenglen's play. From the other side of the net, Browne noticed, "some of the balls hit by Suzanne came so slowly that they seemed to float over the net. But as you approached them with confidence to kill them, something seemed to go wrong. The returns went into the net or floated back beyond the baseline. She seemed so vulnerable," Browne observed, because of that margin of safety. Yet she was invulnerable. She knew when you were coming in to volley—she read your mind. And when you went for the score off a volley she knew just where you would hit it and she had it back at you instantly. Against Lenglen the serve-and-volley game was not only ineffective, it could be suicidal.

Perhaps the player who knew Suzanne Lenglen best was Elizabeth

Ryan, her regular doubles partner. Ryan beat Lenglen when she was
fourteen in singles, and tested her at Wimbledon in 1924. Asked about
her game, Ryan told sportswriter Bob Considine that Suzanne was the
best ever. "She owned every kind of shot, plus a genius for knowing how
and when to use them." "She never gave an opponent the same kind of
shot to hit twice in a row. She'd make you run miles . . . her game was
all placement and deception and steadiness. I had the best drop shot anybody ever had, but she could not only get up to it but was so fast that
often she could score a placement off it. She had a stride a foot and a
half longer than any known woman who ever ran, but all those crazy leaps
she used to take were done after she hit the ball. Sure, she was a poser,
a ham in the theatrical sense. She had been spoiled by tremendous adulation from the time she was a kid. . . . But she was the greatest woman
player of them all. Never doubt it." Billy Johnston, the American who
won the Wimbledon singles title in 1923, told Edith Cross, a ranking
American player of the time, that "Suzanne could beat any woman any
day by any score she wanted. She was by far the best woman player ever."

The Lenglen mind impressed most of those who watched her or who
played against her. Both Browne and Tilden compared her mind to that
of a chess master. She forced opponents to play her game, controlled the
board from the first move, and used her intelligence and incredible will
power to bend and then to break the game of women who challenged
her. Lenglen explained that on the court she let her mind do the running for her, and then she slipped easily into the proper position for
each shot. She seldom scrambled, and she said she even disliked the word
because it rhymed with "gamble." Browne found that she calculated two
and three strokes ahead during a game. "She can draw you into a position despite everything you do to avoid it," Browne complained. "She
can make three or four plays and tell you where she will end her point.
Just as John J. McGraw can tell you in advance the position of his men
on bases as the result, say, of a single, a sacrifice and a double." Another
knowledgeable observer concluded that Suzanne was very simply "a flawless machine, directed by one of the most analytical minds in tennis. She
made tennis a mathematical science," he said. "The mastery of her strokes
and style was phenomenal."

Commander George Hillyard, secretary of the All-England Club, noticed that Lenglen always hit the ball in the dead center of her racket.
And she always returned it to just the right spot on the opposite side of
the net. An informed observer might point out during a match when a
player had played a wrong shot, Hillyard said. But "one of the most
striking aspects of the Lenglen game in singles was that you never see
her commit an error in judgement in this respect. Her instinct to make
the correct counter to every adversary's attack, or in her own turn to
attack at the right moment and at a most vulnerable point, is quite
extraordinary, and is the outcrop of genius in her play that impresses

me beyond all her other qualities." Hillyard conceded that the Maid Marvel did make some errors, both from the baseline and from the net. "But it is always clear that the intended destination of her shot was correct—even though the actual execution was faulty."

Suzanne Lenglen was asked often about the secret of her success. And out of impatience she sometimes replied, "Oh, there isn't any real secret"; or "practice." But, she confessed sometimes, in the back of her mind she realized that beyond the essentials like practice and natural aptitude there was indeed a secret to her success, a fundamental one. "Willing to win is good psychology and good tennis requires good psychology," she believed. "I never for a minute permit myself to entertain a doubt. Confidence is not egotism. If your mind is in doubt, your muscles will be also . . . when you are wavering . . . the nerves will not convey to the muscles the exact impulse which must be imparted." During match play, Suzanne said, "the ball is coming at you like a bolt. Somehow you instantly sense what it will do. Your mind seems to decide, almost without your knowing it, that you must return it deep to the sideline, it must be hit right there—not an inch further. Then comes your stroke. Everything in the world is a blank to you, except that exact spot where the ball must go. It must go there! Do you think if at that second a doubt flashed through your mind that your strokes would be unwavering? That is what I mean by confidence and the will to win."

Lenglen said that she never meant to imply that with confidence alone one could perform athletic miracles. "But without it, without the will to win that allows no doubts, you cannot expect to be a consistent winner. . . ." The enemy of the athlete was uncertainty and doubt. She knew that bitter truth from experience. And when one began to feel doubt, it was always nice to have an undoubting Papa on the sidelines.

One of Suzanne Lenglen's favorite doubles partners on the Riviera, Englishwoman Phyllis Satterthwaite, believed that in addition to the will to win Lenglen possessed extraordinary speed. She always took the ball at a full arm extension and always before the ball reached the maximum height of its bound—in other words, she hit the ball on the rise with a half volley. In this way, she felt, she gained a fraction of a second every time the ball crossed the net. Thus she was able to hurry and harry an opponent and more easily catch her out of position. Satterthwaite also praised her remarkable ability to conceal the direction of her shots until the last moment before the ball left her racket. She was like a gifted baseball pitcher who can deliver a wide variety of pitches from the same motion, confusing and confounding the hitter. If Lenglen's opponent committed herself one way or another, shifted her weight and indicated that she was getting set for this or that return, Suzanne could seemingly stop the ball and transform her shot into a chop or a lob. And to many spectators this was the most uncanny and spectacular part of her game, a maneuver that seemed something like sleight-of-hand or sorcery.

For Satterthwaite, Suzanne Lenglen was the eighth wonder of the world. And "not the least of her charm is the fact that she is able to produce her game without any apparent severe concentration and with an entire absence of that dreaded 'tennis face' which is so very unattractive and at the same time so very easy a habit to fall into, when all the muscles are strained to the utmost attention and each stroke seems to be made with a visible and at times painful amount of effort." None of that for Suzanne. She was always bubbling over, always effervescent, always smiling, always winning. After the most difficult rally she could be seen to look around and beam at Papa or at one of her friends among the spectators, Satterthwaite observed. She was seldom unsmiling, seldom lost her concentration. After all, winning was wonderful fun.

Suzanne Lenglen sought by way of articles and in books to provide advice for others on playing tennis. But there was inevitably an oversimplification in her directives and descriptions. They were not unlike Pavlova or Nijinsky explaining the magic of ballet by providing foot patterns on the floor. The physical genius of the artist just could not be communicated by the printed word. In Suzanne's magic there was a divine spark, a soul, that could never be contained in photographs or in drawings. There was an irreducible quality to her movement that could be summed up with one word—"genius."

Control of the ball and accuracy were the secrets of tennis, she believed. "I never had a wicked service; my forehand drive is not nearly as powerful as Miss Wilis's, but I have always been able to place the ball within inches of where I wanted it."

"Her only weakness," Mary K. Browne summed up Suzanne Lenglen, "was that she was not a man. If she were a man, I would back her to defeat Tilden."

After years of rigorous training supervised by Papa, it was not surprising that Suzanne tired of daily conditioning and exercise. She found training more and more a nuisance and convinced herself that it was not really necessary. "I could lay off six months and get in shape again in two days," she believed. "I do not have to train. I eat pretty much what I please in moderation. I smoke a little and cigarettes do not hurt me, though of course they would if I smoked too many. I sleep until noon every day." In 1920 she told an interviewer that she drank no wine or alcoholic beverages of any kind. Yet it was well known that she took "stimulants" and "tonics" before and during matches in the form of wine, champagne, and generous gulps of iced cognac. These were to provide her with quick energy, she believed. And as the years passed she used heavier and heavier doses of stimulation, whether or not she played tennis. By the mid-1920s, she enjoyed the night life on the Riviera as much as any free-spending tourist. She danced until the early hours of the morning, smoked regularly and drank champagne like a trooper. Yet on the following afternoon she could play as marvelously as ever; her play seemed totally unaffected by her dedication to night life.

She also accepted without question all the fine perquisites of her position. In doing so she put the amateur rules of athletics to the test and stretched them far beyond conventional interpretation. The Lenglens were rewarded by several special financial arrangements while Suzanne remained an amateur. Her presence in any tournament meant a certain lucrative guaranteed gate—in most cases a sell-out. No one ever knew for sure how much, if any, of the gate found its way into the pockets of Papa. In some cases friendly wagers were offered Papa prior to a tournament. A club official customarily wagered one thousand francs, betting Papa that Suzanne would not appear for the local club tournament. When she did arrive, as scheduled, Papa was paid his winning share.

French rules concerning amateurism were far more liberal for the time than those governing English and American players, and the rules for amateurs playing on the Riviera were nearly non-existent. American visitors to the Riviera wondered how Suzanne Lenglen could possibly live in such resplendent style and actually continue to consider herself an amateur athlete. The Lenglen family fortune had never been great—Mama and Papa were "petits rentiers," deriving their income from modest capital investments. By the mid-1920s Papa's most profitable business investment was his daughter. Through Suzanne the family expenses were paid. Her activities paid for the travel and hotel accommodations and the stylish clothing she wore. Her friends provided her with generous amounts of spending money. The Lenglen Riviera home, the Villa Ariem, was financed by the Nice Tennis Club. Papa was the secretary of that organization. No one was sure what guarantees or arrangements had been made between the Lenglens and the club officials for the financing to have been offered. Suzanne's refusal to play against Molla Mallory anywhere on the Riviera but at the Nice Tennis Club may have been part of the arrangement. She always participated in the club's winter tournaments, providing substantial gate receipts for the organization. Indeed, soon after Suzanne retired from amateur tennis, the club went out of business.

Tourists on the Riviera bought tournament tickets in order to watch Suzanne Lenglen in action. They also spent large amounts of money in the restaurants, hotels, and casinos of the region. Several local players were on the payroll of the hotels and casinos, and there were rumors that Lenglen was subsidized by some of these organizations. The tycoons and the shadow powers behind those interests, it was intimated, controlled the press releases concerning the Goddess and assured her of only the most favorable media coverage. Suzanne was an official and allegedly unpaid outside mannequin for Patou. She never responded to questions concerning the prices she paid, if any, for the costumes he created for her. But she was a style-setter and annually introduced the public to the latest creations of this exquisite and prestigious house. Lenglen also collected royalties from a novel she wrote, *The Love Set: Being the Life Story of Marcelle Penrose,* and she was under contract to do newspaper and magazine articles for spectacular sums of money. As an amateur she was permitted by the French Tennis Federation to endorse commercial products like the Lenglen Tennis Shoe, manufactured by Best and Company in England.

Tournament directors on the Riviera were only too willing to go along with the clandestine financial agreements necessary to get name players to appear at their clubs. And the name of Lenglen heading the list of competitors guaranteed a profit. Some club owners learned the importance of Suzanne's presence the hard way. When the secretary of the La Festa Club in Monte Carlo annoyed her, she scratched her name from the tournament, and the club lost 50,000 francs in admissions as the result of her pique.

Riviera tournaments incorporated the well-known *bons* system to reward title winners. By that system, amateur players could support themselves for the season. When a player won first or second prize in a tournament he was awarded a *bon,* which was an order on a local store for a thousand or so francs. It was expected that the winners would exchange the *bons* for some article of jewelry, perhaps inscribed with the tournament name. But more often than not they were exchanged for cash. The generous *bons* from the numerous tournaments she won along the Riviera no doubt provided additional financial support.

Journalist John Tunis contended that Lenglen had been a professional in everything but name long before she signed a professional contract. And he insisted that the French Tennis Federation was not unaware of the situation. But they dared not act to penalize or punish her because of her enormous popular appeal. In France she was sheltered by her fame not only from criticism but also from disciplinary action. One French tennis official confessed that she was a great international symbol for her nation and to punish her or to deprive her of the right of representing France in amateur sporting contests would be nothing less than cataclysmic. "We know perfectly well she is a professional," the official told Tunis. "Have we not a file—so—so big?" he asked, holding his hands far apart to demonstrate. "But what can we do? After all she is our champion." Tunis only concluded that the situation was "delightfully French."

Yet Lenglen remained adamant in her denials of having accepted money illegally in exchange for her appearances and victories. "Please spike this talk for all time," she advised inquiring reporters. "I have never received a sou either at Wimbledon or the French championships or at the modest little Riviera clubs. I know I have a reputation for becoming fabulously rich. People could not believe that I was not making and spending fortunes." After she officially abandoned amateur athletics, Suzanne confided to friends, "I was such a boob (*poire*) to do this for nothing."

The constant pressure of staying at the top of the tennis world, competing in all of the major European tournaments and facing challenger after challenger, as well as accommodating legions of journalists and dignitaries, gradually took its toll on Suzanne Lenglen. Consequently, her attitude toward competition and crowds changed. She became more moody and petulant as the years passed. Her refusal in 1920 to obey the dictum of the French Tennis Federation was merely a first act of rebellion. Such episodes became common, and her mercurial temperament became legend. Americans never really appreciated her behavior, but she dismissed it all and concluded that the Americans were simply incapable of comprehending the fiery Latin spirit. Her apologists explained that the Goddess had the soul of an artist. And such a soul could never be confined within the rules of a game or the chalk lines of a tennis court. It bubbled over and defied convention on the court and off. She just found it impossible to emulate the studied insouciance of Anglo-Saxon phlegm that English and American audiences seemed to value so highly. And so she regularly indulged herself with explosive emotional displays when things did not go as planned. And, extraordinary as it seems, the French crowds favored the Maid Marvel during such exhibitions and seemed to sympathize completely with her frustration.

When Suzanne Lenglen disagreed with a line call, she glared at the linesman or snapped at him between points or stopped and stamped her foot on the ground. When her partner failed to play up to expectations, Lenglen defaulted and left him on the court alone. Following a questionable line call made against her during a Riviera match in 1925, she threw down her racket in protest. The referee then declared a foot fault against her as a penalty. That only enraged the Goddess more, and she loudly cursed the linesman. She was informed that her protestations were in vain because the linesman was hard of hearing. She screamed that his hearing was not at issue. It was his vision she questioned. Was he blind? The match was delayed still further while Lenglen had her complaints written down for the offending linesmen and the tournament officials. This was done with mock dignity, and when the linesman was finally shown her written indictment—he could see well enough to read—he left the match.

Suzanne Lenglen was indulged in such behavior because both she and the officials realized that the crowds had come to see the Goddess perform and not to watch linesmen make questionable calls. Such calls merely interfered with the show. And given the choice between Lenglen performing and a linesman making calls, both crowd and officials sided with her. The presence of the linesman was simply an inconvenient and sometimes obtrusive formality when Suzanne Lenglen played before a French gallery.

During an exhibition match in Austria in 1925, Lenglen was paired with one of her favorite doubles partners, Count Ludwig Salm von Hoogstraten, the most temperamental of the male players on the Continent. But she outdid even the temperamental Count when it came to emotional pyrotechnics. When he played poorly and missed a shot, she hurled her racket into the net, glared at her partner for several seconds, and then stomped off the court. Her exit was accompanied by sympathetic applause. She refused to return to the court despite earnest apologies from her partner and pathetic pleas from tournament officials. After several hours a default was announced.

Behind Lenglen's explosive displays of temperament was an awareness of certain unpleasant realities. Time did not pass her by. Her dominance in tennis could not last forever. Sooner or later on some sunny afternoon it would all end, probably without warning. Some young upstart would come along to unseat the Goddess, and her time in the sun would be over. But not quite yet. Not quite yet.

She continued to defend her titles successfully as her health deteriorated. Her flights into illness were now often the real thing. She suffered from two types of jaundice and from pernicious anemia. She caught colds more easily. And she taxed her fragile constitution by overeating for weeks at a time and then going on severe starvation diets. At times she seemed to be bulimic. Helen Wills noticed that Suzanne Lenglen dieted so severely at times that she ran out of energy on the tennis court. In late 1924 she suffered from a severely strained tendon that made her movement on the court during the next year extremely painful. She had always been high strung and extended herself time and again to the outermost limits of her physical and nervous capabilities. At times she crossed those limits. By the mid-1920s she experienced regular hysterical fits of crying followed by uncontrollable laughter and then the meaningless babble of logorrhea. She fluctuated between emotional highs and lows. She suffered several nervous breakdowns, or, as they were referred to by her closest friends, *crises de nerfs*. Before important matches she became withdrawn and sullen and then, at times, hysterical. Off the court and on, she was playing against herself.

Lenglen's severe physical and emotional problems in the mid-1920s were exacerbated both by the French financial crisis and by Papa's lingering serious illness. Just when she began thinking of retirement and rest, playing and winning became increasingly important. It was a final cruel irony in her career. The family fortune began to slip away. Lenglen recalled, "Our money began to decrease in value and its buying power began to grow smaller and smaller. My father began to find that the very comfortable income which we had once enjoyed, although unchanged in size, had considerably decreased in value. Luxuries which we had once enjoyed gave way to mere comforts." Financial solvency depended more and more upon Suzanne.

Beginning in 1926, there was a renewed earnestness to her play and even more grimness about winning. There was something far more important at stake in the play than a simple game of tennis. People continued to watch her win and marveled at her skill and analyzed her tactics but they could never know what it all meant to her. They saw the show, the façade. Only a few knew of the emotional storm within.

It was tragic for the Lenglen family, also, that Suzanne had been unsuccessful in establishing herself either in a comfortable marriage or in a financially rewarding career outside sport. After amateur tennis, what would the world hold for her besides memories? Tennis was her life. She could never support herself as a novelist or as a professional journalist— as a writer she was a good tennis player. And although she had been a close associate of royalty and aristocracy for years, and although there had been scores of suitors and dozens of delicious rumors concerning romance and marriage, no man ever requested the privilege of sweeping her off to a comfortable country estate. Her closest friends and confidantes, after Mama and Papa, were all women. When she took a brief rest away from home and vacationed in Switzerland or Italy or Spain, she was accompanied by female companions. That fact, too, became a source of intriguing rumor. And some of Suzanne's fellow players insisted that she was in fact interested in men only because of her overwhelming dedication to Mama and Papa and their desire for respectability. Part of the emotional storm that unsettled her may have been due not simply to her inability to find a husband, but to her actual lack of interest in finding one.

And so Papa's little girl never found that shining prince who might love her and support her and make her happy and bring security and financial stability to the family. There remained but one man in Suzanne Lenglen's life—her Papa. Now Papa's health was failing, and there was no man to take his place. He still sat beside the courts every day, the shell of the man he once was, wrapped in blankets, pale, watching his daughter. She had become his dream girl, the ideal he had once envisioned. But still there were non-believers. The Americans. Molla Mallory was gone for good, but now the American newsmen sang the praises of yet another pretender—Helen Wills. And now they had dispatched their American girl to France. She was to arrive in January 1926 and to seek out Suzanne on the Riviera. Despite what the Americans or anyone else might believe, Papa Lenglen knew that Suzanne was the greatest tennis player the world had ever seen. And in 1926 she would prove it one last time.

CHAPTER

II

THE AMERICAN GIRL

"A sunny day, white balls, fresh white tennis clothes,
a good-natured opponent, and a brisk game—this
spells heaven for the one who loves tennis."
                                        —Helen Wills

"A mask, a perpetual natural disguiser of herself,
Concealing her face, concealing her form,
Changes and transformation every hour, every
    moment,
Falling upon her even when she sleeps."
                                        —Walt Whitman
                                        "Visor'd"

"She was What America Needed; the antithesis of
the gaudy, gin drinking, John Held, Jr., flapper.
She neither smoked, drank, nor used cosmetics."
                                —Helena Huntington Smith
                                The New Yorker, August 27, 1927

"When she steps on a tennis court, all but the game
ceases to exist."   —William "Pop" Fuller

NONE of the other passengers knew her name. A few thought they recognized her face but could not remember where or when they had seen it. There was something vaguely familiar about her. She was obviously someone of importance because half a dozen reporters were running around her asking questions and scribbling down her answers. It was clear that they were enchanted by her. But who was she? Had they seen her picture in the newspaper? Was she a movie star returning to Hollywood? Was she a model, perhaps, who endorsed a product and whose face was on boxes of cereal or soap?

Someone overheard her say to the reporters, "Some day I'd like to meet a celebrity." When asked what she meant by "a celebrity," she said, "I'd just like to meet some of the people that everybody is reading about," apparently unaware that she herself had become one of those people.

"Do you intend to travel to France next year to play against Suzanne Lenglen?" she was asked.

"No," she replied. "I plan to attend the University of California to study art. I have no plans to go abroad."

"Will you be studying any foreign languages at the University?" another reporter asked.

There was a momentary pause and then the young woman betrayed just the hint of a smile and replied, "Yes. French."

The reporters all laughed.

The informal press conference took place in the LaSalle Street Station in Chicago as the young woman waited to board the train. The other passengers watched with fascination as she finally pulled away from the persistent newsmen and stepped up into the train. They saw that she also attracted a certain interested look from the porters and from the young men standing nearby. But if she noticed their attention at all she gave no sign. She was cool in her behavior, with a diffidence that made her avoid looking anyone directly in the eye. She was uncomfortable being the center of attention in the station. And she stayed close to her traveling companion, an older woman she was heard to call "Cass."

The train she boarded on this August morning in 1923 was the celebrated Overland Limited, the finest machine on wheels west of Chicago, and those booking passage on it knew they would travel to the Pacific Coast in style. "There was something about the train that struck on the chords of imagination," the young woman wrote years later in her autobiography. And there was something about the young woman herself that struck the chords of imagination of the passengers on the train and of the American public.

Along the way on this particular trip the other passengers learned that the young woman was not a movie star and not a model. She was an athlete—a tennis player. Her name was Helen Wills and her traveling companion was her mother, Catherine, and they were returning to their home in California. Some of the passengers might have seen her face in the paper earlier in the week after she had won the national singles tennis title at Forest Hills. At seventeen she was the second youngest woman champion. And it was clear to anyone who followed tennis that this young woman was by far the most attractive titleholder in the history of the sport. Heads turned when she passed.

Americans in 1923 were not accustomed to the notion that a female athlete could be beautiful; they tended to agree with writers like Paul Gallico, who said that pretty girls did not participate in sports. Girls who excelled in sports, Gallico suggested, were simply trying to compensate for their lack of beauty. Athletics was their way of getting attention. If Suzanne Lenglen were really beautiful, for instance, she wouldn't be running around like crazy on the tennis courts of Europe. She would have been quietly at home, happily married. Athletics provided a refuge and a last chance for the desperate female ugly ducking. Or worse.

Until Helen Wills. After she appeared public attitudes changed. She was an athlete—a great athlete. And she was beautiful, far more beautiful than most film stars. She had bearing and class and intelligence. And once having seen her, even Gallico abandoned his way of thinking and joined the enthusiastic chorus of citizens who sang her praises.

As the seven-car train pulled by a powerful brace of locomotives passed across the Great Plains, passengers saw something else unusual along the way: small delegations of men, women, and children standing at many of the crossings and stations. As the Overland Limited rumbled past they waved or pointed, straining to get a glimpse of someone on board. When the train stopped in Ogden, a group of local citizens bearing bundles of California poppies came aboard. They were accompanied by half a dozen reporters. "Where is she?" they all asked at once. "Where is our girl champion?" They were directed to the observation car, and there they found Helen. They presented her with the flowers, and several of the young women in the group asked for her autograph. Someone asked how it felt to be the champion. "It seems just the same to me as it did before I won the honor," she said. "Remember, I have been playing tennis for four years and have worked hard to win the title." Before the group left the train, one of the men told her: "We are proud of you. We are particularly proud that a Western girl has won the national championship."

When the delegation was gone, Catherine Wills asked that for the remainder of the journey no one be told where Helen's compartment was. She just wanted to be left alone. Yet, after the train was ferried across the Carquinez Strait in California, a gaggle of sorority sisters from the University of California boarded and found Helen. They surrounded her and chattered away excitedly telling her of the advantages of their organization. Helen smiled and listened. She was told that there was a huge crowd awaiting her arrival in Oakland. Local politicians were eager to welcome her home. And there was a band.

But Helen and Catherine Wills spoiled the reception awaiting them in Oakland. When the train stopped in Berkeley, Helen and her mother decided to become fugitives from fame and got off. But some reporters who were already there followed them to a waiting automobile, shouting out questions all the time. Columnist Harry Smith of the *San Francisco Chronicle* ran down the tracks toward the observation car looking for Helen after a porter directed him that way. Smith found that the porters were accustomed to this sort of thing. All he had asked was, "Where is she?" and the porter pointed to the observation car. As he was running down the tracks Smith realized he hadn't even mentioned Helen's name. "Smart porter," he thought. But he missed his interview with Helen, who had already escaped.

Smith returned to his office in San Francisco, frustrated. He wrote a few lines in praise of Miss Wills. He had hoped for more. He said she had made all Californians proud. She was talented and she was beautiful. She was a young woman whose head had not been turned by success. At the time, Smith could not know that he would be writing words like that about this tantalizing young woman for the next fifteen years. And in those years he would use several popular titles to describe her—"Helen of the Pigtails," "The Wonder Girl," "Little Miss Poker Face," "The Girl of the Golden West," "Our Hope," "Our Helen," "Helen of America," "The Ice Queen," "Big Helen," "Queen Helen," and the one that best described her place in the hearts of her fellow countrymen, "The American Girl."

--◄{ 2 }►--

Helen Newington Wills was born in Centerville, California, in Alameda County, on October 6, 1905. Her father, Clarence A. Wills, a native Californian, was born and raised in Antioch and had graduated from the University of California Medical School. In 1923 he was a surgeon at the Alameda County Hospital in Oakland. Helen's mother, Catherine Anderson Wills, was born in Stanhope, Iowa, and raised in Winters, California. She also was a graduate of the University of California, where she majored in social science and was trained as a teacher. Her only student was to be her only child.

Helen was kept out of the public school system until she was eight years old. Before that time she was tutored at home by her mother. Mrs. Wills did an unusually good job in instructing her daughter. Helen excelled in her studies and would have graduated from the exclusive Anna Head School in Berkeley at the age of sixteen, had she not insisted on being held back a grade because of difficulties in math. At the University of California, Helen earned her Phi Beta Kappa key and was awarded an academic scholarship.

The bond between Helen and Catherine Wills was special and powerful. They were more than mother and daughter. They were best friends—or, in the idiom of that time, they were "chums"—and often secret sharers. After Helen joined the Kappa Kappa Gamma sorority at the University of California she continued to live at home. And reporters who snooped around the sorority house were told that Helen had no very close friends in the organization. Her best friend, they were told, was still her mother. Catherine Wills sat at courtside in Berkeley while Helen practiced and went with her daughter to all of her tournaments in Europe and America from 1921 until 1930. At courtside she fulfilled the role Papa Lenglen played for his Suzanne, but with a major difference. Catherine Wills encouraged Helen by her quiet presence alone. She said nothing during a match, sent no signals, made no gestures, gave no advice, volunteered no criticism. She was simply present. But that was enough to give Helen extra strength and resolve. She also provided solace and companionship and guidance and strength between matches and during the long days of traveling on the Overland Limited and countless other trains and ships. Helen, in turn, provided her mother with pride, companionship, and escape. Helen was her mother's best friend.

Helen Wills, who became an avatar of health and strength as an adolescent, had not been a robust child. Her father initially tried to interest her in outdoor activities in order to strengthen her fragile constitution. She took up swimming, which helped. Her father bought her a horse, and riding helped too. Helen accompanied her father hunting quail and duck and loved it. Finally, almost as an afterthought, Dr. Wills turned to tennis to provide Helen with a regular exercise.

Dr. Wills bought his daughter a tennis racket when she was eight years old and played with her on the dirt courts adjacent to the Alameda County Hospital. He hit with her every afternoon and tried to teach her the fundamentals of the game.

She was annoyed at first, she recalled, by the rules that required a player to hit the ball between chalk lines drawn on the court. She preferred to hit the ball straight up in the air or to sock it up into the highest branches of the trees. And she still loved to play other games, too, less serious games where the only parameters and rules were those of the imagination, games lik Cowboys and Indians and Tarzan of the Apes. Her love of tennis was not love at first sight. It developed into real love only over a period of time. "I spent most of my time until thirteen outdoors running with dogs, playing Cowboys and Indians, riding horses," she wrote later. "There was nothing formal in the way of athletic training and there was no attempt to direct me toward one game. As a matter of fact, I was especially keen about nature and liked to hunt wild flowers as much as I liked to play any games at all."

Only when she took up tennis, however, did Helen start to develop physically. "It is more strenuous than swimming, more vigorous than horseback riding, and if there were any way of measuring the output of energy in the different forms of athletics, tennis, I believe, would prove to call for more stamina than any other, except perhaps rowing," Helen later claimed. Part of the reason she found tennis a demanding sport was the racket most commonly used in those prewar days. Helen learned her tennis by swinging a 15-ounce wooden racket with a 5½-inch handle. And though in later years she would switch to a lighter racket, she still preferred the large handle.

It seemed only natural that Clarence Wills would sooner or later turn to tennis in order to get his daughter interested in an outdoor sport. While Helen was growing up, tennis had become the most popular participation sport in California. Numerous tennis clubs operated in the state, sponsoring tournaments and exhibitions by top players, and a public parks tennis program gave youngsters a chance to play without cost whenever they wished. Tennis in California had also become a popular spectator sport, and large crowds turned out regularly for the various city, county, state, and regional championships.

Tennis developed in California without any of the genteel affectations or staid traditions of tennis on the East Coast. Everything about the game in California, the courts, clubs, the sporting attire, and the attitude and background of the players and fans, was unique. And Helen was to be a beneficiary of the differences.

Tennis courts in California were almost exclusively hard courts—cement or asphalt—because the hot and dry summers killed off lawns. When tennis was introduced to the state in the 1880s, grass courts were constructed. But to maintain those courts during the summer it was necessary to water them often, which softened the ground and made them nearly impossible to use. As a result, dirt was next used, then asphalt and concrete. Climate and the hard courts meant that Californians could play tennis year round. This gave them an advantage over their eastern and midwestern counterparts, an advantage that begin to tell early in the twentieth century. One New York sports writer, trying to account for the dominance of the westerners, concluded, "Of course they play well out there, where it is always June."

One California writer at the time, however, claimed that the idea that the weather alone created California champions simply was not true. It wasn't nature but rather the democracy of the California game that produced western dominance, he said. And the democratic quality of the sport in the state was made possible by the fact that hard courts, unlike grass courts, were inexpensive to build and maintain. Almost every city and town in the state built public courts in parks during the last decade of the nineteenth century. The courts were open to everyone free of charge, so thousands of Californians took up the new sport. "Here it has never been necessary to have fifteen suits and the membership card of an exclusive club to enjoy the best tennis," Robin Baily wrote in 1917. "Municipal courts are available for all. Any one with enthusiasm, a pair of shoes and a racquet can meet opponents of his own standard of skill, whatever it might be." In one public tournament held in the spring of 1917 in Golden Gate Park in San Francisco, 350 people played, including a sixty-year-old grandfather and a boy of twelve. "The sight of this happy-go-lucky free-for-all competition is visible throughout the year from dawn to dusk," he wrote. Baily concluded that "the history of the sport proves that to obtain athletic genius it is necessary to tooth-comb the whole population. The privileged class is never sufficiently numerous to yield world champions."

In California anyone with an inclination and a racket could play. "And from the thronging thousands are thrown up the Maurice Mc-Loughlins, Billy Johnstons, and May Suttons who are the delight of the crowds and the despair of opponents." To that list he might have added, after 1923, the name of Helen Wills.

The California galleries were different, too. Beginning in the 1890s the western galleries included numerous cheering groups, and organized cheers and yells by spectators punctuated the play. Groups showed up at matches decked out in club or park colors. The California Tennis Club, for example, as early as 1892 had its own organized cheering section with rhythmic cheers to encourage its top player, Will Taylor, who won the state singles championship that year. The Pacific States Lawn Tennis Association was organized in July of 1890, and had within two years sixteen clubs on its membership list, each with its own cheering section. When Helen Wills played in Paris in 1924 a University of California cheering group showed up to encourage her. As a result of the noisy enthusiasm at courtside, the Californians developed better concentration and adapted to the demonstrative galleries, unlike many of their East Coast and European counterparts.

There was an element of aristocracy to American tennis on the East Coast in the early decades of the century. Tickets for matches were expensive and the gallery small. The common herd was kept away from the carefully tended grass courts of the casinos and clubs. The only aristocracy in California tennis was that of talent. And the culling of the common California herd produced the players who became the darlings of the democratic crowds.

California tennis was also more emancipated than that of the East. In 1891, California clubs and associations began using female scorers and line judges. There were few complaints, and the women were a decided success. The women's game also caught on in the 1890s. And about the time Helen Wills was introduced to tennis, Maurice McLoughlin, the "California Comet," pointed out that there was "scarcely any place of importance in California where the ladies events are not treated as of equal importance with those of the men. This can scarcely be said of any other section of the country. As a result, it stimulates both interest and keen competition, which is so absolutely essential to the development of a high-class tennis player." And, he observed, the women often practiced against men, "a matter of invaluable assistance to any girl in the development of strokes, for she learns to adapt herself to the faster shots of the men, which naturally has the effect of making the strokes of other ladies easier to handle."

California women quickly took up the so-called California game of the men, with more volleying and more derring-do than in the East. As early as 1891 the first female volleyer appeared on the coast—Ethyl Bates— and showed that women could play an adaptation of the men's game in California, and do it fairly well. As evidence of the democratic and coed nature of California tennis, writer James Archibald referred to it in an 1892 article in *Outing* magazine as "the royal sport of the people."

In the first two decades of the twentieth century, California tennis players took their expertise east to win national titles. Hazel Hotchkiss, Mary K. Browne, May Sutton, Maurice McLoughlin, and Billy Johnston all became national champions, and Sutton won two Wimbledon singles titles. And when Molla Bjursted, a Norwegian immigrant who had won the National Indoor Tennis Title and the Women's Metropolitan Championship in New York, and who for eleven years had been the woman singles champion of Norway, came to California to play in the Panama-Pacific International Exposition tournament in 1915, she was beaten by Anita Meyers, holder of the California state title. Later that summer May Sutton beat Mallory twice. The emergence of these new heroes and heroines of the court popularized tennis in California even more.

Maurice McLoughlin was the first male player from California to gain a national reputation, winning the American singles title in 1912 and 1913. And he became an inspiration for Helen and for thousands of other California youngsters. When McLoughlin competed at Forest Hills, sportswriter John Kieran wrote, it was the democratic West against the aristocratic East. The democrats won hands down. Billy Johnston followed in McLoughlin's footsteps and became the second of many of the state's celebrated totems of democracy in action on the tennis court.

In 1909 California had but one male player ranked in the national top ten. But in each succeeding year for the next several decades there were three or four Californians in the top ten.

Clarence Wills took Helen to see the exhibitions by Meyers and by the Sutton sisters of Pasadena and by McLoughlin, Johnston, and others. Helen watched in fascination, and her interest in the game increased. McLoughlin was the first nationally ranked player she saw in an exhibition, and he left an indelible impression on her. "There is no other player in tennis history that I would rather have seen than McLoughlin at his best," she wrote after seeing him. She remembered the afternoon distinctly, and "how thrilled I was when I took up a tennis ball for his famous signature."

In 1917 Clarence Wills entered the U.S. Army. He served as a physician for one year in Europe with the AEF. During that time Helen and Catherine Wills moved to Vermont, where Helen attended a private school, Hopkins Hall, and Catherine served as a house mother for the institution. Helen brought her tennis racket to Vermont but couldn't play because the courts at the school were being resurfaced. As a result, "we spent much time playing Tarzan in the trees. The Tarzan books were beginning to come out, and although they were proscribed in the school, they were smuggled in." Helen took up ice skating and field hockey during her year at Hopkins Hall.

After the war the Wills family returned to California and took up residence in Berkeley, the community built around the University of California. They bought a house on 1200 Shattuck Avenue, near Live Oak Park, a wooded region of the town. Helen once more played tennis with her father and competed on the public courts at Live Oak Park. She improved, hitting the ball more carefully, moving around the court better, and learning the logic of the game. She played against many of the neighborhood youngsters and almost always won.

She began to play more seriously, she said, when she found that "life was like tennis, with rules and lines and scores," and that she could not play make believe all of her life. "I wanted to play at something," she recalled, "and I discovered that in tennis—as in all sports—is to be found a counterpart of the imaginative play of childhood—much less thrilling, of course, but better than nothing." And so "tennis was exchanged for the games of childhood, and I am very happy that this happened." Yet, she remembered, tennis remained just a game for her. "There was nothing deadly serious about the way I played. Nor has there ever been, for tennis always has been above everything else, a real pleasure for me. Neither was there any training, so called, any strict routine to be followed. There were just a comparatively few simple suggestions which my father, a physician, thought fitted to my needs."

It was while she was playing at Live Oak Park that Helen was spotted by William C. "Pop" Fuller, who supervised the junior tennis program at the Berkeley Tennis Club. Fuller found his tennis pupils on the public courts of San Francisco and the East Bay. Some playground instructor or player was always inviting him to watch some promising youngster. And Fuller could never turn down the invitation. "Like gold," he believed, "tennis players are where you find them."

Someone told him about a little girl with long pigtails who was beating all of the boys on the courts at Live Oak Park, so he went to see for himself. He was impressed. Fuller watched Helen play for a while, then he spoke with Dr. Wills and suggested that a junior membership in the Berkeley Tennis Club be bought for Helen so that she could get some better competition and have the chance for formal instruction. In August 1919, Clarence Wills presented Helen with a junior membership in the club as an early fourteenth birthday gift.

Helen's skill developed so quickly that Clarence Wills began to think it was possible for her to win some titles. And shortly after joining the club, Helen confided in some of the other junior members that she intended some day to become a "world champion."

Fuller didn't use a tennis racket in teaching Helen Wills for fear that she would copy his own faulty style. He wanted her to develop her own strokes and her own game. He confined himself to throwing balls to her to allow her to practice almost endlessly hitting the same shot over and over again. He had a box that held ten dozen balls, and he emptied and filled the box and and again day after day tossing balls to Helen, offering words of encouragement. He also got her practice partners and matches with other players.

"Helen was among the first to stand up against my new-fangled barrage," he recalled, "and though I have found out since that most of my girls have to overcome a curiously feminine fear of a thrown ball, I didn't notice that Helen-of-the-pigtails batted an eyelash at my unusual procedure. Even then she was the 'Little Poker Face' that the world called her subsequently."

It was that lack of emotion—the poker face—that struck so many spectators and opponents and caused them to wonder how Helen could concentrate so deeply. But Helen later provided a different reason for her sober demeanor on the court. Sportswriter Will Grimsley visited her in the late summer of 1977. She laughed with him about her reputation for being poker-faced and said it was because of her father's advice. "My father, a doctor, always told me not to wince or screw up my face while I was playing. He said it would put lines on my face."

After each long session of drills, Fuller arranged practice matches for Helen. At first she played against the other girls in the club. Then, when they provided little challenge for her, Fuller had her play against the boys. And after she had beaten all the boys, he arranged for her to practice with some young men from the University of California tennis team who played regularly at the club.

Fuller found that Helen already had a grasp of the basics from playing against her father. He said that Dr. Wills "appreciated the fine points of the game and acquitted himself well at it" and was "keen about his daughter's potential ability and future in the field." Dr. Wills, Fuller discovered, "had faith that Helen would go far. So had her mother." Catherine Wills accompanied Helen to the Berkeley Club almost every day and sat patiently through the coaching sessions. "I think that her parents' interest and unfailing encouragement were the most important factors in her climb to supremacy," Fuller said later.

Helen was a superb student. She had extraordinary coordination and stamina along with mental alertness and self-control. "From the day when she was Helen-of-the-pigtails, I never saw anyone more determined and cool about winning success nor more indifferent to failure. She has always carried out Kipling's idea of treating them both as 'twin impostors'." Fuller was even more impressed after seeing Helen in one of her first tournaments at Golden Gate Park. She was beaten in an early round. "Her father and I, who had gone to see her play, began to console her," Fuller recalled. " 'Oh, that's all right, Daddy!' she said. 'Now give me some money—I want to ride on the merry go round.' " Fuller said that she never mentioned the loss again. "She forgot it utterly. It is part and parcel of her to concentrate absolutely on the business in hand and forget what has gone before. What a gift that is in tennis! Helen is one of those rare players who never think of the shot that is made if it is a poor one. Her whole mind is on the shot to be made. Everything else is excluded, even the audience watching.

"The only way that I was ever able to tell when things were not going to suit her was by watching the fingers of her left hand. If they were held close together, all was well; if they separated, it was a sure sign of emotional disturbance," he said.

Without knowing of Charles Lenglen's method for developing the accuracy of Suzanne's strokes, Fuller independently came up with the same exercise. He placed a handkerchief first in one corner of the service court and then the other and Helen served until she hit it consistently. "I can still remember how little Helen-of-the-pigtails forgot her 'poker face' when she hit the mark!" he said. Fuller found that Helen's most serious early problem was her insistence on hitting every shot with all her strength. She never varied her strokes and never hit soft shots, and so Fuller attempted to teach her patience and to teach her to use a little finesse in her stroke production. He failed. Not until the late 1920s would Helen brag that her game was at its peak, because, as she told a friend, she at last could use "finesse."

After a time, Fuller used Helen to play a joke on new club members. "I used to get a big thrill out of matching some new male member of the Berkeley Tennis Club with her," he said. "The fellow would laugh at the idea of playing a child and a girl at that. But as the game warmed up he would get a worried look on his face. And in the end he'd be amazed. "The vanquished males used to come into the clubhouse and say, 'I wish she were a boy—it wouldn't look so damned bad.'"

Although many champions came out of Pop Fuller's junior tennis program at the Berkeley club, Fuller would always be most closely identified with the rise of Helen Wills. And when he passed away in 1956 he was memorialized as "Helen Wills's tennis coach."

Helen disagreed with that claim, however. Fuller had not been her coach or her teacher, she said. The credit he heaped upon himself was the result of a fantasy. She insisted that she was a self-taught natural athlete. "What I know I have learned through observation of others and actual practice or contest," she said. "My father was the only person who told me what to do in tennis that I really believed. I was stubborn, perhaps because I made up my mind to appear to be listening politely to what other people said, but not really to do what they suggested."

Fuller remained loyal to Helen all of his life. She had been, he said, the best player he had ever "coached" and the best player he had ever seen.

In describing the development of her game, Helen said, "I played for fun. I practiced by playing games, not by drilling on strokes. I never bounced the ball against a barnyard door. I played against those who could show me the simple principles of position and strokes, and then I worked out my own technique. I was early impressed with the importance of footwork. I found that my serve was about the hardest thing for me, and I worked quite hard on trying to perfect it. But I did not do this by serving a lot of balls over the net at once. I did it in games as I went along. The result was that I never noticed any sudden mastery of a special stroke, but just found my game improving gradually, strengthening as I continued to play."

Her method of self-instruction was simple: observation, concentration, and imitation. Helen watched carefully the play of champions like Mc-Loughlin and Johnston; she tried, as best she could, to analyze their games by concentrating carefully on their movements, their strokes, their tactics, and even their stance; then she sought to imitate them. But adolescent imitation was always imperfect due to physical and emotional differences among players. And so in the imitation there was personal adaptation and unconscious interpretation as Helen found her own peculiar strengths and weaknesses and worked with them, through them, or around them. Helen even whispered to herself sometimes while playing, "Now I'm Johnston. Now I'm Johnston," trying through those words to become "Little Bill," copying his extreme western forehand grip and attempting to duplicate his trademark cannonball service, his blistering forehand drive, and his daring volleying techniques, none of which worked very well for her. So she shifted to a less severe western grip and stayed on the backcourt developing an ever more powerful forehand drive as the centerpiece of her game.

Other California players imitated and adapted and interpreted the games of others, too. The California tennis courts became little laboratories of pragmatism. Whatever worked for a particular player was right and was kept. Whatever didn't work was wrong and was discarded. The result was that some of the creativity of each player was manifested in his or her game. Not surprisingly, a wide variety of semi-original and personal strokes and tactics was seen that had never been seen before and not been seen since. And this made for interesting and sometimes amusing confrontations as players learned to work around a weak service or awkwardly struck forehands, backhands, and overheads and to adjust to unexpected tactics. Players commonly ran around bad strokes and teased opponents into hitting to their strength. There were few clones, despite the efforts to imitate Johnston and McLoughlin and Hazel Wightman and the Sutton sisters.

Helen Wills was especially attracted to speed and to power. She said later of her early development, "Nothing is more fun when playing than to hit the ball hard and see it go flying over the net. Speed, even with greater risk, has a certain fascination and charm that cannot be equalled by anything else in the game. If I had my choice I would much rather be the fastest player in the world than the most accurate, if to be the most accurate demanded slower play."

She also liked the scrambling part of tennis when she was young, going for every ball, no matter how desperate the effort—Boris Becker style—even to the point of stumbling and turning a somersault on the court during one of her early matches as a junior, much to her consternation and to the shocked delight of the gallery. She felt it was not improper to go so energetically for everything. She said that "to slide, lunge, and dive does not conform to good style in tennis, but there is the dignity of sincerity in the scramble."

Eventually Helen Wills developed superb abilities of anticipation and, like a good baseball player, she seemed to know just where a ball was going as her opponent moved to make a return. Then she was in position and ready with her own reply. As a result, she was seldom rushed and had no need to scramble, slide, lunge, or dive. To some observers this power of anticipation in turn made it look like Helen was slow on her feet, and she acquired a reputation for having bad footwork. But her opponents always pointed out, "You will notice that Helen seems to move slowly, yet she always gets to where she wants to be in plenty of time."

The combination of tremendous power and uncanny anticipation had a devastating impact on her opponents. Edith Cross, who played often with Wills in the late 1920s, remembered her thinking ahead and knowing where a shot would cross the net and where it would fall. And there were times when she became impatient and wanted to finish a rally. She would would glide in toward the net, sometimes moving just in front of the service line. Cross remembered that when she saw Wills move forward she knew the point was about to end. "But oh my God the fun of playing against Helen. She was the master of every stroke and it was always an honor—and I mean that—it was always a real honor to face Helen across the net, no matter how inept or awkward she made you feel by her own abilities."

Anna Harper remembered that Helen Wills hit so hard that the ball seemed to have been dipped in concrete after she hit it. It was hard to stop it and put pace on the return. You could feel the impact of the ball up your arm and into your shoulder, she recalled. And so Helen tired weaker opponents quickly. Every stroke carried that same tremendous pace, again and again until she broke you down by taking away your best shots and making you play her game. You fought just to stay on the court, let alone make points. "Those shots of hers, coming one after another after another without relief—well, after a game or two when you found out how hard this was going to be, she either broke your confidence or she broke your arm."

In the process of inventing her powerful game, Wills got her stance wrong. She hit both her forehand and backhand drives from an open position—she faced the net as she made the strokes. A coach concerned with producing a perfect textbook game would have insisted she face the side of the court with her shoulder toward the net while making her strokes. If Pop Fuller found her stance awkward, he did nothing at all to correct it. From that open stance and a big windup, Helen generated all her power.

Journalist Al Laney watched Helen Wills over the years and wrote that her forehand was "a resounding whack at the ball, not taken too early, not pretty, but absolutely certain, fluent and severe." He found something awkward in her backhand, however, and he wrote that it was "as safe as could be—she could hardly be made to miss with it across the court, the shot she played nine times out of ten whatever the situation, but it was often taken off the wrong leg. . . ."

Yet, despite her unorthodox stance and the fact that she hit her backhand off the wrong leg, there was genuine grace and beauty in her movement on the court. Everything worked together in perfect harmony and efficiency in her strokes, and she glided back and forth on the baseline sending explosive drives back across the net, operating with the ease, rhythm, and perfection of a powerful machine. As to the aesthetics of her movement on the court, there was no denying the fact that Helen Wills had successfully married sheer power to sheer beauty. The legions of male admirers at courtside wherever she played were testimony to this. One journalist described her as "a miracle of motion," and Charlie Chaplin, in 1930, when asked to name the most beautiful sight he had ever seen, said without hesitation, "the movement of Helen Wills playing tennis: it had grace and economy of action as well as a healthy appeal to sex." Paul Gallico concurred and wrote that one of the images from the 1920s that he could never forget was "the gleam in the eyes of Helen Wills looking up at a tennis ball in the air during her service, and her lovely neck line."

--◄§ 3 §►--

Helen Wills's name first appeared in local newspapers in the summer of 1919 when she won the Bay Region Tournament in her age group. She received notice again in the fall of 1919 when she competed in the California State Tennis Championships. Although she was defeated in her match by Marjorie Wale by a score of 10–8, 6–4, she was, nonetheless, applauded by the gallery for her play, which was said to resemble in style that of another prominent Californian, Hazel Hotchkiss Wightman. Six months later, in the spring of 1920, Helen met Wightman for the first time.

Years later Wightman liked to recount the story of her propitious discovery.

I'll not soon forget Berkeley in 1920. There were children playing everywhere, slamming the ball around, having a great time. But very few were playing real tennis. Most of them were merely amusing themselves.

There was one little girl who attracted my attention at once. She was about fourteen years of age, very pretty and prim in her pig tails. She hit the ball with definite skill and earnestness that stamped her as far superior to the others. Her figure, her concentration, her poise were remarkable in a child so young.

I made suggestions to her during play and it was an absolute delight to see the little girl put the suggestions into effect at once. She was possessed of a great desire to learn and an unswerving will to accomplish whatever new idea I was able to demonstrate.

Helen and I played most of that day and I was simply amazed at the power behind her drives and the finesse in many of her returns. I sensed that there was a coming star but I never dreamed she would attain the greatness she achieved in later years.

Because of this little girl I prolonged my visit to Berkeley to three weeks. We had a regular routine of three hours a day, four days a week. We would spend hours on serves, volleys, smashes, and other strokes.

She found Helen's footwork slow. She tried to give her drills to get her to run around the court faster, shouting as she did, "Run, Helen, run." When Helen made a mistake, she remembered that Hazel "simply looked away, her face assuming a patient but hopeful expression. But when I won a well-played point, she beamed so brightly that I wanted to please her every time."

Wightman's method was based on earning the points you made. There were hours of hitting the ball "until it does what you want." She found Wills to be shy, and so gave her special attention. "I have a special feeling about the awkward and shy ones," she said. "By doing something well that other people admire, they can gain confidence. It can be the difference between a frustrated life and a dull one."

In addition to the strokes and tactics of tennis, Wightman taught the girls she worked with proper decorum on and off the tennis court. She believed that a female tennis champion was in fact a model for other impressionable girls and so carried a responsibility in her behavior. She let Helen know this. But, she said, Helen took it a little too seriously, perhaps.

Helen Wills had a reputation as early as 1921 as a very serious young woman. And her serious demeanor was interpreted by some journalists and spectators as arrogance. She paid no attention to those around her, on or off the tennis court. There was even an air of severe formality to her walk. "There is no motion of her upper body when she is in movement. The effect is curiously like that of a West Point cadet after considerable military training," one newsman said. She behaved as though she were almost alone in the world with her thoughts. "I was not curious about people, nor did I wonder why they behaved as they did. I was possessed of a self-centered calm, which made me incapable of any feelings of nervousness. I had no nerves—least of all in a tennis match," she wrote later.

And she had extraordinary self-confidence. "It never occurred to me that if you once did get into action and tried your hardest, you would not be rewarded with victory. If by chance you did not win, nothing could prevent you from winning eventually," she concluded. "It was a marvelous thing to be imbued with the feeling of certainty."

That cold, hard exterior melted in the presence of Wightman. The trick, Hazel said later, was to treat Helen Wills like an unqueenly and imperfect human being. "Helen was really an unconfident and awkward girl—you have no idea how awkward.

"I remember one morning . . . Helen came banging down the stairs violently enough to shake the whole house apart. I asked her to go up-stairs and come down again, and this time to walk rhythmically and lightly. It was almost as bad as before. 'You try that once more,' I told her, 'and this time lay those nine double-"A's" of yours down with just a suspicion of femininity.' She came down pretty well that time. You see, where I differed from most of the tennis crowd was that I thought of Helen as an honestly shy person who was bewildered by how difficult it was to please most people."

Wightman worked with Helen Wills as teacher, amateur psychologist, and finally doubles partner. In tournament competition the team of Wills–Wightman was never beaten. "Nobody has ever derived more genuine pleasure from the rise of Helen Wills than I," Wightman affirmed years later.

--◄ 4 ►--

In 1920 Helen Wills won the Bay Counties tennis title and became re-gional champion in the private school competition. Hazel Wightman returned home and told her friends in the East that there was a rising star in California. And Paul Gallico wrote that "somebody said there was a leggy kid out on the Pacific Coast who wore her hair in two long, brown braids, named Wills or something, who would bear watching."

In 1921 Helen Wills won the California State Women's Championship and then made her first trip east to play her first matches on grass before an eastern gallery. In the Agawam Hunt Club Tournament in Provi-dence, Rhode Island, she was put out of the singles in the second round by Marion Zinderstein Jessup, but in the mixed doubles she made it all the way to the finals with fellow Californian Wallace Bates before losing. It was the first time she had played on grass. Then she won the National Girls Championship at Forest Hills. She was impressive, but hardly a new Maid Marvel. She stood a little over five feet tall, and she hit as hard as she could and ran as fast as she could and won more points than she lost. She had a long way to go, however, before she would be a top-ranked player. Her game was still developing.

Following her victory, she saw Suzanne Lenglen for the first time. "My first glimpse of Mlle. Lenglen was on the clubhouse veranda at Forest Hills," she wrote later. "She wore a yellow organdie dress, a large hat, and a white lapin coat described as ermine by the newspapers. The fur coat on a hot day made me ask why. I was told that she had a cold." Helen and her mother were given seats at the end of the court in the middle of the front row for the match. "At the time when I saw the Mallory-Lenglen match," Helen recalled, "my game was in the transition stage. Seeing the best women's tennis in the world concentrated in one match was an invaluable experience. After that I knew the goal for which I hoped to aim, the kind of tennis I wanted to play."

While Suzanne Lenglen impressed Helen Wills and other American spectators by the exotic quality of her costumes, Helen received attention for the contrastingly commonplace appearance of hers. She appeared for her matches wearing her school uniform: a long cotton skirt, a middy blouse with a broad collar down the back, and white stockings rolled above the knee. She wore her long hair in two thick braids that reached to her waist. Her trademark, however, became the white visor that shaded her eyes. The shadow it cast across her face gave her just a hint of mystery—she was like someone always looking at you out of interesting and mysterious shadows. Whatever its origin (Helen insisted that all California players wore one) it was soon referred to everywhere as the "Helen Wills visor."

In 1922 Helen Wills won the California state title again and then defeated Helen Hooker of New York in the National Junior Tournament held at the Philadelphia Cricket Club. She was then beaten by Leslie Bancroft, a left-hander from Boston, in the Women's Middle States Championships at the club.

She played in seven more tournaments in the East that summer, the most important one being the National Women's Singles at Forest Hills where, to just about everyone's surprise, she won her way to the finals and then lost 6–3, 6–1 to Molla Mallory, who one year earlier, on the same court, had beaten Suzanne Lenglen. After Mallory had beaten her she offered no excuses. In fact, just before taking the court she told reporters, "I shall do my best, but I hardly expect to win."

Wills was more successful at Forest Hills when she teamed up with Marion Jessup to defeat Mallory and Edith Sigourney in a three-set match, 6–4, 7–9, 6–3, to win the national doubles title. One week later Helen Wills shocked the tennis world when she took a set from Molla Mallory in a tournament at the Nassau Country Club in Glen Cove, Long Island.

Ten days later at the Longwood Invitational Tournament at the Longwood Cricket Club in Brookline, Massachusetts, Wills came close to beating Mallory. For the second time that summer she took a set from Mallory and then moved ahead 5–4 in the final set but could not hang on to win, losing the close match, 3–6, 6–3, 7–5. The crowd was pro-Wills, going so far as to applaud Mallory's errors. They objected loudly to several line calls that went against Wills, despite the fact that the calls were unquestionably fair. The umpire tried but failed to quiet the crowd. And the *New York Times* noted that the crowd "laid aside its manners for the afternoon." At the end of the match Mallory, the tough competitor, was almost in tears because of the treatment accorded her by the hostile gallery. For the fourth time in 1922 Helen lost to Molla at the Rockaway Hunting Club in Cedarhurst, Long Island. Helen took the first set 6–3 and then lost the next two at 1–6, 3–6.

Suddenly, she was the young sensation of the day. She won the hearts of the audiences of the East, and when she left the court the crowd stood and cheered. Helen Wills had acquired a public. And although she was the darling of the crowd she seemed unaware of that fact. Spectators found her to be serious, earnest, and totally absorbed in her play. She was expressionless throughout a match, never smiling, never frowning, never betraying any emotion at all. A visiting British writer said she looked and acted like a Quaker. She disposed of her opponents as quickly, dispassionately, and as impersonally as possible. She had a childlike ability to concentrate completely on the task at hand and to block out all else, much to the fascination and amusement of the crowd. She was just like the Little Engine That Could as she huffed and puffed her way through the early rounds of the national tournament. And following each match she left the court and joined her mother and then was seen no more until her next match.

Ed Sullivan, who wrote about tennis for the *New York Evening Mail* in 1922, interviewed an English tennis authority who said that Helen Wills reminded him of a player in a card game—poker. The reference stuck in Sullivan's mind when he was trying to find an expression to describe Helen, he came up with her most famous nickname, "Little Poker Face." Arthur Guiterman of the old *Life* magazine later composed a verse using it—"The journalists, a ribald race, Have named her Little Poker Face"— and was credited with inventing it. But Sullivan, himself a poker-faced journalist who later became the poker-faced host of a successful television variety show, was the first to use the term, which other journalists immediately adopted.

Wills's concentration involved a mantra that she repeated quietly to herself over and over on the court. In place of "Now I'm Johnston, Now I'm Johnston," she now said to herself, "every shot, every shot, every shot" to remember that only the shot being played existed or counted and once it was played only the next shot counted, and so on. This led her to pay no attention at all to the score of a match, and there were times when she was unaware that a game or a set or a match had been completed.

It was the way she used to escape from the noise and confusion of the California crowd. She played every shot. One shot at a time. Never worry about the score. Repeat the mantra. Remember the feet. Every shot.

"What indeed does anything matter, either during a match or after, if you have done as well as you are able on every shot?" she pointed out.

To her opponents and to members of the gallery she often seemed cold when she walked onto the court and went into her concentration, and this in turn was described as her iciness or her coldness. She was called by some writers, "The Ice Queen." And reporters said that she waged a war on the courts—a cold war—that often spooked the younger and less-experienced opponents, who must have appeared to be gracious victims led to the slaughter, more concerned about not being hit by one of her powerful drives than by earning points. She was not unlike Gene Tunney or Joe Louis in her approach to her sport. She was methodical.

One writer noticed that she never smiled at her opponent or exchanged words when changing courts, and he asked her about it. She responded, "I do not believe in encouraging my opponents in a tournament contest. I want it to be understood that we are in a battle, not a social affair." Another Californian, May Sutton, said something like that at the turn of the century: "Remember, tennis is not pink tea!"

She carefully and thoughtfully planted her feet in position, her body correctly poised and balanced so that a stroke could be made and contact with the ball could be perfect and the follow-through correct. She studied the ball as it approached her and never took her eye from it until it hit the racket—perfectly in the center. Half a century after she retired from tournament tennis I asked her if she thought that a larger racket might have improved her game. "No," she replied after a moment. "I always hit the ball right in the middle of the racket. I don't see how a larger racket would have made any difference to me." But she was particular about her rackets. From the day of her first tournament she played with only the very best rackets strung with only the very best gut. The rackets were hand-picked and strung for her throughout the 1920s by Gus Feibig of the Berkeley Tennis Club, who became a family friend.

Despite the efforts of other players to get Wills to lighten up, she remained set in her ways. Because of that, Grantland Rice observed that Helen at sixteen was "intensely serious, unemotional, stoical—not only for a girl of her age, but for a human being of any age." She represented, Rice wrote, the power of youth, but not the romance of youth or its light and less serious side. She masked all of her emotions in the contest, he found, "curbing any tendency to show elation or nervousness or worry." That was what others believed, he wrote. But the fact was, he concluded, that she "had no great emotions to mask. Her set, determined unsmiling face was a natural part of her being. She was attempting to suppress nothing—nothing but the enemy in front of her."

Rice also was first to write that Helen had a "killer instinct," and pursued her game with the feeling that no quarter should be given to an opponent. On the other hand, she abhorred alibis and excuses for her own play.

Rice was sure that there had been some days when Wills did not play well when she should have cancelled or postponed a match. But she apparently had a rule, he wrote, that if she went onto the court then there were to be no excuses. If she played she was not ill. And if she had been beaten that day there would never have been a suggestion from her camp that she was not in the best possible physical condition. In that she was the complete opposite of Lenglen. She had totally neglected what Rice called "the art of the alibi." On the court it was all business in a period when American business and the business ethic seemed almost deified. Here was suddenly a businesslike, no-nonsense player who was the perfect example of American energy and determination and efficiency and know how. In the age of the Big Bull Market there was also Big Helen, the American Girl.

Looking back at her youth, she would smile at her uncommon seriousness. She confessed that she "must have been an oppressive young person" who did not enjoy life as much as she should have. But there was also a melancholy side to Helen that she did not discuss openly. She wrote later that there was always "a restlessness which seems to be continually in my heart." Tennis and painting were her means of responding to it. That was why she concentrated so hard on tennis, she said. "By working steadily on the thing that I like I can remove from my mind momentary spells of sadness or irritation or anger, and afterwards feel happy and almost peaceful." "For me," she wrote, "life is interesting, entertaining and happy, if only I can have some activity for the restlessness that is in my heart."

The public and the press found in Helen something complete and solid. She had the future in her. And there was a secret quality to her, also. A hidden something, a mystery of potential, like America itself. Paul Gallico wrote, "I promise you she was one of the most astonishing creatures ever to froth to the top of our great American melting pot." She was gifted, imbued, and at the same time common. She was a goddess in the form of an American girl, unlike Suzanne Lenglen, who was a goddess in the form of a vamp.

At the close of the 1922 season Helen was ranked third among American women by the USLTA.

In the spring of 1923, when asked about promising young players, Billy Johnston pointed to Helen Wills. In 1922 she seemed to tire easily in extreme heat in the East, he said, and she also seemed inclined to be uncertain on the court. The problem, Johnston suggested, may have been the soggy grass courts. Helen was not accustomed to the surface. But she had worked hard on her game since then and she was in good physical shape. She just might win the national title in 1923 he said. Hazel Wightman agreed. Helen was going to be unstoppable in 1923, she told reporters that spring.

But Wills seemed to have other things on her mind in the spring of

1923. She was graduating from the Anna Head School, and she had enrolled for the fall term at the University of California in order to study art. According to the press reports from Berkeley, Helen planned "to shove tennis into the background and woo the muse." "Miss Wills claims that tennis is merely an avocation and she has decided upon art as her life work," one report said.

In the spring of 1923 Wills repeated her victory as private school champion for the Bay Area and then with her mother went east once more. Helen did not enter the Junior Championship Tournament in 1923 because "the girls are pretty small, and I don't want to be, what is it you call it, a 'pot-hunter.' " And before she departed for Forest Hills that year she told a local reporter that "I play tennis because I love it" and not to gather trophies.

Her appearance at Forest Hills that year was a revelation because of her dramatic physical change. She had grown five inches between 1922 and 1923 and had put on twenty-five pounds so that she now stood just over five feet seven inches and weighed nearly 150 pounds. Along with the bulk she had added substantial strength. Her game seemed to have improved, especially the power of her ground strokes. And she now played what was referred to as the "man's game." She came to the net often and volleyed, even when it seemed a reckless maneuver. And she had acquired a more powerful service than any other woman. In 1921 she had been promising. In 1922 she had been promising and accomplished. In 1923 she was awesome.

Grantland Rice was deeply impressed when he watched Wills in 1923. He said that her strokes were a marvel of "peacefulness and perfection, regardless of the level from which they were hit. I saw her . . . hitting the ball from the back court as hard as most men can hit it, and placing it time after time within a few inches of where she wanted it to go. It required a combination of tennis genius and amazing patience and long, hard practice to get this result. No woman player today would have even the slightest chance against her, for no woman player could come close to matching her power and control. Any good male player would have trouble beating Miss Wills from the back court—as several have testified. As none of the women has a first-class net game they are all forced to meet her where she is stronger and almost invincible, where she has all the excess in both power and control of power. So the result is usually as expected."

On her way to Forest Hills, Helen stopped off in Chicago and won the Illinois state women's singles title without the loss of a game. Then, on the East Coast, Wills entered several small tournaments in order to accustom herself to the grass surface. She was beaten once by Molla Mallory and once by Eleanor Goss. Bill Tilden, a close friend of Molla, said that "Helen has no chance against Mallory." But Tilden was wrong about Helen, as usual. Helen had simply been getting practice in those preliminary tournaments. And now Molla had no chance against Helen. Hazel Wightman selected Wills to play in the number 2 position on the first American Wightman Cup team in 1923, and the matches were held at Forest Hills just prior to the national championships. She played in the singles in the American-British competition and beat both Kathleen McKane and Mrs. B. C. Covell as the American team swept the matches, 7–0.

Then, as in the national singles competition tournament, 5000 turned out to see Helen Wills crush defending champion Molla Mallory, 6–1, 6–2, in just thirty-three minutes. Accustomed to the hard hitting of the men she had played against, Wills now used Mallory's strength against her, blasting back drive after drive to the champion. After only four games it was clear that she was in command of the match, and Mallory was already talking to herself in frustration at the way her shots were coming back and she was losing points.

Mallory tried to force Wills to play her game, the backcourt duel. But she came to the net again and again and caught Mallory's shots for winners. At times in coming forward a bit late she made winners off half volleys as well as volleys, hitting both forehand and backhand.

Helen Wills became the first American-born champion since 1919, when Marion Zinderstein of Boston interrupted Mallory's string of victories. But in 1923 the "Norse conquest," as sportswriters called the rule of Molla, came to an end.

The crowd showed uncommon enthusiasm and cheered wildly at the closing points. They cheered for Helen Wills, and they cheered against Molla Mallory. Whenever Mallory missed a shot the crowd cheered, and several times Molla stopped the match and asked the umpire to address the crowd and ask for quiet. At the end of the match Helen's stern poker face had disappeared, and she was crying and smiling through her tears.

Newspaper writers now described Wills as a true genius of the court. Samuel Brookman of the *New York Herald* called her "marvelous" and said that "no milder adjective can truthfully tell of the brilliance and sterling worth of her play."

The fact was that Mallory was not just the American champion. She was the all-time American woman champion who had won the national title six times since 1915—seven, if one counted the special wartime tournament she won. She was called "Iron Molla" and was the player who in 1921 had shattered Suzanne Lenglen's hopes of an American title at Forest Hills by battering her off the court. Now she had in turn been battered by a seventeen-year-old California girl, culled from the democratic crowd on the coast.

Only one American champion had been younger than Helen Wills. In 1904 May Sutton came through with a similar triumph at the age of seventeen, but a few months younger than Helen. At that time the prediction had been made that her performance could never be duplicated.

Critics in 1923 were saying that the quality of all players was better than it had been nineteen years earlier. And the quality of Wills's play in particular put her on an almost equal footing with Lenglen. Another season or two of play, and she would no doubt be the best player in the world. One of the few female sportswriters of the day, Eleanor Carroll of the *New York Evening Post,* praised Wills's off-court behavior. She noticed that when Helen was not on the courts smashing winners she was seen on the club grounds or in the streets of Forest Hills, and she was always accompanied by her mother. "It is a game of doubles that she plays continually." Helen and her mother, whom she called "Cass," "make a happy, invincible team; there seems to be no one in the town whose love they have not won."

"It seems to me that California, especially, raises a race of real sports and comrades," Carroll wrote. "Mrs. Wills and her daughter are hauntingly like the most successful mother-daughter partnership that I have ever met."

She was impressed by Helen's shining brown hair, which she wore in long rope braids over her ears. She noticed the "firm brown arms that ripple with power" and said that they could not have had a lovelier setting.

Helen now took all of the credit for teaching herself tennis. She told reporters:

I have never had a professional lesson in my life, nor any help from really good players, either. . . .

I play every afternoon when at home in Berkeley. I love it. I have no theories of how to go about learning the game. I never have read any. And I don't want any. Just play the game; play hard, for pleasure—and let the technique and variety of strokes take care of themselves. They come to you, I suppose, but they don't really matter. The thing is to have a good time.

The reporters swooned. Everyone wanted to know how she played the game. Was there a difference between the man's and the woman's game? "I suppose that women do, on the whole, play a safer, slower, baseline game," she said. "But really it's much more fun to run to the net and try some smashing volleying shots. They seem to call that a 'man's game.' But I don't. I just call it fun."

The *New York World* referred to her now as "The Girl of the Golden West" and asked if she might not defeat Suzanne Lenglen if they met. Helen was of "championship calibre," but Suzanne was "a genius." A match between the two would be "the most sensational match in the tennis world, not, of course, from the standpoint of actually the best tennis, for, as in other games, the men excel the women. Yet, on the side of universal appeal what could be of such interest as the meeting of the brilliant temperamental Lenglen and the marvelous slip of a girl from Berkeley?

"Youth is always engaging, and when it is coupled with virtuosity, it becomes irresistible. Long live the girl queen!" the paper concluded.

The *New York Tribune* mused that in France, Suzanne Lenglen must be saying to herself, "I have beaten them all but this Helen Wills, and she has beaten all but Suzanne. Next year, perhaps, she will pay us a visit. Then we shall see." Already, the paper was dreaming of a confrontation between this new American heroine and the French goddess.

France had Suzanne Lenglen. And now, in 1923, Paul Gallico wrote that we had "Our Helen," America's own little girl.

---⋅⋙ 5 ⋘⋅---

Helen Wills established her national reputation in 1923. In 1924 she established an international reputation as a representative of the United States in the Wightman Cup competition in England and in the Olympic Games in France. She also competed for the first time as an individual in the championships at Wimbledon. Her endeavors abroad in the summer of 1924, as she brought laurels to her country as well as to herself, made her, thanks to a press hungry for heroic materials, not only one of the most highly publicized women in the United States but also one of the most admired.

No sooner had Wills won her first singles title at Forest Hills, than reporters and promoters, who knew a great story when they imagined one, began drumming up excitement for a Wills-Lenglen contest. The public was gradually caught up in the excitement, and a few Northern California sporting speculators started gathering cash in order to place early wagers on Helen when she did play Suzanne. In New York, in Chicago, and then in California, the talk was of the new American champion traveling to Europe to tackle the old world title-holder. Nobody stopped to ask *if* it would happen. Of course it would happen. What they wanted to know was *when* it would happen. How soon? Since 1924 was the year of the Olympic Games in Paris, and since tennis was an Olympic sport, and since Suzanne Lenglen was the defending Olympic gold medalist, it seemed certain that they would clash there. Or perhaps they would meet even earlier, in early July at Wimbledon, where Lenglen would go for her sixth straight singles title. Even though Wills insisted that she wished only to be a university student in 1924, surely she could not turn down the chance to play on the Wightman Cup and Olympic teams, and that would entail going abroad. Whatever the case, it was clear that 1924 would be a year of destiny for Wills and Lenglen as they inevitably drifted toward a clash.

Helen Wills entered the University of California in the fall of 1923 to study art—she continued to insist that "art will be my life" and that tennis was simply a diversion—and Suzanne Lenglen undertook an exhibition tour of Spain and Portugal, where she played against the leading male and female players of those countries. Then in January 1924 Lenglen started her regular Riviera winter round of competition and delighted the press when she said she felt just marvelous and intended to compete at both Wimbledon and the Olympic Games.

Optimism swelled in America when accounts from California suggested that Wills was practicing daily against some of the best male players on the West Coast and that she was regularly taking sets from them during some fairly rough-and-tumble practice sessions. But Blanche Ashbaugh, writing in the *San Francisco Chronicle*, cautioned local readers that it should be "clearly understood that the score in these matches means nothing and proves nothing except the generosity of the stars in giving their services to Miss Wills to help in the development of her game for her meeting with Mlle. Lenglen in the Olympic Games in June." Wills practiced daily with Bud Chandler and Gerald Stratford, two hard-hitting University of California classmates, and Billy Johnston and Howard Kinsey came to Berkeley from San Francisco at the request of Pop Fuller and went onto the court against Wills with instructions to feed her certain shots purely for practice and with no thought of trying to beat her. Johnston was asked to hit everything as hard as he could right at Wills to see if she could return his shots. She could. Kinsey, on the other hand, fed her all chop shots with a low bound, and she took a set from him.

On the Riviera, Lenglen won one title after another in her usual fashion. She defaulted in a tournament at Cannes because she said she had a cold. But then at her home club in Nice she took the singles, mixed doubles, and the women's doubles for a triple title. All three victories were won with comparative ease, but the field against her was not exceptionally strong—there were no ranked players and few serious challengers—precisely the type of tournament Lenglen loved. In mid-March she again won the championship of Southern France. It was reported that she was playing in top form. But the reports were not true.

Suzanne Lenglen began to experience serious problems in March. It was announced that she was suffering from a slight case of jaundice contracted during her Iberian tour. But this was part truth and part subterfuge. She was also suffering from the onset of another crisis of nerves due to her terrible conditioning and the anticipation of another highly publicized match against an American champion. She had put on weight, too much weight, during the winter. And her coordination suffered seriously. Her timing was off and her strokes had lost much of their crispness. She was slower on her feet and she tired quickly. She started to make excuses.

The Riviera system still worked to her advantage, however. In a tournament at the Gallia Club a foot fault was called against her. Lenglen blew up and quoted a Riviera rule that the first foot fault must result only in a warning. She stopped playing and sat down at courtside until the linesman left. By failing to give her a warning the linesman had demonstrated his lack of understanding of the rules, she said, and he was quickly removed. No more foot faults were called against her during the afternoon. And she won her match. But later it was pointed out that the matches at the Gallia Club were played under international rules which did not require a warning and that she was wrong. Yet no amends were made and no apologies given. Suzanne, heavier and slower, still ruled on the Riviera and made up her own rules as she went along, if she so wished. When Suzanne was tired, and she wanted to remain in a tournament, it was not unusual for club officials to impose upon her scheduled opponent to default. The record book then registered a Lenglen win. This was good for the clubs, good for Suzanne Lenglen, good for French tennis, and good for France, it was assumed. Even a goddess had bad days and had to be indulged.

Yet she eventually saw the seriousness of her situation, and went on another of her anorexic bouts in order to prepare for Wimbledon and the Olympic Games and her expected matches with Helen Wills. She starved herself and became even more self-pitying and temperamental. In early June she chose not to compete in the singles championships of France, and her title was taken by Didi Vlasto, France's second-ranked player.

Helen Wills left for England the day after she completed her final exams at the university. She arrived in England on May 20th and was immediately lionized by the British press. A dispatch in the *Evening Standard* stated that "the first thing that strikes one about her is that not a single photograph that has been published in England does her striking beauty anything like justice. No lovelier or more striking girl has ever been seen on the historic courts here." Blanche Ashbaugh took note of the stories in the British press and asked, "What must be the effect on Suzanne's sick mind when she reads—and she must be reading—of the wonderful impression California's 18-year-old tennis marvel is creating on the staid English critics?"

Helen Wills practiced against men, much to the delight of the British press. She defeated a top British club player and come within two points of defeating D. M. Grieg, who was ranked among the top twelve British amateurs. The set was 9–7, after British reporters insisted that Wills would be lucky to win a single game from a man. They were referring to her now as the American girl—not yet with capitals. Her blistering service aces were especially enthralling to the British newsmen, since very few women ever had been capable of winning points off a service.

Meanwhile, in Paris, Suzanne Lenglen told a correspondent from *Matin*, "I am all right again, as you can see for yourself. Please deny the imaginative stories current about my health. The doctors have authorized me to begin training again. I shall do so in a week's time and without the slightest doubt shall take part in the Olympic Games." She then set out for England a week earlier than usual in order to see for herself the talent of her new American challenger. She arrived in time to see Helen Wills compete in the Wightman Cup competitions. Watching those matches restored Lenglen's confidence. She felt better. She lost her fear. She could eat again.

A big crowd turned out to see the highly touted American girl in her first English matches. But Helen Wills was the major disappointment of the competition. She was beaten in the first round of play by the second ranked English player and in the second round by first-ranked Kitty McKane, who was not even considered a serious challenger to Suzanne Lenglen. Molla Mallory was also beaten twice in the singles.

Lenglen saw both of Wills's matches, and as McKane battered the American competitor, observed "with a satisfied smile," according to press reports. The odds in favor of a Lenglen victory over Wills soared.

After her defeat by McKane, Wills offered no excuses. "I feel fine," she said. "The ball, racket, and court did not bother me in the least. I did my best, but took a bad beating. There is no use worrying about the past, but I still have the greatest hopes for the future. I plan to take a good rest before Wimbledon and then hope to redeem myself."

American newsmen lauded her no-excuses attitude. That, too, they suggested, was admirable in her. She was candid and generous and, unlike the French goddess, gave credit where credit was due. From California, Pop Fuller said of the loss, "You have to expect those things" and suggested that as soon as Helen made the necessary adjustments to playing on English grass she would win and keep winning.

A decade later, writing her autobiography, Helen Wills did attribute her loss to illness. She pointed out that she went abroad before the rest of the Wightman Cup team in 1924 in order to get extra practice. She entered one tournament and then scratched at the last moment, opting for playing practice games rather than real competition. But then it rained for several days and prevented her from practicing at all. The rain was followed by very warm weather. The rest of the Wightman Cup team arrived, and she practiced with Molla Mallory. "I felt later in the afternoon as if I had had a sunstroke," she wrote. "I had all night an intense headache and the feeling of a temperature. But I did not tell any one for fear they might not let me play in the matches which were the next day."

The only bright moment for the American team in the competition came in the victory by Wills and Wightman in the doubles. During that match Wightman often yelled at Wills, "Up!" "Mine!" "Yours!" and most often, "Run, Helen!" much to the absolute delight of the crowd. The command "Run, Helen!" caught the fancy of the British crowd, and for years after that whenever an Englishman wanted someone to get moving faster, he was likely to shout, "Run, Helen!"

Helen Wills believed that Wimbledon would be her real test in 1924, and the American press was inclined to agree with her and write off her collapse in the Wightman Cup matches. But here again her performance was far less than perfect. And most disappointing of all, there was no match with Suzanne Lenglen.

Lenglen started out well enough in the 1924 Wimbledon competition, but then in the round of eight on June 30 she was forced into a grueling three-set match with Elizabeth Ryan. There was a period in that match when it looked as though Lenglen would not only lose her first set at Wimbledon since 1919, but that she was likely to lose the match, too. But she managed to reverse the trend in the play and win. After the match she had nothing but praise for Ryan, saying that she was proud of her doubles partner and that she had played the best match of her career.

Yet Lenglen was nervous, and her skin was dappled under her caked-on makeup, and she had used up all her reserve strength. Papa had remained in France, and Suzanne did not want to go on. There was suddenly too much risk to it. Better to make excuses than to plunge ahead and lose, she believed. The Forest Hills experience still haunted her. She was scheduled to play McKane in the next round and then probably the American challenger in the final. She lost her confidence and lost her nerve. She became hysterical and on July 1st announced her withdrawal from the tournament, shocking the officials and the public and the other players. She insisted that she was suffering from jaundice contracted during her Spanish journey and even came up with a physician's report to back up her allegation. Her friends elaborated on the lie and said that the romantic Suzanne had contracted jaundice when she visited Spain to with her secret Spanish lover—consequently, the ever-romantic Suzanne was a victim of love. But there were few believers among the Americans. And the general American attitude was summed up by Pop Fuller when he said that he was not at all certain that Suzanne Lenglen had jaundice, but he would not be surprised because she certainly looked yellow to him.

The Wills-Lenglen duel was now postponed, it was assumed, until the Olympic Games at Paris in mid-July.

As a result of Lenglen's default, Kitty McKane moved into the final round of the tournament rested and fresh. Wills won her way straight through the tournament, defeating Phyllis Satterthwaite in the semifinal round. Again, the American press expected an easy Wills victory. But she stumbled in the final and lost.

The 1924 final was played on July 4, the tenth anniversary of Maurice McLoughlin's unsuccessful effort to win against Anthony Wilding on the Centre Court. Queen Mary came to watch the match along with the Duke and Duchess of York (later King George VI and Queen Elizabeth). It was not a long match—it took just seventy-five minutes for McKane to beat Wills in three sets. Helen took the first set 6–4, and then pulled ahead in the second set 4–1, and was three times within one point of taking a

5–1 lead in that set but failed. McKane recovered and won five games in a row and the set and then the next set, 6–4, to win the match.

Helen Wills approached the umpire's chair after the tenth game of the third set and asked George Hillyard for the score. He told her the match was over. She seemed genuinely shocked. She shook hands with McKane and then, a moment later, according to press reports, she burst into tears.

McKane became the first British woman since 1914 to hold the title. The reign of Suzanne Lenglen and of France was over temporarily. She also took the mixed doubles crown with her husband that year. Helen Wills accounted for her loss in the finals against McKane by saying she had lost her concentration. "I saw the end before it arrived," she said later. And then the end didn't arrive, at least not in the way that she'd envisioned it.

Wills redeemed herself in the women's doubles when, partnered once again with Wightman, and to the steady command of "Run, Helen!," the unbeatable American duo defeated McKane and Mrs. B. C. Covell, 6–4, 6–4, for the title.

The American Olympic tennis team crossed the English Channel together. The water and the weather were rough, and all the members of the team became a little ill, with the exception of Wightman and Williams, "whom nothing ever bothered," Wills remembered. But Williams had experience in this sort of thing. He was a survivor of the *Titanic* disaster. Williams took photographs, though Wills remembered, "nobody wanted to be pictured in a state of momentary misery."

While Helen Wills had been very worried about her matches in England, she was relaxed in France and had no apprehension at all about her Olympic competition. "Perhaps it was because I found that being on the Olympic team was fun," she recalled, "or it may have been the air of Paris." And six decades later she said she could still remember the summer of 1924 "just as though it was yesterday." "You must remember," she told me, "it was not just my first Olympic Games. It was my first glimpse of Paris." And when she recorded her impression of Paris in her autobiography she described the city in 1924 in almost the same way that American newsmen had been describing her: "Perfection along with simple homeliness. Sophistication, and deep-rooted common sense."

An American tennis team had not competed at the 1920 Games in Antwerp. The reason given was that it would be unfair for Americans to compete with players from nations that had been devastated in the World War. But there was another reason, also. It was thought too expensive to send an American team abroad for such an unimportant competition. In 1924 the USLTA asked tennis clubs and state associations to raise money for an Olympic tennis team by assessing their members a small amount. There was some disappointment when two premier players, Bill Tilden and Billy Johnston, announced that they would not play on the Olympic team. Tilden resigned from the team over his continuing controversy with the USLTA concerning his amateur status and his career as a professional journalist, and Johnston said he simply could not afford the time away from his job in San Francisco as an insurance salesman.

Helen Wills, as the national champion, was selected as the number one player on the American women's team. Molla Mallory, who was ranked second by the USLTA among American women, was not allowed to represent the U.S. She had participated in the games of 1908 and 1912 for her native Norway and so under an Olympic rule could only compete again for Norway—despite the fact that she had become an American citizen. Norway consequently invited Molla to be the number one player on their national team, and she accepted. Since the Norwegian team lacked funds to send players to the game, Mallory agreed to finance her own journey from London to Paris. Her trip to England was financed by the USLTA so that she could compete there as the number two player on the American Wightman Cup team. So Molla Mallory in the summer of 1924 played on two different national teams in two months.

Hazel Wightman was chosen by the USLTA to serve as captain of the women's Olympic tennis team. The other players were Helen Wills, Eleanor Goss, Edith Sigourney, Lilian Scharman, and Marion Zinderstein Jessup.

The men selected to represent the United States were Vincent Richards, Frank Hunter, Richard Norris Williams, and Watson Washburn. Julian Myrick was selected as the non-playing captain of the men's team.

In April a fund-raising effort had been initiated in San Francisco in order to place a bet on Helen Wills against Suzanne Lenglen in the Olympic Games. A pot of $15,000 was gathered by the clubmen of San Francisco, and one of their number was assigned the not unpleasant task of proceeding to Paris to place the bet on Wills, no matter what the odds. It was expected that the odds would be heavily against Helen and that the clubmen would make an enormous profit from their wager. The same group placed a bet earlier in the year on American golfer McDonald Smith to win the British Open at odds of 150 to 1 and had lost when Smith was beaten by just two strokes. It was close enough for them to believe that they could now recoup their loss by betting on Wills.

The actual site of the 1924 games was Colombes, a manufacturing district on the edge of Paris. Hazel Wightman recalled that "if they had hunted for an uglier place for the Olympic Games, it could not have been found." The approach to the site of the competitions was along factories, rough, cobbled streets, small depressing-looking dwellings, and dirty corner cafés. The stadium for the field and track sports was in the middle of a large open space, overgrown with weeds, and full of burrs that got into the players' stockings.

The red clay and sand that was to be used to construct the tennis courts was still in little piles and pyramids around an empty field when the American team arrived. There was no place to practice. The weather, moreover, was oppressively hot. And the tennis courts were finally constructed in a small depression in a field that seemed to hold the heat. No sooner had the courts been completed than the 10,000-meter race was run in 113-degree heat and several of the runners succumbed to the heat and "sun stricken, staggering, vomiting and fainting," dropped like dead men around the outside of the tennis courts, where the sun was "furnace hot."

Helen Wills was protected perfectly from the sun and the heat by her visor and by her cotton middy blouse and long cotton skirt. Wightman noted that the large collar on the blouse protected her shoulders and back from the heat of the sun. The other players, the French women in particular, dressed stylishly, but wilted quickly in the heat. Helen, the schoolgirl, appeared to have a special dispensation and was always cool in her school uniform.

Within a week of withdrawing from Wimbledon, Suzanne Lenglen withdrew from the Olympic Games as well, disappointing millions of her countrymen and dozens of California gamblers. The favorite of the competition then became the Wimbledon champion, Kitty McKane. Wills, if there had been a seeding at the time, would no doubt have been given number two. She and McKane were placed in separate brackets so that they might meet in the final if all went according to expectations. And if there was to be a final.

There almost wasn't. Julian Myrick, president of the USLTA and captain of the men's team, surveyed the facilities provided the players and immediately threatened to boycott the Games unless "civilized facilities"—such as running water and towels and a place to rest—were provided for the players. During the initial matches there was no running water anywhere near the courts, so the French provided bottled water for the competitors. There was no place for players to sit except in the bleacher seats. The tables that were supposed to be used by the press were given to the tennis players to sit on, while the reporters worked under the stands or on the steps of the bleachers. The dressing room was nothing more than a large wooden shed with a tin roof and a shower that, when it worked, provided one sharp needle of cold water.

It is unimaginable that the authorities would have expected Suzanne Lenglen to accept such facilities. But with Lenglen absent, almost no attention at all was paid to the comfort and the requirements of other players. But none of this seemed to bother Helen Wills. She was in heaven. She wandered alone around Paris sightseeing, visiting the museums, walking along the boulevards, browsing in the bookshops and galleries, worrying not at all about the tennis competition or about any other events in the Games. She had fallen in love with Paris.

When the tennis courts were completed, she was amused by the distractions nearby. In the distance she watched wrestlers practicing on a platform and gymnasts gyrating about on a framework of rods. "It was a Surrealist scene, and very funny. All the time, roars were coming out of the big stadium across the field, but about what we did not know. The captain of our Olympic team and our officials were very cross." Helen went to watch the track events one day in the stadium but didn't enjoy it. "Everyone appeared to be in a violent state of mind," she recalled. "No one seemed pleased when a race was won, and pistols were being fired all the time. I couldn't see any Americans."

When the courts were completed, she played some practice matches on the hard clay and announced to American reporters that she was ready. She found that the heat and the bright sun dried and hardened the clay courts and made them more like the California hard courts. By the time the competitions began they were perfectly suited to her hard-hitting game. "I am in good condition and playing as well as I ever did," she said. Then with characteristic modesty she added: "I can't say whether I will reach the finals or not. If it were possible to tell in advance it wouldn't be much fun for the others."

The stadium where the track and field events were held was right next to the tennis courts, and there was no knowing when a pistol would suddenly go off or a band would start playing a national anthem or a loud cheer or boo would go up. The ball boys hid under the bleachers to escape the heat and often refused to come out to get a ball, forcing the players to do that work. The Eskimo Pie was introduced to Europeans during the Games and throughout the competitions it was disconcerting to the players to hear the vendors crying out, "ES-KEE-MO, ES-KEE-MO!" One old female vendor went through the stands crying out, "Oranges, bananas, glaces" over and over again until Norris Williams asked her to stop. Jean Borotra also had to ask her to stop. The officiating was poor, at best. Several times only the umpire showed up for work, and line judges had to be recruited from the crowd for some matches. In at least one important contest, when McKane played against Didi Vlasto of France, the partisan crowd helped decide the line calls.

But Helen Wills would remember only the pleasant moments of the 1924 games. "It was the best team I've ever been on in my life," she told me. "We had so much fun and it was so pleasant. And of course I was so very young then—and young for my age, too. I enjoyed it. No, I loved it. I really loved it. It was my first glimpse of Paris—my first time away from America. I remember it all very clearly today, just as though it was yesterday."

Under a fiercely hot sun the competitions began on the morning of July 14. The players were introduced to the audience by a little man with a very large megaphone who shouted "Allo! Allo!" to get the attention of the crowd. This got the Americans in the crowd to laugh and to greet each other around the stadium with a loud "Allo! Allo!" followed by sophomoric laughter. When the announcer introduced Helen he pronounced her name "Meese Veels."

Lilian Scharman was beaten in the first round by Lili d'Alvarez of

Spain, and Marion Jessup and Eleanor Goss lost in the doubles. Helen Wills drew a bye in the singles and then faced a formidable British opponent, Phyllis Satterthwaite, a close personal friend of Suzanne Lenglen. Molla Mallory, playing for Norway, beat a French player in the first round with some difficulty and a Dutch competitor in the second.

On the third day of the competition more Americans were put out of the race for the gold medals. Hunter was beaten by a Belgian. Eleanor Goss won on a default when her opponent did not appear for play on time, but she was beaten in the next round by Didi Vlasto. Wills beat Satterthwaite. The press reported that Wills looked spectacular in her victories and that her play was now "quicker, cleaner, and more finished than it had been at Wimbledon." Suzanne Lenglen was in the grandstand studying the play of the American girl down on the hot clay of Colombes. When it became clear that she would win, Lenglen said that it was too hot and she did not feel well. She left early. All eyes were on Suzanne when she was present, and her reaction to the play seemed as interesting to the crowd as the play itself.

On the fourth day of the competition Helen Wills gave her most spectacular showing yet, beating Molla Mallory, 6–3, 6–3. Mallory took a 2–1 lead in the second set, but that was the only time she threatened to take the match. It seemed, some spectators noticed, that Wills was just practicing, experimenting and testing new strokes and tactics against Mallory in order to get ready for her next match against her Wimbledon nemesis, Kitty McKane. That was why Helen gave up the three games, most on unforced errors. While Molla stayed along the baseline, Helen proved adventurous and followed her shots to the net, a dangerous and often foolhardy tactic on clay, but she was determined to force the play, and at the same time she amazed the audience and became their favorite for her apparently daring tactics.

McKane in the other half of the draw beat Mrs. Jessup, 6–2, 6–0, on day four but on the next day was surprised by Vlasto and the extremely hostile French crowd and was beaten in a strange seesaw match, 0–6, 7–5, 6–1. When there was disagreement over a call in the second set, members of the audience loudly threatened the life of the linesman. The match was held up again and again by the shouting and disagreement. This so frustrated McKane that she lost her concentration and her rhythm and blew the match after being far ahead. In the semifinal round Helen Wills defeated Mrs. Golding of France, 6–2, 6–1.

In the doubles Wills and Wightman had no difficulty and won their way through the competition easily and beat McKane and Covell in the final on July 19 for the gold medal. Mrs. Wightman again directed Wills on the court with "Run Helen" and "Yours," as she had at Wimbledon, and the cries now became a humorous historic idiom for the French spectators.

The singles final between Wills and Vlasto was unusual right from the start. The French gatekeepers at the courts had been rude as only the French could be and time and again had refused entry to anyone without proper credentials. Sometimes, when competitors who had left their proper identification in the dressing room, sought entry to the courts to play, they were kept out, even when it was obvious to all who they were. Henri Cochet, the French champion, was kept from his match in the finals when he forgot his pass. He was sent like a child back to his dressing room to retrieve his pass while the crowd and his opponent, Vincent Richards, waited impatiently. When he finally returned with the pass, the gatekeeper let him through but did not apologize for the intrusion. Cochet lost his match.

Then Vlasto forgot her pass, too, and her entry was delayed. The day was very hot, Helen Wills recalled, and she was ready to play, but her opponent hadn't shown up. Under the hot sun the crowd grew impatient. President Domergue of France was seated in the gallery along with Suzanne Lenglen. People began to stamp their feet and shout out protests and questions. But the gate-keeper would not let Vlasto into the stadium. She argued for several minutes with him and finally forced her way past him. When the two players finally walked onto the court they were greeted with boos and with hisses. Then a contingent of University of California students, some of them members of the American track team, stood up and gave a UC cheer for Helen that began "OSKI-WOW-WOW." Wills understood it as an encouraging American cheer. But Vlasto, who spoke little English and had no acquaintance with American college customs, didn't know what to make of it. And she started the match still wondering what strange spell part of this audience was trying to cast on her with their arcane chant.

Whatever it was, it seemed to work. Vlasto was one of the last female players to use an underhand service in international competition, so it was not difficult for Helen to beat her. Wills fed high bounding balls to her backhand, heavily topped, so she was drawn far off the court and had to make an awkward high-backhand stroke to hit them. Wills followed this again and again with a hard forehand winner. Part of the crowd began to boo this tactic. They seemed to think Helen was unfairly taking advantage of Vlasto's weaknesses and wanted Helen to play to her opponent's strength. Wills was actually intimidated by this a couple of times and hit to Vlasto's forehand and then came to the net when she shouldn't have and was passed. Then she decided to beat Vlasto from the backcourt with ground strokes. At one point in the match Wills received a line call that much of the crowd thought should not have been given. The match was interrupted with prolonged booing again. Helen Wills, newsmen thought, purposely gave away the next point, to the absolute delight of the French crowd. But then she served two quick service aces, much to the consternation of the pro-French gallery. Vlasto's misery did not last long, for Wills won quickly, 6–2, 6–2.

The American fans at the match had their own victory cheer. And when she was shaking hands with Vlasto after the match, many of them stood together in a section of the bleachers and shouted out:

"Allo! Allo! Allo!
Es—Kee—Moe!
Colombe, Colombe, Colombe!
Helen Wills!"

Helen Wills remained placid and poker-faced through the play and betrayed emotion only when it was all over and she approached the net to shake hands with her opponent. Then she smiled. She had become the first American woman to win a major singles title abroad in seventeen years.

Vincent Richards beat Henry Cochet in the men's singles, and Richards and Hunter won the men's doubles. Norris Williams and Wightman won the mixed doubles for an American sweep.

Helen Wills's performance in the Games was noted in the press, especially in the California press. The *San Francisco Chronicle* called for a special match between Wills and Lenglen to determine who was now the best player in the world. The Mayor and the City Manager of Berkeley sent a telegram congratulating Helen on her victory.

The American success in the Games produced a good deal of bad will abroad. An American spectator was beaten by a Frenchman in the crowd for cheering too loudly. The British press in particular demonstrated a distaste for the American athletes, who, it was pointed out, put too much emphasis on winning. "There is something unhealthy in the organization of amateur athletics in America today we are profoundly convinced," one British journalist wrote.

The behavior of some American athletes was far less than sporting. Especially disturbing was the plan of the American runners in the 100-meter dash, led by Charlie Paddock, to make false starts in order to confuse and tire Englishman Harold Abrahams and to produce an American victory. The plan went awry, and Abrahams won.

After the games Helen Wills alone among the large American contingent at the Games was praised by the American press and the American public. The matches themselves were reported throughout the world. For the first time the young Berkeley player was on the front pages of many newspapers. The whole world began to take notice. She had star quality but at the same time she was an innocent and fresh and decent young woman of modesty, humility, simple taste and dress—a schoolgirl champion discovered on the public courts of California, self-trained, determined, strong, level-headed, pretty, generous in victory and defeat. She was an American ideal, a democratic icon. Not many writers had believed that a woman like this existed anywhere anymore. And certainly none expected such a young woman to have such extraordinary skills in athletics. The contrast with Suzanne Lenglen was remarkable. While it seemed so many other women in England and France tried to look and play like Suzanne, Helen never seemed to give the goddess a thought. She lived and played to a different drummer.

After the competition Helen Wills walked around Paris again looking in book shops and clothing stores. She used her scholarship money from the University of California to buy fifteen pairs of evening slippers. "I suppose I was supposed to buy something intellectual," she told me. "But you should have seen them. Those slippers were exquisite and I loved them."

During her shopping spree she lost all sense of time. She was out on the streets when the American team prepared to leave by train. When her mother finally found her, after a frantic search, and told her she must hurry, Helen remembered, "a most curious feeling of happy indifference came over me." And as her taxi raced toward the station, Helen said, "I hoped we would miss the train." But they did not. They arrived just as the train was about to leave. The team members were leaning out the windows watching her dash down the platform. Myrick later presented Helen with a watch, engraved to commemorate the event and to remind her in the future to be on time.

Until she arrived in New York aboard the *Aquitania* with the rest of the Olympic tennis team, Helen Wills was not yet aware of how she had been transformed into a media star by the American press. And so she was surprised when a small army of reporters and photographers—the *New York Times* referred to them as "a veritable horde"—stormed aboard the ship as soon as it docked. They were accompanied by an equally large crowd of "utter strangers" who simply wanted to see the woman they had been reading about through the summer.

The *New York Times* reporter found in her something that the American press and the American public was to celebrate about Helen Wills for the next decade. He found that "she looks a bit older. She is of the athletic build and broad shoulders—and her face, too, is broad with a rather wide mouth and excellent teeth and lips which bespeak vitality and energy, and teeth—a perfect set of teeth—which indicate determination, firmness. She is perhaps as perfect a specimen of the outdoor girl of twenty-two or thereabouts as this country can produce."

And when the reporters questioned her—only her, among the athletes on board the ship—they eventually pulled her aside and continued shouting questions at her, and she confessed that this had never happened before and that "this sort of thing upsets me." Was there something about the trip, she was asked, that impressed her especially? "No," she answered. "Nothing especially. It was all wonderful." Asked if she had seen Suzanne Lenglen play, Wills said that, yes, she had watched some of Suzanne's play at Wimbledon. The Lenglen questions then came, always more

Lenglen questions. She was asked to evaluate her play. She said that she noticed no weakness in Suzanne's game. "Her tennis was wonderful. It was—it was, well, it was just wonderful tennis."

And would Helen like to meet her in a match? "Oh, yes. Certainly, I should like to meet her in a match at any time." Then a reporter asked if Helen thought she could beat Suzanne. There was a moment of silence. Wills glared at the reporter. Then she began to blush brightly, right through her rich summer tan. Her blue eyes seemed to become hard and cold, reporters noticed. She did not answer. She just glared. After a long awkward pause, Julian Myrick intervened and said that the question was really out of order: "In as much as in amateur sports the question whether one contestant could outplay another is a matter for determination only upon the field." The reporters did not distinguish, he complained, between amateur tennis and other sports. This was not, after all, prizefighting.

The reporters also quizzed Catherine Wills. They got more information. Yes, she and Helen had talked about returning to Europe to play a match against Suzanne Lenglen, she said. Helen would go to France in 1926 for that match, she told reporters. But primarily, Helen would be going abroad to study art and to continue her education rather than to pursue an athletic challenge. In the meantime there were plenty of capable opponents for Suzanne Lenglen.

During the interview session that followed, the newsmen discovered that all of those wonderful stories about her filed from England and France were in fact true. And one of them wrote that she was still just "a shy, modest, schoolgirl, although international laurels rest now upon her brow." They found that, when she described her accomplishments and her titles, she was not like the other athletic champions or stars or celebrities or politicians. The *New York Times* reporter observed that she described her European adventure "in a detached manner, as if she had lived through a world of dreams and seen those dreams come true and was still aghast at the fulfillment of her dreams, still wondering how it was that to her, of all persons, had come a fulfillment so complete, so almost overwhelming."

To Californians she was primarily a "California girl" and a "Girl of the Golden West." But to the *New York Times* and the rest of the country she was being transformed slowly into what would be termed "the American Girl."

Following her triumphant return to the United States, Helen Wills successfully defended her national singles title and then won both the national doubles and mixed doubles title for a triple crown. At Forest Hills she played through the tournament without much difficulty until she faced Molla Mallory in the final once more. On her way to the title she dropped one set in the semifinals to Mary K. Browne, former national titleholder of 1912, 1913, and 1914. Wills lost the set, it was said, after a misunderstanding jogged her service rhythm on Browne's set point. Against Mallory, Wills did a little better and won 6–1, 6–3, in just thirty-five minutes. It was the third straight time that the women faced each other for the national title and the second time Wills came away the winner. But there was never any doubt, never much suspense, as to who would win. From the moment Helen took the first point on a pretty placement until the final winner, she had the former champion on the run. Then she paired with Wightman on the same afternoon and won the national doubles title.

A week later, at the Longwood Cricket Club in Brookline, Massachusetts, Wills and partner Vincent Richards won the national mixed doubles title by beating the defending champions, Mallory and Tilden.

On her return to California Helen Wills detrained in Illinois and stayed long enough to play an exhibition match at the Skokie Country Club against Jack Harris, a ranking Chicago player. She split sets with Harris. It was becoming standard practice to have Wills play against men in exhibitions in order to show her real ability. Then she boarded the Overland Limited and returned to California. A large crowd greeted her at the Berkeley station. Newsmen found her to be still "the shy sweet school girl" who had departed four months earlier. She reminded reporters that she had gone to Europe not for herself, 'but for the people of this country who sent me and who had so much faith in me." Her head had not been turned at all by the attention and praise she had received abroad. She was still the same unaffected Helen with "no frills and no furbelows." She was greeted officially by Mayor Frank Stringham of Berkeley, the head of the Chamber of Commerce, various representatives from the state tennis association, and a large and noisy contingent of Kappa Kappa Gamma sorority sisters. There was no band, but there was a parade of cars with honking horns.

When Helen Wills was told that a special collection had been taken up to buy her a new car as a sign of the city's appreciation for her, she said it was too good to be true. "It is awfully good of them, but I do not deserve it," she said. "Everybody has done so much for me now that I do not think I should be given anything more."

A week later she played an exhibition at the Berkeley Tennis Club against May Sutton Bundy, beating her in three sets. When she came onto the courts the crowd took up the cry,

> ALLO! ALLO! ALLO!
> ESKEEMO!
> COLOMBE, COLOMBE, COLOMBE!
> HELEN WILLS!

Following the match Helen was presented with a new Buick. "Why an automobile?" someone at the ceremony asked. "Because it is something she can keep and remember," he was told. And there was no question at all that this might compromise her amateur status. She was given the automobile not for her tennis, it was said, but for her fine representation of California.

Harry Smith saw the exhibition and the giving of the car and wrote in the *Chronicle* that more than an ordinary amount of space had been devoted to Helen Wills over the past many months not just because she had achieved spectacular things in tennis. She had transcended her sport and become a star. She had "set herself up as a news source of general interest" and her adventures and successes in the East and abroad could be reported not only on the sports pages but on the front pages of newspapers. People who knew nothing of tennis and who cared nothing for tennis now were committed deeply and interested in Helen Wills he found. She was a Californian who had won world renown, and now everybody wanted to know everything about her. She was more than a mere champion. Helen had become an American heroine.

In late September, at an exhibition, Helen Wills again played against a top ranked male player, Phil Neer, in San Jose at an all-comers tournament. Playing what was now referred to as a "man's game," she defeated the NCAA champion 6–4 in a single set. More than 800 people showed up at the San Jose exhibition to see her. They filled the bleachers and all the empty spaces around the bleachers and climbed onto the roof of nearby Jefferson school and into the trees to see the Berkeley star defeat Neer. When I asked Neer about the match, he told me that he played his best against Helen and she beat him. He insisted that she was the best female player ever. Other men, however, who played against Wills in exhibitions insisted that "the only men Helen Wills ever beat in a tennis match were real gentlemen. Phil Neer was a gentleman."

Wills started her sophomore year at the University of California in the fall of 1924 and continued to practice tennis daily at the Berkeley Tennis Club. She had no plans to travel abroad in 1925. The Wightman Cup matches were scheduled for Forest Hills, and there was no Olympic competition. Unless Suzanne Lenglen decided to travel to America—and that was unlikely, then Helen Wills would cruise through the entire season playing only American and English challengers, consolidating her reputation, waiting for 1926 and the confrontation with Lenglen.

--◄{ 6 }►--

One of the things that interested the press and the public more and more about Helen Wills following her return from Europe in 1924 was the fact that she appeared to be such a spectacular anachronism. In an age of flappers and flasks, Helen was something of a sweet, old-fashioned girl. In an age of flaming youth, she was an ice queen. And yet, ironically, there was nothing about her that seemed awkwardly out of style. She appeared to be completely comfortable with herself, her dress, her values. When asked about jazz, on her return from Europe, Helen said, "Oh—I can't say anything at all about jazz, because, you see, I've never jazzed around at all." She answered the question without apologizing, in a straightforward way, the reporter noted, as though it was the most ordinary statement in the world for a typical college sophomore to make. But it wasn't ordinary at all. It was, in fact, quite extraordinary. In an era of excess, there was not a whisper of excess about her. Young women like this didn't often make the news. Young women like this didn't often attract public attention. Young women like this weren't supposed to exist anymore in the Roaring Twenties. Yet here she was. There was something solid about her, like a principle, something that transcended the style of the moment or the latest rage. There was almost something timeless about her, something classic. The press and public could recall no one like her, and they never could have predicted her appearance.

Helen Wills was celebrated by the press and the public more and more as "a model of the ideal maiden to be evolved out of the flapper." The contrast between her and the typical flapper was dramatic. One columnist listed the differences and pointed out what Helen did not have: bobbed hair; cigarettes; beaded eyelashes; boisterousness; "freshness"; jazz. What she did have was: Modesty; Dignity; Simplicity; Athletic wholesomeness; "Good Fellow."

By her victories and her behavior, Helen Wills proved herself to be more than an athletic champion, he wrote. She proved "the clean-cut superiority of the new American girl."

"You can't flap and be an Olympic champ," another reporter pointed out. "And while not every girl aspires to be an Olympic champion, yet every girl knows that the Olympic Games stand for the highest all-round development of that topnotch ideal of young womanhood today.

"The Olympics have done more to put the flapper into discard than all the sermons preached against her. A new type is on the horizon and the new type is the sort which Helen Wills personifies." Naturally, the writer pointed out, Helen would not admit that because of her modesty.

"Take one look at Miss Wills," a writer for the Newspaper Enterprise Association suggested, "easily balanced in the midst of a volleying drive, every muscle on the alert, her face flushed with exercise and abounding health, her clean-limbed figure as lithe as a panther's, but without anything sinister in her makeup. Then take a look at the typical flapper, with her cocktail, her cigarette, her boyish haircut and her killing walk. And then—choose."

Well, there just wasn't any question which one would be chosen, of course. Helen was to "the average flapper what the Wings of the Morning are to the grasshopper. And it's the girls of the Helen Wills type that young Miss America is taking today as her pattern."

And the pattern was a striking one. "Her broad face is saved from plainness by the splendid color with which it is always flushed," another reporter described her, "and by the big, clear, bright-blue eyes. Her firm red lips do not look as though a cigarette had ever touched them."

When she was asked about the youth of the day Helen Wills said, "I hadn't thought about them very much. It was a perfectly splendid crowd of young people that went over to the Olympics; congenial and fine and full of good sportsmanship, especially tennis players."

Helen Wills did not appear to worry about what others thought of her or about her destiny or about the destiny of her generation. The criticism or praise of others, she pointed out, just sort of rolled off her back.

"She spends her days in study and athletics, and in the endeavor to make something of herself in one or the other of these lines," another writer found. And she did not try to make herself conspicuous. She wore her hair, which was bronzed by the sun and thick, in braids wound neatly around her head and "done up so carefully that even in the most violent tennis match no strand of it flies loose."

Yet "this new American girl was not reverting to a mouse-like timidity or the super-ladylike seclusion of the good old days when hoopskirts were rife and no girl stirred abroad without a duenna." In fact, "Nothing could be more free than the new girl. In her knee-length tennis skirt, battling for a championship, with a thousand spectators applauding her every move, the new Miss America is anything but a retiring and suppressed personage."

Another writer used a political allegory to describe the appearance of Helen, not as a sweet, old-fashioned girl, but as "the newer girl." What interested modern sociologists and psychologists, he suggested, was that between the flapper and the newer girl there was the same difference as between Bolshevik Russia and the French Republic. "Having gone through the Bolshevik stage, where she felt compelled to hurrah for her freedom till the welkin rang, to trample on tradition and generally make herself a large sized blot on the landscape, the modern girl has now acquired enough freedom so that she can afford to be dignified."

Helen Wills, the writer pointed out, was willing to sacrifice many things in order to improve her tennis game and keep it supreme. But her general attitude toward life was the one toward which most young women seemed to be turning at the time. "Not long ago the goals of the typical American girl seemed frivolous—dancing and drinking and smoking and jazz music seemed goals in life, not simply diversions. Now there are other things. Helen seems to be showing the way."

"Helen Wills doesn't use mascara. She doesn't bead her lashes. She goes to bed at 9 or 10 nearly every night of the year, and she has breakfast at 9 in the morning. She watches her diet, too; not in a finicky way, but in the way of the sensible girl who would rather forgo a rich dessert than her healthy color."

To understand Helen, another writer said, you had to picture her on the court at Forest Hills before an enthusiastic filled stadium, with newsmen, cameramen, and radio broadcasters all around. Before such a crowd, the nerves of most flappers would show. "But Miss Wills has steel nerves, where the flapper has only brass nerve. Following her victories, Wills gives a faint smile, shakes hands with the other players, poses for photographs, signs autographs for the ball boys and others, all gladly and without much reluctance. With dignity, with all the poise in the world, and with a championship, Helen Wills disappears at last behind the doors that lead to a shower and bath and rest.

"Perhaps you can imagine how the typical American girl of—well, even of a year ago—would have taken such honors. 'Ohhhhh, my d-e-a-r! It was too thrilling.'

"For some time now," he said, "the flapper has been 'old stuff.' She piled so many thrills, so many shocks, one atop another, that after a while people ceased to be thrilled or shocked at all. For the last few months, people have only been amused, then annoyed, and finally alienated. The mannish flapper is not a thing of the past. But her popularity is.

"Remember the good old days, about a year ago, when people wondered what this younger generation was coming to, and what, since parents and preachers and police had failed, would intervene to save it from perdition?

"The Olympic games are the answer to both questions. After bolshevism, a newer sanity. After the flapper, Helen Wills and the welcome young American whom she typifies."

Helen Wills not only symbolized a new incarnation of youth and womanhood in America, but she also gave a tremendous boost to athletic activity for women. After the Olympic Games, golfer Glenna Collett commented, "the tomboy has come into her own in America." She said that Helen seemed to be a throwback to the pioneer days of America in her attitude toward vigorous exercise. Physical fitness, she pointed out, was "the rightful heritage" of the American female. Helen was helping restore that heritage.

Following Wills's return to America in 1924, many journalists began re-examining notions of health and beauty. She was helping to alter the popular misconceptions of beauty and athletic activities for women. America was not only starting to "glow with pride" for this unusually talented young woman, but it was doing some serious thinking about what she represented. Many schools that had dropped women's tennis as a sport had reincorporated it into their athletic programs following the rise of Helen Wills.

--◄ 7 ►--

Throughout 1925 Helen Wills played tennis against a ghost. The ghost was Suzanne Lenglen. Everywhere she played in America in that year, against any opponent, the question always was, "But how would she do against Suzanne?" Each set and each match and each move was simply a solo exercise that evoked the memory of the French goddess. No American gallery had seen Lenglen since 1921. But anyone who read the newspapers knew that she was back in form winning one tournament after another, setting records and setting European hearts aflutter. Yes, she faltered in the summer of 1924 and never came face to face with the new American champion. But Helen Wills had also faltered in Europe; she had lost three important matches.

Suzanne Lenglen opened her 1925 campaign, as she had begun her other victorious seasons, in the winter tournaments on the Riviera. She demonstrated early that she had recovered completely from whatever ailed her in 1924. Helen Wills was not present to haunt or threaten her, so she began running up a string of victories against the usual winter opponents and in front of the usual winter crowds. The year 1925 would prove to be the greatest in her long career.

Without a similar circuit to play in on the West Coast, Wills began the year as a sophomore at the University of California and participated in a series of fund-raising exhibitions for the various associations and clubs in the Bay Area. In early January she played against Phil Neer at the California Club. She played and won an exhibition in San Mateo against Eleanor Goss. She beat Goss again in an exhibition at the Burlingame Country Club in February. She played in the North-South matches in Los Angeles and won there, too, and she won the Hotel Huntington Tournament in Los Angeles at the end of February. She played against May Sutton in the tournament before 2500 spectators, and the scrappy southern California veteran took the first set, 6–1. The crowd was surprised and apparently so was May by the ease with which she took six games in an early ambush. But Helen Wills settled down and took the next two sets, 6–2, 6–2. Sutton got tired of running around and even asked herself during the match, "Why I am running around like this?" Then she turned to pick up a ball with her back to Helen and ever so politely flipped up her skirt. The crowd was aghast for a moment, and so was Helen, not knowing what to make of it. But then there was laughter because May Sutton had pleased the crowd once more, even though losing the match in the process. May was never the American Girl, but she was always a good-humored favorite of the crowd. In March Wills continued her busy schedule and played a charity exhibition for the Mt. Zion Hospital in San Francisco. In May she went to Sacramento and easily won the championship for Central California. And then in April she played an exhibition at Golden Gate Park for the officers and enlisted men of the combined Atlantic and Pacific fleets. A crowd of 3500 came out to see her easily defeat Pacific Coast champion Charlotte Hosmer.

At the end of June, in a significant exhibition, Helen Wills drubbed the national junior champion, Helen Jacobs of Berkeley, 6–3, 6–1, at the Pacific Coast Championships held at the Berkeley Tennis Club. The press was already referring to Jacobs as "Little Helen" and Wills now as "Big Helen." Jacobs was following in the footsteps of Wills, practicing with Pop Fuller and taking careful instruction from Hazel Wightman. The match was in the regular competitions of the tournament and, it was pointed out, it was by exactly the same score that Molla Mallory had beaten Helen Wills the first time they met at Forest Hills.

In July, at Wimbledon Suzanne Lenglen took her sixth singles title, and won titles also in the doubles and mixed doubles for another triple crown victory there. The most interesting match of the early rounds was that between Elizabeth Ryan and Lenglen. Ryan was expected once more to test her, as she had done in 1924. But it was not to be. Ryan won the first two games of the match and nearly went ahead 3–0. But she could not get that third game. Then the tables were turned. Lenglen began winning and continued to win—twelve games in a row and the match, 6–2, 6–0. Restored to mental and physical health, there was no other woman in Lenglen's class; she was clearly *hors classe* again. In the semi-finals she beat in love sets the defending champion, Kitty McKane, who had beaten Helen Wills twice in 1924. After the match Lenglen was summoned to the royal box by Queen Mary and they chatted for several minutes. It was the second time during the tournament that she had been asked to speak with the Queen, a unique honor. In the finals she easily beat the newest English *Wunderkind,* Joan Fry, in straight sets in just twenty-six minutes. In the tournament she had won ten sets and lost only five games. Borotra and Lenglen won the mixed doubles, Lenglen and Ryan the ladies' doubles. The *New York Times* commented editorially that the gulf between Suzanne Lenglen and all other women tennis players in the world was, by the summer of 1925 after Wimbledon, ob-viously wider than ever before.

Even without Helen Wills or a USLTA-sponsored group of players, the 1925 tournament was the most successful Wimbledon to that time. The All-England Club earned "enormous" profits of £40,000, or about $194,000 in the dollars of that day. No leading American player was in the tournament either. The principal drawing card day after day for royalty and commoners alike was the goddess of grass, Suzanne Lenglen.

After her college classes concluded in the spring, Helen Wills departed with her mother for Brookline, Massachusetts, and the Longwood tourna-ment, which would be her debut in the East in 1925. In her opening match against Anna Fuller, who had been runner-up for the national indoor singles title in 1924, Wills dropped the first game and then quickly won twelve in a row. The score was not what amazed spectators. The time of the match was what was surprising—nineteen minutes. She showed some new weapons in her arsenal. She now had a fast sliced service that Howard Kinsey had taught her. She used it again and again to draw her opponent far off the court and then followed it with a sliced volley for a winner. And she had a new topped backhand that was nearly as powerful as her forehand drive.

Wills at Longwood, just like Lenglen at Wimbledon, was by far the biggest drawing card. Wherever she was playing, the crowds abandoned other courts and games to see her. During one exciting match between two leading male players, more than half the gallery suddenly stood and left to see the start of the semifinal match between Wills and national indoor champion, Mrs. B. E. Cole II. Wills won, 6–4, 6–0.

Helen Wills then moved on to Manchester-by-the-Sea, Massachusetts, to play in the Essex Country Club Invitational. She moved easily through the early rounds and played well with Mary K. Browne in the doubles. Browne beat Mallory in the semis and then was beaten by Wills in the finals, 6–2, 6–1. Wills and Browne teamed up to win the doubles.

Next Helen Wills moved on to Seabright, New Jersey, and won her way through the early rounds of the tournament, losing a set to Marion Jessup on the way. She trounced Molla Mallory, 6–1, 6–0, in the semifinal match and appeared to have regained her full powers. She faced Elizabeth Ryan in the final. It was Ryan's first singles tournament in America in thirteen years, and she had a homecoming surprise for the American girl. She shocked Wills, 6–3, 6–3, in just forty minutes. Four thousand spectators witnessed the match, the biggest crowd ever in the thirty-two-year history of the tournament. Included among them were members of the USLTA Executive Committee and Davis Cup Committee. This was the same court on which Wills had been beaten by Eleanor Goss, and it was her first defeat since she fell to McKane at Wimbledon. It was a good measure of how far she had not yet come. Ryan took Wills again in the doubles when she and Goss beat Wills and Browne.

The wet grass gave Ryan an unusual advantage in the tournament. After a downpour, the Seabright turf, which was imported from England, was extremely heavy, and when the morning match was played was well suited to Ryan's chopping game. Wills was aware of this and worried about it. But she was almost helpless as Ryan again and again left her standing flatfooted in the backcourt. The grass was too slippery for her to move with confidence to the net to volley winners. The *New York Times* commented that the Wills defeat "has come like a bolt out of a clear sky" since it had been assumed that the only player in the world capable of beating her was Lenglen. The weather alone was not the cause of the Wills downfall, the paper pointed out. She had been unable to adjust to the Ryan game.

It was then on to Rye, New York, and the New York State Championship Tournament at the Westchester Biltmore Country Club. Wills drew a bye and then won a match in love sets. Not inclined to be lenient now, reporters found she was determined to redeem herself from the Ryan loss. She passed easily through the fourth round into more serious competition. Then, near disaster again against Molla Mallory. In the finals Mallory took six games in a row and won the first set at 6–3 before losing the next two sets, 2–6 and 2–6. But she had demonstrated that Helen Wills was a slow starter and that a vigorous and forcing opponent could take her.

Helen Wills and Molla Mallory were named one and two on the Wightman Cup team that entertained the visiting British for the second time. And Wills won both her singles matches and her doubles match against the visitors. She won her first-round match against Joan Fry, who had lost to Lenglen in the Wimbledon final. Wills beat her at love in the first set but was extended to a 7–5 win in the second. McKane, who had lost in love sets to Lenglen, beat Mallory in three sets. Then Wills was taken to three sets by McKane before winning, in a very tough match, 6–1, 1–6, 9–7.

An unusual incident at the Wightman competition shocked Helen Wills. She was hissed and booed by an American crowd simply for keeping them waiting for ten minutes. Wills explained afterward that the team captain, Browne, had arranged for a masseuse for McKane and herself. Out of courtesy, Wills let McKane go first. By the time the masseuse began on Helen it was time for the doubles to begin, and Helen was scheduled to play in the doubles. "I would gladly have played without waiting to be rubbed, but the tennis committee and everyone else insisted that I wait until the masseuse had finished with me, so I did," Wills later explained. "I was surprised and hurt when I went on the court and heard the spectators, but I couldn't do anything about it but just play the best I could. I'm trying to forget their actions now. At least I'll never be late again." It was the first time Helen Wills was so treated by an American audience.

As soon as the Wightman competition was over the National Tournament began at Forest Hills. On August 17, Wills defeated an unseeded opponent, 6–2 and 6–2, disappointing those who expected her to be completely overwhelming. The exciting player in the tournament proved to be May Suton Bundy, who knocked off Charlotte Hosmer in the first round of the tournament in a tough three-set match. It was twenty years after Bundy had won her first Wimbledon title and she was now thirty-seven years old. But in the third round Helen Wills beat her, 6–3, 6–2. Bundy led in the first set 3–1 only to lose five games in a row at that

point. She forced five games in the second set to deuce only to lose to
Wills's greater power and stamina.

Kitty McKane, Wills's former conqueror, moved ahead in impressive
style, too. She beat Elizabeth Ryan, who was considered by many to be
Helen's most serious opposition, on August 20 in three sets, 3–6, 7–5, 6–2.

There was yet another surprise in the semifinals when Molla Mallory
fought through a hard three-set match with McKane and lost 4–6, 7–5,
8–6. And Wills was carried to three sets in her match with Goss, losing
the first again at 3–6 and then winning 6–0, 6–2, consolidating her reputation as a fine slow starter—but hardly a competitor for Suzanne. Her
victory made McKane the first foreign female player to advance to the
final round of the American championship.

Once more in the final round Helen Wills lost the first set and then
beat McKane in the next two for the match, 3–6, 6–0, 6–2. She explained
the loss of the first set as the result of an accident just prior to the match.
While Helen was having lunch with her mother and a friend, a huge
chandelier broke and fell into the middle of their table. Helen was badly
shaken, and had to go out onto the court a short time after this. It took
time to settle down, she said.

In the moment of her victory over McKane, Wills again cast aside her
somber poker face. She tossed her racket high into the air and "jumped
for joy" as cheers from the gallery cascaded down on her. She laughingly
acknowledged the congratulations of those around the court. Then 7000
people rose and cheered for her again as she waved the large victory cup
over her head and then skipped out of the stadium. The Championship
Cup that Wills retired bore no name but hers. Molla Mallory retired one
cup with three victories in 1922 and now Helen Wills had won three in
a row herself.

An hour later she returned to the court to win the national doubles
title with Mary K. Browne. Wills announced she would not play in the
mixed doubles tournament at Boston and would return to California
and the University immediately, forfeiting the mixed doubles title she
held with Vincent Richards.

When Helen Wills arrived in Berkeley on August 31, there was the
customary large crowd waiting to greet her, and reporter Blanche Ashbaugh wrote that Helen remained the "same, sweet, unaffected girl who
came back to California with her first championship." And Pop Fuller,
"who claims all the credit for making Helen the great player that she
is," was there early to meet her.

Dr. Clarence Wills set himself up as a protector for his daughter when
she returned, trying to assure himself that she now lead a "normal" life.
He complained to a friend about the amount of mail that Helen was
receiving and that he was throwing it away. And he complained about
the many civic organizations and product manufacturers who discovered
suddenly that linking the name of Wills to their product would be good

for business. "Every organization and commodity from the Dons of Peralta to the Star Chewing Tobacco Company suddenly realized what fine advertising her name is equal to," he told a friend. "Add to this a large mass of crank letters (her mail has to be censored before she reads it) and the poor girl's life is made miserable." Dr. Wills asked that everyone just leave Helen alone for a time and let her enjoy the normal life of an American girl.

Earlier in the year Grantland Rice, like so many other American journalists, believed that Helen Wills's talent was so prodigious as to be virtually unchallengeable. He wrote a verse about her power that went:

> "If seven men with strength and skill
> Met Helen Wills this year,
> Do you suppose," the Walrus said,
> "They'd play her without fear?"
> "I doubt it," said the Carpenter,
> And grinned from ear to ear.

She had played seven men with strength and skill in 1925 and had beaten them in exhibitions before enthusiastic galleries. But she in turn had been beaten and had been extended by players who had been easily beaten by Suzanne Lenglen. She had been booed by an American crowd. Her reputation for invincibility had not been enhanced in 1925. Already, she seemed to be wavering at the top and, in 1926, might fall back, down with the other American players.

Writing for the *New Yorker* in late August 1925, John Tunis pointed out that Helen Wills alone of all the American women playing tennis had the potential to develop the game that could beat Suzanne Lenglen. "It makes no matter how often the child is beaten," he wrote, "in our opinion she has the extra ounce of talent—the last sixteenth—the thing they pay Babe Ruth the extra $50,000 for." But Lenglen could never be beaten by any player who had even the slightest weakness in her game. Helen's major problem, Tunis felt, despite her losses and her three-set victories in 1925, was that she was so good, so far superior to any other American player, that she sometimes became blasé on the court. She could afford not to pay close attention to her opponents, and she often didn't, and that was why she lost sets and matches. She dispatched most other female players with impersonal ruthless virtuosity. "And were we one of those who have her destiny in hand, we would ask her please to remember that the Mademoiselle of France plays admirably from the back line or the net, it matters not which, either on one foot or two, or lying down or standing on her head as the exigencies of the match require." If Helen hoped to beat Suzanne someday—and Tunis hoped she would—then she had better start paying attention to details and learn to adjust and to play every shot and every angle and every player, because Suzanne could hit every shot and every angle and could play every game on the court imaginable and some that were not imaginable. Only in that way could the American Girl bring down the Goddess from France. Only perfection could challenge perfection. And Helen was not yet perfect. Not quite.

Meanwhile, Suzanne Lenglen danced from title to title in Europe, unafraid and unchallenged. The only victory that would mean anything in tennis anymore was a victory over her. The only way Helen Wills could continue to excite enthusiasm and admiration was if she played Lenglen. And although she had not said so publicly and was embarrassed when she was asked about it, she had long questioned the skills and the reputation of the goddess.

Helen Wills firmly believed that if you wanted something, and you worked hard enough to get it, then nothing could stop you. It took merely energy and a willingness of the heart to accomplish anything. Even miracles. More and more she was feeling a restlessness in her heart now, and she came to realize what she must do. A few weeks before the end of the fall semester at the University, Helen made up her mind to travel to France. She said she would go to study art. And perhaps she would play a little tennis, too. And when she played tennis she would try her hardest. And, she believed, if by chance she lost a match or two, there was nothing that would pervent her from winning eventually if she could just get into action and try her hardest. That was, after all, the American faith. And she was an American Girl. She was confident.

CHAPTER
---⊰ III ⊱---

BALLYHOO

"Suzanne Lenglen's game is the greatest height to which present-day women's tennis has soared. She showed by her truly beautiful and consistent play what women's tennis could really be. In her wake, then, followed a flock of younger players whose eyes had seen the newer game."   —Helen Wills

"When my time comes I will meet defeat smilingly and with a word of congratulations for the victor— but it will not be this year."
                                        —Suzanne Lenglen, 1926

"Now, I take it that what we're all put on this earth for—every one of us—is to rise up in the world—to reach out."   —"Girl of the Golden West"
                                        David Belasco

O N the morning of January 15, 1926, more than a thousand people crowded the train platform of the Gare St. Lazare in Paris to await the arrival of the boat train from Le Havre. Included in the gathering were scores of newspaper reporters and a sprinkling of formally attired officials of the French Tennis Federation. Pierre Gillou, the leader of the FTA delegation, clutched a small piece of paper on which he had scribbled florid phrases of salutation. Gillou betrayed his nervousness by frequently glancing down at his notes and then quietly mumbling parts of the short address to himself.

It was remarkable that so many people had assembled to welcome a young American to France. Americans were more often castigated than celebrated by the French in early 1926. In fact, only a few days earlier a story in the *Paris-Midi* had described Americans as "degenerate and rotten, physically, intellectually, and morally. They offend our eyes, our ears, and our nostrils." Crowds of Frenchmen on the Place de la Concorde had recently taken to stoning buses of American tourists, whom they blamed for the fall of the franc. And the most popular review in the city, *Quel Beau Nu,* included a lengthy diatribe against Americans that concluded each evening with the audience rising to chant, *"A bas Americains! A bas Americains!"*

Yet the American arriving on this morning, to be sure, was an exceptional individual on an extraordinary mission. Helen Wills, the reigning

American queen of tennis, had come to France to challenge the suzerainty of Suzanne Lenglen. Helen was, to the French, a gracious and accommodating sacrificial lamb. Her impending inevitable demise at the hands of the unconquerable incomparable French Goddess would no doubt provide more than symbolic revenge—a revenge for Carpentier in America, for Suzanne in America, and for all of the economic woes of France attributed to the selfish and provincial policies of the United States. Yes, Helen Wills was to be welcomed with open arms. Her imminent humiliation, like that of Molla Mallory three years earlier, would become a source of French pride.

When the morning train arrived and rolled slowly to a stop, the waiting crowd pressed forward impatiently to get a first glimpse of the American Girl. Then, suddenly, there she was in the doorway of one of the last cars. There were cries of recognition, sporadic clapping and cheers, and even a few gasps. My God, she's white! A few reporters, unacquainted with the American Girl and with sport outside France, had come to the station expecting to greet a black woman—a Josephine Baker of American athletics. Wills, they believed, was the sister of Harry Wills, "The Black Panther," a leading challenger for Jack Dempsey's heavyweight title. That mistake would for years be a source of humor for the American Girl.

Photographers poked and elbowed their way forward, using their cameras and tripods as wedges, while a dozen reporters broke into an indecipherable chatter of questions as the statuesque American stood silently above them on the steps of the car looking quite bewildered by it all. Pierre Gillou suddenly added to the bizarre confusion of the moment by stepping forward and beginning his welcoming speech, almost oblivious to the fact that his words were lost in the competing chorus of reporters' questions. And then from the back of the crowd came the thunder of a familiar welcoming voice: "Hello, Helen! Welcome to France."

Helen Wills looked up and gave a slight smile of recognition. Gillou stopped speaking and turned around to see "The Bounding Basque," Jean Borotra, the most outgoing member of France's popular Four Musketeers of tennis, ploughing his way through the crowd. "Hello, Helen!" he continued to shout. "Hello, Helen!" until he stood beside Gillou and gallantly offered his arm to Helen. Borotra's magnificent aplomb restored some semblance of order, and the awkward welcoming ceremony and press conference proceeded smoothly.

Gillou completed his formal remarks. Then Helen Wills submitted good-naturedly to the demands of the photographers and walked to the end of the station platform, where the light was much better for picture-taking. She answered a score of questions about her intentions. Yes, she intended to play against Suzanne on the Riviera. "What will you do if Mlle. Lenglen beats you on the your first meeting in tennis?" she was asked. "I shall try again," she responded. Then, saying she was exhausted by the travel, Helen begged the reporters not to talk to her of tennis for ten days.

Earlier in the morning, after disembarking from the *De Grasse* at Le Havre, Helen Wills had submitted patiently to the countless questions of another crowd of newsmen. She was surprised by their insistent and bold curiosity, by their apparent desire to know about every aspect of her life, every detail. She was cautious and answered in as few words as possible. Someone asked her whether she would rather be tennis champion of France or have her paintings displayed in the Salon. She replied that tennis was one thing and painting was another and that in her life the art of the brush came before the art of batting the ball. She had come to France primarily to paint, she told the questioners, and she expected to complete several watercolors in the coming weeks. At the same time, bystanders noticed that Helen kept a close eye on the bundle of eighteen tennis rackets she had brought along. There were no paints or brushes anywhere in sight. She was, they concluded, delightfully modest.

Helen and her mother were escorted from Gare St. Lazare station to a limousine that whisked them away to another station, where they were scheduled to board the Train Bleu for the final leg of their journey to the Riviera. The reporters rushed back to their offices with stories and pictures.

In the newspaper accounts that appeared the next day, it was quite clear that French newsmen had been deeply impressed by the American girl. Some, it seemed, were simply overwhelmed by her. She was so completely unlike any other American woman they had seen. And she was not at all what they expected. She was certainly no flapper. Her hair was not bobbed. She wore no makeup at all. She did not chew gum. She lacked that pugnacious punch-you-right-in-the-nose athletic look of Molla Mallory and May Sutton Bundy. Helen Wills was a tall woman who exuded both femininity and strength. She had a certain bearing, a presence, that caused heads to turn. She possessed an understated imperiousness. Yet there was a simplicity in her dress and in her demeanor, an ingenuousness that was both surprising and refreshing. The young American beauty wore a simple gray coat, a black fur piece, and a red scarf. Her only jewelry was a glass-bead necklace. The newsmen had become accustomed over the years to the Lenglen panache, to the furious mugging for the cameras, to the carefully calculated photo opportunity. Now, suddenly, the opposite: understatement and timidity and courtesy. Here was genuine humility. Helen was supposed to be the villain of this story. She was here to take a celebrated and symbolic fall. But the stories of her arrival did not quite put it that way. Helen Wills was not like other Americans. And it would really be too bad if her journey to France merely repeated the Mallory debacle of 1923.

In the twenty-four hours following her arrival in Paris Helen Wills made an impact on French clothing styles. Aboard the boat train she had worn a small close-fitting velvet toque with only the suspicion of a brim. The hat was devoid of trimming except for a small University of California button attached in the front. A milliner from a shall shop on the Rue de Rivoli had seen the American girl at the station and was so impressed by her hat that he rushed back to his shop and worked all night creating a duplicate. In place of the UC button the milliner placed a small dark button. The next morning the "Helen Wills Toque" appeared in his window, and in the following days it became the fashion in the French capital.

Newspaper accounts of the arrival also brought about a heated international exchange between France and England. Wills had been asked if she intended to play in the World Hard Court Championship at Saint-Cloud in June. She replied that she had previously obligated herself to play in the Wightman Cup matches in England at that time. That simple announcement outraged officials of the French Tennis Federation. How could the English have possible arranged matches so as to steal this American girl from the French? Younger members of the FTA called for a boycott of Wimbledon—this on the fiftieth anniversary of the tournament and with the defending male and female singles champions being French. How would the British like the absence of the defending champions? Or why not organize an alternative international contest in Paris to be played the same week as Wimbledon and thus steal the publicity and the prestige from the All-England Club? A spokesman for the French Tennis Federation immediately fired off a note with the tone of an ultimatum to the English Lawn Tennis Association. He threatened the organization of a French-Spanish or a French-Italian tournament while the Wimbledon competition was played unless the English compromised on the American girl. Within a few days the conflict between France and England was resolved peacefully. The FTA was informed that the dates of the Wightman Cup matches were not yet official. There need be no conflict tournament dates and no boycott of Wimbledon. The French could keep the American Girl for the hard court tournament in June.

During this war of words between Paris and London, Helen and Catherine Wills traveled south aboard the Train Bleu to the Riviera and the Kingdom of Suzanne. The journey was much more than a mere geographic transit. Suzanne Lenglen herself had written that the Côte d'Azure was the "happy hunting ground for tennis players" and referred to it in her novel *The Love Set* as having the historical significance of the Rubicon. Traveling to the Riviera was for any tennis player "one of the landmarks of life from which there could be no retreat." Certainly, in the case of Helen Wills the train that carried her to the Riviera crossed that Rubicon dividing her past career and her future. In the next weeks she would be thrust quite unexpectedly into an entirely new world of fame and achievement.

When the Train Bleu arrived in Cannes, another large crowd of reporters and spectators was waiting to see the American girl and to question her. But this time there was no press conference and no formal welcoming speech. A representative of the FTA rescued Helen and her mother from the crowd, ushered them into a waiting limousine, and drove them to a modest pension for their stay.

Helen Wills discovered an utterly enchanting and exciting world on the Riviera in 1926; a world where the most important business appeared to be pleasure. "It was like a dream in which things were happening with the extravagance of a grand opera," she found. The Riviera was a winter playground and a source of pleasant diversion and sin for the titled and monied melancholy herd of postwar Europe. During the day there were constant rounds of tennis in tournaments sponsored by the dozens of clubs along the Côte d'Azure. In the afternoon and the evening the casinos and the sumptuous restaurants of the grand hotels catered to the formally attired pleasure-seekers. Helen was awed at first by the number of women dressed in the latest creations by the leading Parisian couturiers, the number of chauffeured limousines, the servants and footmen, and the generous sprinkling of real royalty. There were wealthy industralists from throughout Europe with their wives and families, and in the clubs there were unctuous gigolos and slim adagio dancers vying for the attention of the wealthy, bovine matrons. "I had supposed people like that existed only on the screen," Helen confessed. "Certainly you did not see them in Berkeley, California."

Even tennis, the dominant formal sport of the region, was unlike the tennis Helen had seen anywhere else in the world. Tennis in the south of France seemed to be dominated by the English. Most of the players, officials, club members, and spectators were English. The language used in calling out the scores was English. The rackets and balls were provided by English manufacturers. Suzanne Lenglen had learned her English here in order to participate in the big tournaments. There was also the unusual *bon* system of the region that mixed professional rewards with amateur sport. And it was well known, also, that many players were affiliated secretly with equipment manufacturers and were lushly subsidized in return for refusing to play in any tournament in which the products of their patron were not used. The clubs of the region offered generous inducements in order to draw leading players of the world into their tournaments. On the Riviera, in other words, sport was serious business. Not only could an aspiring tennis champion make a reputation here, it was possible to make a very good living also.

Since 1914 the Riviera had pretty much been Suzanne Lenglen's private preserve. Each year thousands of faithful followers of the French

goddess came to the Riviera to see her began another campaign in quest
of the supreme tennis laurels offered in Europe. As a matter of course
she defeated all of the challengers in the region before moving on to
Saint-Cloud, Paris, and then Wimbledon. On the clay courts of the
Riviera, Suzanne never disappointed the ardent partisan fans.

But all was not well in Suzanne's kingdom in early 1926. Shortly after
word was received that Helen Wills was coming to France, troubling
rumors began circulating along the Côte d'Azure. In early January the
wire services carried reports that Suzanne had suffered yet another nervous breakdown. She had dropped out of a tournament in Cannes and
returned to her home in Nice. She was said to be very seriously ill this
time. There could not possibly be a match with Helen Wills on the
Riviera this year!

Those reports were followed by furious denials that anything at all
was wrong. A family friend explained, "Suzanne gets around quite a lot
on the Riviera and it was just at New Year's time. Before going on the
court that day she felt as if she had an attack of *mal de mer*. But she
will watch her step when it comes to meeting Helen," he predicted.
Suzanne herself denied the reports of a nervous collapse. "I am neither
neurasthenic nor have I had any attack of nerves," she told newsmen. "I
intend to play in the Nice championships in a few days and will be
ready to meet all comers after that." When asked directly if she would
play Helen, Suzanne responded, "I shall have just as much if not more
pleasure in trying conclusions with Miss Wills as with Miss McKane,
Miss Ryan, or Mlle. Vlasto. But I must tell you," she confided, "that
Miss Wills coming here is the least of my cares. My father, who has been
seriously ill, has just undergone a severe operation and Mama and I
have been terribly anxious about him lately."

Lenglen then added that she believed Wills's visit "is certain to give a
great boost to the French winter tennis. Miss Wills is the finest type of
sportswoman and a great tennis player," she said. However, she cautioned, "my winter campaign was all mapped out before I knew she intended coming to France and her coming will not interfere with the
schedule I have outlined for myself, which consists of playing singles in
three tournaments and doubles and mixed doubles in all the winter
tournaments as I have been doing for the last three or four years." Then
she concluded, with a twinkle in her eye, "Please tell your American
journalist friends not to say that I quit or that I am afraid to meet her
if I should not be entered in the singles in some tournament in which
Miss Wills takes part."

A reporter asked if Helen had a chance to defeat Suzanne if the two
met this season on the Riviera. "When my time comes I will meet defeat
smilingly and with a word of congratulations to the victor," Lenglen
said. "But it will not be this year." She then gave reporters and spectators
something to think about. She returned to the tournament in Cannes and

won the singles, doubles, and mixed doubles without losing a game in any match. Opponents of the Maid Marvel confessed that they detected no sign whatever of a nervous breakdown or any other disability. In fact, they said, Lenglen had never played better in her life.

With Wills's arrival in Cannes, everyone began to speculate about the where and the when of the first match between the Goddess and the American Girl. Doubtless, there would be a whole series of confrontations between the two—in Cannes, Mentone, Monte Carlo, and Nice. But the first match would be the most dramatic. And Suzanne and Papa would more than likely insist that it be played at the Nice Tennis Club, like the Mallory match. Lenglen had crushed Mallory before the home-town crowd there in the winter of 1923, and she would probably seek to duplicate that performance. There were two big differences, however, between what had taken place in 1923 and what was taking place in 1926. First, the promise of a match between Wills and Lenglen already had much more public attention and appeal than did the Mallory match. Second, Helen Wills was not Molla Mallory.

In Cannes, meanwhile, Wills had already demonstrated her innocence of the way things worked on the Riviera. There was some amusement among regional tennis officials and players when Helen and her mother moved into a small pension. That would never do! On the morning following their arrival the Wills women were invited to move into a suite at the Metropole, one of the finest hotels in the region. They were to be guests of the hotel and to use it as their headquarters so long as they stayed on the Riviera. Helen and her mother were flattered by the offer and immediately made the move.

Wills later admitted that she had no knowledge whatever of the way things worked on the Riviera. She asked few questions and simply accepted the accommodations. Other players in the region, she was told, accepted similar arrangements. One big advantage of the move was that it gave her the chance to practice on the courts of the Metropole Club. And only hours after taking up residence in the hotel she was practicing her ground strokes on the soft pink clay courts of the Metropole Club with a local professional, seeking to regain her equilibrium and timing after the long journey from California.

On the following morning, her third day on the Riviera, Wills attended a tournament at the New Courts in Cannes in order to get a glimpse of Suzanne Lenglen. Helen had watched the Maid Marvel in competition twice—once at Forest Hills in 1921 and again at Wimbledon in 1924. Both competitions had been on fast grass surfaces, and in both Lenglen had defaulted from the tournament. Helen was curious to see if the celebrated sorcery of the French woman was more apparent on the slower clay surface of the Riviera. She was escorted to the club by a small entourage of Englishwomen who had volunteered to show her the city. Arriving late in the morning, the group was informed that they were too early—Suzanne never made an appearance on the Riviera courts before noon. Helen elected, nonetheless, to stay for a short while and to watch the match in progress between local favorite Henri Cochet and an English opponent. While she watched there was a great amount of excitement and commotion a short distance away as a sleek chauffeured limousine glided to a stop at the club entrance and Suzanne Lenglen emerged. The goddess was in full costume, wrapped in a white lynx coat with a huge standing collar high enough to frame her entire head in white. She was accompanied by Mama and by a bevy of stylishly attired, chattering sycophants. When Lenglen was told that Wills was on the club grounds, she immediately asked to be formally introduced.

Wills was uneasy at this initial meeting. She was aware that Lenglen had already told reporters that she considered Helen's invasion of the Riviera a bit "cheeky," and Wills suspected that the French star could not have been pleased in reading the many newspaper articles announcing the American girl's intention of taking away Lenglen's tennis titles. Helen was, as a result, quite surprised by Suzanne's genuinely pleasant demeanor. "I hope you had a very good crossing," Suzanne said in English in her deep throaty voice. She extended her hand to Helen. The American girl shook hands and replied that her crossing had been very rough. Then she exchanged a few pleasantries about the weather and the city and the local tennis. The two women, accompanied by their followers, then drifted off in different directions. Reporters caught up with Suzanne and asked her for her impressions of the American girl. She had, they found, nothing but praise for Helen Wills. "I admire Helen in every way; she is such a sweet child. I simply love her," Suzanne bubbled with a certain flippant lack of conviction. And those who understood the nuances of Suzanne's peculiar idiom understood right away that the Goddess had taken the measure of the American Girl and she was not afraid. This was going to be another romp.

Lenglen invited Wills to watch her play later that day. But Helen left the club soon after meeting Suzanne. Had she stayed she would have seen Lenglen in her glory, winning two matches and dropping only three games in the process. Wills left the club and strolled with her companions along the Mediterranean. She spoke very little. She was thinking about what to do next. She had shaken Suzanne's hand and looked her in the eye. Her own confidence increased. She felt healthy and strong. She was anxious for action, tired of waiting, tired of talk and idle chatter and watching others play tennis. She had originally planned to practice for at least a week before entering any tournaments. But a week was too long. Within a few hours, contrary to the expectations of journalists following Helen Wills and contrary to the American girl's earlier stated intentions, Helen announced that she would play in a tournament that very week. She sent her official entry to the Metropole Club for the women's singles competition. Lenglen had already entered that tournament, but in the mixed doubles only. And so the champions of the old and the new worlds would be on the same tennis courts on the same day, but they would not play against each other. They would provide the opportunity, however, much sooner than anyone had hoped, for spectators to evaluate and compare their styles and expertise and to estimate the chances of the American Girl against the Maid Marvel. And to bet.

Journalist John Tunis, who had followed Helen Wills to the Riviera for the expected confrontation with Lenglen, reported on daily events in the region for both *American Lawn Tennis* and *The New Yorker*. Tunis knew Helen's game well, and he was deeply disturbed now by her apparent impulsiveness in entering a tournament so soon after her arrival. Tunis knew the ins and outs of the business of tennis on the Riviera (he had been there before as a reporter and a player) and he sensed that Wills was being subtly manipulated, pushed along by certain commercially motivated but unseen interests. Who they were and what their intentions were, Tunis did not yet know. He did know, though, that players were entered or not entered in various tournaments in order to stimulate public interest, betting, and potential gate receipts. Wills attributed her entry into the Metropole tournament to simple restlessness. "I could see that there was nothing that I especially wanted to do," she wrote, "except play tennis." She was not unduly concerned with her lengthy absence from competition. And she seemed clearly underwhelmed by the local competition. Tunis was, however, skeptical. First came Helen's move to the Metropole Hotel, and now her entry into the Metropole tournament surely indicated that someone was counseling the American ingenue. Tunis began watching Helen more closely in order to discover who was guiding the American girl through the Byzantine maze of Riviera sport and gambling and business.

In preparation for her premier Riviera appearance, Wills went through several intense practice sessions with a veteran English player, Major Randall. Afterwards, Randall was asked by reporters to evaluate her play. She was in excellent form, he volunteered. And her volleying and ground strokes were very effective. Unfortunately, Randall concluded, she would not disturb Lenglen in the last. Lenglen had much more finesse and she was "half a second quicker in her head and on her feet" than this American challenger. "I think, though," he said, "that Helen will beat everyone else down here."

Wills opened her campaign of 1926 on January 19 in a match against Miss E. M. Green, an experienced English player who was known for her steady and competent play from the backcourt on clay. She was a player of the old style, though, underhand service and all.

The crowd that turned out to see Wills play was the largest that had ever attended a match on the Riviera, an extremely promising sign for whatever club landed a Wills-Lenglen duel. The club grounds were packed, and photographers and reporters pushed their way up to the very edge of the playing surface itself. With so much excitement and animated disorder all around, whatever there had once been of Miss Green's game deserted her now. The Englishwoman managed to win only eight points in twelve games as Helen breezed her way to a love-love victory. The match took less than thirty minutes to complete. Since Wills had not yet warmed up by the time she had won twelve games in succession, she rallied for a short time with the club professional after Miss Green made her exit. The crowd appeared to be as interested in watching Wills practice as they had been in seeing her in competition, and nearly the entire gallery remained to watch until Helen finally left the courts.

Although the Green match hardly provided a typical display of Helen Wills's capabilities, one aspect of her play on this day intrigued nearly all of the spectators—her absolute serenity and her lack of expression. She was a stark contrast to Suzanne Lenglen. Her sober countenance was like something set in marble. Nothing seemed to faze her in the least. Little wonder the American press dubbed her Miss Poker Face.

Reporters also pointed out the "masculine" qualities of Wills's play. She hit with all of the power of the male players, and she came to the net to volley winners whenever the opportunity presented itself. She was not exceptionally fast on her feet, it seemed, but she always got to the ball in plenty of time to launch thundering drives back at her opponent. She was not Suzanne Lenglen, to be sure. But she was definitely a crowd-pleaser.

Wills's attire for the match was also a stark contrast with what other Riviera players wore. Almost all of the women on the Riviera emulated Suzanne Lenglen, wearing silk designer creations and matching bandeau fastened with an expensive bejeweled pin. Helen, however, wore her customary plain white cotton skirt and middy blouse—a schoolgirl's uniform. And instead of the Lenglen bandeau she wore her eyeshade. She also refused to wear makeup on the court and was the only woman among the thirty-two in the Metropole tournament with unbobbed hair. When asked why she didn't bob her hair, Wills responded, "I'm too old-fashioned." That remark utterly delighted many spectators, and one elderly British countess remarked to reporters at the match, "I love Helen Wills because she has not sacrificed her beautiful hair to foolish fashion!"

The local Riviera press was also enthralled by the almost unbelievable simplicity of the American girl, by her ingenuousness. They had never seen anything quite like this before. The *Eclairer de Nice,* the most important newspaper in the region, referred to Wills as *"une petite jeune fille de province,"* and, indeed, to many she did give the unmistakable impression of being a beautiful and healthy young girl from the country. Yet a clearly imperious quality was mixed with her simplicity. And it was that surprising combination of royalty and provinciality—Marie

Antoinette as a milkmaid—that made her almost irresistible to the men of the press.

In the second round of the Metropole tournament Wills gave reporters more to think about when she beat one of England's most highly touted young tennis players, Peggy Saunders. Newsmen at the match credited the English girl with putting up a "plucky struggle" before going down to the hard-driving American girl, 6–1, 6–2. Wills followed up this win with an equally impressive victory over a fellow American, Leslie Bancroft Aeschliman, a left-handed player who had beaten her several times in junior competitions in America four years earlier. But now, on the Riviera, Aeschliman was clearly no longer in Helen Wills's class.

The vast amount of publicity about the activities of the American girl was fast making her the best-known personality on the Riviera. And local residents, who shared the general French antipathy for all things American, found themselves taking a real liking to this exceptional young woman. She was, it seemed, everything that Americans were not supposed to be—polite, kind, old-fashioned, deferential, quiet, and cultured. Helen Wills was actually surprised by the quick popularity she gained with the local folk when she first discovered it quite by accident. Following the Aeschliman match she drove to Nice with a fellow Californian, Fred Moody, who was vacationing on the Riviera. The young couple intended to get away from the crowds and the inquiring newsmen and to relax and enjoy an American movie. But when they entered the theater, Helen was instantly recognized. There were shouts of delight and cheers from the audience and then a rousing standing ovation. Demands were made for Helen to make a speech. She demurred for a few moments but finally stood and announced, "I hope to play in your town in early February." Her words were quickly translated by a dozen enthusiastic volunteers, and the crowd again cheered. After several more minutes of applause the movie began.

Suzanne Lenglen, meanwhile, also progressed without serious challenge through the doubles and mixed doubles divisions of the Metropole tournament. Newsmen and fans eager to compare the skill of the two champions were in general agreement that she appeared far more polished and accomplished than her American challenger. If Wills were really to test Lenglen's game on the Riviera this year, then there would have to be a dramatic improvement in her play—and soon.

As for herself, Helen Wills never overestimated her own capabilities or underestimated the expertise of the Maid Marvel. She was an interested observer at every one of Lenglen's matches, sitting as inconspicuously as possible in a corner of the bleachers, studying every move of the French woman and then meticulously recording her observations in a small notebook. She betrayed no emotion while watching and writing. She remained calm and inscrutable and studious. When someone asked her what she thought of Suzanne's game, Helen replied, "She is really wonderful. I have seldom before seen such tennis." One local reporter wrote that no matter how much Helen studied Suzanne's game, she would never find a weakness in it. Papa had taken care of that. The Maid Marvel's tennis was simple perfection.

Although Lenglen glanced in Wills's direction several times during her matches and appeared to be more than normally self-conscious in the presence of the American observer, the two stars did not exchange words when the play was completed, not even when they stood only a few feet from each other at courtside.

The most exciting matches of the Metropole tournament were the semifinal and the final rounds of the women's singles. In those matches Wills played the fifth- and second-ranked French stars. Here, then, was her first real chance to show her stuff against accomplished players in France. And in the two matches she did not disappoint.

In the semifinal match she defeated Helene Contostavlos, France's fifth-ranked woman, 6–3, 6–4. The match gave Wills a chance to demonstrate her deadly volleying skills, for play had not progressed far before it became clear that she would have great difficulty in beating Contostavlos with ground strokes alone. Consequently, Wills added pace to her service and followed it to the net in the dashing Borotra style that had transported French crowds in the past several years in men's competition. On the slow clay, which neutralized much of her power, the serve and volley tactic was particularly dicey. But Wills made it work. She was passed several times after moving forward, but she was, nonetheless, very effective at the net.

Following the Wills-Contostavlos match, an umpire cautioned reporters, "Don't let this score mislead you! Constostavlos played sterling tennis. And don't let yourself be influenced by Contostavlos' repeated defeats by Lenglen in straight love sets. That's another story. There would have been another story to tell had Lenglen played against Contostavlos today." Despite such evaluations, Wills's play was clearly still far below the quality of Lenglen's on clay. And as if to prove it, the Maid Marvel streaked through the doubles and mixed doubles competition winning most of her matches at love. She attended the Wills-Contostavlos match and showed her partisanship openly by shouting enthusiastic approval several times after the French girl made successful passing shots. After the match Lenglen uncharacteristically refused all comment.

On the next afternoon, in the finals of the Metropole tournament, Helen Wills played Didi Vlasto, France's second-ranked player and the woman she had beaten in the Olympic finals in 1924. Wills gave up eight games in beating Vlasto on this day, 6–3, 7–5. She played throughout the match as if this were merely a practice session. She stayed in the backcourt and with her powerful ground strokes pounded away mercilessly at Vlasto. Wills at times seemed to be doing her imitation of a human backboard, refusing to go for outright winners and letting Vlasto lose on her own errors. As the match progressed, she actually appeared to grow stronger. She closed out the match by winning four straight games and coming back from a 3–5 deficit. In those final four games she sent the ball exploding off her racket back into Vlasto's court, grinding down the strength of the French girl and neutralizing her game. When the match ended Wills appeared to be untired. Vlasto, on the other hand, was so completely undone by the play that she had to be helped from the court. Her exhaustion was so complete, in fact, that she was unable to play with Lenglen in the finals of the women's doubles later that same afternoon. The pair requested and received a postponement of their match. When the announcement was made that the Goddess would not appear on the courts that afternoon the mood of the capacity crowd at the Metropole Club quickly turned ugly. There was a good deal of shouting and booing and cursing of club officials. Many people hurled their seat cushions or other small objects onto the court, and hundreds of others demanded their money back. Suzanne Lenglen was still the star attraction on the Riviera.

Despite the pounding she had taken from Wills, Vlasto's evaluation of her game was less than flattering. "When I play Suzanne I never have a chance," she pointed out. "But I showed the crowd here that I always can give Miss Wills a good game." Wills responded immediately to Vlasto's remark with a cold mechanical smile and the observation that "Mlle. Vlasto has greatly improved. But my game was far below form." She was learning. Suzanne Lenglen remained uncharacteristically close-mouthed about her own feelings concerning Wills's game. She would say only that "Helen has made progress."

On January 26 public attention turned to the next big Riviera tournament at the Gallia Club in Cannes. Wills entered the singles competition, while Lenglen again entered only the two doubles categories. As in the Metropole tournament, the two feature attractions of the Riviera would be on the same court on the same day but would not face each other across the net.

The opening matches of the Gallia tournament provided unmistakable evidence of the rapidly growing journalistic obsession with the progress of Helen Wills on the Riviera. Swarms of reporters and photographers now trailed behind Wills wherever she went. From the hotel to the tennis court and then back again to the hotel, she could not escape the constant dogged barrage of questions concerning her feelings about Suzanne, about her opponents, about her game, about the local courts and the local weather and the local men and the latest fashions. Questions about anything and everything. What Helen said and what she did not say became front page news in more and more newspapers throughout the world. Helen Wills's pursuit of Suzanne Lenglen was fast becoming the big media event of 1926.

Not long after Helen's arrival in Cannes a mass migration of newsmen to the Côte d'Azure began. Editors from every part of Europe and from North and South America had begun to see the almost unlimited possibilities for publication of stories dealing with the slowly unfolding drama in the south of France. The very best reporters and features writers and photographers were dispatched to cover the action. From the morning Wills disembarked at Le Havre the French press had run daily accounts of her activities. By the end of January the name of Helen Wills had become a household word in France. The relative talents of "notre Suzanne" and "Mees Veels" was a source of daily discussion not just along the Mediterranean coast but on the boulevards of Paris and in every other city in France. Not only had the French public become intrigued by the quiet American, but they also had come to like her. The friendly response of the movie theater crowd in Nice was something that might have been duplicated in just about any city in France at that time. And what was most amazing to Helen was the fact that she need only be herself to become the toast of the Continent. Remaining unaffected by all the hoopla, however, became more and more difficult as the days passed.

Helen Wills and Suzanne Lenglen were, in fact, fast becoming the beneficiaries of a phenomenon known as "ballyhoo." Journalist Frederick Lewis Allen found that the newly consolidated newspaper chains and news services of the 1920s were becoming increasingly prone to blow any number of "tremendous trifles" far out of proportion in order to arouse public interest and increase circulation. When no really important news stories developed, news was invented—"pseudo events" were covered. Consequently, relatively unimportant or obscure people or events were snatched up regularly by a hungry press and bloated into major media events for days or weeks. It worked wonderfully, just as it had worked earlier for the successful tabloids. Soon the public came not only to expect, but to demand arousing stories from the media. Helen Wills's quest for the laurels of Suzanne Lenglen was a natural for the media concerned with boosting circulation, and it was quickly recognized as one of the "good shows" that the public expected and embraced.

Helen Wills's quest, however, differed from most previous journalist ballyhoo explosions in that it had nothing at all to do with violence or corruption or degeneracy or homicide or mayhem or evolution or bizarre feats—the staples of public interest. Her adventure seemed, indeed, a reaffirmation of American ideals and American visions. In a world in which the most sordid and salacious and scandalous events usually made the biggest headlines, here was good news for the front pages and for the parlors and the pulpits and the pride of the democratic masses. It was good to discover that there were still young women like Helen Wills out there, and the public responded almost ecstatically to the news. She was in Europe all alone, the stories went, in quest of a contest with the most celebrated female athlete of the century. Here was a young woman worthy of public attention and public adoration.

Americans had always been prone to hero worship of one kind or another. And in America in the 1920s, following the disclosures of seedy political corruption in Washington, sports figures were fast emerging as the most easily marketable brand of hero. There were no more Theodore Roosevelts or Woodrow Wilsons around. The press played up the myth that athletic champions were special because they had been, in a sense, transformed—cleansed and sanctified—in the great white heat of competition. Consequently, they were different because they had achieved a certain nobility of character by being tested and thus were truly worthy of public awe and esteem. But time after time those noble cleansed heroes tarnished their public image in the unashamed pursuit of the buck. Babe Ruth, Jack Dempsey, and Red Grange were in sport not for the sport itself, but for the money they could make. They were, in fact, merely a cut above any money-grubbing businessman or politician. But Helen Wills! Ah, Helen Wills was different. Much different. Her quest was not for riches or fame but merely for a match with the champion, the newsmen wrote. A match with the champion. She was motivated by an ideal, by the love of the game. And, after all, wasn't that what sport was supposed to be all about? In one of the nation's most materialistic decades, here was an American girl totally unswayed by material motivation who could remind all of us of our real spirit and our ideals.

Helen Wills, however, presented a special difficulty for American journalists. In the past the sporting heroes of the nation were males. Here was our first sporting heroine. The precise language and symbolism for such a phenomenon was as yet undeveloped. France already had Suzanne Lenglen—the Goddess. But by what mythic title might a democratic heroine be dubbed? She was already known to sportswriters and tennis fans as "Little Poker Face." But such a sobriquet would hardly do for one bearing a heavy symbolic burden so far away from home. And so writers and editors tried out new references to Helen. Thus, she became The Girl of the Golden West and Helen of California and The Girl of the Golden Gate. But she hardly belonged now to a single state or region of the country. She belonged to all. She became Little Helen. But that wasn't right either because there was nothing little about her muscular five-foot-seven-inch frame. Then she became Helen of America and Our Helen. But the most accurate appellation was one that reporters had already been using automatically without giving it much thought. She was a refreshingly simple middle-class girl, the kind of girl everyone dreamed of living next door to but didn't. She was The American Girl. And that was what many of them now conscientiously called her in their stories.

Editors and columnists went to work examining the virtue and the meaning of Helen Wills's adventure in Europe. The French had come to hiss the American girl, one of them wrote just as Suzanne had been hissed in America. They did not want to like Helen Wills but were unexpectedly seduced by her charm. "Helen Wills has won Europe," one American reporter wrote home. And Allison Danzig of the *New York Times* wrote with enthusiasm of her deportment on the Continent. She had behaved perfectly in the face of "the most flattering reception that has probably ever been accorded a woman athlete bent on foreign conquest," he concluded. "That a whole nation should have been excited to the point where everything else but her became somewhat secondary for a time and where even the hat she wore created a vogue might easily have turned the head of an older woman. . . ." But Helen's head was not turned. She maintained her poise and conducted herself on the courts perfectly and "with rare wisdom" refused to be drawn into any controversy like that caused by the bitter feeling on the arrival of Suzanne in America five years earlier.

One young sportswriter sent to cover Wills in Europe was Al Laney. He arrived in Cannes and found the city nearly overrun with newsmen. He was forced to neglect Helen's activities for a day while he sought a room in the city. Eventually he found quarters in a nearby village. Then back in Cannes he found all of the talk was of tennis and of the impending meeting between Wills and Lenglen. Every major press association now had its top reporters in Cannes and there were writers from every major European and North and South American newspaper present. Laney was determined to write nonfiction exclusively for his paper, no matter how difficult that might be. And it was very difficult, he found. He discovered that the competition for information on the two players was bitterly intense. Many journalists ended up interviewing each other, while others just gave up trying to get reliable stories and used their creativity in composing their articles. A stringer for *Time* magazine composed a fantasy diary for Helen Wills and published it week by week, revealing what he guessed to be Helen's innermost thoughts and dreams. Actually, James Thurber had established a precedent for American correspondents on the Riviera. He was living in Nice at the time editing the Riviera edition of the *Chicago Tribune*. The newspaper was quite unusual, since Thurber and his wife simply wrote almost all of its daily contents out of their imaginations. For hard news Thurber merely provided an English translation of reports in the local French newspapers. The remainder of his stories were pure fiction, but good fiction, so nobody seemed to mind.

Laney became part of the entourage that tried as politely as possible to get Helen Wills to speak out. As protection from what she considered harassment by the press, Helen, for a time, gathered around herself a staff of young American male volunteers who served as spies and reported the best available routes for escaping the press. Her daily routine came to involve an elaborate game of hide and seek with reporters, who referred sneeringly to Helen's helpers as "Wills' Boy Scout Troop."

But the more experienced reporters easily outwitted the guard and headed off the American girl on the streets of Cannes. She responded to their questions very reluctantly at first and gradually gravitated toward almost total silence, even refusing to say "Hello" to many of them. That attitude, Laney remembered, at a time when everything she did from the moment she got up in the morning until she retired in the evening was newsworthy, caused Laney to develop a feeling of resentment toward Helen, a feeling, he confessed, he maintained through the later years of her career. Her "rudeness," be believed, was not really part of her nature, but was rather her response to the increasing chaos on the Riviera at the time. Nevertheless, Laney was unable to erase it from his memory over the next several years.

Part of Wills's reluctance to hold news conferences or to cooperate fully with all American correspondents, Laney learned later, stemmed from an agreement she had signed with the International News Service which provided that she would not give interviews or pose for cameramen from any other news agencies. Wills was, at the time, writing several of her own tennis articles for the INS. As a result of her agreement, many of the reporters found themselves pumping INS correspondents for inside information. But whatever the INS arrangement, all of the wire services and syndicates demanded stories. And so the less solid the information reporters got, the more they were forced to guess or create. By cooperating a little more with some of the writers, Helen might have exerted a certain degree of control over the information coming out of Cannes. In that way she would have contributed enormously to the veracity of Riviera reporting.

On the opening day of the Gallia tournament Wills showed dramatic improvement in her game, defeating an English opponent 6–0, 6–1 and dropping only six points in the match. With each of her subsequent victories speculation on her chances in the Big Match gave her an increasing chance to take a game or two from the Goddess. Looking at the schedule of tournaments, reporters guessed that Suzanne and Helen would more than likely face each other in singles at the Nice Club during the first week in February. But no sooner had those predictions been printed than Lenglen announced that "circumstances beyond my control" might prevent her from entering the singles competition at her home club that week. She refused to elaborate, and nobody knew anymore just what her plan was concerning Wills. Some guessed that the gate for the big match would not yet be big enough during the first week in February and that Suzanne and her financial advisers wanted more time for public interest to build. Others said she was just afraid.

During the Gallia tournament Suzanne and Helen again came face to face in the presence of an army of reporters. The two women, accompanied by friends, could hardly avoid exchanging pleasantries. And so again they commented on the weather and on court conditions. Suzanne's Belgian poodle, Gyp, to the absolute delight of reporters, met an attempt by Helen to pet him with ominous low growls. Suzanne observed, "He's too old. He does not like young people." There was a patter of laughter, and the two stars disengaged and floated off in separate directions.

Helen Wills was becoming increasingly uneasy in the highly charged atmosphere of Cannes. "It was all rather extraordinary to me," she wrote, "concerned with my forehand drive and with padding happily about the courts, it seemed out of proportion, rather crazy, in fact." The UPI had just published a report claiming that "the boys in the boxing game would refer to the Wills-Lenglen match as a 'natural' and a promoter like Tex Rickard would hang up around $100,000 for the privilege of handling the tickets."

Helen escaped from the reporters once again during the first days of the Gallia tournament and went on a scouting expedition with Fred Moody to Nice. The young couple visited the Nice Tennis Club and examined closely the playing surface of the courts and the club facilities. If any Wills-Lenglen confrontation was to take place on the clay of Nice, as everyone expected it must, in early February or later, then Helen wanted to be familiar with the place. She found the courts of the club very pink and beautiful and fast. While she and Moody were on the terrace of the clubhouse overlooking the grounds, Suzanne Lenglen suddenly called to them from the Villa Ariem across the street. Lenglen then came to the club and escorted them around the grounds, showing them the court where she had whipped Molla Mallory so decisively. Before Helen and Fred could leave, Suzanne ordered champagne and toasted the health of the young American couple. The Goddess seemed more open and cordial in this semiprivate setting than she was in the presence of the reporters and the spectators in Cannes.

Soon after her visit to the Nice Tennis Club, Wills's name was officially entered in the club tournament scheduled to begin on February 1. Here, at last, on Lenglen's home grounds, the challenge had been delivered by the American girl. Unless Lenglen backed out now, the Big Match would take place under the most advantageous of circumstances for the Maid Marvel. But Suzanne suddenly surprised everyone, including Helen, and announced that she had decided not to play in the singles in the Nice tournament—her first refusal to play in the tournament at her home club since anyone could remember. "My program is unchanged since I made my statement on December 10th," she said. "I will play in the singles of three tournaments, as I planned previous to Miss Wills' arrival." The Nice tournament would simply not be one of the three.

Suzanne Lenglen's statement of her intention not to play in the singles in Nice brought an immediate outcry from the American newsmen on the Riviera, who accused her of shamelessly refusing to give the American girl a well-deserved shot at her title. Then the Nice Tennis Club announced that the new Slazenger grooved tennis ball would be used in the tournament. The ball adoption brought an even greater burst of protest from the American Riviera press corps. The "groover," as it was called, was of a revolutionary new design with a corrugated cover. The ball had a low, sharp bound, even lower than the other English tennis balls commonly used in Riviera tournaments, which were much less lively than the balls used in the United States. What this meant was that the combination of the groover and the clay courts would successfully neutralize most of Wills's power. And it would give an enormous advantage to the soft-stroking placement game of the French and English players. What the American correspondents suspected was that now Suzanne Lenglen would change her mind and make a dramatic announcement that she had decided after all to play in the Nice tournament.

They were right. But before Lenglen did, Wills withdrew her own entry from the singles competition in Nice. She was already having some difficulty in adapting her game to the clay courts and the slower English balls, and the use of the new groover was simply an added disadvantage she was not yet ready to deal with, at least not in singles. No sooner had Wills announced her withdrawal from the singles than Lenglen announced her entry.

In America, editors and columnists across the country denounced the Lenglen tactic in unrestrained terms. A *San Francisco Chronicle* editorial suggested that "the man who introduced the trick ball for use in an international match of this caliber ought to be shot at midnight. Sunrise is entirely too far away." And Harry Smith of the *Chronicle* wrote that the American public was sick and tired of Suzanne dodging the American girl. Suzanne Lenglen owed it to the tennis world to play against Helen Wills in Nice with a fair tennis ball so that the question of just who was the best tennis player in the world could be settled once and for all. Smith pointed out that Helen had traveled to France not in any spirit of braggadocio but rather "for the good of the sport," and consequently Suzanne should do everything possible to arrange a singles match with her. Smith even alleged that Lenglen had withdrawn from the 1924 Wimbledon tournament not because of illness but rather because of her overwhelming fear of meeting Helen Wills. More and more Americans were concluding that Lenglen was just plain scared of the American girl.

The *New York Times* commented editorially on Lenglen's actions and condemned her apparent effort to drum up greater commercial interest in a confrontation with Wills. Suzanne's activities placed "a new and far from pleasing light on the tennis situation in Cannes. The tennis powers of the area, including Papa Lenglen, appear to look upon tennis tournaments less as sporting events than as devices for attracting large crowds to spend enormous sums of money," the editor wrote. The adoption of the groover, he felt, was "a shabby device."

For several days in late January 1926 the talk in tennis clubs, on the streets, in barber shops, schools, and around diningroom tables throughout the United States concerned the adoption of a grooved tennis ball for the Nice tournament. Many journalists were utterly amazed at the pervasive public interest in the continuing saga of the American girl on the Riviera. Smith of the *Chronicle* wrote that while traveling by train he found his interest aroused by seeing so many people studying the newspaper. When he looked more closely he found that everybody seemed to be reading the sports page all of a sudden and they seemed chiefly concerned with stories about Helen Wills. Moreover, he noticed, the people he watched didn't simply read the headline and then glance at the first few paragraphs. They started at the top of the column and went down to the bottom and then turned to the next page to get the remainder of the story. "Some days back," Smith wrote, "we had a story from a sports enthusiast who insisted that the story of Helen and Suzanne was one of the really big stories of all time. Rather thought he was stretching the facts of the case. Now I'm coming around to the conclusion that he was more nearly right than a lot of us conservatives."

Later, Helen Wills said that she could not even remember entering the Nice tournament. Apparently the club committee had taken it for granted that she would play in their tournament, since she had played singles in the two preceding Riviera tournaments and had visited the club to look at the courts. But Helen said that her mother had not wanted to move to Nice for one week and then back again to Cannes for the next tournament at the Carlton Club. By entering only the doubles competition in Nice, Helen could play in fewer matches and could commute from Cannes daily. Still later, however, in her autobiography, Wills wrote that "my thoughts at the time might have been, 'Why meet Mlle. Lenglen on the court that she knows best in the whole world?' Or I may not have thought anything. I was definitely entered in the mixed doubles with the Swiss champion, Charles Aeschliman. By this time I was being followed by the press, who wanted to find out when the long-awaited-for match was going to take place. I did not know any more than they."

One of Wills's favorite correspondents on the Riviera that winter, Don Skene, told her that the betting odds were seven to one that Suzanne Lenglen would beat her when they met. A Greek syndicate that had ruled supreme for three years over the baccarat tables in Deauville and Cannes announced that it had 5,000,000 francs it would wager on Lenglen against 1,000,000 on Wills. Even money would be accepted on bets that Helen would not take five games from the Goddess when they eventually played—Lenglen had lost just five games on her way to the Wimbledon title in 1925. When told the odds for a match with Wills, Lenglen said that she was pleased to be the favorite. Wills's response to the news was one of annoyance. "I suppose you cannot prevent gamblers from betting on anything," she said. "But it seems rather incongruous that the tennis activities of two young women are treated like a race track feature or a boxing match." Yet even with the odds at five to one, few bets were placed. Too many people had watched the American girl play, and they found her game far inferior to that of the Goddess. Lenglen would wait for the right moment, pick her spot, and then make the kill both athletically and financially. There was some enthusiastic talk among Americans on the Riviera about Helen Wills's holding back and concealing her real talent until she finally faced Lenglen. But that was passed off by the majority as merely wishful thinking.

John Tunis was intrigued by the war of words that raged over the singles entry fiasco in the Nice tournament. He was sure that most American correspondents who believed that Lenglen was afraid of Wills were way off base. Rather than being afraid of the American girl, Suzanne and Papa were confident that Helen could be beaten quite easily. And so Suzanne avoided meeting Helen in Nice in order to let public interest in their meeting continue to snowball. The commercial possibilities of their match were enhanced almost daily. Suzanne and Papa acted at the behest of the business interests on the Riviera and in England, Tunis concluded, interests that would milk the meeting of the two athletes for all it was worth. What was happening—who Helen played and when and where—was a part of a carefully orchestrated master plan. Helen's opponents and the sequence in which she played them were supposed to be determined by a blind draw, Tunis wrote, but there was certainly something contrived even in that.

Several commercial interests had their hands in the tennis works on the Riviera, Tunis found. Certainly the casino-hotel moguls were privy to plans for the Big Match. And certainly the English tennis ball and equipment manufacturers had an important say in the events. It was well known now that three English tennis equipment companies were making their influence felt in the region, subsidizing clubs and players and seeking the exclusive adoption of their products in various tournaments. In January a fourth manufacturer had entered the competition and the bidding for the players. For several weeks charges had been thrown back and forth of large amounts of money passed under the table and of players and club owners bought and sold by the companies. One of the English tennis ball manufacturers had even recently been accused publicly of "contemptible dishonesty" in its business dealings by the Lord Chief Justice of England. How pervasive was the influence of the English companies? "If I was told that one company owned the Leviathan and the Statue of Liberty and had paid Senator Borah a hundred thousand francs for his good will," Tunis wrote, "I shouldn't be astonished."

What made matters even worse, Tunis feared, was that the upright and untainted American Girl was innocently and unknowingly being sucked into this cesspool of commercial intrigue. It was bad for Helen Wills and it was bad for tennis, the last bastion of amateur sport, Tunis believed. Tunis loved tennis. It had long been the only purely amateur sport and the only honest sport around, he insisted.

Tunis insisted that Suzanne and Papa already knew when and where the Goddess would play Helen. And she was playing a little tournament tennis and practicing daily at the Nice Tennis Club with the kind of balls that would most certainly be used when the two faced each other. Any chance of victory for Helen under these incredible circumstances was, at best, remote.

Tunis intensified his sleuthing efforts on the Riviera in an attempt to get hard facts and figures on what was happening in the process of putting Wills across the net from Lenglen. Eventually, after two days of running around and questioning insiders, he sketched in the details of what had happened in the arrangements. Originally, he found, it had been planned that they would play each other at the Nice Tennis Club on the same court where Molla Mallory had taken her shellacking. Financially this would be an enormous boon for the Lenglens' home club. But Papa Lenglen, who wanted the confrontation at the Nice Club, had been overruled at the last minute by the group of businessmen, casino and hotel owners, and tennis manufacturing interests who really ran the Riviera. They feared that Wills was not yet ready to play Lenglen and that the beating she would surely take would destroy any interest in a rematch. The Nice Club would benefit, of course, but all of the other clubs and hotels along the Riviera would lose out. There had to be a play for time so there could be more beneficiaries of the match. If, when they finally met, Helen Wills did moderately well and won a few games, then there might be a series of matches and a subsequent increase in profits. The two women were kept apart in Nice, and Suzanne Lenglen's honor was preserved by the simple tactic of adopting the new Slazenger groover. As a partial compromise, Lenglen entered the mixed doubles in Nice and thus provided at least a remote possibility that she and Wills would face each other with partners and drum up some extraordinary gate receipts.

Helen Wills was surprised at the reports that she was being exploited for private commercial gain. "I think I was not," she objected, "since I was seeking nothing but some good and interesting tennis." But Tunis pointed out that Helen was "wholly ignorant of the ins and outs of sports in this section of the Mediterranean Coast" and that she was being "engulfed innocently, but none the less completely" in a web of intrigue.

Years later, in describing her experiences on the Riviera, Helen Wills confessed, "The South of France engenders intrigue. It was not surprising that tennis fell heir to a certain portion of it." She concluded that she might have been better off "under the protective wing of the United States Lawn Tennis Association." But that was impossible. She had come to France in outright defiance of the wishes and advice of the leading officers of the association. And so, "being blissful in ignorance," she wrote, "I played through tournament after tournament, enjoying the tennis keenly. And why not? Because, after all, what went on behind the scenes did not really affect me." Why worry when everything seemed to proceed so well? "The courts were pink perfection in their rolled smoothness," Helen wrote. "The days were sunny and the tournament committees were models of good manners and pleasantness. Why really ran the tournaments, whether the clubs were real clubs or privately owned, why the balls were changed for every meeting, why some players went to one tournament and not another, where the gate went— I cared not at all, nor was I curious enough to ask. I was delighted with the courts and with the games. It was interesting to play against all these people from different countries, many of whom I had never seen before. The tournaments were well run, and everybody that I had anything to do with had good manners and was extremely pleasant."

And so the American Girl proceeded merrily along on her Riviera adventure, winning all the way. Crowds of reporters and tennis fans followed her everywhere, people on the street turned to stare when she walked past, and women sought to imitate her style of dress and her cool behavior. Americans wrote home from France that they were proud of Helen Wills and that she was fast becoming the most popular young woman in France.

Correspondents also reported that Helen was fending off scores of suitors. There were unconfirmed rumors that she had already received two marriage proposals on the Riviera, one from an English aristocrat and another from a plebeian professional tennis player. Both offers, the public was advised, had been rejected. When Helen was asked to confirm or deny the news of the proposals, she said simply that marriage was not in her present program. "I won't deny that I have had offers of marriage," she said. "And I won't confirm the rumor. But if you are a betting man please lay odds that I shall return to California single if not singles champion."

The loyal French press responded to the romantic rumors concerning Helen with rumors concerning Suzanne. It was said suddenly that she had become engaged secretly to the Duke of Westminster, who had recently divorced. Her close friends began addressing her publicly as "Duchess," but Suzanne Lenglen laughed and denied the rumors. She was always at her sparkling best when called upon to deny romance. "I am getting ahead," she told newsmen. "The last time I denied I was engaged it was reported that my fiancé was a count. This time it was a duke. But there is no more truth in this report than there was when they had me married to Count Salm."

Meanwhile, Helen Wills tried to concentrate on her matches in the Gallia tournament in Cannes. But even before she stepped on the court for her first match in the competition, the French press opened a new controversy involving the American girl, one that threatened for a time to end her amateur career.

American reporters had been zeroing in on Suzanne's alleged ties to commercial interests on the Riviera, and had intimated that for years the Maid Marvel had been a professional in spirit and in deed. The French press suddenly countered with the accusation that Helen Wills was clearly violating the player-writer rule of the USLTA during her Riviera sojourn. The governing body of American tennis had years earlier formulated a rule to prevent tennis players from enriching themselves by capitalizing journalistically on their athletic prowess. Big Bill Tilden had run into serious problems with the USLTA over this matter in 1924, and the hard feelings resulting from the dispute influenced Tilden's decision to refuse to participate in the Olympic Games of that year for the United States. That same year a special committee of the USLTA clarified the player-writer rule by stating that it was all right for a tennis player to write about tennis as long as he did not cover an event in which he was himself participating. The French newsmen now pointed out that Helen Wills had signed an agreement with the INS before coming to Europe, an agreement under which she would write a series of articles about her matches in France. One French editor wrote that "it is quite possible that before Miss Wills has an opportunity to meet Mlle. Lenglen that the United States Lawn Tennis Association will take measures against this youthful representative as it did against Tilden, also a newspaperman in his idle hours. What could not be tolerated from Big Bill cannot be admitted from Little Helen."

Before leaving for France, Helen Wills met with representatives of the USLTA in order to get sponsorship from the organization for her journey. Not only did the USLTA decide not to sponsor her campaign in France, but she was advised not to go alone to the Riviera. The USLTA wanted her to stay in the United States and travel later that spring with a special American team to play in an international tournament it sponsored. In that capacity alone could she be considered a representative of her country and receive sponsorship. Wills decided to ignore the advice of the USLTA. She sought and found corporate spnsorship for her trip. She signed an agreement with the INS to write stories from the Riviera. And she decided also to sell some of her sketches from the region in order to pay for the trip. In her display of independence she was doing exactly what Suzanne Lenglen had done in 1920 in seeking independence from the male-dominated national governing body of her sport. But the governing body had means of enforcing its wishes and means of warning those who defied its dictates.

Although Helen Wills had not as yet published any newspaper stories with the INS dealing with her Riviera adventure, the question of her amateur status was suddenly called into question. In New York, President Jones W. Mersereau of the USLTA announced that he would launch an immediate investigation of Helen Wills's activities on the Riviera. And he warned that if the investigation found that the player-writer rule had been broken, then appropriate action would be taken. Americans abroad had to abide by the USLTA rules just like those at home, he said. This was a sudden surprising and ominous reminder to Helen Wills of the long arm of the USLTA. Hadn't officials of that organization specifically advised her not to go to the Riviera in 1926? Hadn't she disregarded their advice? Now her amateur status and her entire athletic career—her future—were in jeopardy because of her little act of rebellion.

Although Wills had not yet published anything with the INS when the Gallia tournament opened, it was known that she was at work on "literary efforts" dealing with the tournament at the Metropole Club in which she had been a participant. The player-writer rule stated specifically that no reports from a tournament in which a player had participated could be reported under the player's byline until at least three days after the conclusion of the tournament. Whether she had broken that rule was yet to be seen. Mersereau pointed out that even if Helen Wills had written a general observation of the tournament and published it before the three-day waiting period she would have endangered her amateur status. But, he added, he had faith that the American girl would not knowingly have violated any rules of the USLTA and pointed out further that the affair was one between Helen and the USLTA.

When asked about the player-writer rule and her contract with the INS, Wills replied, "I am perfectly satisfied that I am living up to the spirit and the letter of the player-writer rule. The articles I have been writing do not contain a single reference to the Metropole Tournament. My stories are intended to assist young players to learn the technical points of the game. I am not reporting matches in which I am engaged in over here. I only ask you to let the American public judge for themselves when my first article is published."

Yet Wills was very deeply disturbed by the charges of violation of her amateur status. One local Riviera newspaper displayed the Mersereau statement in bold type, and the paper was handed to her just as she was on her way to a match at the Gallia Club. The news shattered her concentration, and she found herself unable to get into the match against an unranked English player, Mrs. R. E. Haylock. As a result, Helen Wills came close to losing a set, falling behind to 4–5 and love–thirty in the tenth game. She managed, through the use of defensive lobs, to save the set and the match, eventually pulling it out at 9–7, 6–2. In the same afternoon, when she appeared for the doubles competition with her partner George Hillyard, word had spread through the stands of the psychological difficulty under which Helen was playing. Consequently, the sympathetic crowd gave the American girl a standing ovation.

While the USLTA investigated Wills's writing for the INS—and eventually exonerated her—there was a quiet controversy involving the drawings she was selling to finance her journey. There was no USLTA rule governing drawings by tennis players of other players, no so-called player-artist rule, so Helen seemed safe in this endeavor. Yet several journalists questioned the ethics of the way in which she smoothly marketed her art work.

Wills's special interest in art had been explored by American journalists long before the American girl traveled to France. She had studied art at the University of California and was in France, ostensibly, to further her art studies. The *New York World* in its coverage of the Riviera adventure managed something of a ballyhoo coup when it succeeded in buying a series of Helen's sketches and then printed them with a narrative describing Helen's devotion to art, "a devotion that has rivaled her devotion to the game on which her fame is based." Her drawing of other well-known tennis players were undistinguished in every way. What gave them commercial value was the signature scratched in one corner—Helen Wills. But she chose to believe that the value of her art work lay in its artistic merit and almost completely overlooked the fact that she was actually capitalizing on her reputation in sport to sell art. So she continued doing her drawings to make money, more money, in fact, than most established working illustrators of the time made. "The quality of these sketches by Miss Wills will surprise most people," the *World* commentary suggested somewhat ironically.

Paul Gallico remembered how his own newspaper, the *New York Daily News,* was taken in at the time by the shouting and the excitement surrounding Helen Wills's quest and how it "eventually did something that looked rather silly in retrospect." Several years after the great Riviera ballyhoo, while writing his memoirs, Gallico found over his desk a "curious memento" of the winter of 1926—"an amateurish pencil drawing of Suzanne Lenglen sketched and signed by Helen Wills." Gallico's paper had paid $500 for it—a significant sum in those days even for a pencil drawing by a well-known artist. Gallico's editors apparently believed that in making the purchase they were buying an exclusive drawing by Helen Wills of her famous opponent to be. Technically, it was, Gallico wrote, but "ethically it was a sell." It was well known that she was an art student and that one of her drawings would have enormous value and fit well into the ballyhoo of the Riviera madness without disturbing her amateur status under the "conveniently amateur interpretations" of the USLTA. The *Daily News* sent a correspondent to France specifically to make the arrangements. Helen Wills accepted a commission for the drawing—cash in advance amounting to the full purchase price. But because she was so quiet about her feelings and her business dealings, she failed to mention that the *New York World* had also paid for drawings, and before the *Daily News*. The *World* had, in fact, purchased and run an entire page of drawings soon after the *Daily News* paid its advance. So, by the time the *Daily News* received its drawing, "it wasn't worth the postage it took to carry it overseas because the *World*'s page had already appeared. It lost all value as news, and it certainly had very little as art," Gallico found. And he concluded that "the girl caught us very neatly because theoretically we weren't buying it as news, but strictly as a drawing. If we chose to be suckers and pay five hundred dollars for something worth fifty cents, that was our look-out business."

Such were the wonderful commercial possibilities that the world of sport opened to the American girl during her campaign in France. Not only was the sporting world at her feet, but now, too, the worlds of journalism and of art openly courted her. Success seemed not a terribly difficult thing, suddenly. She had earlier concluded that if one tried hard enough in any endeavor, then failure was, in the long run, impossible. The power of the will, she concluded, was limitless. And so it seemed to be on the Riviera in the winter of 1926. Helen Wills was learning something else that Suzanne Lenglen had learned long ago—fame could provide things that dollars and francs could never purchase: doors suddenly swung open; the world was only too happy to accommodate one so alluring, so ingenuous, so talented, and so beautiful.

After her shaky beginnings in the Gallia tournament, Wills quickly recovered her old form and proceeded smoothly. On her way to the singles titles she again beat Helene Contostavlos, but this time the score was 6–2, 6–3. Wills and her partner George Hillyard lost in the mixed doubles, but the press was in general agreement that it was Hillyard's fault; the veteran English player had given a miserable account of himself in the couple's defeat.

With the completion of two Riviera tournaments Wills appeared to be progressively improving and growing stronger and more confident every day. A correspondent for the *New York Times* calculated that the American girl had played 248 games in two tournaments, winning 187 and losing 61 and fourteen of the fifteen matches she had played in, "A performance," the correspondent concluded, "seldom if ever equalled." She had won nine sets at love and six sets by a score of 6–1, and had been extended in only two sets. Yet Wills knew that the competition was not as stiff as she would have liked, and that the matches were hardly tests and she needed to push herself constantly in order to prepare for the final assault on the Goddess.

Just prior to the opening of the Nice Club tournament, American newsmen and photographers were given a totally unexpected revelation. One morning when several photographers begged Helen to pose for them, she threw up her arms and asked them to wait: "Don't take my photograph today, gentlemen. Wait until Wednesday. I am getting some new French dresses made and they will be delivered on Wednesday.

I want my California friends to see how good I look in the French models." The reporters were then told she would meet with them on the following morning at the marble and onyx shop of Jean Patou.

From the moment Jean Patou had seen photographs of Helen Wills in Paris and had read of her poise and her stature, he had been interested in designing clothes for the American girl. He had long been unhappy with the flat-chested, slim, and hipless look of the flapper, and Helen Wills was a wonderful physical contrast to the prevailing popular figure. She was tall and muscular, athletic, and with a full figure. She was in the classic mold. Patou saw that she might provide the vehicle for altering fashion. Her figure was heavier and more rounded than the young Latin women for whom he had previously designed. "The rounded figure is not only a more beautiful one," Patou now announced, "but it is a healthier one." And so he invited her for several fittings of some of the new fashions he had created with her in mind. Eventually, Wills received five dresses and a coat from Patou, clothing valued at about 35,000 francs.

When Helen Wills emerged from Patou's shop on the following morning to face the crowd of photographers she was attired in her new clothes. Reporters were very surprised at the transformation. They had become quite used to the shy, sober, and expressionless athlete in the plain costume on and off the court. Now here she was suddenly beaming and laughing and smiling broadly for the cameras. She seemed to have no tennis worries at all. Al Laney saw that she was like an eager young schoolgirl trying on a new dress. "And for the first time the reporters saw that Helen really was beautiful," Laney wrote of the Riviera press corps. "I don't think any of us had realized it before. We didn't see much of the schoolgirl after that, but from time to time we saw some of the new creations which were especially designed to accentuate Wills' fine features."

There was disagreemnt over just how much Helen had paid for the Patou creations. Reporters wanted to know if she, too, was to be an outside mannequin for the great designer. Had Patou given her the clothes without charge? Helen denied accepting the clothes in return for advertising Patou. And Patou himself responded to questions about the price Helen paid by replying curtly, "You know I never gave anything away in my life!"

In the Nice Club tournament a good deal of speculation centered on the chances of Wills and her doubles partner Charles Aeschliman reaching the finals. Should they make it that far they would no doubt run up against Suzanne and Baron de Morpurgo, "the sheik of Trieste." At first Wills and her partner were given little chance of making it to the finals, but they won their early matches and seemed to work well together, and daily the probability increased of a Wills-Lenglen match in the mixed doubles.

In the women's doubles Helen Wills played with Eileen Bennett of England. When the Wills-Bennett team appeared on the courts for their first match, the entire Lenglen entourage turned out in force to study the play of the American girl close up. Papa Lenglen sat right at courtside, haggard and wasted after major surgery and a lengthy illness, wrapped in several blankets. Suzanne sat at his feet. Papa carefully watched the movements and the strokes of the American girl, evaluating her play, planning Suzanne's attack. It was clear that the presence of the Lenglens and their crowd of sycophants disturbed Wills and caused her to misjudge many of her shots. She and Bennett lost the first set and then recovered enough to win two sets and the match. Wills and Aeschliman also dropped a set before winning their first match, and her performance before the Lenglen troupe brought a cloud of gloom to her friends on that day. Suzanne Lenglen was playing "in the best form she has displayed in years," according to Riviera habitués. What did Papa Lenglen think about Helen's chances against Suzanne? Not much. In fact, after the match he told reporters that he thought a match between Suzanne and Helen was out of the question for the immediate future.

But Papa's announcement demonstrated that he was no longer privy to negotiations taking place for arranging the Big Match. Fading physically and losing touch with the real powers on the Riviera, he was also losing his control over Suzanne's career. Even as Papa predicted no Lenglen-Wills match in the immediate future, final arrangements were being made in Cannes for the staging of that match at the Carlton Club tournament, which was scheduled to begin the following week. Negotiations for the match involved the Carlton Club owners—an Irish threesome of Tom Burke, the first professional player in France, and his two sons, Albert and Edmund—along with two representatives of the Dunlop Company, F. M. B. Fisher and Jacques Brugnon. Fisher was a New Zealand politician and businessman as well as an agent for Dunlop. He was also a former Davis Cub tennis player. Brugnon was one of France's outstanding Four Musketeers of tennis. Fisher and Brugnon promised that the Lenglen-Wills match would be staged in Cannes if Dunlop balls were used in the tournament. Adoption of the Dunlop product would also involve a generous financial subsidy to be paid directly to the Burkes. The gate receipts from the Lenglen-Wills match would, of course, be enormous. And if the Burkes went along with Dunlop and the staging of the match was a success, then a Lenglen-Wills rematch might be arranged for the Carlton Club and profits could be doubled. When club members were drawn into discussions over the use of the Dunlop product, several of them resigned in disgust. The Burkes, nonetheless, agreed. The match was on.

The next day it was announced in Cannes that Helen Wills and Suzanne Lenglen had sent their entries in singles to the Carlton Club. Their names would be placed in opposite sides of the draw so they would meet in the final. Along with the announcement came the further notice that Lady Wavertree, an intimate associate of Lenglen and Fisher, and Sidney Beers, who had just won $200,000 on the baccarat tables in Cannes, had donated a large gold cup for the winner of the women's singles competition in the Carlton tournament, a cup described as the most magnificent ever awarded a winner of any Riviera sporting event.

With the announcement of the Carlton Club entries, Suzanne Lenglen changed: her polite conduct was dropped and she became openly hostile to the American girl. She appeared at courtside on the next day to watch another Wills-Bennett doubles match. Wills and her partner again were forced to fight to a three-set victory. But after the two dropped the second set of the match to a pair of unranked players, Lenglen stood and announced loudly enough for spectators and players alike to hear, "Isn't this comical?" and left the match for tea. Later, when she was told that Wills and Bennett had won, she laughed, "A real champion always beats second-rate opponents quickly."

During the doubles play with Lenglen on the sidelines, Helen Wills tried hard to keep her poker face, but it was obvious that again the presence of Suzanne bothered her badly. Reporters, of course, loved the cool animosity Lenglen displayed and promised that, given her growing dislike of the American girl, the match in Cannes would surely be a "knock-down drag-out battle for blood with no holds barred." No other prediction could have sold tickets better.

While Wills and her partners struggled through the doubles competitions in Nice, Lenglen breezed her way through the singles. She beat Mrs. Haylock—the player who had extended Helen in Cannes—in love sets. Papa watched the match from courtside while his champion danced her way to victory. When the match was over, the Duke of Connaught approached Papa. "Your daughter played superbly," he observed. "Yes, little one is in great form just now and will be hard to beat," Papa responded weakly.

"Little one!" Suzanne quickly interjected. "Little one! Papa, you forget that I shall be twenty-seven next May!" She seemed slightly agitated when she spoke. Papa was still looking at her as his little one, the dancing pixie with the big racket. But the years had passed. Younger, stronger tennis players were appearing. Suzanne was no longer a "little one," and she could not be expected to play as she did forever.

In the next days, despite her reminder to Papa of the passage of time, Suzanne played as though she were still the little one and thrilled the hometown crowd at the Nice Club by winning sixty straight games in singles. Not one of her games even went to deuce. She was still the sorceress.

Wills, meanwhile, prepared meticulously for her meeting with Lenglen. She practiced each morning on the courts of the Carlton Club against the resident professional, Roman Najouck, before starting out for her doubles matches in Nice. Several reporters entered the grounds early one morning and found her earnestly practicing her volleying and overhead smashes with Najouck. Wills had the professional repeatedly hit the ball high over the net to approximate Lenglen's famous "margin of safety." She came forward quickly, time after time, to volley the high drives for winners. Then she had Najouck come to the net, while she practiced top-spin lobs. She largely ignored her familiar hard-hit ground strokes. Some of the observers expressed concern at her practice routine, declaring that Lenglen could easily neutralize reliance on volleys or lobs. Only the steady pounding ground strokes already used so successfully had any chance of success against the Maid Marvel. Wills should hit with all of her strength and wear down the French champion. Yet, here she was, morning after morning, working on tactics that could not possibly succeed. Unless, of course, she knew something the reporters had missed in their observations of Lenglen.

Wills surprised just about everyone in Nice by winning her way to the finals of the mixed doubles with Aeschliman. Their opponents for the championship match, as expected, were Suzanne Lenglen and Morpurgo. And although betting odds ran heavily in their favor the prospect of a one-sided contest kept few people away from the match. A standing-room-only crowd at the Nice Tennis Club witnessed the first match in which the Goddess and the American Girl faced each other across the net. The crowd, the largest that had ever attended a Riviera tennis match, was, despite the presence of many pedigreed and titled aristocrats, unabashedly and rousingly partisan. And seated in the midst of the cacophony was the pathetic figure of Papa Lenglen, nearly buried beneath heavy blankets.

In the finals in Nice, Lenglen was in her glory, basking in the friendly applause and cheers of thousands of people who had watched her grow up and fulfill her father's dreams. She pranced out onto the court on her toes—still an incredible thing to American correspondents—like a high-strung, high-stepping show horse, twirling this way and that and mugging for the cameras, adjusting her bandeau and placing her hand on her hip for a sudden dramatic pose and then pirouetting and skipping from one corner of the court to the other while newsmen and photographers scurried about obsequiously at her feet, begging her to turn this way or that.

Wills, on the other hand, walked onto the court almost unnoticed. It was her second appearance in a match this day—she and Eileen Bennett had won the women's doubles title earlier. When newsmen finally noticed the American girl they steered her quickly onto the court and pushed her up next to Suzanne Lenglen for a picture session. The American and French champions stood beside each other without exchanging a word while cameras clicked away. Everyone noticed the sharp contrast between the two women now. Helen was dressed in her familiar prim schoolgirl middy blouse, starched and pleated white skirt, and her eye-shade. She walked flat-footed. Suzanne, always on her toes, was attired in her playing silks and wore a matching salmon pink sweater and ban-deau. She was painted with heavy powder and makeup. Suzanne was laughing and debonair, while Helen remained grim and determined and all business. Suzanne seemed every inch the great artiste, bowing and smiling and waving to her adoring subjects. But a few spectators noticed behind the smiles and the bravura gestures, there was a hint, a slight shadow, of anxiety and self-consciousness. Suzanne kept darting momentary glances at the serene American girl, looking for something, trying to make eye contact, failing, and then becoming even louder and more exaggerated in her gesturing. Helen seemed to be completely un-interested in Lenglen's behavior at the moment. Helen was already deep in her zone of concentration, shutting out everything but the coming contest.

Lenglen and her partner won the toss and elected to serve the first game. Morpurgo served the game to deuce and then made two good placements for a win. Wills served the second game to deuce and then lost it. In that second game, Aeschliman, who stood six feet four inches and was nicknamed "The Swiss Giant," played aggressively at the net, but alone was no match for the expertise of the Morpurgo-Lenglen team.

Lenglen served the third game. Wills and Aeschliman surged back with real determination in the game, came to the net quickly after each service return, volleying expertly and taking four consecutive points and leaving Lenglen with the loss of her own service at love.

Just when the Wills-Aeschilman team was showing signs of coming alive, a dramatic change in play by Helen Wills in the fourth game proved to be a turning point in both the set and the match. Instead of continuing to blast hard ground strokes and to volley whenever possible, as she had been doing in the third game, she began lobbing and at-tempting to force Lenglen and Morpurgo back to the baseline. But most of her lobs fell short at mid-court and were fired back at the feet of either Wills or her partner. Morpurgo's racket actually exploded into pieces when he hit an overhead with all his strength. Lenglen also proved to be deadly accurate with her overhead shots and was not bothered even in the least by Wills's lobs. Suddenly, what had been an interesting contest began to take on the trappings of a practice session for Lenglen and Morpurgo. At first the spectators believed Wills was merely experimenting with her lobs and that she would abandon them when they proved ineffec-tive. But she doggedly kept lobbing, so Aeschliman was stuck with the unenviable task of imitating a moving target for the Maid Marvel and her partner. Helen Wills and her partner lost the first set, 1–6.

The second set held one surprise for reporters and spectators alike— Helen Wills's service. In the first set she merely put the ball in play on her service, using little power. But when she served at 1–1 in the second set, she used more pace and alternated a fast flat service with a sharp slice. In her first service to Lenglen, Wills arched back gracefully and then launched a cannonball that kicked up chalk, took a crazy high bounce, and nearly decapitated the Goddess. Suzanne smiled and spoke a few words to her partner and tried to appear unfazed by the shot. But Helen served to her again, and again she scored an ace off a cannonball. Tremendous applause and cheers came down and Wills, for the first time on the courts of the Riviera, lost the poker face. Walking back to the baseline she glanced up at the crowd screaming its appreciation, and a deep blush spread over her pale face. Then she showed the flicker of a smile. In the next two games Suzanne Lenglen was guilty of more errors than she made in the rest of the entire match.

Despite Lenglen's errors and Wills's service aces, the Maid Marvel and her partner won five straight games by continuing to kill Wills's persistent and ineffective lobs. Following the final point, Suzanne skipped smilingly to the net and offered her hand to Helen. The American girl murmured a faint "thank you" and left the court, refusing to accommodate reporters who insisted that she pose again with Lenglen. Of course, the bubbling victorious Frenchwoman was only too happy to pose alone.

Because most American correspondents on the Riviera accepted without question the fact that this mixed doubles match was a momentous event, and because they had been building up the confrontation of the Goddess and the American girl for weeks, many of them now struggled to find bombastic phrases to wire back to their readers in America in order to describe with the proper color what they had just seen. In newspapers the match became a war between "the New World and the Old"; "youth against age" ("Papa, you forget that I shall be twenty-seven next May!") despite the fact that but six years separated the celebrated contestants. Don Skene wrote that Lenglen charged around on her tip toes "like a high-strung racer, while Miss Wills walked flat-footed—like an Indian or a detective." And while Helen wore a poker face, Skene wrote, Suzanne wore "a fixed frozen smile like a toothpaste advertisement." Helen was "the Coolidge of tennis"; she was "stolid, silent, white-faced as a ghost"; and, of course, "she fought with lion-hearted courage." Yet she was no match for the "slashing, flashing Suzanne."

Lenglen was anxious to talk with reporters after the match. She told them that "the first two games of the first set were the hardest I have ever seen played in my entire career. I am happy I scored such an overwhelming victory over Miss Wills, who is a splendid player, a great champion, and a fine sportswoman. The score really does not indicate how close and how hard fought every point was," she exaggerated.

Later in the afternoon in an interview granted to Don Skene, Wills told Skene that she found Lenglen "a marvelous player—just as great as I have been informed from reading and hearing about her. My partner and I played our best and fought for every stroke, but we could not win."

And years later, after reading the thrilling and often hyperbolic press accounts of her mixed doubles match in Nice, Helen Wills observed: "I thought it a very peaceful match, in which Lenglen made the best of her opportunities through placing the ball exactly and precisely and her partner the best of his, with his fast service and his powerful overhead. We did not have as good team work as they, for they had played in many more tournaments together, nor did I know the doubles game as Lenglen did." She never mentioned her reliance on lobbing in the match.

With the completion of the tournament in Nice the crowds moved to Cannes and the Carlton Club for what was looking more and more like the tennis match of the century. Reporters and photographers were everywhere in the city and ballyhoo reigned supreme. Everywhere the talk was of the match. In the United States stories of Helen Wills's progress had moved from the sporting page to the front page. Helen believed that "no tennis game deserved the attention this one was receiving. The main reason was that in the United States there was, at the moment, no other sports in progress. Spring athletics had not yet gotten under way and the football season was over. There was a February lull in the sports pages and details of this encounter were welcome." Then she added that "of course, there was the indisputable fact that Mlle. Lenglen was the great genius of the tennis court and a spectacular figure in the world of sport." And there was also the indisputable fact that Helen Wills had been transformed by the American press from a mere national tennis champion into an ideal and the perfect symbol of young America. Everything she did now was newsworthy and described in glowing, near-mythic terms.

The Carlton Club tournament opened on February 8, a Monday, and Wills made her premier appearance in the singles that afternoon before another standing-room-only crowd. Once again she displayed tremendous power and appeared to exude unwavering self-confidence in dispatching an English opponent, Ethel Fischer, in two love sets. The entire match lasted only fifteen minutes. Many of those watching the match were struck by her strength and by the businesslike manner in which she went about crushing her helpless foe.

Suzanne Lenglen arrived in Cannes for the opening of the tournament but did not attend Wills's first match. Instead, she pranced and preened her way around the club grounds and out along the Croisette, attired in a stunning new sports ensemble created for her by Patou. In the afternoon she eliminated her first victim in the singles competition.

Following the initial one-sided victories by the two star attractions in the Carlton Club tournament, it rained in Cannes, providing a welcome rest for the players. But for the newsmen, and particularly for those making news films, inactivity on the court ushered in a frantic period of debate and bargaining off the court. Even when the players relaxed, the ballyhoo went on.

In all previous Riviera tournaments the gates were thrown open to all newsmen and filmmakers who paid a standard admission price. But now came an announcement that the old system was no longer in operation. It was time for ballyhoo to benefit someone besides the newspapers and the players. The proprietors of the Carlton Club, the Burkes, sent out word that exclusive film rights were to be awarded to a concessionaire through a secret bidding system. Shortly after this first announcement it was rumored that a high bidder had stepped forward, and film rights for the tournament had been sold for the extraordinary sum of $100,000. When Thomas Burke was asked about the sale of the film rights, he admitted that for the semi-final and final matches in the tournament no newsreel cameramen would be admitted to the club free of charge. Each would have to bargain with the film concessionaire. "This is a plain business proposition," Burke stated.

Newsmen discovered that an American, William Blumenthal, also known as Willie Methal, had been granted exclusive film rights for the last two rounds of the tournament. Blumenthal was not a newsman; he was a well-known gambler. Newsmen were then informed that Blumenthal would sell part of his franchise to any news service agreeing to pay $25,000 per camera allowed on the club grounds. Several tennis officials on the Riviera were openly upset at this open intrusion of business into sport. George Simond, a well-known referee of Riviera matches, stated that it was hardly less than a crime to allow profit-takers to become involved in the match and "to place the almighty dollar over the net as a guiding power for one of the few remaining amateur sports." Simond compared the practice with ticket-scalping, another enormously profitable enterprise now booming around the Carlton Club.

The sale of exclusive film rights was, however, hardly unprecedented in France. American newsmen now remembered the 1924 Winter Olympic Games in France when a French news agency had purchased exclusive film rights for the games and the French military police had used fixed bayonets to chase away free-enterprising American newsmen in order to protect the lucrative French monopoly.

But this match was already much bigger than the Olympic Games. And the American news services were not about to accept the mixing of commercialism with news-gathering. The various news services now announced their intention to refuse to pay for filming the match. They said they would set up their cameras on balconies in nearby hotels and on the roofs of buildings surrounding the Carlton Club. Emil Barrier, a well-known photographer and president of the Anglo-American News

Photographers Association in Paris and a man who knew very well where ultimate power was exercised on the Riviera, declared that he had written the strongest protest possible to Eugene Cornuch, the alleged boss of bosses of the casinos of Cannes and Deauville, and had protested against the proposed news monopoly. Barrier predicted optimistically that justice would be served and that no money would be paid speculators for the right to film a Wills-Lenglen contest.

Four American newsreel companies with representatives on the Riviera—Kinograms, Fox, International, and Pathé—drew up a statement of protest and dispatched it to the USLTA in New York. Their statement read:

The Undersigned, exhibiting news events in every motion picture theater in America, wish through the United States Lawn Tennis Association to protest vigorously at the exclusion of their representation from the Lenglen-Wills match. Such discrimination is a violation of the rights of news organizations to cover events of universal interest. Moreover, showing through our products is the only possible method for millions of Americans to see pictures, as films taken by private concessionaires, positively, will not be purchased by any of the undersigned. We respectfully urge the transmission of our protest to the French Association.

The newsreel companies represented in the protest claimed a weekly viewing audience of more than 100,000 people in the United States. These people would be deprived of seeing the American Girl in action if the charge of $25,000 per camera was held to.

The threat by the movie men to film from surrounding buildings was successfully countered when the Carlton Hotel, which had no connection with the club, but which towered over the club grounds, issued an ultimatum stating that no movie cameramen would be allowed to rent rooms in the hotel or to occupy the room of any guest during the match. The owners of villas and hotels surrounding the Carlton Club indicated to American newsmen that they dare not let them on the premises to take pictures in defiance of the Carlton Club, "one of the strongest members of the Riviera tennis trust."

Members of the news services also turned now to the individual whose fame they had nurtured—their American Girl, Helen Wills. They came, almost literally, on bended knee to Helen to ask her to intercede in the dispute. It was an awkward moment both for Wills and for the newsmen. She was asked to make a public objection to the sale of the exclusive film rights. Helen Wills's extreme diffidence was mistaken by many of the newsmen who had never before spoken with her as a sort of unexpected aloofness. The Riviera stringer for *Time* watched her closely while she spoke with the newsreel representatives, and recorded her imaginary thoughts: "Moving picture men! They are just the same here as they are in California. They all ask you very politely whether you mind their cigarettes—and they drop the ashes on the carpet. One of them (a French Jew) hadn't been in the room five minutes before he called me 'Helen.' I wonder why I don't dislike them more."

Despite the guesses of the *Time* writer it was never revealed exactly what the newsmen told Helen Wills or what she thought about their request. Several statements and thoughts were attributed to her following the meeting. Wills later remembered that "I felt that all newsreel companies had equal rights to take pictures at an amateur sporting meeting, since such events were, in a way, public property." But she gave no official statement for public release. This did not deter the newsmen. One of them reported that she said, "I am terribly sorry that such a thing has happened. It seems to be a shame that a game of amateur tennis between myself and Mlle. Lenglen should be distorted into a money-making scheme to enrich the commercial speculators who are hoping to make huge sums of money from our tennis match, played in the finest amateur spirit. I promise the American photographers my full support to smash this unfair monopoly. I am thinking of scratching my name from the tournament which has been so commercialized and violates the amateur code." The threat, reprinted in all of the local Riviera papers, demonstrated that the American Girl was, at least in the rich imagination of the reporter who wrote the story, also the champion of free enterprise, the free press, and amateurism. She was a female trustbuster walking softly and carrying a big racket.

In the *New York Times,* Allison Danzig questioned the lack of a clear tennis policy in the tournaments in the south of France. The French Tennis Association should immediately take charge of the proceedings, he said. The bidding and the betting and the general circus atmosphere surrounding the Carlton Club tournament would simply not be tolerated by the USLTA or by the All-England Club, he suggested. Lenglen's visit to America in 1921 had, of course, its unfortunate aspects, but they were all in the aftermath of her default and were not part of a pre-match ballyhoo, he said.

The Regional Riviera Tennis Committee did attempt to step in and exercise some control, particularly in the sale of the newsreel concessions. But legally, officers of the committee reported, the Burkes were entirely within their rights to dispose of the exclusive motion picture rights and the tennis governing bodies in France could take no action to stop them.

The arrival of Blumenthal on the Riviera brought additional confusion. The gambler had initially put up only a small retainer for his control to the film rights of the Wills-Lenglen match. He informed the Burkes now that he did not have the $100,000 in American currency to pay them in advance for his concession. He had expected, he said, to pay the Burkes out of the receipts received from the payment of the camera fees by each of the major newsreel services. But once they had announced their boycott, Blumenthal was stuck without funds. As a result, there was another frantic effort by the Burkes to sell filming privi-

leges to the press. The man selected to carry on the negotiations was
F. M. B. Fisher.

John Tunis was fascinated by Fisher, whom he described as "the
Tex Rickard of Riviera tennis." Fisher was "a heavy-set man with a
large frame and a big paw which he extends cheerily when he meets
you," Tunis wrote. He was "a facile and mellifluous conversationalist,
and at the present moment is in the employ of an English tennis ball
company." Fisher had known weeks earlier where the Wills-Lenglen
match would take place, Tunis believed, since his employer, the Dunlop
Company, had placed advertisements with magazines indicating that the
contest would take places in Cannes at the Carlton Club.

Fisher called a meeting of all newsmen to take place in the Carlton
Hotel. Suzanne Lenglen was then given a room adjoining the one where
negotiations took place, no doubt because of her own financial interest
in the match. At the meeting, Fisher announced that Blumenthal had
forfeited his retainer of $1200 and had given up his exclusive rights.
And now, "in the interest of clean amateur sports," Fisher requested that
all of the newsmen be "good sports" and pay the Burkes $125 each to
enter the club grounds during each day of the tournament. When loud
protests met his suggestion, Fisher lost his temper and shouted right
back, "You can pay this or stay out!" The newsmen continued to hoot
at Fisher, and several of them shouted that they would not pay a single cent of tribute to Fisher or the Burkes or to anyone else. Freedom
of the press was at stake here, they insisted. And besides, as one reporter
pointed out, charging $125 per newsman was illegal in France because
the price was stated in American rather than in French currency denom-
inations. Fisher, somewhat embarrassed, cooled down and changed his
offer. Now he suggested that each newsman purchase 25 tickets for the
final match for 300 francs (about $12) each. This offer was also met by
jeers. Fisher stormed out of the room and into the midst of another
crowd of newsmen in the hall. They wanted to know if a deal had been
made yet. Fisher paused long enough only to respond, "Tennis is a business and those Burke boys must get their money!"

In the adjoining room Lenglen listened impatiently to the shouting
match between Fisher and the newsmen. When a reporter from the
Associated Press entered her room, she asked excitedly, "Have they come
to an arrangement? Do they all work?" When told of the deadlock and
the failure to reach an agreement, Lenglen exploded and denounced
the Burkes, Fisher, and the newsmen. "Well, I am going back to Nice
if they don't fix this matter before tomorrow. I will scratch," she warned.
"I don't care whether they say I am afraid of Miss Wills or not."

For her own part, Wills had serious misgivings about the commercial
takeover of tennis in Cannes. She cabled Julian Myrick, chairman of the
Committee on Foreign Affairs of the USLTA in New York, and asked
for advice concerning her amateur status in the midst of all the bidding

and gambling. Cleared of any conflict with the player-writer rule, she was now anxious to avoid an embarrassing investigation of the sale of the film rights to her matches. Myrick cabled right back, "Answering your cable, as you are receiving no financial consideration for moving picture rights, there can be no criticism. By all means play and do not worry."

Relieved by the reassurance by Myrick that her amateur status was secure, Wills spoke with several American newsmen and eagerly answered all of their questions concerning her plans. When asked how she thought her match with Lenglen would end, she replied, "I don't think I will win. But I am going to make a good fight. Win or lose, I am going to stay here some time longer." In fact, she revealed, she had already entered the singles competition in the next two Riviera tournaments in Beaulieu and Monte Carlo. Consequently, there would be a chance for a second and a third contest with Lenglen. Wills also said that she would stay on the Riviera at least until the end of April. Then she hoped to put in a month in the Latin Quarter of Paris studying art before moving on to play in the French and English championships.

Wills also indicated that she was aware of the nationalistic surge of public opinion in the United States supporting her efforts to meet and beat Lenglen. She assured reporters that she would try her hardest "to give the United States a victory."

With thousands of newsmen now swarming in the streets in Cannes, no individual was safe from being approached concerning his or her opinion of the big match. Brand Whitlock, the former American diplomat, was vacationing in Cannes at the time. Reporters questioned him about the length of the skirt Helen Wills wore for her matches. Somewhat perplexed by the nature of the question, Whitlock volunteered that he believed Helen's skirt was "decently long." And what about Suzanne Lenglen's skirt? The former ambassador replied that he thought it acceptable that her skirt "kissed her knees from above."

Following three days of rain, tennis resumed in the Carlton Club tournament. Both leading ladies received roaring ovations each time they appeared on the court. They remained, nonetheless, a study in contrasts in their public behavior. Helen Wills remained quiet and shy and slipped away quickly after each match. Suzanne Lenglen stayed at the club after each of her matches and seemed to welcome being mobbed by society folk, by men kissing her hand, and by bejewed dewlapped dowagers kissing her on both cheeks and clucking their approval.

Both women easily won their way through three rounds of singles and doubles. Both maintained perfect records in the singles not losing a single game until the quarter-finals. There Wills dropped two games before beating Eileen Bennett, 6–2, 6–0. In her own quarter-final match Lenglen was awesome, winning not only in love sets, but allowing her helpless opponent only three points in twelve games. Wills sat quietly watching Lenglen's quater-final massacre, her eyes riveted on every movement of the Goddess. She nodded to friends and smiled occasionally, but said nothing at all to reporters concerning her impressions of the match. Lenglen was bubbling over her incredible victory and told the newsmen, "I want to reach the finals without the loss of a game. If I am going to lose a game in this tournament they will have to get it out of me at the point of a gun."

"Does that mean you intend to beat Wills in straight love sets?" she was asked.

"I am talking about the tournament and not the finals," was her bitter reply. "I wish you would not keep pestering me with questions about Miss Wills."

During the quarter-final matches the Carlton Club was crowded with photographers and newsreel crews who stood only inches outside the playing area taking pictures. Their presence in such great numbers indicated at last that the struggle over film rights had ended and the Burkes had been beaten. The Burkes had, in a desperate last ditch effort to squeeze money out of the media, sought a flat fee of $800 from each of the news services. That proposal, like all of the previous ones, was flatly refused. Consequently, the Burkes simply caved in and gave up all hope of using the press as a major vehicle for cashing in on the public excitement over the Wills-Lenglen contest. The Burkes would have to look to gate receipts and subsidies alone for the profits from the match.

In her semifinal match, Wills played against Didi Vlasto, France's second-ranked player. Thanks to Vlasto's notoriously undependable backhand, Wills expected to win an easy victory. But this time Vlasto proved to be a game competitor and forced Wills to struggle for each point. No one expected the American girl to lose, naturally. And Vlasto admitted the pressure was on her to lose, for a victory would be nothing less than a catastrophic disaster at this stage of the tournament. "I would be cursed all around the earth," Vlasto laughed, "and I never would be forgiven for cheating thousands of fans out of a sporting event they have come thousands of miles to see."

In the first two games of the Wills-Vlasto match, each player held service once. Then Wills ran off five straight games and won the first set. Her deep hard drives, crossing the net exactly at mid-court and just high enough to clear the tape, kept Vlasto behind the baseline and on the defensive. The capacity crowd was obviously thrilled by the performance of the American girl and gave enthusiastic standing ovations several times after Wills blasted booming winners past the French defender. At one point in the match feelings ran so high that a small section of the crowd near the edge of the court shouted insults and booed when a linesman gave a decision against the American. The match was actually stopped for several minutes while the perplexed umpire stood and pleaded for order and quiet. Reporters covering the match referred to the bleachers as "ringside seats."

In the second set Vlasto played with newfound inspiration. She ran up a 4–1 lead against Wills. But the American girl remained calm and steady, eventually finding her length and running off another series of five straight games for the set and the match.

In that second set something did take place that was to have more than a little impact on Wills's play in the final against Lenglen. Running hard across the court to cut off one of Vlasto's drives, Wills lost her footing on the sandy clay and fell hard to her knee, dropping her racket. She insisted, after rising and brushing herself off, that she had suffered only a scratch. Yet there was clearly a deep cut in her right knee, and blood from the cut started to stain her white stocking. Following her victory over Vlasto, Wills tried to hurry through the shouting reporters on her way to get medical attention. To the persistent questions of reporters who blocked her path, she finally replied impatiently, "I have no statement to make before my match with Mlle. Lenglen and I think it unfair to ask me to make one." Then she added, "I'm naturally going to play the hardest game I possibly can, but I do not want to say anything before we meet on the courts. After the match I will make a statement."

Helen Wills then hurried from the Carlton Club with her mother to seek treatment. But it was the noon hour and most doctors' offices and drug stores were closed. Helen and her mother and a small group of concerned friends spent nearly two hours in search of medical attention. Eventually they found an open drugstore, and the proprietor offered help. He applied a disinfectant and dressed the open wound. Helen attempted to keep her injury and the time spent on medical attention from both tournament officials and the press. She apparently never entertained any thoughts of seeking either a postponement or a default in the final. In none of her memoirs did she mention the injury. She would use no excuse to explain her play on the next day.

Lenglen suffered in her semifinal match also, but her injury was a psychological rather than a physical one. The Maid Marvel became extremely irate when three successive line calls went against her. She appeared almost completely undone as she shook her finger at the offending linesman and rattled off a lengthy denunciation. Then she had foot fault troubles on her service. The calling of the foot faults seemed to jog her concentration and timing and left her visibly on edge. Despite these difficulties, however, she succeeded in defeating Helene Contostavlos without much difficulty, 6–0, 6–2. Contostavlos, it was noted, took her two games, not at the point of a gun, but by outplaying Suzanne at the start of the second set.

After the final point of the Lenglen-Contostavlos semifinal match spectators were brusquely escorted from the Carlton Club grounds. Even as they exited, a small army of carpenters hurried into the club and began work on the construction of new bleacher seats, seats that would greatly increase the admission revenues for the Burkes. They were accompanied by a local building inspector who made the requisite perfunctory remarks of approval as they worked. Anyone could see, however, that the carpenters' work was more rapid than sturdy.

While work on the bleachers progressed, outside the Carlton Club was a scene reminiscent of World Series games back in the United States. Scores of people who wanted unreserved (and unbuilt, as yet) bleacher seats for the final match were already standing in line outside the gate of the club. Others had hired stand-ins to hold a place in line for them through the afternoon and night. Tickets for the bleacher seats were not scheduled to go on sale until the next morning at nine.

Ballyhoo was completely triumphant by the afternoon of February 15. The match between the Goddess and the American Girl, scheduled to take place on the following morning, was front-page, banner-headline news throughout the Western world. The several news services competed feverishly with each other now not only for colorful information on the players but also for colorful writers to convey that information. An American newspaper chain deposited $1500 in a Nice bank to be paid to Suzanne Lenglen after the match for a 1500-word report on her impressions of the confrontation. Lenglen's compensation for writing, it was pointed out, was more than President Theodore Roosevelt had received for providing *Scribner's Magazine* with an account of his lion-hunting safari. This match, obviously, was a much more exciting story.

The International News Service signed up the Spanish novelist Blasco Ibañez, author of *Blood and Sand* and *The Sheik,* to cover the match. Ibañez was guaranteed an extremely generous salary for his story despite the fact that he knew next to nothing about tennis. Ibanez stated, however, that he understood psychology, and it was the psychological aspects of the contest that he found most interesting.

Most other editors and reporters concentrated on the temperamental differences between the two players. Blanche K. Ashbaugh, tennis writer for the *San Francisco Chronicle,* predicted that when the two women walked onto the court, Helen would be her usual calm and stoical self and Suzanne would be all aflutter and beaming with smiles. If Helen could only get the drop on Suzanne in that first game, Ashbaugh believed, and take the offensive and sock the French woman with those hard-hit drives and shock her self-confidence, then Suzanne would start to make her nervous errors. And then "the game will be over, the match will be over."

Writing for *Collier's,* Grantland Rice also focused on the dramatic temperamental differences: Helen cool and calm and collected; Lenglen with a tightly adjusted nervous system and pronounced excitement during a match. But, Rice pointed out, when Lenglen became upset by an incident in a match—an extraordinary shot by her opponent, for example— she was at her best. Then her nerves worked for her and gave her power and accuracy. No one could possibly predict how Suzanne might react if Helen came on strong in that first game. She had collapsed once or twice in the past. But on hundreds of other occasions she had risen to heights of expertise and had crushed her most earnest and competent opponents.

One of Lenglen's regular doubles partners on the Riviera, Phyllis Satterthwaite, who was also in the pay of one of the local hotels as a tennis player, believed that the match between Suzanne and Helen was much more than a clash between two women. It was a clash of nations, a war on the courts according to the civilized rules of sport. "Apart from the tennis, which will be of the best," she said, "we shall see the French national temperament, volatile, quick and utterly intelligent, as opposed to the calm security and dogged determination of young America."

Satterthwaite had no doubts, however, what the result of the contest would be. Suzanne would win, naturally. And she would win because of her "natural" athletic genius. The American girl, on the other hand, was a "made" tennis player, not a natural genius. Helen had nothing but power. She was unable to change the direction of her shots at the last minute, as Suzanne could. She was too immobile. She could not move quickly from a standing start, could not anticipate and get into position as quickly as Suzanne. Of course, Helen was a scrapper and a fighter, and she had fought her way through many three-set matches to victory. She had "the true fighting spirit and she will go full out until the last stroke has been played," Satterthwaite believed. Helen never tired. But she would, nonetheless, lose because the Goddess never failed.

While almost all American newspapers focused attention on the Wills-Lenglen contest, at least one, the *Boston Globe,* offered a negative assessment of what was happening. One of the chief editorial writers of the paper, James Clarke, using his popular pseudonym Uncle Dudley, suggested that it would be extremely fortunate if in the midst of all of the Riviera confusion and hoopla and wheeling and dealing, young Helen did not suffer from a nervous collapse. After all, from the moment she set foot in France there had been an absolutely breathtaking whirlwind around her, a whirlwind not merely of publicity but also of intrigue. She was a simple and unsophisticated American girl, and she was unprepared for all of this.

Worst of all, Clarke wrote, despite the word bloat of ballyhoo, most of the men all over the world were really snickering at the spectacle of these two young women moving toward a match with each other. Men were saying that the unfolding events had showed how really incapable women were of spirited give and take, how lacking they were in the true spirit of sport. Here they were, for all the world to see, scratching like mad cats at each other's psyche.

A growing number of American women interested in physical educa-tion programs were starting to wonder if the Wills-Lenglen episode was not an object lesson teaching that low visibility was essential in any proper conduct of athletics for women, Clarke pointed out. Most of the trained female physical education directors had become determined to have no part in creating an overemphasis on sports for young women. Placing too much importance on athletic competition between women would play into the hands of male sports writers and would, in the end, discredit all female athletes.

Just look how the Riviera tournaments were being reported, Clarke suggested. Helen Wills and Suzanne Lenglen were being picked apart by nationalistic partisans. But neither woman was really privy to plans being made for their meeting. "The Riviera tournaments are scheduled and managed by men, as are the hotels and the casinos and the clubs that sponsor them and the tennis ball manufacturers and their repre-sentatives," Clarke pointed out. "The only women in this news are the players and the readers. If this were really a woman's party there might be reason for sneers on one side and anxiety on the other," he wrote. "Only it is most emphatically not a woman's party. The fiasco at the West Side Tennis Club in New York in 1921 when Mallory beat Lenglen was also arranged and officiated by men. There was a dollar motive which demanded that the French champion play, even though she was not in proper condition to stand any such strain. A new stadium had been built and the interest on it had to be paid." The story was the same on the Riviera, he said. "The bright idea of selling the film rights was a man's idea, so was the notion of getting players to insist on certain brands of balls. When Wills felt obliged to refer the situation to Ameri-can advisers, she communicated with a body absolutely controlled by men."

What were the ramifications of the Riviera ballyhoo? Well, Clarke wrote, almost all of America's women's colleges had suddenly become hesitant about extending their competitive athletic programs. There was an increasing distrust for the tradition which "men and money" had combined to make. A few women golfers were now taking a stand by which they laid claim to the direction of their own affairs. For any woman who was to take her rightful place in the world, the editor wrote, there was much that could be learned from competition and team play. But the focus of public attention on the Riviera tended to pervert the real value of what Helen Wills and Suzanne Lenglen were doing.

In the patriotic brouhaha pitting the American girl against the wiley Gallic champion, almost all American journalists sang the praises of Helen Wills. But two writers had misgivings about the values repre-sented by Wills and Lenglen and the American public's preference for the stolid American girl. Heywood Broun shocked millions of readers when he came out squarely behind Suzanne and announced that he hoped she would win. Poor Suzanne, Broun said. She was attacked by the American press because she was not a "good sport." Broun agreed that in fact Suzanne was not a good sport at all in the American sense of the term. But, he said, the whole idea behind the term was repulsive to him because it sounded too much like the concept of the "good soldier." Just as the good soldier was to lose his own feelings and beliefs within a conformity imposed from the outside, so the good sport was an individual who adopted "an artificially fostered attitude." Not that this was all bad. Everyone, Broun conceded, must at one time or another "tincture their conduct with tradition and some of the restraints which it imposed." And there were some conditions under which an individual must become a good soldier.

But in using the term "good sport" Americans were making a big mistake. Sport, Broun said, was play and ought to be free and unrestrained. The goal of sport, after all, was to release the individual from his inhibitions. Many people were able to live peaceful and productive lives simply because the powerful and destructive urges inherent in the species had been released through vigorous participation in sport, Broun contended. "Games seem to me to be the very activity in which the participant should follow his natural inclinations." So "why shouldn't losers grumble and winners swagger? Games are substitutes for bloodier conflicts, and if you drain out of them all rudimentary emotion, the purpose of the effort is all but nullified." Too many sports enthusiasts—especially in America—had perfected the "facile hypocrisy" of pretending not to care whether they won or lost, Broun complained. "But cut the heart out of the most flamboyantly chivalrous and you'll find as much bile in it as Lenglen ever showed under adversity."

Broun said that he hoped Suzanne would beat Helen and all other challengers. Why? "Because she is by such a margin so much more the romantic figure," he claimed. "She has played in hundreds of tournaments over the course of many years and she has almost entirely escaped the blight that befalls most veteran performers and champions. She has never become a good sport nor yet an athlete. Mademoiselle Lenglen never once suggests the wholesome outdoor girl. She keeps her pallor even in the middle of the most strenuous campaigns. Her health is by no means 'annoyingly excellent'," he found, as was that of her American challenger. Americans liked their champions to look healthy. And youthful. And charming. Broun did not. He liked Suzanne, who "even on the court seems like one who for a little while plays truant from lights, music, gaeity, and the pace which kills. She moves through one of the most exacting of all strenuous games and remains in appearance morbid."

And, in the end, Broun concluded, that was her triumph. Therein lay her real greatness. Many other tennis players might cover the court better than Suzanne, or slam the ball with more power and authority. But none of them had, like Suzanne, made a trick of tennis. None else had made it seem so much like sorcery. "It is not an exercise when she plays," he wrote," but a subtle game." When she won "the spectator goes away impressed by the finesse and shrewdness of which the human mind may be capable. He does not say, 'Ah, yes, after such an exhibition of physical prowess I must take thought and do my daily dozen each morning at the same time being much more cautious in the matter of nicotine and alcohol.' No, indeed. Suzanne is the finest of all champions." Broun observed, "for she wins and wins and still avoids the reproach of being an ideal or a good example to anyone.

"There she stands," he concluded, "every inch a Borgia, even though God's bright sunlight and cleansing wind seek to make her one of nature's noblewomen."

Paul Gallico also had mixed feelings about the match on the Riviera. He realized that the press ballyhoo had actually created an icon—an American Girl—that in too many ways did not honestly represent Helen Wills. He never quite got over Helen's stinging the *Daily News* with her sketch. And he had seen Helen in various tournaments earlier and concluded that she was a "spoiled and somewhat calculating little lady." But now it was too late to write anything like that. She was the American Girl. The public would believe only the best of her. And so Gallico went along with the ballyhoo in 1926, "swallowing or conveniently forgetting all I knew about the girl . . . and contributing my bit to the general press hysteria with a meandering and touching column or sports editorial to the effect that tomorrow a little American girl beloved by all Americans was going to her greatest test in a foreign country, far from home, and that she must win because she was a fine American girl that everybody loved, and so give a thought to Helen Wills, folks, the highest type of American girl, and our very own, in this her hour of trial, etc., etc. etc. . . ."

It was just such writing that aroused and sustained public sentiment in support of the American Girl. Columnist Harry Smith concluded hours before the match, "We are facing today one of the biggest events in the history of the sporting world. As we go back over our sports history we can pick out here and there an event that stands above its fellows. Such is the Helen Wills-Suzanne Lenglen match that has worked its way through much turmoil and discord to the final match that should tell us which of these girls holds supremacy in the tennis world. No event to which I can look back has stirred interest in general as has been the case with the prospective tennis match. We have had our Dempsey and Carpentier in the fistic line; we have either watched or read of international horse races and of golf; yet the forthcoming match slated for today, if weather and fate are kind, has attracted interest that may well nigh be called unanimous.

"For a year or more this match has been in the making," Smith wrote, "accumulating widespread attention as the days have rolled by and in much the same manner that a monster snowball is built. Americans are united in their prayers for Helen's victory."

Paul Gallico recalled that countless letters arrived at newspaper offices from people signing themselves "Mrs. J. Basutio" or "G. Carmichael," saying, in effect, "Last night I said a prayer for our Helen to win her victory over there in France the way our boys did." And the night before the match there was "a generous outpouring of sentiment and deep heartfelt prayer for Helen in France. Prayers for her victory ascended from the hearts of millions of Americans."

Helen Wills saw no good reason why those prayers should go unanswered.

CHAPTER
IV

THE MATCH

"When we have match'd our rackets to these balls
We will, in France, by God's grace play a set,
Shall strike his father's crown into the hazard,
Tell him, he hath made a match with such a
   wrangler,
That all the courts of France will be disturb'd
With chases."
                              —William Shakespeare
                                Henry V

"A simple game of tennis, yet a game which made
continents stand still and was the most important
sporting event of modern times exclusively in the
hands of the fairer sex."   —Ferdinand Tuohy
                                     Cannes, 1926

ON the evening of February 15, 1926, Helen Wills went to bed early. Several days earlier she had decided to block from her mind all the confusion and bluster surrounding her on the Riviera. To a remarkable degree she succeeded. She was not nervous at all, she felt good, healthy, confident. With her mother, Helen had enjoyed a dinner of steak and potatoes and had capped the meal with her favorite dessert, cake and ice cream. Later, after turning down an invitation to a party, Helen was lulled to sleep by the faint strains of an orchestra somewhere near by playing the romantic "Valencia," the most popular song of the day. Outside, on the streets of Cannes, there was a carnival atmosphere as thousands of visitors to this spot on the Côte d'Azure danced and laughed and tipped their glasses and passed the last few hours before the beginning of the long-awaited match with Suzanne Lenglen.

Suzanne Lenglen, on the other hand, was not so fortunate. She faced yet another major crisis in her career on the night before the big match, and she did not sleep at all. Later she would tell reporters that during the match she suffered from "physical weakness through private worry." But few people knew that on the night of February 15, 1926, Suzanne reached a turning point in her career. During the course of that evening she was compelled to make her declaration of independence from Papa.

As his illness became increasingly severe in late 1925 and early 1926, Charles Lenglen gradually lost control over Suzanne's affairs. The major

commercial interests on the Riviera had vetoed an earlier match between Suzanne and Helen at the Nice Club—a match Papa Lenglen
wanted very much. And then, without seeking his prior approval, the
match was awarded to the Carlton Club in Cannes. For a while Papa
Lenglen had gone along with the way things were arranged, but enough
was enough. And on the evening of February 15, he simply said, "No!"
Suzanne must not play at the Carlton Club. Out of touch with those
handling the arrangements for the match, Papa was suspicious. It might
be another Forest Hills. Who knew what they were plotting? Suzanne
would again be humiliated and humbled. So Papa Lenglen intervened
to protect his little one from the slings and arrows of outrageous newsmen and promoters. Suzanne must scratch from the tournament, he
said. She must stay at home with Papa and not play in Cannes.

An uproarious argument followed Papa's pronouncement. Suzanne
had been given an agent now, an American, Major Charles Willen.
Introduced to Suzanne by F. M. B. Fisher, Willen was to take over
Papa's role and look after her personal finances. Willen now insisted
that a scratch or a default at this stage would be utterly disastrous for
Suzanne's career. She would never recover from it: she would be branded
a quitter forever; she would go down in history not as a champion but
as a coward and a chump. Willen said that she could defeat that American girl easily, perhaps even in love sets. This was no set up. Suzanne
was going to win. But if she scratched at this final moment nobody would
ever take her seriously again. She had to play. It was just too late to back
out now.

Papa remained adamant. He shouted and railed and denounced Suzanne and Willen. The cries and the pleading from the Villa Ariem were
so loud that pedestrians passing by were distracted by the bitter wrangle.
Mama Lenglen burst into tears and sided with Papa. Suzanne must not
play. Suzanne became hysterical and pleaded for her father's blessing.
She had to play, and he had to be there at courtside. But he refused.
Willen intervened and told Papa that it was absolutely essential he be at
courtside for the match, the most important and the most profitable in
Suzanne's career.

The next morning, exhausted and emotionally enervated, Suzanne
made her choice: she would play. With or without Papa's blessing, she
would play. She dressed for the match, carefully caked on makeup to
cover her pale, heavily lined face, and faced Papa one last time. In place
of a blessing, Papa cursed her. Moments later Suzanne, Mama, and
Willen stepped into the sleek black Voisin which transported them in
silence along the coastal road toward the Carlton Club and the waiting
American Girl.

The Carlton Club. Before the Lenglen-Wills contest was scheduled to
be held there, few newsmen paid much attention to its facilities. Now,
when they examined more closely the club where the highly touted ten-

nis match was to be staged, they were, in a word, shocked. John Tunis accurately described it as "a tawdry little excuse for a tennis club." The Carlton Club consisted of six clay tennis courts, a small grandstand, and a hut that served as a clubhouse. It was located a short walk from the Croisette and directly adjacent to the grand Carlton Hotel, which loomed up over the palms bordering the club. The club courts had been constructed carelessly with an apparent disregard for the angle of the winter sun. Consequently, except for the hours from about 11:00 a.m. to 1:00 p.m., one player or another faced directly into the distractingly bright champagne sunshine. Adjacent to the number one court—the Burkes euphemistically referred to it as *le court d'honneur*—was the small concrete grandstand. And behind the grandstand rose the blank wall of a large garage and warehouse. Across the street on another side was a sawmill, and the buzzing and rasping sounds from the mill provided another unwelcome distraction for players and spectators alike. The clubhouse provided for the players was a small wood structure enclosing one room seventeen feet by eleven feet. The room included two dozen lockers, a shower that never worked, several washstands with cold water only, and nothing else. There were no towels provided and no electric lighting.

These facilities had been adequate in the past for the winter tournaments on the Riviera, and they seemed only a cut or two below the facilities of other small clubs in the region. Once or twice during the winter tennis season the stands would be filled with several hundred spectators when Suzanne Lenglen played. But during matches between less noteworthy contestants only a sprinkling of spectators occupied the Carlton grandstand. Special accommodations for the press had not been necessary in the past, nor were they provided by the Burkes for the finals of the 1926 tournament.

Yet, despite obvious inadequacies, the Carlton Club had won the right to stage the first Lenglen-Wills match. All the necessary business and financial arrangements had been worked out carefully between the Burkes and the various interests represented by F. M. B. Fisher. The only snag in the preliminary dealings had been over the sale of the exclusive film rights. And even with the collapse of the attempt by Fisher and the Burkes to milk the media, rumors persisted that an enormous profit was to result from the wildly enthusiastic public interest in the match. John Tunis tried to follow the money to find out exactly who was making how much from this match.

Tunis calculated that 3000 tickets were sold for the finals of the Carlton Club tournament at an average price of 200 francs each. That was, however, a low estimate. Other reporters guessed that as many as 4000 people would pay admission to the final match, and a large number of those tickets were sold for as much as 3000 francs. Using a low estimate, nonetheless, and disregarding funds from ticket sales for the preliminary matches, Tunis estimated that the Burkes would take in about 600,000 francs. About 100, 000 of which would go to the French government in taxes; another 100,000 for expenses such as advertising and building new seats for the final. Where would the remainder go? Fisher responded to Tunis's inquiry by suggesting that the Burkes would make only 100,000 francs on the match. And where did the other funds go? Tunis simply did not know. He pointed out that the amount of "leakage" from the admission money was substantial. How much of that leakage found its way into the coffers of the Lenglens was anyone's guess. Suzanne insisted that she profited nothing from the match. Most American newsmen believed she was lying.

Money was to be made from this match by ticket-scalping also—an illegal enterprise that boomed during the final hours before play began. There was simply no upper limit as to how much many people were willing to pay for a good seat at the confrontation between the Goddess and the American Girl. Tunis found, though, that attempting to buy a ticket at the last moment was like trying "to buy a Pullman reservation to heaven." And just as expensive.

And why shouldn't there be such a mad rush for tickets? The match had been played up for weeks as though "it was a cross between the French Revolution and the Battle of Gettysburg."This was not a game of tennis. This was an international incident. This was history. And millions of people wanted to be part of it. In America, one newsman noticed, people who had never before seen a match or were without even a passing interest in tennis now talked glibly on the street about the chances of Wills against Lenglen. Men and women who could not tell you the difference between a game and a set were now offering to risk cash on this match. Paul Gallico found it difficult to keep what was happening in Cannes in any perspective: "we were whooping it up in those days and it was ballyhooed into the battle of the ages, with the cool peaches-and-cream skinned, clear-eyed beautiful Helen fighting for the forces of youth and light, democracy and right, against the unattractive Suzanne, a foreigner representing the menace that is always met and defeated by our fine American manhood and womanhood."

In northern California scores of Helen's supporters were outspoken in their conviction that the American girl would bring off the upset of the century in this match of the century. All-night parties were arranged by several organizations so that celebrants could wait together for the good news from Cannes. San Francisco radio station KPO prepared to come on the air early in the morning to broadcast the first bulletins from Cannes. The presses for the morning editions of the daily newspapers were stopped and space was reserved for the first wire-service reports.

And then there were the last-minute predictions. George Wightman, former USLTA president, said he believed it was still "anybody's match. If Miss Wills is on her game she cannot be beaten except by a player who can hit harder than she can. When Miss Wills plays her drive with all the speed she is capable of, no woman and indeed few men players can withstand the withering pace." Big Bill Tilden and Sam Hardy agreed. Helen's hope for victory against the more experienced and uncannily talented Suzanne lay in the awesome power of her attack. Relentless aggressiveness would, they believed, shatter Suzannne's defense, upset her control, erode her self-confidence, and bring victory. Molla Mallory insisted that Helen could win only if she went at Suzanne like a lion, using all of her strength on every shot. It would be difficult, but it could be done. In fact, it had been done, Molla pointed out. Once. At Forest Hills in 1921. And it could be done again.

Most Riviera clubs scheduled final tournament matches for the early afternoon. But the women's singles final at the Carlton Club, due to the awkward play of the sunlight on the courts in the afternoon, was scheduled for 11:15 a.m. It was the best time. Helen found on the morning of February 16, 1926, a Tuesday, that "the sky was blue and the air fresh and the sunshine sparkling—a perfect day for tennis. Heaven had looked after the weather," she wrote, "and the Burkes had looked after the arrangements, which were partly good and partly bad." After a light breakfast with her mother, Helen dressed in her white pleated cotton dress and heavily starched middy top, and white shoes and stockings. She adjusted her white visor over the light net covering her hair, pulled on her red wool sweater, and carried her heavy winter coat. She carefully selected from her array of rackets four that felt right. Then, shortly before 11:00 a.m., she walked with her mother the short distance to the Carlton Club.

All around the club, since early in the morning, pandemonium prevailed. John Tunis had expected a huge crowd, so he left his hotel room two hours before the match was scheduled to start to avoid the inevitable final rush for seats. But he was completely unprepared for what he found. Hundreds of people had been standing in line all night waiting to get in. The Train Bleu had arrived from Paris packed with fans eager to see the match, and the roads leading into Cannes were jammed with cars carrying partisans. Tunis found a line of people four across stretching from the gate of the club all the way back to the Croisette, some five hundred yards away. And it was growing steadily, stretching down the street and around the corner and out of sight. Near the entrance the line was flattened out into a large seething, shouting, milling mass of people. Many seemed to have no tickets and tried frantically to thrust bundles of francs into the hands of club officials standing guard at the gate. People around the gate jostled each other and pushed and shoved as they tried to make their way into the club. Just inside the gate Tunis spotted F. M. B. Fisher and Albert Burke trying to maintain a semblance of order and to admit only paying customers.

Tunis was directed to a club entrance reserved for the press. He hurried to that gate but found it resembled the foyer of the Tower of Babel. There was another impatient mob, some with tickets and most without. Many were shouting that they were friends of the Burkes or friends of Fisher or friends of the players or reporters or photographers—a confusing mishmash of professions and a profusion of languages. It took Tunis half an hour of maneuvering and pushing before he was finally squeezed through the gate and onto the club grounds.

Al Laney had similar problems making his way. At first he found it absolutely impossible to push his way through the crowd and into the press entrance. Laney eventually teamed up with a group of photographers and reporters who formed a solid flying wedge and successfully stormed the gate. Once inside the group was directed to a special press section of the bleachers. But in the mad scramble for seats Laney missed the press section, as did most of the reporters. The entire atmosphere was one of confusion and of unrestrained individualism. It was, he observed, as they used to say at Ebbetts Field, "everyone for theirself!"

Tunis found—with only 90 minutes remaining until the start of the match—carpenters were still busy constructing bleacher seats. As they worked away frantically, those fortunate enough to make it into the club surrounded them. And as each section of the new bleachers was completed and a board dropped down, people clambered carelessly and fearlessly around the carpenters to take their seats. Many dropped all restraint and ran for their seats. Tunis was amused by a rather pathetic situation he witnessed that seemed to sum up the utter insanity surrounding this event. He saw a man with a ticket in his hand staring up into space. The man's bleacher seat was still in the process of being built, but at the moment was just air. The man stood there, patiently, as the carpenters hammered away creating the place he would perch on to observe this historic clash of the Goddess and the American Girl.

Tunis examined the stands and the thin boards used for scaffolding and the two-by-four braces and supports for the bleachers. When he pushed against some of the boards to see how solidly constructed they were, there were instant cries of protest and frightened shouts from those already seated. When a member of the Carlton Club tennis committee came by, Tunis stopped him and asked, "Has this been inspected by your local building inspector?" The man was annoyed by the question and replied, *"Mais, mon vieux,* do you not see that it is only just being finished?"

"Yes, but what if it falls down?" Tunis asked.

The official simply shrugged his shoulders "with a delightful Gallic gesture" and responded, "Ah, the club is assured—." Then he dashed off without finishing his comment. Tunis spotted a nurse in uniform sitting in the referee's tent and had no doubt as to why she was there. Tunis consequently climbed very cautiously up to his seat as the boards wavered beneath his feet. "And the mere fact that the Carlton Tennis Club would have to pay nothing to my heirs in case I was buried in the wreckage did not reassure me in the least," he said. After finding a reasonably stable slot, Tunis sat down and then looked around to see what other foolhardy souls had ascended this jerry-built contraption.

Tunis saw groups of reporters sitting together in various parts of the bleachers. If there was a special press section nobody seemed to have found it. He spotted Blasco Ibañez, the Spanish novelist who was being paid 40,000 francs for his account of this match for the INS, sitting with a few "mere journalists." Max Eastman was there and so was Stanley Doust of the London *Daily Mail* and Powell Blackmore of the *Express* and Sparrow Robertson of the Paris *Herald* and Tom Topping of the Associated Press. A few journalists had carried in typewriters, and they tried to balance them on their knees while being squeezed into the mass of fans ever more tightly with the constant flow of new arrivals.

Al Laney seated himself behind Tom Topping, who was writing out his reports in long hand. Topping wrote quickly and then handed his completed pages back to Laney, who corrected the copy, put a paper clip on it, and then dropped it to a man standing behind the bleachers. That man in turn passed the page over the fence to a runner who rushed it off to a wire service for transmission to America.

Laney was struck by Topping's anxiousness in scribbling off descriptions of the club grounds and the crowds, but Topping explained it all to him in a few words. "You know where this wench comes from?" Topping asked. "Berkeley, California. You know what time it is in Berkeley, California? Three o'clock in the morning. Some of the AM's are holding for this, and the guy gets there first gets his stuff in the paper." Looking around, Laney saw that the other wire service writers were working just as frantically as Topping, racing to keep up with events.

While the newsmen settled into their cramped quarters the gate was finally crashed successfully by what Tunis called "French flappers." The gate was blocked again, and the crowd outside became larger and ever more threatening. Thousands of people were pushing their way forward and yelling and swarming around like enraged bees in their effort to get inside. Some of those who saw no chance at all of making it inside climbed a large eucalyptus tree just outside the gate. But when the club officials saw this group of nonpaying arboreal customers they shouted orders to a policeman to get the climbers down. Tunis observed that "as a tree climber he was a good traffic cop." He scaled the tree while solemnly ordering the climbers down. They, in turn, simply climbed higher. Finally, deciding that enough was enough, the policeman slid back down amid jeers and cheers from the multitude.

Across the street from the club were several small villas with red tile roofs. The owner of one of them, after seeing the crowd of people, hit upon a way of making money. He stood at the door of his house and sold places at one of his windows to fans who had given up all hope of crashing the gates. For 20 francs each tennis fan could gather around a small second-story window and look down on the courts. The window spots were sold out six or seven times over. The entrepreneur's wife rushed downstairs and shouted that the rooms were full and that people were complaining they could not see. Yet there remained room for an additional profit. The roof of the house, like that of many Riviera villas, was constructed of clay tiles placed across beams. The tiles could easily be removed from within. The owner of the villa began dismantling his roof. Men and women paid at the door and carted chairs to the attic, stood on them, removed tiles, and then poked their heads out. The villa quickly took on a surrealistic look as human heads suddenly filled holes in the roof. This profitable venture gave residents of other nearby villas ideas, and heads began protruding from other rooftops across from the club.

Then, much like a group of smartly attired marines making an alpine assault, there appeared a crowd of men and women climbing carefully up over the wide sloping roof of the garage behind the Carlton Club. They found comfortable places to stand or sit and perched rather precariously in their makeshift open-air balcony. Still other enthusiasts, who concluded wisely that they could never fight their way inside, rented ladders and leaned them against the fence at the end of the section of the club near the street. Next a large bus pulled up to the fence and parked. The people inside who had hired it for the afternoon scrambled out and up onto the hood and roof so they could peek over the fence and watch the match. Long before match time the roofs of most buildings within sight of the club were thick with spectators, and the balconies and windows of the Carlton Hotel were filled with onlookers. There were in fact many more spectators for this match outside the club grounds than there were inside. And no wonder. Ticket prices during the morning had skyrocketed. Scalpers on the street were getting as much as 1200 francs—44 American dollars—for each ticket. And that was for an impossibly narrow seat in an unstable bleachers. That was about twenty-two times what one might expect to pay at Forest Hills to see a final match between Bill Tilden and Bill Johnston, the most popular American male players. For 1200 francs one could buy a good suit, a pair of shoes, a train ticket from Paris to Cannes, and room and board in a grand hotel on the Riviera for one day. Or, for that same 1200 francs one might buy—if one were very lucky—one ticket to a tennis match in Cannes at 11:15 a.m., February 16, 1926.

During the long wait for the appearance of the featured players on this morning, newsmen seated in the newly constructed bleachers watched the better-known members of European high society stroll to their reserved seats in the permanent gallery. Among the most easily recognizable figures of that elite group were Grand Duke Cyril of Russia, King Gustav of Sweden, Manuel, ex-king of Portugal, the Duke of Sutherland, the Count de Bourbel (president of the Tennis Committee of the Riviera), Baron de Graffenried, and the Rajah and Ranee of Pudukota. The American diplomat and author Brand Whitlock was also there along with what John Tunis guessed was "half the Russian and English nobility." When the army of newsmen weren't scribbling notes on the background for the big match or scrutinizing the stands across the way for somebody who was somebody, they joked and jostled each other. Many of them were a little giddy and somewhat embarrassed by the necessity of assaulting the gates in order to get into the club two hours before match time. They were disappointed at the lack of facilities available for their creative efforts, and what remaining pretense of sophistication they possessed once they battered their way to their seats was squeezed out of them by the crush of the crowd. They laughed hysterically at every trivial incident. They howled with delight when fashionably attired young women stepped across rooftops and the sun behind them made their clothing suddenly transparent or when the gendarmes undertook their tree-top pursuits and tried to coax fans down from the palms. The entrance of each new celebrity into the club was hailed by newsmen as on a Broadway opening night and then followed by jokes and wisecracks. All of this went on while carpenters continued their feverish hammering and sawing while propping up more bleachers.

Shortly after eleven o'clock the officials for the match walked to their stations round the court. Commander George Hillyard had been selected as umpire, and the linesmen included Lord Charles Hope, Cyril Tolley, Roman Najouch, the residential professional of the Cannes Club, Victor Cazalet, Sir Francis Towle, and R. Dunkerely. These officials, ostensibly, had been approved previously by both players. Some newsmen noticed what they guessed was an oversight in the selection of the match officials. There was no foot-fault judge. Yet, considering the difficulties Suzanne Lenglen had experienced with foot faults called against her in the semifinal, it seems not unlikely that the Goddess or one of her concerned partisans among the officials had suggested just such an omission. The French champion would not suffer from distracting accusations of rule violations in this critical contest.

The three-ring circus atmosphere in the Carlton Club—the shouting and the loudly expressed partisanship of the fans—shocked traditionalists. Tennis had never before been played in such an explosively exciting setting. Troubled by the reported behavior of the crowds at courtside in Cannes, an editor for the *New York Times* reminded his readers that "tennis is nothing if not a game for gentlemen and gentlewomen. To degrade it by outbursts of rowdyism is to put at hazard something too fine to be carelessly thrown away." Overlooking the pivotal role of the press in drumming up the extraordinary excitement for this match in the first place, the editor concluded that "things seem to have been carried to an intolerable excess at Cannes. If this sort of boorishness is allowed to continue, the game of tennis will soon be in urgent need of being saved from its patrons and professed friends."

Meanwhile, in Cannes, the patrons and professed friends of tennis were much more interested in seeing than in saving tennis. In the last few hectic moments before the big match was scheduled to start, it seemed that the swirling crowd would burst right through the fences and flood out onto the courts and make any confrontation between contestants impossible. The Carlton Club had become a besieged sports Bastille under assault by an army of energetic and determined fans. There were regular charges at the gates by organized wedges of impatient people, and the constant roar of the crowd outside rose and fell almost ominously, like the deep reverberations of ocean waves beating against a beach. Then, just after 11:00 a.m., the noise outside suddenly stopped. There was an odd—even a frightening—moment of quiet. Why? A few of those inside instinctively stood to peer out over the fence to see what was happening. But before they could relay back any information the quiet was shattered by an ear-splitting eruption of shouting and screaming and ecstatic howling. And above that mad din, one single word could be heard again and again—"Suzanne!" The Goddess had arrived! The Goddess was here! "Suzanne!" the people shouted and sang. "Suzanne! Vive la Suzanne! Vive la belle Suzanne!"

The French champion was quickly escorted through the sea of cheering partisans that parted with almost religious obeisance before her. She proceeded triumphantly through that human corridor into the Carlton Club. Just inside the gate she saw the American girl waiting for her in silence.

Helen and Catherine Wills had walked the short distance from their hotel to the Carlton Club. When they arrived at the gate they found an impenetrable crowd blocking the way. Fortunately, a club official spotted the pair and made his way through the crowd. He then led the Wills women through the confusion to another entrance where there was yet another impatient mob fighting to get inside. At first those around the entrance refused to budge and make way despite the threats and the pleading from the club official. But then, gradually, many of them recognized Helen and began to move back to make room for her to pass. They stared in silent wonder as she glided past them like a phantom. If she was excited or appalled, she showed no sign. She seemed very shy and perhaps a bit embarrassed as she was swallowed up in the crowd whose actions seemed more like an enthusiastic outbreak in a madhouse than a celebration of tennis. Helen was not accustomed to such behavior, to such demonstrative enthusiasm. Tennis, in the course of only a few weeks, had become show business and big business. And Helen Wills was now a star. Just inside the gate she was welcomed by club officials and by a small army of photographers. Only seconds later Suzanne made her perfectly timed arrival.

Helen Wills wore her red sweater and her customary costume. But Suzanne! Ah, Suzanne Lenglen was fully attired for this festive occasion. She wore a rose bandeau and a matching wide-knit rose sweater over a short white pleated silk dress. And over all of this she wore her white ermine coat.

After the two women exchanged a perfunctory salutation they turned to face the familiar phalanx of photographers. The cameramen, lined up in a triple row, shouted commands and requests to the two women. Suzanne smiled a lot and placed her hand smartly on her hip. Helen, on the other hand, remained quiet and unemotional, as unemotional, one man described her, as "a Methodist minister at a funeral." Helen looked around at the sea of faces turned towards her, strange and foreign faces, she thought. And she believed that many of them reflected a dislike of her. Suzanne seemed comfortable with the crowd. She executed some bravura gestures and blew kisses to friends in the crowd. When she moved in front of the cameras, she was like a feather dancing in the wind, turning and prancing here and there to the absolute delight of the cameramen. When the picture-taking session had almost ended there was a squawking commotion just outside the gate and everyone turned to see a policeman trying to drag someone down from a tree. The photographers laughed. The two women laughed. But Helen noticed now that Suzanne's laugh was unusual. It was dry throated and forced—almost a nervous cackle.

At a signal from a club official, the picture-taking session ended, and the two women were escorted towards the court. Suzanne virtually danced her way onto the clay. Close behind her and to one side came Helen, walking with a flatfooted padding cat-like walk and a demeanor that seemed to whisper to those watching, "I really am quite a modest little girl, much too modest for all of this."

As the two women walked out onto the court they were preceded by several reporters and photographers walking backwards, hoping to get the very last word or picture before the match was under way.

There was continuous shouting and applause inside the club now. It was already a magnificent and thrilling and wonderful show. In the bleacher seats there was a sudden speeded up rapid machine-gun chatter of typewriters as correspondents tried frantically, frenetically, to capture all of this on paper in order to relay it to runners who would convey it to the wire services who would send it to cities around the world where it would again be printed on paper and read by tens of millions eager to envision this spectacle. But those readers could never experience the rush of excitement felt by the correspondents and the spectators that sunny morning next to this clay court beside the beautiful azure sea in a sparkling city in the south of France where the two greatest women tennis players in the world were about to test each other.

The correspondents strained for the right words to express pride and awe. The phrases and adjectives poured out steadily again—Our Girl of the Golden West, the American Girl, Helen of America, Our Helen, Our Hope. Even Little Helen—Americans could easily envision that. Little Helen out to slay the Gallic Goliath. There was only one thing wrong with that description. Helen was obviously taller and heavier than Suzanne. Yet her serenity and quietude seemed to make her somehow look smaller than the bouncing, bubbling Suzanne. The Little American. And so in their mind's eye, newspaper readers could envision a racket-swinging diminutive Mary Pickford off to do great things for her country. To bring down the hard-hearted villain. And make no doubt about it, Suzanne was the villain. And what a story it was. Helen stood there like, well, like a little Calvin Coolidge about to deliver a humble homily. The images and the descriptions were important not for their accuracy but to convey contrast. Surely, few athletes engaged against each other in the same sport ever contrasted more than this pair, this Goddess and this American Girl.

Helen Wills had already noticed something unusual in Suzanne Lenglen's behavior. Something was not right. The Goddess appeared to be trembling slightly. Helen felt it first when she grasped Suzanne's extended hand after the French woman's grand entrance into the club grounds. And when Suzanne smiled, her lips quivered as though that bright smile might in a moment reassemble itself into a miserable frown. Suzanne was clearly struggling to seem happy. She was wavering even before the contest began. She was, perhaps, even a bit frightened. Helen wondered at this since it was obviously the challenger who should be more anxious. The thought of Suzanne's emotional vulnerability gave Helen a little more confidence. She became even more relaxed and emotionally placid as she walked out onto the clay court to play.

From his seat Al Laney could see Lenglen's face clearly. Laney was a bit surprised by her appearance. There were dark lines on her face, and her eyes seemed drawn. She looked like she had not slept. "She did not look well," he observed. And although the sun was nearly directly overhead and it was getting warm, Suzanne kept her sweater on. As she proceeded out onto the court, the dark French woman further betrayed her uneasiness. Her smile disappeared. She snapped her fingers impatiently at the ball boy and was quick and jerky in her motions. She did not like the noise of the crowd, and she did not like the carpenters. She was tired, and she had a nervous tic in her right arm. In her preliminary rally with Helen she struggled inwardly to relax, to arouse her confidence. She practiced her strokes carefully, not rushing after any ball, staying right in the middle of the baseline and taking only the forehand and backhand shots that came directly to her. At the same time she studied Helen's movement, analyzing the mechanics of the motion, measuring the pace of the shots. Did Helen hesitate on any shots? Where was her weakness today? And why did she remain so flatfooted?

As the two women warmed up, the final arrangements for the match were made. The carpenters were escorted from the club. The officials settled into their places around the court. Commander Hillyard climbed up into the umpire's chair. The cheering and the noise continued. Suzanne seemed particularly annoyed by the chanting of a group of spectators outside the fence standing on the top of a bus. She gave them an impatient look, a pleading look, but a look that made no difference at all in their behavior. Despite her obvious wishes to the contrary, the crowd outside continued its enthusiastic demonstration.

During the warmup Helen was trying hard to think of nothing but the game, of the drives and the angles and the spin and rebound of the ball. The position of the sun and the effect of the dry clay were taken into consideration and analyzed. She betrayed no emotion. She seemed to have shut out the noise of the crowd completely from her mind. Al Laney noted that she was "placidly unemotional" and stolid, still the Coolidge of the courts. He also noticed for the first time what large capable-looking hands she had, and he wondered to himself if she was actually as talented a painter as she was supposed to be. Hard to believe. At the moment she looked more and more the dedicated and superbly coordinated athlete.

As Helen Wills focused her concentration, everything—the crowd, the cameras, the background commotion—faded into silence. There must be nothing but the game. Nothing but the game. And, as always, she began to repeat her secret mantra to herself over and over again: "Every shot. Every shot. Every shot." She studied the ball and thought of every shot.

Suzanne won the spin of the racket and elected to serve the first game. As Helen moved back to receive service several reporters noticed a stiffness in her knee. There was still a bandage dressing covering the wound incurred in the semifinal match. But Helen had made no mention of it, not on this day or after. No apologies. She had come to play tennis, come to win. And she believed she could win. Despite that knee.

Suzanne Lenglen blew softly into her right palm and then carefully wiped both palms on her skirt. Then she turned to the ball boy who tossed out three balls in quick succession—she liked to hold all three at once in order to speed up the game. She did not bounce the balls. She merely turned to signal that she was ready to begin. Hillyard signaled for the match to commence. Suzanne tiptoed up to the baseline, paused for just a fraction of a second, and then gracefully lifted the white ball high into the air above her left shoulder. With a familiar incomparably fluid motion she arched backward to watch the ball and then leaned forward while bringing her racket up and over her head to strike the ball and send it gliding straight and flat and without spin deep into the corner of Wills's service court. The American girl skipped from the baseline to make a solid forehand return. The crowd of 4000 spectators inside and the equally large multitude outside became silent. The match of the century had just begun.

Lenglen stayed on the baseline to take Wills's deep service return, and she launched it back again diagonally across the court to Helen's forehand corner. The American girl's forceful forehand reply sailed well beyond the baseline. The next three points were pretty much repetitions of the first one: service, short rally, and Wills hitting long. Lenglen took her own service at love.

As the women changed courts at the end of that first game a ripple of whispers went through the crowd inside the club. Another walkover for Lenglen. This had all been set up by the casinos, some of them said. Those betting on Wills, even with long odds, were going to be fleeced— American lambs paying for their patriotic fervor.

Wills served the second game. Her service was harder hit than Suzanne's, and it struck deep in the service court. But it did not bother Lenglen, yet. The women each took a point, and then Lenglen jumped ahead to 15–30. But Wills now appeared suddenly to come to life and to play with more confidence. She took three straight points off forced errors, winning her own service. The score was one all.

Wills continued to assert herself in the third game. Lenglen dropped back to 15–40, then fought back to deuce with some brilliant placements. Helen surged again, revealing surprisingly tremendous power off both her forehand and backhand drives. She earned two points with quick, crisp forehand shots. Lenglen didn't touch either one. The very last shot of the third game surprised almost everyone. Suzanne hit a drive deep to Helen's backhand. The shot pushed Wills back beyond the baseline. Lenglen stayed back for the return. Wills moved with perfect grace toward the ball, pulled her racket back, and then rifled a sharply angled backhand shot that dropped several feet in front of Lenglen and passed safely beyond the range of her racket. There was an explosion of applause following the winner. What made it extraordinary was the fact that Lenglen's shot had been placed so well. No other player in the world could possibly have scored off the Lenglen shot. No other player, that is, but this one, the American girl. Throughout the bleachers people jumped to their feet to cheer. Suzanne seemed for an instant taken by surprise, left flatfooted. Helen was hitting with her, hitting with the Goddess. She was sending lightning bolts back, and the French woman was reeling from the shock. Helen broke Suzanne's service and moved ahead to 2–1.

The cheering outside the club grounds did not stop as Helen Wills prepared to serve. Shouts of encouragement and chants of enthusiasm filled the air. Hillyard asked those outside to be quiet—to no avail. Charles Aeschliman, who was sitting on a bench with F. M. B. Fisher at courtside, stood and addressed the crowd both in English and in

French, asking for quiet. He was booed. Lenglen walked back to the fence and begged the mob standing on the top of the bus and peering over the fence to restrain themselves. They did, but only for a few moments. It all reminded John Tunis of a boxing match in the old Madison Square Garden in New York, except that no boxing match was ever as badly organized as this tennis match. And at courtside Mama Lenglen had now begun her usual bitter tirade. "You shouldn't lose a game," she shouted at her daughter. "You should win easily." Tom Burke, one of the club's proprietors, tried unsuccessfully to calm Mama.

Despite the loss of two games, Suzanne Lenglen was not shaken. She had, in fact, gained some confidence herself. The nervous tic had disappeared. And during the first games she had studied Helen, her mind had been racing, analyzing the movement and the shots of the American girl. She concluded that the American knew only one game—the power game. Helen Wills could pound away almost endlessly to wear down any opponent. Power and speed, but no finesse. No backup game if power and speed did not work. Suzanne had plenty of finesse and resourcefulness. She was the fox who would foil this lioness, would run circles around her. She had dropped two games in the process of learning about Helen's game. But now she knew.

Lenglen had also found a serious flaw in Wills's power game. And several journalists noticed it now also. Helen's backhand drives always went across court from corner to corner. She avoided firing the shot straight down the line to Suzanne's forehand. Those backhand drives were "immaculate in their purity of execution," one newsman wrote. And they were launched with a touch of top spin so that they dropped quickly. But they always came to Suzanne Lenglen's backhand. Al Laney believed that any other day Helen Wills's reluctance to vary the direction of her backhand shots would not have been of overwhelming importance. She could easily use it to overpower other women and drive them far off the court. But not against Suzanne and not on this day. On this day the lack of variety was to be something of a fatal chink in Helen Wills's otherwise perfect armor. Lenglen saw the weakness. Now she would exploit it perfectly. Her chess mind was calculating. She would play now to Helen's backhand, would feed her backhand, would challenge her to change the direction of that shot. And if Wills refused to take the bait and hit the shot she feared—the shot down the line—then Lenglen would herself hit the backhand down the line short. She would draw the American girl up to the net on the forehand side and then she would pass her or drive her back again to the backhand corner. She would run Helen Wills endlessly or pass her easily. But in either case she would take her apart.

In the fourth game Lenglen seized control of the set. She exchanged long backhand drives with Wills, staying behind the baseline on her backhand side, clearly tempting her to go for the easy winner down the forehand side. But Helen Wills did not go for those winners. She hit ball after ball deep to Lenglen's backhand. Suzanne suspected that if Helen decided to go for the forehand side she would try to run around her backhand. And in that case Lenglen would see the shot coming and would be on top of it in plenty of time. She caught each of Wills's long drives perfectly in the center of her racket and slightly undercut the returns so that the ball bounded just in front of Wills and stayed low. She gave Wills little speed to use in making those long drives. After several backhand exchanges Lenglen suddenly dropped a backhand shot straight down the line, sharply sliced. ("A favorite shot of mine is the backhand down the line!") This brought Wills hurrying forward reaching desperately to save the point. But her speed across the court was not great enough to turn Lenglen's drop shots into winners. Every time she came in and stayed at the net after a save, Lenglen passed her easily. Suzanne earned her points off purely executed passing shots that left Helen stretched out along the net trying awkwardly to get her racket into the ball as it floated an inch or two beyond her reach. Then, in the next rally, Wills again would be drawn into exchanging backhands. One newsman wrote that Helen Wills played as though she believed Suzanne Lenglen's weakness was her backhand. It wasn't. Nonetheless, the American girl attacked Suzanne's backhand with all of her strength and determination. But it was a futile and useless attack. Lenglen took ten straight points and she won them by playing against the American girl's best shots. Wills played as well as she had ever played. And she hit as hard as she had ever hit. And still she lost. It was clear she would have to alter her game now, mix up her attack. But before she abandoned her old game plan she was behind. Suzanne Lenglen took two more games for a 3–2 lead.

When the women changed courts at the end of the fifth game, Suzanne Lenglen's compatriots on the roofs and balconies and in the trees around the club shouted madly, joining those inside the club grounds in a thunderous salute to the resurgence of the Maid Marvel. They continued their roar as the sixth game began and as Lenglen took the first two points of that game off Wills's service. The umpire made another futile effort to quiet the crowd. His pleadings seemed more useless than before. The hooting and the hoopla continued.

Lenglen let Wills pull up to deuce in the sixth game, but then took two more points for the game and a 4–2 lead. It was time for Wills to shift her tactics, and she did just that in the seventh game. She tried to hit her service returns deep and then followed them to the net. Then she cut off Lenglen's drives with volleys or half volleys. She became surprisingly aggressive, even reckless. The first time she came in she won a point with a softly tapped volley just out of Lenglen's reach. She anticipated the direction of Lenglen's unsuccessful passing shots, intercepted them without difficulty and broke her service at 15, being passed but once. The score stood at 3–4. Now it was vital for the American girl to hold her own service in order to draw even.

But Wills could not hold her service against the Goddess. Lenglen made her own adjustment. Instead of going around the American girl at the net, she went up and over her, using perfectly arched offensive lobs. Wills raced frantically after the high shots and then came in behind her own ground strokes, only to be forced back again. She earned only one point on her own service, and Lenglen gave up only one on her service to win the first set at 6–3. The contestants received a standing ovation.

As the women changed courts, Suzanne paused for a moment in front of Mama's seat. Mama opened an emergency kit and handed Suzanne a small glass of iced cognac. Suzanne took two deep swallows and handed back the frosted glass. With the liquid she seemed to drink in renewed resolve. There was a noticeably new spring in her walk as she returned to the baseline to receive Helen's service.

Many Americans in the crowd had lost their optimism during that first set. Wills had played well at certain moments. Lenglen had played better. After taking the 2–1 lead Helen seemed to suffer from a momentary collapse. She relaxed and lost 10 points in a row and seemed for a time to have lost much of her spirit. Maybe it was the injured knee! It had begun to bleed again, and it appeared to slow her movement on the court. Yet she did not complain, nor did she take any stimulants between sets. But she was clearly relying too much on her power and too little on her footwork. She would have to raise the level of her game if she were to take the second set. She must change. Now.

Helen Wills found the first set uneventful. "There was nothing spectacular in it," she remembered later. She had lost first sets before. She had, in fact, lost first sets often in the previous season. In America she was still regarded as a brilliant three-set player. She warmed up slowly, got into the match only after several games. She could lose a first set and then come on like a completely new player in the remaining two sets, crushing her overconfident opponents. A brilliant three-set player. She still felt she could win. She found Lenglen's shots were not hit too hard and certainly they did not carry the pace of other women Helen had beaten. In fact, throughout the first set, ironically, she found her confidence increasing. The match was not over yet. Not by a long shot. She was hitting the ball well. Her ground strokes were going where she wanted them to go. She sensed how close she was to hurting the Maid Marvel. Wills was not overawed at all. She was breathing right down Suzanne's neck. And she suspected that Suzanne knew that, too.

Wills found Lenglen's steadiness somewhat disconcerting. She was placing the ball with "a precision that seemed almost unbelievable." But Suzanne was also concerned—even overly concerned—with conserving her strength. Wills had done most of the running in the first set, up and back, mostly. She was obviously exploiting Wills's lack of speed up and back, between the net and the baseline. Now, if Helen could make Suzanne do some of the running, she could grind her down, wear her out. Wills was young and strong, and she could run all day if she had to. But Lenglen could not. Run her, Helen was thinking. Run her. Even with the little running that the Goddess had done in the first set, she was already growing weary. When they passed at the net at the end of the first set Helen could see the toll the games had taken on the French woman. Some of her curls had escaped from beneath her pink headband and were slicked with perspiration on her forehead. The veins in her temple stood out clearly.

Wills served the opening game of the second set. She sliced her first service wide to Lenglen's forehand, drew the Maid Marvel off the court, then moved in quickly and took the return with a winning volley to the backhand side. The crowd loved it. She took three more points in rapid succession and without much difficulty. The last point of the game was nearly unbelievable: a beautiful topped backhand shot straight down the line. The shot completely outwitted Lenglen and left her standing flatfooted in the backcourt. Wills had raised the level of play once again.

If Lenglen was going to win she could not coast. She could not expect Helen Wills to beat herself, lose on her own errors. Suzanne would have to win the game on superb play. And so that magnificent computer in her mind continued to click away analyzing the movements and the strokes of the American girl. Her mind was working overtime, working at a furious pace, analyzing the feel of the ball on her racket, analyzing the increasing fatigue in her arms and legs and the slight congestion in her chest. She was carefully estimating the amount of reserve energy she might call up in a moment of crisis, keeping her nerves under control, keeping her confidence strong and hearing again the warnings of Papa and the persistent complaints from Mama on the sideline. Mama on the sideline. Mama could only whine. Papa might shout encouragement or strategy. But Papa was not present at courtside, now. Yet Suzanne could sense his presence. Could sense what he might be saying at this moment. She must continue. She must win. Suzanne was feeling the heat. The sun was almost directly overhead. Yet to remove her sweater would indicate that she was working hard to win. She must not allow Helen's partisans that pleasure. The sweater stayed on. Suzanne was perspiring heavily now, and the makeup was cracking and running down her cheeks and staining the silk of her dress. The little dark half moons under her eyes appeared from beneath the makeup and gave Suzanne the weird appearance of having aged years during the course of the match.

Across the net Wills had become acutely aware of Lenglen's calculations. She could feel the force now of the Lenglen mind. Suzanne was trying to save her strength—"making her mind do the running instead of her feet." Helen still felt strong. "I felt I could run as far on the court and for as long a time as Mlle. Lenglen," she later remembered. "This was a consoling thought. I felt that I could meet enough of her balls so that the rallies would be prolonged. . . ." She struggled to make Suzanne play her game, to make her run. At the same time she sensed the working of the Lenglen mind. She could almost feel that mind functioning every minute, every second, every instant. It was working to crush her. And she could sense Suzanne's fright in the second set. Could see her increasingly morbid visage. She could feel Suzanne wavering. And she stayed cool and thought again and again, "Every shot. Every shot."

Suzanne Lenglen served the second game of the second set and concentrated on recapturing the momentum of the match. She pulled ahead by two points and then let Helen Wills catch her. Then she managed to take two more points from deuce to win the game. But that American girl was leaning into her shots, battering them across the net with incredible pace. And the ball was getting heavier, and Suzanne could feel in her arm and shoulder the force of Helen's drives. She must win quickly.

But she could not win quickly. Wills held service in the third game by following her deep hard drives to the net and volleying for winners. Lenglen took two points in the game before dropping it to the aggressive and seemingly tireless American. When Suzanne served in the fourth game Helen continued coming to the net at every opportunity to drive home winner after winner. Lenglen started to scurry along the baseline, retrieving Wills's thunderous ground strokes and trying to transform them into deft passing shots. But she failed. Wills's anticipation had improved. She was waiting near the net for every shot, and she broke Lenglen's service in the fourth game. The American girl pulled ahead 3–1.

At the start of the fifth game Helen Wills walked to the baseline to serve but then had to wait. The Maid Marvel walked to the stands for a momentary conference with Mama. She asked for the emergency kit. Mama again quickly poured a glass of iced cognac. Helen stood watching in silence. Thousands of spectators watched in silence. With shaking hand, Suzanne tilted the small vial to her lips. Her hot breath instantly turned to ice crystals along the edge of the glass. Then she snapped her head back and poured the potion down her throat. An unsympathetic writer for *Time* magazine wrote that "as her cells took up the liquor, courage spouted through her veins, empurpled her falcon face. And her strength and spring seemed to return. Her cat cunning footwork began to work again."

Wills was also feeling the heat now. She sensed the increasing toll on her arms and legs and felt the stiffness in her injured knee. She was hitting every shot with all of her strength, unleashing all her reserves on every service. Power was her most reliable weapon, she believed. She was almost trying to bludgeon her way to a victory in this set. There was no thought at all of finesse. And no need for it. Power was the name of the game now. But power was becoming costly. She needed a moment's respite herself. And so in the fifth game she sought to save her legs. She stopped following her service to the net and tried instead to match Suzanne Lenglen on ground strokes from the baseline. But it did not work. That was the Maid Marvel's game. No one could best her at it. No one. Suzanne appeared to regain her confidence and her timing now, and her shots fell true one after another. It was a critical game, and Lenglen knew that she dare not fall behind to 1–4. Helen Wills's hesitation was the window of opportunity for her, and she capitalized on it by using sharply angled shots and long drives to force the American girl up and back, up and back. She broke Wills's service at 15 and then took her own after giving up one point. And in winning those two games she drew up to an even 3–3 in the set.

Each player desperately wanted the seventh game. Each seemed to sense the importance of moving ahead at this point. And so the seventh game of the second set was the hardest fought and perhaps the most important game of the match. Wills quickly fell behind on her service to 15–40. But then she surged back brilliantly. She appeared to have profited from her rest in the previous two games, and she unpacked some unpleasant surprises for Suzanne, who expected the soft backcourt game to continue until the end of the match. Wills again whirled herself into her shots, charging the net to cut off Lenglen's high drives and volley them back. She took three quick points to pull ahead. But then she hit an easy drive into the net and let Suzanne back into the game. Then Lenglen hit a drive long, and Wills missed an easy overhead smash off a desperate and short Lenglen lob. Helen became even more aggressive and assertive now, charging in, blocking an intended passing shot down the line and chopping a short volley that angled across the net and stopped in the forehand court on the opposite side. Then Suzanne hit long again on an attempted passing shot, and Helen had that seventh game. Fourteen points were fought over in the seventh game, the longest in the match. One writer called it "the most thrilling and terrifically fought game of the afternoon."

Lenglen was once again in jeopardy. She could not drop behind to 3–5. And although she had lost the seventh game, she could see that Wills had used up much of her remaining strength in winning it. Reporters on the sidelines heard Helen choking for breath now as she rushed back and forth from the net to the baseline. She needed a breather. But Suzanne would not give it to her.

Before serving the eighth game, Suzanne Lenglen took another gulp from her emergency kit. Then she served and won the first point. But Helen Wills again came back and took two points and the lead. The fourth point of the game involved an exceptionally long rally. Then Lenglen returned one of Wills's long forehand shots with a powerful forehand angled return. Helen moved for the ball near the juncture of the service line and the sideline. But then she held back on her swing and watched the ball bound well outside. Newsman Don Skene, sitting near

where the ball came down, watched it hit wide by "three inches at least."
Associated Press correspondent Ferdinand Tuohy also had no doubts
about the ball. "It struck far outside," he wrote. Wills watched it bound
away but did not hear the linesman call it out.

Cyril Tolley, the line judge, remained silent. Helen Wills stood for a
moment near where the ball went down, listening for the call. Then, in
an extremely rare gesture, she abandoned her silence and her serenity and
her poker-faced look. In a loud and clear voice, almost a desperate shout
that betrayed her anger, she demanded of Tolley, "What did you call
that ball?"

"Inside," he responded. "The shot was good!"

Helen Wills spun around at the linesman's words and threw her hand
into the air in a desperate gesture of ire at the linesman's blindness. A
score of voices in the crowd burst forth in a staccato chant, "Out! Out!
Out!" and cries of protest rang out from all corners of the club. Tolley
and Wills again exchanged glances. He seemed uncertain now. Helen saw
it in his eyes. Had he really seen the ball fall out? Helen suspected he had
not. Charles Aeschliman jumped up to assure the protesters that the linesman's call was correct. But Fred Moody, Helen's regular Riviera escort,
was sitting near the line too, and he knew that ball was out. He had no
doubts at all. "The ball was out and Helen was robbed," he told me.
"That Tolley call," as it became known in the years after the match,
"really burned her up," Moody remembered. "And I think that right
there the match was decided."

Now, in addition to being exhausted, Helen Wills was upset. Years
later, when she remembered this match, Helen emphasized the Tolley
call and her feelings about it. She was no longer certain which game it
occurred in or the precise circumstances of the call. But she did remember
its critical importance.

Despite her efforts to concentrate on every shot, the memory of the
Tolley call lingered in the back of Wills's mind. She could not shake it
off, that call that kept her from moving to one point away from a 5–3
lead. She continued to think about what might have been and played
without much spirit and dropped the next point and the eighth game.
Four all.

Wills pulled herself together in the next game. She held service after
letting Lenglen draw up to deuce. But Suzanne came right back to hold
service at love. Five all.

In the tenth game several newsmen noticed Wills's slackened pace of
play. She was once more banking her fires when she was ahead. She had
become somewhat tentative and was clearly holding back. Wallis Myers
also saw the change and saw how Suzanne Lenglen recognized it and exploited it. John Tunis saw disaster in Wills's lapse. "One fact is certain,"
he wrote in the *New Yorker*. "Could she have shaken off the unfortunate
habit of curbing her zeal just when its expression was most necessary, of

hauling in sail when the harbor was in full sight, could she have maintained a continuous and not a spasmodic pressure, there might well have been another ending to that most dramatic and intensely exciting encounter on the Riviera." Al Laney also wondered about Helen's "strange quietude" which was obviously allowing Lenglen to seize the momentum of the match again.

During the tenth game, the Goddess and the American Girl played an exceptionally long rally during which Wills ran to all four corners of the court and back and forth from the baseline to the net several times, only to lose the point. When she returned to the baseline to receive Lenglen's service she bent over and leaned heavily on her racket for several seconds. Suzanne stood behind her own baseline waiting for Helen to stand up and lose. Helen remained bent over breathing heavily. Finally, impatiently, the Goddess called out, "Service!" and Helen Wills looked up, then straightened up and readied herself. Suzanne tried to disguise her own physical exhaustion but was only partially successful. In the eleventh game, following a long rally, Wills hit a forehand drive that bounced good on the baseline and kicked away from Lenglen. The French woman was only a fraction of an inch from getting her racket into the ball. But she missed. She looked up quickly at the linesman for deliverance from the lost point. But there was no word from him. He was silent. The ball was good. And so Lenglen returned to the agonizing work at hand.

In the eleventh game Lenglen managed to transform her agony into victory. She broke Wills's service at thirty and appeared to be in control of the match. She now led 6–5 with her own service coming. Then, with renewed confidence she jumped out to a 40–15 lead and double match point in the twelfth game. At last Suzanne sensed the end. She hit her first match point down the middle to Wills's backhand and then stayed back for the return. There were several long exchanges as Helen tried to pull Suzanne into the forehand corner with some powerful crosscourt blasts. Eventually, Wills sent a sizzling drive deep into that corner. Lenglen moved over for the return, hesitated, and then stopped. Then she heard a wonderful wonderful wonderful sound as a loud and clear voice roared "Ouuuut!" Suzanne Lenglen flung the remaining two tennis balls she held high into the sky and skipped quickly to the net, a smile of relief on her face, her right hand extended. Helen Wills met her at the net and grasped her hand. The women looked into each other's eyes only for a moment, then turned and marched quickly toward the umpire's chair.

Photographers rushed onto the court and began snapping pictures. But the most famous photograph of that instant shows the two women meeting at the net and a hand extended toward the photographer from the corner of the picture. Someone seemed to be signaling the photographer to stop taking pictures. But why? Something was not right.

The tennis court was almost instantly engulfed by a mob and flowers seemed to arrive from everywhere, a riot of flowers. Suzanne's followers had prepared for this moment, and they were madly turning the court into an altar, a coronation ceremony had begun. Huge bundles and sprays of blossoms were carried onto the court. Photographers and newsmen swarmed around the two women, and there were delightful squeals of triumphant ecstasy from Suzanne's sycophants and camp followers. Demands were shouted out for the two women to stand side by side and to look this way or that, to smile and to shake hands again.

Meanwhile, from the far end of the court Lord Charles Hope frantically fought his way through the crowd, swimming through the shouting celebrants to the umpire's chair. When he was within a few feet of Commander Hillyard, he shouted out a shocking statement. "The shot was good!" he said. "I didn't call it out!"

There was suddenly a stunned silence as Hope's words were relayed through the crowd. Aeschliman and Fisher, who were standing next to the two contestants, instantly accepted the truth of Hope's declaration. And once Hillyard was certain that he had heard Hope right, he turned apologetically to Suzanne. "The match is not over," he said cautiously. "That ball was good."

Suzanne Lenglen gave the umpire a stunned look as the remark registered. Then she responded in a calm and deliberately measured tone, "Then we must go on." She turned and walked through the cheering throng back to the baseline. Those who had been standing near the umpire's chair and who understood what had happened now raced back to the stands shouting the incredible news. "The match is not over! The shot was good! The shot was good!"

Now there were screams and shouts of "Yes!" and "No!" from the crowd. But Lenglen did not hesitate. She was ready to go on. She was ready to accept the decision without question. The game was not over. She would accept what fate had in store for her.

One writer compared the false "out" call to the false armistice announcement on November 7, 1918, when millions of Americans reacted hysterically to a report that the World War had ended. There was still a good deal of confusion and indignation around the court and the stands. Lenglen was handed the tennis balls she had thrown away only a minute ago, her racket was retrieved and handed to her, and she stepped up to the baseline to serve for the match. Yet for several minutes she was forced to back away and wait while people found their seats or ran madly along the edge of the court. Part of the audience had risen to voice their opinions, and many people were waving their arms in protest, trying to stop the match. The whole incident, James Thurber wrote, made this contest "one of the most grotesque and thrilling and momentous games on record."

Helen Wills sensed that the part of the audience that understood tennis had become furious with the part that did not. Part of the crowd seemed to be calling for silence and another part continued hissing and protesting. The uproar and protest were so great that Helen suspected it might never subside. The scene was simply unparalleled. And for several minutes Helen felt removed, felt, she said, like an observer of some bizarre and phantasmic spectacle rather than a central participant in it.

What would the effect of this long disruption be on the players? It would take a moment or two to find out. And in those few moments Helen Wills appeared to come back strong. She saved the second match point and brought the game to deuce. Then with her hard drives and sharp crisp angles she took two more points and the twelfth game. Six to six.

But Lenglen had been distracted only for a few minutes. She was not yet beaten. She had not given up all hope. And John Tunis watched her recover now and wrote that "never in her long and luminous career did Suzanne Lenglen so justify her claim to greatness as at that moment."

Wills served the thirteenth game, and she hit her serves with all of her remaining strength. She leaned heavily into her shots again, took a full windup on her ground strokes and hurled forehand and backhand shots at the dancing Goddess. She came down hard on each service, as though she were pounding nails into the coffin of the Maid Marvel. And in a very real sense that is exactly what she was trying to do. But Lenglen stood up to the battering bravely and with incomparable expertise. She robbed Wills of three points and carried the game to love–40. Helen was surprised by Suzanne's sudden recovery, at the continuing control of her emotions. "She was a fine match player," Wills found. "Better than people realized. She had an astonishing amount of control and determination."

But so did the American Girl. She blasted her way back with three very hard-earned winners and pulled even at deuce. And then from deuce she continued her battering of the Goddess and moved to advantage. But Lenglen hung on tenaciously, never giving up, never giving in, never letting go. She pulled back to deuce. And then following two long rallies she hit two winners and took the game. Seven to six. Lenglen now serving.

Suzanne Lenglen served cautiously in the fourteenth game, placing each service with meticulous calculated care. The game see-sawed back and forth. Lenglen took the lead at 30–15, but then Wills took two points for a 40–30 lead. Again Suzanne showed her steadiness, earned a hard point and pulled up to deuce again. And then at deuce she double-faulted. There was a murmur from the crowd. This was terrible. Suzanne Lenglen double-faulted so rarely. And when she did it was a sign of trouble. She had double-faulted at Forest Hills and then had walked off the court. But she maintained her composure and pulled back to deuce. Finally, with one of her pretty placements she arrived once more at match point. This was fifteen minutes after she believed she had won the match.

She served to Wills's backhand once again and took the strong return with her forehand, punching over a drop shot just to the left of the center line. Wills responded with a running desperate save that was high over the net. Too high. It hung there for an instant. Hung there deliciously inviting as Lenglen gracefully danced forward concentrating on that ball. She caught it near the service line, shoulder high and slapped it back at an angle across the court for a winner. The match was over.

Now, for the second time the crowd rose to its feet and again exploded in cheering and applause that spread from the club grounds to the crowd outside and then down the streets of Cannes and to the rooftops and windows of the towering hotels. The hosannahs for Suzanne Lenglen filled every quiet place in the seaside city and echoed in the mountains behind the city and along the Croisette and into the casinos and in the alleys and the streets of Cannes.

This time Suzanne Lenglen did not run forward with her hand outstretched. She had been delivered. She had been given a respite. She had looked into the valley and had survived. As if by sorcery, she had been spared. She stood now as if stunned by it all in midcourt in a trance. She was quickly engulfed by the enthusiastic crowd. She was approached by bearers of flowers again, baskets, endless baskets of flowers. It was as if the earth were pushing up hills of flowers to fill the club. Suzanne was half carried and half pushed to the side of the court, where she collapsed onto a bench. The flowers were dropped around her nearly burying her. Soon only her wearied and wan face showed above the scented mounds erected in her behalf. Supplicants were offering flowers to their Goddess. Yet, at this moment of victory, Suzanne seemed completely heartbroken. She was visibly shaking. Lords and ladies and titled nobility from throughout the world fought their way through the crush to touch Suzanne, to offer their congratulations. Helen Wills was pushed up beside Suzanne Lenglen for a photograph. Then she was pushed past the Goddess and behind her. She stood for the photographers only for a moment. Then she was suddenly forgotten. The crowd pressed in around her to look at Lenglen. Wills was caught in the crush with no room to extend her arms in order to pull on her sweater. In fact only the long arms of Charles Aeschliman saved the two women from being squeezed in the crowd. And as Helen Wills watched, she saw more and more flowers arrive. There were floating continents of carnations and orchids. And there was a large pile of American beauty roses. Helen looked down on the Goddess and saw her suddenly break into convulsive sobbing.

Helen Wills felt strangely isolated from all of this. She felt almost invisible. Once again she was merely a spectator in a madhouse. She watched with both detachment and fascination. Suzanne was comforted now by Mama and by several friends. They helped her stand and then moved slowly in a sad almost funereal procession toward the sanctuary of the clubhouse. Helen watched. Gradually she became aware that she was standing entirely alone at the edge of the court now beside the crushed flowers that marked the way cleared for the exit of the winner. She turned her thoughts inward. She realized suddenly that she did not feel sad. She suspected that she should. She felt, instead, strange. Strange being alone on the court. When she turned to look for her mother, someone touched her arm softly. It was Fred Moody. "You played awfully well," he whispered. And then he escorted her toward the exit.

While the ecstatic crowd swirled and eddied and swallowed up the victor, Cyril Tolley moved cautiously to the edge of the court where a few games earlier he had seen a tennis ball fall near the line. He stood near the spot and poked around with his cane looking for the exact place where that ball had fallen. He studied the clay both inside and outside the line. After a few minutes he gave up his search and walked away. He never told anyone if he had found the mark he was looking for and which side of the line it was on.

James Thurber summed up the end of the match and wrote that Helen Wills, "the girl in white," walked silently from the throne that the crowd was quickly constructing for Suzanne Lenglen. She detached herself from the maelstrom. "Helen Wills had been defeated and was going home."

"She went home quietly, directly, without looking around, as she always did when a match ended." Helen did not speak, not even when she was spoken to now. She just looked ahead and walked from the court. "The only color that relieved the whiteness of her face and her dress, a whiteness so pathetically odd against the silver and red and pink colored scene, was a bright flush on her cheeks. But it wasn't a flush that comes from being ashamed or crushed," Thurber suggested. "It might well have been a flush of pride. At any rate," he concluded, "to the crowd that watched from the stands it was a sort of red badge of courage with as much significance as the glory that broke about the victorious head of Suzanne Lenglen."

And although he did not say it, Helen Wills had been to play the Great Lenglen and had found her not much greater than herself. The memory of this match would fade like the flowers around Suzanne Lenglen. Yet Helen Wills could remain sure of one thing on this day. She had played like the champion that she was. And she knew it. There was no shame in this loss. She had forced the Goddess to play her very best. And she had pushed her to the outermost limits of her endurance. Following the match, Suzanne looked like a Goddess in pain. As Jean Borotra assessed Lenglen's accomplishment, "It was a heartbreaking victory."

Thurber wrote that Helen Wills had bet "the greatest woman tennis player in the world since the time when Helen was fondling dolls, fought her with everything she had, smashed with her, drove with her, volleyed with her until she had the French champion so greatly on the run that at times it seemed like the baseline on Lenglen's side of the court was a dropping off place." To beat Helen the next time they met Suzanne would have to play even better. Helen had met "a baptism of fire which was strange and new to her: she encountered a variety and brilliance of technique that she had never encountered before. And having come through it so superbly, the unfinished sentence on everybody's lips was 'the next time.' . . ."

One reporter ran to Wills and asked for a final comment on the match. She provided him with a prophetic remark that he scribbled down to be wired around the world. "There will be other tennis matches," the American Girl said. "There are other years coming."

Newsmen and photographers broke from the crowd and dashed to the wire service offices and the telephones. One small clique of journalists chartered an airplane to stand by on an airstrip just outside the city. They hoped to get their photographs and stories to London before their competition. But some of the competition chartered another plane. Both planes took off within minutes of the conclusion of the contest. Neither, however, made it to London. One fell in the Durance Valley after developing engine trouble, and the other came down near Lyons a little later. A third group of journalists boarded the express train north, and they became the first newsmen to reach Paris, Le Havre, and London with photographs of the match.

Meanwhile, in the cramped clubhouse of the Carlton Club, Suzanne Lenglen stumbled into a table where part of the day's income was being counted and tens of thousands of francs were scattered on the floor. She then collapsed onto the money and rolled back and forth on the paper currency carpet moaning and whimpering. It was a fitting private finale to the most profitable sporting event ever staged on the Riviera. Exactly how many of those bills would be carried back to the Lenglen villa, no one could ever say. It remained a well-guarded secret.

When the singles match was over, newsmen struggled to come up with precise closing paragraphs for their melodramatic narrative accounts of the contest. What should be remembered of this confrontation of the Goddess and the American Girl? The correspondent for the London *Times* concluded that Suzanne Lenglen had used extreme care and perfect judgment and had played her "characteristically beautiful game" throughout the morning. She had not made more than half a dozen mistakes or bad shots in the entire match. What Helen won, he said, she had earned. "It was coolness and experience that won in the end."

Al Laney left the club and made his way to a seat in a quiet and unhurried section on the Croisette. There he sat and reflected on the incredible performance he had just witnessed. He would think about the match, reflect on it, again and again in the coming years. His conclusions in the future would be no different from his conclusions on this day. He believed that had the conditions been more normal, Suzanne Lenglen would have won by a more comfortable margin. If the two women had met again a year later, then Lenglen would have won again, but not as easily as on this day. And if they had played against each other regularly, Suzanne would have eventually been overtaken and beaten by Helen.

But Lenglen was still at her peak on this day, Laney believed, and she was better than Wills. Perhaps, he suggested, she was even slightly past her peak. Perhaps she was going into a decline. After all, for more than six years she had reigned as the queen of tennis. That was a very long time for a champion in any sport. Helen would eventually discover for herself just how difficult a six-year reign might be for a champion.

Laney believed that on this warm morning in Cannes a pair of tennis stars from different generations had clashed. Destiny was carrying them in different directions, one up and the other down. For a moment in Cannes their paths had crossed. Lenglen had won. But in a short time she would burn out. It was rare for two such stars to meet, for the best player of one generation to play against the best player of the next generation. Had they met again in the next years, the world would have had the thrilling chance of seeing an incomparable series of tennis contests.

In San Francisco, Blanche Ashbaugh reported that "we" were far from being beaten. There were indeed other years and other matches coming. "Helen may have been defeated in the first match, but she is never beaten. She is a glutton for punishment. She plays better when she is down than when she is on top. She will come back for more and more until eventually she wins out. It is up to the French girl to give her a chance." And, like many Americans, Ashbaugh believed that Helen had lost the match because of "an unfair line call" that had broken her concentration.

In New York there was considerable enthusiasm for the match and officials of the USLTA, and leading American players waited anxiously for news of the outcome. Molla Mallory was disappointed in accounts of Helen Wills's play and thought she could have won had she taken the fight more aggressively to Suzanne Lenglen, had she relentlessly pressed the French star. "You can never beat Suzanne playing a soft game," Molla concluded. "We all told Helen before she left to carry the game to Lenglen and smash the ball all the time."

Bill Tilden was disappointed at being upstaged by two women, but he did offer a brief statement to the press. "I don't like to comment on a match I didn't see," he said. "However, I am glad they played and sorry Helen lost." René Lacoste called it "a great victory for Suzanne," but said it was also "a glorious defeat for Helen."

In Paris, journalist William Shirer read of the match and listened to reporters' analyses of the play. His conclusion contrasted with that of Al Laney. "Wills, I am sure, would certainly have blown her off the courts the next year," he wrote. "In women's tennis the day of the graceful elegant player who won by shrewd placements was over. The future belonged to the slugger with the blazing serve."

In the *New York Times,* Allison Danzig concluded that a myth had been shattered and "a precious jewel added to the champion's crown" when the two women played. Suzanne Lenglen was no longer the unrivaled queen of the tennis world. She had only demonstrated that she still held the championship qualities of courage and a fighting heart. But she was no longer beyond comparison with any other woman. She had lost a good deal of prestige in her match. Without doubt the American girl was a player to be reckoned with. To Helen Wills belonged the honor of breaking the spell that the name of the great Suzanne Lenglen had cast over so many opponents for so many years, Danzig wrote. Critics on the Riviera who had laughed at Helen's chances for victory now acclaimed her as a dangerous rival. And many of them were so impressed that they predicted an entirely different outcome the next time the two women met.

News of the match was received in Berkeley, California, at 4:16 a.m. In thousands of homes and in clubs where all-night parties were held, the bulletins from Cannes were read and analyzed. Newspapers throughout the country began to roll their presses with special editions. Clarence Wills, father of "America's hope on the courts," according to the *New York Times,* said that he was proud of his daughter's accomplishment in extending Lenglen in the second set. "She made a wonderful fight and she will play better over there because of this taste of defeat," he predicted. In a few weeks, he said, his daughter would be in top form. And at Wimbledon in June he was sure she would take Suzanne.

In Paris, public opinion along the boulevards seemed surprisingly pro-Wills. Most commentary pointed out how little difference there really was in the prowess of the two women. No one was willing to express confidence in Lenglen's ability to repeat her victory. And the editor of *L'Echo des Sports* wrote that "one can say that Helen is the greatest tennis player in the world after Suzanne, but far from definitely solving the problem of superiority, this encounter complicates it. We had grown to consider the French champion as a class apart; that short of accident her position could not be threatened by any rivals. Yesterday's match proves that Suzanne is not in a class of her own above all others; that her defeat can be classed among the possible if not the normal eventualities."

The British public seemed fully as interested in the match as were the Americans and the French. For weeks English papers were filled with detailed reports of the wanderings and the words of the women stars. The result was that the match was followed as enthusiastically as the Derby. Several papers eventually deplored the "boosting" that had been given the match. It had all been quite degrading, they said. The *Westminster Gazette* complained about the contemporary "tendency to magnify the difficulties incidental to all sporting competitions and so turn them into front-page sensations." "Seldom has any sporting event aroused so much interest beforehand," the correspondent for the *Daily Mail* reported, "and seldom has such interest had such a thrilling climax. Both victor and vanquished had won fresh laurels." "Everybody wanted to see Miss Wills make a good show," said the correspondent for the *Daily Chronicle,* "and that she unquestionably did." "In acclaiming Mlle. Lenglen's latest victory," the *Morning Post* said, "we must not forget to give our heartiest congratulations to Miss Wills, who in one point of the game, at any rate in the severity of her hitting, excelled her opponent and made a glorious fight of the match."

"The strain of the match must have been exhausting," the *Daily Telegraph* reporter said. "We are not inclined to take too seriously the expression of disgust with which Mlle. Lenglen is credited. [Suzanne had told correspondents following her win, "Now, for God's sake, will you English and Americans leave me alone for a moment and accept my supremacy, however much it may be getting boresome?"] It is more pleasant to recall the sportsman-like comment of Miss Wills that 'Mlle. Lenglen is just as good as I thought she would be.' That is the spirit in which games should be played even for championships." The *Evening News* reported that "it seemed as if the earth itself would pause in its rotation, as if all the international excitement would end in an appeal to the League of Nations. Anything might have happened, including a war between the United States and France." But after the match, the same paper happily concluded, "The universe can now go on as before."

Columnist Harry Smith of the *San Francisco Chronicle* saw the bright side of Helen Wills's performance. "It was a defeat," he pointed out, "not without its happier side. The scores indicated how bitterly contested was the game and what wonderful resistance was offered by the little miss from Berkeley." And then there was the knee injury. "Whether or not the injured knee had something to do with the outcome would be hard to say," Smith claimed. "Certainly, as good sportsmen, we of America will not be anxious to offer that as an alibi," he wrote, introducing it as an alibi. "We much prefer to stand upon the result and await the future. Helen and Suzanne may meet again this season. It is quite questionable whether our Helen would be returned the winner. Yet I am sure that another year might tell the story. Sooner or later, I am sure, Helen Wills will be waving the Stars and Stripes from the top of the heap."

Smith realized, though, that what had happened was one of the biggest sporting shows in the world, ever. People stayed up until 3:00 a.m. to get the news and newspapers held back their presses in order to put the results of the match on page one. Men and women who had never seen a tennis match in their lives suddenly discussed the details of this one. Thousands of people left their "listening sets" turned on in order to be awakened by the first news bulletins. And thousands of others besieged newspaper offices with telephone calls requesting the scores. "It may be many a day before we have a situation resembling one that has passed into history," he wrote. "Even a return match in the summer would hardly have the same tenseness."

And what changes it had produced for the sport! Smith found that multitudes of people in northern California were now venturing out into the sun each day and facilely counting "fifteen-love, thirty-love and so on." Before hearing of Helen Wills in France, these same people never both-erd to inquire into the technique of tennis and now they wanted to know all about the sport. In short, tennis had gained tens of thousands of con-verts in the days since Helen traveled to France. And countless others had their curiosity aroused by the drama in Cannes and they were now look-ing for tennis stories in the newspaper.

And what did Suzanne Lenglen think of the match? Shortly after her victory she retired to a room that had been reserved for her in the Carlton Hotel. There she spoke with Ferdinand Tuohy of the Associated Press. She said that her tennis had not been distinguished on this day because of her concern for Papa. And the noise had distracted her. She did not like to beg an audience to be quiet. She believed that she would improve in the following days and would turn back all challengers. All. What about the American girl? "Helen showed more intelligence than I imagined," Suzanne said in a backhanded compliment. "She has style and production of strokes. She will improve." Tuohy wanted a more charitable assessment of Helen's abilities. Suzanne did not provide one. Suzanne Lenglen's friend Baron de Morpurgo volunteered that Suzanne had played far be-low form. She had not put any of her placements exactly where she wanted them. When asked if Helen's play might have been at least partly responsible for that, Morpurgo conceded reluctantly that such just might be the case.

In their excitement, many reporters and fans missed the other final match of the Cannes tournament. It was too bad, because it again pitted Helen Wills against Suzanne Lenglen, and it gave the spectators who re-mained in the club an additional revealing look at the relative talents of the Goddess and the American Girl. The finals of the Carlton Club wom-en's doubles championship began shortly after 2:00 p.m. The crowd had thinned since the completion of the singles match. But those who re-mained in the club seemed even less restrained in their enthusiasm than the morning crowd. They were willing now to make demonstrations be-fore, during, and after every point. And, once again, their expectations of another great match were fulfilled.

In the women's doubles final, Wills and Lenglen faced each other with partners. Helen was paired with Helene Contostavlos and Suzanne with Didi Vlasto. Helen Wills appeared now to be completely loose as the match got under way. She had nothing to lose by playing a daring and almost reckless game, and she was noticeably more dashing in her play. She felt free to attack on every point and to use all of her remaining power. Her knee had been rebandaged during the interval between the matches. And she seemed fresh and energetic, almost as if this were her first match of the day.

Almost all of the newsmen had left the Carlton Club to file their stories or to complete their accounts of the singles match. And so coverage of the doubles was sparse. Most tennis fans never even knew the match had been played. And that was unfortunate because it might well have altered their predictions concerning the outcome of future contests in singles between Helen and Suzanne.

In the doubles contest Helen Wills advanced quickly to the net on every point, daring Lenglen and Vlasto to try to pass her. She hit every stroke with all of her determination and might. And, whenever possible, she aimed her shots directly at Lenglen. Wills was clearly trying to challenge the Goddess again and to show her own superior skills to the crowd. She was almost brazen as she played for blood, and the crowd loved every minute of it. The effect of this strategy on Suzanne Lenglen was devastating. Every time Wills came to the net she blasted picture-perfect volleys for winners. Vlasto and Lenglen played everything they could get right at Contostavlos, lobbing over Wills and hitting awkward shots crosscourt and out of her reach. Helen Wills started to poach almost shamelessly, at times seeming to forget that she had a doubles partner.

The match went to 6–4, 8–6, one game longer than the singles final. Lenglen and Vlasto won. But they appeared to have beaten Contostavlos and not Wills. Their strategy was focused on playing keep-away from the American Girl.

Wills's ferocious versatility in the contest crushed Lenglen both physically and psychologically. The Goddess was near complete collapse in the second set, and she had to depend on Vlasto to produce the final push for the victory. And when it was all over the crowd stood and hooted and yelled their heads off for Wills and then they engulfed her as they had Lenglen only a few hours earlier. In the midst of this partisan outburst, Suzanne collapsed and fell to the clay and had to be carried from the court. Wills shook hands with Vlasto but did not even look in the direction of Lenglen. Nor did she ask about Suzanne's health. She just left. And as she walked from the club to her hotel she was followed this time by a mob of screaming, worshipping fans who now believed that Helen Wills was indeed the best player in the world. They had seen it demonstrated in the doubles. God pity poor Suzanne should they ever face each other in singles again. Next time, everyone was now saying. Next time. Next time.

When Suzanne Lenglen was escorted from the Carlton Club, some reporters heard Mama bitterly chastising her for losing so many games to the American girl and her partner. Suzanne listened to this tirade and then slashed back: "There will come a time when I cannot explain losses of games or even of sets, matches and tournaments. Get ready!"

And what were Helen Wills's conclusions about all of this? Later, somewhat philosophically, she wrote, "On one of the best courts in the South of France I played a match which happened to draw a larger gallery than usual. I was defeated because my opponent had played a better game. The arrangements, umpiring, court, and so on had been perfect. My youth was certainly not blighted by the result." She did not mention the score of the match. And she did not mention the doubles match that followed. And she did not mention the name of her opponent.

CHAPTER

⋯⋙ V ⋘⋯

OTHER MATCHES

"There will be other matches. There are other years
coming."   —Helen Wills, February 1926

"They bury me too soon. I am not finished yet."
                    —Suzanne Lenglen, February 1926

"ONE little vagary of fate," the novelist Vincente Blasco Ibañez wrote
of the Wills-Lenglen contest in Cannes, "and the result might have been
different." Until the last ball fell beyond the baseline there had been the
possibility of the match swinging suddenly to the underdog American
Girl. All of the post-match celebration and shouting could never disguise
the fact that Suzanne Lenglen had not so much triumphed as escaped. Unable to fulfill her expectations of crushing the young challenger quickly
and convincingly, the victorious Suzanne ironically suffered in the aftermath of the match from a serious case of severely diminished prestige.
Moreover, many of the observers and writers at courtside in Cannes insisted that the colorful encounter represented merely the opening act of a
compelling drama whose conclusion was yet to be disclosed. Suzanne Lenglen had obviously not proven beyond a reasonable doubt that she was
the best female tennis player in the world. And although she had defended
her popular title successfully this time, her throne had been rocked and
her post-match perch appeared to be alarmingly precarious.

One little vagary of fate and the word sung over the long-distance telephone line between the Carlton Hotel in Cannes and the Villa Ariem in
Nice early in the afternoon of February 16, 1926, might not have been the
sweet sounding "Victoire!" But the gods had been kind, and Papa Lenglen
had been wrong this time, so Suzanne telephoned the bittersweet news of
her victory to Papa soon after she had staggered from the clubhouse of the
Carlton Club. During the rest of the afternoon hundreds of congratulatory
telegrams were delivered to the Villa Ariem, and beneath that flood of paper praise Papa's misgivings and warnings about the clash in Cannes were
buried and forgotten. Suzanne's dramatic win cleared the way for a tearful
and melodramatic reconciliation. She was welcomed home that evening
with open arms and sonorous statements of compassion and clemency. Suzanne's American adviser, Charles Willen, was unceremoniously dumped.
Once more the French Goddess was safe within the protective embrace of
Papa, and all was right with the world.

In the next few days several French journalists demanded some sort of official governmental recognition for Lenglen's Cannes performance. An editor for *Le Journal* suggested that Suzanne be awarded the Legion of Honor without further delay, and other editors chorused approval. Yet the journalistic conjubilation lacked the conviction and the certitude that had characterized previous celebrations of the feats of the Maid Marvel. The troubling specter of Helen Wills now haunted those who sang songs of praise for Suzanne Lenglen. Oh, if only Suzanne had ground Helen into the clay as she had Molla Mallory! Then there would be no cause for moderation in the celebration. But in Cannes the American girl had actually gained in reputation and stature. She had lost, but she had not been broken. There would have to be another test, it was obvious. The press knew it, and the public knew it, and Suzanne knew it. The lingering doubts about the relative talents of Helen and Suzanne must be addressed and answered convincingly. But where and when? Perhaps in Nice. That was where Molla had been dispatched once and for all. But no matter the place, they must play again and this time Suzanne Lenglen must play as all of France knew she could play and as they had seen her play before— like the Goddess that she was.

For several days after the Cannes match the Lenglens lived an almost reclusive existence in Nice. The dark cretonne curtains of the Villa Ariem were drawn and visitors kept to a minimum. There was concern for the emotional and physical condition of Suzanne, who had suffered much more than a loss of prestige at Cannes. She was utterly shattered by her winning experience. Her collapse on the court following the doubles match in Cannes represented only a glimpse of things to come. In the next several days at home she was completely overcome by a recrudescent depression. Mama and Papa put up a good front and pretended that little was wrong, that Suzanne was merely physically exhausted. In fact they were gravely concerned about Suzanne's deep, dark despair. Visitors to the Lenglen villa wondered whether the administration of last rites might be more appropriate than an award of the Legion of Honor.

One of the favored few admitted to the Villa Ariem at this time was Ferdinand Tuohy, the Riviera correspondent for the Associated Press, who had interviewed Suzanne right after the singles match in Cannes. Tuohy was the only American correspondent Lenglen considered to be objective and well informed. She had, nonetheless, turned on him after her victory and denounced him for his doubts concerning her ability to win. Now she asked to see him. Tuohy was greeted at the door by Papa and advised, "Poor Little One; she is very tired, but she wanted to see you; she wants to talk with someone who has been impartial. She will see you."

Suzanne was still in bed recovering, and Tuohy was led into her presence there. Her "cozy little room," he found, was furnished in a Louis XV style and glittered with scores of silver and gold cups won by Suzanne.

The Goddess was attired for this meeting in a simple blue kimono trimmed with Bruges lace. Hundreds of telegrams and messages lay strewn about the room. The first thing Suzanne asked about was Helen Wills. When Tuohy confessed that the American girl was also exhausted and had requested and received a postponement of her opening match in the Beaulieu tournament, Suzanne could barely conceal her elation. "Poor little girl," she said of Helen. "I know how it feels. Look at me! I have stayed in bed all day. But I am getting to be an old woman," the twenty-six-year-old Goddess insisted. "She is a mere child." Then Suzanne added some kind words for the American challenger. "She is a good sport," she said, "a nice little girl."

Lenglen then spoke of losing her titles some day and suggested that she would rather lose them to Helen Wills than to anyone else. But such talk visibly unsettled the Goddess, and Papa interrupted. "Be quiet; don't get excited," he counseled. "You are a good little girl; you are all right. Don't cry," he said when he saw tears well up in Suzanne's eyes. Lenglen then apologized for her bitter remarks to Tuohy in Cannes. "Please don't be angry at what I said yesterday after the match," she asked. "I was nervous and excited when I said I knew you would have to congratulate me on the victory. Please do not think I am so conceited that I do not know I must be beaten some time. But it was the crowds, environment, and reaction—I don't know." She had been very nervous before the match, she said. And she had not slept. "Was there ever a match advertised as much as mine with Miss Wills?" she asked. "Were we not treated like two prizefighters, from cinema rights down to the bill posters?"

Papa once more interrupted and drew the covers, soothing her and softly whispering, "All right, all right, my little one. I think you had better try to sleep now." Suzanne, "a vision of desolation and despair," then turned and buried her face in her pillow and sobbed. "She did not, at the moment, exemplify the fame and splendor of a world's champion as generally pictured," he observed.

Papa tried to explain the situation to the newsman. In Cannes she had faced enormous difficulties in playing against his advice and before such an unruly crowd and with incompetent officials and without the reassuring presence of her Papa on the sideline. It would not happen again, he vowed. She would play Helen Wills again, probably in Nice. She would win, and there would be no excuses. Papa did not like the fact that Helen had complained about the tennis balls used in Nice earlier, and he particularly objected to suggestions by the press that undue influence had been used to get the adoption of the grooved ball that would give Suzanne an unfair advantage on the court. Suzanne needed no special advantages. "We have given orders that the kind of ball with which Miss Wills always plays in America shall be bought for our tournament in Nice in March," he said. "Suzanne is not satisfied with the score she made against your champion on Tuesday. She feels that she can do better and asserts that she played below form. Her most intense desire is to meet Miss Wills again and show that the score of 6–3, 8–6 was wrong."

Papa also discussed the family concern with money. The franc was in deep trouble, and the Lenglen family was in deep trouble. "Poor child," he said of Suzanne. "I would like to assure her future against want. We were comfortably off, but not rich. I am getting old." An American promoter had offered Suzanne $20,000 to turn professional and tour the United States, he revealed. "Twenty thousand dollars is a lot of francs; it would be wealth for my little girl." Yet, despite the attractive offer, "We cannot turn professional; this is not boxing. She won't hear of it."

There were widespread rumors that Suzanne need not turn professional because she had received a generous cut from the gate receipts of the Carlton Club. No doubt such stories were spread by the American press in a concerted effort to discredit and shame the French woman, Papa believed. And Suzanne suffered deeply from such accusations. After the match Suzanne visited an antique shop in Nice and purchased a small statue of St. Luke. The shopkeeper asked 400 francs for the statue but Suzanne bargained with him and bought it for 300 francs. He then asked her why she was bargaining "after all the money you made!" Suzanne shot back that she had received no pay for her play in Cannes. But her reputation was stained by talk of sharing the gate, particularly when she was compared with the American girl, whom the press continued to portray as a pure and unmonied character.

When a film of the Cannes match was shown in a theater in Nice on February 18, Lenglen ventured from her bed to see it, but walked out of the theater before the film was half completed. She appeared greatly agitated and disturbed, and when asked what was wrong, replied, "I played too bad for anything. It makes me sick just to look at it."

The only really encouraging news for Lenglen in this post-match period came from the United States. There, three of Suzanne's compatriots—René Lacoste, Jean Borotra, and Jacques Brugnon—humbled America's best male players and left the French standing proudly atop the tennis world. In the U.S. Indoor Championships played at the 7th Regiment Armory in New York City the French trio defeated Bill Tilden, Vincent Richards, and Frank Hunter. The first to fall was Richards, who was beaten by Lacoste, "the small Frenchman whose face shows all too clearly his partiality for the vices that infect his country and capital city," *Time* magazine reported. The galleries apparently expected that another clean-living American would never yield to such an opponent. But they were wrong again: Richards, playing well, lost to Lacoste, who played better, 6–4, 6–4.

Then it was Bill Tilden's turn. Big Bill entered the court clearly set to avenge Richards's loss. It was the sort of setting and situation the lanky melodramatic American champion adored. In the first set, Borotra and Tilden held their own services through twenty-two games. The crowd thought it was wonderful that Tilden would give his feisty opponent such a chance by toying with him. Surely the Frenchman, who lived in a country without prohibition, would not have the stamina to match the healthy teetotaling American. But then something unexpected happened. Borotra broke Tilden's service and held his own service to take the opening set at 13–11. Tilden was exhausted by the long set, and Borotra was not. The Frenchman beat Big Bill in the second set, 6–3.

Brugnon was considered the weakest member of the French trio. With his small rakish moustache and his pale face, he looked, *Time* reported, "like a man who would be much more at home at a cafe table than on a tennis court." Frank Hunter, on the other hand, was the epitome of fine young American manhood. America could be vindicated at long last. But again it did not happen. Brugnon outplayed Hunter from the opening service and took him 6–4, 6–4. The French then celebrated Washington's birthday in New York City by playing against one another in an all-French final in which Lacoste beat Borotra.

But the American men had one more chance. A special exhibition match was arranged for the next week, again in the Seventh Regiment Armory. This time around, it was hoped, the American men would show their stuff. But once more they did not. Lacoste beat Tilden. Richards gained some pride for his country by beating Borotra in three sets. The USLTA, meanwhile, concluded that enough was enough and refused to sanction another exhibition between the Frenchmen and the faltering American men.

The news of Tilden's double defeat at the hands of the French players was a bracing tonic for Suzanne Lenglen. She remembered Tilden wishing her ill when she played against Molla Mallory. She told reporters how he had actually "lured" her into a match against him just so he could beat her before a crowd of journalists. Now at last, she said, she was simply delighted that she had lived long enough to see the despicable American champion humbled before an audience of his own countrymen by a French player. It was a glorious day, indeed.

Lenglen continued to spend most of her time in bed in the Villa Ariem recovering. She was scheduled to play in the women's doubles in the Beaulieu tournament with one of her regular partners, Mrs. Phyllis Satterthwaite. In deference to Suzanne, the opposing women's pairs in the early rounds of the tournament were persuaded to default in order to make the route to the title a bit easier for Lenglen and her partner and to prevent the embarrassing necessity of a request for postponement. She had not, of course, entered the singles competition, where there was a good chance she would run into Helen Wills. Capacity crowds turned out to watch the play of the two women and to evaluate their chances in the next big confrontation. What the crowds saw was both surprising and shocking.

After being granted a postponement of one day, Helen Wills appeared on the courts for the Beaulieu tournament on February 18. She was pale and her face was drawn, yet she played with her old familiar power. She won her opening matches in both the singles and the mixed doubles with her partner, Charles Kingsley of England.

At Beaulieu, Helen quickly captured the attention and the adulation of the audience. She acted as though the match with Suzanne Lenglen was like any other and seemed completely unbothered by the loss. Even if she was not yet the queen of Riviera tennis, she was certainly behaving like a queen and playing like one. She fully expected to meet Suzanne again soon, and this time she would be even better prepared. Helen Wills and Papa Lenglen agreed on at least one important point: the score of that first Wills-Lenglen match did not accurately reflect the relative talents of the two women. In the second match the result would be dramatically different.

After winning her opening singles match and giving up only fifteen points in two sets, Wills spoke with correspondent Don Skene. The day of rest had done wonders for her, she said. And although her injured knee was still giving her some trouble, it was healing nicely. She also said that she liked the Beaulieu courts better than those of the Carlton Club. The light was much better here she found; she confessed that she had been badly bothered by the odd angle of the light at the Carlton Club, like so many other visiting players over the past several years. Helen also had encouraging news for her fans. She said she was staying for another month on the Riviera and announced that she would in fact play in the singles competition at the Nice Club—Suzanne Lenglen's home club—in the second week of March. And since it was assumed that Suzanne would certainly defend her singles title in that tournament, it was likely that a second meeting between the two women would take place there. And Helen welcomed that probability. In fact, Don Skene reported, no sooner had Wills sent her entry to the club than construction work on a 10,000-seat gallery was begun by the management.

Charles Lenglen affirmed the fact that Helen's entry had been received, and he assured American newsmen that he would do everything possible to provide her with everything she needed to play her best in Nice. "You may rest assured," he told the press, "that Miss Helen Wills will get at Nice a square deal and the best welcome of her Riviera sojourn. I will go out of my way to make it pleasant for her. I would not want anyone to believe that I would take advantage of my position with the Nice Club to favor my daughter."

On February 19, Wills played two more rounds in singles on the Beaulieu courts. Her performance this time was stunning, and she gave the Lenglen entourage something serious to cluck about. In two matches she gave up but one game. She did not leave the court between matches but elected to stay on the clay rather grim-faced and await her next victim. Helen won her first set of the day in the incredible time of nine minutes; the second took slightly longer. Helen dropped one game in the second set of her second match because she experimented with her game, playing a rather daring serve and volley game on the slow, heavily watered French clay. She concentrated on her power service and then followed the ball to the net in order to volley any return. She also experimented with a heavily sliced service to the deuce court that pulled her opponent far outside and opened up a rich opportunity to cut off the return with a winning volley. Helen toyed with her opponent, who had no defense for such a game—a game played on the Riviera by only one other player, the bounding Basque, Jean Borotra.

Reporters and fans alike were intrigued by Wills's serve-and-volley der-ring-do. Why had she adopted it at this point? She responded good hu-moredly, "All you gentlemen have been saying that I am weak at net vol-leying. Then, of course, you must be right. I am trying to improve my playing in this particular weak spot." Reporters found her serve-and-volley game on clay to be both splendid and deadly, and they doubted that there was a female player around—any female player—who could stand up to the quick rush and the pounding that Wills gave with her powerful combination punch volleys.

While Wills sailed on to victory after victory, the Riviera world awaited the return of Lenglen in order to see how the Goddess had recovered from her victory over the American Girl. When Suzanne finally made her ap-pearance in Beaulieu, it was clear why she had delayed her return to ten-nis. Don Skene reported that "a ghastly pale, almost hysterical woman who once was the flashing spirited Suzanne Lenglen made her first ap-pearance on the tennis courts this afternoon since her historic struggle with Helen Wills last Tuesday. Hovering on the brink of a nervous break-down and playing erratically, the ghost of the world-famous French tennis tigress wobbled through to a victory against a pair of unknowns in the women's doubles and then withdrew from the Beaulieu tournament." That, in a nutshell, summed up Suzanne's comeback.

The embarrassing episode was explained by several of Suzanne's close friends. The Goddess had started for the Beaulieu tournament early in the morning but then suffered from one of her periodic nervous collapses in her automobile on the way. She was rushed back to Nice. A physician was summoned. He examined the champion and advised her not to play. He then administered stimulants, and Suzanne, buoyed up by those stimu-lants, again set out for Beaulieu. She was accompanied this time by Mama Lenglen and by a close friend, Lady Wavertree. Unfortunately, on her sec-ond attempt she made it to Beaulieu.

Why had Suzanne Lenglen acted against her doctor's orders this time? Apparently, the Lenglen family financial situation along with the increas-ing pressures exerted by the Riviera tennis, hotel, and casino interests in-fluenced her to get up and play. Papa thought the play would aid her re-covery. The applause from the friendly gallery would quickly restore her confidence and her nerves, he believed. But instead, Suzanne's appearance on the court was disastrous and resulted in a further setback to her health. Even in the warm-up Suzanne mis-hit the ball constantly. Once the match was under way, the opposition centered their attack on Lenglen, a reversal from every previous doubles match in which the Goddess had participated. Lenglen, reporters found, played like a rank beginner, and spectators who had followed her on the Riviera for several seasons concluded that she probably had come to the end of her career. She was finished. They had never before seen her in such bad shape, nor had they seen her play so pathetically. The broken figure on the clay at Beaulieu bore little resemblance to the Suzanne Lenglen they had watched over the years.

Suzanne's response to her own incompetent play was to screw up her face and twist her features in a grotesque and hysterical fashion. The thick makeup covering her deathly pale skin began to crack. She looked like a very sick celebrant on the morning after a drunken party, exhausted, tired, nervous, and badly hung over. Satterthwaite comforted Lenglen, talking to her softly throughout the match like a therapist leading a dizzy patient through a difficult routine. Suzanne gave every indication of being near a complete breakdown. The crowd watched in total silence and with fascination as Suzanne Lenglen self-destructed before their eyes. When the match had ended Lenglen announced her withdrawal from the tournament. She left the club without speaking to newsmen and returned immediately to Nice. Later in the afternoon she announced that she would not play in the Monte Carlo tournament scheduled to begin the following week.

Helen Wills, in the meantime, proceeded without much trouble through the singles and the mixed doubles of the Beaulieu tournament and was applauded enthusiastically by capacity crowds that came to see her play against anybody. In the semifinal round of the singles she played Satterthwaite. After losing the opening game on her own service, something happened to Helen, and her game suddenly came together in an almost supernatural way. She cut loose in the second game with a terrific attack and took six games in a row, giving up only a few scattered points. One amazed correspondent said that Wills's driving was like a siege gun, and she simply smothered Satterthwaite's shots with fiery winners. Helen then dropped the first game of the second set before again turning into a roaring tiger and taking six more games in a row from the woman who customarily took two or three games from Suzanne Lenglen during the course of their competitions.

In the finals of the singles competition at Beaulieu, Helen Wills was dazzling. She showed a mastery of every shot in her win over Eileen Bennett—hard, deep drives, deadly volleys, terrifically paced overheads, and a complete and spectacular array of services to confound her opponent completely. In the mixed doubles final Wills's partner became merely a superfluous presence as the American Girl took over. She covered all parts of the court, making impressive gets and hitting a series of incredible winners. She might well have played alone and won the match. In fact, in all but the strictly technical sense, she did precisely that. Her partner, Kingsley, obviously didn't mind becoming just another spectator during the contest.

What was most impressive to the overflow crowd at courtside, however, was the transformation in Wills's attitude toward tennis. She was no more the grim reaper and the stolid, methodical tennis steam engine. The tight-lipped, poker-faced Puritan who had turned play into serious business seemed to have gone on vacation. That had been Helen of Cannes. Now the American girl was moving more fluidly with more grace and more glide and with more confidence. She was very visibly in high spirits. She smiled. And she seemed almost to be bubbling over with enthusiasm and good humor and good will and self-assurance. The crowds loved her all the more for it. The collapse of the French woman seemed to lift a heavy burden from the shoulders of the American girl. There was a new spring in her step on the court. The galleries adored this latest completely unexpected incarnation of the California challenger.

In Nice, meanwhile, Suzanne Lenglen's personal physician, Dr. Roger Castelli, advised the Maid Marvel not to submit to the physical and emotional strain of singles play for several months. Any trying contest, he predicted, would severely, and perhaps permanently, injure her health. Yet Lenglen disregarded his advice and assured her French patrons and fans that she would play a return match against the American girl in Nice in early March, "if I feel I have regained my full strength." She hardly had a choice. The business pressures on both Suzanne and Papa for a spectacular rematch in Nice were snowballing. It appeared that in one way or another—in good health or in bad—it was imperative that Suzanne appear on the courts in Nice opposite the American Girl again. A minimum gate of $80,000 was expected from the rematch. An enormous grandstand with special press boxes for 100 correspondents was already under construction, and $40,000 had been committed by the Nice Club to the new facility. The Villa Ariem was, of course, financed by the Nice Club, and any serious financial setback of the club might bring about serious readjustments in the manner in which the Lenglens were accustomed to living. The commercial interests of Nice never dared assume that Suzanne Lenglen would not play. She must. By an act of will her health and mental resolve had to be restored. The French woman was not merely the key to financial prosperity for the Nice Tennis Club; suddenly she was the agent of financial survival for dozens of other Riviera enterprises too.

Wills's vigorous exhibitions in the Beaulieu tournament did nothing to ease Lenglen's troubled mind. When Lenglen loyalists returned to Nice with glowing reports of the American girl's one-sided wins, Suzanne arranged for a week's retreat in a secluded mountain resort. She also gave her fans cause for hope when she affirmed that she had changed her mind about the Monte Carlo tournament. She would play in the doubles of that competition with one of her favorite partners, Didi Vlasto.

With Lenglen gone from the singles play in the Riviera tournaments—at least for the time being—Wills was left without a worthy foil. Her opponents, it was all too clear now, were little more than a series of ciphers. There was no way for her to demonstrate her true dominance and supremacy in face-to-face confrontations with these inept surrogates for Lenglen. Helen very quickly realized that in the eyes of the Riviera crowds from now on she would be hitting against the ghost of Suzanne. She would have to beat Lenglen's records and she would have to shatter the memory of Suzanne Lenglen if she could not beat the Goddess in the flesh. And since Suzanne had made a habit of trouncing her opponents in endless numbers of love sets, Helen would now have to do likewise. And so she redoubled her efforts at scoring wins without allowing her opponents to score. Every stroke became important now, a matter of record. She would crush all comers and make it look easy. Only in that way could the crowds become true believers in the American Girl. And at the same time, her accomplishments would have a profound effect upon the Goddess in her mountain fortress. Lenglen would either be so frightened by Wills's skill that she would refuse to return to the courts for a rematch, or she would become so enraged she would return prematurely and be humiliated once and for all. In either case, Wills realized, it just might be possible to deliver a mortal blow to the Goddess long before confronting her again face to face in a match.

Wills's life on the Riviera by now had become comfortably routine. She lived what was referred to by reporters as a well-regulated sixteen-hour day. She arose in the morning at eight, and after a light breakfast sketched until ten. Her tennis matches began at 10:30. Then, after her victories, she met briefly with newsmen, fashion writers, movie-makers, perfume manufacturers, shoe salesmen, automobile advertisers, and the like, all wishing either for an exclusive interview or wanting to inflict their wares upon her gratis. She was at last getting a bracing dose of the type of tempting treatment that had been extended to Suzanne Lenglen for so many years in this region. But to all of the solicitors Helen Wills turned a quiet almost inscrutable smile, choosing—as reporters intimated she had faithfully promised her father—to remain "independent" in Europe. When she was required to play tennis in the afternoon, as was often the case, Wills lunched first with her mother and then enjoyed a rest period during which she wrote letters or sketched. Then, again the interruption of tennis and another lopsided win. Tennis was followed by tea and dancing, which Helen enjoyed thoroughly. She seemed to have no shortage of handsome and dashing young men—many of them in uniform—pursuing her and requesting the pleasure of partnering her on the dance floor. After that came dinner and an early retirement. Every other evening Helen Wills indulged herself and left her hotel for one small party or another hosted in her honor. "Who can deny," one American journalist wrote home, "that Helen Wills is drinking in life to its utmost and as only a young girl can do?"

Following her Beaulieu victories Helen Wills moved on to the La Festa tournament in Monte Carlo. Interest in that tournament focused in two areas. In the upper half of the singles draw was the popular Elia de Alvarez, the young Spanish prodigy who had appeared first on the tennis scene only three years earlier. She was, however, the player many experts picked as the European successor to Suzanne Lenglen. It was likely now that she would meet Helen Wills in the finals of the tournament. And in the competition for the coveted Beaumont Cup in doubles, both Wills and Lenglen were entered, so there was the likelihood here also of a foursome meeting in the finals that included the Goddess and the American Girl on opposite sides of the net.

When Wills appeared for her opening matches in Monte Carlo a large crowd was on hand to cheer her on. In the singles she won easily in love sets, but her play lacked the dash that the crowds had applauded a week earlier. Part of the problem was the adoption of the slower English balls in the tournament, which tended to neutralize a good part of her driving power.

In the opening doubles competition, Helen Wills and her American partner, Leslie Bancroft Aeschliman, met an English duo, Dorothea Lambert Chambers and Mrs. E. H. Harvey. The match almost didn't take place. Prior to play Aeschliman had wanted to scratch because of illness. But without Aeschliman, there would be no chance for Wills to meet Lenglen in the tournament, so the American girl had, according to news reports, strongly urged her partner to go on the court despite his poor health, and her partner acceded to the request. Wills was apparently of the persuasion that she could win the Beaumont Cup with any partner who would simply move over once the ball was in play and let her take charge. The newsmen, particularly the French writers, found something less than admirable in this overwhelming drive and unswerving and insensitive ambition to win. During the course of her long and brilliant career this singular and unbending will to win would regularly trouble writers who believed that Wills invested too much importance in tennis. In this case, she seemed willing to risk the health of a reluctant partner in order to win a cup.

Oddly, Lambert Chambers and Harvey came in for little criticism when they centered their attack on the ailing Aeschliman. By avoiding Wills they succeeded in winning the first set. But in the second and third sets Helen became ever bolder in her poaching, covered the entire court by herself, and turned the match around. She and Aeschliman won in three sets. Wills received a standing ovation when she walked from the court.

When Lenglen was told of the enthusiastic applause that followed the brilliant play of the American girl in Monte Carlo, she was outraged.

Having just returned from a recuperative rest in the mountains, she certainly did not want to hear that the largest crowd in the history of the La Festa Club tournament had turned out to see Helen Wills win. "They bury me too soon!" Suzanne responded to the news. "I am not finished yet! I will show them in Nice!" Her vow brought a new thrill of hope to the Nice Club officials and to her own loyal French fans. Suzanne Lenglen would come back. In Nice she would show the world that she still had plenty of the old Lenglen magic.

While Wills was charged with having little regard for the health of her doubles partner, she was seldom accused of not looking after her own well-being. On the second day of the La Festa tournament she requested and received a one-day postponement of her matches. Immediately, reports circulated that Wills, like Lenglen before her, had at last succumbed to the pressure and the strain of the bitter Riviera rivalry. But the truth was that after her unstellar opening performance in the singles Helen felt she was getting stale from the continuous competition. So she took a day off. She drove with Fred Moody to San Remo on the Italian Riviera, lunched there and dodged reporters, and then returned to Monte Carlo looking relaxed and refreshed. The short break did wonders for Helen Wills, but Leslie Aeschliman was still ailing. As a result the Wills-Aeschliman team was eliminated from the Beaumont Cup competition in the next round.

But the news in the second round of the La Festa tournament was not the elimination of Helen Wills and partner in the doubles, but the appearance again of Suzanne Lenglen on the courts. Paired with Didi Vlasto, Lenglen made her usual grand entrance and then in less than grand fashion won in straight sets against an unranked English team. What was surprising to the crowd was not the win, which was expected, but Suzanne Lenglen's hesitant and lauckluster performance. She stayed on the baseline throughout the match and was flatfooted and spiritless during the rallies. She looked tired even before play began. And she seemed uncharacteristically frightened and intimidated by the attention of the crowd. When, on the next day, Lenglen and Vlasto won their final match in the Beaumont Cup competition, Don Skene reported that Suzanne was "a pitiful spectacle" and that she literally "staggered" her way through the match, depending on her partner for every winning point. Lenglen was wracked by a hacking cough during the play and several times appeared to be in great pain. Play was stopped at one point in the second set when Suzanne, who could not stop coughing, seemed near collapse. Mama carried a container of iced cognac to her, and that was enough to restore her strength temporarily. But it was obvious to nearly all present that the Goddess was seriously ailing. Her play was a source of additional consternation to the La Festa Club officials who had taken the liberty of engraving the names of Lenglen and Vlasto on the victory cup three weeks before the tournament began. It would have been a significant embarrassment to present the cup so engraved to another winning team.

After that slim victory, Suzanne Lenglen told reporters that she was determined not to pick up a tennis racket again for at least three months. She would not play in Nice, and she would not play in another Riviera tournament during the remainder of the spring. There was a remote possibility, but only a remote one, that she would defend her French national title in Paris in June. But it was more than likely that she would not play competitive tennis again until Wimbledon in July. When she was reminded of the financial investment of the Nice Club in new facilities in anticipation of a second Wills-Lenglen battle there, Suzanne shot back, "My decision is irrevocable. I am not at the beck and call of promoters, like professionals. I need a rest and I will take it." And she added that, no matter what kind of stories reporters printed about her decision not to play, she would not be provoked this time into returning to the courts before she was completely recovered. "They can say I am afraid to meet her; let them," Lenglen said. "Those who know me intimately are convinced that I am not. I have proved that."

Lenglen's personal physician Dr. Castelli seconded Suzanne's resolve to rest and recuperate before playing any more tennis. "I take the entire responsibility for my patient's decision," he said. "It is not a question of tennis with me or world championships, but merely one of safeguarding her health. Should she change her mind and play in Nice, she does so against my advice. I refuse to assume responsibility for the consequences."

Suzanne Lenglen's surprise decision was nothing less than cataclysmic for the management of the Nice Tennis Club. The club was already more than one million francs in debt. The only way that the organization could be saved financially, it was assumed, was through the scheduling of a second Wills-Lenglen battle at the club. Posters advertising such a match, in fact, had been ordered, and construction was already well under way for the glorious new grandstand that could accommodate the anticipated record crowds that would pass through the gates of the club daily to see the two female stars play their way toward each other in the final bracket. But now, suddenly, Lenglen had withdrawn and left her home club in a very desperate situation. Leon Garibaldi, president of the club, ordered all construction work on the new grandstand stopped immediately when he received news of the Lenglen announcement. The hundred men who had been building the structure for several days were sent home.

In Monte Carlo, Wills was questioned about Lenglen's decision. "I am sorry to hear of Mlle. Lenglen's poor health," she said. "I hope she recovers sufficiently to play in June. I have plenty of time. I feel better than ever."

In the finals of the singles competition against Alvarez, Helen Wills continued her familiar winning ways and gained an easy victory, 6–2, 6–3.

During the match she never found it necessary to leave the baseline, beating her highly touted Spanish opponent on ground strokes alone. Alvarez later apologized to newsmen for her performance. "I need one hard tournament and will play better in Nice next month," she promised. "Please don't mention me in the same breath with Miss Wills," she requested. "Yet."

In the open doubles competition for the Connaught Cup, Wills won again with her partner, Didi Vlasto. And before departing for the next tournament, in Mentone, she summed up her feelings for American reporters: "Thirty-nine victories and one defeat mark my Riviera tennis this far. I am quite satisfied."

In Mentone, Wills faced the problem of merely staying in condition since there was no longer any serious opposition for her. The German and Austrian champion, Frau Nelly Neppach, had arrived on the Riviera shortly after the Carlton Club final and attempted to capitalize on the interest in the Wills-Lenglen duel by claiming her right to face the winner. The claim seemed outrageous since Lenglen had crushed the pretentious diminutive woman and allowed her only two games in a match the previous fall in Austria. Neppach got her big chance in the second round at Mentone and failed miserably. Wills beat her easily, 6–0, 6–3. After the match Neppach emphasized that she had won three games, so she tried to turn that fact into a victory of sorts. "That is one more than I scored against Mlle. Lenglen," she exclaimed excitedly. Neppach could not decide, though, whether Lenglen or Wills was the stronger player. "They are both wonderful," she concluded.

There was no more drama for Helen Wills in the Mentone tournament. And as she won her way easily through the competition she complained to newsmen of Lenglen's decision to abandon Riviera tennis for the season. "I feel disappointed that I cannot meet her until Wimbledon," Helen said. "Don't you think she should have given me a return match here?"

Wills competed in two doubles competitions in Mentone, losing in both. Partnered with American James Van Allen, Helen lost in both the Cup of Nations competition and the International Challenge Cup competition. In both categories the American team fell to the French team of Henri Cochet and Didi Vlasto. Wills redeemed herself with ease in the singles and again beat Alvarez for the tournament championship.

With the completion of the Mentone tournament, Alvarez and Neppach decided that they had taken sufficient drubbing from the American Girl for one season. Both women retired from Riviera competition for the rest of the winter, leaving Wills with even fewer competent opponents for the remaining tournaments. The Nice Club was left with just one star— Helen Wills. And that was not enough to save the organization. Without suspense and excitement in the tournament, what was left was merely a Wills exhibition. The hoped-for crowds would not come out for a solo performance. And when it was learned that some of her close friends on the Riviera were urging her to scratch from the Nice tournament—and thereby, perhaps, financially sink Suzanne Lenglen's home club—officials of the organization became frantic. But their worry over a complete collapse of their tournament was eased when Wills reaffirmed her earlier entry in their tournament. Sightseeing and sketching and rest in Italy did sound attractive to the American Girl—that is what some of her friends suggested she do now. But she had promised earlier to finish out the Riviera season, and she would keep that promise.

There was one more force keeping Helen in France—Fred Moody. He was a handsome young man with a Continental education and a confident cosmopolitan savoir faire. Born in San Francisco, Moody spent much of his youth with his family in Switzerland, and he wintered on the Riviera. His family's yacht was anchored in Cannes. Moody knew the region and guided Helen on several sightseeing tours, providing her with the valuable opportunity to escape the pressures of tournament competition. He became her regular escort for the receptions and the gala dinners given in her honor by royalty, semi-royalty, and ex-royalty. Newsman Al Laney saw how Helen enjoyed the attention of the Riviera habitués and particularly the attention of Fred Moody, and he wrote, "All in all, Miss Wills seemed to be having a merry time of it in a quiet way, and I have often wondered if she did not look back upon those weeks along the enchanting Azure Coast, following the great Cannes match, when life was at morning, as among the most enjoyable in her life."

Before leaving Mentone for Nice, Helen Wills and Fred Moody spent an incomparably romantic and beautiful evening together. That night, without telling either their parents or their closest friends, they made a secret promise to be married. Moody recalled later that it was Helen's idea to keep the engagement a secret. He never knew precisely why, he told me, but he agreed. And for the next three years the American girl and her American fiancé made regular denials to the press concerning their infatuation with each other and their plans for the future.

Wills opened her Nice campaign on March 10, 1926, with three matches. She gave the fans a display that they would never forget and in so doing delivered another solid blow to the reputation of Suzanne Lenglen. In view of Helen's flawless play, it became even more difficult to avoid the conclusion that Lenglen had fled before the advance of an American conqueress. Wills won all three of her matches and lost only two games of the thirty-eight played. In twenty-five games of singles she lost only one game. And in the mixed doubles with her English partner, Charles Kingsley, she lost one game. On the second day of the tournament Wills continued her complete dominance, and after forty-eight hours in Nice had run off sixty winning games while losing four. In fact, Wills was so much better than her opposition that her matches became almost boring. Fans began to wander off to watch the earnest hacking go-

ing on in the celebrity handicap matches. Large crowds soon gathered to
stare at King Gustav of Sweden when he appeared on the court, and
Prince Chichibu, second son of the Emperor of Japan, who demonstrated
his uncanny ability for slamming the ball over the fence and outside the
Nice Club grounds. The circus atmosphere of the French Riviera in
1926 seemed at last to have found its most appropriate contestants—the
royal clowns.

Meanwhile, Papa Lenglen fumed over the favorable and uncritical
press coverage given Helen Wills and the unfair coverage given his
daughter. Reporters simply could not refrain from intimating that Suzanne had fled because she was afraid of Helen and that her illness was
faked. "From now on Suzanne will refuse to grant interviews to American
reporters," was Papa's response to such accounts.

For a few hours during the tournament there was a good deal of excitement due to an announcement that Lenglen would return from her
mountain hideaway in Italy in order to play an exhibition match and
thus aid the tournament financially. But such news represented merely
more wishful thinking. Suzanne Lenglen did not return. And Helen
Wills continued to dominate. And the Nice Club continued to sink into
debt.

The very last hope of Nice Club officials was for an international contest in the finals of their tournament so they might exploit the element
of nationalism to build up interest. They fully expected Helen Wills to
meet Englishwoman Eileen Bennett for the championship and in that
way stir up some healthy Anglo-American rivalry. But even that was not
to be. In the semi-finals an unranked American, Isabella Lee Mumford
of Boston, beat Bennett in three sets. The prospect of an all-American
final on the French Riviera was of almost no interest at all to the fans,
who stayed away from the club in droves. Wills wanted to get the final
over quickly, and so she did. She came down on Mumford hard with
her serve-and-volley game. A *New York Times* correspondent summed
up the match by reporting that Mumford "was compelled to race all
over the court for the privilege of being decisively beaten. Helen lost
the second game of the second set while experimenting with her service."

There was a little more public interest in the finals of the mixed
doubles. Willis and her partner played the defending tournament championship team of Cochet and Vlasto. A very partisan pro-French crowd
watched the American Girl and her partner go down to defeat in three
sets, 6–4, 5–7, 11–13. The Nice crowd seemed to be almost desperate in
its desire to see Wills beaten at least once in Lenglen's home club. They
were nearly deprived of that pleasure, though, as Helen Wills poached
aggressively throughout the match and almost single-handedly beat the
French duo in the opening set. To many observers the match looked like
a fight between the French team and the American girl with the Englishman simply standing around watching from the best seat in the house.

The contest took two and a half hours, and when it was finally over, incredibly, Wills was not tired and was hardly even perspiring. Vlasto stumbled from the court in a near faint, and Cochet also showed the effects of a long, tough contest. When asked what she thought of the match, Helen observed dispassionately, "It was a long match."

Financially, the tournament was a disaster for the Nice Club. Gate receipts totaled a mere 75,000 francs. The meager figure produced a good deal of bitterness and regret not only among the club officials but also among the casino and hotel interests who also suffered severely from Lenglen's abdication. When rumors circulated in Nice that Suzanne had decided to abandon amateur tennis once and for all and was about to sign a professional contract with an American promoter, Papa Lenglen bristled with indignation and outrage. The American newsmen had actually printed those rumors, Papa found, and one columnist in particular—Westbrook Pegler—embellished his account of Suzanne's decision to become a professional with details of the contract. "The American newspapers have printed such vile lies about Suzanne that I will not talk to any American reporter," Papa vowed. Then he unleashed a storm of picturesque French expressing his unmistakable contempt for the low creatures covering Lenglen for the American newspapers. With trembling fingers he displayed a sheaf of clippings from American newspapers—all contained lies about his daughter, he said. He expressed an overwhelming desire to find Pegler and to give him "three healthy blows of the foot" in the seat of his pants. The newsmen thoroughly enjoyed listening to Papa's wrathful denunciations and his defense of Suzanne's courage and sportsmanship, and they reported the episode in humorous detail.

Helen Wills, in the meantime, returned to the place where her Riviera conquest had begun. She entered her final tournament of the season in Cannes and give the fans there one last chance to see her do her spectacular stuff. Helen's opponents in the tournament were again mere ciphers who hardly gave her practice, let alone serious competition. In the first four rounds of the singles she won forty-eight games and lost two. By the time she had won the singles title she had won seventeen sets at love. In the mixed doubles, played at last with Henri Cochet rather than against him, Wills won another title.

And so Wills's seventy-day Riviera campaign came to an end in Cannes. Her record of achievement in that campaign was stunning. She had met nearly forty different opponents in singles matches and had beaten all save one. She had beaten several challengers repeatedly. She had played singles in nine tournaments and had won eight of those tournaments. She had played 800 games of tennis and won 650. The most dramatic event of her "raid on the Riviera," as the *New York Times* now referred to her French adventure, was "her causing of Mlle. Lenglen to seek the balmy breezes of the Italian lakes when Suzanne ordinarily would have been stunning Riviera habitues by a series of walkovers."

"This evening Helen surveys the field like a Waterloo with almost the entire tennis troupe not anxious to meet her for some reason or other, either physical or mental," the Riviera stringer for the *New York Times* reported from Cannes. "Helen leaves with one thing proved—that she is as far ahead of all she met here as Mlle. Lenglen may be of the majority of her rivals. Those who have watched the unfolding of events on the Riviera this season do not doubt Helen's potential for beating Lenglen in the near future, perhaps the very near future. Even perhaps now."

Personally, Helen Wills left nothing but good impressions everywhere she traveled on the Riviera, the *New York Times* correspondent wrote. Her continued modesty was remarkable and admirable. That she was a girl with a magnetic personality was evidenced by the complete upset she made of the Riviera. And the way in which she steered through difficult seas had been generally recognized in the area as downright extraordinary. Due to her popularity, the price of her drawings had increased by 300 percent since her arrival in France.

On the other hand, Suzanne Lenglen's behavior on the Riviera became curiouser and curiouser. She returned to Cannes from a short rest in Italy. She looked well. In fact, reporters found her dancing a furious Charleston in one of the clubs soon after her return, and they observed that she was behaving as though she had just completed a victorious season in the Riviera tournaments. She pretended that the region still belonged to her alone, they wrote, and she appeared to be not bothered outwardly at all by the praise and publicity given the American girl.

Lenglen's behavior was a reminder of the way she had carried on during her disastrous visit to the United States. Obviously, playing tennis against Helen Wills was one thing and staying up late at night dancing and drinking another.

The French press did not remain silent in the face of the American newsmen's unsympathetic observations of Suzanne Lenglen. They considered the American assault to be more than simply unkind—it was petty and it distorted the truth concerning the fragility of a living national treasure. The reports of Suzanne's activities printed in the American newspapers also represented an indirect affront to the French public that had worshipped the Goddess and her great accomplishments over the past several years. In response, French journalists took some parting shots at the American Girl. They reminded their readers that Helen Wills had insisted again and again rather disingenuously that she had undertaken her trip to France in order "to study art." Yet, she began playing tennis the day after she arrived on the Riviera and she had played almost every day and in every tournament since then. At the same time Helen and her mother had freely enjoyed the best suites and the best meals of the Grand Palace Hotels along the littoral from Mentone to Cannes. One spiteful French journalist, emphasizing the broad gap between Helen's stated intentions and her actions, published an imaginary interview with the American girl upon her departure from France. "Yes, I've been perfectly delighted with my stay upon the Riviera," he quoted her as saying. "I've made one little sketch and have played tennis only to amuse myself and quite by chance. For before everything else I am an art student."

John Tunis was also bothered by certain aspects of Helen Wills's stay on the Riviera. He found a good deal of hypocrisy and of patriotic myopia in the reporting of the American newsmen, particularly in their avoidance of discussing the perquisites made available to the Wills women in France. Tunis suggested that on the Riviera there was no little "confusion" over the difference between an amateur and a professional tennis player. A professional in one of the clubs in Cannes ironed out the definition for him, Tunis wrote. "See, it's like this," the man explained. "A professional tennis player is a simp who pays his own expenses from New York to Cannes to compete in a tennis tournament. An amateur player is a gentleman—or lady—who comes from New York to Cannes to compete in a tennis tournament, has all expenses paid, is lodged in Grand Palace Hotels and eventually goes home with fifty thousand dollars picked up on the side by the sale of his—or her—very valuable name." The inference to Helen Wills's Riviera sojourn could not be missed in the statement, particularly after a reference to the soaring prices paid for sketches by Helen and the great scramble by the various news services bidding for her journalistic efforts. Thanks to the blossoming fame of the American Girl, her career also was getting curiouser and curiouser.

Helen Wills and her mother departed for Italy on the morning of March 25, 1926. Fred Moody had gone on ahead to make arrangements. Helen told reporters, without even a hint of irony in her speech, that she was undertaking a three-week tour to view Italian art and architecture. And, since Benito Mussolini had expressed a strong interest in seeing the American girl perform on the tennis court, she planned to play a little tennis during her stay.

CHAPTER
❧ VI ❧

TRIUMPH
AND DISASTER

"After all is said, you must remember that I am
only a girl."   —Suzanne Lenglen

"If you can meet with Triumph and Disaster
And treat those two imposters just the same."
                    —Rudyard Kipling

"When sorrows come, they come not single spies,
But in battalions."   —William Shakespeare
                                 Hamlet

"—what at last but One's self is sure?
With the Soul I defy you quicksand years, slipping
under my feet."   —Walt Whitman

THE French Riviera was breathtakingly beautiful in the spring of
1926. Italy, on the other hand, was absolutely divine. That, at least, is
what the Italian Fascists were proclaiming shortly before Helen and
Catherine Wills arrived in Milan on the morning of March 25, 1926.
The official Fascist news organ, *L'Impero,* announced that Italy was divine and that all living Italians were reincarnations of the Imperial
Romans who had once conquered and ruled the world. Furthermore,
L'Impero trumpeted, the lowest Italian was worth one thousand for-
eigners; Italians possessed an absolute monopoly on creative genius; the
Italian landscape was unquestionably the most beautiful in the world;
and every foreigner entering Italy could not help but fall under a religious spell.

Helen Wills proved to be something of an embarrassment for the
crowing Fascists. She did not find Italy divine, and she did not fall under a religious spell during her brief sojourn there. And in tennis the
American Girl demonstrated that her talents were far greater than those
of any living Italian—male or female. As a symbol of democratic America she fractured the fantasies and pretense of the posturing bullies who
ruled Italy and left them, like the French, both charmed and awed by
her incomparable combination of beauty and athletic genius. Although
the editors of *L'Impero* might have been sorely tempted to do so, they
did manage to refrain from claiming that Helen Wills was Italian.

Wills traveled to Italy at the invitation of Benito Mussolini himself. Il Duce had followed the widely publicized successes of the American Girl in France and announced that he would like to see her confront some of Italy's best tennis players in Rome. She had whipped the premier players of England, France, Germany, and Spain, and she had sent the French champion of champions packing. Ever on the lookout for advertisements for his new order in Italy, Mussolini found Helen Wills a useful phenomenon. Her appearance alone on the courts of Rome would draw attention to his Fascist regime. Win or not, some of the limelight that constantly illuminated Helen's activities now would fall on Italy and the Italian players and even on the Italian strong man himself.

Helen Wills's Italian adventure began in mild confusion. Shortly after leaving Cannes it was discovered that both her tickets and tennis rackets had been left behind. There was a sudden frantic search for the missing items, which were located in Wills's hotel in Cannes and delivered to her in Milan. From Milan the Wills women proceeded to Florence, where they stayed in a large villa owned by a fellow Californian. Helen later wrote in her autobiography that during her stay in Florence she "saw everything that was famous and historic" because she was "being 'educated.' " She was taken on a tour of the Pitti Palace and the Uffizi Gallery, but she confessed that she had a limited ability to appreciate the wonders of the art she saw there. In Florence and later in Rome, she discovered, the beauty and the grandeur that should have made a deep impression seemed instead simply beyond her grasp.

The art and craft of tennis, on the other hand, was something else again. This Wills understood and appreciated. And in this Helen was both master and masterpiece. In Italy she showed large crowds of curious spectators a type of athletic artistry they had never before dreamed possible. Since there were simply no Italian women capable of competing effectively against Wills, in Rome the American Girl was scheduled to play against the top-ranking male players of the nation. Although Mussolini did not attend any of her exhibition matches, a large cross section of Roman society showed up along with a contingent of American divinity students studying in Rome. The American ambassador and his wife were also present along with the entire embassy staff and the British ambassador.

In her initial exhibition match Helen Wills played against the defending Roman champion, Clemente Serventi. After a hard-fought set that featured some rousing rallies, Serventi downed the American Girl, 7–5. Wills was relaxed during the set and played exclusively from the baseline, fighting it out with her opponent with ground strokes alone. After twelve games she appeared as cool and fresh as when she had begun the set—in dramatic contrast to her perspiring and winded opponent. Serventi seemingly pulled out all the stops to beat the American

Girl, while Wills remained unhurried and unworried by the contest. Following a brief break, Helen Wills and a young male partner, Giullio de Stefani, played Serventi and Countess Gianuzzi, beating them easily. Helen's net game in this contest brought a steady outpouring of gasps and applause from the crowd both because of its daring and its deadly effectiveness.

On the next afternoon Wills displayed her power in a second exhibition before another distinguished and fashionable Roman crowd. No male player could match her on this day, and she beat two of Italy's best. She made almost no errors and had both more control and pace than on the previous afternoon. In the end her male opposition looked inept as she hit winner after winner leaving her foes either flatfooted or making desperate hopeless stabs at her superb placements. Wills received a standing ovation when she finished her sets, and many spectators exclaimed that they have never before seen such tennis played by either men or women.

Roman newsmen were as lavish and unrestrained in their praise for the American girl as had been the American newsmen on the French Riviera. They delighted in her success at joining athletic expertise and femininity—two qualities that would be central to praise in the future for the American girl all over the world. "She is an example beyond words of the wonderful womanhood that uses sports to enhance womanly charm instead of to affect artificial masculinity," one Italian journalist wrote. "Helen represents the maximum attainment in sport and still remains a woman," another observed. She was a bridge between the genteel feminine tradition of the past and the more active and assertive and aggressive future. In her was a perfect link, the Italians found, between the best of yesterday and the promise of tomorrow. She was the New Woman, the avatar of the ideal female—an ideal become real.

American newsmen in Italy, on the other hand, after detailing Wills's athletic conquests for several weeks, now concentrated on the romantic side of her life. They rediscovered Fred Moody, Helen's Riviera companion who had preceded her to Italy in order to make reservations and arrangements for her visit. Again Moody was present at Helen's matches, accompanying her to and from the clubs and escorting her to social functions. Curious newsmen now wanted to know if Wills and Moody were engaged. Were they planning to be married? Helen blushed deeply at such questions and offered diffident denials. Then her embarrassment turned to annoyance, and she refused to respond to any questions about Fred Moody. When Moody also evaded answering their questions, several reporters simply reverted to their Riviera brand of journalism and began composing fiction. Thus, one newsman wrote that Helen and Fred had been close friends since their childhood days around the Golden Gate and that Fred had been an admirer of Helen since he had first seen her play tennis in California. All of this was, of course, not true.

Cannes, February 1926. Suzanne and Helen face the press before their big match. Suzanne reflects concern; Helen, to the press, betrayed no emotion. (Author's collection)

Suzanne Lenglen playing in Nice in 1913. (Photo by Jacques Henri Lartigue)

At Wimbledon in 1921, Suzanne, not yet wearing her bandeau, impressed the crowd by her tenacity and grace on the English grass. (Author's collection)

Suzanne hits a backhand shot from the baseline, about 1925. (Author's collection)

"The Goddess" ready for another match, about 1925. (Author's collection)

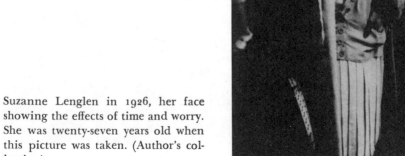

Suzanne Lenglen in 1926, her face showing the effects of time and worry. She was twenty-seven years old when this picture was taken. (Author's collection)

Suzanne in repose, about 1921. Her attire on and off the court set fashion trends. (Author's collection)

The "Lenglen-trail-a-winding" outside Wimbledon, waiting to see Suzanne in 1921. (Author's collection)

Helen Wills, The American Girl, in 1926. All of the
young men in America were a little bit in love with her,
the *New York Times* noticed. (Dorothy Wilding)

Seventeen-year-old Helen Wills at
the Berkeley Tennis Club, April
1923, before she traveled to Forest
Hills and won the Women's National Singles title by beating Molla
Mallory. Helen is wearing her familiar school uniform. (Wide World
Photos)

"The American Girl" during a quiet
moment in Paris in 1926. (Author's
collection)

In the semi-final match at Forest Hills in 1928, Helen Wills defeated her good friend, Edith Cross, 6–0, 6–1. The camera caught Helen in this rare awkward moment on the court that day. (Wide World Photos)

Helen Wills on the courts of the Essex County Club in Manchester by the Sea, Mass., July 20, 1931, pushing all contenders aside. She was, at this time, in the middle of her incredible winning streak. Between 1927 and 1933 she lost no sets in singles competition. (Wide World Photos)

Helen, wearing make-up, ready to play tennis again during her 1938 comeback. (Wide World Photos)

Helen Wills, "The American Girl" and National Champion, in 1923. (Author's collection)

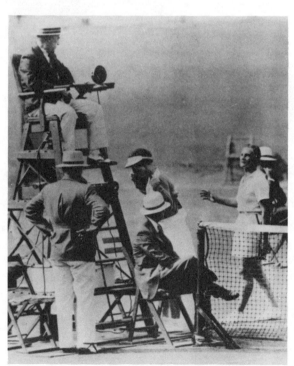

Helen Wills walks off the court at Forest Hills in 1933 in her default to Helen Jacobs.

Helen Wills and Fred Moody pose for photographers in San Francisco following the announcement of their engagement in 1929. (Wide World Photos)

Fred and Helen clowning at Senator Phelen's estate, Villa Montalvo in Saratoga, California, in a light moment, 1929. (Edith Cross Jansen)

Helen Wills Moody displaying three of her oil paintings as she opened her "one-man" show at the Grand Central Galleries in New York in 1936. (Wide World Photos)

Helen at the ceremony marking her final
singles victory in a major tournament,
the Irish National Championship, Dublin, 1938. (Author's collection)

Helen Wills Moody Roark in 1981 at her induction into the Northern California
Sports Hall of Fame. (Cheryl A. Traendly)

May Sutton, about 1907, one of America's first successful international tennis stars. The English-born, American-raised woman won twice at Wimbledon and was a favorite of the American crowd before Helen Wills began to play tennis. (Author's collection)

Suzanne Lenglen with Molla Mallory just before their final match at Wimbledon in 1922. (Author's collection)

Betty Nuthall, the English woman who made history by taking a set from Helen Wills in 1933. (Edith Cross Jansen)

The 1924 U.S. Olympic tennis team going home on the *Aquitania* in August
1924. *Front* (seated): R. Norris Williams. *Second row:* Julian S. Myrick, Edith
Sigourney, Hazel Wightman, Helen Wills, Eleanor Goss, Marion Jessup, Lillian
Scharman. *Back row:* Australian player Norman Brookes, Watson Washburn,
Sumner Hardy, Frank Hunter, Vincent Richards. (Dorothy Wightman, author's
collection)

The two Helens pose for photographers before their dramatic match at Wimbledon in
1935. (Wide World Photos)

The "Black Helen Wills," Ora
Washington, second from right,
still competing in doubles in 1947.
Left to right: Margaret Peters,
Roumania Peters, Ora Washing-
ton, Doris Miles. (P. H. Polk,
Tuskegee Institution, Ala.)

Helen Wills Moody follows through on a typical backhand: cool, balanced and powerful.

Seen from her rival's court as she hits an overhead, Helen Jacobs seems all arms and legs.

(Wide World Photos)

Helen and Suzanne face the press just before the start of their dramatic match in
Cannes in February 1926. (Author's collection)

Outside the Carlton Club, climbed atop ladders to get a glimpse of the Goddess
and the American Girl. (Author's collection)

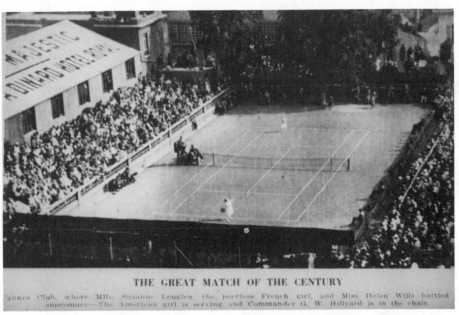

THE GREAT MATCH OF THE CENTURY

Cannes Club, where Mlle. Suzanne Lenglen, the peerless French girl, and Miss Helen Wills battled supremacy—The American girl is serving and Commander G. W. Hillyard is in the chair.

The Match of the Century in Cannes, February 1926. (Author's collection)

The premature conclusion of the Lenglen-Wills match in Cannes, February 1926. Notice the man with the raised hand, partially concealed at the right, signaling the photographer to stop. (Wide World Photos)

But it made, nonetheless, pleasant reading for the folks back home, and it seemed harmless enough at the time. Whatever the truth of the matter might be, newsmen found the young Moody an engaging character and approved heartily of him, calling him in their stories "the dashing Fred." He was deemed the proper prince for the uncrowned queen of American sport.

It was noticed also that the two mothers, Mrs. Wills and Mrs. Moody, were often spotted conferring with each other, and anxious reporters moved in closer to eavesdrop. They overheard nothing but an exchange of pleasantries between American tourists abroad.

Back in Berkeley, Dr. Clarence Wills was besieged by reporters inquiring about the blossoming European romance between the American girl and the American boy. The kindly physician similingly denied the rumors and the speculations about an engagement and marriage, but in his denials he was something less than flattering to his daughter. Helen was simply not possessed of a romantic nature, he explained to newsmen. In an almost clinical fashion he elaborated, stating that "her disposition is just as cold as the attitude that has made her famous in every net tournament where her name has been entered. In fact," he went on, " 'Little Poker Face' fits her nature as well as her conduct." Consequently, Dr. Wills gave no credence at all to stories of either romance or an engagement between Helen and Fred. Furthermore, he said, Helen never mentioned young Moody in her letters, and certainly if the young man was making any impression at all it would have found its way into her correspondence.

Despite the adulation of the Italian crowds, Wills was not completely comfortable in Fascist Italy. She found something vaguely forbidding in the atmosphere of the place. One evening while visiting the Coliseum with Fred, Helen was overcome by a sense of imminent danger. She and Fred left the structure immediately, and within a few days the Wills women returned to the more relaxing and relaxed atmosphere of France.

Fred Moody had his own good reasons for wanting to leave Italy. He, too, was uncomfortable, but not because of any uneasiness with the violence that lay close beneath the surface of the Fascist social order. Rather, he recalled years later, he was upset with "the phoney counts and dukes who swarmed around Helen like flies," he said, using an ironic half metaphor. "And I had to keep them off. They all wanted to marry an American girl, all this royalty, you know." In time some of the annoyance of fighting off the pseudo-royal suitors would disappear, and Fred would look back on the relentless romantic attentions focused on Helen with a certain delicious degree of humor.

Wills played one final exhibition set in Milan and then entrained for Paris. Shortly after Suzanne Lenglen arrived in Rome to provide her own exhibition matches, intending to dispel any lingering doubts about the relative abilities of the two competing athletes. The result, however, was yet another bitter disappointment for the Goddess. The crowds that turned out to see Suzanne were noticeably smaller and less enthusiastic than those that appeared only a week earlier to see the American Girl. Mussolini was absent, further detracting from Lenglen's intended Italian media splash. Like it or not—and she certainly did not—Lenglen would have to play against Wills and not the memory of Wills. Accepting the inevitable, Lenglen rested for several days in Italy and then boarded a train and followed Wills's path to Paris.

On April 5, Albert Canet and a score of other luminaries from the French Tennis Federation gathered in the Gare de Lyon in Paris to welcome Helen Wills back from her Italian journey. There they received very bad news. A telegram arrived informing them that her departure from Italy had been delayed, and she wished her name scratched from an exhibition scheduled for the wooden-surfaced courts at the Tennis Club of Paris. Wills had been paired with Jean Borotra for the exhibition, and an eager Parisian sporting public had looked forward to the chance of seeing two superb serve-and-volley players in action against another team. Certainly, it was expected, the Wills-Borotra combination would be more than exciting to watch—they would also be absolutely unbeatable. But now Wills's decision not to play in the exhibition unnerved the FTA officers, who feared that she might scratch from two other tournaments she had entered in Paris and subsequently cause them a substantial loss of ticket revenues. And so Canet and his somber entourage showed up again one week later at the Gare de Lyon to welcome the American Girl and to escort her wherever she wanted to go, satisfy her every whim, and above all else to gain assurance that she would play in their two tournaments—the International Tournament between American and French teams and the World Hard Court Tournament which was open to all amateur contestants. No sooner had Helen Wills stepped from the train than she confirmed her original plans to play in the two tournaments. Hearing that news, the welcoming committee smiled more easily and breathed a sigh of relief.

Suzanne Lenglen recovered her health soon enough to confirm her own entry in both the International and the World Hard Court tournaments. And so, excluding another crisis of nerves or an unforeseen physical collapse, FTA officials could go ahead with their plans for seating capacity crowds that would pay substantial sums to see Helen Wills and Suzanne Lenglen face each other in two more Matches of the Century. Financially and psychologically, that was exactly what the FTA needed.

In preparation for their approaching matches, both Lenglen and Wills practiced daily now on the clay courts of the Bois de Boulogne—Helen in the morning and Suzanne in the afternoon. When the French woman first appeared on the courts with professional Albert Burke of the Carlton Club, a score of reporters was waiting for the chance to see her hit the ball and to assess her recovery. They were pleasantly surprised.

There was nothing wrong anymore with the Goddess. Nothing, at least, that they could see. She moved easily and gracefully, they found, and hit with all of her former authority, accuracy, and confidence. She was ready. Following her brief practice-exhibition session, Suzanne spoke with inquisitive newsmen. She complained again about the great Cannes match. She had not been herself in Cannes, she said. The absurdity of the ballyhoo atmosphere, the unruly and noisy gallery, and the incompetent officiating combined with her own poor health to undercut Suzanne's tennis. Now she was playing the sort of tennis she was famous for. But still there was the pressure both from tennis associations and from clubs and from the press. She objected to the fact that her career had been taken over by others and that she was virtually ordered where she must play and when, regardless of her emotional or physical health. "Playing tennis is almost slavery," she concluded. "If I didn't resist all suggestions, offers and prayers made of me, I would be playing tennis from January 1 to New Year's Eve every year. Therefore, I have to limit my engagements, but I will most certainly play in the coming international championship and will meet my 'rival,' as you call her." When the newsmen persisted in asking about Lenglen's attitude toward Helen Wills now, the Goddess broke off the interview and left with her friends.

Following her own practice sessions each morning, Helen Wills enjoyed a rich social life and managed to get in a little writing. She had switched her journalistic allegiance from the International News Service to the United Press, and she had agreed to write a series of articles on the International and World Hard Court tournaments. Because of the USLTA's odd amateur player-writer rule, though, Helen Wills was forbidden from reporting directly on the matches in the tournaments in which she was a participant. As a result, Helen agreed to compose reflective "literary work" while Al Laney was to report the details of the early matches leading toward the expected second Wills-Lenglen singles clash.

When Wills was not practicing or writing she enjoyed dancing and socializing. Reporters watched the American girl while away the afternoons dancing with handsome and interested young men who seemed only too eager to win her away from the ubiquitous Fred Moody. Still defensive over the attentions paid his fiancée, Moody sought to protect her from the more aggressive young men who constantly inserted themselves into her life. He challenged one young suitor to a duel, and Helen really feared for a time that he would go through with it and kill or be killed in defense of her. But in the end nothing came of the bitter exchange between Fred and one of Helen's more forward French admirers. Helen and her mother and Fred also spent several afternoons with ex-Senator James Phelan of California, who had been traveling in France with a group of friends. Phelan had invited Helen to visit his estate, Villa Montalvo, in Saratoga, California, before she departed for

France. He had provided her with letters of introduction to influential Americans living in Europe. And he had become infatuated with her. Now, like millions of other men, Phelan was under her spell and he sought, whenever possible, to make her European adventure as pleasant as he could by entertaining her and introducing her to his friends in the worlds of art and journalism.

The public attention that had been focused on Helen Wills for several weeks now began to produce some changes in her behavior. She confessed that she had become much more interested in dressing fashionably since she was constantly in the public eye. And it was important that she live up to her responsibility of representing young American womanhood in a positive way. And so she attended afternoon showings of Paris designers and purchased several new outfits from her favorite designer—Patou. Attired in the latest fashions, Helen Wills discovered that they were not enhanced by her unstylishly unbobbed hair, which she wore in three tight buns. Her refusal to cut her hair to match the current fashion initially won admiration for her on the Riviera, where she was the only unbobbed woman athlete. Helen had taken a certain pride in the portrayal of herself as a self-confident, independent, sweet, old-fashioned girl. But the time for a change had arrived. Following a conference with her mother, Helen went to a hairdresser and had her hair bobbed fashionably. And so she became a self-confident, independent, sweet, new-fashioned girl.

Wherever Wills went in Paris she was followed by a persistent phalanx of young newsmen. The French reporters, most of them sensitive to the American public's concern with Suzanne Lenglen's questionable and arcane financial arrangements, carefully kept track of Wills's enjoyment of the perquisites accompanying international amateur celebrityhood. And gradually, they came to conclude that Helen Wills was not dissimulating when she mentioned her constant attention to the amateur rules of the sport as defined by the USLTA. She appeared to have no suspicion at all that the acceptance of the hospitalities of the Riviera resort hotels and casinos in any way at all compromised her stringent interpretation of what amateurism entailed. And, most amazingly, she really did believe that the sale of her drawings and articles had everything to do with the inherent merit of those efforts and nothing at all to do with her fame as a tennis player. They concluded that she was either unbelievably innocent or incredibly stupid or calculatingly disingenuous. Or perhaps a convenient conscious combination of all three, which would have made her characteristically American! When she attended the races at Longchamps, she was approached by a Parisian journalist, who asked her casually in passing, "Winning much?" Wills turned to him as though he had made an indecent proposition. And in one sense, he had. Her face colored deeply, and she snapped, "Why, I never even bet. Betting is the bane of amateur sports. I do not encourage it anywhere." The journalist, who had followed the tremendous ebb and flow of treasure bet on the Lenglen-Wills match in Cannes, waited for the flicker of a smile to cross Helen's face. There was none. She was deadly earnest in her denunciation of betting. He was stunned by that realization as Helen turned and walked away. How little she seemed to see! How easily she seemed to forget!

In the midst of the journalistic sniping at the two international stars, the Franco-American team tournament was staged. The competition was expected to be a hands-across-the-sea kind of contest in which international harmony could be fostered. But at the last moment there was disagreement over the women's competition in the contest. The French Tennis Federation, following the arrival of the American team, decided to conserve the energies of the top French women, including Suzanne Lenglen, for the more important World Hard Court tournament. The suggestion was offered that, since only male players had competed in the earlier Franco-American matches in the United States, now only the males should compete in the contest in France. But the Americans insisted that the French also field a women's team to play the visiting American women. The French refusal to play against the American women involved what they considered to be a slight by the Americans. The USLTA had not, after all, sent the two top American males—Tilden and Johnston—with the American team. As a consequence, the expected French triumph would obviously be compromised. And although the promise of another Lenglen-Wills match would produce a significant financial windfall, the FTA was willing to forego that windfall to uphold French honor. Eventually, however, the French found a way to return the American slight and at the same time provide opposition for the visiting American women. They assembled a team that conspicuously exempted their three top players—Lenglen, Vlasto, and Contostavlos—from that group. The French newsmen sided with the FTA and dubbed the tournament a "farce" and suggested that the American victory would now be "hollow and utterly negligible"—which it was. So instead of advancing Franco-American friendship through athletic competition, once more athletic competition produced deep feelings of resentment and narrow, nationalistic animosity.

For the leading French female players, exemption from the Franco-American competition proved to be something of an unexpected blessing. The weather for the matches was terrible. It rained lightly throughout several matches and put a temporary stop to others. As a result, a severe strain was put on several players who were forced to play two or three matches in a day in order to make up for lost time. The American men split with the French: Howard Kinsey and Vincent Richards each winning and losing a match against Paul Feret and René Lacoste. In the women's competition, Elizabeth Ryan, Marion Zinderstein Jessup, and Helen Wills all won their matches, and Mary K. Browne and Ryan

won the doubles. The gallery was filled for the Wills match against Simone Mathieu, a promising new French competitor. Wills won the
match, 6–3, 6–4, on a slow wet clay court that almost inhaled all of her
hard-hitting power, and the victory seemed to be more difficult than
expected for the celebrated American champion.

In the World Hard Court Tournament, which began as soon as the
Franco-American contest had ended, the FTA escalated their undisguised
hostility toward the American players, for the French press and public
once more closed ranks behind Suzanne Lenglen in the face of what
was suddenly considered unfair American journalistic sniping. The FTA
insisted on complete and exclusive management of the tournament. This
was Paris and not the Riviera. Cooperation by non-French players and
officials was neither wanted nor invited and was openly resented when
offered. Umpires and linesmen were French, and nobody else need apply. Efforts by visiting players to get an English-speaking linesman ended
unsuccessfully. One American player asked an internationally known
English official to call the lines for an important match. But when the
official started to walk onto the court he was stopped and ordered off.
When he hesitated in order to protest, a gendarme appeared and quickly
escorted him away. He did not try to return, and he was not shot. Play
on the center court was monopolized by the French players in the early
rounds of the competition, and all visiting players, especially the Americans, were exiled to outlying courts. Moreover, all calls were made in
French, even when both players were English-speaking. During one
match an umpire obliged an audience made up almost exclusively of
Americans and Englishmen by calling out the scores in English. The
official was solemnly warned to speak French, since this was a French
tournament and the official language of the host country was the only
one permitted in officiating. American players complained about the
line calls, which appeared to favor French players, but in this case, too,
no change resulted from the protestations.

Attention in the tournament naturally focused almost exclusively on
the Goddess and the American Girl as they progressed through the early
rounds of play. Newsmen reported a lively business in betting as the
odds shifted almost hourly for the anticipated rematch of the two women
in the finals of this tournament. Lenglen, in her opening matches, demonstrated beyond any lingering doubt that almost miraculously she had
fully recovered from her victory over the American girl. Before a highly
partisan and noisy crowd she dispatched an almost helpless Hungarian
opponent in love sets. Wills, by way of contrast, experienced difficulty
from the very first. Her opponent in the opening round was Mme. Golding, formerly France's second-ranked player and a medalist in the 1912
Olympic Games. But following the emergence of Lenglen, Vlasto, and
Contostavlos, Golding had slipped to fourth in her ranking; she remained, however, a competent if not a formidable player. On the slow

wet clay Wills took the first set from Golding, 6–3, but her play seemed clearly uninspired, and she double-faulted three times on her way to the win. She took the opening game of the second set before a heavy downpour brought a suspension of play. Wills objected and said she wanted to continue in the rain, feeling that she had at last found her stroking rhythm and could finish off her opponent in only a few minutes. Yet, in fairness to Golding, the officials cleared the court. Then, when the match was resumed, thirty minutes later, Wills seemed to have lost both her concentration and her timing. She appeared not very interested in the match any more, and her stroking was erratic. She dropped three games in a row, one of them at love on her own service. She took two games to pull even at three all, but then suffered another lapse and dropped two more games. In the ninth game, the game that should have given Golding the set, she dug in once more and became visibly more determined. The game went to deuce six times, and the American Girl finally broke through for the win. She then continued her winning ways with a vengeance and gave up only two points in the final three games of the set and the match.

After the victory Helen Wills sought an explanation for her uneven play. She was confused. The damp court had obviously absorbed much of her power again and had slowed down her footwork. The strongest parts of her game had been neutralized, and the interruption due to the rain had further hurt her. But beyond that, she simply did not feel well. Newsmen studying her progress in the tournament had not been told that for almost a week Helen had complained to her mother that she was ill. She suffered from dizzy spells and from a general indisposition. But she had entered the tournament despite her ailing condition. She was not a quitter. She refused to talk about her health to anyone but her mother because she wanted very badly not only to finish this tournament but also to win it, and to win it without excuses for the way she played. On the Riviera she had seen Lenglen use the excuse of bad health to cancel out of various matches and to explain away her mistakes in the matches in which she did participate. On the Riviera, Wills had decided not to use any similar excuses. She was in this tournament to play. And she would play even if it killed her. And in this instance, it almost did.

On the second day of the tournament, newsmen learned that Catherine Wills had called tournament officials and requested a twenty-four-hour postponement in Helen's scheduled match with Kea Bouman of the Netherlands. In Europe such postponements were periodically extended to female players, especially in the early rounds of play, and so the request was no cause for either unusual attention or for alarm. In fact, the American newsmen welcomed the postponement, which gave them a chance to escape for a while from the tyranny of their deadlines.

Later that same day, Catherine Wills contacted the office of the United

Press in Paris, Helen's employer, and informed the director that Helen would not be able to write her article for the news service that day. Unlike other sports figures of the time, Helen Wills really wrote her own material. Many reporters and editors confessed that they thought this was both eccentric and unwise. Nonetheless, she employed no ghost writer "as other sports figures did when they went literary for a price," Al Laney observed. When the UP director out of simple courtesy asked if Helen was feeling all right, Catherine Wills replied that she was not. In fact, she said, Helen had become violently ill and had been rushed to the American Hospital in Neuilly.

The news hit like a bombshell. Correspondents from every American paper and news service in the city began scurrying around trying to drum up a few details on this dramatic and unexpected development. Earlier in the morning, it was revealed, Helen had become violently ill in her hotel room. A French physician was summoned. He quickly diagnosed her illness as acute appendicitis, and he ordered an ambulance to transport Helen to the hospital for immediate surgery. Even as the news of the fate of the American girl went out over the wires, she was undergoing an operation for the removal of her diseased appendix.

In their race for the inside story, newsmen again turned to fiction when they could not get the facts. And so the world was informed that Helen Wills had concealed her illness because she was a Christian Scientist and conferring with a physician was against her religion. Only when her life appeared to be endangered, the newsmen asserted, had she turned to professional help.

Suddenly, Helen Wills was again front-page news. An army of reporters converged now on the American Hospital and sought word of Helen's condition. The world waited expectantly for several hours to hear how the brave American girl would fare in this new and deadlier contest as she went "under the knife." Would she emerge once more as a consummate embodiment of the American spirit? Yes. She would.

At the American Hospital, Helen Wills was examined by Dr. Thierry de Martel, one of the most renowned surgeons in France and a member of the attending staff of the hospital. He concluded that Helen should undergo surgery immediately. She underwent the ether, he reported, "pluckily and calmly," and the operation was performed. Nurses told newsmen that, while Wills was being prepared for surgery, she expressed regret that she would now be unable to continue playing tennis in the World Hard Court Tournament and that there could be no rematch with Lenglen this year in France. The nurses found Helen's disappointment and depression from this to be profound. Helen herself recalled later her consternation at having fallen ill. Even as she waited to be wheeled into the operating room she had trouble drawing her mind away from tennis and the match with Lenglen that would not take place. She looked out a hospital window and saw the cloudless sky and noted that it was perfect tennis weather—at last. Perfect tennis weather! She was thinking about that perfect tennis weather when she was wheeled into surgery.

Despite Wills's regrets, in at least one way she had defeated Lenglen. She had captured the attention and sympathy of the world. She had won a long string of victories since her loss to Lenglen in Cannes, and Suzanne had appeared to be frightened of another contest with her. Now the public, for a while at least, would have to imagine what might have been in Paris. And Americans preferred to believe that the American Girl would have clobbered Suzanne Lenglen this time around and would have avenged the Cannes loss in spades. Poor Suzanne, meanwhile, no matter how well she was prepared for a second Big Match, she would now play against that glowing memory of Helen Wills. And no matter whom she defeated in the current tournament there would be a chorus of doubters who would remind her that she had not beaten Helen Wills again. For the remainder of the season, the American Girl, lauded by a sympathetic and compassionate public, would remain untouched and unthreatened by the Goddess.

American newspapers, meanwhile, went on another ballyhoo binge, this time flavoring their standard bombast with a dollop of melodrama and sentimentalism. "A twenty-year-old American girl lies stricken in a French hospital and the feelings of the entire nation undergo a complete change," the *New York Times* reported. "Helen Wills, in the full vigor of health, compelled the respect of French tennis followers for her power with a racquet, but by this token she was a menace to the supremacy of France's idol and so was in hostile territory. Today France has only sympathy and affection for the brave spirited girl who crossed mountains and seas to have the opportunity of meeting Suzanne Lenglen." The *Times* exercised little restraint in praising the behavior of the American Girl. "One hardly knows which to admire most—the lion heartedness with which Miss Wills sought a second meeting with her rival after being beaten or the Spartan stoicism with which she underwent the knife. It was characteristic of the fiber of the American champion that the only tears she shed in her hour of danger were tears of disappointment over the fact that she would not be able to continue in the tournament to meet Mlle. Lenglen."

Catherine Wills confessed to reporters that Helen had refused to talk about her ill health with anyone except her mother because she wanted so badly to compete in the World Hard Court Tournament. Helen was willing, Catherine Wills said, to play Suzanne Lenglen under even the most unfortunate and dangerous physical conditions in order to have the chance to beat her. Helen's determination and will power were so strong that she really believed she might overcome any physical incapacity and win against the Goddess. She had, after all, pursued Lenglen halfway around the world, and she was not about to let her prey escape merely because of an infected appendix. Only when she could no longer stand up and when the pain was absolutely excruciating did she even request a postponement in her matches. And following her surgery as she was coming out of the ether her first words were, "When does the game start?"

These, naturally, were the kinds of facts that the American press and public cherished. Whether or not she ever picked up a tennis racket again, Helen Wills, the gritty American Girl, was a real champion!

Lenglen's response to Wills's misfortune came in two parts. At first she summoned up what seemed to be genuine concern and compassion for the ailing American. She called at the American Hospital twice and left flowers. When questioned by reporters she said, "I hope to be the first to visit Helen's bedside. I understand the sorrow of illness in a foreign land, for I have experienced it. I thought Helen was not up to form in the last few days, but I didn't think it was anything grave."

But then, a short time later, perhaps annoyed by the intemperate praise heaped on the American player by both the American and the French press corps, Lenglen offered a second observation that included a less-than-subtle bitter reminder of her own treatment in America in 1921. "I am sure that France will be just as sympathetic and kind to Miss Wills as America was to me when I was ill in a foreign country," she said. For several American newsmen the remark was vintage Lenglen, and it reminded them how much she had become the woman they loved to hate.

In fact, France was extremely sympathetic and kind to Helen Wills during this emergency. News of her rapid recovery following surgery was flashed on movie screens in local movie houses in Paris, and audiences went wild at the news, shouting "Bravo! Bravo! Bravo, Helene Veels!" And when her picture then appeared on the screen it was the signal for even more tumultuous celebration and demonstration. Also, truckloads of flowers for Helen were delivered by French florists to the American Hospital. So many flowers, in fact, that they became a problem. Eventually, once all of the wards in the American Hospital had been adorned with flowers, the delivery trucks were directed to other hospitals in the city to make their deliveries in the name of the American Girl.

Right after the surgery, which took only a few minutes, Helen Wills felt quite well and suffered only a small amount of pain in the toes of her right foot. Despite this rapid recovery, she was protected from her admiring and impatient public. Suzanne Lenglen and a contingent of American tennis players were kept a safe distance from Helen's room. When a battalion of bold photographers and reporters prepared to storm the wing of the hospital where Wills was housed, the hospital staff formed a human barricade and successfully defended the privacy of the American Girl. There were no casualties in the battle of the American

Hospital. For four days following the surgery Wills's attending physicians kept her in bed. On the fifth day, Helen walked. Fred Moody came calling soon after that and took Helen to a garden in the Bois de Boulogne, where the young Americans relaxed in the sun and enjoyed the quiet beauty far from the pursuing newsmen.

Privately, right after her surgery, Wills seemed unusually optimistic. She confided to close friends she expected to be able to play competitive tennis again in only four weeks. This was possible because of the skill of her surgeon, Dr. Martel, who had performed Helen's appendectomy without cutting a single muscle fiber. Within a few days she spoke not only of defending her American title at Forest Hills in late August but also of challenging Suzanne Lenglen at Wimbledon. She revealed that she had not allowed her name to be scratched from either the singles or the doubles competition in the English tournament. Eleven days after the surgery Wills left the American Hospital and prepared to depart for England. Reluctantly she had abandoned the dream of playing in the singles at Wimbledon, but her name remained entered in the mixed doubles. She confessed to some American correspondents, however, that she might have to wait until the end of the summer to resume competitive tennis. She had been advised to exercise more patience and allow sufficient time for healing in order to prevent permanent impairment. She would, nonetheless, wait until she had been in England a few days before making a final decision on playing or not playing in the mixed doubles at Wimbledon.

Among the voices raised in praise at this time for the American Girl were those of the physicians who had performed her surgery. It seemed that Helen Wills had made history not only in sport but also in medicine. Dr. Gabriel Maurange disclosed that the superb muscular development of the American Girl permitted the removal of an appendix for the first time in the history of French surgery—and perhaps for the first time ever—without the cutting of a single abdominal muscle. Maurange, who assisted Dr. Martel, explained that an incision one inch deep had been made and that no fat whatever was found in Helen's abdomen. As a result, Dr. Martel was able to pry aside abdominal muscle and reach the swollen appendix without trouble. Previously, surgeons had been obliged to make a horizontal incision in the muscle, Maurange explained, but in Wills's case this had not been necessary. He concluded that Helen was "physically a 100 per cent perfect specimen of girlhood, one whom all women of the world could wisely copy." He praised "her moderate life, her quiet temper and her devotion to sport," all of which had "made her body remarkable." Dr. Martel was equally impressed. He told reporters that he had never seen another woman with the physical perfection of Helen Wills. It was extremely rare, he said, even among athletic men "that such harmonious development of body muscles is to be found. Like her whole body, they were marvelous. He concluded that the American girl was "a splendid example of what sport can do for women. It should encourage all girls to do two things: first, select some sport and play it moderately; second, seek to cultivate such excellent calmness as hers, which is largely responsible for her quick recovery." Martel predicted that she could be playing tennis again in four weeks.

The sudden withdrawal of Helen Wills from the World Hard Court Tournament, meanwhile, was accompanied by a dramatic surge forward by Suzanne Lenglen. The absence of the threat of another confrontation with Helen, at least in this tournament, seemed a sort of tonic for Suzanne. Her play in the final few rounds of the tournament was nothing short of spectacular. And several newsmen who watched her performance in Paris in 1926 concluded that she was without doubt a picture of pure perfection. She was every inch a goddess and her recovery of her touch and style was a source once more of pride and honor for the loyal sons and daughters of France.

Lenglen swept all before her on her way to her sixth World Hard Court title. In the final match of the tournament against Mary K. Browne, she reached the high point of her long career. Her play on that afternoon on June 12, 1926, was simply flawless. She won the match, 6-1, 6-0, and spectators had trouble remembering exactly how Browne had won that single game (it happened after two of Lenglen's long drives struck the net cord and dropped back into her own court.) What everyone did remember was a rally in the third game of the second set that electrified the crowd. Everyone had seen it happen, but few could believe it because Suzanne appeared to have invoked the gods and received their intervention during that rally. She had accomplished something that was impossible. During an extended exchange, Browne had fired a fast low backhand drive that hit the baseline in Lenglen's backhand corner. Lenglen moved well behind the baseline to retrieve the ball, while Browne moved to the net quickly to intercept and volley any return. Lenglen was forced to run quickly and to stretch out awkwardly in order to get her racket behind the ball and block it up and back for a desperate save. But her shot was short, and it came down just across the net exactly where Browne stood waiting for it, her feet planted firmly and her racket back for an overhead winner. Without letting the ball bounce, Browne blasted it with all of her might just in front of the baseline in the far forehand corner on Lenglen's side. Suzanne recovered from her own desperate save, pivoted and stayed low, like a runner, while flying back across the baseline to the opposite corner of the court. Her silk skirt was flying high above her knees as she shot like an arrow over the clay, her feet hardly appearing to touch the surface of the court. Once again she lunged for the ball, which was only ankle high as she neared it. But this time she did not block it. She instead caught it in the center of her racket and then smashed it with all of her strength straight back down the line. The ball cleared the net by only a fraction of an inch and was far beyond Browne's reach. It kicked up chalk as it skidded on the far baseline and then rolled to a stop against the wooden wall behind the court. For a moment spectators were silent, and Browne stood in her forehand service court staring in disbelief at the ball. Then there was an explosion of noise—exclamations of disbelief and shouts of praise and hurrahs for the Goddess, again. As the audience came to its feet to acknowledge Lenglen's incredible shot, Browne was heard to mutter, "She's just too damned good! She's just too damned good!" Sportswriter W. O. McGeehan, who watched Suzanne execute the shot, found her a picture of "swooping grace—swooping at the ball, like a falcon into a flock of pigeons, killing and killing." Here was the Lenglen the French had worshipped for seven years. And McGeehan wrote, "I can see no chance for Miss Wills to beat Suzanne either here or at Wimbledon. There is no woman player who can beat this champion."

Lenglen gave up four games while taking the World Hard Court title in 1926. She felt badly about that—those four games—and she felt she could have done just a little better. She had hoped and expected to win all of her matches at love. But there was yet another chance to accomplish that feat—to win a world title without giving up a game in the process—the Wimbledon Jubilee Tournament—the Fiftieth Anniversary of the greatest tennis competition of them all. As in 1919, Lenglen departed for England in 1926 with great expectations.

2

Suzanne Lenglen knew that her 1919 victory over Mrs. Lambert Chambers on the Centre Court at Wimbledon had signaled her real emergence into the world limelight. Since that time Wimbledon had been very special for Suzanne—her favorite tournament. She had won six singles titles there and in 1926 she expected to win her seventh and thus to tie the record of Mrs. Lambert Chambers. And then in 1927 she would, no doubt, take her eighth and record-setting title there. And so on for several years.

But then everything went wrong. It began to go wrong, ironically, because of money. For the Jubilee Tournament the All-England Club management altered the way in which money was expended on visiting players. Previously, money had been allocated to the various national associations to finance the travel of the top players of a nation to England. Some of the money, of course, trickled down far enough to be pocketed by the players most in favor with the national associations. Suzanne Lenglen was one such beneficiary. But in 1926 the All-England Club management announced that the qualified players would be invited to the tournament and in England would be the "guests" of the club. All financial arrangements were to be made and executed by the English themselves. There would be no travel money to sweeten Lenglen's journey this year, and since in England she stayed during the tournaments with her very special friend, Lady Sophie Wavertree, she would receive no benefits from the All-England Club's provision of quarters. Financially, the Jubilee Wimbledon Tournament was to be a losing proposition for Suzanne Lenglen, who produced the greatest amount of gate revenue for the sponsoring club.

At the same time the French Tennis Federation pressured Lenglen to play doubles at Wimbledon with a French partner rather than with her regular doubles partner Elizabeth Ryan, who represented America in the Franco-American matches in Paris. The FTA wanted Lenglen instead to play with Didi Vlasto and through her anticipated victory to glorify further the athletic reputation of France. Lenglen strongly objected to the request. She favored playing with Ryan, a superb doubles player with whom Lenglen had never experienced a defeat. Only very reluctantly did she finally concede to play with Vlasto. But then when the draw for the tournament was announced, there was further bad news. In the opening round of the doubles Lenglen and Vlasto were to play against Ryan and Browne. And in the opening round of the singles she drew Browne. Although she had just beaten Browne easily in Paris, she knew the American player was capable of pulling off surprises during tournament matches, fighting tenaciously, and wearing down the opposition on occasion. Browne was never a walkover for another player on grass, no matter how accomplished or divine the player. And so in the tournament that Suzanne Lenglen expected to be the greatest triumph of her career she was playing with a doubles partner not of her choice against the best doubles player around. And she was meeting potentially stiff opposition in the opening round of the singles. Even before the opening matches of the Jubilee Wimbledon, Suzanne Lenglen sensed trouble.

And then there was Helen Wills, who continued to divert public attention that might otherwise have gone to Suzanne. Up until the very last moment Wills kept her name on the tournament list at Wimbledon in the mixed doubles and kept reporters guessing as to whether or not she would participate. Her close friends and several concerned newsmen advised her not to play. Her response to their advice was blunt: "I think I have to judge these things for myself."

Finally, on July 19, Helen Wills did judge for herself and announced that she would not play at all in the Jubilee Wimbledon. She did tell newsmen, though, that she would get in some good vigorous practice sessions on the outside courts of the All-England Club, practice that was sure to attract an interested gallery and prove a bit disconcerting to Suzanne Lenglen by reminding spectators of the big matches that were not to take place. The American girl continued to hound the Goddess, even when she was not on the official roll of players. "You see, I really thought I would be able to play here," Helen explained of her belated withdrawal. She had made the final decision to withdraw only after receiving a request from her father to do so. She planned, however, to defend her title at Forest Hills later that summer. Catherine Wills added that Helen was deeply disappointed at not being able to participate as a player at Wimbledon. Then she disclosed with a knowing smile, "Helen is just like a child and we did humor her for a while, but now she knows we must not take any strenuous exercises and we are sure that she will soon be her old-time self again." Helen Wills insisted that she felt in tip top shape, but newsmen noticed that she still had something of a convalescent pallor.

Instead of playing, Wills wrote about the tournament in a series of articles for the United Press. She also took time out to sketch the various participants. She was especially interested in the on- and off-court performances by Suzanne Lenglen. Now, perhaps at last, without facing her across the net, Helen Wills could see more closely the moves and the artistry that had placed Lenglen at the pinnacle of her sport.

On the opening day of the Jubilee Wimbledon, Queen Mary was present to distribute special commemorative medals to the former champions. Suzanne Lenglen, as the defending champion, was the last to receive her medal. She waited patiently at the end of the long line of celebrated veteran players, and when her name was called she tip-toed forward daintily and then curtsied before the Queen. Of all the great players present on that day, Lenglen received the loudest and the longest cheers and applause from the crowd. Following that solemn ceremony the courts were cleared, and an exhibition doubles match was staged for the royal family and other notables and spectators in attendance for this historic opening. In the exhibition match, Kitty McKane Godfree of England and Kea Bouman of the Netherlands played the undefeated team of Lenglen and Ryan. And to the shock not only of Lenglen and Ryan but of just about everyone else in attendance, Godfree and Bouman won. It was the first loss ever in doubles for the Lenglen-Ryan team, and Suzanne knew that it was a bad sign. Aiming at the performance of her life—winning Wimbledon without losing a game—Suzanne Lenglen had suddenly begun by losing a match before the royal family. Papa had been too ill to attend this tournament—another bad sign—and so Suzanne now had to reach within herself to find the strength to resist the resurging doubts about her abilities. In a matter of only a few hours she had to gather up her mental resolve once more, put this defeat out of mind, and proceed with the task at hand. Nonetheless, she could not help but suspect that some sinister force was at work to dethrone her at what should be the greatest moment of her career.

On the next afternoon Lenglen played the 35-year-old American veteran Mary K. Browne, whom she had just beaten on clay in Paris. Now she wanted to beat her in love sets on grass, where Browne was more experienced and more dangerous. But it didn't happen. Lenglen suddenly seemed uncertain and to have lost much of her keenness. She faltered several times during the match and failed to display any of her usual dancing vitality. She beat Browne, to be sure—but in the process of winning surrendered five games—the same number she had given up during the entire Wimbledon tournament the previous year. Her perfect Wimbledon was gone. After the match Lenglen was nervous and mentioned that she did not feel at all well. She had arranged to see a local physician, she said. She was coming down with something, she feared. She wasn't sure what it was.

When Lenglen left the tournament grounds following her win over Browne, she believed that her only match on the following day was a doubles contest in which she and Didi Vlasto would play Ryan and Browne. The match was listed for 4:30 p.m. No one told Suzanne that the posted schedule was not the final schedule and that changes might still be made. And later that afternoon, changes were made. The tournament referee, F. R. Burrow, added a 2:00 p.m. singles match for Suzanne Lenglen against Mrs. Evelyn Dewhurst, the champion of Ceylon. The match was scheduled because Queen Mary, an ardent and faithful fan of Lenglen's since 1919, wished to see her play in the singles, and the royal family had already made plans to be in attendance the following day. The revised schedule was published the next morning in London newspapers, but it was not seen by Suzanne and none of her friends called her attention to the change.

In the past Lenglen had been contacted each evening during the tournament by Commander Hillyard, secretary of the All-England Club, who reminded her of her matches on the following day and confirmed the final schedule for her. But Hillyard had been replaced in 1926 by Dudley Larcombe, who did not consider it his duty to inform the Goddess personally of schedule changes. Larcombe believed that it was the responsibility of the players themselves—including defending champions—to know the schedule and to appear promptly for their matches. Hillyard, who was present at the Jubilee tournament, no longer considered it his personal responsibility to keep Suzanne informed of the match schedule. In fact, even had he remained as secretary of the All-England Club he probably would no longer have gone out of his way for her. Ever since the match against Helen Wills in Cannes, Hillyard had been *persona non grata* with the Lenglens. Suzanne had acquired a deep dislike for him because she considered his decision to continue the match in Cannes after the false "out" call had been both unwise and unfair. She believed the false call should have been ruled a "let" rather than a point for Wills. And many fans and officials agreed with her. But Hillyard ruled the shot in question a point for Wills. Because of his insensitivity and his stupidity, she believed, she had almost lost. His action had endangered her supremacy, her health, her career, her name, and her future. And she still burned with resentment over the incident. She would never forgive Hillyard or Lord Charles Hope or Charles Aeschliman because of their failure to rescue her at a particularly critical and pivotal moment in her life.

Late the following morning Didi Vlasto told Lenglen of the schedule change and Suzanne immediately sent word to Burrow at the All-England Club that she could not possibly play at 2:00 p.m. She had a doctor's appointment at that time; she was not feeling well and needed to be treated before she could play. She would be present for her match at 4:00 p.m. Lenglen did not doubt for an instant, as the defending champion of the tournament and as the champion of France and as the Goddess, that her request for rescheduling of the already rescheduled singles match would not be honored. What she did not know, though, was that her message was never received by Burrow. The man who said he delivered the message to Burrow was Jacques Brugnon. Burrow said he did not receive it. Both men held to their stories over the years. Whatever the truth of the matter, the result was tragic.

On the following afternoon, Queen Mary arrived to watch Suzanne Lenglen. Suzanne did not appear. The Queen waited in her box beside Court No. 1 with her hands folded primly on her lap, her pale eyes looking politely down on the grass where nothing much seemed to be happening. A ground crew rolled the court and rolled it again and then rolled it again. The tournament committee was frantic and tried to dream up excuses for the delay. Several times the Queen was told that the Goddess would appear shortly, but the assurances were based upon wishful thinking and fervent prayer. Suzanne did not appear.

At 3:30 p.m., Suzanne Lenglen arrived at the club. Before she could proceed to her dressing room she was summoned to the club offices and there faced a group of enraged and embarrassed club officers. They demanded to know where she had been. What had she been thinking? Why had she not telephoned the club? Hadn't she seen the schedule of matches? Didn't she know that the Queen was waiting? How could she do this to her hosts? Immediately, Suzanne answered the emotional accusations of the men facing her with her own emotional pyrotechnics. She shot back at them in a low and then a high and loud tone verging on hysteria, chattering away like a mad machine. How dare they be so presumptuous? How dare they accuse her, the Great Lenglen? How dare they be so rude? How dare they? She made this tournament what it was, and she had brought in those crowds, and she had made possible the construction of the very building they were standing in. How dare they be so ungrateful? Had they already forgotten those Lenglen-trails-a-winding? Had they forgotten who she was? Why were they so stupid? How dare they? Papa would hear of this!

Lenglen turned her back on her detractors and marched from the office to her dressing room. There she collapsed in tears and suffered a severe *crise de nerfs*. They were all against her. Papa was gone. The ground seemed to be giving way beneath her feet. Everything was sliding away. Everything. There was nothing to hold on to any longer. Jean Borotra was called. He found Suzanne completely distraught in her dressing room. He asked politely if she would play, and she screamed back at him, "I can't even stand on my feet!"

During the long wait for Suzanne Lenglen, Helen Wills sat quietly in the gallery wondering what might be taking place behind the scenes. Finally, sensing that something must be drastically wrong—she remembered that Suzanne had a reputation for punctuality—she walked to the locker room. There she found an unusual amount of confusion, commotion, and hysteria among a small circle of women. Suzanne and Lady Wavertree and Mama Lenglen and Didi Vlasto were all there. From behind the white door of the dressing room marked "The Lady Champion" Helen heard sounds of weeping. She left immediately. Wills did not comment further on the incident except to observe that "people usually have a reason when they cry, and the reason must have been a real one, because Wimbledon meant much to Mlle. Lenglen."

Eventually, Borotra was chosen to convey the bad news to Queen Mary. Suzanne, he explained, was indisposed and was unable to play tennis on this day. The Queen listened politely and then expressed her concern for Suzanne's health and her hope for a quick recovery. A few minutes later she departed with her entourage.

Suzanne Lenglen's opponents for the afternoon were given the chance to accept a default for their matches. But in the singles and in the doubles competition, Lenglen's competitors refused to accept defaults and instead arranged for rescheduling of the postponed matches, to be played the following afternoon.

Meanwhile, Lenglen suspected that some sinister force was at work at Wimbledon to humiliate her and bring her down. Before coming to Wimbledon for her dressing down by club officials she had undergone electric shock treatments for severe pains in her neck and shoulders. She was running a temperature, and yet she had decided to participate in a tough doubles match. Out of sorts and already feeling mistreated, she was then emotionally browbeaten by the club officers. Why, she wondered, did they choose this moment to attack her? Why did they turn on her in what she thought was an unjust and ruthless way?

What had happened, and what had made possible the sudden lashing out at Suzanne Lenglen was a combination of developments—none alone particularly fateful for her but in combination proving to be a menacing and explosive concoction. First, there was the fact that the male officials not only of the All-England Club but also of every major club and association in western Europe had an unusual love-hate relationship with Lenglen. In England she had made both the Wimbledon tournament and the All-England Club financially sound after 1919, and she had put the women's competition in every tournament she played in on an equal footing with the men's competition. Indeed, in the finals competition, whenever Lenglen was defending her title or going for a title, the women's competition was an even bigger and more exciting event than the men's. Queen Mary came to Wimbledon, it was not overlooked, to see Suzanne Lenglen and no one else. When Suzanne did not play or when Suzanne had finished playing, the Queen departed. Ryan, Browne, Mallory, McKane-Godfree, Lambert-Chambers—none of them made scarcely any impression on either the Queen or the crowd unless they were paired with or played against Suzanne. Who, after all, could remember whom it was the Dorothea Lambert Chambers had conquered on her way to seven Wimbledon titles? But who could not remember the woman who had beaten Lambert Chambers in 1919? The other female players, accomplished and talented as they might be, were, after 1919, merely supporting figures for Suzanne's starring role in a compelling drama that seemed created for the French Goddess alone.

All of this the All-England Club management found well and good and financially profitable. What they abhorred and what eventually brought the storm of their wrath down on Suzanne Lenglen was the fact that the French woman knew her worth in this sport—a sport previously dominated by male players and still totally managed by males. Lenglen, the various managers, officials, lords, and grand panjandrums of the game discovered, behaved like no prior female player. Part of this, to be sure, was due to Papa Lenglen's ambitious and creative management, and part was due to Suzanne's recognition of her own outsize value to clubs whenever she played. Before the Great War when an invitation was first tendered to the Lenglens to appear in England, the Lenglen response had been: "What is the proposition?" Nobody had any doubts about the meaning of that ambiguous question. Always, the Lenglens let it be known that Suzanne was playing first for the Lenglens and then for France and then for the crowds. If the clubs were to be the financial beneficiaries from her appearances they must cough up certain perquisites, and that, after all else was said and done, was the proposition. And so the clubs did just that, Suzanne receiving nothing but the best and the most. But the clubs did not bend to her demands ungrudgingly. Suzanne Lenglen, no matter how big a star, was still, in the eyes of those who ran tennis, just a woman. She could make her demands, and she could call the tune, and she could lead the dance, but she could not make the men of the clubs and the associations love her—and they did not. From the very day she won her first tournament and the crowds adored her, Lenglen had been a major threat to the male domination of men's and women's tennis. And few of the men who dominated the sport doubted that some day somewhere Suzanne Lenglen would have to be put in her place or the entire comfortable established structure of national and international competition would crumble. That fateful sometime and somewhere just happened to be in 1926 at the Jubilee Wimbledon.

The man who led the resurgent assault on Suzanne Lenglen was F. R. Burrow, the referee of the tournament. It seems simply incredible that Burrow did not receive Lenglen's request for a postponement of her match on the second day of the tournament. Brugnon, Suzanne's close friend, insisted that he had delivered the message to Burrow. And Burrow, just as adamantly, insisted that he had never received it. Subsequently, acting on the allegation that he had not been notified of Lenglen's inability to appear for her match before the Queen, Burrow and a group of officers of the All-England Club went after her on the principle that no player was bigger than this tournament—and Lenglen had, in refusing to acknowledge that, been an insult to the game as well as the tournament. The fact of the matter was that for a long time now Suzanne Lenglen had indeed been bigger than this tournament, as the gate receipts demonstrated. Prior to 1926, Burrow and his cohorts would have been financially destroying their tournament had they threatened Suzanne enough to drive her away. But now they dared to give voice to their resentment and to take a gamble financially.

Two people other than Suzanne Lenglen were responsible for Burrow's bold action. First, by his serious illness and subsequent absence from Wimbledon, Papa Lenglen emboldened the English referee. Papa had always been Suzanne's crafty and unbending guardian. In his prime, club officials would no more dream of standing up to the outspoken male leader of the Lenglen family than they would have thought of not charging admission for Suzanne's matches. When Papa asked them what the proposition was, they did not argue long with him. He held the winning cards and knew it, and they knew it. But Papa had been slowly fading from the scene for some time now due to his failing health. He had been unable to make the 1926 trip to England, and so Suzanne had come with only Mama to provide encouragement and advice. Mama had failed her at Forest Hills, and Mama failed her again. Also, Suzanne had perhaps made a mistake and revealed her vulnerability by traveling to England under the Jubilee Guest System, a system that did not provide her with the previous cash incentives delivered to her through the FTA.

Second, there was the enigmatic but promising figure of Helen Wills, sitting in all her quiet majesty and mystery in the gallery at Wimbledon, sketching and taking notes and watching and waiting while the crowd watched her. In Cannes, Lenglen had won a very costly victory over this American girl—and the costs were still being tabulated at Wimbledon. Helen had also exposed some of Suzanne's vulnerabilities. Following the Big Match, Wills had returned to the courts to win again and again, but Lenglen fled. Helen Wills was very much the rising star now, the worthy, attractive, and crowd pleasing successor to the French Queen. She waited in the wings, literally, at Wimbledon, while Suzanne Lenglen did her own imitation of the croaking swan. Burrow and the other All-England Club officials were encouraged both by Helen Wills's presence and by her seemingly traditional attitude toward the lords of the game. Wills was not one to rock the boat, and that knowledge was also a source of encouragement for Burrow. If Helen Wills represented the future, then the future looked very good indeed for amateur tennis and its managers.

The first reports of the episode in the English newspapers were sympathetic toward Suzanne. The London *Daily News* observed that "by being indisposed, Mlle. Lenglen had created a bigger sensation than if Poincaré had publicly embraced Caillaux." But within hours the story went out that Suzanne had been faking it again, that she had actually feigned indisposition again—as she had done at Forest Hills and as she had done time and again—because she wished for some perverse psychological reason to slight the Queen of England. The newspapers picked up quickly on the story and naturally took the side of Queen Mary and Burrow and the other All-England Club officials. Before the night was over, Suzanne Lenglen had been transformed by the English press into the Black Queen; she had lost both the newspapers and the English public. Once again she sensed the ground giving way. Papa was not present, and she had no reserve forces, and everything was happening too quickly, and she had no real friends.

On the next afternoon Lenglen appeared with Vlasto to play the rescheduled doubles match against Ryan and Browne. Her request that the doubles be played before the singles had been granted. Lenglen had expected Ryan and Browne to be tougher competitors than Dewhurst and wanted to face them first. And they were tough—tougher even than she had imagined. As a result, Suzanne and her partner accomplished the unexpected—they lost. And they lost after arriving at double match point in the second set and then letting almost inevitable victory elude them. While Vlasto's play remained fairly consistent throughout the match, Lenglen's fell apart at the most critical part of the contest—at double match point—and she was unable to play with the needed drive and command during the remaining games. Ryan and Browne took the second set 9–7. In the third set the teams each held service until the Americans led, 3–2, with Lenglen serving. At a crucial point in the game a foot-fault was called against Lenglen—the sort of call she had avoided in Cannes by insisting that no foot-fault judge be present. Now the call visibly upset her, so she double-faulted and foot-faulted away the rest of the game. And then, still obsessed with the judging of the match, she began to hit wildly and missed easy shots, shots that she was capable of putting away though blindfolded, on one of her good days. But this was not one of her good days, and the third and deciding set went to the Americans, 6–2.

What was doubly disturbing to Suzanne Lenglen about the match was the behavior of the crowd. The English crowd had become a bunch of turncoats. Their loyalty was gone, fled with the revelations and the intimations in the English press about her allegedly calculated insult to Queen Mary. The capricious multitude that had gathered annually to celebrate Suzanne Lenglen now wildly cheered the American resurgence and victory and appeared to delight in her fall. It seemed that there was not a spectator in the crowd—with the exception of Mama Lenglen—who would risk cheering for the Goddess now. In the past Suzanne had won over the partisan crowds by the brilliance of her performance. But her performance had become pathetic and the crowd was won over no longer.

That afternoon Lenglen played her rescheduled singles match against Dewhurst. She was still not at her best, nor was she playing in anything even remotely like her top form. She beat Dewhurst, to be sure, but the score was 6–2, 6–2. The match was supposed to be a walkover; it wasn't. It was supposed to be easy; it wasn't. It was a chance for Suzanne to show her stuff once more; she didn't.

After the Dewhurst match Lenglen told her friends that she was really ill. Rheumatism in her neck and shoulders had kept her from sleeping, and now she was tired and sore and had a temperature of 102°. Newsmen intimated that she was faking it, and so Jean Borotra rushed to her defense and confessed, "She is very ill . . . she cries all the time . . . her mother cannot pacify her."

In addition to all of this, the press reported a snubbing of Suzanne Lenglen by Queen Mary after the doubles loss to the Americans. On her way back to the locker room after the match Suzanne had stood aside for a moment as Queen Mary made her exit. The Queen passed within a few feet of Lenglen but appeared to ignore her. The press delighted in this and played it all up as a royal snub in retaliation for Suzanne Lenglen's action on the previous day. In fact, however, there had been no snub. Queen Mary had simply not noticed Suzanne, and she had inquired about the French woman's health. But word of the Queen's inquiry was not conveyed either to the newsmen or to Lenglen. The individual who had been requested to deliver the message was, unfortunately, no friend of hers. Mme. De Fleuriau, the wife of the French Ambassador, was, in fact, somewhat envious of Lenglen's popularity in England. And so she withheld from the Goddess what might have provided encouragement or solace and instead became one of Suzanne's principal critics. Eventually she advised Lenglen to cancel the planned presentation at Buckingham Palace because the slight of Queen Mary had made Suzanne *persona non grata* with the English royal family. The statement was a complete fabrication, but, having read the newspapers and experienced the hostility of the gallery at Wimbledon, Suzanne accepted it as fact.

The next afternoon Suzanne Lenglen appeared to play her mixed doubles match partnered with Jean Borotra. The general atmosphere was again unfriendly, and the crowd greeted her with hissing and booing as she walked to the umpire's chair to put down her extra rackets and sweater. Al Laney saw that the noise had a visible impact on Lenglen and wondered if she might not burst into tears at any moment and run from the court. Borotra partially saved the afternoon by providing some comic relief—he served his first two serves wildly into the stands and gave an expression of astonishment, pretending not to understand why the balls were behaving so crazily. The crowd laughed, and the atmosphere became less hostile. But Lenglen did not play as she had in the past. She could not dance to hisses. She moved about the court without spirit, listlessly. Nevertheless, she and her partner beat the English team of H.I.P. Aitken and Mrs. B.C. Brown, 6–3, 6–0.

Referee Burrow now had come to expect Suzanne Lenglen to default at any moment. The Monday schedule—the doubles match had been played on Saturday afternoon—included a short statement announcing that Suzanne Lenglen would play "if well enough" in the singles against Miss C. Beckingham. On Monday what Burrow had expected to happen did happen. Lenglen sent a message to Burrow in the morning—a message he received without any short-circuiting—stating that she was not well enough to play any longer and so wished to retire from the singles competition. She elaborated and explained that early in the morning she had felt well and was ready to play anybody in the world, but then she began to feel stabbing pains from neuritis in her shoulder and found herself unable to hold a racket and so could not compete. "I'm sorry," she apologized. "I tried as hard as I could but it was impossible. I thought until the last minute that I would be able to play. But suddenly a terrific pain seized my right shoulder and my right arm became dead. I cannot even lift it. It goes well for ten minutes and then I find I cannot use it." On the following morning she sent another message to Burrow announcing her retirement from the doubles competition.

Burrow received her messages with a mixture of relief and regret, he said. It was unfortunate that she could not have brought herself to these decisions earlier. There was now very little genuine sorrow over her departure. Had she dropped out earlier perhaps she might have saved a great deal of "misunderstanding." Burrow attributed her physical and emotional ills at Wimbledon to a combination of unexpectedly tough competition and the excitement of the Jubilee year. He also said that a large part of her problem was due to having too many advisers, some of whom had misled her into believing she was sufficiently powerful, even at Wimbledon, to say when she would or would not play. Suzanne Lenglen had simply been given some very bad advice. The public, Burrow insisted, believed that Lenglen had in fact been treated far too leniently in the past. "The championships are greater than any champion," he moralized. "But it was a pity that it should have been the Jubilee meeting at which this axiom should have needed expression." He suggested that in previous years "possibly too much attention had been paid to her wishes." In the past she had been treated with all of the deference "due a champion and a lady. But in 1926 she presumed too far on her position in the tennis world." And so the right time had arrived to put Suzanne Lenglen in her proper place.

While many newsmen doubted Lenglen's story of illness, the *New York Times* was quite charitable in its coverage of the episode. Suzanne was a woman of great natural nervous energy, the paper pointed out, and there was no reason to believe that anything other than ill health had been responsible for her withdrawal. But when Molla Mallory was asked for her evaluation of the Lenglen action, she was not generous. "What can I say?" she responded. "What is there to say?" She merely reminded everyone of Lenglen's 1921 default at Forest Hills and suggested that in the past she had used the excuse of ill health as a ploy when things were not going her way. How could anyone doubt that she was once again up to her old tricks?

Writing of the episode for *American Lawn Tennis,* Stephen Wallis Merrihew referred to it as "l'Affaire de Lenglen" and said that "at first it was regarded with indignation—but then people were led to see the whimsical, even the humorous side of it. And ultimately it came to be viewed in the light of one of those visitations that are fated to happen, given circumstances that lead, logically and inevitably, to a situation as unpleasant as it is unnecessary." And he agreed with the action by the Wimbledon officials. "It was an irony of fate," he wrote, "that the institution of Wimbledon should be tested during the Jubilee Wimbledon. There, more than anywhere else, the game is the thing and the players are part of it." He had no sympathy at all with the French sentiment that Suzanne Lenglen had been badly mistreated by the very individuals for whom she had, over the years, done enormous favors.

"I am awfully sorry to see Mlle. Lenglen out of the tournament," Helen Wills told newsmen. "I know what it means to sit on the sidelines to watch players strive for the championship that you have set your heart on winning. I wish Mlle. Lenglen the speediest return to health and hope we both some time, somewhere, will get well enough to play a return match."

Her close friends were, of course, outspoken in her defense. "Poor Suzanne," Didi Vlasto said to newsmen, "suffers such dreadful pain. She cannot sleep from the pain and is obliged to wear her arm in a sling. She is unable even to grasp a racket and couldn't possibly fulfill any of her engagements. It is quite unlikely that she will be able to play for several months." Suzanne would continue her electrical shock treatments and remain indoors, Vlasto explained. And she was now most anxious to return home to her Papa to rest. "It is all very tragic," Vlasto observed. "Everybody is kind, but it is not very gay for a girl to be sick in a hotel. We and other friends are trying our utmost to keep her cheerful."

It was, indeed, not very gay at all for a girl to be sick in a hotel room, and so Suzanne decided not to be. Following her defaults she attended the Jubilee tournament and watched a semifinal match between Howard

Kinsey of the United States and Jean Borotra. She stayed in the gallery for four hours but then left before the start of the women's doubles competition. Newsmen who saw her noticed that she did not look ill.

With both Wills and Lenglen out of the Jubilee Wimbledon competition, the singles title went to Kitty McKane Godfree, who beat Lili de Alvarez in three sets, 6–2, 4–6, 6–3. This was Alvarez's debut on the Centre Court, and the great expectations aroused by her appearance prevented the tournament from becoming a financial disaster after Suzanne Lenglen defaulted. Alvarez was hardly spectacular, however, and her play was several levels below that of Wills and Lenglen. The crowd at courtside was disappointed, and the Spanish woman confessed after her loss, "Ah, when I am good, I am good. But when I am bad, oh, I am damn bad." Ryan and Browne won the women's doubles, Brugnon and Cochet the men's doubles, and Borotra the men's singles. Had Lenglen remained in good health and in the good graces of the officials of the tournament, there is very little doubt that French players could have swept the titles at this special Wimbledon.

For a time after Lenglen's default it was expected that the French champion yet might be presented at court and a kind of meeting of the Queens take place. In fact, she had purchased a special elegant gown for the presentation and had described it in glowing detail to newsmen. But then Mme. Fleuriau succeeded in convincing her that her behavior at Wimbledon constituted an affront to the royal family. Consequently, she was no longer welcome at court. Publicly, Lenglen explained her action by explaining that "no girl would like to be presented amid all that splendor with her arm in a sling." The English press and public were critical of her cancellation and seemed to believe it was her way of scratching back at the English for the mistreatment she had received from Wimbledon officials. But shortly after she departed for France Lenglen reminded English newsmen, "After all is said, you must remember that I am only a girl, not a medieval warrior who thrives on disturbance. To me all this commotion about my playing or not playing is most upsetting. I have been a most miserable girl for the past few days."

The spectators who had seen Lenglen play at Wimbledon in 1926 never suspected that they were witnessing her last appearance in the tournament. Even Burrow expected that the Goddess had merely been put in her place and that she would return in the future, a more agreeable and pliable player. After all, what else could she do? But in fact Lenglen's brilliant amateur tennis career had at long last come to an end. She had wanted badly to win Wimbledon in 1926 and thus to tie the record of seven singles victories set by Mrs. Lambert Chambers before Lenglen dethroned her in 1919. But that was not to be. Her record at Wimbledon was completed in 1926. But what a record! Since 1919 she had won six singles titles in the tournament. She had suffered defeats in the mixed doubles only twice and in the doubles only once—in 1926. In the singles she played 32 matches and won them all. She played 66 sets and won 64—losing one to Lambert Chambers in 1919 and one to Ryan in 1924. Of the 66 sets she played she had won 59 by a score of 6–2 or better. She had taken 29 sets at love.

Between April 1922 and July 1926 she had won 155 straight matches. And before she traveled to America in 1921 she had won 114 matches in a row starting in 1919. And so in the eight years between 1919 and 1926 she had won 269 of 270 matches, and she had won eight major tournaments without surrendering a game.

In addition to those incomparable statistics she left the memory of her brilliance and her artistry etched indelibly in the memories of tens of thousands of fans in England and on the Continent. There was no doubt about it, Suzanne Lenglen was a tennis player and a woman the likes of which the fans at Wimbledon would never see again.

When the Jubilee Wimbledon was finally over, Helen Wills returned to the United States aboard the *Majestic*. As the ship approached New York harbor several tugboats filled with flowers pulled alongside. The flowers were for Helen from some of her fans. And then a special welcoming committee from the USLTA boarded the liner to greet Helen. When the ship docked in New York a familiar mob of newsmen and photographers and fans were waiting. Everyone had praise for her accomplishments in Europe. Before saying goodbye to her, the cabin boys told her how strongly they had favored her in France and how much they wanted her to go back in 1927 to play Suzanne Lenglen again and to win. Helen Wills patiently answered the barrage of inquiries from the newsmen. The voyage home, unlike the voyage to France in January, had been calm, and Helen said she felt fully rested. Asked if she planned to defend her national singles title, Wills said, "I do not wish to do anything foolish." She planned to return to the courts to practice and then to assess her capabilities and her recovery before committing herself to play at Forest Hills. She did say, however, that, no matter how rapid her recovery, she did not plan to travel abroad in 1927 and so there would be no rematch with Suzanne Lenglen in Europe next year.

Helen Wills discovered in New York that her name had become a household word in America in the past several weeks. Everyone, it seemed, now knew almost everything about her. She had made the white tennis visor the fashion rage, and imitations of that sporting attire were now worn by millions of "shop girls, street sheiks, idlers, bummers, city park loungers, and knickered liberated female motorists," *Time* magazine reported. Someone gave her a newspaper clipping from only a week earlier describing an incident in Hartford, Connecticut, where a laborer wore a white visor to work and was called "Helen Wills" by one of his fellow workers. So he smashed a shovel over the man's head. Helen saved the clipping and reprinted it later in her autobiography.

Helen Wills checked into the Forest Hills Inn with her mother. And a few days later she returned to the grass courts of the West Side Tennis club and hit with Paul Heston, the assistant professional of the club. The practice session was light and lasted only twenty minutes. She didn't run, but rather stayed on the baseline and tried to get her rhythm and form back. Reporters who came to watch the practice wrote that she had lost very little of her touch and that she hit as hard as Heston and with remarkable accuracy. She was, in fact, a picture of health on the court that morning and, with her eyeshade and long white cotton skirt and middy blouse, she seemed just like the Helen Wills of old. After completing her practice she posed for a dozen photographers and talked about her plans. If she continued to feel well, she said, she would play at Forest Hills. "It hardly seems that I have had appendicitis," she declared, and the newsmen agreed that she appeared to be in tip-top shape.

The next morning Wills again practiced with Heston and then announced that she had entered two tournaments in order to test herself and to prepare for the defense of her title.

She returned to competitive tennis in the first week in August when she played in the Maidstone Invitational Tournament in East Hampton. All attention in that tournament, naturally, focused on the American girl. Three hours before she was scheduled to play the gallery was filled with a fashionably attired well-heeled crowd. Before the match the referee approached Wills and notified her that he would be willing to postpone the match at any time if she felt even the slightest discomfort. Wills said she was ready. And then, in a little less than thirty minutes on the court, she dispatched her first victim, Mrs. Edward Raymond. In her win, Helen gave the wide-eyed and appreciative crowd only an enticingly small sample of her real capabilities. She conserved her strength during the match and stepped from the baseline only when it was absolutely necessary. She did not race after several of Raymond's returns, and she gave up five games in the match. Although she won, 6–1, 6–4, there was some concern over her stamina and her ability to stand up to a really accomplished and energetic foe.

In the second round of the tournament she played Mrs. Edna Rosser and won again, but her play was inconsistent and see-sawed back and forth between unparalleled brilliance and something a little more commonplace. The second set of the match went to 9–7, a bad sign for Wills, and she was only barely saved from the exhaustion of a third set. She left the baseline more often now and volleyed effectively. This was probably necessary because her ground strokes were neither very steady nor hit with much effective pace. Power, the mainstay of her game, was simply not there during this match.

In the finals of the Maidstone tournament, Helen Wills met her first real test since her illness—Mary K. Browne. She rose nicely to the occasion and ended for a time the concerned talk of her early retirement. Now she seemed to show that she was truly ready to defend her national title. She used her straight hard deep service to put Browne back and then kept her back with deep accurate and low ground strokes. When Browne came in to the net to volley, Wills pounded her to pieces or defty lobbed over her head. From the opening service, she controlled the match, and in 45 minutes she beat Browne, 6–3, 6–2.

It was an effective and convincing display, and the crowds came away satisfied that the American Girl was unstoppable. She appeared to be in perfect shape, and it was Browne who was exhausted at the end of the match. Most spectators failed to notice that Helen Wills was hurting by the end of the second set. Between points she placed her right hand against her side and pressed hard to stop shooting pains. After she had won, she tried to leave quickly and was slowed down only momentarily by a mass of well-wishers who blocked her path and shouted praise and encouragement to her. In her dressing room she felt the strain and the pain of the win. Following her victory over Browne, she said later, "I faded gradually from the scene."

Despite her health Wills remained entered in the tournament at Sea-bright the next week and made her way through the early rounds with little trouble. Nobody pointed out that her opponents were anything but first-rate players. In the semifinal round she beat Eleanor Goss, 7–5, 6–4, and the match consumed all her available resolve and energy. In the finals she played Elizabeth Ryan, who had beaten her on the same courts one year earlier. Ryan outplayed her both from the backcourt and at the net, and in only 38 minutes crushed Wills again, 6–4, 6–1. In the final minutes of the match the crowd—the largest ever for the tournament, due to the return of the American Girl—was moved almost to pity for the pathetic stroking of Helen Wills who could only pat soft returns over the net and then wait for Ryan to blast winners. Everything happened so quickly, it was almost an anti-climax. "A game, another game, a set and before you knew it the match was over and the players were being photographed with the victor of 1925 holding still another trophy and the national champion trying to hide her disappointment as she walked off the court amid applause," one reporter summed it up. Helen Wills gained some glory in the tournament, however, when partnered with fellow Californian Edward Chandler, she beat Bill Tilden and Molla Mallory in the finals of the mixed doubles competition.

Although the newsmen continued to praise Wills's play and to make excuses for her, many of her close friends were advising her to discontinue play for the rest of the season. Temperatures were high, humidity was nearly unbearable, matches were played on fast grass courts, all took a dangerously heavy toll. She nonetheless entered another tournament—this one at the Westchester Club in Rye, New York—in order to get more practice before Forest Hills. Again she made it through the early rounds without difficulty. Then she confronted Molla Mallory in the semifinals. The result was Mallory's first victory over her since 1922. The match took 90 minutes and was intense throughout—but Mallory came away with a three-set victory. Near the end of the match Helen Wills found that she had no more energy, no spring in her toes, and no desire to continue playing tennis. The long campaign of 1926 had finally come to an end. After the match Wills announced she would not defend her national title. She left for California, and her decision to stop playing tennis for the next several months, Allison Danzig wrote in the *New York Times,* was "approved by a sympathetic and admiring public."

Molla Mallory's win over Helen Wills marked the beginning of a short dramatic comeback for the former champion. Mallory won the national title at Forest Hills that year for a record eighth time. She was thirty-two years old, and her victory gave her the greatest number of wins in singles in any major tournament in the world for women—one more than Mrs. Lambert Chambers's record of seven wins at Wimbledon. And she did it against enormous odds. In the final she beat Elizabeth Ryan, who had beaten her in every one of their nine previous matches. But this year there was no stopping Mallory, and she took her former nemesis in a tough three-set match, 4–6, 6–4, 9–7.

Helen Wills came home to California before the Forest Hills matches began. She was sorry she could not defend her title, she said, but she was not sorry she had played in three preliminary tournaments in order to test her physical stamina. Before leaving New York she wrote to a friend, "I know now that you were right when you cautioned me about playing, but I'm glad, anyway, that I tried because now I cannot say to myself, 'Well, I might have been able to have played if I'd only tried.' I am looking forward to a long breath of California air—it seems here that you can't really enjoy the air at all, it's so heavy."

When Wills's train arrived in Berkeley, it was clear that she was still "the idol of California." There was the familiar large crowd that included Helen's sorority sisters and another army of photographers and reporters. Although Wills was exhausted by her journey, she still cooperated with newsmen, patiently answering their questions and posing for the photographers. One reporter wrote admiringly that Helen was "just a brave little soldier who stood up before the firing line. She made not one single protest but breathed an audible sigh of relief when it was over."

Back in Berkeley, Helen sensed certain changes in herself resulting from her European adventure. "The sight of foreign lands, the loss of my long hair (and, perhaps, my appendix), the dresses from Patou, a bit of romance, the disappointment of not playing at Wimbledon, had all had their effect," she found. "I had lost some of my square sturdiness and the brilliant color that used to be there had gone from my cheeks, never to come back."

And she had become famous. She had learned in France the extraordinary pleasures and privileges that came with being well known. There were suddenly millions of people interested in every detail of her life. Everything she did was news. People wanted to do things for her. She was royalty. She was suddenly first in the hearts and minds of her countrymen. And she liked that.

In Europe and the United States Wills had both won and lost in 1926. And, not surprisingly, she found that winning was better and that she did not like losing at all. And so she decided—just as Suzanne Lenglen had decided early in her career—never to lose again. It seemed an impossible goal, but it was a goal that Helen came very close to achieving.

CHAPTER
VII

PROFESSIONALS

"The fact that people hated her was enough for
me. People will pay to see anybody they hate."
                                                    —C. C. Pyle, 1926

"I could see that she was no schoolgirl tennis star
who could be salved with one of those what-you-
owe-the-sport arguments."
                                                    —William Pickens, 1926

"Fireworks! Believe me, I will show them fireworks
in the United States."
                                                    —Suzanne Lenglen, 1926

IT was raining in Los Angeles. And a small group of men gathered in
the lobby of the Biltmore Hotel to escape the downpour and talk about
the news of the day. It was a February afternoon in 1926, and the news
they talked about centered on events on the French Riviera, where there
was no prohibition law and the sun was shining and hundreds of lucky
journalists and thousands of spectators followed the machinations and
maneuvers of Suzanne Lenglen and Helen Wills as they breezed their way
through minor tennis competitions and approached their anticipated
clash in Cannes. What did it all mean? What would happen next? Would
they ever really play each other? How good was Suzanne Lenglen, anyway? Hadn't Molla Mallory mashed her at Forest Hills in 1921?

The man most outspoken in the discussion was Damon Runyon. Like
everyone else, he was following the drama unfolding on the Riviera. It
really was a terrific story, he felt. The American newsmen in France were
writing it up as a mythical good-versus-evil confrontation, and the American public was hooked. Runyon especially liked the evil character of the
piece—Suzanne Lenglen. She had the ability to do things that pushed
politics and catastrophes off the front pages of newspapers. And although
every American didn't love her, every American did seem to love to read
about her. And if people loved to read about her, he asked, wouldn't
they gladly pay to see her in the flesh? Hadn't Hollywood shown beyond
any reasonable doubt that bad girls were big box office? Why, Suzanne
Lenglen was a potential box office bonanza, he said. In fact, he was sure
of it. And somebody—some American—with a little imagination and know

how and some cold cash could capitalize nicely on her delicious infamy and on the controversy she cultivated. Runyon didn't know at the moment who was profiting most from her activities—the club and casino owners or the tennis equipment manufacturers or the Lenglen family or all of those groups. But surely, he said, someone in this country ought to be savvy enough to transform Suzanne's notoriety into some good hard Yankee dollars.

After all, the American public was on a sports binge. There had already been million-dollar gates for boxing matches, and record crowds turned out for baseball games and football games and car races and horse races. And people came out by the tens of thousands in Europe to see Suzanne Lenglen. Not just to see her play tennis, mind you, but just to see her. She had been a financial boon for Forest Hills in 1921 and a windfall for Wimbledon ever since 1919. Maybe with the proper promotion, she could ballyhoo tennis into the biggest spectator sport of all. Anyway, somebody ought to take a stab at it.

Runyon addressed his advice on commercializing Suzanne Lenglen to the man sitting next to him in the Biltmore lobby. The man was William Hickman Pickens, one of the more successful promoters of the day. Pickens made money by exhibiting the bizarre, the exotic, the unusual, the dangerous and the outrageous before crowds of wide-eyed provincials who were hungry for the brand of carnival-like excitement he brought them. He'd initially made his reputation as a promoter in San Francisco in 1915 when he put together the world's first "indoor flight" by an airplane. He'd hired a friend, Lincoln Beachy, to fly an airplane in the Palace of Machinery building, which was only 900 feet long, during the Panama-Pacific Exposition. Beachy did it. Runyon asked Pickens why he didn't grab Suzanne Lenglen and "exhibit her" in America. It was a hell of a lot safer way to make money than flying an airplane indoors.

"I wasn't much interested at first," Pickens later said. "But Runyon kept ribbing me and finally convinced me that Suzanne would be a wow in our big cities."

At the time Pickens was working as a front man for another promoter, the legendary C. C. Pyle. Pyle's principal concern at the moment—and Pickens's—was the profitable career of professional football player Harold "Red" Grange. Pickens suggested that Runyon tell Pyle his thoughts on Suzanne Lenglen. Runyon said he just might do that.

And so he did. In late February, Runyon was in Chicago, where he met with Pyle and told him that Suzanne Lenglen could be the biggest show-biz attraction in the country. As Pyle listened to Runyon make his pitch, some of the other men present disagreed. But Runyon was adamant in his insistence that Suzanne would be a big hit in America.

"No she wouldn't," someone shot back. "People hate her." When he heard that remark, Pyle instantly made up his mind to sign Suzanne Lenglen to a contract. Runyon was right. Absolutely right. Suzanne was indeed a hot property. "The fact that people hated her was enough for me," Pyle said later. "People will pay to see anybody they hate."

Nobody knew better than Pyle what people would pay to see and what they would not pay to see. And when he decided that people would pay to see Suzanne Lenglen, he put in motion a scheme that he hoped would destroy the entire existing system of amateur tennis. He planned to revolutionize tennis and all other amateur sports. But his revolution could succeed, he believed, only if Lenglen served as the figurehead representing liberty and justice for all athletes.

He was an American original. Like Suzanne Lenglen, Charles C. Pyle, whose initials were said to stand at some times for "Cold Cash" and at others for "Cash and Carry," was a legend in his own time. If he had never been born, Mark Twain would have invented him, and W. C. Fields would have played him in the movies. In the era of ballyhoo, bombast, and boosterism, Pyle was king. He was the booster's booster, the promoter's promoter, the huckster's huckster who mastered the barker's art of chewing more than he bit off. He was as close as the decade of the 1920s would ever come to combining the talents of P. T. Barnum, Don King, Col. Tom Parker, and the Oral Roberts. He was a dreamer and a preacher, a door-to-door salesman in the age of the mass media who used the press and the radio to pound on every door in the country at the same time. Had he picked a slogan to convey his business philosophy, it would have been, "You ain't seen nothin' yet."

Pyle made a profitable career out of conning both urban and rural yokels and sophisticates from one end of America to the other into slapping down cash—piles of it—to see his extravaganzas, exhibitions, and personalities. He was a public-relations genius who believed that lying was a fine art and that the only man who told the truth was one who lacked imagination. And Cash and Carry Pyle did not lack imagination. He did not lack energy or audacity either. He was an apostle of the main chance, who believed that a fool and his money are soon parted and helped to make it come true. One journalist said that money talked to Pyle, and it usually said, "Hello, brother" and "Open, sesame!"

Pyle, the son of a Methodist minister, was raised in a religious household in Delaware, Ohio. His mother wanted him to be a minister like his father, and so she sent him off to Ohio State University. After a year he left school. He never went into the ministry but he inherited his father's talent for preaching.

With his discovery of Suzanne Lenglen he was getting back to his roots. The first thing Pyle ever promoted was a sporting event. When he was sixteen he sponsored a bicycle race between Barney Oldfield and a local youngster. Oldfield got twenty-five dollars for taking part in the race and Pyle got seven. Because he was an amateur, the local youngster received nothing. From that moment Pyle had a deep affection for amateurs. He became an advance man for a traveling drama company, posting bills, painting, repairing, and moving scenery, playing a tuba in the band, taking tickets, doing a drunk act, making hotel and stagecoach reservations, and serving as a drama critic for the group. His "temperate and thoughtful reviews" were given away free to local newspapers as he traveled with his fellow actors through Oregon and California. Then Pyle started his own drama company. To cut expenses, he became his own leading man. And he gradually increased his profits by cutting down the size of the company. As a result he became an extraordinarily resourceful performer. He staged *Uncle Tom's Cabin* with a cast of four, and he performed *The Three Musketeers* with a single musketeer. There were times when a single performer had to take five or six roles in the same play. These productions were big profit makers for Pyle, who usually left town in the middle of the night right after the final show.

In 1908 he came to the conclusion that the future was in movies. Pyle bought a projector and some films and started to travel again. Two years later he went broke in Boise. He sold his lens to buy a meal. He decided the future wasn't in movies. By 1910, however, he was back in the movie business in Chicago. In the next sixteen years he built up a chain of theaters in the area. One of them was in Champaign where, in the mid-1920s, an extraordinary young athlete named Harold "Red" Grange, "The Galloping Ghost," was becoming a legend while playing football for the University of Illinois. Pyle read about Grange and watched him and decided that he wanted to promote the young star. While Grange was still playing in college, Pyle became his manager and press agent. He gave out interviews in behalf of Grange and arranged for a professional football contract for him. Grange eventually signed with the Chicago Bears for $100,000, an amount not to be surpassed in sports until Joe Namath signed with the New York Jets forty years later.

But the Grange enterprise created a controversy. The Illini alumni said that they didn't like the idea of the Galloping Ghost signing up with a flim-flam promoter just to make a hundred thousand dollars. They argued that he had denigrated himself and the university. They wanted him, instead, to go into business and make his money there rather than in sport. Alumni organizations from other universities sponsored scores of resolutions denouncing any athlete who signed up with Pyle. Pyle enjoyed the controversy. "Publicity means only one thing," he said at the time. "Controversy!"

With Red Grange, Pyle became "a peddler of personalities." While other promoters of the period, like Tex Rickard, stressed the contests they staged, Pyle pushed personalities. His first personality was himself. He promoted himself to townsfolk throughout the West when he was a dramatist. Then he promoted himself to Red Grange. Grange became his second personality. Suzanne Lenglen was to be his third.

Pyle was still promoting Grange when Runyon arrived in Chicago and suggested that he get into the Suzanne Lenglen business. Pyle wired

Pickens in Los Angeles and ordered him to stop everything and catch the next train to Chicago. Then in a secret strategy session in Chicago he ordered Pickens to proceed to France and get Lenglen's signature on a contract for a tour of the United States. Pickens suggested that the price for landing Suzanne might be high—as high as $15,000, in fact. Pyle didn't wince at that figure. "Sign her," he said. "Just sign her." And so Pickens departed for France.

Before sailing, Pickens stopped in New York long enough to receive discouraging advice from two individuals. Edward Moss, secretary of the USLTA, told Pickens that his organization would never sanction a professional promoter joining the ranks of respectable amateur tennis. Even if Lenglen did agree to a contract to play tennis in the United States, Moss said, she would have to be managed by the USLTA from the time she arrived until the time she departed.

What Moss did not tell Pickens was that at that very moment there were ongoing negotiations between the USLTA and the French Tennis Association regarding a possible American tour for Suzanne Lenglen and an accompanying French team. The tour was to include her participation once again in the national singles tournament at Forest Hills in August with the probability of another dramatic clash between Lenglen and Wills, but this time in America and on fast American grass courts. Some of the negotiation involved opening up the Wightman Cup matches—an Anglo-American competition exclusively—to the French. The French would send a Wightman Cup team to the United States that would include Lenglen. As Allison Danzig of the *New York Times* observed, however, the successful "consummation of the plans" for the matches hinged upon the decision of Suzanne Lenglen. And the FTA simply would not commit itself to sending a team to America unless Suzanne agreed to be on it.

Pickens then approached Georges Carpentier, the prizefighter, who was in New York and who was a close friend of the Lenglen family. Carpentier assured Pickens that if the issue of professionalism ever came up, Suzanne would simply break off the discussion. She would never leave the ranks of amateur tennis. It was simply too profitable for her.

Pickens proceeded to France, nonetheless, with that discouraging advice ringing in his ears. He recalled several years later, "I didn't mind Moss so much, but I had wasted a good cigar on Georges."

After hearing of Pickens's unpromising meeting with Moss, Pyle contacted the USLTA and requested the sanctioning of matches for Lenglen in the United States in anticipation of her signing a contract with him. But when Suzanne was told of the request, she said that she had no intention of playing tennis in America ever again. "I play for my own pleasure and am completely free to do so when and where I desire. This is merely another one of the canards launched by the so-called sports writers in the United States who seem to take pleasure in inventing all

kinds of unpleasant and untrue things about me, cooking up matrimo-
nial prospects and similar nonsense every week. Why they do it is a mystery to me." Moreover, she said, she had no desire to go to a country, to
play tennis, "where many people deliberately malign and misinterpret
my very nervous Latin temperament. I will never play in the United
States again." She pointed out the climate, unlike that of the Riviera,
did not agree with her. And if ever she came to an American tennis tournament again it would be as a spectator and not as a player.

The USLTA took a firm stand against Pyle's proposals: they would
not sanction matches by Lenglen in America when they were played for
the profit of Pyle. The situation of a promoter bringing an amateur tennis champion to the United States under a contract and expecting the
USLTA to lend its approval to her appearing in exhibition matches
struck one official as "ludicrous." The USLTA position was clear: it was
not about to split its profits with an upstart lowbrow promoter.

A few reporters sensed that Pickens was up to something big for Pyle.
And they tried to find out what. So Pickens fed them tall tales. He said
at first that he was going to arrange a European tour for Red Grange.
And he also suggested that he was going to deliver an autographed football to the Prince of Wales. In Paris, Pickens stopped to speak with Victor Breyer, editor of *L'Echo des Sports*. Breyer was surprised that Pickens
had traveled so far just to try to sign Suzanne Lenglen to a professional
contract. He was also shocked, he said, by Pickens's "temerity." "I looked
temerity up that night in my vest pocket dictionary," Pickens recalled.
"It meant gall, which made me a millionaire in the temerity business."

Pickens spoke with several other French journalists, each of whom assured him that there was no chance whatever of Lenglen abandoning
amateur tennis to become an object for exhibition. And besides, they all
agreed, amateur tennis paid well in France. Pickens also found that every
Frenchman he met claimed to know Suzanne Lenglen very well and to
understand her thinking well enough to predict precisely what she would
do when confronted with the chance to become a professional tennis
player.

Pickens tracked Lenglen down in Nice. But before he could speak with
her he saw a copy of the Paris edition of the *New York Herald,* which
carried a large front-page photograph of Pyle and a story claiming that
Pickens was in France to sign up Suzanne as a professional for $200,000.

When Papa Lenglen saw the *Herald* story he became enraged. American reporters on the Riviera who tried to question him about the matter
found that he was hostile to all Americans. "If I were a younger man I
would give a magnificent kick in the seat of the pants to all those so-
disgusting American journalists who have written such filthy things in-
sulting my daughter's honor," he roared. "The American newspapers
have printed such vile lies about Suzanne that I will not talk to any

American reporter." Papa held up a fistful of newspaper clippings sent to him by Suzanne's friends, all of them indicating that Suzanne would turn professional. He insisted that he had never heard of either Pyle or Red Grange and had received no offers for a contract from Pickens or Pyle or from anyone else.

The Pickens mission was denounced as "unethical," and the FTA issued an "authorized statement" from Cannes stating that there was "not the remotest chance" of Suzanne Lenglen agreeing to leave the ranks of amateur tennis players. The statement was signed by Suzanne, and it asserted that no matter what the proposition Suzanne would not abandon amateur tennis "for years, if ever."

One reporter cornered Lenglen for a moment and asked her if it was true that she had been offered a professional contract worth $10,000. She was astonished not so much at the rumor of the contract but at the puny amount suggested for her services. She responded by saying that, no, she had not been approached by any promoters from Scotland.

On the next morning Pickens telephoned the Villa Ariem and spoke with Papa Lenglen. He said that he was Pickens, the representative of Pyle, and he was there to talk with Suzanne. Papa hung up on him. Pickens then contacted Don Skene to find out how to approach the Lenglen inner circle. Papa was ill, he was told. And the best way to get through to Suzanne was to go directly to her. So, on the following day, Pickens traveled to Monte Carlo to see Suzanne perform in an exhibition match. Pickens had never seen her before and wasn't sure what to expect. She gave a convincing demonstration that she had come a long way since her collapse after the Wills match. "Her skill, grace and rhythmic movements on the court were amazing," he found. "I figured that she would be a sure-fire in America and from that moment I never permitted myself to nurse a doubt about her signing the books."

He tried to meet her after the match, but she left before he could speak with her. In fact, he found, she rushed to the sidelines and tossed her rackets to an attendant, hurried to a limousine, and left without any hesitation at all. Pickens was impressed. "The expensive gondola cheered me up," he said. "For only amateurs with large incomes can afford those carts." Pickens hurried to his rented car and followed Suzanne back to Nice. On the next day he was told that it would be impossible to see her because she had deported for a vacation in Italy with her friend Lady Wavertree.

As news reports trickled out of France during the Pickens visit, the figure of $250,000 suddenly appeared in the papers as the offer made for Lenglen to play tennis professionally, and $100,000 for her to appear in the movies and maintain her amateur tennis standing. Papa Lenglen refused to meet with Pickens or to discuss any proposal. When the newspapers started throwing around such big numbers, Mama Lenglen became

interested in speaking with Pickens. When he called the Villa Ariem
again, Mama answered the telephone and listened politely to Pickens's
proposal.

"No one has ever written about Mama," he said. "It was always Papa
Lenglen this or Papa Lenglen that. She assured me that she was Suzanne's business manager." Suzanne would return at the end of the
week, Mama said, and Pickens could speak with her then.

At the end of that week Pickens went to the Villa Ariem and met Suzanne Lenglen for the first time. He would never forget his first vision of
the Goddess at home. "She was dressed in negligee, reclining on a chaise
longue and holding a Pomeranian in her arms." Suzanne said that she
would represent herself in the discussions. "I could see that she was no
schoolgirl tennis star who could be salved with one of those what-you-
owe-the-sport arguments."

Pickens had planned carefully. Suzanne Lenglen, he believed, would
be attracted by money but at the same time repelled by the idea of abandoning her amateur status. And so in preliminary discussions he avoided
the use of the term "professionalism." And he presented himself as simply an individual who wanted to represent her in all of her pursuits except tennis. He said he wanted her to tour America as a great artiste.

He countered her tearful tale of the misfortune of 1921 by reminding
her that she had only seen New York and "the tennis cliques of Long Island." She had not yet seen the "real" America. And all of the "real"
Americans were interested in seeing her and would pay for the privilege.
Suzanne Lenglen seemed interested in the proposal. He told her that
C. C. Pyle was different from the New Yorkers. He was a gentleman. And
he would never criticize Suzanne. This pleased Suzanne. In fact, Pickens
told her, if there had ever been any doubt at all about the American
reception of her, Pyle would never have risked any money on the enterprise. They were going to love her this time around. Pickens based his
proposals on one central lie. He said that he and Pyle had in mind a plan
that would absolutely protect her amateur tennis standing. They planned
to make her the star of a movie that would be shown all over the world.
Suzanne glowed at this. Pickens said that they would syndicate her newspaper articles and sell them on the international market, and they would
handle the sale and the marketing of her novel *The Love Game*. And they
would market all books she wrote in the future. Pickens also disclosed
Pyle's intent to put Lenglen on the stage and to star her in a musical
comedy!

Then, in a sobering aside Lenglen suggested that her features "were
not suited for such work." Pickens told her that dentists could work wonders. Everything would be all right. Pickens played to Suzanne's monumental vanity and buffeted her ego with gentle breezes of flattery. Her
resistance crumbled. She was fascinated, utterly fascinated by herself. She
could become a film star. She *would* become a film star, Pickens said.

She could not help but become a film star. The world demanded it. She might become the new Renée Adoree. It was even intimated that she would star in "a romantic film story."

"I talked of everything but professional tennis and smeared plenty of icing on the beautiful birthday cake I was baking by offering her a substantial cash bonus with an absolute guaranty of the entire amount to be named in the contract," Pickens confessed later. Pickens knew that he was merely doing a little "verbal shadow boxing" in the discussions of a contract. What he was looking for was some indication, some hint as to the amount of money that might interest her in coming to America for a tour. He learned that the amount she had in mind was large—very large. She told Pickens that after the Armistice of 1918 and before she had even played at Wimbledon she had been approached by someone who offered her $200,000 to play professional tennis. Pickens did not blink when Suzanne mentioned that amount. But he thought to himself, "That's a lot of money, even when you say it fast!"

Pickens accepted the $200,000 as a working figure and said he would put it in an agreement that would protect Suzanne's amateur status. Suzanne could have it all, he told her. She could become a very wealthy woman and at the same time continue to play amateur tennis and bask in the attention and adoration of the tournament crowds on the Riviera, in Paris, and at Wimbledon. At this point in the discussions Mama Lenglen entered the room and sat down. Suzanne and Pickens and Mama drank a toast to Suzanne's prospective new career—as an international artistic celebrity. Pickens then drew up an agreement with the $200,000 figure in it. Suzanne signed. Pickens put the agreement in his pocket, kissed the outstretched hand of Suzanne and then of Mama, and quickly departed.

Pickens stopped on the way back to his hotel to wire the news to Pyle. But he harbored grave doubts about the dollar amount in the agreement. It would never hold up, he believed. "I knew that old Doc Pyle would slice that sum right down the back," he later wrote. "Suzanne was worth $100,000 for an American tour," he was absolutely certain. "But not in motion pictures or on the stage. She would have to do her stuff on the tennis court." But if she did her stuff on the tennis court in America while signed to a contract for a fixed sum of money that was to be paid over the table, then she would forfeit her amateur status. And there was no way under heaven that the Goddess would give up all the financial prerogatives and fringe benefits that went with playing amateur tennis, especially on the Riviera.

Before he could figure out how to get Suzanne Lenglen to turn professional, Pickens received a call from Suzanne. She was frantic. She had to see him at once. She wanted him to bring the contract back. She wanted to go over it again. Then she changed her mind. She asked him to stay where he was. She would come there. He should get out the contract again. She wanted to be sure that he would be there when she arrived. She was on the verge of a hysteria. Minutes later Suzanne arrived. This time she was accompanied by an American. She introduced him as "my manager, Major Charles Willen." Willen had been Lenglen's manager during the Wills excitement at Cannes. Now he was present to protect her interests once again.

"The Major was an American," Pickens learned. "And while he was telling me about himself, I was figuring out methods of easing this new managerial menace out of the picture." Willen wanted to see the contract Suzanne had signed. Pickens refused to produce it. He lied. He said it was being photoduplicated and promised that Willen could see a photographic copy on the following day. Willen asked Suzanne to leave the room while he talked with Pickens but then had to call her back into the room again to repeat that Willen had complete and absolute authority to negotiate any and all contracts for her. Suzanne concurred in this and then went into the hall again. Willen said that he, too, had been planning for a long time to take Suzanne on an American tour. "There is a lot of money waiting for her over there and I am not going to allow you or Pyle to put anything over on her," he warned. Pickens assured Willen that neither he nor Pyle wanted to put anything over and that everything would be legal and fair. All the money that she eventually signed for, he promised, "will be deposited in a weatherproof bank."

Pickens and Willen conned each other back and forth, arguing over who had the rights to sign Suzanne Lenglen. Finally, the two men signed a new contract that required Pyle himself to come to France in August and to conclude any financial agreement directly with Willen and Suzanne. "There was no doubt that the Major was the real manager of Suzanne," Pickens concluded despairingly. "I didn't mention outright professionalism to the Major, but hinted that Suzanne's success in the movies would depend on the publicity acquired by plenty of tennis playing."

The situation became further confused when on April 9, Pickens announced that there would be a Wills-Lenglen match staged for charity in California on New Year's Day, 1927. Pickens said that when Suzanne agreed to come to America to make movies she agreed also to bring along her tennis rackets in order to play charity exhibitions. And one of those exhibitions would be against Helen Wills. Pickens never wavered in his conviction that the key to Suzanne Lenglen's success would be her appearance in the United States as a paid professional tennis player. And he still had grave doubts that she would ever agree to play as a professional as long as amateur tennis paid so well. But neither Pickens or Pyle could have foreseen the Jubilee Wimbledon disaster. It changed everything.

A London correspondent for the *New York Times* wrote that 1926 was Suzanne Lenglen's "unlucky year." Indeed, it was her unluckiest year. Papa Lenglen had advised his daughter earlier, "Of glory and the price, the higher up the scale you go, the harder your work becomes, the more difficult for you to retain your place. When you are champion, you have become the legitimate prey for those beneath you. Your weakness will be grossly exaggerated. The hour of your failure may be eagerly looked forward to. The slightest variation in your play will be interpreted as a signal of your decline. Do not permit yourself to be carried away by congratulations or flatteries or eulogies. Receive calmly the applause of the public. They will undoubtedly forget you on the morrow. All this is ephemeral. When the day comes that you will go down to defeat, you will taste the bitterness of your own disillusionment, but glory is often worth the price one pays."

And so he had advised her that defeat would come and the crowd would turn against her and she should be prepared. But neither Papa nor Suzanne expected it would come at the hands of tournament officials rather than other players. The attitude of the All-England Club managers and of the English crowd and the English press was a tremendous blow to Suzanne's confidence. She believed she had been wronged, just as she had been in America in 1921. She had been humiliated publicly, and no one had come to her rescue. After all she had done for the All-England Club and the Wimbledon tournament, in the end, it meant nothing to the English. They treated her as just another tennis player. And if there was one thing that Suzanne Lenglen was not, it was just another tennis player.

So she did what she had done after other unlucky days and disappointments of consequence in her career: she became despondent; then suffered a nervous collapse; then went into seclusion; and then plotted revenge. She cancelled all tennis dates, including an appearance at a charity tournament sponsored by her very special friend Lady Wavertree. She even dropped her plans to play in the Irish Championships in Dublin, one of the few European titles she had never won.

And, of course, she dissembled. She said that she was suffering from an attack of neuritis, so severe that she would be unable to play tennis for months. She said she had to return to Paris to be under the care of her personal physician. Then she went shopping.

One of the things that bothered Lenglen in this crisis was her knowledge that other players, too, had been late for appearances in the Wimbledon tournament and had not been reprimanded or suffered official disciplinary action. Vincent Richards and Howard Kinsey had been so late for their second-round match in the men's doubles that, for a time, it was assumed that they would be forced to forfeit. The American management at the tournament offered the opposing English team a forfeit, but they refused to accept. Later it was explained that the problem was a misunderstanding regarding scheduling. Richards and Kinsey finally did show up and won their match easily. The difference between this episode and Suzanne Lenglen's was the fact that Richards and Kinsey had slighted only the usual crowd of tennis fans, while Suzanne had slighted the Queen. As a result, Lenglen felt that she had been robbed of what should have been her greatest moment—being crowned queen of the Jubilee Wimbledon tournament.

Suzanne Lenglen's friend and fellow countryman René Lacoste noticed that so long as Suzanne was sustained by the English crowds and by their admiration and affection, nothing could wound her pride and her confidence for long. She had suffered previous setbacks but she always came back. And the English crowds had always welcomed her back. But then came the collapse of 1926, and suddenly everything around Suzanne crumbled. The English crowd—her crowd—and the English officials who owed her so much turned against her.

She went home. Then she retreated to a remote mountain resort, just as she had after her costly victory over the American Girl. She conferred with a few friends. She listened to Papa. She listened to Mama. She made her usual vows and threats, and she raved to her friends about the English lords of Wimbledon, the English officials, the English press, and the English crowds. But what could she possibly do about it? This time there was no opposing player to crush. Following the Forest Hills fiasco of 1921 she had vowed never to return to America. She did not need America, and she did not need Americans. But she needed Wimbledon. She needed it badly. It was the greatest of all tournaments and awarded the greatest of all titles. How could the queen of tennis forfeit the greatest tennis title year after year and still expect admiration and respect? But to go back to Wimbledon would mean once again submitting to the schedules and the demands of the ruling tennis association and even to some of the same people who had been responsible, she believed, for her persecution.

Suzanne Lenglen faced this dilemma: she needed amateur tennis as much as amateur tennis needed her. She could not exist as a great national celebrity without the amateur tennis system. She had not transcended the system. She must still submit. The queen was still a subject, too. There was no way out. Off the court she could be little more than a former champion, a fallen goddess. She would suffer the humbling experience of sitting in the gallery with the other forlorn former champions and watching someone else—perhaps watching Helen Wills—win all the titles that she could and should still win. She would see her laurels and her crown awarded to others. She would see others, less worthy than she and less talented, lionized by the press and pampered by the clubs. And she could not suffer that. She needed the tournament titles and the love of the crowds. She needed to hear the applause and to pose for the cameras and to wave to her subjects. Without all that she felt she was nothing. Papa had told her that since she was a child. And she believed it.

But the men who ruled English tennis, although they appreciated the financial advantages that Lenglen provided, did not appreciate her dictates and demands. She behaved as though she was in charge. And she was not. She was like a movie star who thought she was a director. They were the directors. And they were the producers. They were in charge. It was their tournament, their stadium, their game. She was merely a performer—a great performer, to be sure, but still just a performer. They had long objected quietly to her behavior. And in 1926 the chance came to discipline her. And they did. And in doing so they demonstrated that they were in charge of the game.

While Suzanne Lenglen tried to figure out exactly what she might do to redeem herself, how she might once again arrange odds in her favor and triumph over the narrow-minded male officials who had ridiculed her at Wimbledon, C. C. Pyle came up with an alternative strategy.

Pyle arrived in Pourville near Dieppe in late July. And Suzanne was now more open to his suggestions. The one way out for her was professional tennis, he told her, an organization in which she would be beneficiary and in which she would decide for herself when to play and when not to play. As a professional she could be her own boss. Pyle's song of professionalism became a duet in August. He brought along with him on the trip his attorney William Hayward. Hayward wasn't simply a lawyer. He was also an unofficial ambassador of good will. The French government had awarded him the Legion of Honor for his service in the Great War. He was a member of a wealthy New York family and a prominent figure in New York's social set. During the Great War he put together the 15th New York National Guards, which became known by the designation 369th Infantry. The 369th was an all-black unit with both black and white officers. The men of the unit referred to themselves as the "15th Heavy Foot" and were the most colorful American regiment in the war. Hayward was a dashing figure, and the artist James Montgomery Flagg painted several portraits of him. He was a showman, much like Pyle. Unlike Pyle, he was also an officer and a gentleman. When the war was over Hayward led his black troops up Broadway while the regimental band played "Won't You Come Home, Bill Bailey." The crowds went wild.

The official slogan of Hayward's black regiment, never printed, was "God Dam, Le's Go." That might well have been the slogan of Hayward and Pyle when they arrived in Pourville. In any case, it perfectly summed up their advice to Suzanne Lenglen. Pyle and Hayward drove to Pourville, and negotiations took place on the porch of the Lenglen summer cottage. "Miss Lenglen turned out to be quite a good business woman," Pyle later reported.

Suzanne had never met Pyle before and had never even seen a photograph of him. She found him to be an impressive physical presence. He was a tall man, with a broad ruddy face, a high forehead, graying blond hair and a little mustache. He had a powerful athletic build and spoke with a deep authoritative voice in an unwavering and direct manner. He had large blue eyes, and he stared straight at Suzanne as he preached his new evangel of professional tennis and as Hayward hymned in occasion-

ally with a strategic amen. Every few minutes during the negotiations
Lenglen darted into the house to seek counsel with her parents and her
uncle.

In the discussions with Suzanne Lenglen in Pourville, "Pyle did some of
his greatest manipulating," Pickens said later. Suzanne could make a lot
of money touring America, making stage appearances and writing articles
and books, Pyle said. But the real money, he insisted, was in tennis—
professional tennis. Should Suzanne abandon amateur tennis and become
an out-and-out professional—playing for money—then her tour could be
a triumphant procession, enriching her and everyone associated with it.

Pyle found that it was not Lenglen's reluctance to leave amateur tennis
that was the main sticking point of the negotiation. "Her great fear," he
said, "was lest she should forfeit friends and social position. In very good
English she painted for me a vivid picture of her desolation should it
come about that by turning professional she had lost social prestige."
And, mindful of that, he began to soothe Suzanne's fear of becoming a social pariah by turning professional.

"You are not always going to be the star you are today," he told her.
"You won't always be sitting on top of the world. If your social standing
and friends are such that you'll lose them by turning professional you can
console yourself with the thought that the money you'll get will be worth
a hundred times more than the things you'll lose.

"Money never hurt anyone's social standing, anyway. And by turning
professional you can insure yourself enough to enable you to live in comfort all the rest of your life. Ten years from now if you go into a smart hotel and order an elaborate luncheon, you won't be able to pay for it by reminding the head waiter that in 1926 you were an amateur tennis star."

Suzanne responded to each of Pyle's points with a soft thoughtful "I
see."

Pyle produced a contract and left it with her. He drove back to Paris
and on the following day she drove into the city for a conference with
Charles Willen. Then, that evening, Pyle dined with her at the Florida
Cafe in Paris. They chatted, and they danced, and they did not mention
the contract. A few days later Pyle and Hayward again drove up to Pourville. This time they brought along several thousand American dollars.

Suzanne Lenglen could, Pyle and Hayward said, stand the tennis world
on its head by providing the specter of a tennis future liberated from the
traditional aristocratic male-dominated associations and clubs. Suzanne
could join hands with the American promoter and could jerk tennis out
of the hands of the ruling lords of the sport, democratize it. Her action
might mean that in the future money from tournaments would go to the
players who produced the revenues rather than to the clubs and the associations. Suzanne could control her own destiny and make a fortune doing it. She did not have to return to Wimbledon. She could transcend
Wimbledon and the English and French and American Lawn Tennis As-

sociations. She could step out from under the male domination of amateur tennis. And she could show the way for others to do the same. This was better than vengeance. This could be total annihilation of the forces that had humiliated her at Forest Hills and Wimbledon.

There were more discussions, and then a revised contract was drawn up and the original Pickens contract torn up. The new contract was signed by Suzanne and then Mama and then Papa and then Uncle Lenglen and then Pyle and then Hayward and then Willen. So many people signed the contract, Pickens observed, that when they were finished it looked like a petition. Several weeks later it was revealed that Red Grange was a partner in the Lenglen contract, too.

Pyle and Hayward left Pourville this time without the money, but Pyle carried the new signed contract. He told a friend several months later that he had been prepared to do almost anything to sign Suzanne Lenglen. "If I hadn't signed her up last July," he said, "I would have signed her up in August. And if I hadn't signed her up in August,—I'd still be in Pourville."

The signing of Suzanne Lenglen to a professional contract was a push-and-pull proposition. Pyle wanted to pull her into one of his enterprises. But it would have been impossible to do if the All-England Club and its officials had not given her a gentle push, if the English crowd had not turned on her, and if the year had not been a perilous one. Pyle was the right man at the right time with the right contract and with cold cash. He offered her not the chance to end her career in a sort of nostalgic old-timers tour, he offered her the chance for a new gust of fame. Her career would take off and truly soar, and all for her own benefit, he pointed out. He promised to transcend time and make her the star that she once was and to work with her rather than over her on the tour. She was now to be pretty much the master of her own fate, he said.

Suzanne Lenglen had always been a trend-setter, a trail-blazer, an agent of change. She revolutionized women's tennis. She altered the style and attire of the women who played tennis and of women who did not play tennis. She came to embody the New Era of liberation from Victorian constraint. Along with Papa she invented the whole idea of the female athlete celebrity. She used the press to advertise herself, and the press adored her for it. She was great copy. The public in Europe worshipped her. And so the fact that she should decide to play professional tennis was indeed a serious blow to the established order of things in the tennis world. Now she would carry a revolution ahead. Suzanne Lenglen now said that the time had come for tennis to be played not for the benefit of the upper classes who invented and controlled the game. It was time that tennis be managed for the profit and benefit of those who were the common laborers in the sport—the players.

Under the terms of the new contract, Lenglen was to play at Madison Square Garden in New York in the fall. Then she was to go on a cross-country tour to about forty cities of the United States and Canada and finally to Havana. She was also to star in a movie and to make endorsements for a tennis racket and for perfume and for clothing.

"I don't think I'll have any trouble managing Miss Lenglen," Pyle told newsmen. "I found her extremely affable and ready to cooperate." He worried, however, about her appearance because some of her teeth protruded "unhandsomely" from the sides of her mouth. "We'll have to get those teeth fixed up," he said, "for the movies, you know." She promised that if he could find her a good dentist she would get her oversized teeth repaired at once.

Pyle had a good deal of difficulty pronouncing Suzanne Lenglen's last name. The correct pronunciation, she had been saying for years, was a combination of the English words "long" and then "glen." And although she practiced with Pyle over and over again he just could not pronounce it correctly and instead came up with a more comfortable pronunciation of "Leng-lon," which was the way that most Americans eventually mispronounced it.

Pyle now sang her praises to the press. He said that she had extraordinary grace. And that when he danced with her in Paris, "in my clumsy fashion," well he just felt out of place. He was earthbound and she wasn't. She had no doubts about the wisdom of turning professional either, he said. "Now that she has become reconciled to the idea of turning professional," he said, "she is into it hammer and tongs."

"I have tried to be a real amateur," she assured Pyle. "Now I'm going to be a real professional. I have given my life to tennis so far, and I feel I am entitled to derive something from the game now."

And Pyle did not see any reason why the public should resent what she had done. "All I am doing in commercializing tennis," he insisted, "is what the tennis associations are doing. Why, they even make the players pay entrance fees. The present system forces players to sneak a little money on the side. I am giving the player an opportunity to make money doing the thing he or she does best. Furthermore, tennis is a healthy game and more Americans should play it. This tour of Miss Lenglen's will stimulate interest in the game and I believe that the result will be that more tennis will be played in the United States than ever before."

Writer John Tunis objected to Pyle's moralizing about professionalism in tennis. "I am all for debunking sports," he wrote, "but these utterances by professional sponsors, who are freeing tennis from its chains, leave me a little cold. And by the way, why is it that it takes twenty thousand dollars and a signed contract to make amateur players see the great hypocrisy that unquestionably exists in modern sport?"

Suzanne Lenglen issued a simple statement reading, "To whom it may concern: I have just signed a contract with Charles C. Pyle of America for a four months' tour of exhibition tennis. My engagement will start in America on October 1, 1926."

Pyle followed this announcement with one of his own. It was all true, he said. All true. Suzanne Lenglen, the greatest female tennis player in the world, had abandoned amateur tennis and had signed a professional contract. He refused to disclose any of the details about the contract, but someone leaked the figure of $200,000 for a four-month tour to the press, and they printed it, and Pyle didn't correct it, even though he knew it was incorrect. (By way of comparison, Babe Ruth, who was the highest paid baseball player of the era, was paid $70,000 in 1927.)

Pickens pronounced the most appropriate benediction following the signing of the contract when he told newsmen, "Pyle is her manager now, and Pickens is her prophet."

Pyle said that Suzanne Lenglen would play against Molla Mallory in America—in a restaging of the duels that the two fought so dramatically in early 1921 and 1922. He said that Suzanne would also "take part" in several films that were being prepared specifically for her. None of this was true, and he knew it. But it made great copy.

He said that she would tour the United States with a group of other professional players all under his management. This was true. Lenglen verified Pyle's statements. And a controversy began.

There were immediate denunciations from tennis associations in the United States, in France, and in England. Suzanne Lenglen could not possibly make a living as a professional, the lords of tennis announced, because there was no one for her to play against in the United States—unless Pyle intended to teach the game to Pickens. No other ranking American players would turn professional. Not Molla Mallory and not Helen Wills and not anyone else. They wouldn't dare. And no ranking English players would give up their amateur status either.

Pyle remained calm during this initial wild burst from the amateur cartel. "He allowed the officials and the sports writers to nibble this negative bait until it was all chewed up," Pickens observed. "He had plenty of announcements to make, but he was milking one cow at a time."

The signing of Suzanne Lenglen was to be only the opening shot in Pyle's war against amateur tennis. He calmly listened to the salvo of sentiment against him and was very happy. Publicity, he reminded his friends, meant controversy.

Suzanne Lenglen defended herself from France. "The nightmare is over," she announced. And a reporter from the Associated Press noticed that "freed from the always-present thought of having to defend her title, Suzanne appeared five years younger, carefree and happy."

"Some believe I am tied up hand and foot by becoming a professional," she said. "To me it is an escape from bondage and slavery. No one can order me about any longer to play tournaments for the benefit of the club owners. I got great fun out of tennis for a few years after the war, but lately it had become too exacting." And in speaking of her tour of the United States, Lenglen said, "Fireworks! Believe me, I will show them fireworks in the United States. With nothing to lose and nothing to gain I will take chances on shots I never dared take before when each point loomed up as big as the Eiffel Tower and the match might depend on it."

Yet, when asked about her opposition, she confessed, "I don't know and I don't care. I am ready to meet them all. Tell them to come on. I have done my bit to build up the tennis of France and the world. It's about time tennis did something for me." Asked if she would meet Helen Wills again in a match, Suzanne was enthusiastic, "I sincerely hope so! Perhaps it can be arranged. I don't feel that I should be ostracized because I have turned professional. Maybe the United States Lawn Tennis Association will permit a match between us to be staged in America. It would be the fulfillment of one of my most cherished ambitions."

Lenglen also told a reporter from the *New York Times* that tennis had become a full-time business for most of the top ranking players. So there was room for professional tennis. "Now I am going to make some money, to have some fun and to see the world," she said. "I have been working for others for fourteen years, and now I am going to work for myself. When I finish my four months' tour of America next winter, I hope to make plans for a world tour. I think that you will find a good many other well-known players in America and Europe who will follow my example."

When other reporters asked her who she now thought was the best female amateur in the world, Suzanne said that there were many good players. But Papa Lenglen was more specific. "By all means, Miss Wills," he said. "She is the best player in the world just now." Papa forgot to insert the qualifying adjective "amateur" in his evaluation of the American Girl.

Some of the initial shock at Suzanne Lenglen's signing with Pyle quickly turned to anger, and there were accusations that she had abandoned tennis—the adjective "amateur" had not yet been commonly combined with the name of the sport, since tennis was always simply amateur tennis—out of the love of luxury. Interviewed in Pourville right after the signing, one of her aunts lamented that all that Suzanne had acquired in life after eleven years of amateur tennis was "expensive tastes." "Our Suzanne," she said, "likes things de luxe, and with the franc where it is it is not easy for the French people to live de luxe."

Others insisted that Suzanne Lenglen signed a professional contract not out of the love of money alone but out of the fear of Helen Wills. This opinion was most commonly heard in California. One reader wrote to the *San Francisco Chronicle*, that Suzanne "says she has turned professional because of the financial harvest she can reap, but I believe the chief reason is she does not want another contest with Miss Wills, fearing that little Miss Poker Face will 'bring home the bacon.' If she was really anxious to again meet 'our Helen' she could have postponed her action, but she knew as well as we all do what the result would be."

Bill Tilden, who had never lost any love on Suzanne Lenglen, turned on her, too. He had not wished her success as an amateur, and he certainly did not now wish her success as a professional. Tilden announced that he would not turn professional in 1926 or after. He then pointed out that her turning professional was not surprising. It was an evolutionary rather than a revolutionary act on her part. In fact, he said, her "sickness complex" would prevent her from playing through any amateur tournament again. He suggested that she had turned professional actually in April and said that Pyle had shown him a contract to induce him to turn professional at the time. Tilden assured reporters and club and association officers that the only way in which professional tennis could make a successful bid in the United States was if the top ten male and the top six female players joined the ranks of the pros. And he assured them that such a case was not even a remote possibility.

Not surprisingly, there were mixed feelings among the club and casino owners on the Riviera who had always considered themselves not only benefactors but also patrons and fans of Suzanne Lenglen. Suzanne may have created herself in the image that existed only in her father's dreams, but the club and casino owners had paid all the bills. And they felt that they deserved much better treatment than to have Suzanne simply dance away from them as a professional. Trying to make the very best of a very bad situation, the Nice Tennis Club announced that it would arrange exhibition matches for her when she returned from her tour. But the exhibitions were never held since opponents in those exhibitions would have forfeited their amateur status. And as a final insult to the Goddess, as soon as word of her move to professionalism spread along the Riviera, clothing styles were altered. The bandeau, popularized by Suzanne and adopted almost universally by the French and other European players on the Riviera, was dropped by all of the female players. They wore instead the white green-lined visor, symbol of Helen Wills, the American Girl, who remained an amateur. Even this reminder of the Goddess was to be expunged from the Riviera.

Everything possible was done to induce her to break the contract and to return to the amateur fold. Many club officials, formerly enthusiastic followers of Lenglen, now went out of their way to make her career as difficult as possible since she had betrayed them, so to speak, by depriving them of the business they gleaned from her talents. And in their opposition to her, officials and associations simply made her more determined as a professional and more assured in her decision.

Her continued popularity with the common folk, however, was demonstrated on August 16 when she vacationed briefly in St. Moritz, one of her favorite hideaways, where she was treated as royalty. When she arrived in St. Moritz a huge crowd was waiting for her. They greeted her train by cheering loudly, and a large group of local children serenaded her and presented her with Alpine flowers. It was a reception truly fit for a goddess. Following the ceremony, which touched Suzanne deeply at this vulnerable moment when she was studying the public reaction to her actions, she was led to a beautiful coach drawn by four horses and driven to her hotel while some of the crowd ran alongside the carriage just to get a last glimpse at her.

Ironically, on the same train with Suzanne was the Swiss president, M. Haberlin, who was also taking a holiday vacation in St. Moritz. He thought, when he first glanced out the window and saw the crowd, that a special welcoming ceremony had been arranged for him. He straightened his attire, gathered his resolve, and stepped from the train only to find no one there to greet him. The entire crowd—every person—had run off with Suzanne. Haberlin walked alone to his hotel far behind the entourage that ringed the popular tennis player, confused as to what had happened.

But then Suzanne found trouble in St. Moritz, too, and the first of the official assaults against her. Earlier she had sent in her entry form for the St. Moritz tournament, which she had entered almost every year since 1919. But now the tournament committee cancelled her entry. She was informed that in Switzerland she could no longer play against amateurs but would have to confine her playing to exhibitions exclusively against other professionals. Confusion resulted when it was learned that Lenglen's entry in the tournament had been officially accepted months earlier. How could the Swiss Tennis Federation reverse itself and reject her entry? An Italian team had also entered in the tournament. But in response to Suzanne's signing of a contract with Pyle, Italian authorities intervened and refused to let the Italian team cross the frontier into Switzerland. The team was scratched, and the tournament ruined. Then the German players also withdrew after it was known that Lenglen had been allowed to enter. Both the German and Italian players acted in accordance with their federations which barred amateurs from competing against professionals.

At the news Suzanne Lenglen broke down and wept publicly. She was bitter. She said that she was being "persecuted" for her actions and announced that she would quit all European tennis tournaments if the persecution did not cease. She was entered in the Lido Tournament in Italy later in the month. She now received word that the Lido Tournament officials had also rejected her application for participation. Then the South African Lawn Tennis Union joined the fray and announced that she would be disinvited from appearing in South African tournaments to which she had been invited several months earlier. She had never before appeared in South Africa. The chairman of the South African organization said that the attitude of the "lawn tennis circles" toward Lenglen had changed completely since she had signed a professional contract. Now "she is out of court," he said. He added that the original invitation carried the necessary required condition that not only would all of Lenglen's expenses be paid, but also those of her parents would be paid, too, "in order to facilitate her visit." It was bizarre. Payment in the form of lavish services to the entire Lenglen family could be made, but for Suzanne to be paid above the table in cash made her *persona non grata.* The tennis circles were not going to be short-changed when it came to dispensing money.

Other writers and tennis officials expressed doubt that a professional tour would ever take place since there was no opponent for Suzanne Lenglen in the professional ranks. Professional tennis players in the United States and Europe were exclusively teaching professionals and believed to lack a competitive edge and thus considered far inferior to amateur players who competed regularly. The attitude toward teaching professionals in tennis was pretty much what it was toward teachers in general: those who can, do; those who can't, teach.

Pyle and Pickens and the officers of the USLTA all knew that the American public would not dish out hundreds of thousands of dollars to watch Suzanne Lenglen hit a ball against a wall. When the correspondent from *L'Auto* pressed Pyle to learn who the opposition would be, Pyle gave no names but said only that she would play a highly ranked player worthy of facing her. He said he had, in fact, nine ranking players to pit against her. "Every one of them is an amateur right now," he said, "but they will be professionals when they join the Lenglen entourage." He said he would not name the players in order not to embarrass them while they continued to compete in amateur tournaments. But he did indicate that they were among the best players in the world. He repeatedly predicted that the move to professionalism would popularize tennis even more and would be the beginning of the biggest boom the game had ever seen. Pyle said that the professional spirit would spread so that within a month he would put together a professional tennis association and within a year he would stage open tournaments, where amateurs and professionals played against each other, as in golf. Pyle also insisted now that tennis should not remain a game reserved for the rich and their favorites. He said he would make it possible for tennis players who had to work at other jobs and kowtow to the USLTA and the various tournament committees in order to play tennis, to become professional and thus meet, on an equal basis, players who did not have to earn a living. He was out to undermine the aristocratic structure of tennis and replace it with a paid democracy.

Yet there was no sign that the professional spirit was spreading. When news of Suzanne Lenglen's abandonment of amateur tennis was made public the annual tournament was being held in Seabright, New Jersey, and many of the women playing in the tournament expressed surprise at her move. Helen Wills assured American reporters that there was nothing in the world that could induce her to turn professional. And she believed she would never be able to play Suzanne Lenglen unless she were reinstated as an amateur. Molla Mallory, too, insisted that she had no intention of playing tennis for money and that she had not been approached to play professional, despite Pyle's claims to the contrary. Elizabeth Ryan, on the other hand, the second ranking American player, stated that were she offered perhaps $200,000 she would do some serious thinking about signing. But Ryan didn't have to worry. The offer never came. Pyle needed someone more flamboyant than Ryan on his tour.

The other ranking leading female players guessed that Pyle would try to sign one of the Sutton sisters, who were already teaching professionals. Violet Sutton Doeg, was an instructor at the Women's Golf and Tennis Club at Glen Head, on Long Island, and Florence Sutton, her sister, was teaching in California. But he didn't go after the Suttons.

The lords of the USLTA were relieved when Helen Wills gave repeated assurances that she would not turn professional. Helen, as the ruling American power on the courts, was the key to future crowds, future gate receipts, future profits, and future legitimacy for amateur tennis. Gate receipts at Forest Hills had plummeted in 1926 when Wills had to drop out of competition because of illness. Her defection to the professionals would mean future problems. But Helen Wills still received all the necessary consideration and deference to keep her an amateur. She was able to write and to draw and paint and to sell all of her products along those lines and make a handsome profit. Turning professional might not necessarily hold any real financial advantage for her. Amateurism was paying her just fine. She said in August that she had received no offers, but supplemented her statement by saying that she could hardly afford to overlook a fortune if it should drop into her lap. She said she was looking forward to a rest in 1926 and that she would return the next season for regular tournament play.

Years later it was learned that Pyle had, through an intermediary, approached Clarence Wills, Helen's father, and had proposed $100,000 as a payment for Helen to turn professional and play against Suzanne Lenglen. The offer had been rejected almost immediately. And it was not even mentioned to Helen, who would have been surprised to learn that a fortune had in fact almost dropped into her lap.

It seems doubtful that Pyle told Lenglen of this move, since Suzanne was adamant about not facing Wills or Mallory across the net night after night. And she did not want Tilden on the tour either. She hated all three of them, and money or not she could not stand before American crowds and be crushed night after night. She wanted Pyle to sign a player she could beat with regularity and one who had no chance of beating her back. This was her tour, and they were to be her matches and her crowds.

What Pyle hoped to do next was more agreeable to Suzanne: it was what Pickens had suggested in the spring—a big match between Wills and Lenglen in which Wills would preserve her amateur status and the gate could be divided between the USLTA and the various interested associations on the one hand, and Pyle and Suzanne on the other. Lenglen could certainly rise to the occasion in one match, and the contest would fill the Cal Stadium or some other huge stadium with paying customers and make a financial killing in the first degree for Pyle. But he needed the cooperation of the American Girl and the USLTA. The bait was to be cash, and once again Pyle was expected to hear the money whisper "Open sesame!" But the money was silent. The USLTA refused to bargain, and Helen Wills refused to negotiate without the blessing of the USLTA. With Clarence Wills at the gate guarding his daughter's amateur status there was just no way the money could bring the deal off. But Pyle kept up his hopes until the day his tour left California.

Canadian officials volunteered that Suzanne Lenglen would have no trouble lining up opponents in their country. Stars of amateur tennis in Canada could play against Lenglen and still maintain their amateur status so long as they did not accept remuneration for their play. In other words, there were no rules in Canada to prevent open tennis. The problem was that Canada had no top-ranked players to oppose Suzanne.

As late as September 1, Pyle still had not named another player who had signed a contract with him, and he tried to conceal the fact was that he was having serious difficulty in finding a suitable opponent. "I am finding it much easier to land American players of ability and note, both men and women, than I expected in signing Mlle Lenglen," he lied.

Pyle was rebuffed by Henri Cochet and René Lacoste when he asked them to join the tour. Despite a considerable cash guarantee, both lacked faith in professional tennis and said they believed they would not "get a kick" out of playing for money. Jean Borotra was approached, and the sum he was offered ranged from $50,000 to $150,000, depending on the imagination of the person telling the story. His answer was a simple, "Thanks, no! I play tennis for the fun of it."

Pyle was successful in signing Paul Feret to accompany Lenglen on the tour. He was the son of the vice president of the French Tennis Federation and the fourth ranking player in France. He was also a deeply melancholy young man, still under the shadow of the death of his nineteen-year-old bride only four months after his marriage. It was rumored that he accepted Pyle's offer of an American tour mainly to distract his mind.

With only two players signed, Pyle said that the opening night of the "Suzanne Lenglen North-American Tour" would be October 9 in New York City's Madison Square Garden. The seating capacity for tennis in the Garden, it was pointed out, would be 17,000. No tennis match in the United States had yet attracted a crowd anywhere near that size. If Pyle could fill the Garden just for one night of tennis, that in itself would be an extraordinary feat. It would be even more extraordinary if he could sign a ranking woman player to compete against her on that night and for the remainder of the tour. Who would it be?

It would be Mary K. Browne. On September 6, Pyle broke the news that he had signed Browne to a professional contract, the first American player to join the tour. Browne, the sixth ranked woman player in the United States, was from Santa Monica and for fifteen years had been an outstanding tennis player. Browne was, like Lenglen and Helen Wills, an extraordinary natural athlete. She won her first national title in 1912 and repeated as national champion in 1913 and 1914. In 1915 she didn't defend her title, and it was won by Molla Mallory. In the same years—1912, 1913 and 1914—she won in the national women's doubles, too. And in those years she won in the national mixed doubles, first with Johnston and then with Tilden twice. She had demonstrated her staying power by returning to national competition in 1917 and played a series of 21 matches with Molla Mallory, winning 13, in behalf of the Red Cross fund. Her game was called a "Coast" or "California" game. She was strongest at the net and overhead and had "a relatively severe service." (In 1924 she pulled off one of the greatest upsets in sports history by defeating the national golf champion Glenna Collett—the only match that the national champion lost that year. Browne was only an amateur and a novice at golf.) In 1924 she made it to the semifinals of the national tennis championships and was defeated there by Helen Wills.

A contract had not yet been signed on September 6, but Browne and Pyle announced that they would probably agree on specific terms within a few days. While both parties to the agreement refused to discuss money, the *Brooklyn Eagle* reported that Browne's contract called for $15,000 and 5 percent of the net receipts from the tour. Other papers then speculated that Browne would probably pocket between $40,000 to $50,000 for signing the contract.

Browne was a necessary quantity for the tour, for without her, or someone close to her in caliber, there could be no contest with Lenglen. She said that she agonized over the decision for several days after Pyle approached her, describing her action as "a matter of business necessity." She was the captain of the women's team that had just brought back the Wightman Cup from England. And she expressed the opinion that her move was a "pioneer effort to clear the game of the taint of professionalism. It will help to take the hypocrisy out of American lawn tennis," she said.

Lenglen seemed unsurprised that Pyle had succeeded in signing Browne: a fitting foil for the Goddess. Browne was a good energetic player who came to the net often. She always lost to Suzanne and seldom threatened her. "You can say I am delighted and I am going to have such a sweet girl as Mary Browne with me on my tour," she said. "With Miss Browne as an opponent you need not think it's going to be merely a series of exhibition matches. As a tennis player, she's terribly good," Lenglen said of the player she had beaten twice very decisively in 1926.

Pyle had contacted Browne just prior to the women's championship matches at Forest Hills in the fall of 1926. The first approach was simply exploratory. "I was surprised," Browne said later, "for I had never considered the possibility of earning money at the game I had played for twenty years. I was also worried and said to Mr. Pyle's emissary, 'Oh, you shouldn't have come to me while I was playing in this tournament. Why couldn't you have waited two more days? I feel like a professional already."

Browne said that at first she felt "contaminated" and tried to put the thought of professional tennis out of her mind. She didn't sleep at all the night after the proposal was made. And when she went on the court against Elizabeth Ryan on the following morning she imagined that people in the crowd were pointing at her and whispering, "There's Mary Browne; she's considering turning professional. Isn't it shocking what some people will do for money?"

Ryan beat her. And Browne then thought that the defeat would ruin her chances for turning professional. "Now," she thought to herself, "they will not want me to play with Suzanne." And she felt happy and complacent at the thought. But she was wrong. A few days later she was again visited by Pickens, who said that she was in fact still wanted for the professional tour. She was offered what seemed a huge sum of money to play forty exhibition matches against Lenglen.

Browne nonetheless wavered in her decision. She freely admitted that the chance to make money—and perhaps a lot of money—by playing tennis, a game that she loved, was attractive. She had played for twenty years, she said, without any direct financial compensation. She pointed out also that she had always played strictly by the amateur rules. Other ranking players had received money and gifts from the clubs and associations they played for, but she had not. She knew that the public believed that most of the ranking tennis players were paid for their amateur matches in real dollars. "I was never paid for playing tennis, either directly or indirectly, in the twenty years of my career as an amateur," she said. Frequently, she said, her expenses were paid by tennis associations or clubs. But not always. And when her expenses were paid the sum allowed never covered the actual expenditure she personally made to play in a tournament. And with a limited income she did not have sufficient funds to pay expenses for all the tournaments in which she played. She said that in twenty years of tennis she had spent far more from her own pocket—more by several times over—than Pyle offered her to play as a professional. And so when the Pyle offer came it was tempting. "I am still Miss Browne and therefore obliged to take a husbandly view of opportunities," she pointed out to her detractors.

Browne also explained that the tennis game and the galleries were changing and that perhaps the time for a professional organization had come. She said that any person who had performed recently before tennis galleries understood the peculiarities of the masses that were now appearing at the matches. The new public for tennis, she said, was "the masses rather than the classes." They were boisterous and had favorites and villains. They wanted a new idol installed and then were just as eager to see their new idol tumbled. Suzanne Lenglen had been responsible, largely, for this change in the game. She brought people out to the matches who knew little about the game but who wanted an afternoon of colorful entertainment. Suzanne gave that to them. "She has a vital personality which makes a mighty appeal to the mob."

She was eight years ahead of Bill Tilden in holding titles, she pointed out, since Tilden won his first national championship in 1920 and she had won hers in 1912. And she had been winning titles for three years longer than Bill Johnston who didn't win his first national title until 1915. So when the chance came to turn professional, she was at the end of her amateur career, she could see. She had been around and had been winning titles longer than any of the other males or females, including Suzanne Lenglen. "I felt that tennis could spare me and let me, without hard feeling, earn some money. The game has done much for me in the way of creating friendships, besides making it possible for me to travel about this fascinating country of ours, and even abroad." And, she concluded, "Sports is not really a pastime in America. It is an industry, and industry must have its wage earners. After all, what does it matter whether you are an amateur or a professional as long as you play the game?"

Suzanne Lenglen departed from the Gare St. Lazare in Paris on September 22. Hundreds of well-wishers gathered at the station to bid her farewell. She had spent almost all of her free time in the three weeks before leaving in dress shops on the Rue de la Paix rather than on the tennis courts. When someone asked her how her tennis was she replied, "I don't know. I haven't played for months. You should see that black and white evening dress of mine. It's a masterpiece."

Someone asked whom she was going to play in America. "I don't know. Ask Pyle."

But she felt good. "I never felt better in my life," she said," and I think I will be able to give a good account of myself after a little practice."

Although the station was filled with Lenglen's friends, no official of the French Tennis Federation was among the well wishers. Paul Feret was with her and was also booked on the *Paris,* but no one paid much attention to him. Nor would they pay much attention to him during the tour. He was then as later merely a member of the supporting cast. They set sail for America on September 23. Suzanne brought about a dozen trunks and about twenty hat boxes with her. She regretted that Papa would not be on the tour because of his ill health. But Mama Lenglen would be and so would her personal maid, Helene. Suzanne said she would bring along her ukulele—she had just taken up the instrument and wanted to know if there was anyone in America who could teach her to play it.

She occupied one of the best cabins on the ship and as always traveled strictly first class. Pyle had ordered that fresh flowers and champagne be placed in her cabin each day during the voyage. She also took aboard the ship twenty-five new Suzanne Lenglen dolls, all dressed like her and wearing her famous headband. She auctioned them off as souvenirs during the trip.

Pyle scheduled a news conference for September 15 in order to introduce his new professional players to the press. But he cancelled the conference because he wanted to hold his big news about another professional signing until Suzanne's arrival.

Lenglen docked in New York on September 29 and competed well in the newspapers with the World Series. There were about twenty-five reporters and a dozen photographers to meet her, but no officials from the disgruntled USLTA. The reporters found the once imperious Suzanne cordial to them now, and she explained what she had done and why. Red Grange was brought to the ship, and there were pictures taken of the two and some suggestions that they would make a wonderful couple. Everyone laughed, Suzanne the loudest. One reporter noted that her laughter was so sincere that she carried everyone else along with her.

On the evening of September 30, Pyle held a special gala dinner party aboard the *Paris,* which remained docked in New York, in order to introduce Suzanne officially to the American press and to announce another triumph. More than two hundred special guests celebrated in the grand saloon of the liner. During the course of the evening Big Bill Edwards, president of the American League of Professional Football Clubs, of which Red Grange was a member, who acted as the toastmaster, held up his hand for silence during the festive ceremonies for an important announcement. Pyle stood up. There was a short pause, and then a buzz of excited conversation and conjecture as the crowd waited to hear what Pyle would say. But Pyle just stood silent for a moment. Then Vincent Richards—the golden boy of American tennis—and his wife entered the room. It took a few seconds before those at the gathering understood the significance of this dramatic entrance. Then somebody started a cheer that rose and echoed around the room.

Several days before Pyle had disclosed that he had been negotiating with "an outstanding American tennis star" but left the identity of that star in doubt. Now the secret was revealed. Richards was noticeably nervous, but Mrs. Richards was smiling and happy. Richards refused to make a speech after the applause died down. He was seated at the speakers' table with his wife. Attention shifted back to Pyle. But Pyle, too, stayed silent. Later he told reporters that he had nothing to add to the fact that Richards had become a professional.

Mary Browne congratulated Richards. Suzanne Lenglen shook his hand, and he was surrounded by others at the dinner who wished to express happiness at his decision. Later Richards explained: "I have signed a contract for four months and in the contract is a clause giving me the option to sign for two more months if I care to," he said. "I am going to tour with Mr. Pyle's other tennis stars here and in Canada and that tour will take about four months. If, at the end of that time, it is decided to extend the tour I am likely to sign for the other two months." Richards said that the amount of his contract was a personal matter and was not for public discussion. When asked if any other major national stars had been signed, he said he wasn't sure. "I only want to say this in regard to my professional tennis career which is before me. I had to turn professional and now that I am professional I intend to play just as hard as when I was an amateur. I feel very strongly for the professional tennis game and I have no excuses to offer for my action. I cannot see any reason why I shouldn't be getting the money as well as the tennis associations."

"We've got a baby at our house," Richards concluded, "and I've got to make some money." "The fame is very nice," he said. But I have discovered that you cannot feed a wife and baby on old newspaper clippings and pewter cups. Several others have discovered the same thing too late."

Richards, who had been born in New York on March 20, 1903, was considered a tennis prodigy as a young man and was brought to the notice of Bill Tilden at an early age. Under Tilden's tutelage Richards developed into a brilliant player. At fifteen he paired with Tilden and won the national doubles title. In 1919 he defeated Tilden for the national indoor singles title and beat Big Bill and other top players since that time. The third ranked male player in the United States, Richards was a pillar of the Davis Cup team and the reigning Olympic singles and mixed doubles gold medal winner and the national doubles champion. He signed his contract on October 1, after Lenglen, Browne, and Feret. He beat Tilden three times in 1926 and expected to receive the number-one ranking by the USLTA at the close of the season. His 1926 record was marred only by his inability to come through at Forest Hills, which was won by a French player. Nonetheless, it was almost certain that he would be ranked second among the American men by the USLTA at the end of the 1926 season. The lords of the USLTA had expected that, with the fading of Billy Johnston, Richards would carry much of the fight for the United States in defense of the Davis Cup in 1927. Those hopes were now gone.

Like Tilden, Richards did not have a harmonious relationship with the USLTA. He had been suspended once by the organization for working in a sporting goods store that published advertisements stating that he would help customers pick out a tennis racket. That, the USLTA declared, was a violation of the amateur rule. Richards was summarily suspended from all amateur events. He was reinstated when it was proven that the advertisement was written without his knowledge or consent.

To add a light touch to the evening, Pyle arranged some competitive games of table tennis for his new professionals. The scoring for the games was tennis scoring. In a preview of things to come Lenglen beat Browne, 6–1, and Richards beat Feret. In the mixed doubles Richards and Browne beat Lenglen and Feret, 6–4.

In seeking a top-ranked American player, Pyle turned to Billy Johnston, who was ranked second among the American men by the USLTA and was acceptable to Lenglen. Johnston was in New York for the national singles tournament. Elmer Griffin, who worked as a broker on Wall

Street at the time and who was a native of San Francisco, a tennis player, and a close personal friend of Johnston, was asked to present Pyle's offer. But Griffin was unconvinced of Pyle's honesty. He telephoned Johnston, and told him that Pyle was willing to put up $50,000 for Johnston to tour with the group. "Billy, he said, "I think Pyle's as crooked as the day is long. But he's willing to put the $50,000 in escrow—he says." Johnston seriously considered the offer.

Johnston thought about the offer for a couple of days and then turned it down. The decision was celebrated as a victory for amateur tennis and a public defeat for Pyle. But Johnston's decision was made not for love of the amateur game, as the press and the USLTA officials indicated, but because he realized he was near the end of his long amateur career. He also knew he was in declining health and could not withstand the strain of a national tour on which he would be required to play night after night against another top player in widely contrasting climates from New York to California to Havana. The tour would be a rigorous as well as a profitable one, and Johnston just couldn't cut it. And so "Little Bill" Johnston remained an amateur player for one more season.

Pyle turned next to the ranks of the teaching professionals. Harvey Snodgrass of Los Angeles signed with Pyle on October 2. Snodgrass had become a teaching professional in 1925 and accepted a three-year contract as the resident professional at the Palomar Tennis Club in Culver City, California. Snodgrass in 1925 had been the sixth ranked American player and with Walter Wesbrook held the national clay court doubles title. Although the terms of his contract with Pyle were not made public at the time, Pyle agreed to pay Snodgrass $15,000 in installments for the tour with Lenglen.

On that same day, October 2, in San Francisco, Howard Kinsey received a long-distance telephone call from Pyle. Pyle told him of the Snodgrass signing and offered him a professional contract. The next day Kinsey telegraphed his acceptance. Kinsey, was the number six player in the United States in 1926 and had been ranked as high as fourth in 1924. He was doubles champion with his older brother Robert and had beaten both Johnston and R. Norris Williams in singles. He was known as a smart player, a fighter, and a master of spin. In fact, it was said that he was too much addicted to spin and that his game might have improved greatly if he drove harder. He was in business with his brother in San Francisco selling typewriter supplies.

Pyle's successful raid on the ranks of the amateurs inspired the *New Yorker* to describe him as a "cannibal king who devours amateurs as the Minotaur gulped Athenian youths." One of the players the cannibal king did not approach in 1926 was the number-one ranked American player, Tilden. He knew that just as the presence of Wills on the tour would destroy it from within, so would the presence of Tilden. Suzanne hated the man as she hated no other. He had humiliated her in Paris in 1921 and then had coached Molla Mallory at Forest Hills in 1921 and had gloated over Molla's success. When she turned professional he characteristically commented on her "sickness complex." His presence traveling with Lenglen and playing in doubles against her night after night would sink the whole enterprise, and Pyle knew it.

Tilden, however, simply could not swallow the fact that other players were approached, and he wasn't. Others were making headlines, and he wasn't. And so, several weeks after the tour had begun and when it appeared to be a successful venture, Tilden told newspaper reporters that the night before the tour opened, Pyle had come to his hotel room in New York and asked him to turn professional and to play against Vincent Richards. He said that Pyle had offered him $25,000 to sign a professional contract. Tilden said that he shocked Pyle by turning down the offer. He explained his negative reply to Pyle by saying, "I shall not become professional at the present time. I think the movement will be a success and there is a field for professional play. But I believe that my duty is to remain an amateur and to play for my country in 1927. We shall have to struggle for the Davis Cup and we must try to win back the championship we lost last month. Therefore, I am at the service of our association and shall do my utmost to keep the supremacy in the game which we have had for the past six years.

"But even if I were ready to consider an offer to become a professional, I would not consider yours." Then he said, rather kiddingly, "If you really wanted me you would have had to double your offer." Tilden said that Pyle thought he was making a bargain and said, "All right. I'll be back later this afternoon. Will you see me?" Tilden answered: "Sure. But its useless; I have no intention of turning professional."

Later that afternoon Pyle returned and he carried a contract. "Mr. Tilden," he said "I will meet your figure. Here is the contract." He handed it to Tilden. It called for $50,000 for six months on the tour. Tilden said he took a deep breath and said, "Mr. Pyle, you evidently didn't understand me this afternoon. I have no intention of turning professional." He picked up the contract and started for the door and said, "Mr. Tilden, I think you are a damned fool."

"Mr. Pyle," Tilden responded, "I think you are right."

Pyle never said that Tilden was a fool. But he did say, publicly, that Tilden was a liar. He had never approached Tilden and had no such conversation with him concerning a contract. Pyle suggested of Big Bill's claim of turning down an offer, "Tilden should be the last one to make it."

His story was never verified by anyone, not by Pyle or any of Pyle's agents or Richards or any of the other professionals. And there seems more than a reasonable likelihood that it was simply a creation of the imagination of Tilden to enhance his own reputation with the USLTA and the public. If that was the case, it worked. A writer for the San

Francisco *Chronicle* pointed out that "Tilden's reasons for not turning professional are much to his credit and have made him a firm and greatly admired fixture in the minds of the leaders of amateur tennis."

And in the fall of 1927 when Tilden's Broadway show opened, the USLTA responded to his loyalty by pressuring its members in the New York area to buy tickets.

--◆{ 2 }◆--

On October 4, Suzanne Lenglen hit her first tennis ball in America since 1921. She practiced on the private court of Dr. Horace Ayres at Richmond Hill, and only a few friends were allowed to watch. She hit with Paul Feret. To a reporter present she seemed to be "her old sensational self." She played Feret at top speed and full power and held her own. Then at Madison Square Garden in the afternoon of October 5 she practiced on the special portable courts that Pyle had for the tour—cork composition covered by green canvas. The playing area was illuminated by Kleig lights.

Professional tennis à la Pyle/Lenglen had its debut in America at Madison Square Garden on Saturday night, October 9, 1926. Ticket sales for the inaugural were brisk, and it was noted that out-of-towners bought many of the tickets, which ranged in price from $2.20 to $5.50. On the night of her professional debut, Suzanne dined with Jack Dempsey, Estelle Taylor, and Georges Carpentier, then she posed for photographers wearing some of the forty suits she brought along for the tour. All of the suits, she explained, were Patou designs. She had signed a contract with Patou and had agreed not to wear creations by any other designer.

Pyle had last-minute difficulties. The USLTA discouraged its members from attending the exhibition, and officials who worked with the USLTA were forbidden to officiate. The boycott, it was said, was spontaneous. Pyle secured some inexperienced linesmen for the exhibition and hired Nat Browne, Mary's brother, to umpire. Pyle pointed out to newsmen that there was a little change in the terminology of scorekeeping. The word "love" was not used because, he insisted, the average spectator would not understand what it meant. In lieu of "love," Nat Browne used the term "nothing."

A crowd estimated at 13,000 turned out for the matches, probably the largest crowd to that time to watch a tennis match in America. In the crowd on opening night were Governor Al Smith of New York, Mayor James Walker of New York, Bill Tilden, golfers Walter Hagen and Glenna Collett, Ring Lardner, Georges Carpentier, and E. C. Conlin, the famous umpire of Forest Hills, who was there only as a spectator. John Tunis, who was reporting for the *New Yorker,* wished that Conlin had umpired, since the officiating was terrible. And Tunis felt the show was hardly better than the officiating.

The first problem was that the exhibition started late—almost forty-five minutes late. And the crowd was not the typical tennis crowd. They were not polite. A band—a terrible band with a brassy sound—murdered the popular tune "Valencia" over and over and over again as the crowd grew increasingly restless. Programs sold for twenty-five cents and included biographies of all of the players and a simple guide to tennis scoring.

Richards and Feret were introduced and made dramatic entrances, warmed up, and played a quick two-set match won easily by Richards. There was unenthusiastic applause. Then the band struck up something that sounded vaguely like "Marseillaise" and the announcer introduced Suzanne Lenglen. She stepped into the spotlight along with Pyle, who seemed out of place just standing there holding her ermine evening wrap. She was wearing her Riviera costume—an accordion pleated skirt, a sleeveless yellow sweater, and a bandeau to match. She was nervous, very nervous. That was apparent to those who had seen her play before; she double-faulted twice in the first game. But Browne was even more nervous. And the first game turned into a fairly unexciting exercise in conservative ground strokes. The burning question of the set was, "Who can give away points first?" The answer: Mary K. Browne. In the second set Lenglen warmed up and showed some of her sparkle, but only on occasion. On the whole the exhibition was a dull affair indeed. The players stayed on the baseline. When Browne put a drop shot just over the net and caught Lenglen flat-footed, the Goddess paused for a moment, piqued at the applause for her opponent. Then she responded in the form of an ace and won the next point with a perfectly placed drive to the corner. But finding that sort of play unnecessary she returned to machine-like precision. She won, 6–1, 6–1, in 39 minutes. There were no fireworks.

The mixed doubles followed with Lenglen paired with Feret and Browne with Richards. Only then did anyone get a glimpse of the legendary Suzanne. She was a little more confident. And she was the best of the four players on the court. She volleyed at the net and won a dozen points.

"But there wasn't any zip or sparkle or punch or color in the thing from start to finish," one spectator complained. "The sting of real competition was missing. Sadly missing." It was difficult to care who won or lost. "As a foil for the greatest of all women on the court it was well enough. As real sport, it simply did not exist." Also there was the unpleasant experience for Suzanne Lenglen of seeing some of the customers walk out on her. The exits of the Garden were crowded during the mixed doubles. Tunis concluded that "professional tennis is a pretty flat affair." Pyle grossed $24,000 for the evening.

"It is a case of Suzanne being so much bigger than the game that the sense of struggle, of uncertainty, was absent," a reporter for the *New York Times* concluded. And he pointed out that "if Babe Ruth knocked a home run every time he came to bat, it is a safe conjecture that he would lose enormously in drawing power. With Mlle Lenglen it is written beforehand that if she does not win 6–0, 6–1, she will win 6–1, 6–2." What was missing in the tour was what the *Times* called "the freaks of chance." Previously there had always been the possibility of some unknown or underestimated opponent flashing a surprise. Thus there could be a real element of suspense on the tour if Lenglen played someone other than Mary K. Browne night after night. Browne was of fine caliber, but not of Suzanne's caliber.

Mark Twain once wrote that the best swordsman in the country was never afraid of the second best swordsman. But he must always reckon with the unknown fighter. Lenglen was to play forty matches with the second best player, and the suspense was missing. Without suspense and without hope of ever seeing her really tested, the tour was to have limited appeal. The audience would, the *Times* correspondent guessed, have to derive its pleasure from seeing her "pure technique, approximating the satisfaction of seeing Bobby Jones go over the course alone."

With the exception of Pyle and Pickens, the man who seemed most moved by the New York matches was Ring Lardner. "It is obvious to everyone," he wrote, "even the experts that Miss Wills would never beat Miss Lenglen, if they were ever to meet in years to come." Lardner was almost alone in his assessment of Lenglen's performance that night. A different opinion was provided later by Harvey Snodgrass, who watched Suzanne that opening night and on the thirty-nine other occasions when she played Mary K. Browne. He was impressed by her expertise but surprised by her temper. "She was really a contradiction," he said. "Her game was grace and speed, soft shots, well-placed; she was a very well-conditioned athlete. But she was always upset, flaring mad. Sometimes it was hard to understand how the two could be connected. She had the worst temper I've ever seen." Yet despite Suzanne's conditioning, Snodgrass concluded that if Wills had been on the tour, it would have been disastrous for Lenglen. Helen was younger and far more energetic than Suzanne, and she recovered quickly from match play. She came out hitting hard on every point in every game of every set. She never let down and never gave her opponent a chance to rest. She took very little time between points. And the result, Snodgrass was convinced, in a series of matches between the Goddess and the American Girl, would have been that the Goddess would have been gradually ground down. Had she played with her characteristic brilliance, Lenglen would have won the first matches against Wills. But within a week or so, simply because of Helen's youth and power, the two would have been even. And by the time they arrived on the West Coast, "Helen would have blown Suzanne off the court every night."

Only half as many customers showed up for the Sunday night exhibition. Tilden was there again and watched Lenglen beat Browne 6–2, 6–2, in a lackluster affair. The professional troupe then departed on a forty-city, four-month tour that went next to Toronto. No other crowd would be as large as the one in New York on opening night.

Suzanne Lenglen added two members to her entourage following the New York inaugural appearances. William T. O'Brien was to serve as her personal masseur during the next four months, and nineteen-year-old Ann Kinsolving, a reporter for the Baltimore *News,* was hired as her personal press agent for $6000. O'Brien was much more than a masseur. He was a spy on the tour. He studied Pyle's methods and his management and within a few years launched his own professional tour with Tilden, Richards, and others. The travel took an unexpected toll on Suzanne's nerves and she became increasingly irritable and unfriendly. "It was a strenuous tour," Ann Kinsolving remembered. The troupe traveled at night in Pullman berths separated by drawn curtains. Lenglen suffered from insomnia. There was only one compartment with washing facilities, which was reserved for Suzanne. In defiance of the prohibition laws, she brought along French wines, which she drank with her dinners and after her matches. Suzanne insisted that wine consumption, like the cigarettes she smoked regularly, did not affect her playing. Mama helped Suzanne put away the wine.

Toronto welcomed the tour, and Suzanne Lenglen was wined and dined. Journalists attempted to outdo their American counterparts in hyperbolic allusion. On the evening of October 12 an enthusiastic crowd of 3500 turned out to see Lenglen and Browne play. To no one's surprise, Suzanne won 6–0 and 6–2. In the mixed doubles that night Lenglen was hit in the face by a hard drive from the racket of Snodgrass. The play stopped, and it took several minutes for her to recover. It appeared that no serious damage had been done, yet the experience was just another bad one to be listed with the misfortunes that accumulated as the days passed.

A crowd of 5000 turned out in Baltimore on Columbus Day to see Lenglen beat Browne 6–0, 6–0. Then in Boston a crowd of 8000 watched Lenglen batter her again, 6–2, 6–1, in the Boston Arena. In Cincinnati fewer than 1500 turned out to see Browne fall, 6–1, 6–1. The local sportswriters swooned over Suzanne, accepting Pyle's suggestion, that she was undoubtedly better than Helen Wills, who had never played in Cincinnati.

In Philadelphia on October 19, Lenglen triumphed again at 6–0, 6–2. About 3000 showed up for the matches in an auditorium that was freezing. Lenglen seemed uninspired in the city of Brotherly Love. Her service was weak and her placements not extraordinary. The problem was that the court was placed over a hockey rink. Perhaps she was also disturbed by the presence of Bill Tilden.

On October 20, after six engagements, Pyle announced that 41,000 people had paid $83,400 to see "the international stars twinkle." He predicted if the averages held that by the end of the forty-city tour the gross receipts would be somewhere between $700,000 and $800,000. The flat guarantees that he had agreed to for the stars amounted to just $142,500, but he didn't say on what basis the money was apportioned. Pyle concluded that the reception of professional tennis was, so far, "very satisfactory."

The tour then moved on to Montreal, Buffalo, Cleveland, Pittsburgh, and Columbus. As early as the Baltimore exhibition the pace of the tour began to tell on Browne. She was being worn out. Despite the fact that she was winning few games, she was working furiously at losing. She no longer played in the mixed doubles because of exhaustion. And it was rumored that Pyle was trying to sign two more female players for the tour—something that he never succeeded in doing. Pyle tried to do something to make the scores closer. He thought the crowds would be a little more animated if it looked like Browne had a chance to win. But he dare not pursue the most obvious way of doing this by asking Lenglen to throw points to make it look good. So he offered an additional cash incentive to Browne. The more games she won, the more money she would make. Snodgrass too was now given a bonus. He was to get a $200 bonus if he could win seven games in two sets from Richards. Browne was to get a $100 bonus if she won four games in two sets. And she did that. The bonus system was expanded after Chicago. Any player who could take seven games from Richards, Pyle promised, would receive a bonus of $100, and any who might win a set would win $200 bonus. The winning of a match would mean $300. Browne received $300 for a set, five games in two sets earned her $200, and four games in two sets $100.

There was serious trouble when the tour played in Chicago. Lenglen let it be known now that she was tired of it all. The troupe played in the Coliseum before a crowd of 6500. French consular officials and French societies came out in large numbers to cheer for Suzanne. Other fans said they just wanted to see the woman who beat Helen Wills. Before the match began the crowd witnessed a surprising display of Suzanne Lenglen's temper. A group of photographers took several pictures of her and French dignitaries at the match. After Lenglen announced that the picture-taking session was over, one photographer continued to flash pictures of her. She told him to get out, then she screamed at him and cursed him. When a Coliseum official tried to remove the offender, a French official joined in the fray. Then in the midst of the melee Suzanne took a swipe at the offending photographer. The crowd loved it. But poor fragile Suzanne Lenglen was unnerved by the ugly episode and as a result dropped five games in the first set to Browne and two in the second, assuring Browne a $300 bonus. Later that night she screamed at Pyle and said that she had enough and wanted to go home.

Lenglen was starting to have problems with the other players on the tour, too. "She was always saying she wanted to go home," Snodgrass remembered. "She would get all dolled up every night and then fight and argue with everybody. She was always throwing everything out of her dressing room screaming that she wanted to go home. She was a real case, believe me."

"She wasn't a good mixer, either," Snodgrass found. "She was with her mother most of the time. She didn't like men—that was all publicity. She preferred the company of women. She and her mother dined together and they stayed away from the rest of us. That was fine with us."

She complained to Pyle almost constantly. One time in the middle of a match she told him she was not feeling well. She was having her period and she wanted to stop. Pyle replied that the women he had known only complained when they did not have their periods. Suzanne laughed and went on with the match.

Pyle tried to convince the press that Suzanne Lenglen's temperamental outbursts were just a show. He fell back on his belief that people would pay to see someone they hated. "And the whole problem," he said, "was to keep them hating her. Suzanne is charming when she wants to be, and we had to repress that side of her nature. Every now and then she would go pleasant on us, and we would have to jog her a little, and have her make faces at Miss Browne, or get unpopular with the local aristocracy by refusing to meet them. But I will say for Miss Lenglen that she kept her unpopularity campaign going nicely with very little jogging."

There were more problems as the tour neared the West Coast. The Victoria Tennis Club refused to post a $5000 guarantee so the tour re-routed to Seattle on December 2. A few days later in Portland, Browne seemed suddenly to get a second wind, while Lenglen became emotionally and physically more brittle. Their exhibition did not begin the way that all the others had begun. Browne matched her game for game. They went to five all and then six all, then seven, eight, and nine all. At 9–8 Browne came within two points of winning the set—a disaster of tremendous moment for Lenglen. But the Goddess weathered the emergency and won that game and the next two to take the first set, 11–9. But she had struggled through twenty games in one set and had heard the crowd grow increasingly boisterous about Browne's scrappy luck. Before the second set could begin, Suzanne Lenglen walked off the court, leaving Browne standing there. She went to her dressing room and collapsed. A taxi was called to take her back to her hotel, and it was announced that she was suffering from a cold and could not continue the match.

Snodgrass remembered that she again wanted to quit the tour in Portland. She deposited the contents of her dressing room in the hallway. And she screamed that she was finished, absolutely finished with Pyle and the tour. Snodgrass shared some of her disillusionment. He was himself increasingly unhappy with Pyle. "I found him to be dishonest. He was really just a bunch of bullshit, a con artist, always talking about big things. But he wasn't even with us half the time." And if the was not bad enough, Snodgrass began to suspect that Pyle was not going to make enough to pay everyone on the tour. Snodgrass had signed for only $15,000, and he began to doubt he would ever see that much. He was, unfortunately, right. In the end he received only $9000 for the tour and had to sue Pyle for the remaining $6000.

The excitement built for Suzanne Lenglen's California appearances. The entire tour could be made a huge success simply by the California reception. The local press was excited about the native sons and the native daughter on the tour. And Pyle still harbored the hope that arrangements could be made for a Wills/Lenglen rematch in the West.

Prior to the arrival of Lenglen and the Pyle troupe, Pickens and Ira C. Pyle, the brother of C.C., came to San Francisco to make hotel and show arrangements. The troupe stayed at the Palace Hotel and was scheduled to perform in both San Francisco and Oakland. The initial exhibition was to be Tuesday evening, December 7, and the second was to take place in Oakland the next evening. There were also rumors that the exhibition would not take place because of Lenglen's poor health. The USLTA had suggested that its officials not attend the exhibitions and that they make no statements concerning professional tennis. Players, also, were encouraged to skip the show.

On the afternoon of December 6 the Shasta Limited arrived at the Ferry Building in San Francisco carrying the players of the Pyle troupe. It was greeted by a small army of reporters. Someone asked Lenglen if she would see Helen Wills, and Suzanne asked, "Does she live near here?" Then one of the reporters, seeing the chance for a good joke, pointed out the campanile across the bay in Berkeley "as a monument to Miss Wills in her home town." Lenglen was impressed. "It is quite a large monument to so young a girl," she exclaimed with genuine awe. In response to questions about her training, Lenglen said that she exercised each morning to stay fit—she didn't say how—while attired in her "fetching black pajamas," designed specifically for her, naturally, by Patou. She was asked why Browne appeared to be doing better against her as the tour progressed? Lenglen reminded the reporters first that she had beaten Browne twenty-one times in a row. Browne was improving, though, because she "has had 21 lessons from a past master in the art of tennis."

In the next few days during her stay in San Francisco, every facet of Lenglen's life and travels came under the scrutiny of the local press, which tried to satisfy the public demand for knowledge about this woman who had beaten the American Girl in Cannes in February. She was not "a dainty eater," they discovered, as earlier press handouts had alleged. In fact, she loved to eat. She had a voracious appetite. Several reporters watched in amazement as she downed her lunch. As an appetizer she munched on celery sticks dipped in catsup—a favorite light treat, she confessed. Then she consumed a large salad and lamb chops. And, as a special dessert, while Pyle chatted with the press, she devoured his lunch of oysters à la Kirkpatrick.

Pyle offered an exclusive to the reporters and told them that Lenglen had acquired yet another title during the tour. She was no longer just "the Goddess." Now the Pueblo Indians had adopted her as a member of their tribe with the name "Princess Sparkling Water," a tribute, they said, to her eyes. But after witnessing the Goddess eating, the reporters imagined several more fitting Indian titles.

One final effort was made to arrange an exhibition between Wills and Lenglen in San Francisco. Sumner Hardy, president of the California Lawn Tennis Association, sent a hasty telegram to Jones Mersereau, head of the USLTA, asking under what conditions the match could be held. The answer was that the rules prevented amateurs from playing professionals for a prize. And it also stated that no exhibition could be held where a promoter or any other individual received anything. Dr. Clarence Wills said that he would be glad to let his daughter play Lenglen in a friendly match, but not if there were any gate receipts. And so the talk of a match ended at that impasse. What, after all, Pyle concluded, would be the point of a Lenglen-Wills match if there were no proceeds

Helen Wills paid a call on Suzanne Lenglen at the Palace Hotel. But Suzanne's telephone had been disconnected so that she might have some undistrubed rest, and Helen was unable to get in touch with her. Helen was offered tickets for the performance by Pickens, but she "demurely replied" that she had already made reservations and thanked him for the courtesy.

Suzanne Lenglen did her part for charity in San Francisco by graciously giving lessons at the Civic Auditorium to a group of children selected by the city's Playground Commission. She pointed out that she had been among the first to sponsor junior development in France and had always been interested in the proper training of younger players. She also appeared on a local radio station, KPO, to answer questions about the tour and about her amateur career.

Lenglen kept her temper under control in San Francisco. "She certainly can be the gracious lady when she so desires," columnist Harry B. Smith wrote. And on the radio she spoke with quiet confidence and ease, he found. When the program concluded, she said that she would like to broadcast some more, having found it to be a particularly pleasing experience.

In her exhibition match at the Civic Auditorium, Lenglen captured the hearts of the San Francisco tennis fans, a local paper headlined. She again beat Browne, but by a score of 8–6 and 6–2, giving up one less game than she had against Helen Wills in Cannes. And the local fans loved it. The locals particularly liked the way the players were introduced. Instead of simply walking out onto the court, the announcer called out the name of the player, who then skipped out onto the floor. About 5200 people came to see the show—the largest crowd ever to attend a tennis match in San Francisco. Helen Wills was there, having ignored the advice of the USLTA to stay away. She watched the match intently from her balcony seat but had no comment for the press when it was over.

And Dr. Sumner Hardy, president of the California Lawn Tennis Association, was there, too, in defiance of the USLTA. Pop Fuller, Helen Wills's teacher, was also present at the performance. He was seated in a box close to "ringside" and took notes throughout the match. Fuller spoke with the press later and said he had seen Suzanne in 1921 when she stormed off the court against Molla Mallory. He found that she was good, very good. But could she beat Helen Wills? "No chance," he said with absolute certainty. "Helen would win easily enough."

Another spectator who was expected to be awed by the matches was a youngster who dreamed of becoming a professional baseball player with the San Francisco Seals. Alice Marble was taken to the exhibition by her older brother Dan in his effort to encourage her to play tennis rather than baseball. Dan thought that if Alice could watch a really outstanding tennis player at work she might be inspired enough to start practicing the sport on the public courts. But little Alice never got the chance to see Suzanne Lenglen play. Dan could only get seats far from courtside, and, before Suzanne danced out into the spotlight, Alice Marble, who would within the year take up tennis and would in time win twelve major titles at Wimbledon and Forest Hills before turning professional herself in 1941, had fallen sound asleep and could not be awakened.

A California player who was awed by her was Bud Chandler, who also watched the exhibition. Chandler was amazed by her gracefulness. When she came to the net to pick up a ball, he observed, "she did it with a sort of plié, just as though she was dancing. And she remained on her toes throughout the evening. She was just incredible. I had never seen anyone like her, with her sense of showmanship, before. Nor since."

On the afternoon following the exhibition Helen Wills called on Suzanne Lenglen at her new quarters at the Oakland Hotel in Oakland and chatted with her for more than an hour. They talked at length about their meeting in Cannes but did not discuss the possibility of a match in California. That evening Helen attended the exhibition in the Oakland Auditorium and saw Suzanne beat Browne by a score of 6–2, 7–5. About 3000 showed up for the show.

The troupe then traveled to Los Angeles. The press in Southern California was already cheering for Browne and predicting she would win one in Los Angeles for her old hometown crowd. Browne helped stir up local enthusiasm when she said: "when I signed with Mr. Pyle for this tour I knew I would one day defeat Mlle Lenglen. My hour is near. Of all places in the world where I would like to turn the trick, Los Angeles is the one."

But when Lenglen arrived in Southern California there was, again, the possibility that she would be unable to play at all. She checked into the Hotel Del Coronado and was examined by a local doctor. He announced later that it was incredible that Suzanne had not suffered a physical collapse on the tour. "She must have been going on sheer nerve for the past months," he guessed. "It would be very unwise for her to start a tour of the world without first taking a long rest. She would surely break down under the strain."

But Suzanne Lenglen insisted now that her nervousness would not hinder her game. No doubt prodded by Pyle, who was hoping for a killing in Los Angeles, financially, she said, "I play my best tennis when I am on the verge of a breakdown. My nervous condition does not affect my game when I am in a tournament, but I have to pay the penalty after it is all over. It is when I am on edge that I can make impossible shots and drives which the tennis gallery demands." The Los Angeles matches were scheduled for the Olympic Auditorium for the evening of December 28. Suzanne stayed in Coronado in the days prior to the exhibition. Pyle leaked tales to the local press of her working out for several hours daily, frantically polishing her game in order to prevent Mary K. from beating her. After all, Pyle pointed out, the California woman was creeping closer and closer to a win each time they met, and it just might happen in Los Angeles. What a great event if the first defeat since 1921 could be pulled off by a local player right in Los Angeles on the 28th. Who in the world would pass up the chance to see it?

Behind the scenes a controversy was brewing. The USLTA was threatening to discipline fifteen Southern California amateur officials who were accused of aiding Pyle. Far from the clutches of the headquarters of the USLTA, the West, which supplied three of the four American professionals on the tour, didn't take the screams of the USLTA all that seriously. The *Los Angeles Times* championed the exhibition matches and pointed out that the "tennis monarchs" had initially ridiculed Pyle when he came up with the plan to stage professional matches. But now that the tour was more than two-thirds completed and Pyle's pockets were bulging with profits, "the only recourse of the old-line net organization is to threaten local amateurs who agree to officiate in the professional matches."

The players and fans of Southern California took issue openly with the USLTA and believed that the appearance of the Pyle group would be the greatest boon to tennis that the area had ever received. Elliott Church, who volunteered to be one of the umpires, said that "we have no desire to wave the red flag in the bull's face, but it is up to all who have the good of tennis in this section at heart to cooperate and put the Lenglen games over with a bang." The Olympic Auditorium was quickly sold out, and Pyle had the manager of the place install 300 additional seats. Those special ringside perches were snapped up immediately by Charlie Chaplin, Douglas Fairbanks, Mary Pickford, Harold Lloyd, Marion Davies, and a host of other film stars and local celebrities.

The *Los Angeles Times* almost shamelessly ballyhooed the professionals, predicting that Suzanne Lenglen would face "the greatest test of her athletic career" in her contest against Browne, who was at last finally tuned and now ready to win. Another local player was added to the exhibition in Los Angeles—Walter Wesbrook—a local favorite and already a teaching professional, was scheduled to play doubles with his old partner, Snodgrass.

Helen Smithers of the *Los Angeles Times*—one of the few female reporters given the chance to cover Suzanne Lenglen in America—watched her at practice and concluded she had never before seen anything quite like the French woman. "The flying French demoiselle jumps, lunges and whiles. Americans want action and she provides it. La Lenglen has the spring of a panther. She never saves energy; she wastes it. Her one object is to provide action and excellent tennis. She is that rare combination, a great player and a great showman. Some athletes are great performers but lack personality, while others teem with personality, but lack expert talent."

The *Times* dropped a bombshell when it published a highly controversial and surprisingly candid report from San Francisco alleging that Helen Wills had remarked to reporters that she was completely unimpressed by what she had seen of Lenglen in the two exhibition matches in Northern California and she believed that Suzanne had degenerated, pathetically, into little more than a "mechanical doll." The publication of this allegation infuriated Lenglen. "I have done nothing but boost Helen Wills since I defeated her at Cannes nine months ago," she pointed out to newsmen. "Being catty is far from my policy. But when Miss Wills plainly makes capital of her newspaper connections at my expense, I may be pardoned for declaring that it is my opinion that the world would not have heard of Helen Wills had it not been for her being pitted against Suzanne Lenglen as the logical contender for the world's championship."

In a candid interview in Los Angeles, Pyle indicated at last why Wills had not been signed for the tour. "I realized even before I had her turn professional that if she [Lenglen] were defeated by an American girl she would terminate her tour and return home to her beloved France—heartbroken. She would have to listen to the equivalent of 'I told you so' in French."

When the match was played the next night all the words in the world about Browne's determination and Lenglen's illness didn't mean a thing.

Suzanne showed only how completely superior she was to her Santa Monica foil. Before a crowd of 7000, she convincingly crushed Browne 6–0, 6–1. The crowd alternately cheered and was stunned into silence by her incredible virtuosity on the court. In the first set Browne was beaten so quickly there was hardly time for the spectators to figure out what was happening. It was over it seemed almost before it began. Nobody could remember Browne winning any points in the first set, none at all. And in a matter of minutes Lenglen had racked up six games. Browne never had a chance to get warmed up. She played with a little more determination in the second set, but could pull out only a single game. The gate receipts for the night came to $21,000.

The next day the Pyle professionals of the "Suzanne Tour," as they were popularly referred to now, left Los Angeles for the next engagement in San Antonio, Texas. Pyle remained in Los Angeles to arrange professional football games for his new professional league and to handle other business. Pickens was assigned the day-to-day management of the troupe for the remainder of the tour. After San Antonio they were scheduled to play in Dallas, Houston, New Orleans, Birmingham, Atlanta, and then a series of exhibitions in Florida and Cuba.

When the touring professionals left California, they brought along a new member of the group who was not entirely a welcome presence. In Los Angeles, Lenglen met and was wooed by a wealthy California playboy, Baldwin M. Baldwin, grandson of E. J. "Lucky" Baldwin who had acquired a sizable fortune during the gold rush. Baldwin was apparently so enamored of Suzanne that he insisted on joining the tour with her. He was a married man with a family who for another two years did not speak publicly about getting a divorce. In order to make it all look fairly innocent, he appeared in news releases as her manager. The subterfuge may not have been inaccurate. As the days passed it appeared that Baldwin was most interested in the financial possibilities of Suzanne's career, and he questioned her in detail about her agreement with Pyle and Pickens. He began to scheme with her for a new contract or a new tour under a different manager.

With Pyle absent and with Baldwin present and with Pickens running the show, the tour became even less pleasant. Pyle had not yet settled financially with any members of the tour, and there was a suspicion that everything he was doing was not on the up and up. Lenglen was ill more often and complained more often and was even more anxious to finish the tour and return to France. Pickens was not an adept manager of personalities, and he did not get along with Lenglen as well as Pyle had.

In Miami, Lenglen met Molla Mallory again. They were introduced to each other before newsmen at the site of the exhibition. The greetings they exchanged were described as cool. Lnglen said later of the meeting, "Women are not good sports and don't pretend to be. They are too temperamental. I am furious in defeat, but the public doesn't know, because I don't show it."

Richards contracted jaundice in New Orleans and was ill for much of the rest of the tour. In Havana Lenglen was listless and unhappy, and at last let Browne win a couple of sets, far from the prying eyes of American journalists.

Then as the tour wound down, Lenglen demanded different arrangements for her matches along with some postponements. Pickens let her have her way. The appearance of the group in Hartford was postponed in early January because she was suffering, it was said, from tonsillitis. She was placed under the care of a personal physician again. In early February an appearance in Newark was postponed, again because of illness. The appearance in New Haven was rescheduled and then postponed for a week. When she finally did play in New Haven on February 11, she played only in the mixed doubles, and she appeared either so ill or so uninspired that she was a disappointment to the crowd. She was helped from the court by trainer O'Brien. She and Richards won their match simply because of double faults by Browne and Kinsey. This was not the kind of tennis the crowd paid to see. Then on the next night before 4000 and, she said, against the advice of her physician—she and Richards in mixed doubles again defeated Browne and Kinsey. Her singles match against Browne was again cancelled. On the evening of February 12 she played what was billed as her farewell appearance at the Twenty-third Regiment Armory in Brooklyn before a handful of spectators. Again she played in mixed doubles only. She and Kinsey were defeated this time by Browne and Snodgrass in a long three-set match. She was outplayed by Browne—who was now in top form—and tired visibly as the match wore on. When the tour concluded on February 14 with the playing of a rescheduled match in Providence, Browne, whose contract had expired, departed for Cleveland, where she intended to open a sporting goods store. Pickens tried to make the best of the Providence appearance and put together a scaled-down exhibition and advertised the first "mixed singles" match in history: Lenglen against Kinsey. Suzanne was to receive a one-point advantage in each game. But the singles event wasn't held, and instead a mixed doubles match was. Lenglen and Richards lost in an unspectacular doubles match against Kinsey and Snodgrass.

At the end of the tour Mary K. Browne wrote an article on what she had learned from Suzanne Lenglen. She had, she pointed out, won two sets in two different matches during the tour. "We were together four months, and I learned more about tennis and sports in general in that short time than I had learned in all the twenty years before," she wrote.

The professional tour was not simply ending, it was clearly falling apart. Baldwin was trying to horn in on the action now, insisting that

Suzanne Lenglen be given a new and better contract by Pyle, and Pyle was tiring of the Suzanne business. Papa Lenglen telegraphed Suzanne ordering her not to sign any new contract with anybody. He said that there had been a number of offers in Europe, and there were now stories of an offer of 20,000 francs per week for a European tour. Papa's advice now was, "Let us wait and see." Suzanne said she would sign no contracts and booked passage home.

Pyle wanted a monopoly with his players. He now insisted again that if the tour was to continue he would have to be assured that he was the exclusive promoter for the players and that they would not deal with anyone else. The dispute between Pyle and Baldwin became public and increasingly acrimonious. Pickens realized that Baldwin had money but not the knack for promotion. But Lenglen would not listen. She had grown suspicious of both Pyle and Pickens. Pickens relayed her complaints to Pyle in Los Angeles. Baldwin became such an enormous pain that, Pyle warned, if he continued to represent Suzanne, then he—Pyle— would no longer deal with her. Baldwin said that was just fine and announced that he would become Suzanne's exclusive manager and arrange a world tour for her.

On February 16, Pyle, speaking at a news conference in the Hotel Vanderbilt in Los Angeles, announced his withdrawal from professional tennis. The problem, Pyle said, was that Lenglen had asked for more money, and she was, at the same time, negotiating with other promoters. So, he said, he was dropping all associations with professional tennis "until the players make up their minds with whom they wish to play, and realize that they are not entitled to increases in pay."

"Mlle Lenglen and I part company with nothing but the friendliest of relations," Pyle said the next day. "She had a successful tour of this country and would have been equally successful in Japan had we gone through with our original schedule. Shortly after meeting Mr. Baldwin I noticed that she was getting advice contrary to what I regarded as for our mutual best interests.

"I am given to understand by my Eastern representative, W. H. Pickens, that Mlle Lenglen and Mr. Baldwin have decided to map out her future professional program together. I am perfectly willing to step out of the picture."

At the same time Pickens complained that the professional players just don't seem to realize that an amateur who turned professional was worth far more money to a promoter than a professional who had already taken the plunge. The tour needed new blood. And because of that simple fact Pyle could not afford to pay increases to players who were already professionals. In some cases, in fact, as with Snodgrass, he could not even meet past salary agreements.

And so Lenglen and Feret announced that they were going home. Howard Kinsey decided to accompany them to France. Mary Browne was already gone, and Harvey Snodgrass made plans to return to California and to teaching. The tour had come to a close.

Pyle had always been aware of the riches available via endorsements. It was learned only later that Pyle got his cut—a significant one—in all Lenglen endorsements. He got the lion's share of the royalties on the Lenglen racket and the perfume and the dolls and the clothing. He made more than $100,000 personally from the tour. And he confessed in the end that it had never been his intention to establish or even to help the cause of professional tennis. "I was in the Suzanne Lenglen business, not the tennis business," he said.

Just how good was the Suzanne Lenglen business for Suzanne Lenglen? Pickens told inquiring reporters that before Suzanne departed from the United States she had earned $100,000. He revealed the financial details of her contract, stating that she had signed for $60,000 and 50 percent of the gate. Browne received $30,000 and 5 percent. Richards received $35,-000 flat. Total receipts for the tour, including royalties, came to nearly $500,000.

Suzanne Lenglen departed from New York on February 19 on the liner *France* with Mama, Feret, Kinsey, and Baldwin in tow. She did not look forward to the voyage because she could not smoke while crossing the Atlantic. Smoking aboard ship, she said, made her seasick. But she had a remedy for seasickness from causes other than smoking. She drank lots of champagne. "I expect to have a bottle near me at all times," she said. "I am glad that I came to America," she told reporters at dockside. "I am sorry to go. Everyone has been splendid to me."

How much had the American tour netted her? "Oh, I made sufficient money," she said. And although she had received "many offers" to appear in movies, she revealed, she had accepted none of them. She was planning a European tour followed by South American and Asian tours. A South African syndicate in Johannesburg announced that it would sponsor a tour of that country by Browne and Lenglen, but nothing came of it. Asked what she planned to do with her earnings, she responded, "Travel—I never get enough of travel." Would she buy a chateau near Paris? "No, I don't want a big house. I much prefer to travel."

One of the reporters asked about tennis. Why was Suzanne Lenglen so dominant? Did she pray before her matches, perhaps, in the way that some generals were said to have prayed before battles? "Oh, no, indeed," she responded. "It all depends upon physical condition. Suppose both players prayed. Then what would God do? There are more important things for God to do than to take care of tennis players." In conclusion, she said, she believed that she had furthered the game and said that after every exhibition people approached her and said that they were now going to take up tennis.

On February 26 a cheering mob greeted her when the *Paris* docked in Havre. "I have no regrets," she told them. "I am proud to be a professional and after a tour in Europe I plan another professional trip to America." When asked if she had marriage in her future she said, "I don't say never," and gave a sly glance toward—Howard Kinsey! She again refused to say how much she had earned on the tour and asked that French journalists not exaggerate so she would not have problems when she made her income tax declarations.

A limousine took Suzanne, Mama, Kinsey, Feret, and Baldwin to Paris and inadvertently stood up the huge crowd that had gathered at the train station to greet her. In Paris she let it be known that she had changed her mind about the United States. She liked the country and said she planned to return. She even wished she could have stayed longer, particularly in California. The best of all the states, she said, was California, because of its climate.

When the tour was over, Vincent Richards announced that he was satisfied with his career as a professional and had no regrets. In February, Richards said that he was moving ahead on his own with plans for a professional tennis association. He said that his league of professionals would be organized in one of the largest cities of the country, but he was not certain where. When the organization got under way—if the organization got under way—Richards wanted to hold a regular series of open tournaments in various parts of the country.

Richards did put together a national professional tournament in 1927. And he won it. He also won it in 1928. In 1929 the title went to Karel Kozeluh of Czechoslovakia, but Richards won it back again in 1930. Then he announced his retirement from professional tennis and said he was going into business. "I am at the top now," he said, "but my legs won't stand the gaff of nine solid months of play and teaching much longer. I am retiring while I can still break into another field of livelihood. From now on I shall swing a racket only for exercise."

But he changed his mind. In 1931 Tilden, who had turned professional, convinced Richards to come out of retirement and play him in a series of ten matches. Tilden won all ten; Richards again retired. Eventually he went to work for the Dunlop Tire and Rubber Company and did quite well. And two decades later when Tilden was an impoverished and desperate man, Richards provided him with rackets and balls so he could continue playing tennis. In 1953 he even entered a tournament in Palm Desert, California, along with Tilden.

The USLTA took its revenge on the professional players at the end of 1926 when it published its rankings for the year. The rankings were supposed to be based on tournament play during 1926. But the USLTA decided that the rankings for 1926 should not include the names of any player who had turned professional at the end of the season, even though the same individual had played throughout the regular season as an amateur in all major tournaments and competitions. So the rankings for the year excluded Richards, Browne, and Kinsey. Tilden opposed the action, but it was supported and pushed through by Julian Myrick, chairman of the Davis Cup Committee, who insisted that the ranking of all tennis players should be based not simply upon something as objective as proven playing ability in tournaments, but also upon the subjective "meritorious conduct" of each player throughout the year. The same committee omitted Helen Wills from its ranking despite her obvious meritorious conduct throughout the year, stating that she had not been able to compete in enough American tournaments to secure a realistic ranking.

The USLTA had precisely what it wanted—enough ambivalence in its rules and regulations to apply them on a personal basis and thereby reward friends and punish enemies of the established order of amateur tennis. Richards protested. He had expected to be ranked number one by the USLTA and in all fairness should have been. He pointed out that Helen Wills who was a favorite of the organization sold drawings and writings that were worth absolutely nothing were she not a well-known tennis player. She was making good money out of her amateur tennis career and so, under the rules of the USLTA, was a professional. The USLTA chose not to respond to Richards's outburst. After all, why should they? They had not ranked Helen Wills.

This was the last controversy of the Pyle tour. The *New York Sun* compared the action of the USLTA to that of the Russian government, which deprived a player of his national chess championship title because he was lukewarm on Bolshevism. Richards had played the entire amateur season of 1926 and deserved a top ranking for the year, the *Sun* said.

The French Tennis Federation did precisely the same thing, omitting Suzanne Lenglen from its ranking for 1926 along with Paul Feret. The FTA waited for the USLTA to publish its listing before publishing its own and then followed suit. In place of Lenglen at the top of the list was a dual number one ranking for Didi Vlasto and Helene Contostavlos. M. Canet, president of the FTA, announced of the professionals that "these players decided to live their own tennis lives. The French Federation must ignore them for the time being." There was some indication that the FTA would consider reinstating both Feret and Lenglen as amateurs if they were properly contrite and petitioned the organization. But Canet said the organization would be guided in the matter by the USLTA. The USLTA regarded the loss of amateur status much like the loss of virginity. It could not be restored no matter how fervently it was wanted back. The damage was irreversible.

Yet one of the Pyle professionals was, in time, restored to amateur status. Feret, son of the FTA official, copped a sort of "temporary insanity" plea because of the death of his wife and his overwhelming sorrow. He had acted on the spur of the moment while suffering from diminished mental capacity, he insisted. The FTA bought his argument, and he was an amateur again in 1933, after he paid them an amount equal to what Pyle had paid him. But his best playing days were past.

Later that spring the United States Golf Association barred Mary K. Browne from competing as an amateur in golf because of her status as a professional in tennis. The Association said, in handing down its ruling, that Browne had "acted in a manner detrimental to the best interests of golf" by turning professional in tennis.

The Pyle episode did result in demands from some for a more objective definition of "amateur" by the USLTA. One of those calling for such a definition and a strict adherence to it was the president of the Western Lawn Tennis Association, who pointed out that "expense accounts at many tournaments have grown to such proportions that many players are living off the game and still are classed as amateurs. We feel that tournament expense accounts should be held to legitimate expense and private expense accounts forbidden."

When the USLTA held its annual meeting in February to take up this and other issues they chose not to alter amateur rules. The Pyle professionals found themselves on their own when the tour came to an end. Suzanne Lenglen was in a strange new world, no longer the center of attention. She could no longer play in the tournaments that had kept her in the public eye. Helen Wills, on the other hand, had maintained her amateur status and was now the darling of the tennis establishment in the United States and in England.

When Lenglen arrived home in the spring of 1927, Helen Wills was preparing to travel to England for a second try at the Wimbledon women's singles crown. Lenglen had won the title six times. It seemed unlikely, in 1927, that the American Girl would ever approach that record. But she could, perhaps, win it once or twice, it was said. In the absence of the Goddess, Helen Wills might provide some fireworks for amateur tennis tournaments.

Suzanne Lenglen played professional tennis for a few more months— but her exhibition tours were financial failures. She opened a tennis school in Paris and attended matches at Stade Roland-Garros and Wimbledon and on the Riviera as a spectator only. Because she was a professional, she was not given choice seats at Wimbledon, the All-England Club having revoked her honorary membership. She watched herself turn into memories in the minds of her former fans. She was associated with warm afternoons in the champagne sunshine of the Riviera when a dancing youngster enthralled the crowds. She was the Goddess who had barely beaten the American Girl on the Riviera in 1926 in the greatest tennis match in history. She was the woman who dominated the game several years ago and who kept the Queen waiting at Wimbledon. She was a set of numbers in the record book, a faded photograph of a young woman in a pleated skirt and a bandeau, caught in mid-stride above the clay of some vaguely familiar tennis court somewhere several years ago. She was the greatest player who ever stepped onto the court. She was at her best when the going was good. She was Papa's girl. She was the past.

And Helen Wills, the American Girl, was the present. And she was, perhaps, the future.

Suzanne Lenglen hoped still for a rematch with the American girl, her one sure path to regenerate fame and glory. She spoke often of such a match, at first in a challenging way and then, after a few years, in a whimsical way. But she was never given the chance to play the American Girl again.

QUEEN HELEN
1927-1933

"Great ladies can their beauty wear
A little while upon the floor;
But all their beauty turns to air
When Helen glitters thru the door!"
—"Helen," 1932
Edwin Markham

"Watching her on the tennis courts, I have appreciated that she is the nearest living approximation of the old Greek ideal of perfection."
—C. S. Jagger, 1931

"They called Helen Wills 'Poker Face' because no expression of emotion ever crossed that classically beautiful mask while she was on the court. I regard her as the coldest, most self-centered, most ruthless champion ever known to tennis."
—William T. Tilden, III

"It's not a game to the death, and I'm glad Helen didn't place me in the position of taking the championship over her disabled form."
—Helen Hull Jacobs, 1933

IN the spring of 1927, while a Suzanne Lenglen's exhibition tour of England fizzled, Helen Wills's career blossomed. She won no major national titles in 1926, and she had been beaten in Cannes by Lenglen. Yet, ironically, she became the object of enthusiastic international interest. Her reputation had not suffered, as it had in 1925 when she had faced few formidable opponents. The question being asked in the spring of 1927 was, "Can she in fact be a worthy successor to Suzanne? Can she attract the crowds and the loyalty and the attention of Suzanne? Can she inspire the same controversy and the excitement that Suzanne inspired? Can she win the way Suzanne won? Or will she be like May Sutton and Kitty McKane and Mary K. Browne and a whole host of others who had once been promising but then fell back with the pack, winning a few titles and arousing some attention before they became perennial 'contenders'?"

Wimbledon, where Wills had already lost once and Lenglen had never lost in singles, was to be the test. If she could win in 1927 there was hope for her and for amateur tennis and for the associations and the clubs that sponsored and exploited the sport. If she could not win at Wimbledon the search for a successor to Lenglen would go on, and perhaps public attention would switch to favorites in other sports or other activities, and the associations and clubs would languish.

Throughout her career, Helen Wills sought to perpetuate the myth that she was a natural athlete, and that she did not try hard or practice hard for matches. She wanted others to believe that tennis was a mere pastime and not of great importance in her life. Art was to be her career, she said over and over again. In her autobiography she wrote that in late 1926 she did not play tennis for several months, yet in fact she devoted full time in the fall of 1926 to tennis as well as to drawing; the *two* activities, she told a friend, took up all of her time. In the fall at the Berkeley Tennis Club she was allowed to enter the men's doubles tournament for the club championship, the only time in club history that such a thing was permitted. Her play was so far superior to any other woman's in the club that it was considered only fair that she compete against the men. Wills and her partner Ward Dawson lost in the final to Bud Chandler and Tom Stow in a tough three-set match, 3–6, 6–4, 8–6. The papers reported that it was Dawson's fault that Helen Wills was not the men's doubles co-champion of the Berkeley Tennis Club. At one time in the third set Wills and her partner led 5–4 and had match point. But Dawson wavered badly, made several errors, and the game and the match were lost.

In December 1926 Helen Wills dropped out of the University of California for the second time and traveled to New York with her mother to publish a book of her poems and to complete the manuscript of a book on tennis. The book of poetry, entitled *The Awakening*, was published by Dorrance, and the tennis book was published the next year by Scribners. Wills took a job on the art staff of the *New York World*, where she was given a special office and did several sketches for the paper. Her period of service for the newspaper was brief because, as another journalist at the *World* wrote, "she found that regular office hours interfered with indoor tennis practice. It was not that she loved her art less, but that she loved her tennis more. Her sketches had little merit. Unsigned they would probably have appeared nowhere. Signed, newspapers and magazines were glad to buy them." She also interviewed celebrities for the paper—actresses, actors, visiting royalty, traveling adventurers. "I was not impressed by the people whom I met," she wrote later, "whose time I was taking up. I would have undertaken any assignment with assurance." She returned home for several weeks in the late winter, but then set out in the early spring for England and the Wimbledon tournament.

The year 1927 marked the shift in power in men's tennis from the United States to France, as French players captured both the Davis Cup and the American national singles title. But in women's tennis, the retirement of Suzanne Lenglen and the rise of Helen Wills, the year marked an American ascendency.

On May 23, Helen Wills sailed from New York to England on the *Tuscania*. She began her English campaign of 1927 in the North of London Championships at Stamford Hill, where she defeated Elizabeth Ryan, 6–4, 6–4, for the title. She didn't give up a single set in the competition, but, in the early rounds she often lost six to eight games per match against unspectacular competition. It was whispered that she was not in very good form and would have a lot of trouble at Wimbledon. A week later she played in the Kent Championships at Beckenham, "the real preliminary to Wimbledon." She appeared to have improved dramatically. She thrashed Billie Tapscott of South Africa in just eighteen minutes, and on the following day beat Molla Mallory in twenty-three minutes. She had cut ten minutes off the time in which she had first beaten Molla at Forest Hills. The initial set took ten minutes, and Mallory seemed helpless before her drives. British journalists observed that, in winning so quickly Wills had accomplished something that Lenglen had never achieved. Lenglen did not rush through her matches, but often slowed down to toy with her opponents. Wills had none of that. This was a grim business, which, she believed, was best finished quickly. In the final she beat Kitty McKane, now Mrs. L. A. Godfree, 6–2, 6–4. It was a great exhibition of all-court tennis.

The promise of a resurgent Helen Wills was a boon to Wimbledon ticket sales. Once more there were long lines—no longer the "Lenglen Lines" but now the Helen Wills Lines—forming outside the facilities at 5:00 a.m. for tickets, and Wimbledon prepared to celebrate the first of several Helen Wills days. This was the first Wimbledon in which an electronic public address system was used to announce the score and the decision in matches, after it was determined, with due deliberation, that such announcements would not disturb the players.

She was seeded first at Wimbledon. In the second round of the tournament on June 21, an historic event occurred. Helen Wills dropped a set to Gwen Sterry of England, the daughter of Charlotte Sterry, the 1908 champion. Wills won the match, 6–3, 3–6, 6–3. It was to be the last set that Helen Wills lost in singles until July 8, 1933, six years later. In those six years, in fact, she did not lose a set in singles in any tournament anywhere in the world.

In the third round of the competition another historic event took place as Wills, in beating Eileen Bennett, was extended to 7–5, 6–3. She was not extended again in a singles competition at Wimbledon until 1933.

In the finals at Wimbledon in 1927 she played against Lili de Alvarez and won, 6–2, 6–4. "She was the hardest hitter I have ever met both on fore and backhand," Helen wrote later. An English journalist wrote of the Wills-Alvarez match that "this was tennis never seen on the Centre Court before. These were man-like strokes to which the perfect poise of feminine grace was added. They may not have had man-like tactics behind them; in speed and counter speed they were majestic, drawing riotous applause from an enraptured crowd." Duncan Macaulay, the referee for the tournament, write that the match was "a magnificent spectacle" and that it was "an encounter of great speed and beauty in which, for the spectators, the score didn't seem to matter." American journalist Al Laney remembered it, too, as an incredible confrontation. "I doubt if any match ever played by two women could equal it for sustained attack on both sides of the net and the quality of strokes employed over such a long period.

"At the beginning of the second set," he wrote, "Lili brought out a maneuver I never was to see any other girl, with the one exception of Lenglen, attempt against Miss Wills. This was to exchange full-length drives from deep court and then to draw Miss Wills forward with a short, almost insolent flick to the forehand line. With this plan, the señorita went to 4–3 after a series of unforgettable exchanges. But she was at advantage three times before she got the game, and by the end of it Miss Wills, though she had yielded, had caught on.

"Miss Wills now set out to defeat the plan by sheer speed of stroke, which made the final half-volleying coup impossible to bring off. This brought them to the crisis of the match, the eighth game. It was an extraordinary session of tremendous hitting, and the last point of it produced a rally the equal of which I have never seen again in women's tennis. Such sustained hitting and such gorgeous shots by two girls had never taken place on this court or, I imagine, anywhere else. Twenty strokes by each girl were counted, each hit to score, speed countered by more speed, until finally the señorita, perhaps in desperation, attempted once more to trap the other girl with her favorite coup and failed. The backhand half-volley curled out of the court and the score was 4–all."

At that point both players paused and used their rackets for support. Applause resounded throughout the gallery. Wills recovered from the rally instantly. Alvarez did not. And she won only one more point as the American Girl displayed an absolutely dazzling *découpage* of strokes, slicing and pounding the ball, ranging along the baseline, plunging toward the net, winning point after point after point. Alvarez, for all her talent and determination, could never take a set from the American Girl. Not on this day. Not in 1928, when she met Helen again in the Wimbledon final. Not ever. As the two women left the court, at the gate Alvarez stepped aside, smiled, and gestured for Helen to go ahead and said, "Queens first!"

A writer for the *New York Times* found that suddenly there was "praise everywhere for Miss Wills, a simple, unostentatious girl who has won by persistent development of her natural talent." As Laney concluded, "for speed of attack and counterattack, for quality of stroke employed over a sustained period, I am wondering if women's tennis did not here reach its highest point during my time. I have since seen flashes of perhaps similar brilliance by individual girls, but never a succession of games in which two girls played with such virtuosity of stroke at the same time." Laney wrote his evaluation in 1968, almost forty years after he watched the match.

After her singles victory, Helen Wills teamed up with Elizabeth Ryan, Suzanne Lenglen's favorite doubles partner, to win the Wimbledon ladies doubles title. Suzanne watched from the gallery.

Upon returning to America, Helen Wills checked into the Forest Hills Inn to prepare for the national women's tournament. She made a brief side trip to Manchester by the Sea, Massachusetts, where she played in the Essex County Club Invitational Tournament just to warm up for Forest Hills. It was not much of a warm-up, though. She beat young Helen Jacobs in just thirty-four minutes in the final. She kept Jacobs pointless through the first five games of the match.

As she prepared for Forest Hills, Allison Danzig, writing for the *New York Times* watched her and reported that "a healthier and more attractive picture of American girlhood could not be imagined than Miss Wills." At Forest Hills she cut her way through the competition without much trouble. She beat Betty Nuthall in the finals, taking the first set from the newest British hope in just twelve minutes. The *Times* described the match as "a savage struggle." The "furious tempo" of the play made men's tennis "seem tame by comparison." Helen's attack was one of "such withering accuracy as to make a mockery of her opponents efforts to hold her off." And Danzig said she provided "the greatest exhibition of destructive hitting power that has been put on . . . in the forty-year history of the tournament."

In the Wightman Cup matches Wills also won two of her matches and then won in the doubles with Wightman. Writers restorted to jumbles of superlatives to praise her and describe her game because they had never seen anything quite like it before. And at the end of the summer of 1927 Helena Huntington Smith, in an article entitled "Another Glorified Girl," which was published in the *New Yorker,* tried to account for the sudden public obsession with Helen. Smith found the reasons for Helen's enormous popularity to be elusive. She pointed out that if the selection of Miss America were put to a popular vote, "the real Miss America would probably turn out to be Miss Helen Wills." And that Helen "grows increasingly qualified to adorn the roto pages herself."

A New York editorial writer, Smith said, observed that "all the males of America from six to sixty are a little in love with her" and Smith felt the editor was probably right. What was remarkable about such sentiment was that Helen was no "siren of the stage," not one of Ziegfeld's "hothouse orchids," but rather a "lady athlete. She is most closely identified with a class notoriously short on sex appeal." So why the all the excitement over a lady athlete? Because, Smith reported, "she has mastered the trade of amateur tennis with superb skill, seems to have a huge time at the business of living, and is prettier every time she is snapped by photographers. Each year she is more gracious, more stylishly dressed, easier to gaze upon," Smith found. "Annually the reporters rush to their offices and pound out a lyrical column or so about 'Our Helen.' "

And always they ended up writing pretty much the same thing about her. They assured their readers week after week that she was, indeed, still modest and that she had not lost her perspective and that she was always the favorite passenger on the ship or train she traveled on and she danced divinely. But they seldom went beyond that because Helen didn't talk much. She was, for reporters anxious for copy, often troublingly silent.

There were several reasons for Helen Wills's silence at press conferences—the rigors of her sport and training and the fact that she didn't socialize much because of tennis. But also, Smith pointed out, "Helen finds it difficult to say what she thinks, so much so that her friends have sometimes wondered whether she thinks at all. Undoubtedly she does."

Until the summer of 1927 the press also emphasized what a normal American girl she was. They wrote that she was "a nice wholesome girl, with all that this implies of personality and family background. She came from a home similar to thousands of other American homes. She was What America Needed; the antithesis of the gaudy, gin-drinking John Held, Jr., flapper. She neither smoked, drank, nor used cosmetics." Outwardly, Smith found, she was both sophisticated and calm. Yet some of the "schoolgirlishness" still lingered. The articles she wrote, for example, "are naive enough to demonstrate that she really wrote them herself." And as to her art, Smith wrote, "her sketches are, as yet, pretty bad."

Smith found that Helen Wills had flowered into a lovely woman. Yet she remained calm and imperturbable and poker faced. It was said, Smith found, that Helen still represented "the normal American girl. But it is doubtful whether the normal type has ever been so sound in body and so untroubled in soul." Even the French surgeon who had operated on her in 1926 burst out that "she is a model for all young women."

"It is, we maintain, a little hard to see what is meant by the repeated declarations of her normalcy," Smith wrote. "She is still wearing her hair down her back at an age when modern young ladies are supposed to be overcome by alcohol at night clubs." More than anything else Helen was "wholesome, magnificently so. And applied to her, this much abused word loses its sting."

Smith had heard one young man sigh after gazing at Helen, "It would do you a lot of good to see a girl like that once a week." It was a sentiment shared widely in a nation looking for comfortable symbols of normalcy in an age of dramatic and often confusing change.

Helen Wills had become a comforting symbol of stability, a sort of sweet old-fashioned girl who had made the transition to the New Era almost painlessly. And in that respect, she represented what Henry Ford represented and what Charles Lindbergh would come to represent. She had successfully bridged the gap between yesterday and tomorrow, between the past and the future. She had done it seemingly without effort and with singular grace. While she embodied all of of the traditional virtues and values of America, she was something entirely new. She was no petite and helpless Lillian Gish or Mary Pickford, rather she was a big, powerful, hard hitting, and beautiful athlete, a gorgeous Amazon, a woman of independent means who, somehow, was not threatening to American males. She could do almost anything she chose to do. But she chose a traditional mold. She represented a New Woman who was a stark contrast to the Flapper or the Vamp. And she outlasted the Flapper and the Vamp and various other brief incarnations of so-called modernity. In celebrating Helen Wills, Americans celebrated tomorrow— a tomorrow of American ascendancy, of aesthetic beauty, of intelligence, of modesty, of energy, of romance, and of optimism. In her millions of Americans saw a future that was attractive and irresistible and worked. If the American Girl was the American Future, then one could face the confusing changes of the present with confidence and even, perhaps, with a smile. If the American Girl was the future, then you could bet on the future.

Following her 1927 Wimbledon comeback and her return to America, suddenly reporters were writing less about how wholesome she was. Rather they wrote about what she was wearing. Her outfits were described in detail. She now wore "just a discreet touch of lipstick," and she danced in fashionable clubs. And so—encouraged by such praise— Helen Wills sought to move up a notch in celebrityhood, but she did so cautiously, as cautiously as she did when she prowled along the baseline dispatching challengers. For several years Helen Wills, like millions of other young women, had been enthralled by motion pictures and the stars of the silent screen. She pinned up pictures of the stars, cut out from magazines and newspapers, on the walls of her room. Now, having heard the applause in tournament after tournament, she took the journalistic praise seriously. She had become a popular national icon. And if the public loved her, she believed, and if the press loved her, then they would love her even more in the movies.

Helen Wills believed she had at last transcended tennis. She now appeared to believe fully the stories that were written about her. She seemed to believe she could do anything. It was a wonderful youthful naive belief. It was the belief usually harbored by the incredibly romantic, the hopelessly innocent, or the children of the very wealthy. Anything could be had for a price. The price was either money or energy or both. Helen believed the price was energy. The world lay before her to be discovered and won. She now put new energy and effort into becoming a film star. And she called upon her patron and principal aristocratic guardian, James Phelan, to help her.

Wills met Phelan in 1923 soon after winning her first national title. Phelan was born in San Francisco in 1861, the heir to a large fortune. His father had organized the First National Bank of San Francisco, invested heavily in local real estate, and put up the Phelan Building in the heart of the city. James Phelan inherited the valuable property. Phelan received a Ph.D. degree from Santa Clara University and studied law at the University of California. He was first elected mayor of San Francisco in 1897 and then twice reelected. He was named to the U.S. Senate in 1914 but then was defeated in his bid for reelection in 1920. He owned a large estate, Villa Montalvo, south of San Francisco in Saratoga, where he entertained friends and visiting luminaries. Phelan enjoyed the company of poets and writers and subsidized the work of many of them. He published his own poetry and that of other local poets. He was a bachelor. And from the moment he first saw Helen, Phelan was utterly enthralled. For nearly a decade he lavished attention, favors, and gifts upon her and carried on what can best be termed a passionate platonic relationship. She was never fully aware of the depth of his devotion, but gladly accepted his attention, favors, advice, and money until his death in 1930, seven months after her marriage to someone else.

Wills had visited Montalvo on numerous occasions as a guest and as a guest of honor at celebrations and dinners. She played tennis there. Helen told friends after one visit that she found the air and the grounds and the total environment of Montalvo romantic and inspiring. She met famous people there, was celebrated there by the wealthy and the notable. She recalled one evening in 1929, one magic evening, dining with the movie star Ramon Novarro, who sang to her.

In the spring of 1929 she was the guest of honor at the Blossom Festival in neighboring Saratoga, where Phelan described her accomplishments to the large gathering: "Not so many years ago in a city a few miles to the north, a baby girl was born. She grew up and went to school like other little girls and learned to play tennis. Then, while still a high school student, she won the championship of California. Not satisfied, she became national champion, and finally the woman tennis champion of the world.

The girl is Miss Helen Wills. She represents California and the West and the fine spirit of achievement."

Phelan wrote poems celebrating Wills and encouraged others to do the same. At his request Edwin Markham wrote his poem, "Helen." In a collection of poems entitled *A Day in the Hills,* Phelan published one of his own compositions entitled "To Helen Wills," which expressed his own feelings about the American Girl:

> Delightful child, who from the Berkeley nest
> > Took flight—a fledgling native to the skies
> > Thou dar'st the sun—and undimmed are thine eyes—
>
> To hold aloft the banner of the West
> No strangers thou and Phoebus meeting there
> > In Heaven's firmament among the stars.
> Did not they Sun-born state by God-right share
> > Elysian fields divine where nothing mars
> > The calm procession of ethereal days
> > So sprung the motherland for filial praise:
> Fair goddess come, Minerva-like, a Greek,
> > Arched brows austere and lips impeccable,
> Straight-nosed of mein not menacing nor meek;
> > And daughter counterpart delectable.
>
> The Gods are good, the Gods propitiate;
> > Tho' favored, yet thou hast not won by favor,
> > Tho' magical, thy talisman is labor,
> Nor conquest greater than they promise great!
> As pounds the ocean on the shining shore,
> > And peaks spring skyward to a loftier height,
> The generations building up their store
> > Increase they glory and preserve they might.
> > The lists of life are open. Helen first
> > Of hosts triumphant, children of the Sun,
> Olympic Champion crowned: Exultant burst
> > The cry of world devoted, "Helen won!"
> > Historic bygones! Now ascendant Art!
> > Inspired Scions, shall ye do your part?

Phelan carried on an extensive correspondence with Wills and encouraged her to express herself in writing and in art as well as in sport. He recommended books to her, mailed them to her, introduced her to artists and writers and escorted her to the theater and to the opera in San Francisco. In 1926 he traveled to France to see her and boosted her among the wealthy and the influential in California as the epitome of the California Girl.

In the spring of 1930, only a few months after her marriage, Helen went to France to compete. Phelan continued to correspond with her. In Paris she received a final letter from him—he was very ill. His letter stated his final advice to her. "You have the vantage ground of your position and you will be heard and given audience where others will struggle and even fail," he wrote. "Your artistic star is in the ascendent! Take advantage of the moment! . . . by coming out with a slender book of poetry! Don't please give up the idea. The few lines of yours I have seen—too few—indicate to me that you can do it. In idle hours write a verse; or charge yourself with the duty of one poem a week; you will be surprised by your prolific pen and what is behind it! Mail them to me as you write them and I will keep them safe for you during your travels and distractions—will you?"

Then he closed with a poem from his favorite poet, Oliver Saint John Gogarty, entitled "Good-by." No lines copied by Phelan ever better described his feelings for Helen.

> If you saw your face as I
> Saw it when you said Good-by:
> With the hair about it lit
> Where the sun had Titianed it;
> And the eyes that glowed and shone
> With that inner sun,
> Chalices that held a wine
> From the wild immortal vine
> Glowing in the double cup
> That a mortal hand holds up;
> You would know, for you have wit,
> Why I lingered saying it.

Only years later would Helen Wills indicate privately to a friend her warm affection for Phelan and her regret that such a great age difference separated them. Phelan had always represented to her something that might have been but had not been possible to attain.

In 1927, Phelan thought it was only natural and acceptable that she should go into films or the stage. He saw her potential as unlimited. She wrote to Phelan from the Essex County Club on July 28, 1927; that

I think that I should like to do one movie, or perhaps, two, but I should really like to try one—not only because I have the secret idea, that all young girls have about acting—that I might be able to do it! But also because I think it would be a most interesting experience. And, also, because with what I should make from it I should go on with my drawing. I am planning, anyway, to go on with my study, but it would be an immense satisfaction to continue with what I, myself, had made!

But my great difficulty is in discovering what film company is the best, and what one would be trustworthy and reliable in every way.

I feel that I would like the best company or else none, and that I should want the whole thing done in a dignified and restrained way.

The picture in which I was to be cast should have a sensible and logical story into which I would fit. It cannot have any tennis connected with it, as this would violate the Amateur Rule of the American Lawn Tennis Association.

Helen told Phelan that from time to time she had met people connected with the movies. Yet, "I wouldn't want them to think that I am terribly interested, for if they should think that I was not a good film subject, it would be quite easy for them and for me to put the matter aside quite casually."

Helen Wills worried about negative publicity. And she eventually asked Phelan to arrange a private screen test for her. She also asked that no news on the test be released, so if it was not good she would not be asked about it by reporters. She indicated that, once Phelan helped to get the test and she passed it, she could present her father with a *fait accompli,* and he would have to let her become a film star.

Suzanne Lenglen had also wanted to star in films. And she had dreamed of performing on the silver screen as a dramatic and romantic artiste. But those who seemed to take her wishes seriously, individuals like William Pickens and C. C. Pyle, realized that the only thing Suzanne could do in the movies that would hold the attention of an audience was to play tennis. As an object of romantic interest, she was unconvincing and sometimes pathetic. The only movies she could possibly star in had to be tennis movies. Yet playing tennis was precisely what Suzanne Lenglen wanted to escape from. Her only real film success came in her real-life role in the films of her 1926 match with Helen Wills at Cannes. Helen believed she would have more success.

Phelan sought the best agent and director in helping Helen get started in the movies. Reporters were told that she was not interested at all in the movies, but rather was pursuing her art and her writing. It was deft management by Phelan for a woman he adored. Her first problem was her amateur status. She could write a tennis book and sketch players during a match she was participating in and publish them. But if she made movies and was paid she would compromise her amateur status. She could never touch a tennis racket in a movie. The USLTA and the other national associations were scared to death of a star becoming financially independent of them—especially a major star—and so watched to make sure that tennis in no way could be used by a player to raise money independently. Lenglen learned that nobody wanted to see her act. Bill Tilden harbored the illusion all his life that his thespian talents were above normal. They weren't. Those who watched him act in several New York productions insisted that his amateur status had not been compromised.

Phelan initially asked Wills to stop off in Los Angeles for the test, but she did not like the idea, saying since she would be tired after traveling from New York her chances of passing the test would be reduced. Also, her wardrobe would need pressing, and she would be happier if there were no wrinkles in the test, so to speak. And she was afraid her journey to Los Angeles would attract attention from reporters. Phelan contacted Joe Schenck of United Artists in New York and tried to convince him to put Helen in a film immediately. But without a screen test first Schenck refused. Phelan then asked his close friend, A. H. Giannini, president of the Bowery and East River National Bank, to make arrangements for a screen test in New York. Giannini arranged for the test to be made at the Famous Players Studio in Long Island City. But before the test he secured an agent for Helen, Joseph Kennedy, who was president of the Film Booking Offices. Giannini reported back to Phelan that Kennedy was a good reliable Irishman who was a Harvard graduate who had been a pitcher on the Harvard baseball team. Moreover, he was married to the daughter of former Mayor Fitzgerald of Boston. "I am explaining this in detail," Giannini wrote, "because I want you to know that I did not shift her over to an irresponsible person." Giannini asked his close personal friend, director Henry King, to direct the screen test. Giannini reported that King, who usually received from $75,000 to $100,000 per picture, had agreed to do the Wills screen test for no fee at all. King was largely responsible for the success of Lillian Gish, Richard Barthelmess, and Vilma Banky, Giannini said.

King spent three hours with Helen Wills on the morning of September 30, 1927, and used 700 feet of film in making the test. "This was an expensive test and will cost several hundreds of dollars," Giannini reported. "However, it was all gratis. Both Mr. Kennedy and Mr. King feel that they are obligated to me and very gladly offered their services. We will know in a day or two the result of the tests." In the meantime, Wills spoke with Kennedy and gave him story ideas for the films in which she wanted to star. She found him unexcited by the prospect.

When the test was evaluated, the consensus was that, "being an athletic girl, her limbs were too developed and her body lacked the petiteness so necessary for film success. Her face photographed all right, but her feet were indicative of sturdy underpinning rather than feminine charm," Giannini reported. "This is only the opinion of two or three and I have known girls to achieve stardom with seven or eight so-called experts reporting unfavorably," Giannini wrote. Kennedy said he thought the screen test "could have been worse." He told Helen she was just too heavy for the movies and that she might take care of that shortcoming by dieting. When Helen expressed eagerness to shed several pounds, he was still unenthusiastic and said it would be difficult to find a story for her, since she was "a certain type" and the type of story that could be assigned to her would be very limited. He did not want to see her cast in a movie in which she did not belong.

After a couple of days Helen got the idea. She was not going to become a film star. The conclusion drawn, she left New York abruptly without saying either goodbye or thank you to Giannini, Kennedy, or King. Giannini, in particular, was disappointed by her behavior, since he had spent a considerable amount of money and effort to make her stay in New York as pleasant as possible. He concluded from the experience that "she is a cold-blooded business woman and with a good knowledge of bookkeeping, and knows where she stands commercially every minute of the day. I would say that she will know how to take care of herself in a business deal in any company and I would even hazard the guess that she is adept in extracting service and attentions from others and yielding very little gratitude," alluding to her relationship with Phelan. "I am dealing with stars all day long and she is no different from the rest. Portia would have to reconstruct her speech on the quality of mercy. She put the giving and receiving of mercy on a 50 : 50 basis. Helen's geometrical ratio on giving and receiving is about 2 : 98." The American Girl was a sharp businesswoman.

The next year, however, Wills received an offer to make a film from an unexpected source—Arthur Brisbane of the *New York Evening Journal.* Brisbane, who was working on the Herbert Hoover presidential campaign, wanted to make a special newsreel that would influence young American men and women to vote for the Republican candidate for President. Brisbane told Hoover that he thought it would be effective "to make some good talking films with the Movietone, presenting some of your most popular supporters to the gigantic movie picture audience, the other side, of course, having the same privilege." And he believed that "a short talk to young men and women by Helen Wills, who is chairman of the Sports Division of the Women's Hoover Committee, showing her in her tennis costume, racket in hand, would be very effective. I have suggested that to my brother-in-law (Courtland Smith of Fox) who has a good deal to do with the Movietone. I should be glad to write a short speech for the young lady."

In late August, Brisbane reminded Hoover how important the votes of women might be in the election of 1928. That Hoover's appeal to end poverty in America in his nomination acceptance speech would appeal not only to the poor—"often weak and ungrateful"—but also to all "that have any idealism, women especially." And for that reason he wanted Helen Wills to make a speech on film. In order to give equal time to the other side, he suggested that Rosamond Pinchot, "daughter of the well-known radical, Amos Pinchot, who played the part of the nun in *The Miracle,* should also make a speech telling why she is for Governor Al Smith."

The remarkable thing about Brisbane's proposal was that Helen Wills was the only woman he considered approaching to make the campaign film. Helen agreed to make the film, and Brisbane wrote a brief speech for her. Then he advised her to "speak very slowly and earnestly, looking straight into the eyes of the audience. And remember," he told her, "this speech earnestly delivered means many votes." Wearing her tennis costume and holding two rackets in her left arm, Wills appeared on camera and said that she was putting aside her rackets to devote two months to campaigning for Hoover. She said she had been "aroused to active campaign work by Hoover's statements concerning the youth of the nation." She suggested that "All youth can admire Herbert Hoover because of his sincerity, intelligence and great industry. His achievements, in the past, have been marked with success because of his ability for organization and his wonderful powers of perseverance. His life is a story to fire the imagination and admiration of every young person in the country." She concluded, earnestly, "May youth everywhere, by voting for Hoover, show that its ideals are of the highest and that it has the earnest desire to be of service."

With the exception of the films of the match in Cannes in 1926, the Hoover campaign film of 1928 was as close as Helen Wills ever got to becoming a movie star.

Rumors surfaced in 1930 that she was going to star in a film, but they were rumors only. And in 1931 she said that the only thing that would lure her away from amateur tennis was the offer of "a lot of money to sign a movie contract." Again in 1937 Wills did some screen tests for Twentieth Century-Fox. The success of Sonja Henie's *One in a Million* was so pronounced that other sports figures were suddenly being sought after. But again nothing came of the screen tests.

Although she did not make money in the movies, Wills continued to earn an income by writing newspaper stories. She signed a long-term contract with the Newspaper Enterprise Association in 1927 to write a series of article on issues of interest to young womanhood, including articles on sports, beauty, clothes, interior design, exercise, popular books, writers, and movie stars.

Ironically, even though Wills failed to stir the interest of movie-makers enough to get a part in a commercial motion picture, she did inspire some of the best known painters and sculpturers of the 1920s and the 1930s, who found her to be the perfect subject for their work. Alexander Calder created a small wire sculpture of her in action wearing her visor and swinging her tennis racket. Antonio Covarubbias did a famous caricature of her at play in 1927. Today this painting is held by the Humanities Center of the University of Texas. Augustus John painted her portrait in the late 1920s and signed his work, "in affectionate homage." Childe Hassam also painted a portrait of Helen which was eventually acquired by the Louvre. And local artists like Louise Janine and Haig Patigian found her to be inspiring, even if the patronage of Senator Phelan helped stir their enthusiasm. The noted sculptor C. S. Jagger observed in 1931 that she was "the perfect type of womanly beauty immortalized by Greek sculpture. Watching her on the tennis courts," he said, "I have appreciated that she is the nearest living approximation of the old Greek ideal of perfection. She has a supple figure, long legs and a small head, and even her features are the classic features of the ancient Venuses. The only difference is that the old masters generally chose slightly more matronly outlines."

Patigian, who created a bust "Helen of California" under the sponsorship of Phelan, said that he chose Helen as a subject before he was contacted by the Senator, "because of her beauty of face and form combined with intelligence. She is a singularly excellent representative not only of the Greek classic mold of feature and nobility of head, but a splendid type of California beauty and brains." He suggested she was the perfect representative of modern womanhood and a distinctive product of the state. "For some time I have had it in mind to model in clay such a type of womanhood," he said, "and in Miss Wills I found the ideal. The features that have been admired by thousands at tennis matches and in student assemblages are entitled to be reproduced in sculpture and to bear the title I have chosen."

Patigian, who knew of Helen Wills's screen test, described her beauty as different from the popular Hollywood kind. "Hers is the sort of beauty that does not enter into beauty contests," he said. Rather, she was beautiful in the classic sense. "She is an athletic woman of intellect and of physical vigor and her beauty is more than 'candy box prettiness'—for it rises from within." Helen sat for several sessions for Patigian. One of his works in white marble was donated to the Palace of the Legion of Honor collection. Two copies were made in bronze. One went to the San Jose Tennis Club; the other was kept by Phelan.

Four years after Charlie Chaplin described Helen Wills playing tennis as the most beautiful thing he had ever seen, in 1934 sculpture Bryan Baker, who won $100,000 for his Pioneer Woman statue, described Helen as "a perfectly beautiful woman." He suggested that she was the "ideal American beauty" and said she was the most beautiful woman "in 2800 years." She was more beautiful, he said, than either Katharine Hepburn or Mae West. "Miss Hepburn's face is too peaked and Miss West has too many curves. The American girl doesn't really want curves—she likes an attractive athletic thinness."

But by far the most controversial and celebrated portrait ever done of Helen Wills was done by the renowned Mexican muralist, Diego Rivera. Rivera had been approached at the end of the 1920s by an American artist, Ralph Stackpole, with an invitation from the president of the San Francisco Art Commission, to paint a wall in the California School of Fine Arts. At the time Rivera was so involved in his own work in Mexico that he could not accept the offer. Then Stackpole secured a second commission for Rivera to do a mural in the new San Francisco Stock Exchange Club. Architect Timothy Pflueger offered $2500 to Rivera along with $1500 from the Art Commission—the most Rivera had ever been offered for a single work.

Rivera initially had trouble getting a visa to come to America because of his radical political affiliations, but in November 1930, thanks to the intercession of Albert Bindera, a prominent San Francisco art patron and collector, he finally secured his visa. Shortly after that he arrived in San Francisco with his wife Frida, who had long dreamed of visiting the "City of the World," as she referred to San Francisco.

The local response to the commissioning of Rivera was not ecstatic. Rivera was described in the local press as a "famous revolutionist and communist" who had been hired to paint murals in the city. And it was alleged that his radical political sympathies made him eminently the wrong person to paint the Stock Exchange Club, the social hub of capitalism in San Francisco. And there was also the problem of local artists who had been slighted. "Rivera for Mexico City: San Francisco's Best for San Francisco" became the protest cry. The president of the local Art Commission was accused of having committed a "frank betrayal" of the trust of local artists.

From the moment of his arrival Rivera was a front-page item in the local papers. He was welcomed at posh receptions and parties, and Ralph Stackpole's studio was put at his disposal. The wall he was to paint flanked the interior staircase connecting two stories of the Luncheon Club of the Stock Exchange and was thirty feet high. As he planned the mural, Rivera met the woman who was to become the central figure of his work. He was introduced to Helen Wills at one of the receptions and was instantly enthralled. He made an appointment for her to come to the studio so he could sketch her. Then he made daily trips to the California Club where she practiced. Edith Cross remembered seeing him waddle out to the umpire's chair, crawl up rather awkwardly, and then sketch Helen at play. He did this not just once, but several times, she remembered. And Fred Moody remembered him "sort of hanging around all the time." And he recalled, "You know he was a short, ugly little guy." Fred didn't mind the intrusion. Rivera wasn't as bad as the reporters, after all.

When he finally began the painting, Rivera made a frontal portrait of Helen the huge central figure of the mural. He explained his decision to the local press, "I found in Mrs. Moody all that was beautiful in California womanhood. She represented my ideal of the perfect type. Therefore I wished to paint her."

William Grestle, a local art patron and a friend of Rivera, explained, "The beauty of Helen Wills interested Rivera at once. He saw her play, made some sketches of her in action and was struck by her personality even more than by her great fame as a sportswoman. He asked her to pose and made a heroic size sketch, as he did of all the figures in the mural. This is the sketch that was recently purchased by Lord and Lady Hastings and is now at the Palace of the Legion of Honor."

Much to the surprise of both Wills and Rivera, objections were raised when the face of Helen became recognizable on the Stock Exchange mural. No doubt, some of the objections were based upon simple envy. When Rivera said that Helen was a representative woman, others thought they had a better claim to that title. Still others demanded that the head be made "typical of the finest California womanhood but not a portrait of any one individual." One member of the art commission objected to the use of Helen because, as he put it, "suppose she should turn professional?" Some members of the Stock Exchange also objected on the grounds that they did not like the idea that "a tennis player was the model for 'California.' "

Rivera decided to compromise. He altered a few of the features of the central female figure and "generalized" them. But still, even when generalized, it looked like Helen. And the huge nude figure flying on the ceiling, entitled "Helen flying," also bears an unmistakable resemblance.

The finished mural had California symbolized by a large female figure—a woman with tanned skin and "opulent curves," as Rivera described her, "modelled after the rolling hills of the landscape, with one hand opening the subsoil to the labor of miners and the other offering the ripe fruits of the earth."

When he was finished, Rivera told local reporters of Helen Wills, "She was my inspiration, but not the actual model. The figure represents my idea of the idealized type of California womanhood—a type perfectly exemplified by Mrs. Moody."

But in his autobiography, Rivera wrote that "in the central portion of the mural I painted a colossal figure of a woman representing California. The almost classically beautiful tennis champion, Helen Wills Moody, served as my model. In portraying her, I made no attempt to formalize her features but left them recognizably hers. Soon a cry was heard: California is an abstraction and should not be an identifiable likeness to anybody. To this I replied that California is known abroad mainly because of Helen Wills Moody; that she seemed to represent California better than anyone I knew—she was intelligent, energetic, and beautiful; and that, finally I thought her the best model, I had the right to use her."

Helen Wills's popularity with artists was paralleled by the adoration of the large segment of the American public for her in the late 1920s. Each day she received stacks of mail from young women asking her advice on how to dress, what sports to play, how to train, what schools to attend, and so on. And even close friends like Phelan had friends in turn who asked him to solicit advice from Helen for their own daughters about sports and training and proper behavior. Helen tried to answer most of the inquiries.

And she became the object of romantic infatuation for tens of thousands of young men, as journalist Helena Huntington Smith found. Many of those young men were not happy simply with seeing her once, but became obsessed. In Berkeley a persistent young man was arrested for hanging around the Wills house in 1928, knocking on the door and personally delivering his letters to Helen.

Other young men who went on to distinguished careers in journalism or the arts were also deeply impressed and inspired by Helen. Poet John Berryman insisted in his later years that he had once been a ball boy for Helen Wills at Forest Hills, and he challenged his friends to top that. One of the young men most infatuated by Helen Wills was Jonathan Daniels, who went on to become an accomplished historian and journalist. Daniels met her in Paris in the spring of 1930 while he was there writing on a Guggenheim Fellowship and she was playing in the International Hard Court Championships. They met at a dinner given by American Ambassador Walter Edge. Helen was invited "because she was an American luminary in Paris," Daniels recalled. "I was a friend of a friend of the wife of the ambassador. I know of no other reason why an obscure writer would have been asked." Following the dinner Daniels escorted Helen to the opera.

"I think at the time we were both lonely people. My first wife had died a few months before, and I am under the impression that Helen had been divorced for about the same period [actually, Helen was newly married at this time, to Fred Moody, who was in California].

"I remember a long walk we took along the bank of the Seine, stopping at the little book stalls along the way. She asked me to come see her play at Wimbledon, but my $2500 Guggenheim grant could not stand the expense.

"In those days, in Paris, I was always ready to meet any new flame. It was a happy interlude with Helen. I think of us as walking along the Seine in a sort of hand-in-hand laughing relationship. Yet, by the book stalls and the river, we were sometimes very serious young people, too. I don't think either of us expected anything lasting to come of it. I had a book to write and she had worlds to conquer on the court. Of those days with Helen Wills I can say I don't regret one hour and sometimes I think that the times dallied there have served me best across the years."

In 1931 he saw her in New York when he was writing for *Fortune* magazine and she was still a tennis champion. "On this occasion she and I dined together at '21.'

"Obviously, I found her good company," Daniels told me. "Also, I am sure I was impressed by her status in sports—though in those days I was, as I am now, more of a cafe and books man than a sports enthusiast. She was a very beautiful woman. But my feeling long after the time was that she was a Galatea and I was just not the Pygmalion to bring her out of the marble."

She was in Europe alone for the first time in 1930. And she wrote to a friend, "When one travels alone, one discovers how much one loves the people who are important in one's life. It is perhaps good for a young person to travel alone so that he can discover this. I have made a number of discoveries about myself on this journey that are new to me and which would never have come to my attention had I been along with someone. In fact, I don't believe that I have known myself very much until now."

Marjorie Morrill Painter gave me another perspective on Helen Wills. She traveled with Helen and Edith Cross to The Hague and Berlin in 1929. Morrill was then ranked sixth in the United States. "You couldn't have asked for a more thoughtful and considerate person than Helen was at the time," she told me. "She always took the trouble to introduce us to some young men, who would wine and dine us; she helped us plan our sightseeing. She was at the time the center of attraction everywhere she went—all sorts of young men paid homage to her, and with all that adulation she never let it turn her head. Photographers found her in out of the way places, and she was always polite to them—always. I remember in Berlin, I was relegated to answer the telephone as I could speak German quite well at the time. Numerous bouquets of flowers arrived, and many callers who wished to take her out to dinner. She was a very shy person at heart, and though very friendly and fun when no one was around, seemed to put up a very different front when in public.

"Of course, her tennis came first. She kept very strict training, always in bed by ten, but did enjoy very much the attention of the men. I really don't think she allowed herself to get overly friendly with anyone. But, as I say, in private, she told us many amusing stories of her experiences with men."

Helen Wills's male tennis partners also came to adore her. Frank Hunter, who had been on the Olympic Tennis Team in 1924, played doubles with Helen many times in the years after 1924. "In 1928 in Paris I played the mixed doubles tournament with Helen," he told me. "We lost a close final round match to Cochet and Eileen Bennett after which I was very upset, naturally, taking all the blame. So Helen took me aside and said, 'Frank, don't let it bother you. That was just the experience we needed. If you're not already committed, I'd love to play Wimbledon with you next year, and believe me, we'll win it!' I was thrilled beyond words to accept, and you know the result. We played it, and won the event quite easily. Do you wonder that Helen has always been and always will be just tops in my affections?"

Wilmer Allison, a top American player in the early 1930s, recalled spending an afternoon with Helen near Wimbledon crawling around in a strawberry field "picking those big delicious English strawberries" and eating them. "She was always a delight—a pure delight," he told me. "And don't let anyone try to tell you that she wasn't the greatest woman tennis player who ever lived. I watched her, and I watched the women who came after her, and I can tell you there was never anyone quite like Helen."

Don Budge, too, was in her thrall. "I met Helen Wills at the Berkeley Tennis Club during one of the California state championships about 1932," he told me. "I was thrilled to meet such a great champion and such a fine lady. And I thought that if ever I became a champion I'd want to behave just like her. Helen Wills influenced me greatly. Whenever I learned that she would be practicing at the Berkeley Club I would ride up there on my bicycle and watch her hit topspin shots off both forehand and backhand, keeping them low over the net."

At the Essex County Club in Manchester by the Sea in Massachusetts, a young boy named Ben Bradlee, who was born in August 1921, and whose great uncle was Edward Crowninshield, the brother of Frank Crowninshield, the founder and editor of *Vanity Fair* magazine, met Helen in the early 1930s. "We were asked by our great uncles to put up Helen Wills. I was a pretty fair player for my age and weight, and I was a ballboy in one of the matches. I remember being allowed to rally with her for a couple of minutes before one match. An old photographer for the *Boston Globe,* with one of those cameras that you used to look down into, even took a picture of it. She had in fact given me a racket—a Gold Star, I remember—the handle of which she autographed. I played with it, and then after the head started to warp, kept it on. I don't remember ever sleeping with it, but probably I did. I was thrilled. Helen was certainly one of the first women athletes to capture the imagination of this country at a time when there weren't many women competing."

But perhaps the greatest compliment paid to her or to any athlete in that time or later came from the popular philosopher and historian Will Durant. Durant contacted Helen in 1931 and asked her to make a contribution to a book he was putting together entitled *On the Meaning of Life.* The selection of Helen Wills as a contributor to this book of modern philosophy was extraordinary and surprising. She was the only sports figure included and one of only four women. It was even more surprising when one realizes that Durant was not interested at all in sports or in training or even in fame, but rather in the crisis in Western values at the time and a solution to the question "What is the meaning of Life?"

On July 15, 1931, Durant wrote to Wills and asked her to "interrupt your work for a moment and play the game of philosophy with me." What he wanted to know was her opinion on the question, "What is the meaning or worth of human life?"

After he had gathered his responses, Durant wrote that "by far the most interesting reply from a woman was that of Helen Wills Moody." And he found that "her very existence is in itself good reason for living. She has done more than a thousand impresarios of anatomy and millinery to 'glorify the American girl'; and the American girl at her best— or the European girl at her best—is a sufficient achievement of protoplasm to warrant some faith and pride in life. She writes almost as well as she plays," he said.

Helen thought for a time about her reply and then wrote back to Durant explaining her philosophy of life. She pointed out that at twenty-five she was really "not quite certain about anything." And she suggested that if certitude about things in life was a sign of youth, then, indeed, she was not youthful by that measure. What she needed most in life, and what governed many of her actions, was some way of "exercising the restlessness which seems to be continually in my heart." Tennis exercised—and exorcised—that restlessness and so did painting.

In a surprisingly candid disclosure, which she realized would be published, Helen Wills confessed that as a child she had not recognized her restlessness. Yet, "it is the reason why I have played tennis so fast and furiously for many years. It is the reason why I study diligently when at school and even cried when I did not happen to get 100 in spelling." That restlessness she believed was a form of constant hope of "arriving at some degree of perfection."

Wills said that her religion was best summed up as striving and action. Together they were the motive force in her life. By working steadily at something she liked, she could "remove from my mind momentary spells of sadness or irritation or anger, and afterwards feel happy and almost peaceful." She said that "perfection and beauty fascinate me in any field, but most of all in art, and there in the abstract sense."

Helen Wills suggested, moreover, that the restlessness she sensed in her heart was not unique. It was to be found "in the heart of every other young person of my age living in our restless country." For her, she wrote, life was "interesting, entertaining, happy" only when she had activity for that "restlessness" in her heart.

She mentioned nothing specifically about the athletic records she had established or the praise that had been heaped upon her by writers and fans alike. Tennis, she said, was merely a method of exercising her restless heart. Yet never before in sport had a simple restless heart inspired an athlete to such extraordinary accomplishment, such public adoration and obsession, and, in time, such incredible and bitter controversy.

In the spring of 1928, in preparation for her campaign of that year, Helen Wills warmed up in some exhibition matches with her friend Phil Neer, the former NCAA titleholder from the University of California and the eighth-ranked American male player. In a San Francisco exhibition, long before any promoter could capitalize on such a male-versus-female confrontation, Helen beat Neer in a hard fought match, 6–3, 6–4. Other men said Neer had not tried. But Neer told me that this was not true. He did not have the mobility he had had in college, he said, because of a knee injury. But, he said, "I never let Helen beat me." She was an extraordinary player, he said, who beat him fairly. She was matched against Neer because, it was said, there was no female player in the area who could give her a good match.

Wills started the 1928 season, her male practice partners said, at least 50 percent better than she had been the previous year. They were probably right. In the spring she played in France's International Hard Court Tournament. No American woman had ever won the singles title there, just as no European woman—Suzanne Lenglen included—had ever won the American title. Helen won. In the finals of the French tournament Helen defeated Eileen Bennett, 6–1, 6–2. In Holland she won the singles title from the Dutch national champion. In England, while the American Wightman Cup Team lost its matches, Wills won her two singles competitions.

Then she defended her title at Wimbledon. Twenty thousand fans turned out the first day she played to see her easily defeat a French player with what English journalists persisted in calling her "man's game." Her play was now described as "ruthless execution" of opponents.

In her six matches at Wimbledon she lost eighteen games and won seventy-two. She used a "cannonball" service against Lili de Alvarez, her opponent once more in the finals, and won in straight sets, 6–2, 6–3. Alvarez did show some resurgence in the second set, winning the first three games. But that was it. Wills then won six games in a row.

At Forest Hills she continued her dominance, winning the tournament and dropping only thirteen games in five matches on her way to the title—6–0, 6–1 over Mrs. J. Saunders Taylor, 6–0, 6–2 over Anna Harper, 6–2, 6–4 over Mrs. A. H. Chapin Jr., 6–0, 6–1 over Edith Cross in the semifinal, and 6–2, 6–1 over Helen Jacobs in the final. In watching her play, Allison Danzing of the *New York Times* described her performance as "the most devastating power ever applied to a tennis ball by a woman, the power that was described as revolutionizing Wimbledon," and which then won for Helen Wills her fifth national singles title. In the final she beat Jacobs in a little more than thirty minutes.

Following her victory she was presented with a mammoth silver vase filled with American beauty roses, while news cameras, motion picture cameras, and radio broadcasters recorded the ceremony. A radio even furnished music broadcast from a plane circling overhead. The plane, talking pictures, and two or three kinds of cameras represented the modern era of mechanical progress, Allison Danzig wrote, and Helen Wills personified the no-less-"remarkable development of women's tennis. Here before the eyes of the multitude was the player whose annihilating speed has held the capitals of the game aghast and has more closely approximated the destructiveness of the masculine players' strokes than any other woman in the history of tennis."

For two moments in the tournament the crowd suspected that Wills had come up against an opponent who could really test her and give the crowd some thrills. That opponent was a nineteen-year-old young woman from Berkeley, Helen Jacobs. In the third and fourth games of the opening set, Jacobs scored on one beautiful placement after another and took two games in a row to tie the score at two–all. This was a noteworthy and dramatic reversal because Wills had taken the first two games of the set in less than sixty seconds, losing but a single point. But late in the second game, Jacobs came, seemingly, out of the "coma that habitually seizes upon Miss Wills's opponents and galvanized the silent gallery into a cheering, sympathizing, rooting section that found itself looking down upon a stirring battle royal instead of a slaughter."

But at just that point—at two–all—Wills realized the seriousness of this threat and the possibilities of the situation. Then, Jacobs seemed to crack and lose control, and the play reverted to the one-sided character it had assumed in the first two games. Wills won twelve point in a row, all but one of them on Jacobs's errors. She took the next four games with the loss of only two points.

Part of the reason for the Jacobs's collapse came from the relentless pressure that Helen always put on her opponents. She always attacked. She never waited to confront the game of an opponent and then counter it—but with her tremendous power she imposed her game and pushed and pushed and pushed and never gave an opponent either much latitude in the choice of play or time to recover or even to breathe. The games slipped by one after another, and a match ended before an opponent could find her own rhythm. In this match Helen Wills didn't go to the net a single time. Although she could play serve and volley as well as any player in the game, she now chose instead to "put her sole reliance in those battering ground strokes which have spelled the doom of the best players in the world, and they were sufficient."

In just three months' time the American girl had won the national titles of France, Britain, and the United States—the first player, male or female, to accomplish that feat, and she had done it without the loss of a single set. At Forest Hills in 1928 she also won the women's doubles and the mixed doubles for a triple crown—something she had also accomplished in 1924—one of the few players to accomplish that feat twice. But records were made to be broken by Helen Wills.

At the end of the 1928 season Allison Danzig suggested that in the future Helen Wills be entered in the men's division at Forest Hills in order to give the other women a chance. When she played, it was simply true that nobody else had a chance. One of the men supporting a transfer of her name to the men's competition was Grantland Rice, who found himself getting bored with the regularity of Wills wins. After all, he wrote, she hit the ball as hard as most men, as accurately as most men, so why not play against the men and give the game a little excitement and color?

Naturally, there was talk in 1928 and 1929 of finding, somewhere, a worthy opponent for Helen Wills. And the talk turned, just as naturally, to Suzanne Lenglen. But it was still just talk. The opposition to such a match remained staunch—the lords of the USLTA. They would never forgive Suzanne for signing with Pyle and for touring America under the management of a huckster promoter and for taking some of the best players in the world into the professional ranks with her. They would never allow her to make money in America again by playing the nation's number-one star. Never. The whole idea of sanctioning "open tennis" in order to arrange such a match seemed almost obscene to them. It was not the fear that Suzanne Lenglen would win that motivated the supporters of strict amateurism in America; it was, rather, the chilling fear that they might in some little way indicate forgiveness or approval of what Lenglen had done. And that they could never do. So a match or a series of matches between the two women became even more remote and impossible than it had been in 1927 when Wills's record and reputation were not yet so formidable. The more Helen won, the better she was for amateur tennis and for the amateur tennis gate. And the more she won, the more Suzanne, desperately, wanted to face her across the net once more.

A player who did figure prominently in Helen's schedule in 1929 was Fritz Mercur, a top-ranked American player. In 1928 he scored a victory over Tilden at Rye, New York, and in the next year he was defeated by Wills in an exhibition at Forest Hills that caused much comment. The match, naturally, ended up being a terrific embarrassment to Tilden, who had gone out of his way to trounce Suzanne Lenglen but was never able to entice Helen Wills onto a court for a similar licking.

It was on Labor Day in 1929 at Forest Hills when Helen Wills came down from Boston to prepare for the national singles tournament. She needed a good player to practice with. Mercur volunteered, Mercur, an insurance salesman, got into trouble with the USLTA in 1929 when he entered a tournament in Michigan on the condition that he receive several customers for his insurance business. As a result the next year the USLTA stripped him of his amateur ranking.

In the debate over men against women in sport, Wills said that men would always win. Although she beat men again and again in exhibitions or came close to beating them, or seemed to at least, she said that the strength, reach, and speed of the males was so much greater than that of the women that there could never be equality in the sport. So no top female player would ever defeat a top male player. Practice with the men was useful, she said. She learned much from the men and attempted to play their kind of game. But she never expected to challenge their supremacy. But, of the men in the middle ranks and college players, Helen Wills believed that a top-ranking woman like herself could give them a good fight and could, sometimes, defeat them. But this would only be the very cream of women players and the very strongest of those. When she played against men and won, there was always the accusation that the whole thing was arranged as a way of making money for the tennis associations. Phil Neer is one of the very few players who contends that this was not the case.

Paul Gallico remembered when Helen Wills played a match against Fritz Mercur he remained on the baseline and simply exchanged ground strokes with her and got the worst of it. Then news that Mercur had been defeated appeared in newspapers around the country, and Mercur was chided for being beaten by a woman, even though she happened to be the national champion. So Mercur asked Wills for a rematch. And they played again on the number-one court at Forest Hills with a battalion of newsmen standing by ready to chronicle what they saw.

At one o clock the two players walked onto the court, just like a regularly scheduled match in the national tournament. Two ball boys were present. Then, as Gallico wrote, "the best amateur woman player in the world and a high-ranking player went at it hammer and tongs, all restrictions off, a couple of kids testing out which was the better tennis player. It was a grand, heart warming show and the girl apparently had the time of her life. For the first time I was aware of the fact that she loved to play tennis. She let her hair down for this one. Gone was the so-called Poker Face, the grim impassive expression, from her face. She grinned. She laughed. She even giggled. The Queen giggled! Mercur, rushing the net, of course, beat her in straight sets and regained his tarnished honor. But the girl gave him a fine battle, beat him on baseline shots, made him run, ran herself ragged chasing his half volleys and smashes at the net, tried storming the net herself, and for that off-guard hour showed herself to be a gay, sprightly, pleasing young girl who could enjoy herself and be gracious in the process, instead of the cold, superior, emotionless sphinx that evidently was her idea of how a famous lady athlete should comport herself."

Fritz Mercur avenged his defeat at Helen Wills's hands on September 4. He beat her 6–3 and 6–4. He got even for his loss on August 18 at another exhibition at Forest Hills. In a third set in which Mercur agreed not to come to the net, she beat him, 6–4. Mercur ranked fifteenth among American men.

But against the women Helen Wills played more successfully, and she played for keeps. She took her third Wimbledon singles title in 1929 and also captured the mixed doubles crown in England. She also won the International Hard Court title in France. She was presented at court to Queen Mary, an admirer. In that year she won the American national singles title at Forest Hills, as she drew closer and closer to Suzanne Lenglen's incredible 1925 Wimbledon feat of winning a major tournament and dropping only five games in the process. Helen Wills might have broken that record in 1929; she came very close. She opened the tournament that year by winning two sets in eighteen minutes over Katherine Lamarche of New Jersey. Her scores in six matches were as follows: 6–0, 6–0; 6–1, 6–0; 6–0, 6–0; 6–0, 6–1; 6–0, 6–0; 6–4, 6–2. Before the final, she lost just two games in five matches. In the entire tournament she lost eight games and won seventy-two. She won eight of twelve sets at love. And this was the national championship, not some provincial tournament on the Riviera. No longer did anyone even think about Wills winning in anything but straight sets. There was the possibility that in a short time she would stop losing games. How long could this go on? How much better could she become?

Allison Danzig guessed that "it can't be much fun for her to toy with her opponents and it certainly isn't any fun for them. Against Molla she allowed only five points in a set that lasted eight minutes."

She came into the final at Forest Hills having dropped only two games. But she gave up six games in the final. She won the 1929 title easily, playing what one writer called, with "grim relentlessness."

One of the more exciting moments at Forest Hills in 1929 came in the quarter-finals when Molla Mallory upset Betty Nuthall, 6–3, 6–3. The crowd at the match was clearly behind the former American champion as she battered her way to victory over the less-experienced and less-determined English girl. And there was even some faint hope that "Iron Molla," when she played against Helen Wills in the semifinals, would show some of her old form and give the American Girl a first-class fight. But that was not to be. Molla's day had passed.

A storm was approaching at Forest Hills when Helen Wills and Molla Mallory walked out onto the court of the West Side Tennis Club to play against each other in a national tournament for the final time. Donald Gibbs of the *New York World* wrote that the wind howled, but the 5000 faithful fans didn't seem to notice. "They had heard the thunder of Helen Wills's forehand. They had seen her service howl across a surprised court," as Molla Mallory bowed before her, 6–0, 6–0, very quickly and without ever threatening.

In the *New York Herald Tribune,* Fred Hawthorne described it this way. "As was foredoomed, Miss Wills simply smothered Mrs. Mallory, and the match never had the semblance of a real contest. The former national champion could win only five points in the opening set. In the second she did better and gathered fifteen, yet none of those was an earned point, but all the result of the California's girl's errors."

Every time the players changed courts and Mallory walked back toward the baseline to serve or receive service, the gallery applauded her enthusiastically. In the second set, when she was within a point of winning a game, on two occasions, only to fail, the crowd groaned in sympathy.

"And through it all the emotionless Helen Wills, her features an absolute mask of serene austerity, with never the flicker of a smile to lighten them, cut her old opponent down without even the pretense of mercy. It was almost as though a man with a rapier were sending home his vital thrusts against a foeman unarmed." An appropriate comparison, since Helen's foes did on the court often seem to be, "unarmed."

During the match a ball boy ran onto the court, picked up a ball and ran off. But when he tried to stop his feet went out from under him and he fell. The crowd laughed. Molla laughed. Helen gave a faint smile for a moment then served an ace.

W. O. McGeehan of the *New York Herald Tribune* was bothered by the way that Helen won, and he wrote, "You may talk of the 'killer' instinct; you might have observed it functioning perfectly on that verdant stretch of turf in the stadium enclosure. What smiles there were during the match adorned the lips of Mrs. Mallory. Knowing she was doomed to defeat before she went on the court, she, nevertheless, laughed at her own inability to withstand the furious cannonading from Miss Wills' racket." Helen betrayed no emotion at all during the match.

Reporting the crowd response in the *New York Morning Telegraph,* James Harrison wrote that "In their applause for the fair Helen, the customers displayed all the warmth and animation of deceased codfish."

But by now there were increasing expressions of discontent among the so-called poets in the press box. After Helen Wills won the national title that year at Forest Hills, McGeehan in his column "Down the Line" said that although Helen was a great national champion, there was "something in the manner in which she plays the game that seems to typify the American attitude toward sport. There is a tense concentration in her every move, something that suggests the killer-type of fighter. Somehow," he wrote, "she does not seem to be enjoying the game itself. Without impugning the amateur standing of Miss Wills, it strikes me that hers is a professional attitude. She plays without change of expression. Not in any gesture does she seem to feel the joy of playing. Because of the immobility of her features they called her 'Little Poker Face' when she first came to Forest Hills." McGeehan complained that Helen Wills was not "colorful," and the crowds demanded color. "She is powerful, repressed and imperturbable. She plays her game with a silent, deadly earnestness, concentrated on her work. That, of course, is the way to win games, but it does not please the galleries."

Gene Tunney fought much the way Helen Wills played—clear-eyed and with absolute concentration. The difference between the two, though, was that Tunney was a frank professional and Wills was not. Tunney had no particular "zest" for the game according to McGeehan. It was a job for him. "For the galleries he had something like contempt, and the galleries felt that, too. He was playing to win and playing safe all the time, which was what he should have done for it was a business and not a sport with him.

"We know a lot of popular athletes who are a bit uptown toward the customers. They reason, quite logically, that the customers will be as quick to turn against their idols as they are to praise them; you're a hero today and a bum tomorrow.

"But Miss Wills, we fear, has overdone it; and hence it would be over-stating it to say that the tennis world is yearning impatiently for some new heroine to come forward and overpower the imperial Helen."

Many other writers agreed openly with McGeehan's assessment and grew weary of Helen's winning and of her manner on and off the court. Many of the same writers who had lauded her so intemperately in the early twenties when she first came out of the west just as intemperately attacked her. Some of them began to hope to see her tested or even beaten. And some of them tried to explain that it was she who had changed and not them, that the system of tennis had brought out the worst in her and she was no longer the refreshing American girl, but rather was imperious and cold and thoughtless and had taken on the values and trappings of the class that dominated the USLTA and East Coast tennis. She had, they suggested, betrayed her democratic California roots.

And she had drained the sport of drama. Nobody asked any more if she would win. Of course she would win. The only question was how long would it take her to win? How many games would she give up? How many minutes would a new player stay on the court with her? How cold could she possibly be, how business-like in her efficiency? She had become not only a killer of the courts with a killer instinct, but she was a cold-blooded killer with no compassion or interest in her opponents. She had no students and gave little back to the sport, it was suggested. She put no spontaneity or suspense in the sport. Helen Wills had become so efficient that she was not as interesting as Suzanne Lenglen once had been. Helen was strength and beauty, but there was no chance of a breakdown, a crisis of nerves, a sudden collapse in a tournament, and then the long litany of excuses concerning her failures. She never blew up at the officials, never stamped her feet in disgust, never threatened a linesman, never glared at an umpire, never threw her racket onto the grass and walked out, never coughed, never quit, and never toyed with an opponent.

But Helen Wills was not thinking of the impression she would leave, and certainly did not calculate one. She told a very close friend in 1930, after winning four Wimbledon, three French, and six American titles, that "while you can hardly call anything that I have done outstanding, yet I feel that I have the necessary strength to do anything." And she said, "I believe in taking things seriously, if one is trying hard for some-

thing, but there must be moments of fun and foolishness to balance it."
And later—in 1933—she addressed the criticism of sportswriters by writing that "to the contender, written criticism is as wind in the trees."
The sportswriters, however, seemed to be missing those moments of fun
and foolishness. And so did Helen's victims.

Now many of the sportswriters who followed her career became clock-
watchers, recording the minutes or the seconds it took for her to win a
match or a game and then to depart without saying anything praise-
worthy or disdainful about her opponent.

In his memoirs, sportswriter Al Laney recorded that he had seen
Helen Wills in about fifty matches during her long career. But of all of
them, he said, he could remember only those in which "she came feeling
not quite up to strenuous effort, as happens periodically to girl athletes."
Laney described a practice of one sportswriter who covered the women's
events. Powell Blackmore kept a notebook on the female players, "and
he always kindly informed me when Miss Wills's time was due so I did
not miss these interesting occasions," Laney wrote. They were interesting
because she was so good she could win standing still, you might say,
while the other girls ran miles. If there came a ball that was out of
reach and was out to beat her—well, let it. There would be others that
could be dealt with, for Helen, standing in the middle of the baseline
was so persistently accurate and so forceful that she seemed actually to
attract the ball to her racket, to force the opponent to play back to
where she was standing or to miss altogether. "One often wondered,"
Laney wrote, "why the silly girl did not make Miss Wills run, until one
realized that the silly girl had more than she could do merely knocking
the ball down the center. It was certainly interesting to see Miss Wills
operate during these few times of comparative discomfort, but otherwise
I do not even remember the names of the long list of victims she disposed of as easily as shelling peas."

Bill Tilden also turned against her. This was unusual because Helen
Wills had done nothing to earn his animosity—nothing that is except to
constantly beat Tilden's favorite female players, Helen Jacobs and
Molla Mallory, and to upstage Tilden in tournaments and in the newspapers. Tilden could be as peevish and petulant and bitchy as any other
player in the sport—male or female—and in his complaints about Wills
he showed himself at his absolute worst. In a 1947 version of his autobiography, he wrote of her: "They called Helen Wills 'Poker Face' because no expression of emotion ever crossed that classically beautiful
mask while she was on the court. I regard her as the coldest, most self-
centered, most ruthless champion ever known to tennis. Her complete
disregard for all other players and her fixed determination to play tennis
only when she herself wished to and felt it was to her advantage let her
make little or no contribution to the advancement of the game or the
development of younger players. On the other hand, she has always been

a scrupulously fair sportswoman on the court. And I must add that at all times she accepted any breaks against her without a sign of annoyance or irritation. Her peculiar Sphinx-like demeanor has given rise to the legend of mysterious depths. I have sometimes wondered whether it did not actually cover a vacuum. She is the most difficult person to know of any girl champion with whom I have come in contact."

Helen Wills was generous in her assessment of Tilden and even today considers him one of the greatest male players of all time.

Paul Gallico also became disillusioned with Wills in the late 1920s. He did not like what she had become—"an imperious and haughty and cold and heartless crusher of lesser talents"—yet he partially blamed the press and partially the tennis establishment for her transformation. Gallico pointed out that when it came to writing about women athletes, the gentlemen of the press were always just that—gentlemen—and they strengthened the truth or bent the truth or overlooked the truth or tempered the truth in the name of gentility. The result, he felt, at least in the case of Helen Wills, was the creation of a monster.

The problem was, Gallico said, that the press was, in its approach to female athletes, Victorian, reporting only in a genteel way and eliminating all negative aspects of a story. It wasn't popular, he said, to knock little girls who were coming up in sports, or young women. What the editors wanted and what the public wanted was positive reporting. And, on the other hand, the Tennis Establishment—the wealthy Easterners who controlled the game and who used the gate receipts and the rules to embellish and enrich their own clubs and facilities—succeeded for many years in impressing their values on the players. The only genuine threat to them was professionalism.

The Victorian approach eventually worked against Helen Wills. As Gallico recalled, "tennis was always strictly a sissy sport, no matter how many gallons of perspiration were shed or pounds burned away during its play; and one never, especially if he was a tennis writer by profession and wanted to return to write tennis another day, printed, "May Jones, the tennis player, is a discourteous, bad-mannered, ill-tempered little snob who ought to be kept home until someone whales some manners into her," even if true. As a result, Gallico believed, many sportswriters were guilty of making important contributions to turning otherwise nice little girls and boys into selfish egoists. This was particularly true, he concluded, in the case of Helen Wills. She was at first just "a shy, normal, sweet young girl" and did not become "really difficult" until after she had become a champion for a few years, developed into an unbeatable player and was sought after by the "society conscious tennis crowd" and been presented at the Court of St. James's. "And by that time it was too late." She had by then, he wrote, been in the headlines for a long time and become, "Our Helen, America's own little girl."

Gallico suggested that Helen Wills had never been, not even in her youth, "the perfect heroine of the perfect American story. Our Helen," he said, "was not exactly a faultless or always heroic little girl. But Our Helen she became and remained, because when she first arrived in the East to play in the Women's National Tennis Championship in 1922, she was a breathless, pretty, pink-cheeked leggy thing with two long brown braids down her back, with bows on them, that bounced and jiggled when she ran from side to side of the tennis court. She was no more than a child prodigy at that stage, and children are not particularly fair game for baiting under any conditions."

But then, thanks to "the stuffy, social-climbing tennis officials who are to blame for the solemn pall and funereal hush that always characterize an important tennis tournament," the "natural gay and vital girl eventually succumbed to that atmosphere. It is the oldsters, after all, who set the pace, and the youngsters who merely copy them. For many years Helen Wills was a perfect mirror of the collection of stuffed shirts, male and female, to be found running any big tournament."

The incident of Helen Wills's sale of her drawings to Gallico's newspaper left a bad taste in the mouths of the editor and writer, and "serves as an indication which way the wind was blowing." "Ruthlessness," he recalled, "is more or less an essential in any social climb, and the girl climbed high and traveled far from a position of no particular importance as the daughter of a San Francisco [sic] doctor to the world's champion tennis player and everything that went with it."

For Helen Wills, he wrote, the routine of each year, year after year, was always the same. Each spring she would pack up her trunk and her rackets and head east, passing through New York on her way to Wimbledon. Then after Wimbledon would come the Wightman Cup matches, in England or America, and then the women's championships at Forest Hills, through which she would move, dropping a game here and there but rarely a set. No one could extend her. She hit too hard, ran too fast, placed her shots too well, didn't get tired, was too smart. And there was practically a standing headline in every composing room: "Helen Wins Again." The only time there was a new national champion was when she remained on the West Coast for one reason or another and didn't compete.

But in the fall of 1933 Gallico sensed a new outlook on Wills's part. She had been, by that time, a target of the press for some time and of a thorough and often unfair newspaper attack. At the time she changed from "a spoiled and selfish girl" and had become "a rather pleasant human being, as all great athletes seem to do." "But where Ruth or Dempsey had to be brought from rough to smooth, Helen Wills needed to tear away a false, unnatural front that she wore like a cold gray veil. The girl behind it shone through rarely, but when she did she was so bright, gay, sunny and loveable that one wondered how she ever managed to keep it hidden for so long."

"The crowds love Tilden," Tunis wrote, "because he loves the game of tennis. They realize that the game is his life, that he has given himself to lawn tennis, that he loves it, revels in it, that on the court he is the artist supreme. Such an artist will try for a difficult shot at a critical moment of a match merely for the sheer joy of artistry, for the happiness it gives him as an artist to produce this effect.

"Wills, on the other hand, they see as a businesswoman upon the courts, as a mechanical marvel reducing her adversaries to sawdust in as short a time as possible, asking no quarter and giving none. Business efficiency of the twentieth century translated into sport. All this the crowd sees, knows unconsciously and unconsciously also they turn away from Helen Wills to William Tilden."

Tunis and Danzig and Gallico and the other "gentlemen in the press box" missed Suzanne Lenglen and her nervous crises and her flamboyant off-court manner. Helen Wills, who was shattering records every day, had at last become a bore—a big powerful beautiful graceful overpowering bore. They wanted more color. Half a century later Jack Kramer asserted a maxim about sport and color. "You can talk all you want about color," he wrote, "but winning is the real color." Maybe to Kramer, but certainly not to the sportswriters. And certainly not to Gallico or Tunis or Danzig. To them Molla Mallory had color and soul. Mallory demonstrated in 1929 what Lenglen had demonstrated in 1921 and Wills in 1926: losing had a color all its own. And it could be beautiful.

But Wills's quietude, and her brooding and her imperious demeanor on and off the court, was now turning off sportswriters and turning off some fans. Her fellow players in Europe and America pointed out that she could be a delightful woman, but that also she was intensely private. Her shyness off the court was misinterpreted by the press and by the fans. Looking back on the criticism, Helen Wills says today, "I was so young then. I had done nothing wrong and I had won. But they didn't like that, for some reason. I don't know why. But I aroused so much animosity in some of them. Especially John Tunis and Paul Gallico. I just don't understand it. I still don't."

When Wills read what Gallico wrote about her, she was both upset and deeply hurt, so much so, she told me, that she made up her mind never again to read anything he wrote because he was so unfair and so cruel. Today she laughs at that decision and says she was probably a little too serious when she decided never to read him again because she missed out on some pretty good literature. Yet, she says, "You must remember that I was a very young woman at the time and they were writing some very unfair things and they were not true and I did not deserve it and to this day I do not understand why they wrote—especially Gallico—what they wrote."

At the time, Helen Wills let these attacks and criticism pass. But privately they both confused and perplexed her, no doubt, all the more because she could not quite figure the hostility of the press and the coolness of the crowds, although she had seen the crowd turn against Suzanne Lenglen in 1921 and Molla Mallory in 1923.

She responded to them eight years later, in her autobiography. She pointed out that "explanation in the form of defense of yourself accomplishes nothing. It cannot change you. At heart, you simply are as you are. You might think yourself quite beautiful, for example, and the thought might be shared by any one, or you may be convinced that your brain power has a potential elasticity comparable to that of Einstein, and yet this may be far from the truth. Or, for example, I might have thought my appearance was quite pleasing on the tennis court and might have been completely mistaken. Actually, I did not think of this—or indeed anything about what I was putting across to the audience. I had one thought and that was to put the ball across the net. I was simply myself," Helen wrote, "too deeply concentrated on the game for any extraneous thought. I did not think of the impression I was creating then, nor would I today, nor will I in Valhalla, if I am lucky enough to tread those lovely courts."

But the part of the criticism that hurt Helen Wills most and that she could never forgive was the part that said she did not "feel the joy of playing." In fact, she said, that was exactly what she did feel—it was why she played over the course of so many years, "why I was able to learn to play, why I was to struggle to overcome an injury that kept me away from the game for almost two years, why I play now with so much enthusiasm on my home courts."

In early 1929 Helen Wills announced her engagement to Frederick S. Moody, a young, flamboyant San Francisco stockbroker. Moody told me that they had been secretly engaged since the spring of 1926. In describing his life to me, Fred said that he went to sea rather than to college, ten years before he met Helen. "I educated myself," he said. But when they were married she insisted that he not go to sea again, "and I didn't until we were divorced." Moody had been educated in Europe, but then signed on as a crew member on ships sailing to just about every part of the world. Fred was a cosmopolitan young man, with an adventurous streak and he loved to drink—perhaps too much—and bet on the horses. When he went away to sea, he said, of his parents, "I think they were glad to get rid of me."

The announcement of the engagement brought a flurry of excitement. There was that delicious shiver of hope that she would retire from tennis, at least for a time, and confine herself to being Mrs. Moody. But the hope was short-lived. Instead, Fred Moody became, almost inevitably, "Mr. Helen Wills," and Helen continued her tennis almost with a vengeance. She said she was going back to the university to earn her degree, and she would not be taking any classes in domestic science. Then she gave a real shocker to the press when she said, without smiling, "I expect to play until I am sixty, at least. Mr. Moody, I am sure, would not want me to give up my tennis. I am not domestic," she concluded. "There are so many more interesting things—tennis and painting and writing. Those are the things I have always cared about. Why give them up? After all it is the modern way for a woman to carry forward her career, isn't it? Must marriage interfere? I do not think so."

Several of Helen's friends had serious misgivings about her marriage to Fred Moody. Among them were Senator Phelan and his close friend, Gertrude Atherton, the successful California author, who had befriended Helen years earlier and given her friendly advice on improving her writing. Soon after the announcement of the engagement, Phelan told Atherton of his concern. And she wrote back to him, "I agree with you that she should not marry for some years yet. Of course, there comes a time when a girl creases to be a virgin and becomes a spinster. But twenty-eight is quite time enough. If she marries Fred Moody I feel sure it will be for the sake of having some one chaperon her to Europe. Her father objects to paying her mother's expenses on these tennis trips. Moreover, Helen is very anxious to spend a year or two in Europe but cannot afford it."

Wills kept her marriage plans secret all year, but upon her return to California as the triple-nation champion again, she and Moody obtained a wedding license on December 19 and were married less than one week later, on Monday, December 23. It was a small wedding at St. Clement's Chapel in Berkeley, and the ceremony lasted only ten minutes. In the Episcopalian ritual it was noticed that Helen did not promise to "obey" her husband. She only promised to love, honor, and keep him in sickness and in health, forsaking all others. Only a dozen people were present. Helen was happy when they emerged from the church to face a huge throng of reporters and gawkers. There was a short press conference at which Moody appeared nervous.

For the honeymoon the young couple sailed to Mexico on the yacht of Cyril Tobin, which was named, appropriately, *Galatea*. Fred does not remember the honeymoon as a delightful interlude. "Helen was seasick the whole time," he remembered. "So I got to know all of the rum runners in Encinada."

Married and back from her honeymoon, Helen Wills settled in San Francisco. In the spring she left for Europe again. Some players and writers expected her to take some time off. Fred Moody expected her to take some time off. But she didn't.

Before leaving for France Helen Wills Moody played an exhibition

match at Stanford for her school, California. The university had granted
her an athletic letter, a "Big C" for her sports accomplishment, despite the
fact that she had not participated on any school athletic team. She said
that now it was time for her to earn the letter by playing against Stanford's number-one player, a mere man. She was scheduled to play three
matches. In the first she played Larry Hall, captain of the Stanford
squad. She upset Hall in a single set, 6–4. Then she played on the winning side in the doubles and mixed doubles. She was the only woman in
the exhibition.

When Wills played her Stanford exhibition she drew the largest crowd
ever to see a tennis match in Northern California. Close to 4000 people
jammed into the Stanford tennis area. Students hung from the fences
and climbed the walls to see Helen in action. This crowd was twice as
large as the crowds that turned out in the past to see visiting tennis
stars in exhibition matches, and it is little wonder that the professional
promoters were after Helen with so much energy.

In the French Hard Court Tournament, Helen Wills was again irre-
pressible. "Meeses Moody-Veels"—as the French now referred to her—
knocked off all of her opponents easily. In the finals, against Mme.
Simone Mathieu, she won 6–3, 6–4.

In England again she played on the Wightman Cup team against the
English. She played a bit slower than in previous years, now and again,
toying with opponents, taking points whenever she needed them, extending some rallies, it was believed.

In the Wightman Cup matches she had a scare. In a match before a
wildly partisan English crowd of 10,000, Mrs. Phoebe Watson came
within two points of beating Helen Wills in a love set. But Helen's
resurgence and saving of the set demonstrated how calm and collected
she could remain while under pressure. She appeared to lose her concentration at one point, but then found it and surged back. Her friends on
the team that year noticed something new and frightening in her game.
Before 1929 there was never much variety in her play, and her game
consisted of either more power or less power, but always power. Against
Watson, when she started hitting out and making unforced errors and
Watson started scoring well against her, Wills started lobbing, putting
the ball up high and giving Watson no speed to use on her ground
strokes. This was a tactic Lenglen could use so deftly, but one that Wills
had not tried before in tournament. It worked. Watson's timing went
off, she started to miss, she tried to readjust, she tried to play Wills's
game, she faltered. Wills found her game again, and the match was
turned around. Wills won. Again. But reporters didn't notice the
changed tactic, the more intelligent play. All they reported was that
Wills had faltered and that Watson had tested her for the first time in
years. Wills's friends saw something else: she was not faltering, she was
better than ever.

At Wimbledon ninety-six women entered the tournament, and they appeared to be like so many clumsy artisans around Wills. Elizabeth Ryan had reached the final previously in 1914 and had been beaten then by Mrs. Lambert Chambers. She reached it again in 1930 and faced the moment of winning what was the most elusive title for her. But this time Helen Wills stood in her way and was not to be moved. In the final at Wimbledon against Ryan, Wills won with the loss of but four games, 6–2, 6–2.

Following her Wimbledon win Wills skipped Forest Hills and returned directly to San Francisco, saying she missed the city and her husband. There were outspoken hopes and expectations that Helen Wills would certainly play at Forest Hills and set a new record, tying Molla Mallory and winning four championships in a row. But at the time breaking records didn't seem important to Helen. And there was the financial consideration. Despite the fact that the crowds were reported to find her play increasingly boring, and the reporters wanted to see her lose—the crowds still came out to see her play, perhaps now for the chance to see a legend at work or to see a legend stumble. Yet in early August she announced that she would not defend her title. She said she would play now in only local events. There would be no quest for a seventh title and a tie with Molla Mallory, anyway, not this year.

The result, at Forest Hills, was predictable. Smaller crowds. Only about five hundred showed up in this Depression year of 1930 for the early rounds of women's singles. And Anna Harper of California, a friend of Helen's, was one of the favorites to win the title.

This was the last tournament in which the women's national singles championship was played as an event separate from the men's. From now on the matches would be mixed and played in the same week at the same time.

With Helen Wills out of the tournament, Betty Nuthall, the young English hope, won. Her final match against Harper took just thirty-six minutes. For the first time in forty-three years the women's national championship was won by a foreign player.

In 1931 Helen Wills decided not to leave the country to play tennis. Ticket sales boomed again at Wimbledon in 1931 as there was the expectation of Wills arriving to go for a fifth straight title. But she announced she would not play in England. She sent a letter to the secretary of the All-England Club announcing her withdrawal from the competition. She said that the trip was too long. She had traveled enough. She would play only in America this year. She had won four Wimbledon titles and three French titles in succession. With five wins at Wimbledon in a row she could put her name in the record book next to Suzanne Lenglen's, who won five in a row between 1919 and 1923. Yet again, to just about everyone's surprise and disappointment, Wills showed that breaking records was not important to her. She let the chance for the record pass—an almost assured chance to tie Lenglen. She would not even try. As a result, the Wimbledon title went to a German player, Fraulein Cilly Aussem.

Wills did come east in 1931 to play in the Wightman Cup matches. She beat Betty Nuthall and Phyllis Mudford each in straight sets but lost in the doubles when she was teamed with Anna Harper. Nuthall had improved since she last played Wills, it was pointed out. But Helen Wills also had improved since she had last played Nuthall. And Helen had improved more. This time there was no serious English challenge, and Wills won easily, 6–4, 6–2.

She also entered some warmup tournaments in 1931 in the East. At the Essex County Club at Manchester by the Sea, Massachusetts, Wills played Anna Harper in the final and beat her in thirty minutes in love sets. She won eight straight games against Harper before giving up one game on errors. Then she took four more and the match. She had won the tournament three times previously—1925, 1926, 1928. Then she went to Seabright, New Jersey, where in the past she had never won. She had been beaten at Seabright the last time she played there by Elizabeth Ryan. But this time, she broke the jinx and before a capacity crowd of 3000 beat Helen Jacobs in love sets in the final. The first set took eleven minutes. The second took a bit longer, twenty-one minutes. It was not the sort of match that thrilled a crowd. It was like an execution. Without blood. It was like a ten-second heavyweight fight in which a blow to the stomach ends the contest.

Now John Tunis pointed out that Helen Wills obviously should, like Suzanne Lenglen, have HC placed after her name on the tournament programs for *hors classe*. "Her opponents," he wrote, "were so many clumsy tyros ineffectively trying to match strokes with the best woman lawn tennis player in the world today." She had it all, he observed, tactics, shots, strategy. She won her seventh U.S. title in 1931. She restored the national title to an American player again. In the women's national singles tournament, Helen Wills won easily through the tournament and then beat Eileen Bennett Whittingstall in thirty-four minutes in the final, 6–4, 6–1, without expanding much energy. Someone noticed two drops of sweat on her forehead when she changed courts near the end of the match.

—◦◦❦ 4 ❧◦◦—

In 1932 Helen Wills decided to go abroad with Fred for a combination vacation and tennis campaign. Even before she departed for Paris, when she was in New York in late April and practiced at the River Club—just practiced—the stands were packed to capacity by people who paid just to see her practice. The crowd was fashionable New York Society, and her opponent was the club professional, Harry Brunie. Fifty-second Street from First Avenue to the East River was jammed with limousines, while inside the club every seat was filled and people stood in the rows to watch. She practiced against Manuel Alonzo, the Spanish Davis Cup competitor, and he beat her 7–5, 6–3 and was leading 6–5 in the third set when play stopped.

Sydney Wood, the defending Wimbledon champion, also practiced at the club, yet the packed gallery had obviously come to watch Helen Wills. They waited patiently for an hour for two men to finish before she appeared. She was applauded wildly when she walked onto the court. Despite the growing dissatisfaction of the sportswriters and the democratic galleries, Wills remained the darling of the upper crust, those who ran the tournaments and the clubs and watched the games from the best boxes.

In France, Helen and Fred visited galleries. Helen painted and she captured a fourth French singles title and her second women's doubles title—partnered with Elizabeth Ryan—at Roland-Garros. She tried to win all three titles in the tournament, and she would have succeeded if Freddie hadn't plotted against her. Moody did not enjoy tennis much. He would rather be sailing or seeing sights or walking or betting on horses. His most important correspondence with Helen in 1930, while he was in San Francisco and she was in France, concerned placing bets for him on the right horses at the races in Paris. He clowned around at some of the matches Helen entered, and several of her friends complained privately that he was, quite obviously, not of the same "class" as Helen. The sportswriters, of course, loved his company.

In the mixed doubles competition that spring in Paris Freddie made sure that Helen would have trouble. Sidney Wood was asked to play in the mixed doubles with Wills by the president of the French Tennis Federation. It sounded to everyone like a wonderful combination—the Wimbledon male champion and the American female champion playing together against foreign teams. But Wood was much more concerned about the singles and begged off. He was especially worried after Fred found him and threw his arm over his shoulder and said, "Let me tell you something about my wife. She will let nothing stand between her and victory. Nothing. She is determined to win every game she starts. Naturally, in mixed doubles she likes to play with the best available partner. And this year, Sidney, you happen to be hot as a firecracker. Take my advice and don't play with her. She takes the game too seriously. If you have an off day she'll never let you forget it."

So Wood tried to wriggle his way out of the mixed doubles. He told officials he would not play. But the officials refused to allow him to withdraw. Much to his surprise, a few days later he saw his name listed with Helen Wills's in the program in the mixed doubles. They were seeded first.

In the singles Wood was beaten by René Lacoste in a three-set match that left him with cramped muscles and throbbing nerves. After a brief rest, he had to go on the court with Helen. The only way to recover, he felt, was to have a drink. Fred provided him with a bottle of brandy, and the two took several healthy swallows in the dressing room. Then, as Wood recalled later, "I staggered forth to do or die for the fair sex. I couldn't see very well, but I could walk, after a fashion."

The opposition was Fred Perry and Betty Nuthall. Helen and Wood were introduced as "ace glorious Americain combeenaseeon." Wood tried to serve the first game. He tried to throw the ball up but it wouldn't go. It stuck in his cramped fingers. He tried again and still the ball stuck in his hand. Somebody in the crowd let out a long derisive whistle. Wills turned and glared at her woozy partner. "I grinned foolishly and held out the balls," Wood recalled, and said "Here, Helen, maybe you'd better serve."

She did. Wood played net. He swung and missed at the first return to cross the net. Strike one. He connected with the second and hit it into the stands—a home run. The crowd laughed and jeered. Wills glared at Wood.

Finally, Wood scored a point. And from the stands came the happy voice of Fred Moody, "Atta boy, Sid. How's about another brandy?"

As Wood remembered it, at that remark, "Helen put her straight nose up in the air in line with her famous white visor. Her worst suspicions were confirmed; her partner was not only pooped—he was potted."

Wood had so many cramped muscles in his stomach that after his singles match he had taped two glass ashtrays to his gut to keep it flat and to keep the muscles from knotting. Now, as he jumped high for a lob, the adhesive tape broke and an ash tray dropped out of his pants and hit the clay and then rolled at Wills's feet. "That was the end of a beautiful partnership," Wood recalled. Wills didn't say anything to Wood at the moment. And she didn't say anything to him after the match, which they lost. And she didn't say anything to him for two years after the match. And, as Wood pointed out, she also eventually divorced Fred.

Suzanne Lenglen watched the tournament, and again there was talk of the Wills-Lenglen rematch. The amount of money offered for such a match peaked at the end of the twenties around $100,000. But the USLTA ruled that open tennis was "a menace to the game" and still refused even to discuss a Wills-Lenglen match.

There was also some desperation in the Lenglen effort to get Wills to play. Suzanne was having a tough time of it emotionally and financially. Papa Lenglen died in 1929, and Suzanne had lost much of her former enthusiasm for life. And her planned professional exhibitions in England and the Continent had failed. The abortive exhibitions attracted small crowds and Lenglen did not wish to make herself into a carnival act by playing exclusively against men in her matches, as one promoter suggested she do now. There were rumors of her alleged affair with a wealthy Californian and of her efforts and intention to marry. But nothing came of it. She designed clothing and worked for a time as a saleslady for a sporting equipment shop in Paris. In 1930 the wire services carried photographs of female tennis players modeling clothing designed by Suzanne Lenglen. The Goddess was still ahead of her time. She designed tennis shorts for women—called "Suzanne Shorts"—that were popularized later as "Bermuda shorts." They were worn in the winter tournaments of the 1930s on the Riviera by outside mannequins. But they didn't catch on at the time. Finally, Suzanne opened her own tennis school in Paris and began training young French players.

Helen Wills remained uninterested in professional tennis. She didn't need it. She confessed that she had been approached many times by many different promoters, including Bill O'Brien, the masseur on the first pro-tour who signed up Tilden and others for a tour. Helen Wills did come out in favor of open tennis and said she felt that the division between professional and amateur was highly artificial and that something should be done about it. She was sympathetic with those who needed money and took it for playing the sport they loved. But it was not for her. She had been taken care of by her father, by the associations, and by her writing and art and by her husband.

At Wimbledon in 1932 Wills was again successful, winning her fifth title, beating Jacobs in the final, 6–3, 6–1. Suzanne Lenglen sat in the gallery watching the contest. Writing about the match, John Tunis exclaimed, "What a contest—what a lack of variety, what a want of enterprise!"

Helen stayed in Europe with Fred and did not defend her titles at Forest Hills. She said she wished to study art. There was, however, some animosity in this because the USLTA had contributed an unannounced amount to her Wimbledon trip expecting that she would return the favor by playing at Forest Hills. She was badly needed to help make it a financial success. Her behavior seemed thankless to some. There were reports in the press to the effect that if Helen went abroad the next year, she would pay her own way.

Although the Depression had become increasingly severe, the small crowds at Forest Hills were blamed on the absence of a big star. The biggest gallery during the week for women's matches was only 2500 to watch Helen Jacobs win her first national title since she won the girls' national championships in 1924 and 1925. Ever since that time, for seven years, she had been playing in the shadow of Big Helen.

--◆{ 5 }◆--

The issues of open tennis and professionalism were not the only ones confronting the players and associations in the early 1930s. But those were the issues to which most publicity and open discussion were devoted. Other controversies of tremendous import were ignored. It seems that the officials and the stars then, like the officials and stars today, were more caught up in personal concerns more than in public concerns, even to the degree that they were blinded to the larger issues that touched on their sport. Rarely did they recognize certain larger problems, and even more rarely did they speak out on them. The world of sport was a world unto itself. And Helen Wills, despite her writing and reading and her traveling, remained as myopic as any of the other players when it came to the issues of race and sport in the early 1930s.

The world of Suzanne Lenglen and Helen Wills in the 1920s in tennis was a white world. In matters of race the various tennis associations and players accepted the conventional dictum of the time that declared separate playing facilities and associations and strict segregation for all black players. What is unusual is that not a single white player in those years raised a voice of dissent or protest. They accepted the segregation as normal and required and even as good.

In the 1920s and 1930s there was a black counterpart for Helen Wills, a player whom she had never seen and who never saw her except in the newspapers. The woman known as "the Black Helen Wills" was Ora Washington. On the black tournament circuit her victories matched those of Wills and it was reported that it was her lifelong dream to play Wills—a dream confrontation that never took place. Washington's career paralleled that of Wills closely. She won seven consecutive tennis titles in the American Tennis Association's Women's Singles National Championships from 1929 to 1935. She lost to Lula Ballard in 1936, but then came back to regain her title for an eighth time in 1938. (Her record did did not remain for long. Bonnie Logan won seven consecutive titles in the late 1960s and and Althea Gibson won ten in the 1940s and 50s.)

Little is known today of Ora Washington. She was born in Virginia and moved to Philadelphia when she was eighteen. She was born in 1898, and she died in 1971 at the age of seventy-three. She never married. She did not write an autobiography, and white newspapers never covered her matches. W. Eugene Houston, former president of the ATA, told me of her and said, "I doubt if Ora would have gotten a game off Helen Wills." The problem was, he pointed out, the limited ranks of black players to practice against and the limited number of black coaches. So Washington's dream match against Wills never happened. Her last singles title came in 1937. She won ten doubles titles and three mixed doubles titles in the same period of time.

There was an effort on the part of the ATA to alter this. No leading white players became involved in the controversy, though. In December 1929, the NAACP charged the USLTA with racial discrimination. The protest was contained in a letter to Edward Moss, executive secretary of the USLTA, by Robert Bagnall, associate secretary of the NAACP. Bagnall was not making a case for Ora Washington, but rather for two young black male tennis players who attempted to play in the National Junior Indoor Tennis Championships at the Seventh Regiment Armory in New York. He charged that the youngsters were excluded on the basis of race alone.

The two young men were Reginald Weir, a member of the City College of New York tennis team, and Gerald Norman, captain of the Flushing High School tennis team. Both young men applied for the tournament and sent in the required fees. But when the draw for the competition was published, their names did not appear.

The tournament committee supplied no reason for the rejection. Officials of the USLTA, however, said that there were no clauses in the by-laws of their organization which discriminated against black players. To participate in an association tournament, a player must be a member in good standing in the USLTA, as well as a member in good standing of a club belonging to the association. A day later, Moss announced through the Associated Press that the rejection of the two players was in accordance with a USLTA policy. It was the policy he said, to reject black players: "In pursuing this policy we make no reflection upon the colored race, but we believe that as a practical matter, the present method of separate associations for the administration of the affairs and the championships of colored and white players should be continued." And that was that. No player raised a voice of protest at the policy until Alice Marble finally did so nearly two decades later.

The splendid isolation of the American tennis players was demonstrated again in 1933. Almost all the American players were politically comatose and socially hyperactive. On April 1 in that year news reports from Berlin indicated that "the Nazi boycott against the Jews—the greatest organized anti-Semitic movement in modern times—paralyzed the commercial life of its victims today, but passed with comparatively few disorders."

This was but a single day's demonstration against the Jews. Nazis painted indentifying marks on all businesses owned by Jews. Signs like "Danger—Jew Store," and "Attention, Beware of the Jew," accompanied by skull and crossbones, were put up in addition to regulation black and yellow quarantine signs.

Then a little more than one week later, the Davis Cup hopes of

Germany were wrecked by Hitler's ban on Jews, as the German Davis Cup Committee dropped its leading player and former captain, Daniel Prenn.

H. W. Austin and Fred Perry, the leading tennis stars of England, wrote to the London *Times* strongly protesting the exclusion of Prenn from the German team. In the previous year Prenn, before a large crowd in Berlin, won against Great Britain in the semi-final round of the European Zone Davis Cup play. "We have always valued our participation at international sport because we believe it to be a great opportunity for the promotion of better understanding and because it is a human activity countenancing no distinction of race, class or creed," Austin and Perry said. "For this reason, if for no other, we view with misgiving any action which may well undermine all that is most valuable in international competition."

No similar protest came from any individual or association in America. In fact such a protest would have seemed somewhat morally obtuse given the racial policies of the organization with regard to black American players. The Germans were doing what the USLTA had been doing since its inception—segregating on the basis of ethnicity rather than color.

When Germany named its Davis Cup squad on April 23, Prenn's name was missing. Baron Gottfried von Cramm headed the team. And a resolution adopted by the German Association provided that "non-Aryans cannot play in representative matches or official league contests." The association also banned "non-Aryans" from the board of governors. At the same time the German professional Roman Najuch cancelled his contract to coach the Polish Davis Cup Team. The reason was "the Polish anti-German agitations which do not stop at German sportsmen." And furthermore, German players were required to play with German tennis balls only.

On May 7, Nellie Neppach, Germany's best-known woman tennis player, committed suicide following a nervous breakdown caused, her friends said, by the intrusion of Nazi politics into German tennis.

Like Helen Wills in America, Neppach captured the women's tennis championship of Germany seven times and won the championships also of Spain, Austria, Hungary, and Switzerland, and as a national heroine in sport was on an equal footing in Central Europe with Lenglen and Wills. Her suicide brought no remarks of sadness or regret from any player anywhere.

Neppach went into deep depression when the Nazi authorities barred Prenn from the Davis Cup team. She had figured prominently in German tennis circles for several years, but most importantly in 1925 and 1926. She won the singles title of Germany in 1925 and played on the Riviera in the winter of 1926. She played against both Suzanne Lenglen and

Helen Wills on the Riviera, losing to Wills at Mentone, 6–0, 6–3. In 1932 she was ranked seventh among German women in tennis.

Not only was there no official or unofficial protest from any American player or official, but the next year, when the USLTA decided for the first time to hire a professional coach for the Davis Cup squad, the professional they hired was Hans Nusslein, a German. The USLTA was more concerned with hiring someone who had never defied the authority of the organization in this country by turning professional here. Nusslein fit the bill. The fact that he was a Nazi and proud of it bothered not a single soul in the USLTA at all.

Tilden first played tennis in Germany in 1927. He fell in love with the country and said, as late as 1938, "I became and still am, the most ardent admirer of the German people. I would rather play in Berlin than any city in the world." Eventually he was hired as coach of the German Davis Cup team and when that team came up against the Americans in the interzone final of the Davis Cup in 1937—four years after the Germans had segregated their tennis—it was clear that Tilden's heart resided with his paycheck, according to his biographer, Frank Deford.

--◄ 6 ►--

Following the tournaments of 1932, Helen and Fred Moody vacationed in Europe, sightseeing, mountain climbing, seeing the Continent together and escaping, as only the rich could do, from depression America. Helen played tennis on the indoor courts in Paris with Jean Borotra and won a winter indoor title there in the Championship of Paris. Then in Stockholm and Oslo and Brussels she played exhibition matches, one with the king of Sweden.

Wills's friends expected 1933 to be a year of great moment for her. In January she started her campaign with an exhibition at the Palace of Fine Arts in San Francisco before a crowd of 2500. Appearing for the first time on an American court in eighteen months, she played against her regular exhibition opponent, Phil Neer, beating him in one set, 6–4. After that she teamed up with Bud Chandler, the California singles champion, to defeat Alice Marble and Gerald Stratford. During the exhibition, Helen "displayed before a highly appreciative gathering a new and greater assortment of tennis strokes and most convincingly squelched any fear that she was slipping, if any ever existed," a reporter wrote for the *San Francisco Chronicle*. "Her tennis," he found, "was flawless, exceeding anything that she has previously shown here." It appeared to some that her service lacked its usual "zip," yet Neer found it anything but easy to handle.

In April, at another exhibition, she teamed up with Alice Marble to play Helen Jacobs and Anna Harper. They met on March 31, and the local fans were aware of the highly publicized animosity Wills felt for Jacobs. There was the delicious promise of a "real cat fight." More than 3000 fans jammed the Palace of Fine Arts to see the fur fly. They were not disappointed. Wills and Jacobs took the court without the customary greeting to each other. Then to a good deal of delight, the match began with Jacobs serving an ace to Wills. From that moment on, the match became a singles duel of Big Helen against Little Helen, the two women concentrating on efforts to win points off the other, hitting, many fans felt, viciously at each other, trying for intimidation as much as for points. This match was played, fans felt, "for keeps." And Wills was in a class by herself against Jacobs, getting rousing applause with her placements, slams, smashes, lobs, and volleys for winners against Jacobs. Wills and Marble won in two sets, 6–4, 6–1.

A week later Jacobs left for France and her quest for the triple American, French, and English titles.

In late April seating capacity for the courts at the Palace of Fine Arts was doubled to accommodate the enthusiastic turnout for exhibition matches by Helen Wills and Ellsworth Vines. And the *Chronicle* advertised the matches by pointing out that Wills was so good that the national association no longer ranked her with other players. In fact, she was unranked only because she had not played in the United States enough in the previous year to earn a ranking. But such niceties escaped the local reporters.

In May, Wills was still uncertain of a trip to Wimbledon. She entered a doubles tournament with Fred at the California Tennis Club. As to her husband's abilities on the tennis court, Helen said, "I coached Mr. Moody during our stay in France last year, but he plays like all beginners—not very good. I don't think we will last more than one round in the California Club tournament." They didn't.

On May 10 she announced her decision to play at Wimbledon but not in France. She wanted to stay in California for an extra week and enjoy the spring weather, she said. In mid-May she boarded the Overland Limited for the trip east with Fred.

About that same time came a challenge she had been expecting, from Suzanne Lenglen.

It happened that W. O. McGeehan, writer for the *New York Herald Tribune,* while traveling in Europe, ran into Lenglen. He followed her to some courts and watched her play a few sets and reached the conclusion that she was as good as ever, that the intervening years as a professional had not affected her game at all. He wrote a column speculating on the possibility of a Wills-Lenglen rematch. When asked about it, Lenglen said she was in favor of it. In New York, reporters rushed to speak with Wills, en route with her husband from California at the time.

She reminded them that Lenglen was still a pro and that, if the proper arrangements could be made, she would be delighted to play her again. But she would not turn professional. The match would have to be a sanctioned amateur vs. professional contest and would, therefore, have to be endorsed by the USLTA. Newsmen suggested that the match be held in the Yale Bowl in New Haven, where a massive crowd could be accommodated. Jean Augustin headed a group of sportsmen who pushed for the meeting on French soil, and the French Tennis Federation said it would be in favor of the match and thought that the USLTA would be asked to sanction such a meeting within a few days. But again, the amateur/professional division ended any possibilities of the match. This was the last time anyone publicly got excited about the prospect.

Lenglen wanted the match badly in 1933. Wills held five Wimbledon singles titles and would be going for her sixth and a tie with Lenglen at the most important tennis tournament of all. She might have her record equaled by the American Girl, but she wanted the chance, one last time, to demonstrate to her countrymen and to the world that she was still the superior player. If Wills won at Wimbledon she could return to America and play for her eighth singles title there, tying Molla Mallory's record. She could also unseat the defending national champion, Helen Jacobs, in that tournament, which added a bit more luster and personal satisfaction.

Lenglen was practicing again daily on the courts at Stade Roland-Garros. She was losing weight, getting in shape, actively preparing for a match with Wills. She was more animated, more talkative, more optimistic, than she had been in years. Helen was unfazed by this. She said she had doubts about anyone making a comeback—even Suzanne—after a layoff of several years. She said she believed that Suzanne would not be able to lift her game to the heights she had achieved in the early 1920s. She had no fear of meeting her. Lenglen expressed enthusiasm to newsmen about the prospective match. After all, she said, the terms for the confrontation would be simple. When asked what the terms of the match might be, Lenglen answered quickly, "Money terms!"

Lenglen competed as neither an amateur nor a professional. She had been rebuffed in her efforts to get reclassified as an amateur in order to represent France in the 1928 Olympic Games in Holland, and then the tennis competitions in the Games were cancelled. Her hopes for a comeback waxed and waned with the years. The key to it all was Helen Wills, of course. If something could just be done to allow them to play. Just one more time. But the hostility of the USLTA toward open tennis and the refusal of Wills to consider professionalism presented impossible roadblocks on the way back to glory for the Goddess. The years passed slowly. Suzanne pretended to lose interest in Helen and the other women on the tour. She suggested, every now and then, that she was much more interested in her latest hobby—stamp collecting. Papa had been a philatelist and had left Suzanne his collection. But every year journalists spotted her in the gallery at Wimbledon and at Roland-Garros and in the smaller tournaments, unobtrusively sitting there watching. And thinking. And hoping. And dreaming. Over the years, watching countless matches, she gained renewed confidence in her own capabilities and now seemed convinced, much more than in 1926, that she could defeat the American Girl and bring her long winning streak to an end. But with hope gone for her own play against Wills, Lenglen sought a surrogate. And she sought out another Helen—Helen Jacobs of Berkeley—Little Helen, who had been losing to Helen Wills in match after match ever since 1925. And so Suzanne Lenglen, who had never lost to Helen Wills, instructed Helen Jacobs, who had never beaten Helen Wills, on just how to win. First, of course, you had to believe you could win. You had to believe. Molla Mallory, after all, believed that she could beat the great Suzanne. An incredible feat, to be sure. But she did it because she believed. And because the great Lenglen was ill. Molla believed, and Molla won. If Helen Jacobs could be led to believe she could beat Big Helen, if she could be shown exactly how to do it, it could be done. But first she had to be taught to believe. So Suzanne Lenglen showed her how to beat Helen Wills and how to believe she could do it. She could not have picked a better student than earnest, sober, hard-working, tenacious Helen Jacobs.

---◄ 7 ►---

Helen Hull Jacobs was at first an admirer of Helen Wills, one of the many young women who idolized her and was inspired by her and who wanted to grow up to be just like her. She had the unique advantage of living near Wills and being able to see her play and to read the details of her career and matches in the daily newspapers. According to one biographer, James K. McGee, Helen Jacobs "worshipped the ground on which the elder Helen walked." The national champion, in her eyes, "could do no wrong. It was the spontaneous, silent worship of the neophyte for the master." By the time she got around to writing her autobiography, however, Jacobs had cooled toward Wills and denied that she had ever been so passionate in her admiration of the older star.

In time she became a competitor, and, like all other female competitors, lost every match she played against the American Girl. Then she became the principal competitor, the one the press singled out as the most threatening opponent for the champion, and the names of the women were linked in the papers as "The Two Helens." Then she became Helen Wills's nemesis, the agent of her downfall.

There were striking similarities that the two Helens shared. And there were dramatic differences. Both, of course, were named Helen. Both came from the Northern California's beautiful Bay Area—Wills from Centerville and Berkeley, Jacobs from San Francisco and Berkeley. Each was discovered early in her career by William Fuller, and each then became a junior member of the Berkeley Tennis Club. They began their careers by winning local and regional titles, and then each won the junior national title twice. When the Wills family moved from their house on 1200 Shattuck Avenue in Berkeley, the Jacobs family moved in. Jacobs took over the same room that Wills had occupied. Whereas the older Helen had pinned up pictures of movie stars on the wall, the younger Jacobs pinned up pictures of Helen Wills. Both Helens enrolled in the exclusive Anna Head School in Berkeley and then, upon graduation, enrolled in the University of California. Both painted and wrote newspaper stories and books. Each wrote a novel. Each published her autobiography—Jacobs in 1936, Wills in 1937.

But while Wills was cool—The Ice Queen—Jacobs had a reputation for having a good sense of humor, and she was gregarious and generous and outgoing and fair. Wills did not have that sort of reputation. The tennis players, male as well as female, divided along pro-Wills and pro-Jacobs loyalty lines. Most were not outspoken as to why they favored one woman or the other. But some of those who were insiders and who played against both women or saw them play over the years, expressed their partisanship in much the same way that players or fans today express partisanship toward Chris Evert or Martina Navratilova. Wills, they said, preferred the companionship of men and was courted by many men. Jacobs appeared to prefer the companionship of women and was not courted by many men. Each had many friends, close ones, of both sexes. Helen Wills was better for the image of the sport, it was said, and she attracted more players to the sport, despite her shortcomings. Helen Jacobs, a nice and decent woman, was not as good for the image of the sport.

The beauty and grace of Helen Wills was celebrated by poets and painters, and young men swooned over her. The same was not true for Helen Jacobs. Helen Wills cultivated a feminine appearance, carefully selected her clothing and hair style, and applied her makeup meticulously. Jacobs wore a hair net on the court, used little makeup, wore no nail polish, and chain-smoked. In 1936 *Time* reported that Jacobs "has thus far shown no romantic interest in men."

After she matured, Helen Jacobs was several inches shorter than Helen Wills and ten pounds heavier. Many spectators described her as "short and stocky." And if the choice of a Miss America should have been left to a popular vote, there is no doubt that Helen Jacobs would never have been in contention. But she did have a generous soul and a good sense of humor, and many at the Berkeley Club and in the other places she played admired her.

Helen Jacobs began to play tennis in 1922 in San Francisco in Lafayette

Park near her home on Sacramento Street. She received her first racket at the age of thirteen, and tennis quickly lured her away from the piano. Her father, Roland, was her first teacher. After a few weeks of instruction from him she entered a novice tournament and won. Billy Johnston presented her with her first trophy. She based her winning game on that of Wills. "She sought to emulate her poise, her slashing strokes, her service, her concentration," one biographer wrote. While Helen Wills whispered, "Now I'm Johnston," Helen Jacobs dreamed of being Helen Wills.

Helen Jacobs next entered in the state tournament in Berkeley, where she was spotted by Pop Fuller. "I watched her lose the first set of the match," Fuller remembered, "and then saw her come from behind to win the next two." Fuller liked that. So he introduced himself to Helen's parents, said he had coached Helen Wills, and asked if they would allow him to guide their Helen. They agreed. He suggested that they move to Berkeley to be nearer the tennis club where Helen would be playing. They agreed again, and Fuller took care of that for them, too; he found them a house—the house the Wills family had just vacated near Live Oak Part at 1200 Shattuck. That was in 1923, the year Helen Wills won her first national singles title.

Fuller arranged a practice session between the two players. Little Helen recalled years later that she was eager for the test to compare her strokes and her game. But what should have been pleasurable turned out to be humiliating. She planned the day carefully and arranged with her school principal to be dismissed early. Her parents accompanied her to Berkeley to watch her play against the national champion. The contest lasted just twenty minutes. Helen Wills pounded away with all of her might and won twelve games in a row. She didn't care to rally. She just scored. Then Wills said she had homework to do and hurried off the court. Jacobs remained to play some more and to play off her "scarcely tapped energies against one of the club's men players."

Even then Helen Jacobs was puzzled by the behavior of Helen Wills. "I had been used to more informality in practice games," she said, "and even in matches, than the rather stony solemnity of this presumably casual meeting." Jacobs, who was fifteen at the time, wondered "then if the unchanging expression of my opponent's face and her silence when we passed at the net on odd games were owing entirely to deep concentration; or whether they weren't perhaps a psychological weapon." Observations of dozens of her matches over the years followed—with Jacobs across the net from her during many of them. And Jacobs concluded that the psychological bullying was the more important to Helen than concentration.

Because of Pop Fuller's coaching methods, which encouraged each player to find and then perfect her own game rather than to follow certain iron absolutes, Helen Jacobs developed a game that was her own and far different from that of Helen Wills. Big Helen relied primarily on her big forehand drive and on power. Jacobs relied more on a forehand slice and on spin. On grass courts her forehand slice robbed an opponent of power on a return, and it had to be watched carefully by an opponent in order to be struck with any pace. Although her game did not present the breathtaking display of dominance that Wills showed again and again, Jacobs did have considerable success. She was the first player to win four successive singles titles at Forest Hills.

Yet despite those successes, she is best remembered, as are many athletes, ironically, not for the matches she won but for the matches she lost, for the dramatic matches with Helen Wills. For Helen Jacobs stood in the way when Helen Wills wished to set records or to make a comeback. She stood in the way of history, as Wills saw it. And she had to be overcome. She was the proper foil for Helen again and again. And she was, most importantly, a good solid loser.

After Wills beat Jacobs in a tournament for the first time, and a handful of spectators watched the quick licking, the word went out that Jacobs would never test Wills, and that she would never beat her. "They could play every day for the next twenty years, and Jacobs wouldn't take a set." one expert said.

That was in 1925. That same year Jacobs won the junior national title again. That same year she met Bill Tilden. It was just before the finals of the tournament. Tilden met her and Sam Hardy and Sumner Hardy, and he said he would like to practice with her. Tilden and Sumner Hardy hit different strokes to her, helping her practice her slice. The next afternoon she won her title in love sets.

A profile of her that year in *Sunset* magazine called her "Helen the Small" and compared her to "Helen the Great." And the *Sunset* piece noted that among the most striking similarities of the two women was the fact that both had the "stuff" necessary to win national titles and to dominate their sport.

In 1926 Jacobs won both the California and Pacific Coast titles—each left open by the absence of the older Helen. But the next year she found her way blocked by Wills and by a new contender, Englishwoman Betty Nuthall. Jacobs made the Wightman Cup team and then was beaten by Nuthall, although she did take a set from the young English contender.

In 1927 Jacobs had her appendix removed—one year after Wills. The similarities between the women was becoming downright uncanny. The Jacobs family moved to Santa Barbara for Helen's health. But that same year she lost to Wills a second time in the semi-finals at Forest Hills. The score was 6–0, 6–2. She made the natural mistake of trying to play the Wills game—hard hitting from the baseline. And Wills, as with others, lured her into that error and then blasted her off the court.

She became the perpetual number-two player in America; second best was her reputation, the perennial bridesmaid.

The Wills victories over Jacobs were measured not in games but in minutes. In July, 1927, Wills beat Jacobs easily at the Essex County

Club in Manchester, by the Sea, Massachusetts. The match was of prime importance because it was the first meeting of the two on grass, and it also demonstrated how well the younger Helen might hold up under pressure. Wills offered not a single change in emotion as she reeled off game after game against Jacobs. Each player employed the driving game from the baseline, one with top spin, the other with underspin. Jacobs, who had had beaten Mallory earlier in the tournament, seemed helpless.

In 1928 Jacobs traveled to Wimbledon, became ill, and was beaten by the South African Daphne Akhurst. She showed the first signs of heart trouble during the match, and after play her lips were blue. The physician at Wimbledon wanted to rush her to a hospital. He did not understand why she had been allowed to continue the match. But she continued to practice and play and was crushed later that year by Wills at Forest Hills.

The refusal of the USLTA to send Jacobs east in 1929 to Europe was a crushing blow. And the fact that Wills had selected the players was a personal insult. She was the second ranked player in the country and was completely overlooked by the association officials. It was an act and an oversight almost unprecedented in other sports. Yet, as far as the USLTA was concerned in 1929, Jacobs didn't exist. So her friends intervened. They raised the funds for her trip. She went to Europe and lost in both the French and English championships. The season was a disaster for her.

In England she played a preliminary tournament, at the old Gypsy Club tournament in London. She beat Molla Mallory easily, and won the tournament. Then she injured herself in practice, tearing a muscle in her side. She entered the Beckenham tournament "with the understanding that I would default if my doctor thought it advisable." In the quarter-final match, against Evelyn Colyer, she won the first set, and was leading 5-1 in the second, and was at match point when she suddenly defaulted. She played at Wimbledon and lost in the finals to Wills. Some of her friends expected her to win. Among the reasons she did not win, she wrote later, was "because I was so anxious to win it." She then lost in the quarter-final round to Phoebe Watson at Forest Hills.

In 1930 after a disastrous season on the Riviera, defeat by Wills at Roland-Garros, defeat at Wimbledon in an early round, and then defeat in the quarter-finals at Forest Hills by Cilli Aussem, she returned to California. Each year, it seemed, the chances of her ever confronting and beating Wills grew more remote. In 1931 she met Wills for the fifth time, at Seabright, New Jersey, and Big Helen blasted Little Helen in love sets in thirty-two minutes. The gap between the two was growing.

But in 1932 Jacobs won more games from Wills in a set (4) than ever before. She lost at Wimbledon to Wills, 6-3, 6-1, and then won the Seabright tournament and the national title when Wills scratched from both.

Then came 1933. Jacobs started the 1933 season confidently but then was beaten in France and in England, and her chances at Forest Hills, with Wills returning, seemed minimal. Yet she continued to possess what one writer called a "superhuman tenacity to excel." And in watching Wills and in playing against her she thought she had learned how to beat her. Of course, all the women knew how to beat her, what game would be required. They just couldn't play that game. Wills wouldn't let them. To beat Wills, Jacobs found, you simply had to play the same game against her that the men played. You had to come to the net, and you had to hit drop shots that drew Helen in where she was "not naturally agile, very imaginative nor subtle with the volley." But the difficulty in this was "in making the opening to get to the net, for, aware of her limitations in that position, Helen had perfected a defense against the volleyer that required on the part of her opponent a baseline game as sound as the net game."

And to play Helen Wills, Jacobs knew, was to play a powerful machine. There was little conversation during a match, no levity. It was not fun to play against her, Jacobs found. "Matches against her were fun only in the sense that one derives fun from putting one's skills against the champion's: Most of Helen's opponents whom I knew well and played often had the same impression. Yet all had the greatest admiration for her game, and if the indomitable quality of her match play could only be sustained by concentration that must exclude every possible diversion, that was her business, for it is the undeniable purpose of champions to win."

So Jacobs lost her first confrontation in a championship final with Wills. And the saga of "the Two Helens" was born. Newspapermen concentrated on the "cat fight" aspect of the meetings between the two and insisted that they disliked each other personally and that they were carrying on a "feud." Each denied that there was a feud and accused the newsmen of making something out of nothing in order to create colorful copy. Each was concerned primarily with winning. Each was a good competitor. Each was a champion. And each insisted she was above anything like a feud. And, yet, those close to the women knew better. Fred Moody told me, "Helen really hated Helen Jacobs. Don't ask me why. I can never understand women. But Helen hated her like nothing else." And Edith Cross, another close friend of Wills's, laughed when I asked if the feud existed. "Of course it did," she told me. "Helen Wills hated Helen Jacobs. She just hated her."

Cross recalled an event in 1930 when Wills arrived at Wimbledon early for the Wightman Cup matches. She placed her clothing and rackets in the Lady Champion's dressing room. Then the rest of the team arrived, and someone told Jacobs to put her belongings in that dressing room too, for the time being. She did. When Wills returned and found Jacob's bags and rackets next to her own, she opened the window of the dressing room and chucked them out. The other players found them, picked them up, and apologized. Wills never did.

There are many stories concerning the origin of the feud. Some indicate that Jacobs was always right there on Wills's heels in the tournaments, a perennial opponent, and it was only natural that no love was lost between them. Others, however, point to a confrontation between the two players in 1925. Wills believed that one of the women in the gallery at Forest Hills during the Wightman Cup matches when she was booed for being late was Helen Jacobs's mother, who had been outspoken in her criticism of Wills's arrogance. Still others indicate that an exchange took place between Helen Wills and Helen Jacobs with several double entendres which Helen Wills at first did not understand. When she did she was embarrassed and then shocked and then enraged. That exchange and Wills's reaction to it, they say, explain her words to Jacobs at the end of their 1933 match in the finals at Forest Hills. Helen Wills after that never wanted to be alone anywhere at any time with Helen Jacobs. One of Jacobs''s biographers, Charles Johnston, wrote in 1934 that she had been dubbed "the Rattlesnake of the West." It was a nickname, no doubt, that Helen Wills could have given her.

In 1929 the USLTA sent an international team to Europe to represent the United States in a series of international matches. Helen Wills headed the team and was given the partner of her choosing. She chose Edith Cross rather than Jacobs, who was ranked second and was expected to be invited that year. "I could see no justification for the decision," Jacobs wrote, "nor could I understand the tennis association's acquiescence in it, considering the fact that it customarily chose its own teams."

Most of the men writing about women's sports at the time—Al Laney, Grantland Rice, Paul Gallico, McGeehan, among others—shared a strong bias towards women athletes. Laney believed that in women's tennis, for example, the contest was not as important as the personalities—"personalities count as much as skill," he wrote. One of the principal and deplorable maxims of the sports-writing fraternity in the 1920s and long after was that, while the meeting of two well-matched male athletes presented something like "a clash of the gods," or "a classic confrontation," when two evenly matched females met, like Helen Wills and Suzanne Lenglen or Helen Wills and Helen Jacobs, the writers inevitably described it, much to their own delight and to the delight, it appears, of their readers, as "a cat fight." Even Jack Dempsey said at the time that he believed that women were too earnest in their battles with each other, and that female athletes went in too much for "massacres" rather than simple defeats. Laney believed that only when one concentrated on personalities was women's tennis raised to a plane equal in importance and interest with men's—then and only then. The Jacobs-Wills confrontations and animosities were great press because of the contrasting personalities of the two women and because of the shared belief that their hatreds were primal.

In 1929 tennis enthusiasts in San Francisco and Berkeley who believed that Jacobs deserved the chance to play in Europe sponsored her trip to

Europe. And she won her way to the finals of the International Hard Court Tournament, where she again met Wills, who beat her easily, 6–1, 6–2. The line decisions in the match were particularly bad, and most went against Jacobs. As a result, the crowd took its anger out on Wills, who was booed again and again but was not bothered by the response. She remembered that she was so deeply into the match that she could think of nothing else. Jacobs got only to the round of eight at Wimbledon that year where she was beaten by Cilli Aussem of Germany. And in 1930 she was put out of Wimbledon in the quarter-finals by Hilda Krahwinkel. That year neither Jacobs nor Wills played at Forest Hills, and in 1931 Wills won it, and Jacobs won it, in the absence of Wills, in 1932. In 1932 Wills had beaten Jacobs in the Wimbledon final, 6–3, 6–1, and Dorothy Round beat her in three sets in the semifinals in 1933.

In the spring of 1933 in Paris, Jacobs was watching the quarter-finals at the International Hard Court Championships at the Stade Roland-Garros when a woman sat down next to her and struck up a conversation— a conversation that was to lead to a monumental match later that summer at Forest Hills. Before the quarter-final match was over, Jacobs stood to leave in order to get in some practice before dark. Then the woman who sat beside her said, "You're Miss Jacobs, aren't you?"

"Yes."

"I'd like to play with you."

Jacobs realized that the woman addressing her was Suzanne Lenglen. Jacobs had never met her, but she now recognized her from photographs, cartoons, and caricatures. And Jacobs had watched the Goddess from a great distance in December 1926 in San Francisco when her father had taken her to see C. C. Pyle's touring professional troupe. Helen Jacobs had been at the time, just another face in the crowd, a young woman inspired by the great Suzanne who would practice a little harder and dream a little more ambitiously after seeing what a woman athlete might accomplish. "Watching Suzanne Lenglen," she wrote later, "I was fascinated by the artistry of the player who was six times winner of the World's Championship at Wimbledon, losing only thirty-two games in five final matches; and who, before turning professional, had defeated Helen Wills in the Carlton Club Tournament, Cannes." A feat that Little Helen seemed incapable of duplicating. "I felt as I did when Bill Tilden first asked me if I would let him give me some pointers—as anyone would."

"I'd love to play at any time," Jacobs replied. So they agreed to play the next afternoon. Jacobs was excited by the prospect of playing against the "incomparable Suzanne" and so she prepared for the game as if she were playing a final match at Forest Hills, Wimbledon, or Paris. "I think the details of our practice are worth mentioning; certainly, they made a lasting impression upon me," Jacobs wrote years later.

Lenglen and Jacobs played on the court behind the stadium that was visible from the stadium. The stands were filled as word passed among those present that Lenglen was about to play, so a large throng began to follow the two women, more interested in seeing Suzanne play again than in watching the men's competition in the stadium. "Many of them were running to get a front-row seat, and by the time we arrived at the court we had to request our way through the crowd," Jacobs remembered.

Lenglen then explained the point she wished to make. She predicted that Jacobs would be defending her American title at Forest Hills in August. And she would almost certainly play Helen Wills Moody in the final. And she knew how to beat Big Helen. And she wanted to show Jacobs how to do it. "And I was willing to learn, having thus far in five matches against my compatriot been beaten in straight sets." Jacobs recalled. But she was reluctant to take the lesson before so many spectators, "who, I think, would have come to see Suzanne shovel snow." "I wanted my lesson in private. I wanted to concentrate, to ask questions. However, there was nothing I could do about it, so I determined to learn as much as I could under the circumstances."

The crowd troubled Lenglen not at all. They adored her. She was obviously still the Goddess to them. She spoke to Jacobs as though no one else was present, explaining that she seldom played to score but preferred to rally. Then she said, "I am going to fire you a succession of shots, from the baseline to the net along your right sideline. Hit them all to this point," and she pointed with her racket to the right-hand corner of her right service court. "Helen Wills can run forever along the baseline. But she does not like to run up and back, so you must learn to bring your shots low and angled, into the forecourt."

Jacobs began to make straight, low drives crosscourt. Lenglen returned the shots, drawing Jacobs closer to the net with each shot. Jacobs hit as hard as she could, hoping to score. It didn't seem possible to her that someone with a grip like Suzanne's—with her thumb across the broad back bevel of the handle in the continental grip—could hit with such accuracy and pace. But with little apparent effort or movement she hit back shots that Jacobs believed were almost impossible to get. Lenglen outplayed Jacobs. It was a lesson, a teacher and a student. She used variety in her hitting, giving Jacobs every imaginable sort of shot to work with. And she told her, "It is a tennis crime to hit a ball into the net. During a rally, keep it about two feet above the net, and then, when you have made your opening, reduce your margin and hit for the winner." Jacobs remembered the advice as the most valuable she heard that afternoon.

She found herself more tired after the lesson than after any match she'd ever played. For ninety minutes the two players had rallied back and forth without a break. "Suzanne, as nervous and high-strung as a colt at the starting wire, couldn't bear to be motionless. If she wasn't hitting the ball and running, she was bouncing the ball on the court."

Suzanne Lenglen practiced several more times with Jacobs during the following week, talking to her, encouraging her, watching her, imitating

Big Helen, showing how Big Helen was vulnerable. Stressing the fact that Big Helen was beatable. She was beatable. All Jacobs had to do was to see how to beat her and to believe she could.

In March, Helen and Fred drove down to Carmel on the coast, where friends lent them a cottage. Helen remembered later that she was in a hurry to put on her bathing suit, and she lifted a heavy tennis bag from the rumble seat of the car while standing on one foot. Then in the afternoon she carried a number of rocks from the beach to a rock garden near the house. "My back felt strangely weak after that, and I was not to feel really well again, and as I had before, for almost two years."

In May they departed for Europe again. On the boat on the way over she felt strange pains in her back. She concluded that she would be able to work out the pain and play tennis. "I had found the best way to overcome muscular stiffness was not to stop tennis entirely, but to play a little each day until it disappeared."

During a busy social schedule that spring in England, Helen Wills practiced daily, but found herself favoring her back when running down balls on the sidelines. So she altered her strokes slightly, favoring her back, in order not to twist unnecessarily. She cut short on her follow-through. As a result, her shots lost a little power and a little top spin and tended to float more after crossing the net. So she slowed down the strokes more and cut back more on power. She was taking a terrific gamble in all of this; the gamble that if she altered her game she could still win, using her deftness and her mind in place of the power. But she noticed that her "game seemed to have lost some of its snap." She was unsure as to the cause of it and concluded then that it must have something to do with her shoes. She switched from high heels to low heels for the street. But there was no improvement. She began to have a daily massage.

On June 9 she played an exhibition and the next day, before going to Wimbledon to practice, had her back massaged again. Now the pain was nagging and continual, especially, she noticed, on cold days. During practice she gave up altogether on chasing down balls that hit along the sidelines because of the pain of reaching for them.

Wills visited a back specialist, who diagnosed her as suffering from a strained lower back. He advised rest. As a result, Helen skipped the singles in a warm-up tournament at Beckenham, but played in the doubles with Elizabeth Ryan and lost. She blamed the loss on herself; Ryan agreed with her.

Then she played at Wimbledon and, as in the past, won her early matches in straight sets. She seemed to be in top form. She was seeded first among the women, followed by Round and Scriven of England. Jacobs was fifth. She drew a bye in the opening round of the tournament and in the second beat Mrs. J. R. Macready in love sets. Then she moved steadily and easily toward her final match. She gave up two games against young Mary Heeley. Sylvia Henrotin won three games in the first set against

Wills, then collapsed in the second set which Wills won at love. In the round of eight Wills beat Lolette Payot of Switzerland, 6–4, 6–1. She played Hilda Krahwinkel in the semis, while Jacobs played Round. The Jacobs-Round match proved to be an endurance contest won by the English player 4–6, 6–4, 6–2. In the Wills-Krahwinkel match there was little excitement, as Helen reverted to her "tennis machine" tactic—staying on the baseline, returning everything the German woman hit, letting her beat herself with errors. Krahwinkel lost 6–4, 6–3.

Helen Wills then gained the chance to tie Suzanne Lenglen's record of six wins in the singles. She almost failed. And when she almost failed, that was front-page news. She did become the only American singles champion that year, as Ellsworth Vines fell to Jack Crawford, a young Australian. Helen Wills remained America's hope in international sports competition. And although she almost failed, she, in fact didn't fail. She just wasn't perfect any longer.

Her victory over Dorothy Round came on July 8, 1933. Crawford had brought the men's singles crown back to the Empire on the previous day for the first time in eleven years, and now English fans hoped Round could do the same. She was the first Englishwoman to reach the finals since 1926, when McKane won the title.

The first sign of difficulty for Wills in the whole tournament came in the finals. And it was unexpected. Round, a parson's daughter, had already lost to Wills several times before. Today, the newsmen present expected, was just an encore of the same old song.

The day of the match was a curious one, Wills recalled, warm and humid and cloudy with rain threatening. She thought about the possibility of rain and the interruption of the match and the problems that might follow in the interruption of her timing. There was standing room only for the crowd of 16,000.

Then the match was delayed, not because of the weather, but because news arrived that the King and Queen were on their way to the stadium. King George and Queen Mary were fifteen minutes late for the Wimbledon final, and Wills and Round obligingly waited until they were seated before beginning. Queen Mary was especially interested in seeing the match.

The first set went to four all, and then Wills pushed ahead to win 6–4. The set was a long one, and there was a lot of running from side to side, and Round's forehand, Helen recalled, seemed to be working particularly well. Wills remembered of the second set that "it was an unusual one which could perhaps be better understood from the sidelines than by the players on the court. I can remember that I did not know exactly what was happening, since there seemed to be so much excitement." The set went to six all, each player holding service through twelve games. Round then went ahead on her own service, 7–6. But Wills led 40–30 in the fourteenth game of the set. Then came a bad call, and that helped give

Round the game and the set. Round hit a drive that fell a good three or four inches beyond the baseline, most observers agreed. But the linesman said nothing. Helen Wills didn't even try for the ball. Then she looked at the linesman waiting for his decision. He remained silent. Wills seemed astonished for a moment. Perhaps she hadn't heard him. Then after pausing a few seconds longer she turned away, apparently accepting his decision. But then the umpire intervened and called the ball out and gave the point to Wills. He said later that he thought the linesman had called the ball out. The linesman stood up and walked to the umpire's stand and told the umpire that the decision should be reversed. There was more talk with the other linesmen joining in. During this dispute Wills walked back to the wood barrier and waited, as did Round at the opposite end of the court. The argument became heated and took several minutes. The scorekeeper was obviously confused by this time and kept flashing different scores on the scoreboard. Had Helen Wills been given the point, the game would have been hers. Then the umpire made a decision and declared that the shot had been good and that the score was deuce. Round served again. Wills failed to make a return. Round served again and hit a winner off Wills's return and won the set, 8–6.

Round scored many points in the second set by the use of drop shots that brought Wills to the net. Round followed these with lobs that drove her back. And although the tactic won a set for the Englishwoman, the persistence with which she used it helped contribute to her loss of the match. Drop shots "have to be absolutely perfect before they can be entirely effective," Wills observed, "and there is hardly a player who can make a perfect drop shot every time." And in time Wills adjusted to Round's tactic and beat it, hitting the lobs for winners after anticipating them perfectly. Yet Round continued to use them, believing, apparently, that Wills's adjustment was temporary. Round told me of the match, "I used tactics to draw her up to the net, rather than side to side. This could be used today, I'm sure. But playing her was heartbreaking, as she rarely made unforced errors."

The match never returned to normal. Both women were obviously upset. Round hit a drop shot, and Wills never tried for it. After serving or returning service she stayed in the backcourt and hit gentle floating balls to Round, hitting for the corners. She even surprised Round with a drop shot that scored for her. Wills went ahead, but she amazed the crowd by her lack of spirit, her refusal to move from the baseline. She figured that all she had to do to win was to let Round beat herself by making errors. She did that. The final set was not so much won by Wills as lost by Round, 6–3.

In the stands watching the match, studying the play, sat Suzanne Lenglen. She never took her eyes off Helen. She had been right. Now if Jacobs could just believe.

Helen Wills said later that blistered feet prevented her from running very much. So "my head assumed most of their burden, and I mixed my shots and placed them more accurately than if I had been able to charge about."

In the dressing room after the game, Wills had difficulty removing her shoes and socks and found that the soles of her feet were bloody. She poured alcohol on the blisters and then bandaged her feet. Unable to walk, she spent the next four days in bed. She sailed then for the United States.

Helen Wills lost a set in 1933, and the vulnerability of the American Girl was exposed. Her spell—like that of Lenglen before 1921 at Forest Hills—was broken. She was it was suspected, beatable.

Following the match, the London *Daily Herald* published an interview with Wills in which she made several controversial statements. "You may take it from me," she was quoted as saying, "this is the last time—so far as I know now—that I'll defend my singles title in England. I will not be at Wimbledon next year." The statement was construed as a feeling that Helen Wills blamed the English officiating for upsetting her concentration and timing and the subsequent break in her string of set victories.

Back in Berkeley, Dr. Wills insisted that Helen had been misquoted. "My impression is," he said, "that Helen will continue to play competitive tennis as long as she is on top of her game. When I last saw her, there was no indication from her conversation that she contemplated making this her last trip abroad. In fact, it was rather my feeling that she plans to continue until such time as she may feel it better to step aside. Helen truly loves competitive tennis and she will not easily be persuaded to abandon it. "And as regards the so-called disputed point, that was of minor consequence," Dr. Wills said. "I am sure it did not disturb Helen or interfere with her game." In her victory, Al Laney observed, "she had shown signs of fatigue and nervousness." Helen Wills was gradually falling back to where the other players were, just as Tilden had done earlier.

As a sidelight, Helen was, Fred Moody told me, being harassed by a young man in London, who sent notes to her and tried always to catch her eye. He appeared at her matches sitting at courtside. Finally, Fred contacted Scotland Yard, and the young man was detained. He was from a good family, Fred remembered, and should have known better. He stopped chasing Helen, but he had done his damage in upsetting her. She was not sure whether or not he meant her harm; it was another of the distractions faced by the star.

When Wills arrived in America, the usual battery of reporters greeted her. They wanted now to know about the loss of the set to Round. Wills didn't make much of it. She said Round was a good player, had excellent shots, and a good tennis mind and that she herself had not played well. Would she compete at Forest Hills and in the Wightman competitions? "I like to play tennis," she said, "and as long as I feel that way I shall continue playing. Some time the fun will go out of it and then I'll stop.

It's too early now to say whether I'll return to England to play at Wimbledon next year. Wimbledon is a long way from California."

She seemed calm and not at all disturbed by the brouhaha surrounding the loss of a set. She didn't try to change the subject. She showed the reporters the two dogs she brought with her. "They're so gentle," she said to an inquiring reporter who reached out to touch one. "What fine dogs," he agreed, just before one named Bossie jumped up and bit him on the hand. The ship's doctor was called to administer iodine. Helen told no reporters how badly her back was bothering her. And none asked about it.

Fred proceeded on to California with the dogs while Helen stayed behind, tried to loosen her muscles and prepare for the retaking of her national title and for the Wightman Cup matches. Fred urged her not to play any more that season, to return to California with him. But she recalled later, "I said I was there and might just as well stay on for a couple of weeks, that I would be better certainly and that it might be my last chance to play at Forest Hills." But she did not tell Fred how tired she was, "an inexplicable weariness that I had never felt before nor how totally I had lost all confidence in my ability to coordinate, nor how uninterested I had become in playing tennis."

The pains that afflicted her were everywhere, she recalled, "down my back and leg and into my toes of my right foot. My right leg didn't do as it was told, because it seemed numb. I felt uncertain at each step, and this indecision made me think indecisively when in action. The only thing that I was sure of was when I would be all right in a few days."

At Forest Hills, Helen Wills took her usual room in the tower at the Inn so as to be near the courts. Then she visited Dr. Benjamin Farrell of the New York Orthopaedic Hospital, who took X-rays of her back. The doctor prescribed some belts for back support. But by the time of the Wightman Cup competitions, Helen was worse. Farrell now told her not to play and wrote a letter saying so on August 3. The USLTA's Julian Myrick inquired of the physician about her condition, and he was told the details and the doctor's opinion that it would be unwise for her to play tennis for three or four days or until the discomfort and pain in her back was gone. He suggested complete rest.

Wills was expected to be a member of the Wightman Cup team. But on August 4 she bowed out of the competition. Julian Myrick made the announcement. The statement quoted her physician and relieved Helen of the onus of making the decision herself.

When the crowd that gathered for the opening matches heard over the loudspeaker the sober announcement that Helen Wills would not be playing, they listened for a few moments quietly and then as the physician's diagnosis was read, many in the crowd broke into "refined giggling," because, as Westbrook Pegler wrote, "the voice went on to recite the doctor's diagnosis in a lot of Latin, which seemed to denote nothing less than galloping disintegration, but turned out to mean just a pain in the back."

Helen Jacobs emerged as the heroine of the competition, beating Dorothy Round in two sets—something Helen Wills had not done at Wimbledon—and Margaret Scriven in three. Her wins were surprising since she had lost three tournament matches earlier in the season, and many thought her day was past.

A poignant presence at the competition was Molla Mallory, who sat at courtside watching, and when the Round-Jacobs match ended, she stood to leave and was completely ignored by the reporters and broadcasters, who rushed past her to question Jacobs.

Wills sat at courtside when Jacobs played her tough three-set match against Scriven. And she was ready to play in the doubles with Alice Marble if Jacobs lost. But Jacobs won, so Wills was not needed to save the day.

Helen Wills did decide to go for the national title again, and to comply with the wishes of the USLTA. It was hoped a large crowd would come out to see her go for her eighth national title.

Marjorie Morrill Painter, a close friend of Helen's, told me that Helen had told her of the severe pain in her back "but thought she should play at Forest Hills, because the USLTA had sent her all over Europe, and she owed them so much gratitude for what they had done for her, that she should be a sport, as they counted on her for the gate. I want you to understand what she went through. I was playing once and thought someone had thrown a brick at me, I was hit by such a severe pain and I had pulled a muscle. It was horrible."

Many fans came out to see her win, and an equally large number, some sportswriters assumed, came to see her lose. They would have been happy—very happy, many of them—just to see the Queen lose a set. And if, in fact, that was the case, then they were in for a pleasant time.

⁘{ 8 }⁘

The tournament represented something revolutionary. And Helen Jacobs was in the vanguard in this. She was even more nervous than usual because she was about to introduce tennis shorts in the national tournament. The innovator in tennis dress had been, not surprisingly, Suzanne Lenglen. She had introduced the new style in Paris in 1933 at Roland-Garros, where she played an exhibition match wearing what John Tunis described as "a brassière and shorts" against a promising young French player, André Merlin. Today it would be called a halter top and shorts. "Suzanne converted me instantly to shorts," Tunis said. "Now I am not quite so sure about them." Some of the women who adopted shorts at Forest Hills, he said, were "slim, trim and dainty" and so looked very good in the new clothes. But more than once during the tournament, he wrote, seeing the women in shorts had reminded him of a line from Ogden Nash, "But ladies, have you seen yourselves retreating?" But since shorts provided for a better and faster game, he was for it. And the spectators would just have to get used to it.

One player, however, was noteworthy in her staunch refusal to wear shorts: Helen Wills. She elected to play in her white knee-length skirt and white blouse with her red sweater. She never did wear shorts. When I asked about this she said that skirts never bothered her and never ever hampered her movement on the court. Skirts were cool and free flowing, she felt, and she enjoyed wearing a skirt and never even considered wearing shorts. John Tunis wondered about this and said, "To tell the truth, I rather expected that with the added handicap of skirts flapping about her knees, Mrs. Moody would have considerable difficulty coming through against those young Amazons from London and California. Not at all. Can it be that it takes more than a pair of pants to become a world champion?"

Helen Wills mowed down every adversary in the early rounds of the tournament. And Tunis wrote that, although the margin between the Queen and the pretenders was narrowing, there was still a margin, and a large one at that. He wrote the line just before Helen's semifinal match against Betty Nuthall.

Tunis was the first writer to be bothered by something else at Forest Hills in 1933. He found, suddenly, an amazing lack of variety in the games of the younger women players. They were starting, it seemed, to play pretty much alike. They were copying the more successful players, and they were getting coaching. No one seemed to be developing a distinctive individual style any more. Everyone looked and played alike. Everything now, he wrote, "was slug, slug, slug." There was no change of pace, no varying tactics, no back-up game. And watching the newer players, he concluded: "At this rate, there isn't any particular reason Mrs. Moody shouldn't be champion in 1945, if she so desires." Plainly, he thought, Helen Wills was the best player in the country. Helen Jacobs was the second best, just as obviously.

Jacobs introduced shorts in the tournament. She wore pleated shorts in practice several days before the tournament began and on August 15 wore them in her debut. They were, newspapers observed, "the scantiest attire ever worn by a queen of American tennis." But she felt they were an advantage. "Nothing but prejudice has prevented our wearing them for years," she said. "I know they improve my game, and all the other girls say the same. I know I've lost many points through my racket catching in my skirt. Not only that but they're cooler and enable one to get around so much faster. Particularly in the latter stages of a hard match," she said. British player "Bunny" Austin had caused a mild sensation when he appeared in shorts in the men's national tournament in 1932, but no protest was planned by officials this year when Jacobs appeared. Alice

Marble and Caroline Babcock also wore them. Three British players—Round, Heeley, and James—donned shorts in preliminary tournaments but reverted to skirts for the Wightman Cup competition and the national championships.

And so the tournament became one of interest to feminists, too. To them, according to the *San Francisco Chronicle,* the tournament became "the battle of skirts versus shorts." And the feminists, according to another writer, felt that if Jacobs, wearing "charmingly abbreviated pantettes, decisively defeated the skirted Mrs. Moody, the emancipation of womankind would be one step nearer to realization." Sportswear manufacturers were also interested and rooting wildly for Jacobs for less lofty reasons. They believed that if a woman wearing shorts could defeat the beskirted Big Helen, it would bring a tremendous boom—in the midst of the Depression—to the shorts market. Any change in style was lucrative in the women's wear trade.

There were many surprises in the tournament. Among them was rain—persistent rain, during the early rounds. The rain caused postponements and delays, and Helen Wills found herself getting depressed by the weather and felt her muscles stiffen from forced inactivity. It wasn't only the fans who were against her now, but nature too.

Among the women not figured to make it into the final rounds was the defending national champion, Helen Jacobs. It was, the bettors suggested with the odds, to be a Wills-Round final, and a great one. The gate would be substantial. The draw placed Wills and Round in opposite halves, increasing the chance for a great final. The players were seeded in 1933 by nationality. So Wills was ranked number one and so was Round—among the English. The final could see two number one ranked players—another unique situation.

In the opening round she played a highly ranked Californian, Dr. Esther Bartosh. Bartosh crumbled before Helen, 6–2, 6–2.

But her back bothered her after the match. Helen tried to recover. She stayed in bed when she wasn't practicing. When she stood up, she found, the room would whirl about and black spots appear before her eyes until she sat down again. She said she didn't feel like seeing anyone and she told no one how she felt except for Mrs. Louis Carruthers, whose husband was a former president of the USLTA. Mrs. Carruthers had been a close friend since Helen first came east to Forest Hills in 1921.

Helen attempted to will away the pain. She tried positive thinking and tried hard to convince herself that she had no illness. She started to believe that she was just imagining the pain, "because I could not explain to my own satisfaction where it came from." I was convinced that if I gave in to it, I would be bowing to nerves. She hated that idea. She wrote in her autobiography that "after years of the sort of discipline that match competition imposes, not occasionally, but continuously, what would have seemed a matter of course to a sensible person, seemed to me to be heresy. While I may have been wasting effort on something that would seem to others unimportant, it was to me the thing of the moment. I *would* get well, and each morning I expected to wake up feeling all right."

No American had seen Helen Wills lose even a set to another woman since her defeat in Rye, New York, in 1926 when, weakened by recent surgery, she was beaten by Molla Mallory, who went on to win the national title that year.

Wills's strokes looked as good as ever, and the crowd greeted her drives with the familiar "ohs" and "ahs" of years past. But Jacobs also seemed to be playing well, beating Eunice Dean in love sets in the opening round. On the second day the crowds trooped out to see Wills beat Grace Surber, 6–2, 6–1. "It was just another waltz for the peerless Helen," Allison Danzig wrote in the *New York Times*. But she did concede some points she might have made earlier on. She didn't run for some shots. Jacobs eliminated Kathryn Pearson, 6–2, 6–1.

In the next round both Wills and Jacobs beat opponents in straight sets—Wills, Mrs. L. R. C. Mitchell and Jacobs, Freda James. Jacobs wavered in the next round against Josephine Cruikshank of Santa Ana, pulling out an 11–9, 6–4 win. But Wills that day beat Mary Heeley. She won eleven games in a row before Heeley took two, then Wills won one more.

Helen Wills wrote that she was surprised to have reached even the semifinals, the way she was feeling. Betty Nuthall, whom she was playing, was always a difficult opponent for her. And during the match, "My mind would tell me where to go, but there was no answering action. It was curious. Nor could I bend over, as a strange stiffness had taken hold of my right leg and back when I went against it there was a tremendous pain. I learned later that this viselike rigidity was a muscle spasm which is brought on by muscles trying to protect injured nerves and tissue. It was to take almost two years for it to disappear."

With more than 8000 fans watching and expecting little more than a routine clipping of the Englishwoman, the unexpected happened. Playing extraordinary tennis—the best of her life, in fact—Nuthall took the offense from the opening shot of the first game and in just twelve minutes did what only one other woman had done since 1927—took a set from Wills at 6–2. The crowd was both stunned and delighted. Jacobs, who was watching the match, found that Nuthall's quick assault seemed to baffle Wills. And she believed Wills could be beaten. She believed. "Betty couldn't miss," she remembered. And again and again Nuthall left Wills flatfooted as she raked the lines with her ground strokes. Nuthall made no errors in that first set.

It was only the second set Wills had lost since 1927. She seemed only to wave at the balls that hit the chalk lines around her. But she hung on, steadied herself in the second set, and came back to win. Wills won the second set but it included such an extraordinary fluke that through the coming days and weeks writers, officials, and fans alike were at a loss trying to explain how it could possibly have happened. Apparently, Nut-hall's first-set victory put the crowd of 8000 in some sort of daze. Because nobody seemed to notice that in the middle of the second set Helen Wills served two games in a row. The incident is without parallel in American tournament annals.

The umpire for the Moody-Nuthall match was Rufus Davis. Wills was leading 3–1 in the second set with her serve to come from the north end of the court. She lost her service, and then she and Nuthall changed ends. New balls were due, and they had been thrown out in the previous game. The new balls were held by ball boy Paul Nesbit, at the south end of the court. They should have been thrown to the north end, but as Wills was serving from that end, a mistake was made. She lost her service, and the score went to 3–2. The players changed ends of the court. Wills walked to the service line at her end and turned to Nesbit and asked for the balls. Nesbit knew that she should not serve again. But when she saw him hold-ing the balls she turned to him and asked for them. He faced a dilemma. "Should I have told her that she couldn't have them?" he asked later. Then he thought he might have lost count of the games and was mistaken or had forgotten something. Maybe Helen hadn't just served and lost? Maybe the women had not just changed ends of the court. Maybe he had just dozed off for a fraction of a second. Nobody else said anything, so after a moment's hesitation he threw her the balls.

Wallis Merrihew of *American Lawn Tennis* was sitting in a box No. 9 on the south side of the stadium. Suddenly in the middle of the game he sensed that something was wrong and looked at his notes. He guessed what had happened and turned to Manuel Alonso in the next box, and the two men said simultaneously, "She served the game ahead of this." Sarah Palfrey was sitting next to him, and she agreed. But by the time someone got the attention of umpire Davis, Helen had lost again, and the score was 3–3. Then to make matters even more confusing, Davis announced the score again as 3–2 and waited for the women to change ends of the court again.

At that moment, Fred Pond, chairman of the West Side Tennis Club tournament committee, rushed to the box of Dr. S. Ellsworth Davenport II, president of the club, and, as the latter hastened to the umpire chair, the gallery buzzed with excitement. One writer said that Helen Wills serv-ing twice was something like an umpire allowing Babe Ruth to take four strikes in a World Series game. Only a single ball boy seemed to notice what was happening. The extraordinary event, which was not corrected—the women continued to serve in the wrong sequence after that—demon-strated how magnetic Helen was while she played. The gallery and the officials—thirteen officials for the match—watched her, were enthralled and amazed by her, to such a degree that they, just like her in 1924 at Wimbledon, often forgot the details of what was happening. Wills won the next two sets, 6–3, 6–2, and with them the match.

After the last point was scored, a woman in the gallery, overcome with excitement, stood up, screamed, and fainted. It took ten minutes to revive her.

Even after the match Helen Wills was not convinced that she had served twice in a row. "They had better have somebody watch me hereafter," she said smilingly.

While she waited to see who her opponent would be in the final, Wills indicated to one reporter that she was not in good health. She told reporter Michael Foster of the International News Service during a downpour on August 23 while all matches were postponed that on the completion of the matches she would immediately return to the West Coast, "And I'm going to hop right into my bathing suit and get out on the beach when I arrive home. I want to get some California sunshine on my back." Her back caused a good deal of pain, she said. But Foster wrote that "there's no chance of Mrs. Moody's defaulting either in the doubles, where she has reached the semi-finals with Elizabeth Ryan as her partner, or in the singles, where she awaits in the final round, the winner of the Helen Jacobs–Dorothy Round match."

Jacobs, meanwhile, had closely followed the progress of Wills through the lower bracket of the tournament. She was surprised by Nuthall's upset of Wills in one set. Jacobs had played against Nuthall in two successive years of Wightman Cup competition. In the first meeting in 1927 she had beaten Jacobs in three sets by playing precisely the way she played Wills. That was also at Forest Hills. The second time they met, Jacobs won in two sets.

With Wills's victory in the semifinals, it rained, a persistent depressing rain of several days that worked against her. She stayed in the Inn while her rackets warped and the strings broke. She felt her muscles stiffening, and she worried. The other women went to the movies, played bridge, and relaxed. But she continued her daily practice sessions, and on the 24th said "she felt better than she had at any time during the tournament," a statement that contrasted dramatically with what she wrote about the tournament and her activities. Some newsmen suggested that although Helen's back had been bothering her, the rest had given her time for recuperation following the Nuthall match. A real advantage. The other semifinal match, however, was postponed as was the semifinals in the doubles. Jacobs and Round had yet to play. The talk then was of a Wills-Round final. But that was spoiled when Jacobs, the defending champion, using her chop and slice, hit a baffling undercut shot that bounced low and confounded Round. In a long three-set match, Jacobs won 6–4, 5–7, 6–2.

Wills hoped that Round would win. On Sunday, when the match was to be played, Round, a parson's daughter, refused to play. And so the match was postponed until Monday, the 25th. As a result, Jacobs herself had five days to recover from an inflammation of the gall bladder, which had been bothering her off and on all summer for which she had regularly consulted a physician. She attributed her semifinal victory over Round to a windy day and a "low hanging slice, consistently miscalled a chop by the press" and said that Round was a formidable opponent even when she was not at the top of her game.

Just before the singles final, Powell Blackmore's journal indicated that this would be a very difficult day for Helen Wills, indeed. This would be an interesting match, one of those times, some of the reporters realized, when she would have unusual difficulty. Wills tried to remain buoyed up by the belief that she could recapture her crown, crush the upstart champion whom she disliked so much, and return once more—perhaps for the last time, to California. Only a small crowd showed up for the match, expecting a routine walkover.

Jacobs predicted before the match that she would go to the net at every opportunity. There was no sense of waiting on the backcourt to die, exchanging ground strokes, wearing herself down before the Moody assault. She knew though that the net game was not enough in itself. She needed super approach shots, the best she had ever hit, more accurate, more powerful; she knew that Wills would have to feel her presence across the net, Wills's confidence would have to be cracked or shaken. And Jacobs needed to keep her own confidence. But she needed to take away the Wills drives and make her own openings and then slide to the net and cut off those big drives and those attempted passing shots and to smash back those lobs. And she had to believe.

The weather on the day of the match—Saturday, August 26, 1933—was perfect for tennis. There was no wind. It was not hot, and Jacobs found it to be a good day to exploit all the shots and tactics Suzanne Lenglen had advocated—shots that required a perfect touch and little wind interference. And it was, Jacobs found, "a perfect day for the volleyer who disliked more than anything else the drive that cannot be truly gauged, the lob that is pulled suddenly down toward the player by a sudden gust of wind."

USLTA vice president Holcombe Ward brought Wills and Jacobs down the steps to the court. Benjamin H. Dwight was in the chair; Benjamin M. Phillips was the foot fault judge. From the opening shot of the match, Jacobs discovered, Helen was merely going to use her old consistent game, the one that beat Jacobs year after year. She hit to Jacobs forehand and, when Jacobs was off balance, used a short crosscourt drive to the opposite side and then came to the net. But she came too slowly. She came painfully. She came reluctantly. She came without confidence. "The shot was, at its best, a devastating placement, which I was determined to prevent."

To prevent Wills from imposing her game, Jacobs did everything she could in her power and placement of service, with the goal of drawing Wills out of the court for a drive down the opposite side. In the past Wills rifled back her returns, pushing Jacobs herself back, putting her on the defensive, shattering Jacobs's game and her confidence from the opening service. But there was no power behind those returns. The sting was gone. The force was not with her any longer. Jacobs sensed it. She was curious. She was cautious. She remembered Lenglen's advice. And she began to make her cuts, like a picador. She sensed quickly that on this day, before this crowd, after all those years, she was to accomplish what she had never done before.

Jacobs had to take away Wills's shots and impose her own game. She had to hit harder than Wills, make her miss, make her move, make her worry about her own placements. She took care with her service now, trying always to draw Big Helen out of the court, slicing her service in the forehand court, hitting straight and flat in the add court. And she had to keep Wills back from the net or pass her when she came in.

The struggle was fairly even in the first set. Jacobs served first, and the opening three games went with service. In the fourth game, Jacobs broke Wills's service for a 3–1 lead. The loss of that game moved Wills to a driving stonewall defense; she wavered, readjusted her tactics, and began to employ her customary accuracy in corner placements, back and forth, long, harder and harder, coupled with more and more speed. She won the fifth game and then broke back to tie at 3–3. Yet already there were signs of trouble. In the first game Wills had hit a long drive that appeared to be out. It was not called. There was an uproar from the gallery, but the linesman was unmoved. After three games Wills had hit long again, and it wasn't called, and the crowd went wild. This time, Jacobs seemed upset by the call, and referee Louis Carruthers came out and sat beside the umpire's stand. The games went to four-all. Each player then held service until 6–6. Jacobs had never come this far before, had never won so many games in a set from Big Helen.

The Lenglen lessons in psychology were paying off. You have to believe you can do it. Jacobs played like she believed she could win. That bothered Wills. Jacobs earned her way forward, calling up her reserves—reserves not seen on this field of battle before. She raised the level of her game moment by moment by moment. And Wills let some services go by her for aces—services she would have hurled back easily in other days in other years in other matches. Her inability to return some services and the response of Jacobs made Big Helen seem doomed.

In three games in the set Wills had a commanding lead, but let it get away each time. It surprised the crowd. It obviously surprised Big Helen too. Jacobs refused to budge. She refused to lie down and die. The past was gone. History. There was now only the moment, only this tournament, only this afternoon, out of the thousands of afternoons when everything had been far different. Time had caught up with Helen Wills. Her back ached. She perspired. She was dizzy.

In the tenth game of the set, when Jacobs led at 5–4 and 40–30, Wills was serving and took the point and then two more for the game to make it five-all. In the fourteenth game of the set, Big Helen again twice saved set points before dropping the set. Her formerly devastating baseline game just did not punish or intimidate Jacobs the way it had in the past, and she seemed a little confused as to what to do next—her most effective weapon was blunted severely.

Helen Jacobs had let out all the stops, hitting with all of her might on every shot, especially on the service, trying to force Wills away from the net. And she found the safe route to the net for herself. Everything was working well. Then Wills came to the net, and it became a contest to see who would get there first, who would drive the other player back.

Wills forced Jacobs to lob when she came in. Anticipating that, Jacobs had practiced smashing back lobs and now the practice was paying off. The Wills lob had become a feared weapon. Finally it was matched by a new weapon in the Jacobs arsenal: Jacobs broke the Wills service at 6–6 by using sliced drives to the corners and then the volley. She ran out the set on her own service, 8–6. It was the first set she had ever won against Big Helen. It was the second set Wills had lost in this unusual tournament. Jacobs remembered that she had created a record for herself now, winning her first set against Big Helen. But she found it wasn't enough. Not anymore. One set was not enough. She wanted the match. She wanted that title.

There was still a long road ahead. Jacobs knew that. "If I were to win," she wrote, " I must maintain my game at the same level for two more sets, if necessary, and hope that fatigue would impair neither my coordination nor my timing. I did not agree with those who claimed that a woman could not attack the net for three sets. In fact, I found it less tiring to go to the net, volley and smash, than to remain in the backcourt covering twice the ground in pursuit of Helen's magnificent drives."

Wills saw it all differently. "I won the first set, 8–6," she wrote incorrectly, "which was long drawn out, she won the second 6–3. We had long rallies and she was very steady. It would have been a strenuous match for any player. I was trying to meet the competition of the match and the same time was carrying on another fight within myself—one that was between my brain, which was commanding, and my muscles, which were bound in an iron-clad spasm trying to protect the injured nerves of my back."

Jacobs wrote that her winning that first set against Wills 8–6 startled the press at the match into wild activity. "Typewriter and telegraphic instruments clacked furiously from the marquee," she recalled. "To anyone who has watched the great Californian in action in the past it was obvious from the outset that she was not hitting with anything like her accustomed severity," Allison Danzig wrote of Wills. "The speed that subdued her opponents and left them with a feeling of hopelessness even before they went on the court simply was not at Mrs. Moody's command."

In the second set, however, Wills, far from being resigned to defeat, changed her tactics and, as in the past, miraculously turned back the tide.

Instead of hitting for length as she had done in the first set, she now used drop shots, chipping the ball short and then firing deep and then short again, running Jacobs. Jacobs went on the defensive and was kept on the run and trapped again and again. Nonetheless, she went for every ball, no matter how hopeless the effort seemed. And she got some. But most she did not. And she used up a good deal of energy, and she seemed to run out of steam as Big Helen surged ahead 3–0, and the crowd now relaxed somewhat. At 3–0 Big Helen's offensive stalled. Jacobs came back. She won the next three games to put the set at 3–3. But by that time she seemed fatigued.

The most conspicuous incident in the second set came in the seventh game. A point was called against Wills that was clearly, most observers agreed, hers. There was an explosion of protest from the crowd. When the noise subsided and the umpire had sustained the linesman's verdict, Jacobs purposely double-faulted to make the score 15–30. Then she lost the game after a long deuce battle, and then the next two games with them, and then the set as Big Helen applied pressure effectively and won 6–3.

The play in the first two sets was marked by a succession of close line decisions, many of which drew noisy, disruptive demonstrations of disapproval from the gallery. The partisanship seemed passionate in this match, with the crowd heart and soul into the play. And the stadium buzzed with excitement during the ten-minute rest break.

During the break Jacobs was energized. Molla Mallory, who was waiting for Jacobs in her dressing room during the rest period, encouraged her and emphasized over and over again the chance for taking it. Mallory wanted to see her win this one. She wanted to see Wills defeated. She wanted to see Wills defeated at Forest Hills in the same way that Lenglen had been defeated. Jacobs recalled that Molla Mallory was very interested in evening an old score.

During the break Wills became demoralized. Mrs. Carruthers was especially close to Helen Wills and went to the dressing room during the rest period to see how Helen was doing. "Helen was lying on a couch," she remembered, "and she looked utterly spent as any one could possibly be. Her color was almost frightening and there were deep heavy circles under her eyes.

"She has never before taken anything in the nature of a stimulant during a match, but I persuaded her to take some aromatic spirits of ammonia. At the time she complained of a feeling of numbness. During the evening, when I saw her again, the numbness was gone, but she was feeling pain in her back."

The opening game of that third set indicated that Wills's chance of recovering her title were remote. She double-faulted twice. She seemed weak. Jacobs took the game. Jacobs was hitting with confidence and authority and severity and took the second game of the set from 0–30. Big Helen's offense had folded in the first set. Her defense folded in the third. The end was in sight.

In the third game Wills tried almost pathetically to get to the net, to be aggressive, to play the game that produced titles. She made two weak efforts in the game to come in to volley, but each time Jacobs passed her, once on the forehand side, once on the backhand side. On the next point Wills had an easy forehand drive, and she feebly pushed it into the bottom of the net. She was helpless. Trailing 0–3 in the third set, she saw defeat was moments away. And she stopped. The match had gone on for one hour and three minutes.

The score stood at 3–0 when the women changed courts. Jacobs approached the baseline and turned to the ballboy to get the balls for service. She called to him twice, but found him not listening to her or looking at her, but rather staring at the opposite court. Helen Jacobs again asked for the balls and then turned to see Helen Wills standing beneath the umpire's chair putting on her red sweater. Jacobs walked quickly to the chair to see what was happening. She looked at Helen and looked up at umpire Ben Dwight for a sign of what was going on. Some in the audience were shouting, "Don't quit! Don't quit!" Ben Dwight looked at Jacobs and told her she had won on a default.

Mrs. Carruthers saw what was transpiring on the court and wrote later, "When Helen defaulted I wanted to rush out on the court and beg her to try to continue if she possible could. But the decision was too much for me to make. After seeing how spent she looked in the dressing room, I couldn't nerve myself to do it." Carruthers added that "her composure and decision to withdraw deceived observers into believing that she could or should have continued. I hope that sport has not reached the point where our young women must drive themselves on in the face of impending unconsciousness."

There are several accounts of what was said at the umpire's chair.

Jacobs wrote that Wills said to her, "My leg is bothering me. I can't go on."

"Would you like to rest for a while?" Jacobs asked her.

"No, I can't go on," she answered.

"It seemed unnecessary to subject her to this post match ordeal," Jacobs recalled thinking when she saw photographers running out onto the court. "If you're in pain, there's no sense in continuing," she said. "Why don't you leave before the photographers descend on us?" she suggested. Helen then left, escorted from the court by tournament officials.

Yet another account describes a sharp bitter exchange. According to this account, told to me by two of Helen Wills's close friends—who said they heard it from Ben Dwight—Helen said, "I can't go on." Jacobs reached over and placed a hand on her shoulder and asked, "Is there anything I can do?" And Wills turned to her with undisguised hatred in her eyes and said, "Yes. Take your hand off my shoulder and never touch me again."

Whatever the truth of the matter, Helen Wills packed up her rackets and walked off the court, followed by Dwight and other officials. There was hissing from the crowd and shouts at her to stop and play. Jacobs left the court after Wills but then came back to receive the championship trophy. The cheering that greeted her showed the crowd's appreciation of her performance and wiped out some of the disappointment she felt in winning the way she did.

When Jacobs returned to her dressing room, Molla Mallory was waiting for her. A radio commentator had asked Molla immediately after the match to broadcast a statement on what had happened, in view of her own experience with Suzanne Lenglen in 1921 on the same court. "She did," Jacobs recalled, "in biting terms and was still full of it when we met." Very simply Molla Mallory said that Helen Wills quit for the same reason that Suzanne Lenglen had quit. She knew she was going to lose, and she did not want to lose. So she quit. She didn't cough. She just quit and robbed Jacobs of her complete victory.

Jacobs felt afterward that it would have been better for Wills had she remained on the court for the twelve remaining points, had she just stood there and let the ball pass her and had taken the beating. "But what one does under the stress of emotion and pain cannot be calculated in the cold-blooded terms of the spectator." And she concluded that Helen Wills's temperament had always been her most valuable asset. "On this day it was her greatest liability."

Before Jacobs finished dressing, there was another surprise. Elizabeth Ryan came into her dressing room "in a state of wild excitement." Her partner in the ladies doubles—Wills—had announced that she would play in the doubles final. Knowing the probable reaction of the gallery if Helen Wills played after defaulting in the singles, Ryan was determined now to default also in the doubles.

After the match, Jacobs, who was a chain-smoker, smoked furiously as she fielded questions from reporters.

Naturally, gaining the championship through a default was a mixed blessing. And Jacobs reminded reporters that she had not been playing in perfect health either. Her doctors had warned her not to play, she disclosed. She showed signs of nervousness and strain now, brittle words and a suddenly wavering voice. She said she wished Helen had taken frequent time-outs during the game if it would have saved her the final default. "It is untrue that I urged her to go on," she said. "I felt solicitous. I asked Helen if I could do anything for her, but I urged her to leave the court when she said it was too difficult for her to go on."

"The heat is enough to get anyone down. And Helen Wills had the added distress of pain. I know what it is to play in that condition. And I don't believe in making a martyr of yourself. It's vainglory. And tennis is too fine a sport to have to resort to such tactics. It's not a game 'to the death.' and I'm glad Helen didn't place me in the position of taking the championship over her disabled form."

Jacobs tried to concentrate on the happier aspect of the episode. She had, after all, retained her American title and successfully defended her championship. But reporters were interested in other things—in blowing the story out of proportion, she thought. They asked her to make a statement concerning the matter, and it seemed to her that they wanted to make her part of a controversy that simply didn't exist. She refused. Wills, she said, had announced that she felt like she was going to faint. But then she had walked back to her apartment at the Inn and said she wanted to play doubles. That made things look bad to the reporters. They insisted that she refused to lose to Jacobs and would do whatever she could to prevent that from happening.

Tilden found some room for generosity, however, in discussing the default. "I like to think she regretted the decision before she reached the clubhouse," he wrote. Tilden might well have understood Helen's default. After all, it was not unprecedented. On August 14, 1930, Tilden walked off the court in the middle of his match with intercollegiate champion Clifford Sutter at Rye, New York. Sutter won the first set 6–1 and led 4–love, love 15 in the second when Tilden took offense at the heckling of the crowd, said, "I can't stand this any longer," and walked off the court to default.

Suzanne Lenglen sympathized with Helen and suggested that she quit only when she had clearly reached the limit of her endurance. Another of Wills's outspoken defenders in this ordeal was, ironically, John Tunis. Writing for the *New York Evening Post,* Tunis said that "Is it not possible that by her refusal to go on when she was suffering physically and in no condition to play, Mrs. Moody spiked the prevalent idea that a Davis Cup or a national title is a holy grail for which one should risk one's life and if necessary sacrifice one's health? No championship cup, trophy or title is worth such a risk. Congratulations to Mrs. Moody for being one of the first really great American athletes to appreciate this and act upon it. Who knows?—perhaps a sporting America is really growing up." Grantland Rice also defended Helen's actions. "If Mrs. Moody thought she was injuring her health by continuing to play, she was wise to stop, despite the injustices it might have done to Helen Jacobs. Amateur sport is not quite that important."

Dr. Wills felt that what defeated Helen was the ten-minute rest period between the second and third sets. She had warmed up before the match, loosening her muscles. In the second set she had at least become more warmed up and played her usual game. But in the rest period her body cooled down and her muscles tightened. The USLTA was partly to blame, he believed, because "she was persuaded against her better judgement by tennis officials who wanted to assure themselves of a strong attraction."

The British press gave the default front-page coverage for several days. They tended to be more sympathetic toward Wills than the American press and public. The London *Star,* for example, pointed out how she fought back against Dorothy Round to win in England. "Some Americans give her no more sympathy than a Roman crowd gave a defeated gladiator," the *Star* said. "English temperament is more generous." And the *Evening News* said, "It seems a little ungracious that Helen Wills Moody's retirement in collapse from the court should be followed by cries of 'don't quit.' A great figure has gone, if only temporarily from the field of sport. It's better to do her honor." The *News Chronicle,* on the other hand, pointed out that the defeat was really not so sensational, since "Helen clearly wasn't physically fit to play," but the *Telegraph,* under the heading, "End of Tennis Reign," said, "The pity is not that Mrs. Moody failed, but that she failed the way she did. . . . It's almost incomprehensible that Mrs. Moody didn't summon up sufficient resolution, however unequal she felt to the occasion, to finish a set in which she already had lost three games. Even if she had lost them all without winning a point, she would still have gone down like a champion."

Time covered the bizarre events at Forest Hills and opened with a quotation from Wills's autobiographical article in the *Saturday Evening Post* three months earlier. "The American idea is to finish no matter what happens," she wrote in commenting on Suzanne's 1921 default. And time concluded that Helen Wills had forgotten over the years how to lose graciously.

But looking back on the events of 1933, Elizabeth Ryan explained to me in 1977 her feelings about the events. "I did not see the match purposely," she said, "having had a workout in the morning and watching matches just before playing is not good. I was lying on my bed at the Inn reading, then I put the radio on and heard the result of the Moody-Jacobs match. I rushed out and went to where Mr. Pond, the referee was. The first thing he said to me was 'Why aren't you in your tennis clothes?' I said, 'Don't be silly—how can Helen appear after defaulting to Helen Jacobs?' But Pond replied, 'She says she is going to play.'

"And I said that she couldn't play because she would be hissed off the court."

On her way back to the Inn, Ryan saw Helen and Mrs. Carruthers nearly at the elevator, and she called to Mrs. Carruthers. She took her aside and said that she liked Helen too well to go out on the court with her for the doubles. "We must default," she said. And that was done a short time later. "Remember," Ryan told me, "I did it. I was the one who defaulted in the doubles. Helen was willing to play and as far as I could see was capable of playing."

Ryan concluded that Helen Wills had stayed in the dressing room for a time, and composed herself before returning to the Inn. Had she gone directly to the Inn, she would have gotten there sooner. Ryan also added,

"I cannot and will not say anything more about the incident. This time I *will* have peace of mind. I do know many things about it—but no more."

There was a good deal of criticism because Helen Wills hadn't finished the match with Helen Jacobs, and Ryan said that she believed Helen should have stayed on the court no matter what just to show "that she could take a beating—by Helen Jacobs, especially." When Ryan returned to England, she said, she was surprised to find the British press believed that the incident hadn't really happened the way that it was reported in the papers and the American reporters had distorted it and that the Helen, who had won Wimbledon six times, would never have done such a thing.

Later that year Ryan visited California and had lunch with Helen Wills in San Francisco. "All that she said was that the press was down on her," Ryan told me. "She said that the press had done her in.

"I think Helen felt that she ought to play doubles with me, as she had asked me at Wimbledon to play with her, and I at first said no—she was my number-four choice of doubles partners. I said that having won in Paris and Wimbledon I wanted to win at Forest Hills—although we had won at Wimbledon in 1927 and 1930 she was a singles player in a doubles court."

But now Ryan was cheated out of her triple doubles title by the Moody default.

When Helen Jacobs finally made a statement, it was, she found, distorted by journalists who could not possibly have heard any exchange in the umpire's chair. Some of the reporters insisted that they had heard Jacobs plead with Helen to go on. Some said there was a final handshake and others said there was none. In truth, Jacobs recalled, the two women did not shake hands and there had been no refusal to do so and Wills was not assisted from the court. She left under her own power after putting on her sweater. But the two would meet again. Writing in her autobiography of the incident, Helen Wills reversed the winnings in 1933 and had the score all wrong. She said she had won the first set, 8–6, when in fact she had lost it. Then she said she lost the second 6–3, which she won.

"When the match went into the third set, I had to give up, as I knew it was the end when the stadium began to swim around in the air, and I saw Miss Jacobs on the court at a slant."

In 1984, when I spoke with Helen Wills, she recalled the default and stuck by her original action. "I was having trouble with a disc in my back, then," she reminded me. "And it has bothered me ever since." Why did she default rather than go through the motions of remaining for twelve more points and the set and the match?" I don't believe in standing around when you can't move," she said. "Do you? Does anybody? In those days if you were playing for fun you were supposed to play until you dropped dead! But if you were playing for money you could and still can do what you want. Well, I didn't want to play any more and I couldn't. So I stopped playing. I just stopped."

And after the default, with that injury, she never again played so well as she had before.

Clarence Wills blamed the USLTA officials and said that Helen should not have entered the tournament at all. She was persuaded and pressured by male officials who wanted to make more money, he suggested. "Helen never tells me when she is not feeling well," he said. "Nor does she complain. She has always been afraid I would advise her against tennis. You may recall that some years ago, after an appendix operation, she went east for the National tournament and was put out by Mrs. Mallory, whom she had previously beaten. I advised against that trip but Helen has always been courageous and insisted upon taxing herself too severely. I can't tell as to her condition until there is opportunity for a thorough examination that I propose to make."

Fred Moody was reassured after talking with Helen. She was feeling better soon after playing, and the pain was beginning to abate, she told him.

Alice Marble watched the women's final and rooted for Helen Jacobs. "It was highly dramatic," she remembered, "for there had been talk for years about the feud between those two." Alice remembered the excitement when the players left the court at one set all. Then, when Helen Wills defaulted, "she went right past our box and walked slowly but with her head up, toward the clubhouse two short city blocks away. The stadium buzzed with excitement. The officials were stupified." Alice Marble herself was amazed. "I knew that Mrs. Moody's back had bothered her, but it did seem unsportsmanlike to take away what might have proved to be a legitimate victory for Helen Jacobs. Certainly," she concluded, "had Mrs. Moody found the strength to walk to the clubhouse she could have played three more games."

Then Marble overheard an official say to Mr. Carruthers that Wills had telephoned to say she was ready to play her doubles match in half an hour. Carruthers disappeared and upon his return said, "She will not play the doubles."

Alice Marble believes today that if Helen Wills had appeared on the court in the doubles the gallery would not have stood for it. Instead, Marble was again called upon. She and Elizabeth Ryan, were asked to play an exhibition match against Nuthall and Freda James, who won the national title by default. To make things even more bizarre, this match was not completed either. Nuthall hit a fast volley that hit the top of Marble's racket and then struck her in the eye. Alice Marble was carried off the court, unable to open either eye. "The public went home feeling quite cheated," Alice thought.

As to Helen Wills's even consenting to play at Forest Hills, some saw it as an unwise passion to take back the championship from Jacobs. But

Edith Sigourney, a friend of Wills and one of the top-ranked players of the time, gave me another reason. "Helen felt a very strong obligation toward the USLTA," she said, "who sponsored her trips abroad, and so she entered tournaments for them in order to build up the gate—she played as the fulfillment of an obligation that she felt deeply and honored. In 1933 the fulfillment of that obligation was, I believe, a mistake. It was a bad mistake—a very bad mistake." There has never been a convincing explanation of her abortive decision to play in the doubles with Ryan.

Many tennis prophets, after seeing Wills lose that set at Wimbledon to Dorothy Round, wrote that her days as a champion were numbered— thank goodness. And now new blood, they felt, was about to be injected into the upper ranks of women's tennis. And then following the Jacobs victory, those prophets gloated. They had been right. And the press condemned Wills now just as bitterly as they had condemned Lenglen after her 1921 default.

Helen Wills and Suzanne Lenglen shared this, too, at long last. Each saw the crowds and the press turn on them. Each was cheered and then hissed. Each learned the capriciousness of the sporting galleries. Now Helen Wills, too, was branded a quitter. She had cheated a rival out of a clean victory.

Wills tried to ignore the criticism. It obviously hurt her and cut deep. But she did not defend herself or strike back in the press. She did, however, determine from almost the moment she walked off the court that she would be back, clear her name, and one more time prove her mettle. That, after all, was part of the legend of the American Girl. She was not a quitter. And, just like the little girl who was not handicapped by the losing of matches in Golden Gate Park or Live Oak Park in Berkeley two decades earlier, she would be back.

Helen Wills departed for San Francisco on August 27, leaving the controversy behind. She left New York at midnight, with a friend who was also a nurse, Alice Loughlin, within hours of her stunning default. And long after the match was ended, the controversy continued. There was invective heaped on Helen now, and she made it as difficult as possible for reporters to get any stories. Her departure time was a secret to all except close friends. After giving out a perfunctory statement after the match, she maintained strict silence. She refused to see anyone or to consent to any interviews. Her departure, Allison Danzig, wrote in the *New York Times,* wrote finis to the most disastrous expedition she had set out on since as a girl of fifteen she came east in 1921 to win the girls' national championship.

The long glorious reign of the American Girl had at last come to an end.

---⊰ 9 ⊱---

When Helen Wills arrived in Berkeley a few days later aboard the Overland Limited, Blanche Ashbaugh boarded the train and interviewed her. Wills said she felt right in defaulting. "I am sure," Helen said, "that if I had to do it all over again, I would still default. My leg hurt me so badly at the time, I knew I would have collapsed on the court had I remained. The leg was numb clear to the ankle and I could hardly move it. You cannot imagine the feeling of being forced to stand perfectly still and watch a ball go past you. I should not have played at all, but after missing the Wightman Cup matches, I did so want to play. And I thought I could. After all, why go on, when just going on would make a spectacle."

And she told Ashbaugh that she hoped again to meet Helen Jacobs on the tennis court. When asked if she would have beaten Jacobs if her leg held up, she responded, "Tennis is a game that you can tell nothing about. I do not know." She said she would lay off for six months. Then, perhaps, she would play again. But the layoff wouldn't be easy. "It is going to be hard not to be able to play tennis this winter," she said, "but for once I am going to obey doctor's orders. I hope to be able to continue playing tournament tennis for many years.

"You know, I am still young."

After the tournament the financial dreams of the sportswear manufacturers came true. Women's tennis shorts became the rage. A month after Helen Wills's default, according to the *San Francisco Chronicle*, "everybody's wearing shorts. Thousands of ladies from Tacoma to Timbuktu today would just as soon think of wearing red mittens on the tennis courts as skirts. Everyone, that is, except for Helen Wills Moody, who would never wear the shorts and who wore the skirt almost defiantly in 1933."

And the feminists were happy. For, "like the donning of abbreviated bathing suits, shorts on the courts had long been fought everywhere by blue-nosed reformers and old-fashioned people, generally."

CHAPTER

IX

COMEBACK

"Action belongs to youth, and it must be entered into, or forever be looked back upon with regret."
— Helen Wills

"Act Three? Why any dramatist will tell you. Vindication! Queen Helen lives again. Long live the Queen! But what a last act that girl put on!"
— Paul Gallico

"Never be willing to settle for second best, but keep achievement in proper perspective, and recognize that qualities of spirit have far greater value than personal accomplishments."   — Helen Jacobs

SHE was alone again. She was 6000 miles from home, and she was alone again. And she was waiting.

So much of her life, she said later, was taken up with waiting. Waiting aboard trains and ships that crossed continents and oceans taking her from one contest to another, one stadium to another, one crowd to another. Waiting for other matches to end and for her own matches to begin. Waiting for the court to be cleared or for the rain to stop.

Waiting to walk once more out onto those familiar manicured lawns of Wimbledon or Forest Hills or countless other courts or clubs. Waiting for the crowd to rise and cheer and for the first ball to be struck. Waiting to feel the anxiety and the nervousness within her subside as she slipped into the rhythm of the match. Waiting for an opponent's game to fall apart and for the match to end. And then waiting for the next match or the next tournament or the next day or the next week. And finally waiting for that restlessness that drove her to be calmed.

She sat at a table in the dining room of a hotel. It was late in the morning, and there were few others in the room. She gazed out the tall windows and out over the gardens and the red roofs below. Out there in the distance were tall trees. She watched the tops of the trees, saw them bend a bit in the breeze and then stand straight and tall again. The leaves trembled as the light reflected from them in a kaleidoscope of patterns, like light sparkling from the rippled surface of a lake. She realized she was lonely. It was not a new feeling. She had, over the years, become accustomed to it. Loneliness was a frequent unwelcome companion in her life.

It was 1935. Helen Wills sat alone in the dining room of Great Fosters in Surrey. She had moved to the hotel from the American Women's Club on Grosvenor Street, where she stayed only one night. She found it hard to rest in London. Now, at night there was no sound, and she slept, as she remembered years later, "marvelously."

Great Fosters, one of the oldest moated houses in England, had once belonged to Queen Elizabeth. Helen's room had casement windows and a corner fireplace and hand-hewn beams in the ceiling. She slept well. But it was a lonely quiet place. She usually took her meals alone in her room. In the mornings she ran around the spacious garden in order to warm up. There were no others present at the time except the gardeners, who seemed surprised to see this beautiful statuesque American racing energetically around and around the vegetables and through the grape arbors, like a Greek goddess misplaced in time and geography.

The captain of the American Davis Cup team phoned her and said the team's trainers had seen her play and advised her to do some running and to start from a crouching position. It was, he said, a good way of getting off to a quick start in her game. But she had already been doing that for a week, so she was simply encouraged by hearing the advice. She was doing the right thing. She continued running every morning. And it worked. "I was surprised to find that I was day by day developing more confidence in my court covering," she said.

It rained steadily for a week. She had reserved the week to practice and to try to smooth the rough edges of her game. "I needed to play so badly," she thought, "and it seemed as if the situation were now hopeless." The silence of her little room, she felt, was greater by contrast as she waited for the rain to stop. She did a series of drawings for the London *Daily Mail*.

In the afternoons, while it rained and the sky darkened, and she wasn't drawing, she watched three tall trees from her window, poplars that seemed like a living mass of green leaves. They bent in the wind, "as if leaning towards each other for conversation." She ascribed to them her own thoughts, as if they were being spoken by the trees, "but much more wisely and with more understanding." And she thought to herself that this would be the last time she would travel so far alone. This would be the last time she would play tennis, "the game that had held my interest so closely for so many years," in England.

The American Girl had come back to Wimbledon.

--◅{ 2 }▻--

On the day of the final match of the 1935 Wimbledon tournament, Helen Wills had an early lunch in the hotel dining room. And she sat gazing out the windows near her table thinking, "The wind will be blowing up and down the center court. You might easily overshoot when you are on the side nearest the royal box." She wasn't hungry yet she knew she had to eat—food as fuel for the final match. She went through the process of eating mechanically, never really tasting the food. She looked out the window almost lost in reverie. Then, suddenly, she became aware of someone addressing her. She was startled for a moment as she was drawn back to the present. She looked up and saw an elderly woman standing at her table.

"I am Maude Watson," she said to Helen Wills. She was the first female singles champion at Wimbledon. "I won the championship once in the very beginning and I want to wish you good luck for this afternoon," she said. Wills asked her to sit down. She saw the marks on Maude Watson's face, those crinkles in the corners of the eyes of someone who had played in the sun and the wind over the course of the years. She had a strange feeling that she might be looking at a reflection of herself years in the future. "Meeting yourself as an older person might be a rather startling experience," she thought.

The two champions talked. Watson told Helen that she, too, always stayed in Great Fosters during the championships. Wills asked her about tennis in the past. Maude Watson had won the championship in 1884 and again in 1885. She told Helen of the old days in tennis when ladies and gentlemen played the game in their gardens, and some people thought it scandalous to let young women run around in public vigorously swinging rackets at tennis balls. Watson and her sisters were the first women to wear what became the customary white skirts with a bustle to play tennis. She also wore a silk blouse with long sleeves and a sailor hat that flew off when she ran. Her skirts reached to her ankles, she said, and people thought it very short and daring.

They talked about the new styles and the strokes of the game. Watson only played tennis for about four years. Then she became ill from a swimming accident when she nearly drowned. She was ill for three years, and her tennis was finished. "Now I live in the country and ride horses," she said. She never married. She would be watching the matches on this day. She would be sitting in the gallery with an old rival from long ago, Lottie Dod, the youngest Wimbledon winner, who had won the 1887 championship at the age of fifteen.

During the conversation Helen Wills forgot for a while that she had a match to play. One more match. It was time to go to the courts. She said goodbye to Maude Watson. She returned to her room to gather her things for the match. She kept her rackets in the hotel and her dress and shoes in her locker at the All-England Club. Then she was driven to Wimbledon. It was her eighth Wimbledon final, but only the second time she played in the finals without someone from her family watching.

In the dressing room she decided not to read the scores of letters and telegrams left there for her because she was afraid they would tire her eyes. She dressed quietly and then carefully examined her rackets, fearing her favorite might have a broken string. It didn't. She stood and made several practice swings, making a ghostly "whoosh," "whoosh" sound in the room. She examined her shoes again. Then she heard footsteps outside the door and the familiar voice of Ted Tinling. "All ready!" he cried. Wills scooped up her rackets and pulled on her red sweater and stepped out the door. Tinling carried the key for the door leading into the royal hall, through which the two silent figures passed on their way to the door that led outside to the Centre Court. They passed down rubber-covered stairs, past wooden shields where the names of former champions were inscribed. Helen Wills read the name of Suzanne Lenglen on one of the shields. In the lower hall she came face to face with her opponent for the afternoon. She acknowledged her foe with a nod of the head. Then the two women waited for Tinling to lead them outside. She could hear the rumble and hum of the restless crowd. They would stand and cheer, she knew, when she appeared with her opponent.

Her opponent was Helen Jacobs. Again.

Helen Wills had learned patience. It was a virtue forced upon her by circumstance. In the past she had always been impatient, restless, hurrying through matches and tournaments in record time, earnestly bashing her way through practice matches. But time had caught up with her now. And to play at all, ever again, she needed patience. There was no hurrying the healing process. She would simply have to wait until her body healed.

Nobody knew for how long Helen Wills would be out of tennis. Soon after her arrival in California in the fall of 1933 she was asked if she planned to give up tennis. "Give up tennis?" she laughed. "Certainly not! That is, I hope I will not have to." She seemed expansive and optimistic as she predicted that "I am going to rest for six months. If the doctors say I have fully recovered from this injury, I shall play as much as ever. I love the game too much to give it up if I don't have to. My hope is I will be ready for the tournament season next year."

After Wills returned home, her father supervised her medical examinations. Then within a matter of days, after Dr. Wills consulted with specialists, she was admitted to Stanford University Hospital. She was diagnosed as suffering from a "displaced vertabrae."

A special editorial in the *San Francisco Chronicle* pointed out that Helen Wills's admission to the hospital should show the "Eastern crowds" that she had not been faking anything at Forest Hills. "Galleries, strangely unsympathetic to a player whose name and personality have added much to tennis since that day in 1921 when a wide-eyed, pig-tailed little girl, she first appeared in the East, followed her sad, painful, exit from the 1933 tournament with shouts of 'quitter' and 'poor sport.' "

The return of Helen Jacobs to California was far happier than that of Helen Wills. She arrived in California on October 3, after spending several weeks with Alona Friend in Massachusetts, horseback riding and relaxing and enjoying a respite from tennis and having defeated the woman long touted as the greatest American female athlete. She arrived in Berkeley aboard the Overland Limited and was welcomed by a large gathering of friends and relatives. At the train station she was presented with a special flower—the Helen Jacobs gladioli, grown in the Carl Salbach gardens. Dubbed by the press Queen Helen II, Jacobs was described the way that Wills had once been. "She has beauty and reserve and great modesty," Carolyn Anspacher wrote in the *San Francisco Chronicle,* and "lays no great stress upon her achievements in the world of tennis."

Jacobs had only words of praise for Wills. "Helen was right in defaulting," she said. "I don't blame her a bit. If she was ill, there was no reason in the world why she should have played." Jacobs said she planned to remain on the coast for a few weeks before returning to New York to pursue a career in journalism. And she said that she was forbidden by her physician from playing competitive tennis for three or four months. Anspacher noted that Jacobs looked healthy and happy. She was tanned, and her chestnut hair was now highlighted with gold. She was accompanied by Alona Friend, who stayed in the Jacobs house in Berkeley.

When she returned to Boston in November, she was caught up in an ugly incident. She went to the FBI for help after receiving threatening letters postmarked San Francisco. Alona Friend accompanied her to the Federal Building. The newspapers reported that they were inseparable, and they stayed together at the Friend residence in Melrose, Massachusetts. The U.S. Attorney in Boston guessed that the letters were an effort to throw Jacobs off her stride in tennis.

There was yet one more honor for Jacobs in 1933. In December a poll of 180 sports experts of the Associated Press named her the outstanding female athlete of the year. She received 64 votes to only three for Helen Wills. Alice Marble received two. When the USLTA published its ranking list, Jacobs was first among the women, Wills placed second and Marble third. Frank Shields was first among the men, and Ellsworth Vines, who would have been ranked first had he not turned professional at the end of the season, was unranked.

Following the admission of Helen Wills to Stanford University Hospital, Fred Moody told newsmen that her condition was not alarming. Yet she had been in pain constantly since she had arrived in San Francisco, and it was expected that she would now have to spend several weeks in the hospital under close observation. Wills's physicians found her to be in fundamentally good health. The difficulties she experienced, they believed, were merely mechanical ones that could be repaired by time and rest. And patience. She was monitored constantly by her father. He reminded her that rehabilitation would take a long time and that she could not afford to be impatient. Any effort to rush back into her old routine too early would not only risk a setback, but it could be dangerous and bring on a permanent injury. The only way to make a comeback was to do it slowly and to let nature do its healing process. "Be patient," he advised his restless daughter. "Be patient."

Even lying inactive in a hospital, she was still sought out by newsmen. Almost all of them respected her privacy. But one afternoon a man with a camera slipped into her room and snapped a photograph of her. She chased him away by throwing a book at him. She remembered that he tiptoed in and was focusing his camera before she had a chance to react. A doctor suggested to other reporters that "such a fellow is ruthless and probably not a newspaper man. None of you would do such a thing."

At first the forced inaction depressed Helen Wills. She feared that she might not recover from her injury and that she might never play tennis again. But by the time Wills left the hospital she was determined to return to the courts and to play as well as possible. She reminded reporters she met right after her discharge, that she really did love tennis. By mid-October she was on her feet again. She did not return to the tennis courts, but she went for walks in San Francisco.

Zilfa Estcourt of the *Chronicle* interviewed Helen and reported that she walked on "slow feet, that move cautiously as she walks for exericse a few blocks daily with her Sealyham puppy as companion." Estcourt found her morose as she discussed her summer of disappointment and pain. She termed the injury that stopped her at Forest Hills as simply bad luck—she said it was just one of those things that happened to athletes. "It was awfully bad luck. But then I have been lucky for ten wonderful years. I cannot complain now." She took a philosophical view of the future and of the possibilities of a comeback. "I hope to play again some time," she said. "I have loved tennis. It has given me the greatest pleasure. But I shall never try to return to the game until I am confident the injury to my back has been completely cured. It is not a thing to be brought about in one treatment." She pointed out that she was barely able to walk. And she reminded the reporter that active sports were a long way off, for her. In the meantime she would paint and write.

Helen remained in the hospital until October 2 and then returned to her home at 1308 Clay Street in San Francisco. Dr. Wills expressed his doubt at the time that she would ever again be capable of playing championship tennis. "I do not mean that she will never be able to play tennis again," he said. "But whether she will be able to play the kind demanded in championship tournaments is something that only the future can determine." He felt that the back would never be 100 percent again and that the injury that forced her retirement at Forest Hills might recur. She had been placed in a cast and it was removed before she left the hospital. She was able to walk across the room but she needed continued treatment," he said.

There was some solace for Helen in early October when the British tennis writer, A. Wallis Myers, in his annual "first ten in the world," ranked Helen number one and Helen Jacobs number two, the same positions they held in his ranking in 1932.

Immediately after her release, Wills conferred with her father as to how best to prepare for comeback on the courts. There had never been any doubt in her mind that she must return and then vindicate herself in match play. In October she predicted a comeback in 1934. But one month later she found the road to recovery more difficult than she had expected. The injury was more severe than she at first thought. She told inquiring reporters that there would be no comeback in 1934. Perhaps 1935 would be her year, she suggested. But who could tell?

Her father advised her to take up swimming again. He believed it would provide the proper resistance for her muscles, that she could exercise in a pool and at the same time design movements under water to approximate those she made on the tennis court.

She used the swimming pool at the San Francisco Women's Athletic Club, just up the street from the St. Francis Hotel. "I discovered that there was usually nobody in the pool each day at five p.m. So I worked out there, swimming and doing underwater exercises. I didn't play tennis but I did do a lot of exercise," she said. In the pool of the Women's Club she practiced the series of underwater tennis exercises, going through the motions of a match under water. She knew that the other women in the pool must have thought it odd as they watched her go about her solemn practice sessions under water. But she felt it worked, so there was a very good reason for "playing tennis under water in the middle of a big pool." She also swam laps and gradually increased the distance she swam until she was covering a quarter of a mile daily. Then she walked home, up a hill, after her workout. "I walked back up Nob Hill to Sacramento Street alone each night. Walking up the hill was good exercise, too." On some afternoons she took long walks on the hills of San Francisco and familiarized herself with many parts of the city. She also cultivated a garden at home and painted.

She turned twenty-eight in the fall of 1933. And each passing day, she feared, made less likely her comeback and her return to her old form. Her best days were behind her, she suspected. Helen Wills knew that there was, for any athlete seeking to come back, something ominous in the passage of time. "The longer . . . the more unlikely," she believed, and so on until "too late."

There had been a change in her style and approach to the game in 1927, after the surgery and rest in 1926. Then she had been less bold, less daring, came to the net less often. But in the years of her long string of victories, she found she did not have to come to the net or volley or hurry or scramble around the court. It was not part of her regal style. That belonged to little Helen of the Pigtails and not to Big Helen the Queen of the Courts, the Killer of the Courts. She had become a conservative in dress as well as in play, many believed. Slowly, over the following weeks and months she worked and healed. Eventually, looking back on that experience, she concluded, "If people really try, they can work wonders. But it takes time. And you must be patient. And you must be determined."

But she would not be the young Helen Wills again. That player was gone forever. She would not be as great as she once was, she knew. Yet she still would be good, very good. And she still might be better than any other player of the time. She still might win Wimbledon. She still might beat Helen Jacobs somewhere, some time. If time was not on her side, perhaps fortune was.

Wills enrolled again in the University of California in the spring of 1934 and took two English courses to meet the requirements for her A.B. degree. When she registered she gave notice that she would be unable to play in the Wightman Cup matches that summer. And in May she let it be known that she had not practiced and would not practice that year and so was lost for the season. The crowds would be smaller and there would be less excitement in 1934, officials knew now. Alice Marble carried the bad news east for the California Tennis Association.

In explaining her decision she referred to her experience in the East in 1933. It had been strange, she said, because she had always been tired. "I've never been tired before. Playing with a drag took all the fun out of it. I love tennis. I miss it dreadfully now, I know if I start playing before this injury clears up I'll just start it all over. But it's a terrible temptation."

In the spring of 1934 she received an invitation from Stanley Doust of the London *Daily Mail,* asking her to come to England to write a series of articles for the newspaper on the Wimbledon competition. Wills postponed making a decision until April, unsure as to whether or not she would be strong enough to make the trip. On April 11 she decided to go. She agreed to write a series on the tournament for the Hearst chain also.

Being in London during Wimbledon and not playing was a repetition of Helen Wills's unfortunate experience of 1926. She found it difficult to write about the matches—more difficult, she thought, than playing in the tournament. She had to watch most of the matches closely—much more closely than she had in the past. Prior to her own matches she had always, like Elizabeth Ryan and most of the other players, avoided watching a match so as to give her eyes a rest. Now she examined every match closely. And she watched Helen Jacobs closely. She filed stories on the final match in the women's division in which Dorothy Round defeated Helen Jacobs in three sets. But back at Forest Hills Jacobs successfully defended her American title and beat Sarah Palfrey easily in a two-set final match. With this, her third consecutive national title, Jacobs won permanent possession of the Championship Cup, and it was presented to her by Walter Merrill Hall, president of the USLTA. By coincidence, the other two names on the cup were those of the 1930 winner, Betty Nuthall, and the 1931 winner, Helen Wills Moody.

In mid-1934 Hazel Wightman announced that she still believed that Helen Wills was the best female player ever produced in America. She said in an interview that she believed that the greatest woman player of all time was Suzanne Lenglen. But in America, she said, "Mrs. Moody would have beaten May Sutton Bundy, when the latter was in her prime, because of greater speed. May Sutton was the most accurate shotmaker of all; Molla Mallory was remarkable; Helen Jacobs is a finished player; but Helen Wills of a few years ago was brilliant. She was the most versatile of all American players."

Helen Wills's New Year's Resolution for 1935 was printed in a local newspaper. She resolved on January 1, 1935, to try to regain her women's national title at Forest Hills. "But there's a great gap between trying and winning," she said. "I think I will be practicing before the end of January, and I shall certainly be terribly thrilled to be able to swing a racquet again."

Perhaps it was that prospect of the Wills return—sportswriters believed it was—that induced Helen Jacobs in early 1935 to turn down a generous offer to turn professional. A confrontation and a decisive victory over Wills would have enhanced the financial value of any contract she signed. And a match between the two women would equal the gate of the 1926 Cannes match between Suzanne Lenglen and Helen Wills. In fact, it might even make them millionaires or at least very rich if they signed professional contracts. Bill O'Brien had that in mind when he approached Jacobs on January 4, 1935.

O'Brien had traveled with the Lenglen tour as a masseur. He had learned from Pyle, and he was now putting together his own professional troupe and so he approached Jacobs. She told O'Brien that she wanted to remain an amateur at least through the 1935 season. There might be a chance for a rematch with Wills. Jacobs wanted badly the chance for vindication, the chance to prove that she could, in a completed match, beat Helen Wills. She knew and all American players knew that Suzanne Lenglen had been accused of running away from Helen Wills when she had signed with Pyle. Jacobs was not about to make that same mistake. Jacobs also knew that in the past, for the women, professionalism offered only a brief moment in the spotlight, a way of making an exit from tennis. Professional tennis constantly needed fresh faces and novelties to make it attractive to the public. She was not yet ready to retire into professional tennis. A win over Wills would enhance her market value. Maybe then. Maybe at the end of the 1935 season. And she had not yet won Wimbledon. Wills was a six-time winner in the greatest tournament of them all.

In 1934 Helen Jacobs captained the U.S. Wightman Cup team that went to England and lost.

O'Brien had made an earlier less publicized offer to Jacobs in the summer of 1934. The contract he offered her at that time was only for $20,000 plus expenses. But as O'Brien pointed out, the times were bad, and considering the fact that the country was in the midst of a great depression it was a good offer. "But I told him both times," Jacobs reported, "that I was not ready to consider such a move." She did not say that she was against turning professional. Lenglen, after all, made a fortune doing it but made the mistake of turning professional a little too early in her career. So Jacobs decided to wait. She told a reporter for the Associated Press that she could not say that she would never turn professional because "nobody knows what one might do in the future, but please say for me I have not the slightest intention of turning professional this year." Her plans for the year included playing in all the major European and American tournaments. She planned also to play in Cairo as part of a North African tour.

The officials of the USLTA feared that if Bill O'Brien signed the leading female players to professional contracts he could wreck the attraction of amateur tennis, perhaps giving it a blow that would force upon the USLTA open tennis and allow the players a say in their own careers and a share of their own profits. This still could not be allowed, they believed. Pyle had been a threat to tennis, and then Tilden, and then O'Brien. Where would it stop? Tilden had worked with O'Brien to open his professional tour in 1931.

By coming out of retirement, Helen Wills could again make headlines and steal the sports pages from the professionals. There were appeals from England for her to return to the game. And some San Franciscans were privy to the appeals and the pressure.

In mid-January, Paul Gallico visited Helen Wills in San Francisco. She spent the day with him showing him around the city. She talked little of tennis, he reported. But he predicted that she would play tennis again and that she would play at Forest Hills and regain her title. He said that she spoke wistfully and with a far-away look in her eyes when she said, "I want to play in the nationals—very much—if I possibly can."

He didn't know exactly why she wanted that date at Forest Hills. "It is hard to tell," he wrote. "She is a strange, introspective girl."

It had been a pleasant visit, and he wrote to her later thanking her for her hospitality. "I came away strangely convinced that beneath that cool, well-tailored exterior crust, there burned hot fires," he wrote later. "She must have thought of that scene [at Forest Hills in 1933] and of Jacobs a million times, and a million times must have said to herself, 'I'll beat you! I'll beat you! I'll beat you! I'll come back!'"

When he said goodbye to her, Gallico observed that "Something tells me the next time I see her will be in Forest Hills in August. And I wouldn't miss that one for millions."

She rested for eighteen months. Then when she thought she was ready to practice again she found herself afraid to pick up a racket for fear that she would find that her talent had completely abandoned her and would not return. The realization that it was over, she believed, would be even more depressing than the long period of inactivity and then she would be forced to give up. Finally, Dr. Wills said that he thought it might be a good idea if Helen started hitting tennis balls again against the backboard at the California Tennis Club in San Francisco.

And so she went to the club and practiced hitting that backboard. "When I hit some balls it was as if I had been playing only the day before," she found to her surprise. "There seemed to be absolutely no difficulty in connecting ball and racquet. In fact, it seemed so easy that I was rather suspicious. But it must be that one never forgets how to make a stroke nor loses one's unconscious feeling for coordinating eye and muscle."

At first she hit only for ten minutes every day against the backboard. Then she started to rally with Howard Kinsey for a brief time every afternoon. Always, she found, it was easy to get some junior member of the club to practice with. When she found herself getting power behind her ground strokes once more, she started to practice her service. Her father told reporters after her default that he believed that she had altered her service to compensate for a sore back and that the changed service twisted her muscles more and contributed further to the injury, so the service was considered to be particularly dangerous now. But it worked all right. It was not like starting over again. It was rather just picking up and polishing the game that she never lost.

But Wills realized that her game could never be the same. She must be aware of illusions of complete recovery. There were limitations now. She had lost a step or two on the court, and she would never again be as fast. Now she had to think more and to anticipate shots more accurately. She had to use her head. She had to plan and to watch and to calculate carefully. Finesse was now the name of the game. She had to save the big weapon, the big booming forehand winners. She could no longer do as she had done against Alvarez and others, stand on the backcourt and blast away steadily with her drives until she destroyed all the defenses of the opposition and brought surrender. Now she had to play more of their game, accept some of their best shots and then beat them. She had to outsmart her competitors on every shot. Every shot.

She practiced volleying again, came to the net, slipped in behind good approach shots and volleyed winners. But she was less reckless than before, and she tired quickly. She could not use up energy too fast, had to preserve her strength. She would be playing younger and more energetic and more vigorous players, perhaps. Players like Alice Marble and Sarah Palfrey and others. She had to preserve energy and play them from the backcourt and run them.

She felt the strength return to her arms. She had not suspected that the change would be so evident. But the rapid improvement in strength, she concluded, must have come from the conditioning she gained through swimming. She expected as she increased her practice time to feel soreness and stiffness in her back, but it never happened. After a month of practice with Kinsey and junior members she played two fast sets with one of her former opponents, a club member, who played a good fast game. Now she felt the difference. She found that her strokes were pretty much the same in execution, but they lacked power and speed. Starting from a dead-stop set position she was slower. And she had never been known for her speed on the court. She realized that speed work had been overlooked in her practice, and she tried to compensate by running more.

Phil Neer showed up to watch her one afternoon at the California Tennis Club and told reporters afterwards that she would "annihilate the women's field" in any tournament she chose to enter—any tournament.

She played actual games at the club for about three weeks. Then she studied her calendar and saw that Wimbledon was not far off. Maybe, she thought. Maybe.

She made up her mind suddenly. She said that she realized that if she took the train to New York and if she sailed to England immediately she would be there in time for practice in preliminary tournaments and for a week of practice at Wimbledon. She might make a good show of it.

On the other hand, she wrote, common sense dictated that it would be a 6000-mile trip to play in a tournament where the possibility—the probability, some said—existed that she would be eliminated in the first round. Six thousand miles, she reminded herself, to play perhaps just thirty minutes of tennis. Yet she had played at Wimbledon seven times and had won six times—a tie with Suzanne Lenglen's singles record—and the English crowd loved her and the English press loved her—they stood by her when the American crowds and the American press came down on her. They were her staunchest defenders, her greatest fans. And she concluded that "six thousand miles is a short trip, even for the pleasure of looking on at Wimbledon."

She made her decision on May 17, 1935. She indicated later that her mind was really made up for her by some inner sense of reasoning working somewhere in her unconscious mind. "I became aware of it that morning all of a sudden," she recalled. "Some decisions are like this. They decide themselves, and then your attention is called to them, sometimes without warning. I knew that I must go. Even had I been the one warned by the famous words, 'Learn from this, my friend, not to wander from your home too long: for so you find your journey to have defeated itself,' I would have disregarded it, for I would not have understood its wider implication." She had hoped, she said, for days in California that would lose themselves unnumbered. "But at the moment I did not want day to follow day in a sleepy haze of sunshine. Action belongs to youth, and it must be entered into, or forever be looked back upon with regret."

Other players suggested that there were financial inducements for her to return to Wimbledon. There were special favors, they whispered, from the USLTA, who wanted her back at Forest Hills. The Depression had settled in, and crowds were smaller, and the gate was down, and the return of a champion would again bring out the paying customers. Wills's departure from competitive tennis in the fall of 1933 was only the first blow to the game and to the officials of the USLTA who milked it in the depths of the depression. The second blow came on October 9 when Ellsworth Vines, the number-one ranked player in the country, signed a professional contract to tour with a group put together by Bill Tilden, who had also become a professional. Tilden also signed Henri Cochet in Paris. Vines was just twenty-two years old at the time, and rumor had it at the time that he was to be paid $100,000 for signing the pro contract. Francis Hunter, Howard Kinsey, Harvey Snodgrass, Vincent Richards, Charles M. Wood, Frank Boneau, and Allen Behr were also on the Tilden tour. The big stars were leaving the amateur ranks. And the amateur game needed a new star attraction. Nobody had been a bigger draw than Helen Wills. Her comeback could be a trump card at a critical moment in the history of the game. And those who managed the amateur tournaments—whose prestige and power depended on the amateur gate—wanted her back now. And, it was said, they were willing to pay to get her back in the amateur tournaments. Wills denied it. Very simply, she told me, "I didn't do it for money, that's for sure."

Bill Leiser, a columnist for the *San Francisco Chronicle,* wrote that Helen Wills's sudden dash for Wimbledon was not motivated by her own unconscious desire to play there once again but rather came "at the urgent request of tennis officials intent upon thwarting a professional coup that would have stolen all of the appeal of the women's amateur game and turned it completely into a business for attracting box office receipts for the Bill O'Brien organization."

According to Leiser, the O'Brien scheme was to work this way. Alice Marble had already been approached by O'Brien in Los Angeles. Alice's treatment by the USLTA was enough to make a professional offer extremely attractive to her—the offer was not only cash but the ability now to call her own shots and to decide when she would play. The USLTA had forced her into too many matches in 1933 and had caused her collapse and perhaps even permanent injury to her health. If Marble signed, O'Brien believed, he could get some worthy opponents for her. Eleanor Tennant, her coach, was already a teaching pro and was managing Marble's career. She would join the tour also and help some of the other female players improve their games—especially the younger ones. The players were already noted for their beauty—especially Marble—and with Tennant's help and constant practice O'Brien thought he could turn them into pretty good tennis players, combining beauty and athletics, a beauty show and tennis with a little sex appeal, exactly what Pyle had provided in 1926.

Yet the main attraction was still missing. That was to be Helen Jacobs. She would become the biggest star in the game with her victory at Wimbledon—where she had not yet won—coming on the heels of her victory over Wills. When she won Wimbledon and then signed for an American tour, then she was a more bankable product. O'Brien was betting that 1935 would at last be her year—and his. There was nobody around that could stop her, he believed. Nobody, that is, except, perhaps, Helen Wills.

Marble and Jacobs and Wills had all suffered during 1933 because of the rigors of the amateur officials and of the USLTA especially. On the pro tour, with enough women playing, there would be more control of the game by the women themselves, managed by Tennant. They could, to some degree determine how and when they would play. They could do what was best for box office, taking a game when they wanted, dragging one out when they wanted. Whatever was good for the gate. They would marry tennis to entertainment for what O'Brien expected to be a good show revolving around athletic competition. But primarily it would be a show. And the men and women on the tour would be, as Suzanne Lenglen had been, primarily entertainers and secondarily athletes—professional entertainers and professional athletes. And most importantly, O'Brien thought, they could win their independence at last from the male-dominated associations, just as Lenglen and Browne had done nearly a decade earlier.

There was still one person now who could bar the door—Helen Wills. He did not expect her to come out of retirement. And if she did he did not expect her to be anything but a weak foil for Jacobs.

But O'Brien should have known better. In 1926 she had used the threat of Pyle to enhance her own value to the USLTA. She was, with the removal of Lenglen, their big star. And without Helen Wills on the tour now, few would come out to see the women professionals knowing the best player in the world was still in the amateur ranks.

On May 17—a Friday—she played tennis at the California Club until about 1:15 in the afternoon. Then she called her bank at 2:30 and requested a letter of credit and travelers checks. Her passport was current, but she needed to pick up a visa in New York. Her maid helped her pack in the afternoon. She inquired about an air ticket but found that flying arrangements for baggage would not have been adequate, so she decided to take the train—the Overland Limited again. Fred Moody called to ask if she had decided to go and to remind her of a dinner party at six. She called Wright & Ditson and asked that six rackets be waiting for her in New York and the remainder sent to England.

When she had completed packing, Helen and Fred went to the home of a friend for dinner. After dinner they hurried home and picked up Helen's luggage. They then took the ferry across the Bay and caught the Overland Limited in Oakland. Wills was thinking ahead at that time, thinking of her approaching matches and of Wimbledon. She remembered later that she forgot to look back at the lights of San Francisco as she crossed the Bay. Moody said he wished he were going along, and she said she wished he were too. She would be making this trip alone.

In recalling her trip across the continent in 1935, Helen Wills remembered that in Reno there had been a flurry of excitement as Barbara Hutton's railroad car was coupled to the Overland Limited. Reporters and other passengers were excited by the presence of the Miss Hutton and paid little attention to a tennis player trying for a comeback, Wills wrote in her autobiography. But the newspaper reports of the time indicated that as the Overland Limited crossed the country, small crowds gathered at the stations along the way to see the American Girl and to get her autograph—not Hutton's. At Salt Lake City, where Wills changed trains, she was treated by the crowd like a movie star, and she generously gave out autographs. She was still the heroine of the crowd, still the American Girl to these people. She was the public's favorite and there was a delicious shiver that came across the sportswriters and fans alike as she returned to the breach, not just to play again, but to go for the title.

When news of her departure from San Francisco on the Overland Limited reached New York, reporters and columnists went crazy over her once again. They suggested that she was looking for revenge against Jacobs for the Forest Hills embarrassment two years earlier. Gallico wrote that when she left San Francisco this time she showed that she was a fighter. "It raised the short hairs at the back of my neck because she had left her lair like a jungle cat on the prowl. If I had been Jacobs," he wrote, "I should have shaken in my shoes. If ever one woman stalked another, that was it."

Helen Wills was not a "counterfighter," Gallico wrote. She could have waited to play Jacobs at Forest Hills, he believed. But instead, just as in 1926, she went after her adversary. She was a fighter, and she had a sense of the dramatic, and she had shown that in 1926 and again in 1935, and the press loved it. Gallico believed that Helen was afraid she would not catch Jacobs at Forest Hills. If Jacobs won Wimbledon then she would turn professional, and Helen would miss the chance of a lifetime for a comeback. So she had to move quickly. After reading of the O'Brien offer in the newspapers, she knew she had to act soon. "I will bet you all the catgut in the pound that Moody wants Jacobs and she wants her now," Gallico told his readers.

But the Moodys' close friends insisted that such was not the case.

Wills's dedication and her concentration and persistence were, by and large, impersonal. She had things to prove to herself. She had visions and dreams and an agenda in her mind. Her animosity and her disappointment over the loss to Jacobs were not personalized. Jacobs simply stood in her way. Jacobs had become the hurdle over which Helen had stumbled. Now, with practice and conditioning, Wills would, when she came to that same impediment, push it aside and move on. She was not concentrating on a particular person. She was concentrating on internal and external obstacles. Moody suggested to me that he doubted that Helen could even tell you the color of Helen Jacobs's eyes or her hair or her height. She might tell you how the ball felt when Jacobs played it or how her slice bounced or where she moved after hitting a backhand down the line. But the personal things were irrelevant at long last. And they bothered her, she indicated, not at all anymore. She was resolved now to let history take its course. She would come back and she would play. And if the gods were willing she would win. If they were not, then she was finished.

When she arrived in New York, she spoke with *New York Times* columnist Allison Danzig and refused to commit herself on her plans for the season. Would she play at Wimbledon and then at Forest Hills? She could not say. She said that she had brought along enough clothes and rackets to make the trip to England. And she said that Julian Myrick had invited her to join the Wightman Cup squad in England. And she said her back injury bothered her no more. It had healed completely.

Reporters who watched her practice in New York agreed she was back in form. She told them that doctors had told her it was safe again to play tennis. She was not making the trip to England to play against Helen Jacobs, she insisted. But, at the same time, one could never tell who one might meet in the tournaments. Many things might happen.

Gallico didn't believe a word of it. He listened to her and then he wrote, "This time she didn't fool anyone. Wills was on the war path for Jacobs. And how!"

She was interviewed in New York by Grantland Rice. He asked her why she decided to try a comeback, and she told him, "I just had to. I wanted at least one more chance before a gentleman known as Old Man Time starts calling me off the courts. But I doubt that he's a gentleman." Rice said she looked young—perhaps around twenty-one or twenty-two again.

She had time for a single practice session on the courts of the River Club. A crowd came just to see her hit the ball. She played against the club professional who provided her with the sort of shots she could hit to demonstrate again her grace and power. Allison Danzig watched her and wrote that she showed no weakness and no sign of pain. Apparently, he concluded, her injury had been healed. Some spectators noticed the pace she put on her backhand returns now—something that she had not done in her pre-1933 years. One reporter noticed that her backhand was "something to marvel at," and the lower the bound of the ball "the more she appeared to relish it, as she awaited now anyone who dared to try a low bounding chop shot against her." Of course, Helen Jacobs's specialty was the chop shot.

At the Colony Club where she stayed, Helen Wills was besieged by reporters and interviewers who turned out en mass to see "one of the most celebrated woman players in tennis." But most waited in vain, as she had other meetings and other things to attend to.

She had tea with Rollin Kirby, the cartoonist, and his wife, then dinner with some California friends. The next morning Edward Crowninshield picked her up and drove her to the ship. They arrived dockside with only four minutes to spare. Two photographers were waiting. They walked backwards up the gangway of the *Manhattan* taking pictures of her as she boarded. Julian Myrick and Dr. William Valentiner were there. Myrick was surprised at Helen's tardiness again and reminded her of the 1924 Olympic Games when she nearly missed the train home. Her career seemed to have several close calls. Myrick and Valentiner bid her farewell and good fortune.

In England she stayed at the American Women's Club on Grosvenor Street her first night in town and then moved to Great Fosters in Surrey the next day.

By the time she arrived in England she completed her plans for the season. She said that after England she would go to California "without waiting for anything at Forest Hills." American officials and writers let it be known that if she won they felt she surely could not resist the temptation of a comeback at Forest Hills before an American crowd.

She was more careful than ever before, now, about keeping up her training. She entered the tournaments at St. George's Hill and Beckenham to get practice play and to warm up. She remembered that in the past her greatest problems came from lack of practice before matches. Now she could afford no mistakes, no mistakes at all.

Those preliminary tournaments in England where Helen Wills practiced her comeback were not suited for the hundreds of newsmen who scrambled around trying to get a look at the returning queen. The St. George's Hill Club tournament had folding chairs along the edge of the court for observers. It was an informal invitational tournament with a friendly atmosphere about it.

The first tournament in which she played was the St. George's Hill Club at Weybridge, one of the prettiest places in the county of Surrey and with easy access to London. She began her comeback on June 2, some twenty-one months after she walked from the final at Forest Hills. Her first opposition was Jill Notely, an unranked Englishwoman, and Wills beat her 6–2, 6–0 in twenty-one minutes. She appeared to be pretty much the same player the British had applauded in 1927. "Her blazing drives and formidable reputation were enough to subdue her opponent," one reporter wrote.

Wills proceeded, as in the past, through the early rounds. There was some trouble against Mary Hardwick, who forced Helen to three sets, 4–6, 7–5, 6–3, but the American had little trouble in the semifinal against Billie Yorke of England, and beat her 6–1, 6–4.

In the Yorke match, spectators noticed that her greatest problems came from the fact that the strong winds kept ballooning her skirt and raising it up high, and she was constantly holding it down with her left hand or with her racket. She had to hold her skirt down and at the same time hit the ball. There were suggestions that her play might be improved if she switched to tennis shorts like many of the other female players, including Helen Jacobs. Yet Helen stuck to her traditional full pleated cotton skirt.

"In the final round on June 8th Helen seemed unbothered by the unusual energy of her opponent, Mrs. Elsie Goldsack Pittman, and won 6–0, 6–4."

With the conclusion of the Weybridge tournament and the taking of another title, the odds against Wills taking the Wimbledon singles crown for a record-tying seventh time dropped to only two to one. But at the Weybridge tournament, several journalists noticed a change in Wills's game. She had lost her "killer instinct," they wrote. She no longer tried to win all of her games or sets at love. In some instances in the tournament she had let up noticeably in the second set and had appeared to give up several games that might have been taken with the expenditure of a bit more energy. Yet, when it appeared that she really wanted a point she would take it easily with one of her lightning bolt ground strokes. At other times she was patient and willing to wait for her opponent to make an error.

In the St. George's Hill tournament Helen Wills played six matches and lost but one set. She seemed solidly on her way to another Wimbledon title. She won the women's title on courts that were slower than usual due to the rain. Rain not only delayed many of her matches, but also made the grass playing surfaces slippery and uncertain. The surface took its toll on her game, sucked at her feet and sapped her speed energy, and confidence. The elements seemed to have turned against her. This was not her surface—wet grass. Elizabeth Ryan seemed always to beat her on wet grass, and so did Molla Mallory. She had lost some important matches on wet grass, and she began to wonder if she had traveled all that way simply to lose now.

Wills moved on to the Kent Championships in Beckenham for her final warm-up. In the opening rounds of the tournament she played three matches and lost but seven games. She crushed the former English junior champion, S. G. Cutter, in love sets in the opening round of the tournament and beat the former captain of the British Wightman Cup team,

Miss E. H. Harvey, 6–3, 6–1, in the second round. Then she beat Nancy Lyle, 6–1, 6–2, in the third round. But in the fourth round she met with disaster.

There she played left-handed Kay Stammers of Great Britain, one of the most promising of the young British players. One British writer said that Wills's dream "all but dissolved into thin air today," as she was crushed by Stammers. The match was not even close. Stammers won, 6–0, 6–4. Another writer described Wills as "looking more like a tired, muscle-bound matron than a potential champion, the Californian never had a chance to cope with the fiery thrusts of her determined opponent. The crowd of more than a thousand looked on in amazement as the English girl, who recently conquered Dorothy Round for the British Hard Court Championship, matched Wills drive for drive and routed her with stinging placements."

Wills appeared to be almost hypnotized by the left-handed shots of Stammers. She dropped the first three games at love and did not even pull up to deuce in a game until the fourth game. Then the fifth and sixth games also went to deuce, but Wills lost each of them. Helen took a 4–1 lead in the second set and seemed well on her way to making her comeback a success. But then her game just fell apart completely, and she let Stammers take five games in a row and with them the second set. In the last five games she won only eight points. Wills scored only two placements during the entire match.

The loss looked even worse when Stammers was beaten by Dorothy Round in the finals, 6–2, 6–0. Stammers was ranked third in England and Round first. It was surprising and disappointing for Wills also since she came so close to pulling her game together in the second set. But after the match she smiled at reporters and congratulated Stammers on a "marvelous match." But she then hurried to the clubhouse and sat with her head bowed staring at the floor, not moving, for several minutes. She remained in deep meditation for a long time. No one disturbed her or spoke to her or interrupted her mood.

Although she was now committed to Wimbledon, "her admirers who witnessed today's match were about ready to admit she may have reached the sunset of her career," one journalist concluded. Wills's defeat sent the odds zooming again. Now they stood at three to one against her, and Bill O'Brien's plan of putting together a women's professional tour with all of the big guns from the amateur ranks seemed about to succeed.

To her normal routine of playing tennis, Helen Wills now did exercises to speed up her foot work. She consulted with Harry Hillman, the Dartmouth College track coach and trainer for the American Davis Cup team. Hillman had her wear spiked track shoes and do several short sprints each morning. Then he had her place about a half-dozen stakes in a row and run around them in a sprint much like a skier going down hill. There was no doubt that those who watched Wills prepare for Wimbledon believed that she was in earnest in her preparations for the tournament and that her desire to win it this time seemed greater than at any time in the past. She did not play in a tournament she did not expect to win, she had said time and again. And this was another one that she expected to win. She had faltered, it was a bad sign, and she was disappointed, deeply disappointed. She now intended to win.

--◄ **4** ►--

In the spring of 1935 Wimbledon referee Francis Russell Burrow sensed general expectation that, if Helen Wills would not be beaten, then she would be tested in this tournament as never before. After all, she had lost at Beckenham to Stammers and had lost a set to Mary Hardwick at St. George's Hill. "There was not this time, the feeling of hopelessness in going into court against her which had affected nearly all of her opponents in previous years. She was, in fact, only seeded fourth in the tournament. Dorothy Round was seeded first in the tournament, and then Hilda Sperling and Jacobs were seeded second and third.

At the end of the first day of the 1935 Wimbledon competition, Helen Jacobs was presented at court, just as Helen Wills had been in 1929. Jacobs had her opening match transferred to an outside court in order to allow her to get away early to dress for the occasion. Little Helen was still dogging the path of the Big Helen, it seemed, receiving attention, winning titles, gaining honors, making records, but still stalking Big Helen here for that one clear victory, that one bit of proof that she had come into her own and that she was indeed a successor to the Queen and not just the perpetual pretender to the title of champion.

But just as Helen prepared to make her entry onto the Centre Court on the afternoon of June 25, the skies suddenly opened up and a torrential rain fell, accompanied by thunder and lightning. Play was delayed for two hours, and the tarpaulin covers were spread over the grass. The capacity crowd spent that time huddling together gazing impatiently out at the lashing rain. But when the storm passed, it appeared that no one had left the grounds. The stadium was packed again with 15,000 people anxious to see history in the making. There to see Helen Wills. Again.

She had been missed. The English crowd had never seen the American girl default, had never seen her when she was not at her very best. She was still their favorite. They had defended her in her darkest hour in 1933. When she walked onto the lush lawn of that famous arena for her opening match, the entire crowd came to its feet and applauded long and enthusiastically. The extraordinary thing about the crowd was its enthusiasm, newsmen noticed. The awful weather seemed not to have dampened the excitement at all. The match was a special one, and all revenues from the tickets on the first day of the tournament went to the King's Jubilee Trust Fund.

Helen returned to Wimbledon's celebrated Centre Court for her opening round match in 1935 against Mlle A. Baumgarten, a Hungarian player, and easily brushed her aside, 6–0, 6–1. In the second round Wills beat Belgian Nelli Adamson, 6–3, 6–2. But the grass was wet and slippery, and Helen slipped and fell hard twice during the play, a clear reminder that the Queen was a mortal. Yet there were those who still recalled the scrambling stoic Little Poker Face who would dive and lunge for the ball. Helen was trying hard again, reaching way back. Each time she fell she recovered quickly and indicated that she was all right and had not been injured by the fall. After her second fall Helen Wills made the novel move of putting stockings over the outside of her tennis shoes in order to give them more grip on the wet grass. The Duke of Kent arrived in time to see Wills put the finishing touches on her victory.

Jacobs was in another bracket in the tournament, and the only way the two women could meet on the court would be in the finals, initially an unlikely proposition. But if by some miracle of fate Jacobs did make it, she would make possible a dream match for this Jubilee tournament. But the dream match seemed ever more unlikely given Jacobs's performance in the early rounds of the tournament. Against the Dutch champion Rollin Conquerque, Jacobs was taken to six-all in the opening set on the Centre Court. She pulled out the win 8–6. In the second set she won at 6–4, but only after a long grim struggle.

But Wills also had a bit more trouble than ever before with scrappy Billie Yorke, finally beating her by 6–3, 6–1 in a match marked by many long rallies. In the next round she beat Susan Noel, winning 6–1, 6–3.

The first major surprise of the tournament, however, came on July 1 when Helen Wills played unranked Slecna (Emma) Cepkova of Czechoslovakia, of whom little was known at the time, and little was heard of later. But she was the first of many Czechoslovakian players over the next decades to make a memorable mark on Wimbledon. Playing in her first Wimbledon, Cepkova had little to lose. She was expected to be another one of those many nearly anonymous opponents that Wills brushed aside on her way to bigger and more dramatic confrontations. With little to lose, she came out hitting hard at everything, going after every shot Wills gave her, making desperate stabs at balls that should have slipped by—shots that other players, intimidated by the six-times singles champion, would have let pass. But this was Cepkova's day, her moment. She remained pokerfaced through the early games and took away Wills's best shots and made winners of her own out of them. She beat Helen methodically and dispassionately and, most surprising of all, easily. Wills missed shot after shot and fell behind quickly. Cepkova took the first set at 6–3, shocking the crowd. The match was played on an outside court, and suddenly thousands of spectators moved from the Centre Court to the outside court to see the drama unfolding.

Helen Wills recalled later that Cepkova was "a sturdy blonde girl from Central Europe who could run miles better than I, and who had on this day no idea of missing any balls whatever. She was concentrating so keenly that she didn't know when it was her turn to serve." Cepkova was in fact concentrating so deeply on each point that, like young Helen Wills in the 1924 Wimbledon tournament, she lost track of the points and the games. In a daze of excitement, two or three times she forgot which side of the court to serve from, and once she stood on the baseline ready to serve and realized that she had no tennis balls to throw.

Cepkova surged to 3–1 in the second set, scoring frequently off deep hard drives to Wills's backhand, which failed her in this emergency. Yet, finally, after holding her own service and breaking Cepkova once, Wills tied the score at 3–3. But Cepkova took the next game and jumped up to 4–3, and the crowd cheered continuously. This was a test. Helen Wills came through. Not only did she have a generous portion of her old stuff, but Cepkova was not equal to the moment. At that point in the match, the umpire gave Wills a close line call, and the crowd suddenly indicated its disapproval and shouted out protests. Play was interrupted. That decision and the crowd response seemed to confuse Cepkova for a moment. Her concentration wavered, and her confidence seemed shaken. She was confused by the crowd's boisterous response and apparently believed that it indicated disapproval of her own play. No one explained to her exactly what was happening. But from that moment on she was distracted enough for Helen Wills to take advantage, and make her final familiar surge to take the second set and then the third at 6–2.

Wills remembered the linesman's controversial call. Helen considered this to be good fortune, "a lucky break" at the right time and in the right direction. Some in the crowd suggested that Cepkova looked up at the scoreboard midway through the second set, realized that she was beating a legendary player, and seemed all of a sudden to be unnerved by the incredible feat she was pulling off. She probably started thinking about it, they said, and then lost her concentration and her game and her match.

Al Laney saw the Cepkova match and was amazed by it. He wondered what Helen Wills could be doing wrong, if anything. "For she had been open to attack by a girl of no reputation, but one no longer afraid of the great former champion. I remember that this interested me greatly. Perhaps it disturbed me. Anyhow, I had not seen it before and it made me wonder."

Wills advanced now to the quarter-finals. For Cepkova it was the end of the tournament. Her chance to change the course of history had passed. She never returned to Wimbledon.

At this point Helen Wills ran out of rackets. She had used more frames than expected due to the wet weather. A local sporting goods company in London copied one of her rackets overnight and made half a dozen like it for her just for this emergency. One of her biggest problems in 1935 and after was her rackets. Not only did she seem to be somewhat calcified in her defiantly unstylish tennis attire, but she also refused to adopt the new lighter racket used by the other women. She continued to play with a racket with a five-inch handle, and they were simply no longer sold. The new handles were 4⅞ inches. Wills had hers custom made with the old five-inch handle.

And to some she was beginning to look old-fashioned in her behavior, too. One newsman who watched her in 1935 wrote: "she never has been a spectacular person . . . on the courts she walks like a schoolmistress, never hurrying, occasionally plucking a small handkerchief out of her pocket with which she pats her heavily powdered face."

Jacobs, meanwhile, moved through the fourth round in straight sets beating another British opponent.

As Wills and Jacobs advanced, it appeared that Wimbledon would have a dream match this year. So reporters descended on players at the Berkeley Tennis Club, men who had practiced with the two Helens during the past year, and asked for predictions. George Hudson, the professional resident at the club, doubted that Big Helen had recovered enough to beat Jacobs. Her 1933 injuries had been too severe, he said. And for her to win at Wimbledon in a tough match against Jacobs was just asking too much.

But Pop Fuller, who was seventy at the time, disagreed. He said that the Stammers win over Wills was not important and should be disregarded. He said that if the two Helens met in the finals he could not possibly pick a winner. He liked both. When they played at Wimbledon, he said, only one thing was certain: that "Helen will win."

In the quarter-final matches Dorothy Round, the defending champion and one of the two Englishwomen to hold the title since 1924 (the second to hold it since 1914), was beaten by Australian Joan Hartigan. Round played poorly against Hartigan, a player who went surprisingly far without a dependable backhand stroke. Hartigan's three-set victory put her in the semifinals against Big Helen. And it was, to English observers, a free pass for Wills to the finals, since Hartigan was playing way out of her league and was expected to have absolutely no chance at all against the American.

Helen Wills was resurgent in the quarter-finals, beating Rene Mathieu of France, 6–3, 6–0. In the second set of the match, Wills lost only seven points and took three games at love. Jacobs, on the other hand, was extended to 9–7 in the second set of her quarter-final match with Jadwiga Jedrzejowska, after winning the first set at 6–1 over the Polish woman.

On July 4, Wills was tested in her semi-final contest as she was forced to come from behind in both of her sets to beat Hartigan 6–3, 6–3. Wills hammered away steadily at Hartigan's weak backhand and beat her down. She seemed to gain strength as the match progressed, sometimes scoring aces on her second service. She expected to face Hilda Sperling in the final since earlier that spring in Paris Sperling had beaten Helen Jacobs, her semifinal opponent. Wills told friends that she was not looking forward to the impending ordeal of playing the German woman, one of those human backboards who could pop back just about any shot and seemed able to run back and forth along the baseline for hours. Wills was spared that ordeal by Jacobs, who, in beating Sperling in two sets, 6–3, 6–0, showed greater grit and determination than a few weeks before.

The Jacobs-Sperling contest was a dull affair with long rallies terminated, usually, by a Sperling error. Some of the rallies, bleary-eyed fans recalled, lasted for as much as an eternity of sixty strokes.

The 1935 Wimbledon women's final was played on Friday, July 5, and represented the third time that the two Helens met in the final singles match of the championships. Wills had beaten Jacobs in 1929 and again in 1932. In the four sets of those final matches, Jacobs won a total of seven games.

American sportswriters again became very excited before the match. Bill Corum of the International News Service wrote that "one of the bitterest grudge fights in sports will be given a public airing when Mrs. Helen Wills Moody faces Helen Jacobs on Wimbledon's Centre Court tomorrow." And he suggested that "hell hath no fury like a lady tennis player scorched with a disliked rival's service ace, and this surprising meeting of the California Helens shapes up as one of the most dramatic passages at racquets in the history of the sport." Corum also made a prediction. He said he always had felt that Helen Wills was the Gene Tunney of tennis players. "She knows what it's all about at all times and we don't think she would have attempted a comeback if she hadn't been reasonably certain she could regain her old-time form. We think she is going to win."

The English were also excited by the prospect of a grudge match, and British reporters rushed about frantically soliciting final statements and details that might be of significance. Jacobs told reporters, "I have satisfactory memories of Forest Hills," indicating that she believed she would win again. And she later wrote that, on the day of the match, "I had a strong and disturbing feeling that I would win." She never explained why a sense of impending victory should be termed "disturbing" as well as "strong." Wills only told reporters, "I'll try to put up a good show."

Both Kay Stammers and Dorothy Round said that they believed Wills would win. And they pointed out that weeks earlier Suzanne Lenglen, who had shown Jacobs once how to beat Big Helen, had no faith in a second victory for the smaller American. "I choose Mrs. Moody," Suzanne told reporters in Paris. "I choose Mrs. Moody."

For each woman the match was extremely important. For Helen Wills it was the end of a long painful road back. And it was vindication and perhaps even vengeance, possibly, for the humiliation of 1933. Now she had an opportunity to prove herself once more, and to prove that she was as good as people said she was, to prove it by winning her seventh Wimbledon title—one more than the great Suzanne Lenglen. Then, no matter what the critics might write, the record books would indicate forever that she should be ranked as one of the two finest players ever to grace the courts of Great Britain.

And for Helen Jacobs this was an opportunity to move out from the shadow of Big Helen. She could at last be Helen the First, and she could prove that even when Big Helen was in good health she was no match for this formidable and scrappy player who had worked so long and so hard to get to the Centre Court. And she could pave the way for a professional tour for women—women who might then control their own destiny on and off the tennis courts.

An hour before match time, the stadium was full. Several hundred people stood throughout the night outside the gates waiting to get in. The weather for the match was perfect, with only a slight breeze blowing. Nineteen thousand people were packed together in the stadium at Centre Court to see this final between the two Helens. It was called, by some writers, the match of the century, and it was certainly the most publicized confrontation since Helen Wills met Suzanne Lenglen at Cannes.

Just prior to the match Jacobs practiced for about fifteen minutes with Wimbledon's assistant professional. She hit well. She wore her customary elongated shorts with the blue stripe down the side. Wills wore her customary knee-length skirt and a white blouse. She, too, practiced briefly before the match with Don Turnbull, an Australian amateur.

Wills experienced, she recalled later, an unusual high as the match was about to begin. After the preliminary rally, which made her impatient, she experienced, she said, "a sharp feeling of pleasure, almost as if you were a tree with the bark stripped off, feeling the air about you for the first time." It was a good feeling, a wonderful feeling. It was a singular moment in time, and "it belonged so emphatically to the present, that a clarity, unusual to your eye and mind, seemed to take possession of you," she wrote of her feelings that afternoon.

It was on this very same court that a dozen years earlier Suzanne Lenglen had sought and gotten revenge and vindication for her own defeat at Forest Hills by Molla Mallory. Suzanne had won back all of her laurels on that day, and now the chance for vindication and revenge was being played out once more by one woman who had once been a rival of Lenglen, who had herself beaten Molla Mallory and who, just like Lenglen, had been humiliated at Forest Hills by an American player and an American crowd. In hitting ground strokes during the preliminary warm up, Wills noticed that the court seemed to be especially fast on this afternoon, a good sign. A fast court suited her game.

After the spin of the racket for the service, Wills walked to her end of the court. It was 2:30 p.m. "I had the curious feeling that time had been turned back, and that it was the first year," she said. But with two differences. Her opponent was not Kitty McKane; she was not nervous. She noticed that for the first time she was not nervous at Wimbledon.

Wills, having won the spin, chose to serve the first game. She hit Jacobs's return long and lost the point, but then proceeded to hold her service and win the first game. She broke Jacobs in the second game at 30 and went ahead by two. She then held service again in the third game to jump ahead by three. But Jacobs was able to resurge, taking the fourth game on her own service. Then Jacobs made an adjustment in the fifth game. She advanced to the net behind her service return and cut off Wills's return stroke. The tactic worked. She broke Big Helen's service at love. Then Jacobs held her own service at love by forcing Helen to hit long three times. Jacobs knew what she had to do to win, and she was doing it.

At three games all Jacobs clearly had gained momentum, and Wills was on the defensive. Jacobs won the first three points of the seventh game. But Wills pulled up to deuce after three long rallies. The game went to deuce six times, and Wills finally won two points in a row and the game to go ahead 4–3. That game alone—the longest of the match—lasted for thirteen tense minutes. In the ninth game Wills served and ran up a 40–15 lead. Jacobs took the next point, but Wills then served an ace to take the game and the set, 6–3.

Wills continued to roll, taking the first game of the second set. Then Jacobs snapped back in the second game and won it and cut her way through the third game easily, too. Wills tried to move Jacobs from corner to corner, to run her as she had done in the old days. But Jacobs was now hitting hard and accurately, returning long flat drives with her own underspin that kept the ball low on the grass and hurried Wills. The set went to two–all.

Wills took that fourth game by working harder, and she seemed to be zeroing in on the victory in the second set. But Jacobs held her own service in the fifth game, and Wills came back on her service to hold at three–all. Jacobs again held service in the seventh for a 4–3 lead and then broke Wills at love for a 5–3 lead. She held her own service in the ninth game to win the set at 6–3.

The crowd by this time realized they were watching a classic confrontation. As the women changed courts before starting the final set, the 19,000 people came to their feet and cheered like crazy. This was a match they would not forget.

Watching carefully from the stands, Al Laney, who had seen these two women play scores of times, noticed something extremely important about their play in the second set. Wills came on aggressively and confidently as the second set opened and began to serve and volley as she had done in early years, trying to make the match as short as possible. Jacobs came to the net more, behind beautiful approach shots, and she caught and fired back what should have been passing shots. Wills stayed back more, Jacobs now came in more. When Wills came in, Jacobs passed her; and when she tried to lob, Jacobs caught the shots and fired them back for winners. With Jacobs leading 5-2, at set point she double-faulted and lost the game. She came back to break the Wills service and win the next game and the set.

Laney felt that it was particularly important to note that Jacobs faltered badly at set point. And Wills, although uncertain, when uncertain in the past had always recovered. Laney took note of this and wondered if Jacobs ever did arrive at *match* point if she could make it against Wills. The end of the second set, he felt, indicated that she could not.

Except during the actual play, the two Helens appeared to prefer to ignore each other. When they passed at the umpire's chair they did not exchange a word, never looked at each other, and kept their backs turned always. "They didn't play tennis," wrote H. R. Knickerbocker of the INS. "They fought tennis." And he wrote that the two Helens had "hate in their hearts" and a "smile on their lips." Another writer describing it said that, while Wills showed "cat-like grace" on the court, Jacobs showed "bouncing energy." To the newsmen the contrasts were important. Wills showed a "classic profile" and Jacobs "a grimly determined scowl." Wills's lips were "disdainful," while Jacobs's mouth was "a thin hard line."

Journalist Frank Graham believed throughout the first set that Wills would win. But then he saw that the entire complexion of the contest changed abruptly. Wills, in command only a moment earlier, was suddenly on the defensive. She seemed to have lost both speed and power. And she was out of breath, clearly. Jacobs had picked up confidence and energy and used her backhand deftly.

Wills opened the third set well by holding her service in a commanding way and she went ahead by one. But Jacobs stayed in the contest, and in the next game on her own service matched Wills point for point. She took the game. Then she broke Wills in the third game, finding her vulnerable when she came to the net. Wills broke back to 2-2 with some sizzling shots down the line just beyond Jacobs racket. Jacobs then fought hard enough to break Wills's service and hold her own, and she moved the set to 4-2. Wills was slow between games at this point, and she rested on her racket while Jacobs prepared to serve. Then Wills "dragged herself back into position." Jacobs had stepped up the pace of the match, forcing it, sensing exhaustion and vulnerability in her opponent. Jacobs held her service in another difficult game and pulled ahead 5-2. Wills hit hard, but every thundering top-spin forehand drained more energy from her, and it showed.

But Wills did not quit. And she did not let up. She was still into the game and into the match and into every shot. Every shot. Even when it seemed hopeless to many and she was staring at defeat. One game separated her from losing her second match at Wimbledon.

In that ninth game Helen Wills fell behind on her own service to
15–30, and Jacobs stood at just two points from victory. Then Wills drew
Jacobs to the net with a short shot, and Jacobs was there in time to sweep
it up and hurl it back down the line for a winner. Jacobs expected to
hear the umpire call out 15–40 and double-match point. But the umpire
ruled that Jacobs did not get the shot before a second bound, so the score
stood at 30–30. Jacobs took the next point—a point that would have given
her the match had the umpire not made his call—a call with which Jacobs
quietly disagreed. Now, after two winners, instead of celebrating a victory,
she stood at match point. Match point. The noise in the stands now was
a steady hum interrupted by sudden explosions of applause and cheers.
Jacobs came on aggressively now, drove deep and drove Wills off the
court. Wills lunged to put up a last pathetic short lob. It arched high
above the Centre Court and then wavered a little at its apogee in the
breeze. Then it began to fall. All eyes in the stadium were on that ball.
Wills watched from behind the baseline expecting Jacobs to go for an
easy kill, and she tried to anticipate where the smash would hit. It was
not the shot Wills intended to put up. And almost everyone in the stands
knew that the end of the match was at hand.

Paul Gallico wrote that at that moment Wills "looked the end squarely
and gallantly in the face and it was not the end she must have dreamed
of so many many days and nights when she opened those secret places of
her self and read what was written there."

Jacobs skipped in toward the net and kept her eye on that ball, waiting
for it to come down so she could pounce on it, waiting to put it away and
end the match and end the tournament and end the era. She waited. "It
was a shot any weekend tennis player might dream of putting away, could
put away very easily," Gallico thought.

Jacobs had waited a lifetime for this moment, and the three-time American champion who had put away literally thousands of shots just like this
and had been in the finals of this tournament three times and who had
just been presented to the Queen of England, and now she let her nerves
or something get the better of her. The ball bounced and was caught suddenly in a strange down draft. It never came up from the grass quite as
high as Jacobs expected. It hung very low, almost as though enchanted.
As she moved forward, Jacobs made a series of little readjustments in her
stance. She leaned in and began to bend her knees. She was ready for an
overhead smash, but the ball now was too low for that shot. Wills leaned
forward flatfooted from the middle of the baseline ready to move in either
direction. Jacobs was off balance, and her feet were all wrong, and she
stooped more to get the overhead, but the ball was falling again toward
the grass, and she couldn't get it. Jacobs bent her knees to get at the ball,
dipped her shoulder. She went down further and further trying for the
best angle on her smash. She could not get down low enough. By the time
she finally swung and made contact with the ball she was nearly on her

knees in front of the net, still trying desperately, awkwardly for the final stroke of the tournament. But the ball was too low, and her racket was too high, and she could not swing it around for a forehand whip or chop, so she swung at it, and the ball snapped off her strings into the net cord and spun sideways down the net and then slid slowly down the net on her side and rolled off onto the grass and died.

Helen Jacobs did not know what had happened. She didn't understand. She seemed stunned for a moment. The crowd was stunned. Helen Wills was also staring, almost unbelieving. It was some sort of evil magic. Jacobs examined for a moment the spot on the grass where the ball hit. She could find nothing unusual there. Then she walked back to the base-line to play. She kept thinking about the ball and the bounce and the breeze and the ball and the shot and what in the hell had just happened. Her concentration was fractured, and in the next moments, under a renewed battering from Helen Wills's forehand, it began to crumble. Jacobs thought about her sudden misfortune during the next point and lost it. And she continued to think about it during the next point, too, and lost that and with it the game. And she continued to think about it. It wormed inside her mind, and Wills kept winning and pulled even with her.

Helen Wills was now inspired. "It must have seemed to my friends in the stands that I was going to lose the match," she said later. "But this did not occupy my thought, probably because I had not been in the habit of thinking this way during all the years I played in tournaments. Habits of the past are likely to return to one in critical moments." Wills was now again thinking like a winner, thinking positively and with confidence. Jacobs was not. She was thinking about what might have been. Wills was thinking again of what must be.

No sooner had Wills saved that set point than her mind became calm and confident again. She knew now that she would win. She knew. "I have never felt as confident in any match within my memory," she wrote. She did not look ahead to the very end, but she was herself winning each point now, saw the importance again of each individual stroke, just as when she had first come to Forest Hills with her mantra, "Every shot, every shot." And once more like magic it seemed to be working for her. She had, like Suzanne Lenglen, thrown caution to the wind and thought of nothing but the game, and it worked.

Jacobs gradually self-destructed. Helen Wills guessed that Jacobs had lost her perspective, had looked ahead a few seconds and had seen herself winning the point and the set and the match, winning the championship, had visualized everything suddenly at the end and her dream accomplished. And when it escaped her so suddenly, she could not recover her perspective.

"Looking ahead to the conclusion of a match is beyond the demand of the moment," Helen Wills wrote of this match. "The immediate thing was the returning of the ball, and this was the only thought that was in my mind. It may have been that Miss Jacobs looked ahead to the end, which was not illogical, seeing that she was so near to it, and that during the following points she did not regain the perspective of regarding the urgency of the immediate point. I can remember that this was the case in my match against Kathleen McKane in my first Wimbledon final. I saw the end before it arrived."

One linesman recalled that Jacobs played the last three games in a virtual daze. She didn't seem able to comprehend what was happening to her—it was just too unbelievable. "We had to tell her it was her service in the final game," he said. "What a wonderful fighter she is."

Wills held her service in the ninth game and broke Jacobs in the tenth to pull up to five–all. She then went ahead by one on her own service. With the score at 5–5 Jacobs needed one point to break Wills's service and go to a 6–5 lead, but again she drove into the net. She was not given another chance to win. Wills fired terrific drives from the back corner from that point on. She found new strength.

Jacobs was never in the match again. Wills won five games in a row and with them her seventh singles title. In the twelfth game the referee had to remind Jacobs that she was serving, after a long pause. The game went to deuce twice. But after several exchanges, Jacobs hit long, and the match ended. It ended exactly 100 minutes after it began. Helen Wills was again champion of the world.

Jacobs appeared in the last games of the match to be wedded to calamity, playing her familiar supporting role in the drama of the career and life and legend of Helen Wills, the American Girl.

The crowd came to its feet for a long ovation when it was over. Wills threw her racket high in the air, ran to the net, and touched Jacobs's outstretched hand.

When she had completed participating in the closing ceremonies and had been awarded the first prize trophy, Helen Wills ran from the court and grabbed and kissed Sir Herbert Wilberforce, a former president of the All-England Club. "I had always wanted to, because he was so sweet," she said. Then, she said, several of her friends complained to her because of the suspense of the match. Finally, just to make sure this was not a dream, a fantastic dream, Helen stopped the first person she met in the hall of the clubhouse and asked if it was true that she had really won. She not only won, but she won by pulling victory from the jaws of defeat, like the Great Lenglen in 1919. She looked defeat in the eye and did not blink. Like the great Lenglen she played with match point against her in the third set and continued fighting and showed that she too was great, and, like Lenglen, she gave up only when her health was in danger, not when her crown was slipping and the score was against her. It was a perfect win for Helen Wills. Absolutely perfect. It was the best imaginable vindication for the collapse of 1933.

Later Helen Wills told reporters, "I enjoyed the match enormously. I never really expected to do so well after a two-year absence from my game. My heart was in my mouth when Miss Jacobs went set-point but I gritted my teeth and fought on although I felt as though I wanted to cry. I kept up heart although I expected every game to finish my chances."

Wills's seventh singles victory was far more significant than that of Mrs. Lambert Chambers. Wills played through all the championships. Lambert Chambers as champion played only in the final challenge round. Also, Chambers was beaten three times in singles at Wimbledon. Helen Wills had lost only once in eight tries.

Witnesses to the final match remembered it as the most exciting at Wimbledon since the Lenglen–Lambert Chambers affair of 1919. And like that one, the winner of this match found match point against her and saved the point, the match and the day. The parallels between Lenglen and Wills continued.

Grantland Rice was thrilled by the outcome of the match. After commenting on Helen Wills's matches for more than a decade, now he could write, "As the case now stands, Mrs. Moody needs no further proof in her behalf. She has written one of the greatest chapters in the history of sport." Paul Gallico said, "If I tried to write that story as fiction nobody would believe it and no editor would publish it. It seems incredible that a situation should arise which would permit the heroine thereof to score a double triumph and satisfy every dramatic angle. And yet it did. Wills was within a point of defeat and proved that she could take it like a sportswoman. And then when Fate intervened and gave her a reprieve, she went on to show that she was still the better tennis player, had more nerve, courage and stamina, was, in short, a champion."

It was her seventh Wimbledon singles victory, and it tied her with Mrs. Lambert Chambers, a feat that had been accomplished only once before and that prior to World War I. The victory came twelve years after Helen Wills captured her first American singles title in 1923.

For Helen Jacobs it was the fourth Wimbledon loss in the finals. After arriving there four times she had been shunted aside by Big Helen three times and once by Dorothy Round. It was a reminder that Jacobs still had never beaten Wills in a completed match.

No sooner had the match ended than Harry Myers, an entrepreneur from Los Angeles, wired an offer to Wills and Jacobs to play one match in Los Angeles for a purse of $25,000. The players could divide the purse any way they wished, he said. The match would be sponsored by the American Legion. Already Bill O'Brien had competition. But neither woman even bothered to reject the offer.

Local San Francisco papers printed a story stating that Bill O'Brien had promised Jacobs $150,000 as a bonus if she beat Wills. And they reported that betting odds in San Francisco just before the Wimbledon competition began stood at ten to one against Big Helen. Scores of local residents bet for Wills at those odds, only to discover that the bookie taking their money was not legitimate. He took off with the cash. Helen Wills won, and a lot of her staunch California fans lost.

After the match, it was said, the "smart money" in California pointed out that Wills had beaten Jacobs twenty-four of twenty-five times. And they gave Jacobs credit for standing up to so many defeats. She certainly was a good loser. Better than that, she was a perfect loser. Few tennis players could take such a consistent drubbing year in and year out and stand up one more time for another good fight. She was courageous.

Jacobs held her head erect as she walked from the court, side by side with Big Helen, her conqueror again, and the crowd stood and roared its approval for several minutes.

But in the dressing room Jacobs lay prostrate for forty-five minutes, at the edge of tears. Finally, she was heard to say, "Naturally, I'm disappointed I lost. Helen deserved to win. I just couldn't get that match point."

"I thought it was too good to be true!" she told H. R. Knickerbocker. "I just couldn't believe it when I reached match point and then. . . ." Her voice trailed off and she didn't finish the sentence. "She is certainly a great player," Jacobs said at last.

Helen Jacobs was not totally crushed in spirit: "The day must come when I can beat Mrs. Moody. Things may be better at Forest Hills. This is my fourth attempt in the finals at Wimbledon. But I'm not giving up. I feel that some day I shall beat Mrs. Moody."

And Big Helen seemed ready to give her another chance. "Forest Hills is my next plan," she confidently revealed to reporters.

But Paul Gallico thought she should retire now. He advised her to fold and put away her tennis dresses, store her rackets, and give her eyeshade to the Smithsonian Institution as a great American relic and never play tournament tennis again. One thing was for certain, he wrote, "Never again will she ever do anything as perfect, as thrilling, as dramatic and as admirable as winning that Wimbledon world tournament this year."

In San Francisco the victory was celebrated enthusiastically. Mayor Angelo Rossi cabled Wills, "Sincere congratulations on your victory." Fred Moody discovered Helen had won when he was besieged at home with thousands of phone calls and telegrams. He went into hiding at the University Club shortly after noon after talking on the telephone to reporters for three hours. "I never got to work this morning at all," he said. "Every time I started out the front door the phone rang again. Naturally, I am tickled to death that Helen won, as we all expected her to, but I've got a job to hold. I had to give my ear a rest, too."

Dr. Wills thought of the match not only as vindication for his daughter but as a preview of things to come. He predicted that she was now capable of dominating women's tennis competition for at least five more years—taking five more individual Wimbledon titles.

When Helen Wills arrived back in New York at the end of July, she was met by a platoon of newsmen who fired questions at her. Among them

was John Lardner, writing at the time for the North American Newspaper Alliance. Lardner noticed that when the reporters asked her how
she felt about her Wimbledon victory over Jacobs she was not grim or
poker-faced or shy. She gave them a big grin and said, "It was the sweetest
feeling I ever had." Lardner observed that "nobody doubted for a minute
that she was telling the truth."

But after her initial statement on the sweetness of the victory, she
tightened up again and pretty much became her old familiar cool self.
On turning professional and the plans of Bill O'Brien, she said that "I
don't think that fits in with my career exactly." Wills said she planned
only to return to California for a rest. Then, caught up in the glow of
the moment, she said she would return to Forest Hills to play again, and
she suggested that she might play regularly at Forest Hills in the future
and might go to Wimbledon as often as possible—a prospect that delighted the officials of the American and English tennis associations and
drove another nail into the prospects for a successful professional tour
sponsored by Bill O'Brien or anyone else.

By the time she arrived back in San Francisco, Wills was specific about
her professional future. "I will never turn professional," she said in an
interview with the *Chronicle*. "No matter how much money Mr. O'Brien
offers, I shall never turn professional."

Carolyn Anspacher of the *Chronicle* spoke with Wills soon after she
came home and wrote that "a new Helen Wills Moody came home yesterday—exuberant, gay, and wearing false eyelashes." She was no longer
poker-faced. And she had become, Anspacher wrote, "a giggler."

When she stepped from the Overland Limited this time, one reporter
observed that she seemed to have lost about a dozen years of her age. She
appeared to be the same young woman who had escaped from the reporters who approached the train in 1923. She received reporters now at
her apartment on Pleasant Street and giggled about everything from the
latest pocket cameras to Diego Rivera paintings.

When asked if she planned to retire, as Gallico suggested she should,
Helen Wills smiled broadly and flexed her muscular arm. Her blue eyes
glowed as she said, "Retire? I should say not. I feel now that I'm just beginning again. I love tournament tennis. I simply love it. And I have no
intentions of giving it up. And in answer to the hundreds of questions
that have been asked about my health—I feel simply GRAND."

Helen Jacobs arrived in New York on August 6. She told reporters she
had thought about the Wimbledon loss and had analyzed her mistakes.
She said she felt that if she had gone to the net more often, been bolder,
the outcome of the match might have been different. Also, she said, "I
didn't see her play in any of her preliminary matches, so when I faced
her across the net it was the first time I'd seen her in competition in two
years. She's just as steady as ever, although I don't think she's hitting the
ball as hard as she used to." She thought the slower turf at Forest Hills

would give her more time to rush the net and thus a better chance to play her most effective game against Wills.

Hopes were held out for several weeks that Helen Wills would in fact return to Forest Hills and provide at least the opportunity for a rematch with Helen Jacobs. On the grass at Forest Hills, Jacobs would be playing as the defending champion—a title she had first captured in 1933 over Wills and won again in 1934. The USLTA profited only $8000 in 1934. "Not much," the treasurer of the organization observed, "but considerable when you remember the nature of the times." Still, the profit could be increased dramatically if Helen Wills came back to Forest Hills.

Yet on August 16, Helen Wills announced in San Francisco, "I feel that I have had enough tournament tennis for this season. The tournament at Wimbledon and the journey was an effort, and another trip would be more than I feel able to undertake at this time. It would be much more fun just to stay home." She said she intended to continue playing tennis in California and that maybe in 1936 she would return to Forest Hills. The decision seemed a sudden one, like her initial decision to go to England. Less than twenty-four hours earlier she had said that she hoped to regain the national title and planned to leave within the week for New York.

Something had changed her mind. Perhaps another of those fleeting senses that the time was not right and that this was not the tournament to play in and that Wimbledon was enough, maybe even the end. But on this decision she did not waver. She earlier backed out of the Wightman Cup matches, in which she had been expected to be a mainstay of the American team. She was declaring her independence, now, gradually, from organized amateur tennis in America. She was declaring her independence from the USLTA. She would assert herself more and more now with the passing years, leaving a powerful legacy as a strong-willed amateur choosing her own tournaments rather than as a professional leaving the amateur ranks.

When Helen Jacobs was told that Helen Wills was not coming to Forest Hills, she moaned, "Oh goodness. That's terrible!"

The U.S. women, without Wills, kept the Wightman Cup. Jacobs was beaten by Kay Stammers in the competition, and Dorothy Round beat Ethel Burkhardt Arnold. But then Jacobs and Sarah Palfrey Fabyan won the doubles, and Fabyan won her singles, and Jacobs beat Round for the team victory.

In the national singles tournament at Forest Hills, Helen Jacobs defended her title successfully for her fourth consecutive win, but it was not worth as much as it would have been had Helen Wills competed for it.

On the coast Helen Wills participated in some exhibition matches with her close friends that fall and seemed to enjoy tennis without the pressure of tournament competition. She played at the Palace of Fine Arts in a benefit for the NCTA. Her opponent was young Margaret Osborne, who was paired with Gerry Stratford, while Wills played with Bud Chandler. Helen impressed the paying crowd of 1600. Her game was apparently without weakness, and she and Chandler won easily. Wills also played two exhibition matches at the Menlo Country Club. She defeated a leading male club player, 6–4, in a singles match and then was on the winning side in the mixed doubles.

At the end of September Wills planned to play as the leading celebrity in the Pacific Coast Tournament, partnered by the promising young Oakland player, Don Budge. But Budge had already made plans to play with England's Freda James in the tournament. He apologized to club officials and said he would have enjoyed playing with Wills, one of his heroes. His announcement meant that Helen was left in the odd position of being entered in only one category and that without a partner. At the last moment she was paired with Chandler, but in the third round of the tournament Wills and her partner were upset by the doubles team of Henry Culley of Santa Barbara and Nancy Lyle of Great Britain, 6–4, 6–4. The defeat brought to a sudden end the campaign of 1935 for Helen Wills and also removed the star attraction from the tournament.

Don Budge won the mixed doubles with James and he also won the singles title in a four-set match over Bobby Riggs of Los Angeles. The women's singles title was won by Ethel Burkhardt Arnold, and within a month she signed a professional contract with Bill O'Brien.

There was yet another honor for Helen Wills in 1935. In October, A. Wallis Myers, British lawn tennis expert, published his respected list of the top ranking male and female players in the world for 1935. Helen Wills Moody was ranked first among the women and Helen Jacobs, the American title holder, second. In the American list, though, Wills received no ranking because of "insufficient data" due to her scratching from Forest Hills.

And then in late December a sports poll conducted by the Associated Press of sports editors and writers in all parts of the United States named Helen Wills the outstanding female athlete of the year. Helen Jacobs was fifth in the poll and Babe Didrickson ninth. With the award of that honor, Helen Wills's comeback year of 1935 came to an end.

Paul Gallico agreed heartily with her decision to skip the Forest Hills competition. And he liked the idea of her living out her pleasant life on Pleasant Street in San Francisco.

"I can close my eyes again and see that fine lioness licking her chops," he wrote. "It had been a good hunt. There was never a better one.

"She knew when to ring down the curtain."

CHAPTER
X

SOMETHING
TO REMEMBER

"Long having wander'd since, round the earth having
    wander'd
Now I face home again, very pleas'd and joyous
(But where is what I started for so long ago?
And why is it yet unfound?)"
                    —"Facing West from California's Shores"
                    Walt Whitman

"All these were honored in their generations, and
were the glory of their times."
                    —Ecclesiasticus 44:7

"The game may seem to suffice in completing a
world of its own, a world in which its devoted follower may move as in a dream. And, if you have
played your game well, you feel contented."
                    —Helen Wills

HELEN Wills enjoyed a brief retirement in the first weeks of 1936.
Then she decided to give Helen Jacobs and Bill O'Brien another shot.
Sportswriters continued to suggest that Jacobs could never be called a
really first-class talent until she had beaten Wills cleanly in a completed
match.

At the start of the year Wills was practicing daily with Bud Chandler,
Gerald Stratford, and Howard Kinsey and seemed to be preparing for
another campaign in the East. Reporters watched her and occasionally
asked about her plans. She was noncommittal. One morning during a
regular practice session with Kinsey at the California Club, while several
interested spectators looked on, Wills and her partner rallied and continued to rally without missing a shot. Someone at courtside started to
count the number of times the ball crossed the net. For eighty minutes
Wills and Kinsey slammed the ball back and forth, and it crossed the net
2001 times. Finally Kinsey stopped the rally. He had to give a lesson. The
two players laughed and decided to try to break their record the next day,
but rain postponed that contest and the record stood.

The feat demonstrated how intense and energetic Helen Wills's practice sessions could be. She finished the rally by saying that she was not at all tired, but that at about eleven o'clock she had begun to notice some eye strain because of the intensity of her concentration over such a long period of time. Gerald Stratford reminded me that Helen Wills's feat with Kinsey really wasn't unique. He remembered practicing with her in the mid-1920s, each player positioned at a corner of the backcourt and then firing back and seemingly countless backhand or forehand shots, each hitting precisely the same way in the same place "better than a machine could do." Wills could rally without stopping for a break for as long as an hour with her male partners.

She traveled to New York at the end of January to make preparations for an art show. She visited the office of her publisher, Charles Scribner & Sons, and talked with her editor, Maxwell Perkins, about writing her autobiography. Wills felt somewhat uncomfortable with Perkins, who was editor for some of the greatest writers of the time. And he felt uneasy in her presence, too. Perkins thought she was an odd bird and later he told a friend, Elizabeth Lemmon, that he sat and listened patiently to Wills "as she launched into a volley-by-volley account of her recent match with Helen Jacobs."

Looking at her, Perkins thought that "certainly she is beautiful in her way, and strong and healthy, and natural in a way you like to think is American." And although he did not think much of her writing—"Helen Wills can't write"—he conceded that her first book for Scribners, *Tennis,* sold well. Now she was writing her autobiography. Perkins wanted badly to advise her to forget about writing and to have children before it was too late. But then he looked at the sales figures on her book and ordered a new edition. "I don't work properly on that kind of thing," Perkins said of the book, "because it bores me." Encouraged by the meeting, Helen continued working on her autobiography.

The book was published the next year. In preparing her book she reexamined her scrapbooks of clippings and her old letters and photographs, and she thought again of Senator Phelan. And again she recalled in detail—but not for publication—her days at Montalvo and the company of the kind Senator. "I only wish that our lives had more nearly coincided—that I had been born earlier or he later," she told a friend. "This is one of the unfortunate things in life—that a few years make such a difference, and so much sorrow." She passed the gates of Montalvo again in the summer of 1936. And she said after that, "Few people seem to understand that the enduring thing is not so much that which is expressed as that which is felt. That the permanent things are those of the spirit, and not the material." In describing Phelan, she said, what was important was not what he had done. It was the way in which he did it, not his life, but rather the living of it.

When her autobiography was published in 1937 under the title *Fifteen-*

Thirty: The Story of a Tennis Player, John Tunis reviewed it for the *New Republic.* And he concluded that it was an important book, but not important in the way that either the author or publisher intended. "Briefly," he said, "here is the story of what America—or rather the United States—does to its celebrities."

Helen was modest about her career, he pointed out, "so damned modest as to be nauseating." He found the book gave some impression of the ceaseless grind of tournament tennis, which was a consuming and difficult pursuit. Yet Wills insisted that tennis was merely a hobby, a pastime, and that painting and writing and designing were more important to her. And she suggested that when she won tournament after tournament it was often simply because her opponents were having a bad day. Tunis found this forced and reflexive humility and generosity totally disingenuous and distasteful. And he concluded that she loved the game precisely because she won so much. Yet she cloaked her book, he said, with an "air of attractive dumbness." As she put it, "If you are totally helpless, everything seems to be done at once."

Tunis concluded that champions like Helen Wills fooled themselves. They believed what was written about them. They really believed that their articles sold "because they are writers and not because of their name. They imagine their paintings are exhibited on New Bond Street because they are artists." He found the system that enmeshed athletic champions pathetic. And he found that the fault in this lay not with Wills alone. Nor even with the game of tennis. Nor with the people who ran tennis. Rather, the fault lay "with you and me and all the rest of us who insist on pretending that this sort of thing is amateur sport, and are quite willing to allow our champions to pay the price as long as they will continue to exhibit their wares for us at so much a throw."

"John Tunis had a big chip on his shoulder," Helen Wills said of her critic. "He was a thwarted writer. He didn't like me and I didn't like him."

She told a group of New York reporters in late January in 1936 that she had not planned out a schedule for the year. "You know how I am," she told them. "I like to wait until the last minute before I decide definitely I would like to play at Forest Hills and at Wimbledon and I can't say right now just what I shall do."

She practiced at a new tennis facility in New York, the Court House, at 206 East Sixty-fifth Street and hit with David Feron, the local club professional. In ninety minutes of intense tennis witnessed by a group of reporters, Wills beat Feron in two sets.

After the match Feron said that Wills hit twice as hard as she had in the past. Reporters scoffed at the statement, simply because, one of them said, "it is impossible for any woman to hit twice as hard as Helen had hit in the past." Yet Feron did not hedge on his statement. "I have played against Frank Hunter and Vincent Richards," he said, "and without any question, Mrs. Moody's forehand is every bit as hard as Hunter's. I was hitting as hard as I could and the way the ball came back on her drive from deep court was almost unbelievable."

Her game had changed only slightly. She hit the ball flatter now, with less rolling topspin to it, and it stayed lower and closer to the net than in the past. She still had a good topspin backhand. Wills also seemed now to wait longer to take her shots, to wait until they had actually reached their highest bound and had started to come down. She was better able to disguise her shots, too, and caught Feron out of position time and again with shots down the line rather than cross court. Her game was becoming a bit more like Suzanne Lenglen's.

She played against Vincent Richards in New York, too. She was less successful against the old professional from the Pyle tour. He beat her in two sets, 7–5, 6–4. A hundred spectators showed up, including the captain of the Davis Cup team, to watch. The observers seemed amazed at what they saw and the way Helen Wills played so loosely and with such power. They appeared to have forgotten over the years just how incredible the American Girl really was. Now they saw again.

Richards said that "Mrs. Moody is hitting with such abandon and scoring so beautifully with her passing shots" that he had to apply himself strictly to his task "to avert disaster." Richards agreed with Feron. Helen was hitting harder than ever before. Her service return was now an attacking shot, and she hit with more confidence and was looser in her swing.

Helen Wills traveled to New Haven at the end of the month for an exhibition at Yale. She played a match against George Stevens of the Yale team and beat him, 6–1, before a capacity crowd at the Payne Whitney gymnasium.

In April she said she would enter Wimbledon and Forest Hills and some preliminary tournaments. Then she said she wasn't sure if she would compete in any tournaments in 1936. The press and the public waited anxiously. And then on May 25 she said she planned to "definitely make up my mind tomorrow" after a week of suspense and postponements. The French liner *Normandie* was to sail at midnight on May 26th. There was room for her on board. A reporter asked if she would sail on the *Normandie,* and she seemed annoyed and replied, "Oh, I don't know."

He asked her, then, "How could you possibly not go abroad this year when you are playing so well." Wills didn't respond. On the 26th she finally announced that she would not defend her crown at Wimbledon. She said she had decided to play only at Forest Hills this year. Instead of going for an eighth Wimbledon title she would go for an eighth American title. The press thought that England's loss was America's gain.

She had a successful "one-man show" at the Grand Central Galleries on Vanderbilt Avenue in New York. And she told a reporter that now she wanted to be a full-time artist. Tennis was now her hobby. She played tennis every morning and painted in the afternoons.

She wrote in *Scribner's Magazine* that summer, "My future plans do not exist because they have not been made. I have always waited until the last minute before making up my mind about playing in a tournament. When I decided to make the trip to Wimbledon the last time, it was two o'clock in the afternoon and I managed to catch the eight o'clock train that evening.

"I believe that different ages should adjust themselves gracefully, if possible, to pursuits suited to them. One ought not to pursue, year after year, youthful activities if one is past the age, nor should one be, on the other hand, too sober and serious, as I was, perhaps, in my earlier years. But from learning a little partly through tennis, partly because no one can escape learning something, I have decided that the goal is not all important. Equally important is the manner in which it is achieved. To enjoy and to understand as one goes along, should be one's life. Without this, the object of one's efforts becomes, when attained, a hollow victory, as a tennis cup, for example, which is won without the real love of the sport." She stayed at home.

Helen Jacobs at last won her Wimbledon title in 1936, but not against Helen Wills. It was Jacobs's fifth appearance in the finals at Wimbledon. This time she was opposed by Hilda Sperling of Germany in the final. And at a critical moment in the match, Jacobs seemed again to suffer from a loss of nerve. Jacobs took the first set at 6–2 and lost the second, 4–6. Then she jumped ahead 4–2 in the final set. But she allowed Sperling to pull even at 4–4. Jacobs jumped ahead to 5–4 and then lost again. In the twelfth game, leading 6–5, Jacobs stood at 40–15 and double-match point on her own service. But just as in 1935, she found more trouble at that point. It seemed that Jacobs was jinxed at Wimbledon. She could not get those points.

Finally, after several tense points, Jacobs came to match point again in the game, and Sperling dropped a drive into the net, and Jacobs won the title on Sperling's error.

With the Wimbledon crown at last secure on her brow, Jacobs now sought the title when she returned to Forest Hills, a title that might prove to all that she was in fact the equal of Big Helen.

There was the promise of another Wills-Jacobs confrontation at Forest Hills, but on July 27, from San Francisco, Wills issued a statement saying that she would not participate at Forest Hills. Helen said that she had decided not to play in the big national tournaments any more and that she would instead simply play in small tournaments that fit in with her schedule as an artist and designer. This came on the heels of an announcement on July 18th from the president of the Eastern Lawn Tennis Association that Helen Wills had entered her name in the Forest Hills competition. Again, Wills changed her mind.

It was not a Wills year at Forest Hills in 1936, and neither was it a Jacobs year. The four-time American singles champion now intent upon winning a fifth consecutive title, met 23-year-old Alice Marble—"The Girl of the Golden Legs"— of San Francisco in the finals. Jacobs started well, as she did at Wimbledon, and went ahead to take the first set at 6–4. Then she continued her winning ways in the second set and went to 2–0. She was four games from irrefutable greatness when she collapsed. Again. She let six of the next seven games get away from her and lost the second set. Her game then disintegrated completely. In the third set she took only four points in four games. She managed a comeback of sorts and took two games in the final set, but it was only a final desperate gesture on her part. Marble took the set and the match. At the start of the match the demonstrative crowd had clearly been for Marble, the young upstart underdog. By the end of the match they were cheering for Jacobs, who had become, again, an underdog herself.

There remained, however, one last chance for vindication for Jacobs in 1936. If Wills played only in the small regional tournaments, then Jacobs could play there, too. She returned to California and entered the Pacific Coast Championships in the mixed doubles, at the Berkeley Tennis Club. She was teamed with Henry Culley of Santa Barbara, who had won in the division in the previous year. In the lower bracket of the division was Helen Wills, teamed with the player she had been scheduled to partner the previous year, Don Budge. Wills's triumphant 1935 campaign had been cut short by Culley in 1935, so now Helen had a chance for a little vengeance herself. And, naturally, there was Jacobs at Culley's side, adding interest to the match. Budge had been a finalist at Forest Hills, where he had lost to England's Fred Perry.

Budge still recalls that match against Culley and Jacobs. Wills and Budge made it to the finals, and so did Culley and Jacobs. The widely publicized match began late on the afternoon of October 11, 1936. More than 2500 fans crowded into the Berkeley Club to watch—a capacity crowd—and an equally large number were turned away. Special bleachers were set up at each end of the court to accommodate more paying customers. Fans also climbed into the trees around the court to watch—evoking in Helen Wills's mind memories of the Lenglen match of 1926. And, as in that match at Cannes, the crowd in the bleachers and in the trees was not disappointed by the show.

The Wills-Budge team lost the first set—a long, hard-fought battle, 5–7. In the second set Culley and Jacobs went ahead to 5–4. Culley served in the tenth game to a 40–0 score, triple match point.

Wills and Budge dug in at that point and saved the match points. But the game went to deuce five times. The audience went wild as Wills and Budge saved themselves from a succession of five match points. Wills was the star on her side of the net and Culley on his. Finally, Wills and Budge took the set, 10–8, and the match was postponed because of darkness until the following afternoon. On the next day Budge and Wills won the third set, 6–4.

Budge still remembers that two-day match. When the critical game of the second set had ended and the score stood at 5–5, Helen Wills turned to her partner and hugged him and blurted out, "You're a dear!"

"I, along with everyone else, was flabbergasted at this display of emotion," Budge recalled. He wondered after that why they had ever called her "Miss Poker Face."

In 1937 Helen Wills remained in California and concentrated on her art. She again played in local exhibitions and traveled to Los Angeles for some exhibition matches. There was again talk of movies, and there was little doubt that she was interested in a film career. She signed an option with Twentieth Century-Fox, from which she stood to gain $50,000. Yet nothing came of it, no role was found for her.

Helen Wills felt at the time that she would be following in the footsteps of Frank Shields, the handsome young tennis player—and later, grandfather of Brooke Shields—who was one of the top-ranked players, an amateur, and was under contract in Hollywood for two years. He made several motion pictures and maintained his amateur status by not playing tennis in the movies. Wills played exhibitions with Shields and enjoyed his company immensely. Later, she recalled that Shields had always given her generous blocks of time to practice against him, and the time was simply invaluable. He was, she said, "a true gentleman."

The Jacobs jinx continued in 1937. She lost again in France and at Wimbledon Jacobs was beaten in the quarter finals, and Dorothy Round won the singles title. At Forest Hills, Jacobs lost in the semifinals, and the tournament was won by Anita Lizana of Chile.

Earlier that year, as Jacobs prepared for another shot at the Wimbledon title, the American public learned that Helen Wills would travel east this year, but only as far as Nevada and only to divorce Fred Moody.

The divorce itself was a harrowing experience for Helen. Her close friends remember she was devastated by it and said that she attempted to get all of her crying done before she traveled to Nevada. The problem, as Freddie saw it in time, was the traveling and the tennis. Some of Helen's friends insisted that the young stockbroker simply lacked class and said that he drank too much and had little in common with Helen, and that the marriage had been a mismatch from the start. Freddie remembered that he didn't like tennis, and he didn't like the tennis crowd, and he especially didn't like the French announcers at Roland Garros referring to him as "Mister Moody Veels" or "Freddie Wills," and he did not like the English and the Forest Hills' crowds referring to him as "the distinguished drunk from California." But he also said he never had enough time alone with Helen. She was always on the road traveling to or from tournaments. Even, he said, shortly after their marriage she interrupted their life to return to Wimbledon and then did it again and again. Very simply, he said, they drifted apart. "I don't think we really got to know each other," he told me. "It was too bad."

As early as 1933 there were rumors of difficulty. On her way east Helen Wills traveled through Nevada, and there were stories claiming that her friends had arranged for her to stop off there so as to become a resident and get a divorce.

Helen Wills moved in the spring of 1937 to Glen Brook, Nevada, near the shores of Lake Tahoe, in order to gain Nevada residency. On August 23 she received her divorce behind closed doors in a Nevada courtroom. The reason given for the divorce, officially, was "extreme cruelty of a mental nature." Property rights were settled out of court. And so the storybook romance of Little Poker Face and the wealthy young stockbroker had its unhappy end. The divorce was granted in Carson City.

After the divorce Helen Wills told a group of reporters she was returning to California and that she would participate in the mixed doubles at the Berkeley tournament. But after that, she said, she planned to "virtually desert the tennis courts" and follow other pursuits. And it appeared that the curtain had come down at last on an era in American sport. At the age of thirty-one Helen felt she was finished in tennis.

But again she changed her mind. In January 1938 Helen Wills was re-elected to a second two-year term as a director of the Northern California Tennis Association. Gerald Stratford was named president of the organization, succeeding Edward Chandler. The organization had experienced a real financial boom since 1936, thanks to Helen's match at the club with Budge against Culley and Jacobs.

In March Helen Wills and Don Budge were featured in a series of exhibition matches at the Berkeley Club. After those matches Budge said he believed Wills was ready for yet another comeback and capable of winning her eighth title at Wimbledon. But Pop Fuller disagreed. "Helen Moody is not ready for Wimbledon," he said after watching her. Fuller said there was a noticeable loss of speed in her game, and she had less accuracy on her shots. But Budge insisted she could do it. Her game, Budge told reporters, was "wonderful. Three weeks and she will beat any of them," he said.

On March 14, Wills said she made up her mind. "It's pretty definite now," she told reporters. "I'm on my way to Europe in May."

In New York, in the spring of 1938, a writer for *Scholastic Magazine* announced that Helen Wills, "whose name is probably better known than Greta Garbo, stepped off her train without any fanfare." Helen, the writer suggested, was trying to cheat Father Time. Yet, reporters who saw her practice were again impressed by her brilliant play. Several reporters went so far as to predict that she would win the Wimbledon crown again and that she would also win any tournament she entered. The only serious problem might come from Alice Marble or, perhaps, from Helen Jacobs, should the two Helens play again.

In New York on April 18 she impressed a number of representatives of the USLTA and an equal number of newsmen who gathered to see her practice at the Sutton Place Tennis Club, East River and Fifty-fifth Street, for her first scheduled practice session before leaving for England. Photographers and newsreel cameramen swarmed around the club, setting up their equipment and clicking shutters and grinding away before, during, and after the practice. If there was any doubt that Helen Wills was still the biggest attraction among women in sport, this demonstration proved otherwise. The *New York Times* agreed that she was still a headline figure in sport despite the fact she had been in semi-retirement since 1935.

She wore her customary two-piece white cotton tennis outfit and a red sweater and seemed "more attractive than ever with a new style of fluffed hair." She practiced with J. Gilbert Hall. She played three hard sets with Hall, both using ground strokes and coming to the net. Hall won all three, 6–2, 8–6, 7–5. But at the end of the second set he asked whether or not Helen wished to go on, and she chose to play some more. After the practice Hall said he was particularly impressed by Wills's stamina. She played as tough in the third set as she had in the first, hitting equally hard on every stroke throughout the afternoon. And her footwork, which had never been a strong point in her game, now seemed to have a little more spring in it than before.

Also noticeable was Wills's adoption of variety in her hitting, mixing up shots, slicing now and then and going for a short shot. She seemed to be thinking more about her game now than ever before in the rallies. She was not as concerned with finishing points quickly, she had noticeably more patience, although Hall noted that such might not be the case against female opponents. She played again with Hall at the same club on the 19th.

At thirty-two Helen Wills seemed to be playing what many said was her best game. But she saw it differently, and so did some of her opponents. She knew that she had slowed down—she could feel it—and she was thinking about tactics and strategy more. And that fraction of a second, in close matches, could make all the difference in the world. She had stamina as in the past, but she did not have the same power. Yet Howard Kinsey, her practice partner, summed up her play by saying, "Nobody can beat her the way she is going now. She's faster, stronger and headier."

When she sailed on the *Manhattan* on April 20th, she pointed out that, not only would she play Wimbledon and several preliminary tournaments, but she also planned to play at Forest Hills when she returned. So American audiences could expect to see the Queen once more, the first time since her 1933 disaster.

Loaded down with twenty-five new rackets, Helen Wills landed in London on April 27. She examined the English tournament schedule and said she would try to play in two tournaments before Wimbledon. Asked about her return to England, she said, "When you've once been at Wimbledon, it gets into your blood."

The catalyst in Helen Wills's new plans was the Irish poet and novelist,

Oliver St. John Gogarty, whose works she had been introduced to by
Senator James Phelan. In fact, Phelan, in his last letter to Wills had en-
closed a poem by Gogarty. In her unhappiness, Helen turned back to
some of her earlier days and to the memories of the kindness of Phelan.
She recalled that she had been reading one of Gogarty's books entitled
As I Was Walking Down Sackville Street, and she came across a reference
to a "Pleasant Street." [The actual reference in the book was to "Pleasants
Street."] She lived on a Pleasant Street and was tickled by the coincidence.
She decided to write to Gogarty. He wrote back, and they began a steady
correspondence.

Gogarty had friends in the Irish Tennis Association, and when they
learned of his correspondence with Helen they asked him to relay an invitation to her to appear in the Irish National Championship Tournament in 1938. He did. He asked Helen to play in Dublin and to be his
guest during her stay. She accepted.

Helen Wills had never before played in Ireland nor visited there. She
thought about it for a short time and concluded that it would be good to
get away and decided to go. Not only would she play in the Irish championships, she decided, but she would also make another try at Wimbledon. One of the first things she did was to secure for Gogarty and his
daughter tickets for the Wimbledon tournament—tickets that increased
dramatically in value when it was announced that Queen Helen would be
playing again. She sent her entry to the All England Club without fanfare and started preparations for another trip. She again traveled alone.

Wills began her English campaign in the North of London Tournament on May 11th, in an opening match watched by a large crowd that
came out only to see her. She gave up one game in beating an unranked
opponent; in a second round match a few hours later she gave up just one
more game. She continued to win without much difficulty and lost only
one game in each of her first five matches in the tournament. In the final,
however, there was some indication of danger, a portent that reminded
some that Wills was far from invincible. Against an opponent she would
have pushed aside easily in earlier years, Yvonne Law, she won 6–2, 7–5.
In the past that score would have been front-page news. Helen Wills was
slipping, and the slipping no longer surprised anyone. There were young
energetic players in abundance to push her now, perhaps even to push her
down. In London she won twelve of twelve sets in six matches, winning
seventy-two games and losing fifteen.

On May 16 she continued her winning ways at Surbiton, again losing
only a single game in the opening round—but her opponent was unranked. In the second round of the tournament Freda James pushed aside
Anita Lizana, the defending American champion from Chile, in three sets,
ending any chance for a match between Helen Wills and the American
title holder. Wills's winning ways at Surbiton were so routine that report-

ers started asking her about things other than tennis—as in the old days. The questions still bothered her, and she tried to fend them off with as little comment as possible. They wanted to know about any new romance in her life. What about Tallent Tubbs, with whom she had been linked romantically? "I am heartily tired of these stories about me," she told the newsmen, "none of which has any foundation. My visit is being spoiled by these rumors."

Then she dropped a set in the semi-final match to Peggy Scriven. And although she won the match by 6–2, 5–7, 6–3, the headline of the day was that Scriven became one of that select group to take a set from Wills since 1926. Scriven had come on hard in that second set, and, after being down 4–5, won three games in a row to surprise Wills and take the set. Scriven continued her winning ways in the third set for two games, jumping out to a 2–1 lead before Wills found her game again and pulled out the victory. Wills won the match by putting a perfect lob over Scriven's head, while the Englishwoman stood surprised at the net dreaming of a volleyed winner. Helen recovered quickly from the three-set match and the next day beat Margot Lumb in the final, 6–3, 6–4. In the tournament Helen won five matches and eleven of twelve sets, but she lost half of her games, winning sixty-six and losing thirty-three.

Then Helen entered the St. George's Hill Tournament. After taking the early rounds in her customary fashion, she was, after winning a first set, suddenly and surprisingly dispatched by Mary Hardwick, an English player.

Her performance in the English preliminary tournaments appeared to indicate that this year she had unwisely placed herself in more jeopardy than ever before in her career. There was no longer a significant gap between herself and other competitors. She agreed to participate in the Wightman Cup matches as a member of the American team once more. The invitation to play came from Helen's mentor Hazel Wightman, and she could hardly turn down the chance.

From being a pre-tournament favorite for her eighth Wimbledon singles title, Helen was suddenly the long shot and the underdog, while Alice Marble was the favorite. Yet some reporters noticed that Helen Wills was curiously unfazed by her two defeats. She seemed ready to face whatever fate brought her way in the remaining weeks of the spring of 1938, be it a Czechoslovakian upstart, a San Francisco ingenue, or another Helen.

In the Wightman Cup competitions, in her initial match against Margaret Scriven, Wills took a first set easily and then ran out of energy, just pulling back in the second set 7–5. She experienced even more difficulty with her old nemesis, the left-handed Kay Stammers. She beat Stammers but only after dropping a set, 6–2, 3–6, 6–3. In the doubles competition Wills and her partner Dorothy Bundy were beaten by an English team.

Helen Wills also experienced some friction with Alice Marble. Marble

had bad feelings about Big Helen ever since 1933 when she played doubles with the American champion and was expected to carry the duo to
victory because of Helen's immobility and her general lack of energy. All
attention had been given to Helen, Marble recalled, and Alice had been
imposed upon again and again, taking little credit for any victories they
might win and taking all of the blame for their defeat.

But her disillusionment and animosity went back beyond even 1933.
Alice Marble came from a family of modest means in San Francisco, and
she had not been accepted by the same class of people who idolized
Helen Wills. As a youngster, she had gone to see Suzanne Lenglen play
in her professional tour, and she had watched Helen Wills and read
about her in the papers. It was Helen Wills who had inspired her the
most and who had been the example held up to Alice when she, like tens
of thousands of less talented American girls of the time, decided to pattern her game and her court behavior, as much as possible, after the
American Girl.

In 1932 her brother had gotten her a membership in the California
Club in San Francisco, where Wills played each day. "I wasn't very popular there with the snobs," she told me. "I often had to run out to
Golden Gate Park to find a game because my bother would have killed
me if I came home without playing." Alice saw Helen there many times,
but never played with her. "She would say hello three or four times in
the same day, and each time look through me and not recall saying anything earlier. That was, I thought, because she hadn't seen me. Now you
are awfully impressionable at the age of eighteen. And that made an indelible mark on me."

Then came a luncheon at the Berkeley Club in honor of Big Helen.
Pop Fuller invited Marble to the affair. And afterwards he took Alice
over to meet Helen. "And I remember very clearly now," Marble said,
"he said, 'Helen, now that you've won everything in sight, wouldn't you
like to help a young hopeful like Alice here get her start so she can do
what you've done?' It was Pop's way of flattering Helen.

"Helen looked at Fuller—she seemed surprised by what he said. Then
she looked me straight in the eye for just a moment. And then she said,
'No! I wouldn't.' And she walked away.

"Well, Fuller was embarrassed. And so was I. I thought, being a brash
kid, 'That's the god-damned coldest remark I've ever heard in my life.'
And I've thought about it several times since then. I heard that Helen
was kind to her close friends. But I was on the wrong side of her from
the very start and I don't know why, really. But I saw how cold and
cruel she could be to people for no reason at all. You can imagine how
she treated someone like Helen Jacobs if she treated me that way simply
because I was a young upstart.

"I never got to know Helen Wills. And I don't think anybody ever
did. Maybe her husbands did, but I even doubt that. I know, though,

that no woman was ever close to her. She saw us all as competition for attention and that was that.

"She was cold to me off the court and she was cold to me on the court. I think she considered every other player as a rival. Once she and I played in the same tournament and opened some new courts at an exhibition. And the photographers wanted to take a picture of us together after the matches. But she said, 'No, I'm too tired,' and walked away. I never understood her attitude. Maybe she thought it was good psychology. Maybe she was just trying to psyche us out or something. I really couldn't figure it out.

"What I knew at that time was that I wanted to be the very best women's tennis player in the world. I wanted to be the greatest. But I did not want to be anything like Helen Wills. Now that was a complete reversal of my earlier attitude. Because she had always been my childhood heroine and she inspired me to play tennis. I taped pictures of her on my bedroom wall. But that was before I knew her. After that the pictures went in the wastebasket. And so did the admiration."

The next time Helen Wills and Alice Marble were paired was in 1938. By then Marble was prepared to meet Wills some day in the final match on the Centre Court at Wimbledon. "And I had no doubt that when that day came," Alice Marble told me, "I would take her. I was at the top of my game in 1938. And I was eager to play against Helen."

But before Wimbledon there were the Wightman Cup matches. "Mrs. Wightman was captain of the team that year and she was a strong woman. When it came to tennis she had her own set way. And for the practice session she announced the pairings for practice. She said that Dorothy Bundy would play with Sarah Palfrey and that Alice Marble would play with Helen Moody.

"But Helen looked up and said, 'You know, Mrs. Wighty, I never play with the other women.' But Mrs. Wighty didn't hesitate at all, and she said, 'You will tomorrow, Helen.' And when Helen complained that she already had a match on the next day with a male professional, Mrs. Wighty just said, 'Cancel it!'

"So Helen and I had to practice on the next day and she was none too happy with that idea."

The next morning Marble went onto the courts to play her practice sets with her former idol. "The South African and English players were warming up at the time," Alice remembered. "And when we came out to play they stopped and walked over and sat down to watch us. We decided, after hitting for a time, to play a single set. I served."

Alice Marble remembers winning the set 6–2. She was prepared to start a second set, but Helen Wills packed up her rackets and walked off the courts. "Just like 1933 again," Alice remembered. "She never said thank you. She never said anything. And we never talked about it again. That was it. And all I thought at the time was, 'See you in the finals, lady!'

"Little things like that stick in my mind today. She was so cold. So thoughtless. The other girls watching us applauded. They were all rooting for me, I could tell. And Helen could tell too.

"I always thought that Helen Wills believed everything they said about her in the papers. She really believed she was a queen. That is necessary to some degree, of course. You have to believe in yourself or you are not going to get very far. But you have to keep it inside. I lived and talked modestly. But I felt pretty god-damned confident inside.

"After I won that set I never again thought that Helen was impossible to beat. Before that time I did. She could hit magnificent passing shots from almost anywhere on the court. And she had a good dependable defensive lob. But you had to run her to beat her. You had to bring her to the net and kill her there because she was not a prime volleyer. She was weakest at the net and when you got her there, then you had her."

But the other women present and the *New York Times* correspondent who watched the play and Mrs. Wightman remembered it differently. The number one player for the Wightman Cup competitions had not yet been selected. And so Mrs. Wightman arranged for Wills to play Marble for the number one spot on the team. Marble did in fact take the first two games, but then Wills surged back strongly and took six of the next seven games and won the set 6–3. As a result, Wills was picked as number one for the team and Marble number two. Mrs. Wightman was impressed by the play during the set and remarked, "I have never seen Mrs. Moody or Miss Marble play better. Naturally, I am confident."

In her first match in the Wightman Cup competition Wills beat Margaret Scriven, 6–0, 7–5. And in her first match, Marble was beaten by Kay Stammers. On the second day of the competition Wills beat Scriven in three sets, 6–2, 3–6, 6–3.

On June 17, Helen played another preliminary tournament—the London Lawn Tennis Championships. And in the semifinal match she was surprised by Hilda Sperling of Germany, 8–6, 6–3. And as if to make matters seem even worse, in the final round Sperling was beaten easily, 6–3, 6–1, by Jadwiga Jedrzejowska of Poland. With two pre-Wimbledon defeats it was whispered that Wills would now drop out of the singles competition at Wimbledon and admit that her best playing days were past. It was thought she would play only in the women's doubles.

Wills harbored no such doubts. Duncan Macaulay had spoken with her at the St. George's Hill tournament at Weybridge before Wimbledon. "She was quite determined to beat Mrs. Lambert-Chambers' Wimbledon record," he noticed. "She was dedicated in heart, mind and body to this objective."

She played only in the women's singles at St. George's Hill. And after she played each match she went back to her room at Great Fosters. When rain delayed a match one day, Wills asked Macaulay if she could have tea by herself in his office. She said she needed to concentrate. "What for?" Macaulay asked her. "For Wimbledon," she told him, which was four weeks off.

Even before the tournament began, she asked Macaulay to schedule professional Dan Maskell for her to practice with at 1:30 p.m. on the day of the Wimbledon final. Macaulay knew that Wills planned far ahead and what she expected. She knew with whom she wished to practice, he found, before anybody else thought of such things.

Writing of the preliminaries to the 1938 tournament, Al Laney found that Helen Wills was aware that a large number of players were now capable of beating her. She would have to be more cautious than ever before. In 1938, he believed, she risked very much for very little. If she failed she would most probably have to step down from any pretensions of equality with Suzanne Lenglen. And if she succeeded, she would probably at best share honors with Lenglen. "By winning she could only make more secure a position already won." But Helen Wills was willing to take that gamble.

What she did in 1938, Laney found, was to inject an element of drama into what was already one of the best women's tournaments ever staged. Among the men in the tournament was Don Budge, who won the singles title without either drama or much excitement. He did not lose a set in seven matches. So the women's competition overshadowed the men's because Helen was back, the seven-time champion in the midst of a field of hopefuls who wanted to have the chance to knock off a legend. Every young player in the tournament knew that the best way to make a name was to beat Helen Wills on the Wimbledon grass.

---◄{ 2 }►---

Helen Wills was seeded first at Wimbledon in 1938—Alice Marble was second, and Helen Jacobs was unseeded. But as Wills played her way through the tournament it became clear that she was no longer indomitable. A tournament official noticed that she won no match in the old way, "and anybody could see that time was catching up with her." Duncan Macaulay, the referee of Wimbledon, concluded that by 1938 the gap had been narrowed—"if not closed"—between Helen and her nearest rivals. She was beaten twice in preliminary matches and then harassed in the Wightman Cup matches.

Al Laney also found that there was a surprisingly large number of people in that spring who said derogatory things about Wills. Many writers and players asked why Wills had returned when her reputation and her record seemed safe. She told none of them of her agreement with Gogarty and the Irish Tennis Association. In the absence of a clear motivation for her comeback, there were rumors of secret under-the-table financial inducements. Alice Marble heard them and said that several of the players believed that Helen had been provided with "appearance money." Marble said that she and other players had heard that "one of the women" who came to Wimbledon in 1938 received $10,000 in appearance money. But officials of the All England Club denied the allegation then, and today there are no records or verifiable accounts of such a transaction having taken place.

Helen Wills worked her way through the early rounds of the tournament, winning, yet giving up many games to her challengers. In the opening rounds she beat Mrs. Nell Hopman, 6–3, 6–4, and Nancy Glover, 6–4 and 7–5. Then against Bobbie Heine Miller of South Africa, she won in a terrific fight, 8–6, 6–4, after coming back from a 5–1 deficit in the first set. (The crowd was so large for the match that officials had to shut off the standing room area around the Centre Court an hour before the match began.) After the Miller match she appeared to find her stride against Kay Stammers and gave the left-handed English woman a convincing 6–1, 6–2 licking.

In fighting her own way into the finals Big Helen played a long, grim semi-final match against Hilda Sperling. It was a baseline battle that lasted two hours, and the rallies in the match averaged nearly thirty strokes. This was only one week after the lanky German backcourt player had beaten Wills at the Queen's Club tournament.

The first set was extremely long. After an hour the score stood at 9–9, and many fans left the stadium for tea. Sperling broke through in the nineteenth game and in the twentieth had two set points. But Wills plodded on calmly and refused to be drawn in from the baseline and evened the score at 10–10. Then she took the two games necessary for the 12–10 victory. The set took eighty minutes, but Helen Wills kept her sweater on throughout the contest. Later she complained that she could not run because of her blistered feet. From the tenth game on in the first set, she said, she had been in pain. Afterwards she said that she had no idea in the course of the action that she had saved two set points. She was merely thinking of every shot, as she always did. She did not let herself relax. Wills appeared to run out of energy midway through the second set, and Sperling broke her service for a 4–3 lead. But Wills braced herself at that point and took the next three games for the match. Observers suspected that, like Lenglen in the 1926 match against the American Girl, she did not have the energy for a three-set match and had to win the second set simply to survive. Wills was described as both courageous and tenacious for her win, and she refused to let the alternating momentum of the match get her down and finally pulled out the victory. But a correspondent for the *New Yorker* was unimpressed by the Wills performance in the semi-final match and wrote that she "looked vulnerable and a little silly, in her long, boring match against Fru Sperling."

Helen Jacobs, who watched the match from the stands, studied Wills and afterwards described her play as "magnificent." Jacobs told the press she still believed Wills was a dangerous player and might take the singles. And she suggested that Hardwick's defeat of Wills was not important because Big Helen had been suffering from a cold.

There seemed little chance that Helen Jacobs could make it to the finals in 1938. She had a strained nerve in her right arm that kept her out of the play in the pre-Wimbledon warm-up tournaments. And then on her way to the tournament for her third round match with Joan Ingram of England she fainted and had to be carried back to the clubhouse. The match was postponed.

Then she surprised everyone. In a rescheduled match she beat Ingram, continued her winning ways, and played her way through some determined competition. She beat Alice Marble in the semi-finals and became the first unseeded player in history to reach the finals. She did not lose a set in getting to the final round for the sixth time in her career. She also developed a new useful stroke, a flat forehand drive, which she used effectively against Marble's hard-hitting service in the semi-finals, 6–4, 6–4.

But Helen Jacobs considered the costly semi-final contest an anticlimax. Her leg was badly injured. The leg injury came as a result of an earlier shoulder injury. Trying to protect her shoulder, she had changed her strokes and may have strained some muscles. In her quarter-final match against Jadwiga Jedrzejowska, she injured the sheath of the Achilles tendon in her right heel. The match against Marble further aggravated that injury. Then she had strained her leg further during a practice session with Bill Tilden on the day before the final. She saw her physician, Dr. J. J. Dunning, and he wrapped the leg for support. Only then did Jacobs feel fit enough to go onto the court for the final.

With wins in the semi-finals, the two Helens faced each other again in the last match of a tournament 6000 miles from home—their fourth meeting in the finals of Wimbledon.

Helen Jacobs had not planned for this. And on the day before the final she asked Duncan Macaulay to arrange for her to play Dan Maskell in a practice match before the final competition. She found then that Helen Wills had made arrangements weeks earlier. Jacobs, Macaulay recalled, "was incensed and annoyed."

"Why should she have everything?" Jacobs asked.

"Because she has booked everything," Macaulay answered.

And so before the final match, Helen Jacobs had a thorough workout not with Maskell but with her friend, Bill Tilden.

Al Laney remembered that almost everybody he spoke with believed that, based on the way each of the women had played in early rounds in the tournament, Jacobs would beat Wills in the 1938 final. Jacobs at long last would have her certification as a bona fide champion. Wills had to struggle along to make it and was in danger of being knocked off several times. It appeared that a clear-cut victory on the part of Jacobs would seal the rivalry once and for all. Laney didn't know of Jacobs's injury, nor did the other writers and fans.

Queen Mary was present for the match, as were the Duke and Duchess of Kent and other members of the royal family, the Queen of Spain, Clement Attlee, and Anthony Eden.

Bill Tilden recalled that this final confrontation between the two women was pure drama. In the committee box, he said, were all the "old stuffed shirts of English officialdom, while the players' box held every tennis name of note in that part of the world," including, of course, Tilden.

In the final contest between the two Helens there was a strong air of unreality. Few writers had guessed that the women would meet again. Wills had come out of a three-year retirement and had lost twice in preliminary matches, and Jacobs played through the tournament unseeded.

Life showed a series of photographs of the two women walking onto court side by side. Not once did the two look at each other. Wills, almost expressionless, wore a skirt that came mid-knee. Helen Jacobs wore her long pleated shorts with the stripe down the side. Her right ankle was bandaged. The contestants exchanged no words before play began.

Wills began the contest with an impressive burst of power and precision, and the crowd sat up right away in full expectation of a classic fight for the title, a reprise of what had taken place in 1935. The two women exchanged games and played with their characteristic determination, like two fighters exchanging punches in the early rounds of a title fight. Each stood her ground and launched solid brilliant shots at the other. Each showed respect for the other, probing tentatively with skill and power, using years of experience as a guide in trying to find what might work on this afternoon, what solid blow might be landed where, what might cut the contender across the court down, weaken her, confuse her, put her off balance, break her concentration, make her start thinking about losing. Neither betrayed a weakness in the first games of the match.

Then at 3–2, with Wills leading, a questionable decision gave her a service break. But the decision didn't appear to faze Jacobs, who kept on fighting hard, broke back, and then held her own service to even the score at four-all. In the ninth game Jacobs continued playing hard and muscled her way to within break point, 30–40, on Wills's service. Then there was a fast rally, and Jacobs hit to the Wills backhand and came in for the kill. This time there was no defensive lob from the American Girl. This time she boomed back a straight topspin crosscourt reply to Jacobs's backhand side. The shot came at Jacobs from a sharp angle, a beautiful winner if she couldn't cut it off. Jacobs jumped for the shot and twisted her body to make the desperate backhand stab at the ball. It passed just beyond the top of her racket and hit in for the point. When

Jacobs came down from making the jump at the ball, she landed squarely on her right foot. There was a sudden shock up her leg. She had torn the ailing Achilles tendon. The score stood at deuce. Wills had saved the point.

At that moment, however, only Jacobs realized that more than the point had been lost. The game had been lost, and with it the set and the match. Jacobs stood at the net not moving, her back to Wills. She was suddenly very pale.

Tilden was watching her, and he recalled, "Helen Jacobs was still at the net, her face white and drawn with pain. Slowly she forced herself to the baseline to receive. She had badly strained and torn the covering of the Achilles tendon and was practically helpless."

Wills clicked off two easy points now. Jacobs made some slow awkward movements toward the ball. Wills won the game.

Jacobs was nearly immobile. She grimaced. When she moved to change courts, she limped badly. She stopped to tug on the bandage around her leg that was, it seemed, too tight and seemed to be causing her some discomfort. When the women changed ends of the court, she asked Wills if they could stop while she took the bandage off. Wills made no reply to her, and seemed either lost in concentration, cold, or deaf.

That seemed to annoy Jacobs, one tournament official wrote later. "But to be fair to Helen Wills I doubt if she heard anything that anyone said to her when a match was on; and in any case she never paid attention to her opponent when changing courts." The crowd was buzzing now, curious as to what should or could be done.

"Never have I felt so frustrated on a tennis court," Jacobs wrote later. "It was impossible to run for anything, and only those shots that came within my reach could be returned."

Wills steadily clicked off the points now, winning everything easily. She ran out the set. At each change of courts she looked away from Jacobs.

Hazel Wightman came down to the edge of the court where tournament referee Macaulay was sitting and said to him, "One of our players is in difficulty because her leg is hurting her." The umpire said he thought it was reasonable for Jacobs to stop to take off the bandage, which she then did. But while she did, Wills didn't say a word to her or come anywhere near her. Jacobs was so helpless, in fact, that Wightman tried to convince her to default. But she simply shook her head and went on. Wightman said that she feared that Helen might cause permanent injury to her leg if she continued. But Jacobs absolutely refused to stop. She remembered the default against her in 1933. She would not give Helen Wills the satisfaction of a duplication of that event. She would stick it out. Big Helen could have the complete victory. "I preferred to finish the match. It would not, I knew, take long."

Without the bandage the ankle was worse than before, and Jacobs limped badly through the rest of the match. She didn't win another game. "It was a sad end to what promised to be a great match," Macaulay wrote. Hazel Wightman called the match a "tragedy" and a "misfortune."

Many of her friends believed Helen Jacobs should have defaulted, that there was no dishonor in leaving the game when she was badly hurting. But she remembered that storm of criticism Wills had stirred up by walking out on her. And now she refused to quit.

Jacobs managed in some way to get three points in the second set. But it was no contest. And as the *New Yorker* reported, the match was an embarrassment to watch and must have been an embarrassment to play. "But, in sticking it painfully out to the end," *Life* reported, "Miss Jacobs heaped coals of fire on her rival's head. In 1933 at Forest Hills, Mrs. Moody walked off the court just as Miss Jacobs was about to beat her."

Tilden wrote in his characteristically melodramatic style that "Helen Jacobs stood there while the other crucified her." "In the way Helen Wills hit the ball with mechanical perfection to the far corners of the court there was a brutal thoroughness almost sadistic in quality, but far worse was her manner. She never spoke once to Helen Jacobs. Changing courts, if she could, she crossed the net at the other end. When compelled to cross at the same end she walked as far away from her victim as possible."

When asked if any words had been exchanged between her and Helen at the end of the match, Jacobs said that she said to her conquerer, "Congratulations. I'm awfully sorry I couldn't have made a better match of it."

John Lardner remembered later that those who saw the match reported back that there seemed to be a nice friendly spirit between the two Helens. "It was a one-way friendship, launched by Miss Jacobs and dying of exposure five miles off the Grand Banks of Newfoundland."

When it was over, Wills met her at the net and said simply, "Too bad, Helen." Jacobs, with "a look of pleading friendship," according to *Life,* congratulated her conqueror. The match ended in silence. Jacobs limped to the net, her hand outstretched in congratulation, smiling. Wills walked slowly in and without speaking or glancing at Jacobs, Tilden wrote, touched her fingers and then turned away from the court without looking to see if Jacobs followed.

Someone handed Wills a microphone so she could say something. She told the crowd how pleased she was to win. Jacobs didn't leave the court, but sat on her racket waiting for Wills. Wills then gave a brief television interview—the match had been televised in England—while Jacobs stood aside, dejectedly, and rocked with pain. When Big Helen finished and without glancing at Little Helen, she walked off the court to the clubhouse. There was no applause from the crowd, Tilden wrote. The silence was stifling. Caught by surprise, Jacobs limped after Wills a moment after she disappeared. A storm of applause erupted from the gallery.

"Wills left the court eight times World Champion, but Jacobs left it crowned World Champion Sportswoman," Tilden concluded.

So Helen Wills's victory at Wimbledon was tainted by the Jacobs injury. In time the way the victory was won would be forgotten, and the record books would record simply that Helen Wills had been victorious eight of the nine times she played in singles at Wimbledon, a triumph that even the Great Lenglen had not equalled. Nobody knew for sure what the thoughts of Suzanne Lenglen were as she followed in the newspapers the progress of Helen Wills through Wimbledon on her way to an eighth singles title.

On the next day in an interview in the London *Daily Express*, Jacobs said, "The match had to go on. I made the customary remarks afterwards, you always do. I cannot be bothered making an effort to explain inconsequential details." Jacobs told the same reporter that "Mrs. Moody and I spoke in the dressing room. She told me she didn't know what to do when my ankle went." Writing for the *Daily Telegraph,* A. Wallis Myers wrote that "Mrs. Moody was criticized by many onlookers—and probably the public reception of her championship record was cooler in consequence—for her apparent indifference to her adversary's affliction. She offered no sympathy on the court. That is her way, and by this mental detachment and complete abstraction in the game itself she has come to her fame and her record."

Helen Jacobs told me that she did not go to Big Helen's dressing room following the match, nor was it the custom to do so. Following the 1934 Wimbledon final, when Dorothy Round had beaten Jacobs, Helen did call on her in the players' dressing room in order to congratulate her. "But that was purely a personal desire," she said.

In 1938, she said, she got into a hot bath. "I assume Helen did likewise," she said. As Jacobs was waiting to bathe, her hostess, Lady Grieg, knocked on the door and told her that Queen Mary wished to see her. So Jacobs dressed as quickly as she could, and, with one unlaced tennis shoe on her injured foot and one street shoe on her good foot, she hobbled with Lady Grieg's assistance to the Members' Tea Room, where the Queen, the Queen of Spain, and others of the royal family were standing in a row. The Queen commiserated with her on the accident, told her to be sure to soak her foot in hot salt water, and after more light talk she was presented to the others. She hobbled again back to her dressing room, got her tennis clothes packed, and was taken to the Griegs' house at Richmond Park, where a doctor examined her leg and foot again.

"The last time I saw Helen was in 1938 at Wimbledon," Jacobs told me recently. She had forgotten about speaking to her after the match. And she now remembered only that "there was no conversation between us at the time. After we shook hands at the net not a word was exchanged. And I never saw Helen Wills Moody again."

Al Laney was criticized for the way he wrote about the match. One group thought Wills was heartless and wanted Laney to write his story that way, and another group who thought Wills could do no wrong "and their number surprised me," blamed him for not pointing out that Wills had been correct in her behavior in 1933 and again in 1938.

"As a matter of fact I do think Wills was right both times," he wrote. But what maddened the crowd was her refusal to offer any gesture of sympathy in order to show that she was concerned about her opponent. Wills just continued to concentrate on the job at hand, "which was the Wills way." Laney also believed that Jacobs should have defaulted rather than risk further and even permanent injury. "There can be no stigma attached to quitting in such circumstances, and the American notion about it is silly."

Laney wrote the most lenient account of the match from Wills's position. He noticed that Wills "played through calm and detached, but she showed her sympathy for Miss Jacobs in little ways that did not escape the attention of the crowd." Yet the correspondent for the *New Yorker* at the match, on reading Laney's account, said, "I don't know what Mr. Laney means."

That evening when Helen Jacobs appeared on crutches at the dinner given by the All-England Club, the entire gathering rose and cheered upon her entrance.

The following day Jacobs visited Tilden at the Dorchester Hotel. She said she had been trying to escape the press, which had given her no peace since the match. In a conversation with Tilden, she said, "You know, Bill, I don't mind her being a so-and-so, but I object to her being a stupid so-and-so. If she had only smiled when she shook hands at the end and said, 'I'm glad you broke your damn leg'—or something like that, no one would have known how she felt."

When I asked Miss Jacobs about this account, she told me that Tilden, as usual, embellished his prose for dramatic effect. "I am sure he would back track from his statement that I said 'so-and-so' or whatever that was meant to imply."

Anyway, Wills had her title and her record. "It is a record," Laney wrote later, 'that may stand as long as the game is played, certainly until there comes along a girl who can reach the high plane on which we must up to this point place only two, Wills and Lenglen, and this theoretical girl must begin to win titles in her teens."

Duncan Macaulay liked and admired the skills and determination of each of the Helens. But Wills, he noticed, "had just a bit more operational and technical efficiency. Her topspin drives were just that much better than Helen Jacobs's slice, and there was just that little bit more iron in her 'lawn tennis soul.' That was why she won."

Life reported that for Jacobs the match was tragic, and for Wills it was historic. Wills had her unprecedented eighth victory.

Life also reported that Jacobs limped "in tears" to her dressing room.

But the very next week, *Life* ran a letter from Helen Jacobs that asked for a retraction. Jacobs insisted that she did not leave the court in tears and that the pictures of her indicated that such was not the case. *Life* "gladly" retracted the account and said it had been misled by news dispatches. Jacobs was very simply biting her tongue, the editor wrote. She was not crying.

After the match Alice Marble was asked to evaluate Helen Wills's game. "Well," she said, "I do not think Mrs. Moody is the best woman player in the world at all," Alice said. "I know of at least one player who is better, but I am naming no names." Marble also let it be known that she favored Jacobs over Wills. "Miss Jacobs is a swell girl," she said. "I don't see how anyone could help liking her. She is friendly and pleasant and works very hard on her game, which was never better than it was in the final at Wimbledon, until her injury came back. People in the grandstand were actually crying during the second set, when she could hardly get the ball over the net."

A *New Yorker* correspondent concluded that "the Moody-Jacobs rivalry is ancient and complicated, and what happened that Saturday afternoon was probably beyond the understanding of anyone except the two women." As to who would have won the match had Jacobs maintained her playing form, the writer did not know.

When it was all over, at last, Catherine Wills was interviewed in Berkeley. Told that Helen had won once again, she said, "Well, I really didn't expect it. Miss Jacobs has been playing so excellently and Helen has been out of match play for three years. I really doubted if Helen would come through it all. I used to go to her matches with Helen, so I got used to the ups and downs of the tennis game. Of course," she concluded, "it's nice that she won, but it wouldn't have mattered much if she didn't."

Just before the women's singles final commenced at Wimbledon on July 2, it was announced to the capacity crowd gathered to see the battle of the two Helens that word had just arrived from Paris that Suzanne Lenglen was near death. Helen Wills was given the news just before she left her dressing room.

The news touched the historic sunny hour with a cloud of melancholy and sadness. Many in the crowd, no doubt, could remember that magic afternoon nineteen years earlier when the magnificent prodigy from France challenged Dorothy Lambert Chambers for the Wimbledon title, while Papa Lenglen sat in the gallery pounding his umbrella on the ground and sending signals to his daughter.

Papa Lenglen had died suddenly from bronchial pneumonia on March

1, 1929, at his home in Nice. Suzanne never recovered. Her melancholia increased.

Three weeks before his death he spoke with M. Daninos, editor of *Tennis et Golf,* about his life and his daughter. Daninos believed that Papa's only fault was "his infatuation (or blindness) before the prestige of his beloved daughter." Papa spoke at length about Suzanne's signing a professional contract with C. C. Pyle. He deeply regretted that he had given Suzanne permission to sign. Had his health been better, he said, he would have prevented the signing. He was convinced it had been a bad decision, the worst in her career. He told Daninos that "the great tragedy of my life" had been approving the Pyle contract. Had he resisted that, he said, Pyle would never have been allowed to "blemish the white ermine of Suzanne." But he had been worried at the time, he said, that because his health was failing he would not be around much longer to manage the affairs of Suzanne.

Dr. Clarence Wills realized right away the enormity of Papa Lenglen's error in allowing Suzanne to sign with Pyle while she still had worlds to conquer in amateur tennis. And he emphasized in 1927 that Helen would never turn professional. Suzanne was the negative example he pointed out. "No amount of money could make a professional tennis player out of Helen, if I have anything to say about it." If she turned professional, he said, "in a few years she would be forgotten, because I really cannot see how the professional game can last, at least not on the big scale they are trying to introduce it. People might pay the money once or twice to see a prominent player perform, but that is all.

"Helen is young, with ten or twelve years ahead of her to play tennis and she loves the amateur game. She gets lots of pleasure going around to the different tournaments, so why should she isolate herself like Suzanne is isolated now? Any player like Suzanne or Helen who has played in the biggest tournament in the world could not help but feel isolated when she puts herself in a position where she no longer can take part, but must sit inactive along the sidelines."

In early 1927, Paul Feret sought reinstatement as an amateur. It was widely rumored that he was serving simply as a stalking horse for Lenglen. The French Tennis Federation refused to reinstate him, and so Lenglen did not apply for her own reinstatement but instead announced she would never play amateur tennis again. At the end of 1927 Feret was again denied reinstatement as an amateur. In May of that year Lenglen refused to attend the clay court tournament at Saint-Cloud. "I don't believe I have friends there," she said.

In the spring of 1927 she crossed the Channel to organize her own professional tour and announced that she would not watch the women's matches at Wimbledon. "Women's matches never thrilled me," she told reporters.

She tried a tour with Baldwin Baldwin. Karel Kozeluh signed with the tour, he was already a professional. But nothing came of Baldwin's efforts. So Lenglen then signed with another promoter, Charles B. Cochran, an Englishman. Her professional tour of England was a flop. She played against Dora Koring, a former German champion. They played in an exhibition at Henley before a crowd of only four hundred. More seats in the auditorium were empty than filled. On July 5 she beat Koring again before another small crowd in Holland Park Hall in London.

Cochran felt he needed some novelty to make the tour successful. He tried to get Lenglen to play against men. But she balked at participating in doubles with three other men—Charles Read, Howard Kinsey, and Karel Kozeluh. "It is unorthodox," she said, "for one woman and three men to play in a doubles match, and I think it was a stupid idea."

The tour ended after six exhibitions. Suzanne Lenglen returned to Paris. In mid-September 1928 she announced that she was finished with tennis. "I shall never play tennis again, either as an amateur or as a professional," she said. "I have completely given up the game. I do not care whether I ever see another racket." She returned to her villa in Nice and turned it into a virtual fortress to keep out the press. Her mother issued a statement: "She is fed up with newspaper talk about her and only wants to be left in peace."

The French Tennis Federation announced that any former professionals who wished now to be restored to their amateur status could do so three years after applying for reentry. Suzanne Lenglen was insulted by the announcement, and on November 22 she told reporters that she realized that at the age of twenty-nine and with amateur tennis closed to her for three more years by the ruling she had nothing to gain by reentering the sport and possibly suffering defeat and then gradually declining to the status of a second rater. Suzanne would never be second rate. Never. The French Tennis Federation could go to hell. Papa Lenglen reiterated that statement in a letter to the Paris newspaper *L'Auto*.

In November 1928 she came to the United States with Mama and made headlines again by proceeding directly to California. There were delicious rumors that she intended to marry Baldwin Baldwin. But she returned to France in mid January 1929, unmarried. Baldwin Baldwin accompanied her on the return voyage and assaulted a photographer at dockside in New York.

Baldwin again announced plans to promote a Lenglen professional tour. Suzanne announced cancellation of the tour in May. It was said that the exaggerated accounts of Lenglen's American salary had caused other players to ask inflated amounts to sign with Baldwin. She said she planned to open a tennis school on the Carleton courts in Cannes. Baldwin Baldwin returned to California.

On February 7, 1929, Papa Lenglen proudly announced that Suzanne would marry Baldwin Baldwin as soon as the American millionaire's California divorce was completed, but the marriage plans died.

In January 1930 she was rumored to be a saleslady in a sporting goods establishment in Paris. In 1930 she was back in the papers when she invented shorts for female players called "Suzanne Shorts," which came just above the knee; they were later known as Bermuda shorts.

Paul Feret eventually won partial reinstatement by claiming temporary insanity for signing as a pro. The leading French male players attested to his emotional instability at the time he had signed. But nothing ever came of Suzanne Lenglen's inquiries. She remained associated with professional tennis and in 1933 appeared in London to make the award for the Professional Championships of England, won by Dan Maskell. She looked heavier and wore more layers of makeup than ever before. She did not appear to be happy or well.

But she remained a celebrity. When she arrived to watch matches at Wimbledon after her retirement from amateur tennis, the crowd always turned and applauded and paid her tribute by acknowledging her presence. At the Stade Roland-Garros, crowds left the Centre Court matches if word spread that Suzanne Lenglen was rallying with another player on an outside court.

She spent her final years running a tennis school for children in Paris which was state-funded. After she quit competitive tennis, Suzanne Lenglen was still plagued by poor health. She remained high strung and unpredictable in her behavior. In October 1934 she was rushed to the American Hospital in Paris, near death from acute appendicitis. Her appendix was removed and her life saved. Then a sudden downturn in her health came in 1938 after she attended a tennis tournament with friends, who reported that she appeared to be in excellent health. She complained of extreme fatigue on June 15. She rapidly grew weaker, and tests indicated the seriousness of her illness. She still insisted on discussing the Wimbledon tournament with friends and family. She had been suffering from the ravages of anemia again and had gone to bed. There were complications, and her condition worsened. Three attending physicians tried to combat the illness by a series of blood transfusions, but her condition continued to worsen. At first the physicians said that the transfusions had been successful and that Suzanne would recover. But the improvement in her health was temporary. She took another turn for the worse a few days later.

On June 30th, while Helen Wills progressed at Wimbledon, Suzanne Lenglen began the final struggle for her life in a Paris clinic. On July 1 she was transferred from the clinic to her apartment in Paris.

By July 2 she was so weakened that doctors postponed another blood transfusion despite the growing seriousness of the anemia. Special nurses were ordered to take care of her and a special attendant was stationed at her apartment to answer the hundreds of telephone calls from Paris and other cities throughout Europe. She was on a liquid diet and fading quickly. And her friends announced that they had "virtually given up hope." She reached a crisis stage on that day. Physicians said that the next forty-eight hours would determine whether or not she would recover.

During the weekend she still demanded newspapers and asked that the stories from Wimbledon be read to her. She followed the progress of Helen Wills toward an unprecedented eighth singles title. Friends could only guess what she thought when she was told that Helen Wills had in fact set a new singles record at Wimbledon. Suzanne did not speak of that feat to anyone. Her last few hours of increasing feebleness and great suffering left her unable to say more than a few words at rare intervals. But she remained conscious, and courageous, until a few minutes before her death.

On the morning of July 4th she spoke her last words. She awoke from a long sleep and whispered to Mama, "I am at the end of my tether." Then Suzanne dropped off to sleep again. She died in her sleep. Mama was holding her hand.

Physicians attributed her death to a general breakdown and her inability to throw off the affects of pernicious anemia because she had been working intensively for months as the head of a new government tennis school. "The Great Lenglen," they said, "lived for tennis almost to the moment of her death." That account became the one most widely accepted by the French public. Suzanne Lenglen had died because of her love of tennis. She was to have received the Legion of Honor. It was announced that the award would be made posthumously. Mama was officially notified of the award on July 5th. Plans were made for a semi-state funeral for Suzanne on July 6, befitting her position as a national sports heroine and a one-time world champion. The services were held at the Notre Dame de l'Assumption Church and burial was in the suburban St. Ouen Cemetery.

Suzanne Lenglen would have adored the final crowd that came to pay her tribute. King Gustaf of Sweden at eighty years of age was unable to attend, but he sent the Swedish prime minister to represent him. And there were representatives from premier Edouard Daladier and various other government departments. Jean Borotra, Jacques Brugnon, Bernard Destremeau, Christian Boussus, and Georges Carpentier, were among those at the funeral. Borotra, the bounding Basque of the Four Musketeers, delivered the funeral oration. Russell Kingman, treasurer of the USLTA, represented that organization. Crowds of curious onlookers and fans stretched along the route of the cortège. Flowers from tennis clubs and from individuals throughout the world filled three cars that followed the hearse.

At the graveside services Pierre Gillou spoke in behalf of the International Federation of Lawn Tennis and Jean Borotra spoke in behalf of the Federation Française de Tennis. An obituary in the London *Times* called her "the greatest woman lawn tennis player of her time" and announced her death with regret. The *Times* correspondent wrote that "it has become a journalistic custom to hail each successive champion as the best ever, but certainly no woman has played lawn tennis as Mlle Lenglen did." He pointed out that even after Suzanne Lenglen left the game she remained a star and enjoyed every moment in the limelight. She made Wimbledon the greatest tennis tournament in the world."

"It has been truly said of her that she was incomparable," the *Times* concluded.

When the world was celebrating Don Budge's feat of winning three Wimbledon championships in one tournament two years in succession, sportswriters reminded readers that Suzanne accomplished the feat three times. And in 1925 she also won all three events in the national French Tournament at Saint-Cloud, and she won an Olympic Gold Medal in Antwerp in 1920. And she beat Helen Wills.

Duncan Macaulay wrote that "it was agreed on all sides that she was the greatest woman player the game had ever known. And I have never had any reason to doubt that verdict nor do I think a greater woman player has since emerged." He wrote that, to make sure everyone noticed, after writing a paragraph on Helen Wills, whom he considered second to Suzanne Lenglen.

On the following morning the New York *Times* ran a lengthy obituary of Lenglen. "Those who remember Suzanne Lenglen on the tennis courts recall a flashing, tempestuous figure vibrant with life," the writer recalled. "It is pitiful to think of so vivid a woman, still young, as a victim of the enervating process of anemia. But the years of her triumph were gone and her laurels had passed definitely to the most challenging of her old time rivals, 'Little Poker Face,' who only last week won her eighth victory at Wimbledon where Suzanne never won more than five,"—an error—Suzanne had won six, but she would have understood the error, believed it made on purpose by the American newsmen, who forever failed to take her seriously.

"Nevertheless, there are those who say Mlle. Lenglen was the greatest woman tennis player who ever lived. It is hard to refute them. She never had a rival in accuracy and scientific placement." The paper discounted the match at Forest Hills in 1921, and concluded that it was "mere opera bouffe, in which Mlle Lenglen was unexcelled.

"Whether or not she was the greatest in her field, Suzanne Lenglen was by easy odds the most colorful. She could stamp her foot harder, quarrel more violently, cough more appealingly in a declining game and sob more rackingly than any woman she met. . . . But when she chose to play, she played so furiously that few could face her. Perhaps she wrote her own epitaph when she said, 'I just throw dignity to the winds and think of nothing but the game.' "

And the New York *Times* writer also concluded, "It had been truly said of her that she was incomparable." Suzanne would have agreed at last with an American journalist.

She was buried in a family plot at the St. Ouen Cemetery. Suzanne was the fifth family member buried there. For a marker, Mama designed a slab of black marble that still today stands out among the granite. Suzanne's autograph in gold leaf is engraved at the head of the slab.

At the end of her romantic novel *The Love Game,* Lenglen arranged for her heroine, Marcelle Penrose, to marry. Suzanne's heroine feared being alone. So she threw herself into whatever work was at hand. She was, Lenglen wrote, "possessed by the demon of unhappiness." And she used work "as an anodyne for pain." Marcelle's friend advised her to give herself to love. "Give yourself to a man who loves you," she wrote. "After a little while you will find that love engenders love. Oh, Marcelle, if you only knew what a heaven awaits you—what a transfiguration of life when you begin to live for someone else. For in time you will respond—you must respond—to devotion. It is a sweet fire that burns up self—a communion with the loved one. Every moment becomes a separate ecstasy."

Suzanne Lenglen never found the love and companionship that she so desperately wanted. And she was until the end of her brief life possessed by the demon of unhappiness. There can be no doubt, however, that Suzanne Rachel Flore Lenglen, who was known as The Goddess, was loved as no other woman had ever been loved by the people of France.

All of France mourned her passing.

After Wimbledon, Helen Wills traveled to Dublin for the Irish Lawn Tennis Championships. The competition was held at the Fitzwilliam Lawn Tennis Club, which had been founded in Dublin in 1877. W. A. Sandys, trustee of the club, had advised Wills by mail that the Ladies' Singles Tournament had originated in 1877, two years before the same event at Wimbledon and had been won at some time by all of the great players—with the exception of Suzanne Lenglen, who scratched from the tournament after the 1926 Wimbledon fiasco.

The tournament was at first easy for Wills, a welcome surprise after the lengthy tests undergone in the early rounds of Wimbledon. She was tired. And it rained for several days, and she remembered that the Irish courts were like "green moss." Yet she proceeded through the tournament, as expected, without much difficulty.

One young woman recalled that there was a press announcement prior to her matches that she was prepared to play "under any conditions, including rain." "This made a deep impression on the tennis world in Dublin as so many players of lesser stature scuttled off the courts at the first drop of rain."

Oreen Irvine saw Wills in a singles match played with a good deal of mist in the air. "But this troubled her not at all. She came on the court in a beautifully cut frock and her famous eye shade. She looked quite lovely, and at the same time, business like." She won in two love sets, her opponent being quite overwhelmed. Irvine, who was a young Irish player at the time, remembered how Helen Wills overwhelmed her opponents. "I could really appreciate the deadly accuracy of her shots and the strength behind them. The memory I have of this match is as clear as the day I saw it and I enjoyed every minute of it. She was a joy to watch." The enthusiastic Irish crowd, which packed the stands for each of her matches, shared the same awe and admiration for the Wimbledon champion.

Ethel Whiteside, as a fifteen-year-old tennis enthusiast in Dublin went out to see Wills play in the championships. She remembered that Wills arrived for each match in a chauffeur-driven limousine. When she emerged from the car and walked past the side courts and was in full view of the gallery around Centre Court, everyone stopped playing instantly, and the players and the audience turned their attention to her and cheered enthusiastically. The audience always gave her a standing ovation when she walked onto the court. "She deeply appreciated this welcome she received and acknowledged it smiling shyly. She arrived dressed to play and did not have to use the players' dressing room. She wore her white tennis outfit and over it a long green coat," Whiteside remembers.

She played, in one of the early rounds, the Irish Champion, Dorothy Curley. Wills lost the first game against Curley on her own service. She double-faulted several times, but, as Ethel Whiteside remembered, "we thought she did that just to give Dorothy the time to relax. Curley was pleased to have won a game. Then Helen won twelve games in a row without any difficulty. She gave me the impression of being a gracious lady, but shy and reserved, and who had one aim in life and that was to play well and win. Her ground strokes were a joy to watch and she played with ruthless efficiency."

But in the finals she played a young Englishwoman, Mrs. T. R. Jarvis, who seemed untroubled by the surface and who, Helen Wills told me, ran like the wind—"Like the wind, I tell you. And as I was playing her I had to tell myself again and again, 'Now, Helen, you just CAN'T lose here! They've invited you and they expect you to win and you JUST HAVE TO!' "

"Sometimes," Helen explained to me, "you feel you have to win not for yourself, but for your audience. You feel obligated to win. So I won.

But I won only after a terrific struggle. And they gave me a gold watch as a trophy.

"But those mossy courts just did me in. I finally had had enough. I decided right there not to play anymore. I skipped Forest Hills that year. I was through. I'd had it by that time. I was just too tired to go on anymore."

Brendan Arigho, who played in Dublin, remembered that in those days Helen Wills was a great heroine for both the male and the female players of his country. There was no other star who compared with her in inspiring the youngsters to play tennis. To all of the Irish players she was always just Helen Wills—they never tacked on the married name of Moody. "I listened to the radio commentaries of most of her Wimbledon finals but could not afford to travel to London to see her play." He was very excited when he read in the papers that she had agreed finally to come to Dublin to play in the Irish Championship.

The cup presentation took place before the men's singles final in order to allow Wills to get away as quickly as possible since she was traveling at the time on a tour of west Ireland with the Gogarty family.

Following her matches she signed autographs. It was announced that, if members of the crowd left their programs in the club office, Helen Wills would sign them later. She signed her name in those autograph books, once more, as "Helen Wills, 1938." She no longer added "Moody" to her name. She was simply Helen Wills again.

After the tournament she visited the Gogarty home on the west coast of Ireland during the weekend. She loved it and remembers it still. She understood then, she said, why the Irish were such romantics and such poets. The landscape, she remembered, was more beautiful than any painting or photograph she had ever seen. It was a luminous landscape with the mists coming in. There was no other spot on the face of the earth like it, there was no where else in the world quite like Ireland. "And everybody was so kind and entertaining to talk to. Everybody. I just loved it. The Irish people have real charm."

With her victories at Wimbledon and in Dublin Helen Wills remained the center of attention of tennis promoters in America. There were expectations and hopes that the continuing battle of the two Helens would enrich and invigorate the tennis clubs throughout the country and tennis in general, if the continued matches could simply be arranged in a suitable setting. Of course it would be the biggest sporting event in history, promoters said, bigger than any heavyweight prizefight ever held and by far the biggest contest ever staged between two women. One promoter jumped on the bandwagon immediately, a promoter who wanted the two women to remain amateurs and play for charity and for the promoters. Harris Connick, chief director of the World Fair of the West, to be held on Treasure Island in San Francisco Bay in 1939, sent telegrams to the two Helens at Wimbledon after their encounter, requesting that they

accept immediately invitations to play in 1939 at the Golden Gate International Exposition. What he wanted to do, hoped and expected to do,
was to duplicate for the western states the famous final match at Wimbledon, but under more favorable conditions and with a bigger gallery. The
match would be for no title but would rather be an exhibition in February 1939. When Connick also sought the blessing of Wills's friend Bud
Chandler, the former president of the Northern California Tennis Association, Chandler said that his organization would be "glad to sponsor
such a match if the two principals would agree to it."

This was followed by a proposal by Lewis Burton, a New York writer,
who suggested in his column that the Battle of the Helens be staged in
Yankee Stadium where 60,000 paying customers could witness the contest. But Bill Corum, writing for the International News Service, believed that a ballpark site would be impractical for such a match—even
though the crowd that could be attracted would be limited only by the
size of the stadium. He felt it might be as practical to stage the match at
Ebbets Field under the lights at night, just like a baseball game or a
heavyweight title fight. Corum arranged an appointment with Holcome
Ward, president of the USLTA, to present his plan.

But surprisingly and disappointingly to the promoters, neither of the
two women voiced any enthusiasm or even interest in such a contest.
Each returned to the United States and seemed subdued and almost
happy that the pressure was off and that they might not ever have to play
each other again, or face each other again, on or off the court. Like that
match in 1926, there was to be no additional contest. In 1938 the curtain
had at last come down on the two Helens.

For a time Helen Jacobs walked with the aid of a cane. When she returned, she told reporters that she was mending nicely and she would
be ready, she hoped, to participate in the national tournament at Forest
Hills in the late summer. When reporters and newsreel cameramen asked
her to pose with her cane, she refused, saying that she did not think it
would look right. "Let's just forget about it."

She planned now, she said, to continue her writing. And she would
write under her own name. Jacobs's first novel had already been published under the pen name of Barry Court. She had used another pseudonym, H. Braxton Hull, she said, so as not to receive undue publicity
because of her tennis fame.

The reporters were waiting for Helen Wills when she came back to
America at the end of July, shortly after Jacobs's return. Wills was smiling and happy and open and no longer either shy or poker-faced. She
complained that she had injured her back again. While packing for the
trip to the United States she had injured it, she said, and she was again
in some discomfort. She said she was unable, as a result, to practice for
at least a week. But she hoped then to prepare for the tournaments that
were the preliminaries to the national singles tournament at Forest Hills.

Helen Wills also said that she had signed up for a tour with the Feakin's Lecture Bureau and would make a national tour talking about her tennis experiences. She made sure before signing that she would not compromise her amateur status. When asked about the possibility of retirement, she said, "I see no reason to retire now." What about 1939? "Next year? I never plan so far in advance, But right now, there's nothing to it." She also indicated that she thought she was still playing a fine brand of tennis.

Of her confrontations with Jacobs she pointed out that the press had been incorrect in saying that the two women had played each other only twelve times, that in fact the women had faced each other across the net twenty times, and in nineteen of those matches Helen Wills had won. The press had just been a little sloppy in keeping track of the wins of Helen Wills.

John Lardner was present for the Wills homecoming. But his impressions were different from those of the other writers. He found her cold and said that she had "delivered more ice in her time than Red Grange, the Wheaton Ice Man." When she spoke of Jacobs, he wrote, she spoke "in a tone of voice you could skate on." When she indicated that there was no ill feeling between herself and Jacobs, Lardner wrote, her remark "coincided with the end of a recent hot spell."

In late August, Wills again shocked the USLTA. Not only did she announce that she would not be playing in the national singles competition and would thus deprive the tournament once more of its principal drawing card, she also sent a check for $1309.45, the amount given to her by the association just prior to her trip to England. Wills explained in a letter to Edward Moss, executive secretary, that she was refunding the amount given her for expenses in England as a member of the Wightman Cup team and during the Wimbledon tournament. She hoped the check would be accepted in view of her default at the national tournament. Helen Wills let the public know of the return of the money. She said that her inability to play at Forest Hills was due to "a severe attack of neuritis." Moss returned the check to Wills with the remark that the "expenses allowed were a proper charge against the event and your representing us in the British championships."

Moss's letter, released to the press, said her record in international tournaments "has never been equalled and possibly never will be by any other player." He asked her now to keep the money, saying that similar amounts were allotted to the other players on the Wightman Cup team. Since Helen Wills had been an official representative of the United States she deserved to have her expenses paid for that representation.

The nonacceptance of the check was Helen Wills's last kiss off to the USLTA and one in which she defied the organization in much the same way that Suzanne Lenglen had tried, unsuccessfully, to defy the French Tennis Federation and the All-England Club. This was the first time in

American tennis history that an amateur player admitted publicly to having received a payment and then named the amount. While it was assumed by the press that such dealings went on, many reporters were shocked now, in part by the return of the money and making the return public, and also "by the meager evaluation of Mrs. Moody's services."

The return of the expense money opened a line of questioning as to how long this had been going on and which players had been given what amounts over the years. The USLTA, which was openly fighting professionalism, was at the same time, in its policies covertly sponsoring certain players and compromising their amateurism.

Laney wrote that Wills felt she should return the money once she decided not to play at Forest Hills. The suspicious said that the money was not for expenses in Europe but was appearance money for playing in the American championships, and Wills was obligated to return it. In any case, Laney found, Wills did all right financially when she was playing abroad. She wrote for the London papers, the same sort of thing Tilden had done and had been suspended for years earlier. Laney also recalled that tennis champions were paid higher rates for reporting than regular correspondents. And, in fairness to her, he said, "they were very well written pieces and I was assured that she wrote them herself entirely without professional help. I was quite impressed by her literary talent."

Laney also reported hearing stories about a deal that had been made with Wills to play in the Irish Championships. But he could never get straight exactly what it was. He was told that Helen received "social and entertainment considerations besides having her expenses paid."

Neither Wills nor Jacobs competed at Forest Hills, and Alice Marble regained the title she had won in 1936. She came through strong international field, beating Australian Nancy Wynne in the record-breaking time of twenty-two minutes in the final, demonstrating her dominance of the game. She was ranked first among American players by the USLTA at the end of the year.

At the end of 1938 the eighth annual Associated Press poll of sports editors voted that Helen Wills's 1938 Wimbledon win represented the comeback of the year. Jimmy Foxx, in capturing the batting league crown for the American League after a poor 1937 season, came in second. And Joe Louis, who got revenge for his 1936 defeat at the hands of Max Schmeling, came in fourth, after Dizzy Dean.

In the spring of 1939, Helen Wills came to a decision. She would play no more serious tournament tennis. "I was having a nice time in San Francisco," she recalled. "I saw no reason to go again to Wimbledon. I'd done that. Some people, you know, are perpetual undergraduates. They're bores. They are the kind of person who never quite gets over being on a football team or winning a tennis match. I never wanted to be like that. I knew when it was over. I thought it was now. I was done. The time passed. My time had passed. It was a beautiful spring. So I stayed at home."

And so the American Girl's career came to an end with her 1938 Irish victory, seventeen years after her first trip east to play tennis as a junior and fifteen years after her first national singles title at Forest Hills and eleven years after her first Wimbledon singles win. In that time she had rewritten the record books. She had won eight Wimbledon singles titles, seven American national singles titles, and four French singles titles—nineteen titles that would today fall in the Grand Slam category. She had also won the Irish title once. She had also won four U.S. doubles titles, two U.S. mixed doubles titles, three Wimbledon doubles titles, and one Wimbledon mixed doubles title. She was the national girls' singles title holder twice and national girls' doubles title holder once. In Wightman Cup singles matches she won eighteen of twenty matches, and in Wightman Cup doubles she won three of seven matches. She won her first American national singles title at the age of seventeen and her last Wimbledon singles title at the age of thirty-two.

At Wimbledon she won eight of the nine tournaments in which she played, losing only in her first appearance in 1924. She had played fifty-six singles matches on the Wimbledon grass and had won fifty-five. In the doubles at Wimbledon she played sixteen matches and lost none. In the mixed doubles she played twenty-two matches and won nineteen. In all categories at Wimbledon she won twelve titles and won ninety of her ninety-four matches to Suzanne Lenglen's ninety-one of ninety-four.

Between 1927 and 1933 Helen Wills did not lose a set in singles competition anywhere in the world and she won 180 matches in succession. In 1928 she became the first player of either sex to win the singles titles of the United States, France, and Great Britain, and then she won all three titles again in 1929. Wills had also won two Olympic Gold medals and scores of local and regional tournaments. And because of her athletic prowess, she became the first woman to be granted a letter by the University of California for her athletic achievements.

On October 28, 1939, in Las Vegas, Helen married Aidan Roark, a noted polo player. The ceremony was performed by the Reverend Albert C. Melton of the Immanuel Community Church. Helen was thirty-three, Roark, thirty-four. It was the second marriage for both. Helen had been married to Fred Moody for eight years before divorcing him in 1937. Roark listed his occupation as "film writer" and was prepared, he said, to retire from athletics. The couple moved to Rolling Hills near Los Angeles.

--◄{ 5 }►--

Helen Jacobs played for the Wightman Cup team for the 12th time in 1939. She lost to Kay Stammers that year in the round of eight at Wimbledon. She never won another title at Forest Hills. In 1940 she lost in the finals of the tournament to Alice Marble, and in 1941 she didn't make the finals. In 1942 she enlisted in the U.S. Navy. She completed her college credits for graduation at William and Mary and entered Officer Training School in January 1943. And she continued to write, fourteen books on tennis and five instructional books and five novels for girls. She never signed a professional contract. And she never again saw Helen Wills.

In 1939 Helen Wills published her novel, *Death Serves an Ace,* also with Scribners. It was a murder mystery centering on tennis players. And as the *New York Times* reviewer concluded, "In Mrs. Moody's hand the racket is mightier than the pen." Helen later regretted having tried her hand at fiction and advised others to skip it.

Gradually, she eased her way into retirement. In 1940 she publicly supported Wendell Willkie for the presidency. She played tennis—doubles—in local tournaments and practiced regularly with friends.

During World War II she lived in Kansas, near Fort Riley, while her husband served in the army. She took classes at the State College in management and business relations and read a good deal. Each afternoon she took a long walk with her German shepherd. She did not play tennis on nearby courts because the courts were not good, and neither were the other players.

In 1943 she had an accident that affected her ability to play tennis. Her dog, Sultan, got into a fight with a smaller dog, and she broke it up and was bitten on the hands. Her index finger of her right hand was badly mangled and broken, and she spent three weeks in the hospital. The finger was in a special cast for four months while physicians tried to save it. Some of the bone became infected and had to be cut away.

After the war she moved to Pacific Palisades in Southern California. She played tennis with soldiers recuperating in a nearby hospital.

Helen Wills's appearances in publicized tennis matches after 1938 were rare. But occasionally friends and partners wrote about her continued excellent play. In his autobiography entitled *The Game,* published in 1979, Jack Kramer remembered playing in a match with Wills in Los Angeles in 1941. She was thirty-six years old. And she was teamed up with Ted Schroeder for mixed doubles against Kramer and Sarah Palfrey. When some confusion arose in the scheduling, Perry Jones, who was running the tournament, informed the foursome that their match was postponed until the following day. Palfrey, Kramer, and Schroeder said it was all right and began to leave. But when Jones told Helen Wills about it, she simply stared at him and said, "Perry, I came here to play." She wanted either to play as scheduled or default, Kramer recalled. They played. Wills and Schroeder won.

Later, in 1946 Kramer recalled playing doubles with her as his partner and winning against Tom Brown and Pauline Betz, when Betz was at her peak; Wills was in her forties.

Kramer remembered that the first time he played with Helen Wills was in singles when he was just fifteen and she had retired after her eighth Wimbledon title. "I beat her, but Helen had a good game," he wrote in 1979. "She would have run today's women players into the ground."

Mrs. Robert W. Shepard recalled meeting Helen Wills after the war, in the fall of 1945. Mr. Shepard, after the war, had gone to work for the Rexall Drug Company. Justin Dart, president of Rexall, bought Deanna Durbin's house, which had a tennis court and no pool, on Amalfi Drive in Pacific Palisades and lived there.

The Darts were generous, she remembered, about letting friends and neighbors use their court. Helen Wills lived up the road from the Darts, and close friends of the Shepards lived across the way. "You must understand that we all knew who she was but we pretended that we didn't know, partly because we didn't want to appear to be impressed by a celebrity but mostly because it was obvious that was the way she wanted it to be. At the time she was married to Aidan Roark." Everyone called her "Mrs. Roark."

She liked to play at the Darts' court. It was private and nobody made much of a fuss about her playing. "She was Mrs. Roark, a neighbor from up the road."

Several of the Rexall employees played at the Darts, and Helen did too—the men were in their late 20s. They usually played doubles. The teams were always Helen and one young man against two young men on the other side. "Mrs. Roark's side always won. She stayed at the back line, letting her partner play the rare shots near the net while she hit the ball hard and brilliantly placed. She had the young opponents running until they were breathless and dripping wet. She moved back and forth along the back line at a moderate pace, never missed a return shot, never even took off her sweater, never perspired, hardly ever really smiled. She always looked cool and composed and had a rather remote but pleasant expression on her face. The young men took turns playing with and against her—being her partner was something of a rest period. When she had played enough tennis to suit her she gathered up her things and went home. She never stayed around to watch, to have a cool drink or sociable talk."

Sarah Palfrey saw her again in 1967 on the West Coast. "I called her on the phone and arranged a doubles match" with two male friends. "We had great fun with a lot of laughs but still fighting for every point. I could tell that Helen really enjoyed herself."

In 1975, soon after her seventieth birthday, she was living in Carmel Valley, California, and she reflected on her career and her almost countless victories. Asked about her trophies, she said she had turned them into lamps—or as she called them, "active appliances." She remembered playing in nine Wimbledons. She thought of it many times, she said. And "always, when I won a match I was keen to win, I felt a letdown. Wimbledon goes on for two weeks and that's a long time to keep up a certain level of feeling. I think that when people try hard for something, maybe for a while they don't appreciate their good fortune." The part of the good fortune she liked most was "the chance to have been in danger—I mean a big match—and then when it's over it was really nothing. And you had all the fun."

Wills regretted having missed so much when she traveled to play tennis. Especially, she found, this was true in 1938. "I had friends who were members of Parliament. And all they fussed about was the invasion. Hitler was on the move. I'd have lunch with them and all they'd talk about was the Sudeten Deutsch, the Sudeten Deutsch—they'd be so excited—and I didn't realize what it was.

"I never used to see anything because I would rest a lot and then go out and play my matches. I didn't see Pavlova, for example, and she'd be in Paris every spring. There would be her picture on the walls. You'd see them in the streets. I thought, well, I'll sometime be able to see her. But nobody is forever and the time is gone when you could have had that experience.

"I should have gone to see her.

"You know what I thought? I just thought, 'What would tennis be like without me? And how could Wimbledon be going on if I wasn't there?' And then the time came when Wimbledon was going on pretty well and I wasn't there.

"Isn't it strange how you can get so caught up in a thing, so interested in it that you think, 'How can I not be here with these beautiful trees, in this beautiful spot?' Well, there comes a day when you're not there and its the same.

"I don't think anyone is missed and it doesn't matter whether it's sport or life. Do you?"

In a 1981 interview she reflected again and said, "Sometimes I wonder why I tried so hard. When I was doing it, it seemed like so much fun. It was a way of life. It was exciting."

She said she stopped playing tennis in the early 1970s. She divorced Aidan Roark about that time. Both of her parents became invalids, and Helen resigned from the tennis club at Pebble Beach in order to devote full time to their care. She said she thought she was going "to stop my parents from getting aged. I was going to stop the clock." They had done so much for her, she recalled, and now, "I wouldn't permit them to be sick or anything. I tried so hard.

"But you know, you can't really defeat old age, can you? I mean it's a losing game. And that infuriates me."

In the summer of 1984, after a sixty-year absence, tennis returned to the Olympic Games as a demonstration event. Helen Wills wrote a special message which was given to the players in Los Angeles. She pointed out that she was the last living member of the 1924 Olympic tennis team and so wrote a special message from all of those who had played in the Games outside Paris in 1924. "We are very happy not to be remembered as 'the last team'—we now belong to the future. Our message to all future contestants is to carry on proudly the Olympic Tradition of Sport for all Nations—*In Peace*." And she signed her name, "Helen Wills Roark" and drew a small picture of herself at the bottom of the page.

I spoke with Helen that summer just before the Olympic Games. We talked about the comebacks of 1935 and 1938. Why hadn't she simply retired? What made her do it?

"I really don't know why," she told me. "I just wanted to, I guess. It sure wasn't for the money. There was no money in it. I just wanted to do it."

She was struck by the amount of money players make today. "I don't have anything against making a million dollars," she said. "I never did. But I wouldn't have minded making a million dollars. But you would think that with all of that money they would be happy. I had a right to be called Poker Face and to be serious because I didn't earn anything in tennis. So why doesn't John McEnroe smile more with all that money? He's so rich. He's a real genius. And he's lucky. What in the world could he do—where could he earn money like that—if not from tennis?

"Remember, I never took money for tennis. And when I stopped playing I was never approached for endorsements. I think money is wonderful if you can get it for playing. But I was always strictly an amateur. I played all those years, and you know why? Because I loved the game. I really did. It sounds strange today, I know, doesn't it?" She laughed at the thought of it.

"I did *all of that* just because I loved the game."

And what about today's players—players like Martina Navratilova? How would Helen do against them?

"I'm often asked that question," she said. "And it's really hard to know what would happen if I played Evert or Navratilova. But I do believe I could have held my own against the best today. Martina plays very well. I would like to have played her. I can tell you that I certainly would not be afraid of her."

She retired at the end of the 1938 season, she said, because the tournament in Dublin did her in. "I'd had enough," she told me. "I didn't

want to play any more. The Irish courts did me in. I was just too tired
to go on.

"When I got back to California I realized I was tired of traveling, too.
I was having a nice time in San Francisco, and that next spring I saw no
reason to return to Wimbledon. So I didn't. I just decided not to play
any more.

"But I would have gone to Wimbledon again for one reason. I would
have gone to play Suzanne again. Yes, if Suzanne Lenglen had been at
Wimbledon in 1939 I would have gone to play her one more time. You
should have seen her. Words can hardly describe Suzanne. She was really
very special. A unique woman. She was so slender. And so lovely.

"Yes, I would have gone to Wimbledon again just to play Suzanne.
Now that would have been something to remember."

6

Thousands of players—many of them great players—have graced the
courts of Wimbledon, Forest Hills, Flushing Meadow, and Roland-
Garros in the decades since the Goddess and the American Girl stopped
winning titles. And there have been many memorable contests played
since 1938. But none of the players of the past half-century have embodied national values and national pride as did Suzanne Lenglen and
Helen Wills. They were never simply two women who played tennis.
They were, rather, the embodiments of France and America, the Old
World and the New. Lenglen and Wills were extraordinarily talented
young women who were better known and more celebrated in their time
than presidents, kings, prime ministers, artists, writers, or film stars.
They were the glory of their times.

In her autobiography Helen Wills wrote that in tennis she had found
"another world in which there is sunshine, the wonderful feeling of
movement through space and air, speed, the thrill of muscles in action
and the remoteness from everything except the game of the moment.
There are, also, degrees of pleasure, surprise, suspense, disappointment,
and many of the emotions that exist in life itself. The game may seem
to suffice in completing a world of its own," she wrote, "a world in which
its devoted follower may move as in a dream. And, if you have played
your game well, you feel contented."

As she recounted her long career for me and the indelible vision of
Suzanne Lenglen so many years before, it became clear that the American Girl, who had been driven so far by a persistent restlessness of her
heart, knew that she had played the game well and had, at long last,
found contentment.

SOURCES

The following individuals corresponded with the author and provided information used in this study:

France
Jean Borotra
Jacques Brugnon
Henry Cochet
Henri Lacoste

Great Britain
Kathryn McKane Godfree
Major A. D. Mills
Dorothy Round Little
Elizabeth Ryan

Ireland
Brendan Arigho
Oreen Irvine
W. A. Sandys
Margaret A. Towers
B. F. Victory
Mrs. Ethel Whiteside

United States
Leslie Bancroft Aeschliman
Wilmer Allison
Arthur Ashe
Bertram L. Baker
Wallace Bates
Clifford Bissell
Benjamin C. Bradlee
J. Donald Budge
Hugh Bulloch
Edward Chandler
Jonathan Daniels
Allison Danzig
Sarah Palfrey Danzig

Richard Doyle
John Gardiner
Elmer Griffin
Harriet Walker Henderson
Anna Harper
W. Eugene Houston
Effingham P. Humphrey, Jr.
Cranston Holman
Francis T. Hunter
Helen Hull Jacobs
Alice Marble
Edwin McCord
Homer Miller
Frederick S. Moody
Phil Neer
Marjorie Morrill Painter
Bobby Riggs
Mrs. Robert W. Shepard
Edith Sigourney
Harvey Snodgrass
Gerald Stratford
Carolyn Swarz
Dorothea Swarz
Mrs. Ellis Taylor
Ellsworth Vines
Hubert Voight
Dorothy Wightman
William Wightman
Pat Henry Yeomans

Interviews
Wallace Bates
Clifford Bissell
Edward Chandler
Richard Doyle

John Gardiner   Frederick S. Moody
Elmer Griffin   Helen Wills Moody Roark
Anna Harper   Harvey Snodgrass
Harriet Walker Henderson   Gerald Stratford
Dr. Carroll Jensen   Carolyn Swarz
Edith Cross Jensen   Dorothea Swarz
Alice Marble   Dorothy Wightman

Books

Adams, Samuel Hopkins, *Incredible Era: The Life and Times of Warren Gamaliel Harding* (New York, 1930).

Allen, Frederick Lewis, *Only Yesterday: An Informal History of the 1920's* (New York, 1931).

Ashe, Arthur, with Neil Amdur, *Off the Court* (New York, 1981).

Atherton, Gertrude, *Can Women Be Gentlemen?* (Boston, 1938).

Austin, Henry, *Lawn Tennis Made Easy* (London, 1935).

Baritz, Loren, *The Culture of the Twenties* (Indianapolis, 1970).

Berg, A. Scott, *Max Perkins: Editor of Genius* (New York, 1978).

Bernstein, Burton, *Thurber: A Biography* (New York, 1975).

Betts, John, *America's Sporting Heritage* (Reading, Mass., 1974).

Bland, Henry Meade (ed.), *A Day in the Hills* (Saratoga, Calif., 1926).

Boorstin, Daniel, *The Image* (New York, 1962).

Broun, Heywood, *Tumultuous Merriment* (New York, 1979).

Browne, Mary K., *Streamline Tennis* (New York, 1940).

Browne, Ray B., et al. (eds.), *Heroes of Popular Culture* (Bowling Green, Ohio, 1972).

Bruce, Ethel Sutton, *Tennis, Fundamentals and Timing* (New York, 1938).

Buchanan, Lamont, *Story of Tennis* (New York, 1951).

Budge, J. Donald, and Allison Danzig, *Budge on Tennis* (New York, 1939).

Burrow, F. R., *The Centre Court and Others* (London, 1937).

Carter, Paul A., *Another Part of the Twenties* (New York, 1977).

———, *The Twenties in America* (New York, 1968).

Chafe, William H., *The American Woman: Her Changing Social, Economic, and Political Roles, 1920–1970* (New York, 1972).

Chaplin, Charles, *My Autobiography* (London, 1964).

Clerici, Gianni, *The Ultimate Tennis Book* (Chicago, 1975).

Collins, Bud, *Bud Collins' Modern Encyclopedia of Tennis* (New York, 1980).

Cowley, Malcolm, *A Second Flowering: Works and Days of the Lost Generation* (New York, 1956).

Cummings, Parke, *American Tennis: The Story of a Game and Its People* (Boston, 1957).

Davis, Ronald L. (ed.), *The Social and Cultural Life of the 1920s* (New York, 1972).

Danzig, Allison, and Peter Brandwein, *Sports' Golden Age: A Close Up of the Fabulous Twenties* (New York, 1948).

———, *The Greatest Sports Stories from the New York Times* (New York, 1951).

Danzig, Allison and Peter Schwed (eds.), *The Fireside Book of Tennis* (New York, 1972).

Davis, Kenneth S., *The Hero: Charles A. Lindbergh and the American Dream* (Garden City, N.Y., 1959).

Deford, Frank, *Big Bill Tilden: The Triumphs and the Tragedy* (New York, 1975).

Degler, Carl N., *At Odds: Women and the Family in America from the Revolution to the Present* (New York, 1980).

Durant, Will, *On the Meaning of Life* (New York, 1931).

Fass, Paula S., *The Damned and the Beautiful: American Youth in the 1920s* (New York, 1977).

Frank, Stanley, *The Jew in Sports* (New York, 1936).

Gallico, Paul, *Farewell to Sport* (New York, 1938).

——, *The Golden People* (Garden City, N.Y., 1965).

—— and Coswell Adams (eds.), *Great American Sports Stories* (Philadelphia, 1947).

Geismar, Maxwell, *The Ring Lardner Reader* (New York, 1963).

Gogarty, Oliver St. John, *As I Was Going Down Sackville Street* (London, 1937).

Graham, Frank, Jr., *A Farewell to Heroes* (New York, 1981).

——, *It Takes Heart* (New York, 1959).

Green, Harvey, *Fit for America: Health, Fitness, Sport & American Society* (New York, 1986).

Grimsley, Will, *Tennis: Its History, People, and Events* (Englewood Cliffs, N.J., 1971).

Hart, Marie (ed.), *Sport in the Sociocultural Process* (Dubuque, Iowa, 1972).

Hicks, John D., *Republican Ascendancy, 1921–1933* (New York, 1960).

Hillyard, G. W., *Forty Years of First-Class Lawn Tennis* (London, 1925).

Hoffman, Frederick J., *The 20's: American Writing in the Postward Decade* (New York, 1949).

Hutchens, John K., and George Oppenheimer, *The Best in the World: A Selection of Feature Stories, Editorials, Humor, Poems, and Reviews from 1921 to 1928* (New York, 1973).

Jacobs, Helen Hull, *Beyond the Game: An Autobiography* (Philadelphia, 1936).

——, *Center Court* (New York, 1950).

——, *Gallery of Champions* (New York, 1951).

——, *Judy, Tennis Ace* (New York, 1951).

——, *Modern Tennis* (Indianapolis, 1933).

——, *Proudly She Serves! The Realistic Story of a Tennis Champion Who Becomes a Wave* (New York, 1953).

——, *Tennis* (New York, 1941).

Jenkins, Allen, *The Twenties* (London, 1974).

Johnston, Charles H. L., *Famous American Athletes of Today* (Boston, 1928).

Kieran, John, *The American Sporting Scene* (New York, 1941).

King, Billie Jean, with Kim Chapin, *Billie Jean* (New York, 1974).

Kramer, Jack, with Frank Deford, *The Game: My 40 Years in Tennis* (New York, 1979).

Krout, John Allen, *Annals of American Sport* (New Haven, 1929).

Lacey, Robert, *Ford: The Men and the Machine* (Boston, 1986).

Lacoste, Jean René, *Le Method d'initiation au tennis de Suzanne Lenglen* (Paris, 1942).

————, *Tennis* (Paris, 1928).

Laney, Al, *Covering the Court: A 50-Year Love Affair with the Game of Tennis* (New York, 1968).

Lardner, Ring, *First and Last* (New York, 1942).

————, *Some Champions* (New York, 1976).

Lartigue, Jacques Henri, *Diary of a Century* (New York, 1970).

Leighton, Isabel, *The Aspirin Age, 1919–1941* (New York, 1949).

Lenglen, Suzanne, *Lawn Tennis for Girls* (London, 1922).

————, *Lawn Tennis: The Game of Nations* (New York, 1925).

————, *Initiation au tennis principes essentiels et preparation physique* (Paris, 1937).

————, *The Love Game: Being the Life Story of Marcelle Penrose* (New York, 1926).

————, *Tennis by Simple Exercises* (London, 1937).

Leuchtenburg, William E., *The Perils of Prosperity, 1914–1932* (Chicago, 1958).

Levine, Lawrence W. and Robert Middlekauff (eds.), *The National Temper* (New York, 1972).

Lucas, John, *The Saga of American Sport* (Philadelphia, 1978).

Lumpkin, Angela, *Women's Tennis, A Historical Documentary of the Players and Their Game* (New York, 1981).

McCarthy, Mary, *How I Grew* (New York, 1987).

McCoy, Donald R., *Coming of Age: The United States During the 1920s and 1930s* (New York, 1973).

McLoughlin, Maurice E., *Tennis As I Play It* (New York, 1915).

McPhee, John, *Levels of the Game* (New York, 1969).

Macaulay, A. D. C., *Behind the Scenes at Wimbledon* (London, 1965).

Manchester, H., *Four Centuries of Sport in America* (New York, 1931).

Marble, Alice, *The Road to Wimbledon* (New York, 1949).

Merrihew, Stephen W., *The Quest of the Davis Cup* (New York, 1928).

Metzler, Paul, *Tennis: Styles and Stylists* (New York, 1969).

Mewshaw, Michael, *Short Circuit: Six Months on the Men's Professional Tennis Tour* (New York, 1983).

Michener, James, *Sports in America* (New York, 1976).

Minton, Robert, *Forest Hills: An Illustrated History* (New York, 1975).

Mitford, Nancy, *Zelda: A Biography* (New York, 1970).

Morris, Lloyd, *Not So Long Ago* (New York, 1949).

————, *Postscript to Yesterday* (New York, 1947).

Mowry, George E. (ed.), *The Twenties: Fords, Flappers & Fanatics* (Englewood Cliffs, N.J., 1963).

Murray, Robert K., *The Politics of Normalcy* (New York, 1973).

Myers, Arthur Wallis, *Fifty Years of Wimbledon: The Story of the Lawn Tennis Championships* (London, 1926).

————, *Great Lawn Tennis* (London, 1937).

————, *Memory's Parade* (London, 1932).

Myrick, Julian, *et al.*, *Fifty Years of Lawn Tennis in the United States* (New York, 1931).

Nash, Roderick, *The Nervous Generation: American Thought, 1917–1930* (New York, 1970).

Nason, Jerry, *et al.*, *Famous American Athletes of Today* (Boston, 1940).

Navratilova, Martina, with George Vecsey, *Martina* (New York, 1985).

Neuhaus, Eugen, *The History and Ideals of American Art* (Stanford, Calif., 1931).

Noverr, Douglas, *The Games They Played* (Chicago, 1983).

O'Connor, Richard, *Heywood Broun: A Biography* (New York, 1975).

Paret, Jahial P., *Methods and Players of Modern Lawn Tennis* (New York, 1931).

Patterson, Norman H., *The Complete Lawn Tennis Player* (London, 1956).

Paxton, Henry T. (ed.), *Sport USA: The Best from the Saturday Evening Post* (New York, 1961).

Perrett, Geoffrey, *American in the Twenties: A History* (New York, 1982).

Potter, E. C., Jr., *Kings of the Court* (New York, 1936).

———, *The West Side Tennis Club Story* (New York, 1952).

Rader, Benjamin G., *American Sports: From the Age of Folk Games to the Age of Spectators* (Englewood Cliffs, N.J., 1983).

Rice, Grantland, *The Tumult and the Shouting* (New York, 1954).

Rivera, Diego, *My Art, My Life: An Autobiography* (New York, 1960).

———, *Portrait of America* (New York, 1934).

Ross, Ishbel, *Grace Coolidge and Her Era* (New York, 1962).

Russell, Francis, *The Shadow of Blooming Grove: Warren G. Harding in His Times* (New York, 1968).

Scott, Eugene, *Tennis: Game of Motion* (New York, 1973).

Schickel, Richard, *Intimate Strangers: The Culture of Celebrity* (New York, 1985).

———, *The World of Tennis* (New York, 1975).

Shirer, William L., *20th Century Journey: A Memoir of a Life and the Times* (New York, 1976).

Simpson, Eileen B., *Poets in Their Youth: A Memoir* (New York, 1982).

Slosson, Preston W., *The Great Crusade and After, 1914–1928* (New York, 1930).

Smythe, John G., *Lawn Tennis* (London, 1953).

Soule, George, *Prosperity Decade, From War to Depression, 1917–1929* (New York, 1947).

Stallings, Laurence, *The Doughboys* (New York, 1963).

Starr, Kevin, *Americans and the California Dream, 1850–1915* (New York, 1973).

———, *Inventing the Dream: California Through the Progressive Era* (New York, 1985).

Tarshis, Barry, *Tennis and the Mind* (New York, 1977).

Tilden, William T., *Aces, Places and Faults* (London, 1938).

———, *How to Play Better Tennis* (New York, 1950).

———, *My Story: A Champion's Memoirs* (New York, 1948).

———, *Singles and Doubles* (New York, 1923).

Tingay, Lance, *100 Years of Wimbledon* (London, 1977).

Tinling, Ted, with Rod Humphries, *Love and Faults: Personalities Who Have Changed the History of Tennis in My Lifetime* (New York, 1979).

Tunis, John, *The American Girl* (New York, 1930).

———, *The American Way in Sport* (New York, 1958).

———, *Sport for the Fun of It* (New York, 1940).

———, *$port$, Heroics and Hysterics* (New York, 1928).

Twombly, Wells, *200 Years of Sport in America* (New York, 1976).
United States Lawn Tennis Association, *Official Encyclopedia of Tennis* (New York, 1979).
——, *The Official Yearbook and Tennis Guide* (Lynn, Mass., 1941–present).
Wallachinsky, David, *The Complete Book of the Olympics* (New York, 1984).
White, William Allen, *A Puritan in Babylon: The Story of Calvin Coolidge* (New York, 1938).
Williams, Paul B., *The United States Lawn Tennis Association and the World War* (New York, 1921).
Wills, Helen, and Robert Murphy, *Death Serves an Ace* (New York, 1939).
——, *Fifteen-Thirty: The Story of a Tennis Player* (New York, 1937).
——, *Tennis* (New York, 1928).
Wilson, Edmund, *The Twenties* (New York, 1975).
Wilson, Joan Hoff, *The Twenties: The Critical Issues* (Boston, 1972).
Wind, Herbert Warren, *Game, Set and Match: The Tennis Boom of the 1960s and 70s* (New York, 1979).
—— (ed.), *The Realm of Sport* (New York, 1966).
Wolfe, Bertram D., *The Fabulous Life of Diego Rivera* (New York, 1963).
Yeomans, Pat Henry, *History and Heritage of the Los Angeles Tennis Club, 1920–1980* (Los Angeles, 1979).

Documents

Little, Kathleen A. C., "A History of Women's Tennis War from 1873 to 1979" (M.A. thesis, San Jose State University, 1979).
Lumpkin, Angela, "The Contributions of Women to the History of Competitive Tennis in the United States" (Ph.D. dissertation, Ohio State University, 1974).
Miller, Jack C., "California, Cradle of Tennis Champions," M.A. thesis, San Jose State College, 1961.
Application for Admission to the University of California, Catherine Anderson Wills (August, 1899) and Helen Newington Wills (April, 1923), Archives of the University of California, Berkeley, California.

Papers

The Gertrude Atherton Papers, The Bancroft Library, University of California, Berkeley, California.
The James Phelan Papers, The Bancroft Library, University of California, Berkeley, California.
Presidential Campaign of 1928 Correspondence, Papers of Herbert Hoover, Herbert Hoover Presidential Library, West Branch, Iowa.
"Suzanne Lenglen: The North American Tour," Souvenir Program including "Why I Became a Professional" by Suzanne Lenglen, "The Biography of Suzanne Lenglen," by Charles Lenglen and "Professional Tennis" by C. C. Pyle.

Articles

Adams, F. P., "Youngest of the Lochinvars," *Collier's* (Nov. 6, 1915), 26.
Agutter, George, "Learning to Play Tennis," *Country Life* (May, June, July, Aug., 1924).

Andrews, Peter, "The Tennis Racket," *American Heritage* (Aug.–Sept. 1981), 65–73.

Archibald, J. F. J., "Lawn Tennis in California," *Overland* (Oct. 1892), 363–76.

Baily, R., "Manufactory of Champions," *Sunset* (June 1917), 34–35.

Bjurstedt, Molla, "How I Play Championship Tennis," *Ladies' Home Journal* (June 1916), 33.

Bodo, Peter, "The Myth of Sportsmanship," *California Today* (Oct. 2, 1983), 14.

Bongartz, Roy, "Who Was This Man—And Why Did He Paint Such Terrible Things About Us?" *American Heritage* (Dec. 1977), 14–29.

Borotra, Jean, "Tennis: It's a Grand Old Game," *Rotarian* (July 1934), 11–12.

Brewster, H., "Battle of the Courts," *Munsey* (Oct. 1902), 106–13.

Brewster, William, "Helen of California," *Sunset Magazine* (July 1927), 19.

Browne, Mary K., "Fit to Win," *Collier's* (Oct. 16, 1926), 16.

———, "The Girl Who Plays Tennis," *Ladies' Home Journal* (July 1915), 9.

———, "Tennis Pro and Coin," *Saturday Evening Post* (April 30, 1927), 18–19.

———, "What I Learned from Suzanne," *Collier's* (May 7, 1927), 14.

Camp, Walter, "Lawn Tennis, the Queen of Games," *Century* (Aug. 1910).

———, "Tennis Wars of 1923," *Collier's* (Oct. 6, 1923), 18.

Campbell, O. S., "American vs. English Lawn Tennis," *Harper's* (Aug. 27, 1892), 836–37.

Carter, Tom, "The Cradle of Champions," *City Sports* (April 1978), 7–10.

———, "Queen Helen Has Her Day," *City Sports* (April 1981), 15.

———, "Tennis in the Griffin Style," *California Living* (June 8, 1980), 34.

Chase, J., "The Championship Tournament at Newport, 1911," *World Today* (Oct. 1911), 1234–37.

Claudy, H. C., "Getting Ready for Tennis," *Woman's Home Companion* (May 1913), 32.

Collins, Bud, "Farewell to Forest Hills," *New York Times Magazine* (Sept. 11, 1977), 48–50, 58.

———, "Four Cheers for the Musketeers," *World Tennis* (Oct. 1976), 55–59.

———, "Molla Mallory: The Original Mystery Woman," *World Tennis* (Jan. 1983), 56–57.

Cowley, Robert, "The Jazz Age: A Shadow on the Seventies," *Saturday Review* (May 17, 1975), 10–18.

Craig, J., "Sturdy Knights of the Court," *Collier's* (Aug. 26, 1922), 13–14.

Day, A. L., "Tennis for Women," *Country Life* (April 1910), 466–76.

Deford, Frank, "A Head to Heed," *Sports Illustrated* (July 9, 1984), 72–86.

Delehanty, Hugh, "Aging Women Jocks," *California Living* (Sept. 18, 1983), 22.

Dewhurst, E. B., "The Big Four in Tennis," *Outing* (July 1914), 472–77.

Dewhurst, E. B., "McLoughlin, the Champion," *Outing* (Nov. 1913), 188–91.

Durant, John, "A Queen Walked Out," in *Yesterday in Sport* (New York, 1968), 155–59.

Dwight, J., "Court Tennis," *Scribner's Magazine* (Jan. 1891), 99–106.

Eaton, Joan Hodgen, "Profile: Little Miss Poker Face: Wimbledon Champion," *Carmel Coast Gazettte* (May 28, 1981), 1.

Eisenberg, D. D., "The 88-Year-Old Woman Billie Jean King Would Love to Beat," *World Tennis* (April 1979), 92–93.

Eisenhardt, I., "The Dawn of a New Era for Tennis," *Recreation* (June 1934), 148.

Forrey, Carolyn, "Getrude Atherton," *California Historical Quarterly* (Fall 1976), 194–208.

Freeman, Lewis R., "Why California Tennis Players Win," *Outing* (Oct., 1914), 22–30.

Fuller, William C. "Pop," "Girls Are Made of Stardust," *American Magazine* (Aug. 1935), 28–29.

Gallico, Paul, "The Golden Decade," *Saturday Evening Post* (Sept. 5, 1931), 12–13.

Goodwin, A. H., "New Tennis," *Country Life* (June 1905), 185–87.

Gould, G., "Lenglen versus Wills: A Study in Proportion," *Saturday Review* (Feb. 20, 1926), 221–22.

Graves, L., "The Rise of Tennis," *Century* (Aug. 1915), 628–33.

Grimsley, Will, "Tennis Great Helen Wills Doesn't Live in the Past," *Minneapolis Tribune* (Aug. 21, 1977), 11c.

Hawthorne, F., "The Favorite Strokes of Famous Tennis Players," *Country Life* (June 1923), 46–48.

———, "Some Tennis Mannerisms," *Country Life* (July 1927), 53–54.

———, "Who Will Succeed Lenglen," *Country Life* (Aug. 1925), 61–62.

Hammond, J., "Practical Tennis," *Outlook* (Sept. 14, 1895), 427.

Hawk, P. B., "Lawn Tennis Experts of America," *Collier's* (July 16, 1910), 23.

Hellman, Geoffrey T., "Diego Rivera," *New Yorker* (May 20, 1933), 21–24.

Henshaw, H., "Tennis and Its Leaders," *Independent* (June 11, 1903), 1387–92.

Horne, A. "Tennis," *Nineteenth Century* (Feb. 1925), 228–34.

Hulton, C. B., "Lawn Tennis, a Morality Game," *Nineteenth Century* (May 1924), 722–29.

Jackson, N. L., "Lawn Tennis in England," *Outing* (May 1901), 187–91.

Jacobs, Helen, "If I Had a Daughter I'd Like to Help Her Become a Champion," *Country Life* (April 1933), 43.

———, "It's Tennis Time Again," *Good Housekeeping* (March 1934), 36–37.

———, "The Psychology of Tennis Clothes," *Ladies' Home Journal* (June 1934), 31.

———, "Shall I Turn Professional?" *Country Life* (Aug. 1933), 5.

———, "What Becomes of Tennis Champions?" *Country Life* (Sept. 1933), 65–66.

Johnston, Alva, "Cash and Carry," *New Yorker* (Dec. 8, 1928), 31–34.

Kennedy, John B., "Little Miss Poker Face: An Interview with Helen Wills," *Collier's* (Sept. 18, 1926), 10, 32.

Klaw, Barbara, "Queen Mother of Tennis," *American Heritage* (Aug. 1975), 16–24, 82–86.

Lacoste, René, "Advice on Tennis," *Living Age* (July 1928), 1003–5.

Laney, Al, "The Tennis World Watches Wimbledon," *Literary Digest* (June 23, 1934), 32.

Lardner, Ring, "Nice Quiet Racket," *Collier's* (Aug. 31, 1929), 12.

Lawson, G. L., "Lawn Tennis Tactics," *Country Life* (Aug. 1907), 428–30.

Leamy, Hugh, "Net Profits," *Collier's* (Oct. 2, 1926), 9–10.

Lenglen, Suzanne, "My Tennis Adventures in America," *Living Age* (Feb. 11, 1922), 312, 351–54.

———, "Secrets of Tennis Success," *San Francisco Chronicle* (July 4, 1928), 1.

———, "Tennis," *Collier's* (April 10, 1920), 20; (May 15, 1920), 16; (May 29, 1920), 22–26; (July 17), 16.

Lippert, J., "Ladies of the Court," *Scholastic Magazine* (May 4, 1935), 24.

Little, L. L., "Our Leading Tennis Women," *Outing* (Oct. 1922), 24–25.

Little, R. D., "The All Around Game of Tennis," *Outing* (Nov.–Dec. 1912), 244–48.

——, "Attack in Tennis," *Outing* (Sept. 1912), 757–62.

Lucas, John, "Preparations for the First Post World War Olympic Games, 1919–1920," *Journal of Sport History* (Summer 1983), 30–45.

Lupica, Mike, "Ted Tinling: A Beacon of Style," *World Tennis* (Nov. 1978), 36.

Mallory, Molla, "How I Play Championship Tennis," *Ladies' Home Journal* (June 1916), 33.

——, "Shall We Encourage Athletics for Girls?" *Woman's Home Companion* (Sept. 1922), 13.

Marble, Alice, "Making a Champion," *Scholastic Magazine* (May 27, 1939), 36–37.

Marsh, W. A., "Jubilee Wimbledon," *English Review* (Aug. 1926), 217–21.

Marvin, G., "The Davis Cup Stays Home," *Outlook* (Sept. 24, 1924), 118–21.

McKane, K., "Modern Lawn Tennis," *Living Age* (Jan. 8, 1921), 114–18.

McMullen, L. B., "Teaching Girls to Play Real Tennis," *Outing* (June 1915), 332–37.

Merrihew, Stephen W., "The Amateur at Bay," *Atlantic* (Oct. 1924), 497–502.

Messenger, Janet Graveline, "Helen Hull Jacobs," *WomenSports* (April 1977), 14.

Miles, E. H., "American and English Racquets and Tennis," *Outing* (April 1900), 7–12.

"Miss Bjurstedt's Burst into Fame," *Literary Digest* (Aug. 28, 1915), 428.

Mitchell, Sheila, "Women's Participation in the Olympic Games, 1900–1926," *Journal of Sport History* (Summer 1977), 208–28.

Moody, Helen Wills, "The Education of a Tennis Player," *Scribner's Magazine* (May, 1936), 268–72; (June 1936), 336–39.

——, "The Key to Tennis Success," *Saturday Review* (June 27, 1931), 926–27.

Morse, F. B., "Making Tennis Champions," *Outing* (Jan. 1918), 249–53.

Mount, J., "Princesses of the Court," *Mentor* (July 1930), 20–21.

Muller, C. G., "Helen Wills Tells How She Wins," *Parents' Magazine* (Sept. 1932), 18–19.

Munson, Edward L., "Western Athletes—Why They Win," *Overland Monthly* (June 1929), 165–66.

Myers, A. Wallis, "France: The Lawn Tennis Leader," *Atlantic* (July 1929), 87–91.

Myers, A. Wallis, "National Traits in Lawn Tennis," *Atlantic* (July 1927), 37–44.

O'Leary, Theodore M., "The Reluctant Queens of the Court," *Sports Illustrated* (Aug. 20, 1962), w7–w12.

Paret, J. P., "The California Lawn Tennis Invasion," *Collier's* (Aug. 12, 1911), 18.

——, "Good Form in Women's Tennis," *Harper's Bazaar* (June 9, 1900), 341–44.

——, "In-door Lawn Tennis," *Harper's Weekly* (March 30, 1895), 309–10.

——, "Lawn Tennis Twist Service Fallacy," *Outing* (Sept. 1905), 774–75.

——, "New Era in American Lawn Tennis," *Outing* (June 1901), 320–24.

——, "Progress in Lawn Tennis," *Outing* (Aug. 1900), 517–21.

——, "Recent American Development in Lawn Tennis," *Outing* (July 1902), 486–90.

——, "Scientific Tennis," *Harper's Weekly* (Sept. 24, 1892), 922.

————, "Secrets of Lawn Tennis Skills," *Country Life* (July 1906), 305–6.

Pickens, William Hickman, "Accelerating Sentiment," *Saturday Evening Post* (Nov. 26, 1927), 20–21, 133.

————, "Accelerating Sentiment," *Saturday Evening Post* (Jan. 7, 1928), 41, 112, 116.

Pier, A. S., "Lawn Tennis," *Atlantic* (Aug. 1903), 211–21.

————, "Tennis Champions," *American Magazine* (Aug. 1910), 466–76.

Pileggi, Sarah, "The Lady in the White Silk Dress," *Sports Illustrated* (Sept. 13, 1982), 63–79.

Rapoport, Ron, "Little Miss Poker Face Revisits the Golden Age," *Los Angeles Times* (Oct. 28, 1975).

Reed, H., "A Champion and His Challengers," *Harper's Weekly* (Sept. 4, 1915), 226–27.

————, "Champions Don't Merely Happen," *Outlook* (Sept. 26, 1928), 866–67.

————, "High Lights of Lawn Tennis," *Munsey's* (Sept. 1913), 956–65.

————, "How McLoughlin Would Improve Your Tennis," *Country Life* (Aug. 1915), 22–25.

————, "McLoughlin and the Davis Cup," *Harper's Weekly* (Sept. 5, 1914), 236–37.

————, "Mile a Minute Tennis," *Harper's Weekly* (March 11, 1916), 259.

————, "Our Coming Crop of Tennis Stars," *Country Life* (July 1916), 32–33.

————, "Storm Signals in Tennis," *Outlook* (Aug. 1, 1928), 544–45.

————, "Team Work at Longwood," *Harper's Weekly* (Aug. 21, 1915), 186.

Reeve, A. B., "Beginnings of Our Great Games," *Outing* (May 1910), 174–75.

Rice, Grantland, "Big Bill," *Collier's* (June 28, 1930), 24.

————, "The French Are Coming," *Collier's* (Aug. 28, 1926), 10.

————, "Life Is Earnest," *Collier's* (March 1, 1930), 11.

————, "Net Change," *Collier's* (Sept. 12, 1931), 22.

————, "Out Where the Best Begins," *Collier's* (April 17, 1926), 26.

————, "The Rival Queens," *Collier's* (Jan. 30, 1926), 14.

————, "There Ought To Be a Law: A Pro in One Sport Is an Amateur in Another," *Collier's* (Sept. 8, 1928), 22.

Richards, Vincent, "Netting Results," *Saturday Evening Post* (May 15), 10–11; (June 5), 30–31; (June 12, 18–19, 1926).

————, "Never Too Young," *Collier's* (May 23, 1931), 30.

————, "One Is Never Too Young to Play Tennis," *Country Life* (June 1922), 41–42.

Rockman, R., "Playing Tennis with Sarah Bernhardt," *Ladies' Home Journal* (Feb. 1912), 19.

Ryan, Elizabeth, "Lawn Tennis for Women," *Country Life* (Aug. 1923), 63–64.

Satterthwaite, Phyllis, "Beauty on the Tennis Courts," *Good Housekeeping* (July 1929), 40–41.

————, "The Eve of the Tennis Championship," *Outlook* [London] (June 11, 1927), 753–54.

————, "From a Lawn Tennis Player's Diary," *Outlook* [London] (Oct. 1, 1929), 724–25.

————, "Suzanne Lenglen and Helen Wills," *Living Age* (March 27, 1926), 666–67.

Schwed, Peter, "The Unsinkable Mary K. Browne," *World Tennis* (June 1981), 74.

Smith, Marilyn Sode, "Local Color: Uncovering the San Francisco Legacy of Diego Rivera," *Image Magazine* (Dec. 21, 1986), 31–33.

Sohst, T., "Can Women Play Good Tennis?" *Country Life* (July 1919), 58–59.

Sutphen, W. G. V., "National Tennis Championship," *Harper's Weekly* (Aug. 27, 1898), 854.

Thurber, James, "Myron T. Herrick: Master of Ceremonies," *New Yorker* (July 21, 1928), 19–22.

Tilden, William T., "Boys and Girls in Tennis," *Outlook* (April 25, 1923), 759–61.

———, "Some Services That I Have Met," *Country Life* (July 1922), 41–43.

Tinling, Ted, "From Busts to Boom," *World Tennis* (June 1978), 87.

Tunis, John, "American Sports and American Life," *The Nation* (June 25, 1930), 729–72.

———, "Betty Nuthall," *New Yorker* (Aug. 23, 1930), 20–22.

———, "The Amateur Sports Racket," *New Republic* (May 28, June 18, 1930), 34–36, 120–22.

———, "American Sports and American Life," *Nation* (June 25, 1930), 729–30.

———, "Crowds at Court," *Collier's* (June 25, 1938), 18.

———, "That Center Court at Wimbledon," *Country Life* (July 1931), 90.

———, "D'Artagnan of the Courts," *New Yorker* (Sept. 6, 1930), 18–20.

———, "If I Had a Son, I'd Want Him To Be a Champion," *Country Life* (April 1933), 42.

———, "The Great Sports Myth," *Harper's* (March 1928), 422–31.

———, "Impressionists of Sport," *Outlook* (Dec. 18, 1929), 626.

———, "The Lawn Tennis Industry," *Harper's* (Feb. 1928), 289–98.

———, "A Master of Her Art" (Elizabeth Ryan), *New Yorker* (Aug. 22, 1925), 9–10.

———, "Miss Wills and Mr. Tilden," *Outlook and Independent* (Oct. 2, 1929), 168–69.

———, "The Newer Tennis—the Businesslike Lenglen," *New Yorker* (Oct. 16, 1926), 42–43.

———, "Smoke on the Ball," *American Magazine* (May 1933), 5.

———, "To the Ladies," *New Yorker* (Aug. 28, 1926), 28–29.

———, "The Mother of a Champion," *Harper's* (Feb. 1929), 275–89.

———, "Queens of the Court," *Pictorial Review* (July 1930), 18–19.

———, "Tennis the Universal Sport," *Review of Reviews* (Oct. 1927), 390–94.

———, "Why I Think Our Women Will Lose," *Collier's* (Aug. 11, 1923), 18.

———, "Winning Against Time," *New Yorker* (Sept. 5, 1925), 10–11.

———, "Women at Wimbledon," *Country Life* (July 1928), 65–66.

Ward, John William, "The Meaning of Lindbergh's Flight," *American Quarterly* (Spring 1958), 3–16.

Whelan, M., "Temperament in Tennis," *Outing* (Aug. 1914), 521–33.

Wilding, A. F., "The Tennis Outlook," *Country Life* (Aug. 1914), 37–39.

Williams, R. N., "Tennis and Temperaments," *Atlantic* (Oct. 1936), 435–37.

Wills, Helen, "Comeback," *Saturday Evening Post* (Sept. 7, 1935), 22–23.

———, "Emancipated Legs Mean Better Sports," *Ladies' Home Journal* (April 1927), 33.

——, "European Tennis," *Saturday Evening Post* (Oct. 11, 1930), 11.

——, "My Life on the Courts," *Saturday Evening Post* (June 10, 1933), 5; (June 17, 1933), 4–5; (July 22, 1933), 28.

——, "Orchard Maidens," *Sunset Magazine* (July 1925), p. 18.

——, "Organized Tennis," *Saturday Evening Post* (Dec. 14, 1929), 61.

——, "The Spirit of Tennis," *Saturday Evening Post* (June 21, 1930), 8–9.

——, "Sportswomen of Today," *Pictorial Review* (Aug. 1929), 2.

——, "Tennis," *Saturday Evening Post* (Aug. 3, 1929), 6–7; (May 14, 1932), 14; (May 28, 1932), 29.

——, "Tennis: Exercise for Everyone," *Forum* (June 1928), 844–53.

——, "Tennis Impressions," *Saturday Evening Post* (April 4, 1931), 13.

——, "A Wish," *Sunset Magazine* (June 1925), 16.

——, and David MacDonald, "Unforgettable 'Mrs. Wightie,' " *Reader's Digest* (Oct. 1977), 102–5.

Wind, Herbert Warren, "Run, Helen!", *New Yorker* (Aug. 30, 1952), 31–48.

Wood, Sidney, with Philip Harkins, "Mixed Doubles, Double Trouble," *Esquire* (July 1953), 57.

Wright, W. H., "Making Tennis Pay," *Outing* (April 1917), 60–65.

Wright, W. H., "Tempest in the Tennis Teapot," *Outing* (June 1917), 377–84.

The following magazines were used extensively for tennis coverage in the 1920s and the 1930s. I cite some individual biographical articles from the magazines, but hundreds of brief items that were useful are not cited individually.

American Lawn Tennis
Literary Digest
Newsweek
New Yorker
Time

Helen Wills was the subject of two *Time* magazine cover stories, July 26, 1926, and Aug. 1, 1929. Helen Jacobs was the subject of one *Time* magazine cover story, Sept. 14, 1936.

Newspapers
Carmel Coast Gazette
Chicago Daily Tribune
Detroit News
Detroit Saturday Night
Irish Times
(London) *Times*
Los Angeles Times
Minneapolis Star & Tribune
New York Evening Standard
New York Times
New York World
Palm Desert Post
San Francisco Call Bulletin
San Francisco Chronicle
San Francisco Examiner
San Jose Mercury Herald

A revealing biography of Helen Jacobs was serialized in the *San Francisco Call Bulletin* by James J. McGee, during the last week of August 1933.

Obituaries
Edith Cross Jensen, *San Francisco Chronicle*, July 20, 1983.
Molla B. Mallory, *New York Times*, Nov. 22, 1959.
Frederick S. Moody, Jr., *San Francisco Chronicle*, Oct. 11, 1984.

Other

Current Literature
"The Revival of Tennis" (Sept. 1902), 325.

Ebony
"Women in Sports" (Aug. 1977), 62.

Independent
"Professional Tennis" (Aug. 28, 1926), 230–31.

Life
"Remarkable Women" (Special Issue, 1976).
"Sixty-five-Year-Old Tennis Champion" (Sept. 15, 1952), 146.

Literary Digest
"Another Helen of California" (Aug. 25, 1934), 32.
"Behind a Poker Face" (Aug. 24, 1925), 32–33.
"Crowning Queen Betty of Tennis" (Sept. 6, 1930), 34.
"Decided That Champion Tennis Players May Write About the Game" (Jan. 3, 1925), 55–59.
"Decidedly Unconquerable is Mlle. Lenglen, Tennis Champion" (Sept. 3, 1919), 80.
"Eyes of the Tennis World Turn Back to America" (Aug. 5, 1933), 26.
"Getting Old at Twenty-six" (Aug. 12, 1933), 27.
"Girding for the Battle Against Professional Tennis" (May 19, 1927), 72–78.
"Helen II: New Queen of the Courts" (Sept. 3, 1932), 225–26.
"Helen Wills as a Killer of the Courts" (Sept. 7, 1929), 56–61.
"Helens Even Our Score with Britain" (Aug. 22, 1931), 26–27.
"Hope Springs in the Breasts of Tennis Stars" (April 9, 1932), 42.
"How a Sixteen-Year-Old-Girl Made Helen Wills Scamper" (Sept. 17, 1927), 48–52.
"How Molla Mallory Came Back" (Sept. 25, 1926), 58–64.
"How Vincent Richards Became the First Pro Tennis Champ" (Oct. 8, 1927), 69–71.
"New Laurels for the Much Crowned Tilden" (July 25, 1931), 38–39.
"New Tennis Champion Out of the West" (Sept. 18, 1915), 600–601.
"Pro Tennis on Tour" (Jan. 19, 1935), 43.
"Red Head from California" (July 13, 1935), 35.
"Sketches from Helen: A Novel from Suzanne" (Sept. 5, 1925), 12.
"Suzanne and Mary K., Pro Tennis Pioneers" (Sept. 25, 1926), 50–58.

"Tears at Wimbledon" (Aug. 10, 1935), 34.
"Temperament at the Tennis Net" (Feb. 27, 1926), 62–67.
"The Victory of Helen Jacobs" (Aug. 19, 1933), 32.

Living Age
"America at Wimbledon" (Aug. 14, 1920), 426–29.

Nation
"Amateur" (Aug. 1, 1928), 103.
"Nerve and Skill in Competition" (Sept. 9, 1915), 308.
"Proper Sporting Gesture" (Aug. 31, 1921), 220.
"What Is an Amateur?" (Oct. 1, 1930), 340.

New Republic
"Lawn Tennis Today" (Aug. 18, 1920), 324–25.

Newsweek
"Martina: A Style All Her Own" (Sept. 6, 1982), 44–48.

Outing
"As You Like It" (Oct. 1907), 107–10.
"Lawn Tennis Ranking" (Jan. 1904), 487.
"Tennis as We Used to Play It" (Oct. 1917), 10.

Outlook
"International Tennis" (Aug. 22, 1914), 947–48.
"Norway's Woman Tennis Champion" (June 2, 1915), 245.
"The Tennis Tournament at Seabright" (Aug. 1, 1914), 769.

Review of Reviews
"Feminine Laurel Bearers" (Sept. 1926), 314–15.

San Francisco Chronicle
"Exit the Flapper" (Jan. 20, 1923).
"Is She the New American Girl?" (Oct. 10, 1924).
"Science Warns of New Strong Arm Beauty" (Sept. 13, 1925).
"Will Women Athletes Mean Empty Cradles?" (May 13, 1923).

Scholastic Magazine
"Can the Queen Come Back?" (May 14, 1938), 36.

World Review
"Little Miss Pokerface Tells Why We All Should Play Tennis" (May 20, 1929),
    235.

INDEX

455